# www.wadsworth.com

*www.wadsworth.com* is the World Wide Web site for Wadsworth and is your direct source to dozens of online resources.

At *www.wadsworth.com* you can find out about supplements, demonstration software, and student resources. You can also send email to many of our authors and preview new publications and exciting new technologies.

**www.wadsworth.com**
Changing the way the world learns®

# STRENGTHS-BASED GENERALIST PRACTICE

## A Collaborative Approach

SECOND EDITION

**JOHN POULIN**
*Widener University*

with Contributors

THOMSON

BROOKS/COLE

Australia • Canada • Mexico • Singapore • Spain • United Kingdom • United States

**THOMSON**

**BROOKS/COLE**

Executive Editor: *Lisa Gebo*
Assistant Editor: *Alma Dea Michelena*
Editorial Assistant: *Sheila Walsh*
Technology Project Manager: *Barry Connolly*
Marketing Manager: *Caroline Concilla*
Marketing Assistant: *Mary Ho*
Advertising Project Manager: *Tami Strang*
Project Manager, Editorial Production:
   *Jennifer Klos*

Print/Media Buyer: *Emma Claydon*
Permissions Editor: *Joohee Lee*
Production Service: *Buuji, Inc.*
Copy Editor: *Marji Toensing*
Cover Designer: *Andy Norris*
Cover Image: *Richard Cook/Getty Images*
Cover Printer: *Webcom, Ltd.*
Compositor: *Buuji, Inc.*
Printer: *Webcom, Ltd.*

Printed in Canada

1  2  3  4  5  6  7  07  06  05  04

For more information about our products,
contact us at:
**Thomson Learning Academic Resource Center**
**1-800-423-0563**
For permission to use material from this text,
contact us by:
**Phone:** 1-800-730-2214
**Fax:** 1-800-730-2215
**Web:** http://www.thomsonrights.com

Library of Congress Control Number: 2003112638

ISBN 0-534-64151-2

**Brooks/Cole—Thomson Learning**
**10 Davis Drive**
**Belmont, CA 94002**
**USA**

**Asia**
Thomson Learning
5 Shenton Way #01-01
UIC Building
Singapore 068808

**Australia/New Zealand**
Thomson Learning
102 Dodds Street
Southbank, Victoria 3006
Australia

**Canada**
Nelson
1120 Birchmount Road
Toronto, Ontario M1K 5G4
Canada

**Europe/Middle East/Africa**
Thomson Learning
High Holborn House
50/51 Bedford Row
London WC1R 4LR
United Kingdom

**Latin America**
Thomson Learning
Seneca, 53
Colonia Polanco
11560 Mexico D.F.
Mexico

**Spain/Portugal**
Paraninfo
Calle/Magallanes, 25
28015 Madrid, Spain

*To the SWCS staff and students for their energy, creativity, and commitment to strengthening families and communities one STEP at a time*

# CONTENTS

PART 2 | GENERALIST PRACTICE WITH SPECIAL POPULATIONS

CHAPTER 13
## Generalist Practice with Older People   366

CHAPTER 14
## Generalist Practice with People of Color   398

# PREFACE

The second edition of *Collaborative Social Work* is substantially different from the first edition in a number of ways. The book throughout emphasizes building trust as a prerequisite to engaging clients in a professional helping relationship.

A second major change is that the book has expanded its' coverage of macro generalist practice. The coverage of macro practice is now more on par with the coverage of generalist practice with micro client systems. In addition, the coverage of micro and macro interventions has been expanded, especially in the chapter on generalist practice interventions.

The third major change is framing strengths-based generalist practice within a new model of collaborative social work practice. The model specifies the phases of the work, the major tasks to be accomplished, desired inputs, the critical practice skills associated with the different phases of the helping relationship and the desired outputs. The model structures the helping process and emphasizes trusting building and the development of the helping relationship. The addition of core strengths-based practice skills is in itself a major addition to this edition.

In addition to the above changes, Part I of the book has been reorganized so that the reader is introduced to generalist practice and theory in the first two chapters. Chapter three presents the collaborative model and the remainder of Part I (chapter 4–8) cover the implementation of the model.

Part II of the book still focuses on generalist practice with at-risk populations. A new chapter on substance abuse has been added and the chapters on mental illness, HIV/AIDS and natural disasters have been dropped. The chapters on generalist practice with economically disadvantaged people, gay and lesbian clients, older people, people of color, and abused and neglected children and their families and have been updated.

Collaborative Social Work: Strengths-Based Generalist Practice differs from other generalist practice texts in several ways. It integrates the strengths-based collaborative approach to working with client systems and empirical practice methods. The book operationally defines the helping relationship and emphasizes its use throughout the helping process. It also provides detailed coverage of at-risk special populations. These chapter provide the context for generalist practice with the different special populations.

Collaborative Social Work: Strengths-Based Generalist Practice is suitable for use in senior BSW generalist practice courses and for the first foundation practice course in an MSW curriculum. It presents concepts in an accessible manner, using straightforward language that is relatively free of jargon. There are case examples throughout, and each chapter concludes with a detailed case study and discussion questions.

## ACKNOWLEDGMENTS

Many people contributed to this book. I want to especially thank Frann Anderson, Allan Barsky, Martha Dore, Nancy Feldman, Stephen Kauffman, and Norma Thomas for their authorship of the special population chapters. These chapters enrich the book and make generalist practice come alive for students.

I also thank my students for allowing me to try out my ideas, for their constructive feedback, and for their support. I am grateful to Denise Bubel, Jennifer Francella, Leslie Freas, Susan Getty, Dan Lafferty, and Kathleen McCabe for contributing the case examples used in Part I of the book and to Laurie Bluhm, Tony Cousar, Christina Drecher, Louann Kenefick, Sara Kulp, and Pat Mullen for their ideas and help in developing the collaborative model. I also thank the staff and students at Social Work Consultation Services (SWCS)—Pamela Baker, Gina Bottino, Nick Brush, Art Dash, Danielle DuLuca, John Harmon, Christyn Hughes, Joscelyn Keeve-Crawford, Jennifer Marshall, Michelle McCann, Megan Miller, Lauren Nuehart, Dianna Palimere, Cheryl Sadeghee, Linda Santiago, and Pat Stewart—for their help and support.

I am extremely grateful to the peer reviewers: Vicki Gardine Williams, Tennessee State University; Dada Maglajlic, Bemidji State University; Daysi Mejia, Florida Gulf Coast University; Olivia Moreton, University of Alaska, Fairbanks; and Nancy Nystrom, Michigan State University, who provided thoughtful suggestions that substantially strengthen the book.

Finally, I thank my wife, Anne, for her love, patience, and encouragement, and my daughters, Katherine, Jessica, and Claire, for bring true joy to my life.

# ABOUT THE CONTRIBUTORS

**John Poulin** is a Professor at Widener University's Center for Social Work Education, where he teaches generalist practice, research and policy practice courses. He received a BA from the University of Southern Maine, an MSW from the University of Michigan, and a Ph.D. from the University of Chicago's School of Social Service Administration. The former director of Widener's BSW program, he founded its MSW program and served as the dean and director for seven years. He is currently the executive director of Social Work Consultation Services (SWCS), an innovative community based field placement agency developed by the social work faculty in collaboration with a local community human service organization. SWCS (www.swcs-cef.org) provides a wide range for free social work services to low income community residents as well as free capacity building services to under-resourced community based human service organizations. His current research focuses on the helping process and the factors that contribute to trust building in the helping relationship.

**Frann S. Anderson** is the Director of the Licensing and Medicaid Certification Unit with the Delaware Division of Substance Abuse and Mental Health and a Family Therapist at the Rockford Center in Newark Delaware. She received a BA in art and art therapy and a BA in psychology at Carlow College, a MA in art therapy from Vermont College, and a MSW from Widener University.

She is a licensed clinical social worker and certified alcohol and drug counselor in the state of Delaware. She has dedicated her clinical practice to the treatment of individuals with substance abuse, survivors of trauma and sexual minorities.

**Dr. Allan Edward Barsky** has a background in law, social work, mediation, and addictions counseling. He is currently Full Professor at Florida Atlantic University in Boca Raton. Dr. Barsky's book credits include *Alcohol, Other Drugs and Addictions: A Professional Development Manual* (Brooks/Cole, in press), *Conflict Resolution for the Helping Professions* (Brooks/Cole, 2000), *Interdisciplinary Practice with Diverse Populations* (Greenwood, 2000), Clinicians in Court (Guilford, 2002), and *Successful Social Work Education* (Brooks/Cole, in progress). His addictions practice experience includes work with the YMCA Youth Substance Abuse Program in Toronto and the Division of Substance Abuse at the Albert Einstein College of Medicine in Bronx, NY. His addictions research has been published in the *Journal of Drug Education*, *Canadian Social Work Review*, and *Revista Treball Social* (Catalunya).

**Martha Morrison Dore** is currently Visiting Professor of Social Work at Adelphi University. She was formerly Director of Research and Evaluation at Casey Family Services, the direct services division of the Annie E. Casey Foundation. She has served on the social work faculties of Columbia University and the University of Pennsylvania and was Director of Social Work Research at the Philadelphia Child Guidance Clinic. She is currently on the Board of Directors of the Institute for Social Work Research. Her research and scholarship have focused on high risk families with issues of substance abuse, domestic violence, mental illness, and child maltreatment. Her work has appeared in *Child Welfare, Social Work, Children and Youth Services Review, Child Abuse & Neglect, Families in Society, Social Service Review,* and *Family Relations*. She is co-author of a book on home-based services for families whose children have special mental health needs which draws on her research with over 2000 Pennsylvania families.

**Nancy Feldman** is an Assistant Professor at the Hunter College School of Social Work, City University of New York, where she teaches Human Behavior in the Social Environment and Casework courses. She received a BA from Tulane University, an MA in Creative Arts Therapy from Hahnemann University, an MSW from Fordham University, and a Ph.D. from Columbia University. She has worked with children, youth, and families in a variety of settings. Her research interests include strengths-based school mental health services, the process of creating developmental environments, and engaging hard to reach children and youth through improvisational drama.

**Stephen Kauffman, Ph.D.** is an Associate Professor at Widener University's Center for Social Work Education, where he has taught social policy, community practice, program evaluation, and research since 1991. Dr. Kauffman received his MSW from the George Warren Brown School of Social Work at Washington University in 1987, and his Ph.D. from the Graduate School of Social Work and Social Research at Bryn Mawr College in 1992. The two major areas of his scholarly research are citizen participation, and the role of ideology in policy, and he has widely published in these subjects. Since arriving at Widener, he has consulted with several community organizations to evaluate the effectiveness of their programs in education, housing, lead poisoning prevention, and teenage pregnancy prevention. Dr. Kauffman has also served as the evaluator for two HOPE VI projects implemented by the Chester Housing Authority. The HOPE VI evaluation projects, funded by the US Department of Housing and Urban Development research at Chatham Estates, are widely cited as models for housing project evaluations.

**Norma D. Thomas** is an Associate Professor and the Assistant Director of the Center for Social Work Education at Widener University, where she teaches undergraduate and graduate courses. She received a BA in social work from Penn State University, an MSW from the Temple University School of Social Administration, and a DSW from the University of Pennsylvania School of Social Work. She has worked a direct practitioner, administrator, and consultant and sits on a number of boards and advisory groups. Her primary research interests are issues related to people of color and aging.

# PRINCIPLES AND CONCEPTS OF GENERALIST PRACTICE

Robin P. is a first-year Masters in Social Work (MSW) student with a field placement in a public child welfare agency. She is assigned to a unit that provides case management services for adolescents in foster care, their birth parents, and their foster parents. In her role as case manager Robin monitors clients' service plans, provides supportive counseling for adolescents, helps link clients to other services and resources, and advocates for clients who need help from various systems and organizations.

Robin is pleased with her field placement because she is getting experience in working with individual clients and families. However, because the first-year placement is supposed to be a generalist one, Robin is concerned that all her tasks are micro-practice activities. She decides to talk to Mary C., her field instructor, about adding some macro-practice activities to her placement responsibilities.

As she prepares for her meeting with Mary, Robin realizes that she is not sure what constitutes macro practice. What do generalist social workers do that is considered macro practice? How do they work with an organization or community client system? What functions do generalist social workers perform at the organizational or community level? What is the purpose of the helping relationship when one is working with organizations and communities? How do macro-practice activities differ from micro-practice activities? How are they similar?

This chapter provides an introduction to generalist social work practice. The chapter begins with a definition of strengths-based generalist practice and then describes the various generalist interventions and roles. The chapter concludes with a review of social work client systems and the factors that influence clients' willingness to engage in a helping relationship.

By the end of this chapter, you should be able to help Robin

1. Understand the purpose of the helping relationship in working with individual, family, group, organization, and community client systems
2. Identify micro-level generalist interventions
3. Understand the role that the "self" of the social worker plays in generalist social work practice
4. Identify macro-level generalist interventions
5. Clarify the differences among the terms **client system level**, **client system**, and **target system**
6. Classify clients by type and identify factors that might affect their willingness to develop a helping relationship and engage in the helping process

## STRENGTHS-BASED GENERALIST SOCIAL WORK PRACTICE

Traditional agency-based social work practice is problem-focused. Clients tend to be viewed as having deficits and pathologic problems that need to be overcome to improve functioning (Saleebey, 2002). The strengths-based approach, on the other hand, focuses on the client's inherent strengths, resources, and coping abilities. Clients are viewed as being capable of change. They are partners and active participants in the change process. The social worker is not the problem-solver; the client is the problem-solver. The generalist social worker's primary function is to help clients recognize, marshal, and enhance their inherent strengths and abilities (Weick et al., 1989). In the strengths-based approach, the client is the expert with the knowledge and ability to accomplish the needed changes. Social work practice focuses on empowering clients and establishing collaborative helping relationships.

In strengths-based generalist social work practice, a collaborative helping relationship is formed between a professional and an individual, a family, a group, an organization, or a community for the purposes of empowerment and promotion of social and economic justice. The relationship may involve direct work with client systems of all sizes as well as indirect work on behalf of client systems. The professional collaborates with the client or with systems that may benefit the client, all the while focusing on client strengths and resources.

## Types of Generalist Social Work Interventions

A classification of generalist social work practice interventions is shown in Table 1.1. In this conceptualization, intervention tasks are categorized by system level (individual, family, group, organization, or community). Generalist practice often requires simultaneous interventions on multiple levels. In any case situation, you and your client might be involved in a number of individual, family, group, organization, or community change activities.

As Table 1.1 indicates, generalist social work practice entails micro-level and macro-level work. **Micro social work practice** is interventions with individuals, couples, and families (Hepworth, Rooney, and Larsen, 2002). Practice with these client systems is also referred to as **direct practice** or **interpersonal practice** (Garvin and Seabury, 1997). Some authors classify social work practice with small groups as **mezzo-level interventions** (Miley, O'Melia, and DuBois, 1998) and others as **micro-level direct practice** (Hepworth, Rooney, and Larsen, 2002; Pinderhughes, 1995; Shulman, 1999). Because helping relationships with individual, family, and small group client systems share common purposes, this book treats social work practice with small groups as a form of micro practice. Regardless of the client system, the purpose of micro-level practice is to enhance functioning and empower the client. These two related purposes apply to work with individual clients, couples, families, and small groups.

Generalist social workers engage in a wide range of client system change activities with individuals, families, and small groups. Micro interventions commonly used by generalist social workers are divided into two broad groups, counseling and case management (Table 1.1). Counseling interventions include supportive counseling and education and training. Case management includes service linkage, service coordination, service negotiation,

TABLE I.I | MAIN ASPECTS OF MICRO AND MACRO CLIENT SYSTEMS

| System Level | Client System | Purpose of Helping Relationship | Use of Self | Interventions |
|---|---|---|---|---|
| **Micro**<br>Individual<br><br>Family<br><br><br>Group | Individuals<br><br>Couples<br>Families<br><br>Small groups | Enhance functioning<br>Empowerment | Understanding<br>Sensitivity<br>Respect<br>Acceptance<br>Empathy<br>Cooperative intentions<br>Hopefulness<br>Partnership<br>Support<br>Commitment<br>Confidence | Counseling<br>Supportive counseling<br>Education and training<br>Case management<br>Service linkage<br>Service coordination<br>Service negotiation<br>Resource mobilization<br>Client advocacy |
| **Macro**<br>Organization<br><br><br><br><br>Community | Agency leaders<br>Agency task forces<br>Agency committees<br><br>Professional task forces<br>Community coalitions<br>Neighborhood groups | Improve organization<br>Improve services<br>Develop services<br><br>Improve community conditions<br>Empower residents<br>Develop community resources<br>Increase citizen awareness<br>Mobilize citizens | Same as for micro systems | Education and training<br>Program planning<br>Community development |

resource mobilization, and client advocacy. These interventions are discussed in detail in Chapter 8. Table 1.2 briefly describes the more common micro generalist interventions.

Macro-level interventions focus on organizational and community change. Some authors include societal change in the macro practice category and place organizational change at the mezzo level (Miley, O'Melia, and DuBois, 1998). The more restricted definition of macro practice as work with community groups and organizations, program planning and development, and the implementation, administration, and evaluation of programs (Connaway and Gentry, 1988; Kirst-Ashman and Hull, 1993; Specht, 1988) more realistically describes what most generalist social workers do in actual practice.

Typical client systems at the organizational level are organizational leaders, task forces, and committees. The system level is the organization, and the

TABLE I.2 | COMMON MICRO-GENERALIST INTERVENTIONS

| Intervention | Description |
|---|---|
| **Counseling**<br>Supportive counseling | The social worker and client engage in a collaborative therapeutic or counseling process. The purpose of the intervention is to help the client resolve concerns and challenges, enhance coping, and improve functioning. |
| Education and training | The social worker helps the client learn and master new concepts and skills. |
| **Case management**<br>Service linkage | The social worker helps the client identify and contact other programs and services. |
| Service coordination | The social worker coordinates the various services and professionals involved in the client's life to ensure that services are integrated and have common goals. |
| Service negotiation | The social worker helps clients overcome difficulties they encounter with other programs and services. |
| Resource mobilization | The social worker helps the client obtain needed resources, such as housing, clothing, food, funiture, financial support, or health care. |
| Client advocacy | The social worker educates clients about their rights, teaches them advocacy skills, and applies pressure to make agencies and resources respond to client needs. |

client systems that the social worker engages are the decision-makers and decision-making structures of the organization. The worker usually participates in formally organized work groups, such as agency task forces or committees. The client system might also be the organization's decision-makers, that is, administrators and supervisors. Thus, a generalist social worker seeking to change an organization views the decision-makers or the decision-making structures as the client system.

At the organizational level, the purpose of macro-level practice is to improve the functioning of the organization, improve services and service delivery, or develop new services. All three purposes involve change of the organization or agency. Generalist social workers tend to be agency-based and work within an organizational framework.

This does not mean that organizational change from outside the system is impossible (Chavis, Florin, and Felix, 1993). There is a long-standing tradition in social work practice of working for change from the outside. This tradition dates back to the early days of social work and the social reformers of the progressive era (Haynes and Mickelson, 1991; Reeser and Epstein, 1990).

Typical client systems at the community level are professional task forces, community coalitions, and neighborhood or community citizens' groups.

TABLE 1.3 | THREE MACRO INTERVENTIONS

| Intervention | Description |
|---|---|
| Education and training | The social worker sets up organizational and community training meetings, workshops, and seminars. |
| Program planning | The social worker helps in the development, expansion, and coordination of social services and social policies. |
| Community development | The social worker helps improve community conditions and empowers residents to seek community change. |

Often the purpose of community practice is to improve community or neighborhood conditions, empower residents, develop resources, increase community awareness of social and economic problems, and mobilize people to advocate for needed resources and changes. Generalist social workers engaged in community change usually work with professional or community groups. Some groups have both professional and citizen members. Social workers engaged in community practice view the group they are working with as the client system. In other words, the client system is the professional task force, neighborhood group, or community coalition that is seeking to change or improve the community.

Generalist social workers engage in a range of organizational and community interventions. As shown in Table 1.1, macro interventions commonly used by generalist social workers include education and training, program planning, and community development. These interventions are discussed in detail in Chapter 8. Table 1.3 briefly describes three identified macro interventions.

## Use of Self

Use of self refers to the social worker's interpersonal skills and interactions with the client system (Goldstein, 1995; Northen, 1995). Social workers intervene by means of the helping relationship to assist client systems in achieving identified change goals. Research studies have consistently found that the strongest predictor of client change is the helping relationship (Marziali and Alexander, 1991; Russell, 1990). It is through the helping relationship that change takes place. When the social worker interacts with the client system, the quality of the interaction facilitates client change. The social worker uses himself or herself to communicate

- Understanding
- Sensitivity
- Respect
- Acceptance
- Empathy
- Cooperative intentions

- Hopefulness
- Partnership
- Support
- Commitment
- Confidence

## CASE 1.1 | PROFILES OF GENERALIST SOCIAL WORKERS

**Gina B.**

Gina had her first-year field placement at Social Work Consultation Services (SWCS), an innovative agency developed by her graduate school of social work and a community-based agency. SWCS provided generalist social work learning experiences for student interns and social work and capacity-building services for the residents and organizations of an economically disadvantaged community.

At SWCS Gina undertook a range of generalist social work tasks and activities. As a member of the senior services team, Gina provided counseling and case management services for elderly residents of a senior housing facility. Gina met with her senior clients weekly. For some, she provided **supportive counseling** addressing a variety of concerns, such as family relationships, isolation, depression, and a host of loss issues. For other clients, she served as a case manager. She referred clients to other service providers (**service linkage**), negotiated on their behalf with other service providers (**service negotiation**), obtained resources for them (**resource mobilization**), and advocated for them in any way she could (**client advocacy**).

Gina's work on the senior team also entailed a number of macro-practice activities. Gina and two of the senior team interns established a one-day-a-week drop-in center at the senior housing facility (**program planning**) and began holding monthly meetings with local providers who served elderly clients to share information, reduce service duplication, and increase coordination (**service coordination**). Gina helped develop programs and monthly group activities for residents and organized two ongoing support groups. Gina and her team also organized a community service day that targeted elderly community residents (**community development**). The student volunteers provided cleaning and chore services for 125 elderly persons. The senior team provided follow-up and case management services for community residents who required additional services.

Gina also organized a three-day community and university event designed to promote awareness of violence against women (**education and training**). Gina and two other student interns planned, organized, obtained funding for, and implemented the

event. Approximately 200 community residents, students, faculty, and staff participated in the program.

During the year Gina wrote a grant proposal (**program planning**) for additional funding for the SWCS program. She also helped produce the agency's newsletter, developed new program brochures, helped conduct a program evaluation (**program planning**), conducted a series of training workshops for another agency's case managers (**education and training**), served on the agency's executive and recognition committees (**program planning**), and cofacilitated the agency's monthly staff meeting on two occasions.

**Art D.**

Art had his second-year placement at SWCS. His primary assignment was with the functional family therapy (FFT) team. FFT is an intensive model of social work practice for troubled adolescents and their families. Art participated in an extensive FFT training program and worked with five families (**supportive counseling**). He met with the families once or twice a week for about two hours at a time.

In addition to his work on the FFT team, Art, in collaboration with another student intern, developed an eight-week anger management group for adult residents of a local shelter (**program planning and supportive counseling**). Art researched anger management training programs, developed a curriculum for eight sessions, recruited the participants, and cofacilitated the sessions. Art and the other intern also opened a one-day-a-week drop-in day program for homeless adults at a local church (**program planning**). The program provided a warm place for the homeless to spend the day as well as case management services. Art was also a member of the agency's executive committee (**program planning**) and cofacilitated the agency's monthly staff meeting on two occasions.

**Dianna P.**

Dianna had her first-year placement at SWCS. Her primary assignment was the school team, which developed programs and services for schoolchildren and their families. Dianna, in collaboration with a local wellness center, helped expand a peer leadership

CASE 1.1 | *continued*

program for high school students (**program planning**). In this capacity, she conducted a number of
training workshops (**education and training**) for
about 70 high school peer leaders and assisted the
peer leaders in implementing the program.

Dianna also became a member of a community
task force that was formed to address the problem of
teenage pregnancy and promote pregnancy prevention (**community development**). Dianna helped
define the mission of the group and assisted in
preparing a grant proposal (**program planning**) to
help fund the prevention program.

Dianna recognized early in the year that the middle schools lacked a referral system for children who
needed counseling and case management services.
After meeting with school officials and human ser-

vices providers, Dianna developed a referral system
that was implemented in the school district (**program
planning**).

Dianna also cofacilitated a series of workshops
for case managers designed to increase their relationship and case management skills (**education and
training**). She was a member of the team that organized the university-community violence prevention
event (**education and training**), chaired the agency's
recognition committee (**program planning**), and
cofacilitated the agency's monthly staff meeting on
two occasions. In addition to the above-mentioned
macro-practice activities, Dianna provided **counseling** and **case management** services for seven community residents who were referred directly to SWCS
for social work services.

Use of self is traditionally associated with micro-level practice, the social
worker's interactions with individual, couple, family, and group client systems. However, the characteristics described above also apply to work at the
macro level. A generalist social worker can provide support and foster hope
and understanding through interactions at the organizational level with
agency task forces and committees and at the community level with professional task forces, community coalitions, and neighborhood groups. Carrying
out the various intervention tasks involves the use of self and system change
activities. The worker must be skilled in the use of self when working with any
system level. Effective interpersonal skills are needed to facilitate change at the
individual, family, group, organization, and community levels of generalist
social work practice.

## SOCIAL WORK CLIENTS

Generalist practice involves work with client systems of all sizes. The primary
client system could be an individual, a family, a small group, an organization,
or a community. The primary client system is unlikely to be the only client system being helped or targeted for change. Typically, generalist practice involves
working with multiple interrelated client systems.

Strengths-based generalist social work practice uses an **ecosystems perspective**. This perspective focuses assessment and intervention on problematic
transactions between individuals and their environment. These problematic
transactions become the target systems that the client and worker seek to

change (Pincus and Minahan, 1973). A target system can be an individual client or another individual, family, group, organization, or community system within the client's **person-in-environment system.** Any and all systems in a client's environment are potential target systems in the helping process.

Case 1.2 illustrates the person-in-environment perspective, client systems, and target systems in generalist social work practice. In this example, if Alice agrees to work with the social worker, she will be the primary client system. She needs help in assessing her options and deciding on a course of action. Depending on what she decides to do, her parents, her boyfriend, and the school are all possible target systems.

If Alice decides, for instance, that she wants to keep the baby and ask her parents to help her care for the child, the transaction between Alice and her parents becomes the focus of the intervention and the target system. In this situation, the key to successfully assisting Alice is to help her parents respond supportively to her situation. The social worker would probably help Alice prepare for the meeting with her parents, might attend the meeting with her, and might offer to help the parents adjust to and cope with their daughter's pregnancy and the pending birth. In this case, Alice is the client system and her parents are a target system.

It is also possible for the school to become a target system. If, for example, the school has a policy prohibiting students in the third trimester from attending classes, Alice and her social worker might ask the school to develop an alternative plan for Alice to complete high school or even to change the existing policy. The school system would become a target system in the process of helping Alice carry out her plan to keep the baby.

Another possibility is that none of the systems within Alice's environment would become target systems. If Alice decides, for example, to have an abortion and not tell anyone about it, neither her parents, boyfriend, or school become target systems. Alice would be both the client system and the target system.

In any given client situation, all systems within the client's person-in-environment system are potential target systems. Whether or not a system becomes a target system for intervention depends on the specifics of the case and focus of the work.

## Types of Clients

A potential client becomes a client only if and when there is an explicit agreement between the person and the social worker about the purpose of their work together. **Clients** are persons who agree to work with you to achieve a specified outcome. There are three types of clients: voluntary, nonvoluntary, and involuntary (Garvin and Seabury, 1997).

**Voluntary clients** seek out the services of a social worker or social agency on their own because they want help with some aspect of their lives. A young mother who recognizes that she has a drinking problem and seeks help from

## CASE 1.2 | I CAN'T TELL MY PARENTS

Alice C. is seventeen. She has been pregnant with her first child for two months. She is unmarried and very committed to her relationship with the teenage father of the child. They are both seniors in high school and plan to attend college in the fall. Alice's parents are devout Catholics, who follow the teachings of the church. Although quite strict, they have always been loving, and encouraged and supported their only adopted daughter.

Alice is afraid to talk to her parents about her situation. She is concerned about disappointing them and about the shame she will bring to the family. She has not told her boyfriend about the pregnancy, either. She is unsure how he will react.

Alice does not know what to do. She is unwilling to confide in her family and friends, so she contacts the school social worker for help.

---

a professional social worker is an example of a voluntary client. She has made a decision to get professional help and is voluntarily entering into a helping relationship with the social worker.

**Nonvoluntary clients** are being pressured to seek help by someone they know personally. They have not been given a mandate by a court of law or social agency to receive help. A friend, relative, or acquaintance believes they have problems; they themselves may or may not agree. Even if they acknowledge the existence of problems, they are not seeking help under their own volition. Someone in their life is forcing them to seek help. They come to a social worker because "they may suffer unpleasant consequences if they refuse"(Garvin and Seabury, 1997, p. 132). A young mother who is being pressured by her husband to get help for her drinking problem is an example of a nonvoluntary client. She is meeting with a social worker only because her husband has threatened to leave her and seek custody of their child. She is essentially being forced by her husband to get professional help with her drinking problem and is complying with his wishes to prevent him from leaving her and possibly getting custody of their child.

**Involuntary clients** have a legal mandate to receive services. They have no choice in the matter. If the young mother with a drinking problem is arrested for drunken driving, part of her sentence might be a court order requiring her to participate in a twenty-week counseling program. In this situation she is an involuntary client.

Regardless of whether prospective clients are voluntary, nonvoluntary, or involuntary, they must make some sort of contract or agreement with the social worker in order to become clients. They must knowingly and willingly participate in the helping process. Clearly, it is easier to reach an agreement with voluntary clients than with nonvoluntary or involuntary clients. Voluntary clients are motivated to seek help. The others, at the point of initial contact, have probably not made a decision to seek help and engage in a collaborative helping process.

Clients progress through five stages in self-initiated, professionally assisted change: precontemplation, contemplation, preparation, action, and maintenance. "**Precontemplation** is the stage at which there is no intention to change in the foreseeable future" (Prochaska, DiClemente, and Norcross, 1992, p. 1103). Clients at this stage are often unaware of their problems and are not seriously considering getting help. They are reluctant participants in the helping process. They have not chosen to seek help and probably are unhappy about the prospect of being helped. "**Contemplation** is the stage in which clients are aware that a problem exists and are seriously thinking about overcoming it but have not yet made a commitment to take action" (p. 1103). The key here is the lack of commitment to change. Many clients recognize the need to address concerns or problems but need help in making a genuine commitment to bring the change about. "**Preparation** is the stage that combines intention and behavioral criteria" (p. 1104). Clients at this stage have started to address the problem and are motivated to make the necessary changes. "**Action** is the stage in which individuals modify their behavior, experiences, or environment in order to overcome their problems" (p. 1104). During the action stage, clients are engaged in the helping process and are taking necessary steps to achieve the desired changes. "**Maintenance** is the stage in which people work to prevent relapse and consolidate the gains attained during action" (p. 1104). In a way, maintenance is a continuation of the action phase. The client is actively trying to prevent a relapse.

The five stages of change highlight client differences in readiness to engage in the helping process. It is important to recognize these individual differences. Not all potential clients have reached the stage of contemplation or action. Many clients who are referred or have a mandate for service are in the precontemplation or contemplation stage. To become true clients, they must make a commitment to change. In the end, only those who willingly agree to work with the social worker to achieve a specified outcome can engage in a collaborative helping relationship. Nonvoluntary and involuntary clients might go through the motions because they are required to do so, but they will not truly become clients until they decide on their own to engage in a helping relationship.

## THE RELUCTANT CLIENT

Social workers often work with clients who are in the precontemplation stage and are not interested in getting help. In the past, these clients were viewed as "resistant" and often blamed for not cooperating with their social workers (Anderson and Stewart, 1983). The strengths perspective views resistance as a natural and understandable coping mechanism. Many clients, at best, are going to be reluctant to engage in a helping relationship (Rooney, 1992). The following discussion reviews some factors that affect clients' willingness and ability to move beyond the precontemplation stage in the helping process.

## The Experience of Being a Client

A number of factors associated with clienthood affect the helping process. Understanding these factors and the way a person feels about being a client can facilitate the helping process and the development of a collaborative helping relationship. Understanding the client's feelings about needing and asking for help as well as his or her perceptions of what it means to be a client can facilitate the process of reaching an explicit agreement about the purpose of working together. Whether the individual arrives on a voluntary, nonvoluntary, or involuntary basis, the worker's sensitivity to his or her feelings about clienthood is critical to having that individual become a client.

Beliefs and feelings about receiving help from a professional are related to cultural mores. The dominant culture in American society has a strong tradition of individualism (Billups, 1992). Individuals who need psychological or social services are stigmatized and viewed negatively in American society because they are perceived as not living up to the cultural mandates of individual responsibility and self-reliance. This stigma keeps many who need the services provided by social workers from seeking them. Only after everything else has failed are they willing to get professional help.

Most clients have mixed feelings about getting help (Maluccio, 1979). People are uncomfortable about involving themselves in a helping relationship and admitting that they have failed or are unable to resolve their difficulties on their own. Clients may feel shame and embarrassment. They are concerned about what the social worker will think of them and what friends and family will think. Asking for help also raises negative feelings about themselves because they may view receiving professional help as a personal failure. Obviously, the intensity of these feelings varies greatly. However, it is probably safe to assume that every person is feeling some degree of discomfort when he or she asks for help and goes through the stages of becoming a client.

Clients are often afraid of the possibilities of change. Nevertheless, even the most reluctant nonvoluntary or involuntary client has the power to bounce back. The worker uses this resilience to infuse some degree of hopefulness and expectation about positive outcomes. At some level, all clients have what it takes to make changes. They may not know it, but we, as social workers, know it, and that is why we passionately look for a person's strengths when he or she is involved in difficult life situations. Clients may not be aware of their resilience because they are overwhelmed by feelings of failure and stigmatization.

It is only realistic to expect that clients have ambivalent feelings about working with the social worker and receiving professional help. The first interactions will probably determine whether clients decide to engage in the helping process or drop out. During initial meetings, it is critical for the worker to decrease the client's negative feelings and increase positive feelings about seeking help and engaging in the helping process. Empowerment starts during the first interview with the client.

## Prior Experiences with Helping Professionals

Most clients who come to you will have received social services in the past and have had numerous prior contacts with helping professionals. Ignoring the possibility of prior negative experiences or assuming that all prior experiences were positive is a mistake. Clients' expectations about receiving help from a professional are influenced by their past experiences (Gambrill, 1997). Were they treated with respect? Were they given a voice in the decision-making process? Were the services helpful? Were their prior experiences with helping professionals satisfactory or unsatisfactory? Clients whose prior experiences were negative may expect more of the same and approach your work together with reservations, whereas those who enjoyed more positive experiences might be much more willing to engage in the helping process.

Early in the working relationship, preferably during the initial meeting, the social worker should explore the client's perceptions of prior experiences. The worker may not change these perceptions, but recognizing them and learning what clients liked and did not like about earlier experiences is an important step in the helping process.

Clients' perceptions of the agency may also influence their approach to service (Garvin and Seabury, 1997). Does the agency have a negative or positive reputation in the community? Does the agency communicate respect for clients and their cultures in its physical appearance and decor? Are clients greeted at the agency in a courteous and respectful manner? Is the waiting area pleasant and comfortable? Negative agency perceptions can impede the development of a helping relationship and the client's receptiveness to the helping process.

Understanding clients' perceptions of their prior experiences with helping professionals and their expectations for upcoming experiences with the agency is a critical step in the engagement process. Being sensitive to the possibilities of both positive and negative prior experiences enables you to directly address concerns. Communicating empathy about negative experiences and perceptions validates clients' experiences and perceptions. This validation begins the process of coconstructing a more positive mindset regarding the helping process and a willingness to engage in a collaborative helping relationship.

## Expectations about the Helping Experience

Social workers also need to be sensitive to clients' expectations about the helping process and their role as client. "Ignoring or misunderstanding client expectations may result in premature drop out" (Gambrill, 1997, p. 22). Research findings show that clarification of the client role is associated with better outcomes (Orlinsky, Grawe, and Parks, 1994; Yalom, 1995). Client expectations about changes or outcomes should match those of their helpers. Different expectations will affect outcome and client retention.

Clients come to the helping process with various expectations. Some may have little or no hope of making any meaningful change in their lives, whereas others may expect a miracle. Some might be aware of the collaborative nature of the helping process, and others might expect the social worker to fix the problem. Early in your work together, although not necessarily during your first meeting, you need to discuss how you will work together and what your respective roles will be. Clients need to clearly understand the helping process as well as their roles and responsibilities in it. Inappropriate expectations and misunderstandings about how the work will proceed can lead to disillusionment and dissatisfaction. It is important to share your vision of the helping process. It is probably wise to assume that you and your clients have different visions and expectations. These differences need to be reconciled before meaningful work can begin.

## Cultural and Ethnic Diversity

American society is characterized by cultural and racial diversity. Therefore, it is no surprise that social work clients have diverse cultural backgrounds and beliefs. Values and beliefs of different cultural groups might conflict with the values of the dominant culture or with the worker's values and beliefs. Even though social workers and clients often have a great deal in common, the expectation should be one of diversity and heterogeneity. Expect your clients to be unique individuals with different beliefs and values, and expect them to have a belief system that differs from yours in important ways.

The cultural or ethnic background of individuals may influence whether they become clients. Perceived similarities lead to understanding, empathy, and trust. Perceived differences may hinder the development of mutual understanding and trust (Miley, O'Melia, and DuBois, 1998). Perceived differences are barriers to clients' willingness to develop helping relationships. Most people seek out others with whom they feel a connection, a sameness, a likeness. Individuals tend to trust those they perceive as similar and distrust those they perceive as different. The tendency to distrust those who are different makes the task of overcoming cultural and ethnic differences a challenge for all social workers.

The number of potential differences between you and your client is infinite. Differences in values, perspectives, and experiences create barriers to communication and trust. It is your responsibility, as the professional helper, to acknowledge differences directly and communicate respect for your clients' values and beliefs. Rather than viewing cultural differences as threatening, view them as a resource that adds perspectives and options to your relationship with your client (Miley, O'Melia, and DuBois, 1998). Overcoming client-worker differences requires that you acknowledge the differences as well as communicate your understanding of the clients' values, perceptions, and beliefs. Value your clients' differences. Show respect and appreciation of diversity. The differences will remain; what will change is the perception that they are barriers to communication and trust. Directly acknowledging differences early in the helping process increases the likelihood that the individual will become a client. Ignoring cultural and ethnic differences tends to exacerbate the magnitude of differences and hinder the development of trust.

In working with people of color, women, gays and lesbians, and other oppressed populations, it is important to acknowledge that their perceptions and experiences have been subjugated by the dominant culture (Anderson, 2000; Collins, 1990). To understand the experiences of clients, ask questions from a position of not knowing. Be curious, and show a genuine interest in what the client has to say. The client, not the worker, is the expert on his or her perceptions and experiences (Pray, 1991). Client expertise also encompasses cultural, ethnic, and racial experiences and perceptions.

Hartman points out that "in our attempt to become more skilled and more sensitive in our work with people of color, we have sought to gather information about cultures, to learn about difference, to become experts" (1994, p. 29). This approach leads to stereotyping and assumptions that all members of an oppressed group are alike. A better approach is to "abandon our expert role and really listen to our clients and believe and trust their experience" (Hartman, 1994, p. 29). If we listen to our clients, are open to their experiences, and take the position of learning with them and of not knowing, the chances of overcoming our differences are greatly improved.

Another important factor in cross-cultural practice is awareness of self and one's own cultural and ethnic heritage (Greene, Jensen, and Jones, 1996). Being aware of your own ethnic and cultural identity will increase your comfort level in working with clients from different ethnic and cultural backgrounds (Pinderhughes, 1983; Thomas, 2000). A culturally self-aware person is capable of recognizing and acknowledging differences. Social workers who are not aware of their own cultural beliefs and values are more likely to impose their values and beliefs on their clients and to feel threatened by their clients' differences. The more you know about yourself, the more likely you are to want to learn about your clients.

## Client Skills and Knowledge

Clients often seek professional help only after they attempt to resolve problems on their own, with assistance from friends, family, or informal community organizations, or with other helping professionals. First meetings with new clients usually occur after clients have made numerous attempts to cope with their situations. They have a wealth of experience in dealing with their problems. They know what has worked and what has not worked. They probably have ideas about what is making the issue difficult to resolve and what they need to do to successfully resolve it. Be open to and use this knowledge.

Clients bring unique skills to the relationship. Each client has interpersonal skills and competencies. Clients have developed coping strategies and have found ways to get by in spite of pressing life demands and circumstances. They have developed unique ways of adapting to their life experiences. They have been successful, at some level, in coping with their difficulties. They are struggling and need help, but they have managed to survive and cope with challenging situations. All clients bring strengths and skills to the helping relationship.

Clients are empowered when the social worker acknowledges their strengths, knowledge, and skills. They are also encouraged. Clients are given hope when they are viewed as capable and competent individuals. Miley, O'Melia, and DuBois point out that clients' ability to "articulate thoughts and feelings; skills in thinking, planning, and organizing; competencies in giving and receiving support—all are general skills for living that may have relevance for overcoming any challenging situation" (1998, p. 127). Regardless of their level of functioning, irrespective of the severity of their life circumstances, and in spite of the magnitude of the problems that need to be overcome, clients' knowledge and skills can contribute to the resolution of their problem situations. Look for strengths and abilities and expect to find them. It is your job to help clients identify and articulate the knowledge and skills that they bring to the helping process. Recognizing these strengths helps foster collaborative worker–client relationships by increasing clients' willingness to engage in the helping process.

No matter whether a client is voluntary, nonvoluntary, or involuntary, and regardless of the circumstances that bring a client into contact with a generalist social worker, the client has to choose to participate in the helping process. For this to occur, the client has to have progressed at least to the preparation stage of change. The challenge for generalist social workers is to help clients move beyond the precontemplation and contemplation stages, so that clients do not drop out or go through the motions of changing without truly engaging in the helping process.

A number of factors influence clients' ability to engage in helping relationships. One factor is their feelings about getting help and the stigma they feel about asking for help from a stranger. Cultural values and beliefs as well as prior experiences with helping professionals influence these feelings. At best, most clients have mixed feelings about working with a social worker. The social worker must communicate understanding of these feelings and create an expectation that change is possible in order for clients to engage in the helping process. Being sensitive to clients' expectations and their role in the helping process and clarifying the collaborative nature of your work together also help promote client participation.

## SUMMARY

Generalist social work practice involves a wide range of practice skills and interventions. It entails micro-level and macro-level work. Micro interventions focus on individuals, couples, families, and small groups. Macro interventions focus on agency task forces and committees, professional task forces, community coalitions, and neighborhood groups.

The helping relationship in micro interventions is directed toward the enhanced functioning and empowerment of the client systems. The helping relationship in macro interventions at the organizational level focuses on improving organizations and their services as well as developing new services. At the community level, the focus is on improving community conditions, empowering residents, developing resources, increasing awareness, and mobilizing citizens.

Generalist social workers must be skilled in the use of self regardless of the system level of the intervention. The use of self to help individuals, families, and small groups is widely regarded as a fundamental part of direct (micro) practice. It is also a critical component of macro practice. The ability to provide support, increase motivation, foster hope, strengthen commitment, mobilize energy, increase understanding, and facilitate communication is important regardless of the size of the client system. The helping process with individuals, families, groups, organizations, and communities requires generalist social workers who can use the self to help the client make changes.

Generalist practice takes place with individual, family, small group, organization, and community client systems. Thus, generalist social workers are prepared to address both micro-level and macro-level concerns. In addition to working with client systems of various sizes, generalists often work with multiple client systems. Typically, generalists work with a number of different client systems simultaneously. For example, generalist social work with individual clients often entails work with the family system as well as with organizations and community groups within the individual's environmental system. The target systems are those within the client's systems environment that are targeted for change or intervention.

Clients can be voluntary, nonvoluntary, or involuntary. Regardless of the circumstances that bring a client into contact with a generalist social worker, the client has to choose to participate in the helping process. For this to occur, the client must have progressed to at least the preparation stage of change. The challenge for generalist social workers is to help clients move beyond the precontemplation and contemplation stages so that clients do not drop out or merely go through the motions of the helping process.

A number of factors influence clients' ability to engage in helping relationships. One factor is how they feel about getting help and how great a stigma they feel about needing to go to a stranger for assistance play a role. Cultural values and beliefs as well as prior experiences with helping professionals influence these feelings. At best, most clients have mixed feelings about working with a social worker. Communicating understanding of these feelings and creating an expectation that change is possible are critical to having clients engage in the helping process. Being sensitive to clients' expectations and their role in the helping process and clarifying the collaborative nature of your work together also help promote client participation.

# CASE EXAMPLE

The final case in this chapter was written by Leslie Freas, a first-year MSW student placed in an adult partial hospitalization program. The case illustrates the termination process with an individual client who did not want to end the relationship.

---

## CASE 1.3   BUT I'M NOT READY TO LEAVE

### BY LESLIE FREAS

The Senior Care Center is a 16-week partial hospitalization program for individuals aged 65 and over who are experiencing a mental illness. The majority of clients are experiencing depression, often following the onset of a medical condition (i.e., Parkinson's disease, cancer, a stroke) and/or following the loss of a spouse or loved one. Some clients have a long history of mental illness, including major depression, bipolar disorder, schizophrenia, etc. Many of the clients of the Center are either coming out of psychiatric hospitalization or are placed in this program to prevent hospitalization. There are others, however, who are referred by their outpatient psychiatrist, primary physician, or make a self-referral.

The Senior Care Center provides individual and group therapy. The groups consist of psychoeducation, music and art therapy, discharge planning, relapse prevention, and more intense psychotherapy groups. Clients also meet weekly with their social worker for supportive counseling. In addition, the social worker oversees the treatment plan and is responsible for developing the discharge plan.

Mrs. K. is a 77-year-old white woman with a 43-year history of depressive episodes, and has been diagnosed with both major depressive disorder and bipolar disorder. In late 1994, Mrs. K. was diagnosed with Parkinson's disease. Shortly after that she was admitted to the hospital's inpatient psychiatric ward where she received ECT. Following her discharge from the hospital, Mrs. K. was referred to the Senior Care Center for continued mental health treatment and therapy.

After attending the Center for over 3 years, Mrs. K. was told several weeks ago that she is being discharged at the end of March. When she entered the program there was no set time limit on how long a client could stay in the program. Recently the Center was informed by the managed care company that the maximum length of stay would be approximately 16 weeks per client.

Mrs. K.'s biggest obstacle is her physical health. Her Parkinson's has limited her ability to function independently, and it has also started to impair her cognitive abilities, including her memory. In addition, she is suffering from depression. With her medication and the benefits of the Senior Care Center, Mrs. K. has been coping with her depression very well. The concern is that she will fall back into her depression once she is no longer attending the Center.

Mrs. K. still needs to improve her ability to be assertive regarding her needs and wishes. She acknowledges this in her individual sessions with her social worker, and realizes that she especially needs to work on this around the time of her discharge.

Mrs. K., fortunately, also has many strengths. She is a genuinely caring and optimistic person. She is also intelligent and has a wonderful sense of humor. In addition, Mrs. K. is determined to stay active and fight the effects of having Parkinson's disease. She rarely misses her scheduled days at the Center and states that she cannot stand to sit around the house and do nothing. Mrs. K. has a caring, supportive husband and son.

Given her current level of functioning, the treatment team does not feel that her continued participation in the program is justified given the new reimbursement guidelines and policies. Mrs. K., her husband, and their son are upset about her pending discharge. They all feel that she benefits from the treatment she receives at the Center and that after 3+ years the Center has become an important part of her life.

I explored with Mrs. K. her feelings about termination. She was very clear that she did not want to stop coming to the Center every day. She was very fearful of getting depressed again and also fearful about her health deteriorating. I acknowledged her feelings about the termination. Although I could not justify keeping Mrs. K. in the program based on the new guidelines, I felt that Mrs. K. needed the support and stability the program offered. Together we developed the following termination plan:

- Mrs. K., in coordination with case manager, will enroll in the after-care group at the hospital, and attend outpatient therapy at the Center.

- Leslie would investigate the possibility of Mrs. K. receiving physical and/or occupational therapy for Parkinson's through the hospital.
- Mrs. K. will begin attending a Senior Activities Center once a week.
- Mrs. K. would continue to verbalize feelings about being discharged during individual counseling with Leslie and at home with her family members.
- Mrs. K. will verbalize her needs and wishes regarding discharge to the Center staff and her family members.

## DISCUSSION QUESTIONS

1. Discuss the ethics of discharging Mrs. K. and whether or not Leslie is facing an ethical dilemma. What benefits do you see in having Mrs. K. stay in the program? What are the benefits of termination? What are the negatives of staying and leaving? What would you do if you were Leslie?
2. Critique Mrs. K.'s discharge plan. What additional after-care services need to be added to the plan? Would assertiveness training be appropriate for Mrs. K.? (For information on assertiveness training, see Schroeder and Black (1985) and Alberti and Emmons (2001).)
3. List the types of activities you perform in your field placement. For each activity, identify the client system level and client systems. Assess the extent to which your field placement provides micro- and macro-practice experiences.
4. How do the purpose of the helping relationship, the use of self, and the system change activities vary between micro and macro interventions? In what ways are micro interventions similar to macro interventions? In what ways are they different?

## REFERENCES

Alberti, R. E., and Emmons, M. (2001). *Your perfect right: Assertiveness and equality in your life and relationships* (8th ed.). Atascadeno, CA: Impact Publishers, Inc.

Anderson, C. M., and Stewart, S. (1983). *Mastering resistance: A practical guide to family therapy.* New York: Springer.

Anderson, F. S. (2000). Generalist practice with gay and lesbian clients. In J. Poulin, *Collaborative social work: Strengths-based generalist practice* (pp. 357–384). Itasca, IL: F. E. Peacock Publishers, Inc.

Barber, J. G. (1995). Politically progressive casework. *Families in Society,* 76, 30–37.

Billups, J. O. (1992). The moral basis for a radical reconstruction of social work. In P. N. Reid and P. R. Popple (Eds.), *The moral purposes of social work: The character and intentions of a profession* (pp. 100–119). Chicago: Nelson-Hall.

Chavis, D. M., Florin, P., and Felix, M. R. J. (1993). Nurturing grassroots initiatives for community development: The role of enabling systems. In T. Mizrahi and J. D. Morrison (Eds.), *Community organization and social administration* (pp. 41–67). New York: Haworth Press.

Collins, P. H. (1990). *Black feminist thought.* New York: Routledge.

Connaway, R., and Gentry, M. (1988). *Social work practice.* Englewood Cliffs, NJ: Prentice-Hall.

Dorfman, R. (1996). *Clinical social work: Definition, practice, and vision.* New York: Brunner/Mazel.

DuBois, B., and Miley, K. K. (1999). *Social work: An empowering profession* (3rd ed.). Boston: Allyn and Bacon.

Ezell, M. (1994). Advocacy practice of social workers. *Families in Society, 75,* 36–46.

Freire, P. (1990). *Pedagogy of the oppressed.* New York: Continuum.

Freud, S. (1987). Social workers as community educators: A new identity for the profession. *Journal of Teaching in Social Work, 1,* 111–126.

Gambrill, E. (1997). *Social work practice: A critical thinker's guide.* New York: Oxford University Press.

Garvin, C. D., and Seabury, B. A. (1997). *Interpersonal practice in social work: Promoting competence and social justice* (2nd ed.). Boston: Allyn and Bacon.

Goldstein, E. (1995). *Ego psychology and social work practice* (2nd ed.). New York: Free Press.

Greene, G. J., Jensen, C., and Jones, D. H. (1996). A constructivist perspective on clinical social work practice with ethni-cally diverse clients. *Social Work, 41,* 172–180.

Hardcastle, D. A., Wenocur, S., and Powers, P. R. (1997). *Community practice: Theories and skills for social workers.* New York: Oxford University Press.

Hartman, A. (1994). Social work practice. In F. G. Reamer (Ed.), *The foundations of social work knowledge* (pp. 13–50). New York: Columbia University Press.

Haynes, K. S., and Mickelson, J. S. (1991). *Affecting change: Social workers in the political arena* (2nd ed.). New York: Longman.

Hepworth, D., Rooney, R., and Larsen, J. (2002). *Direct social work practice: Theory and skills* (6th ed.). Pacific Grove, CA: Brooks/Cole.

Kirst-Ashman, K., and Hull, G. (1993). *Understanding generalist practice.* Chicago: Nelson-Hall.

Kurzman, P. (1985). Program development and service coordination as components of community practice. In S. H. Taylor and R. W. Roberts (Eds.), *Theory and practice of community social work* (pp. 59–94). New York: Columbia University Press.

Lantz, J., and Lenahan, B. (1976). Referral fatigue therapy. *Social Work, 12,* 239–240.

Lauffer, A. (1981). The practice of social planning. In N. Gilbert and H. Specht (Eds.), *Handbook of the social services* (pp. 583–597). Englewood Cliffs, NJ: Prentice-Hall.

Lewis, E. (1991). Social change and citizen action: A philosophical exploration for modern social group work. *Social Work with Groups, 14,* 23–34.

Maluccio, A. (1979). Perspectives of social workers and clients on treatment outcome. *Social Casework, 60,* 394–401.

Marziali, E., and Alexander, L. (1991). The power of the therapeutic relationship. *American Journal of Orthopsychiatry, 61,* 383–391.

Middleman, R., and Wood, G. (1990). From social group work to social work with groups. *Social Work with Groups, 13,* 3–20.

Miley, K., O'Melia, M., and DuBois, B. L. (1998). *Generalist social work practice: An empowering approach* (2nd ed.). Boston: Allyn and Bacon.

Moxley, D. P. (1997). *Case management by design: Reflections on principles and practices.* Chicago: Nelson-Hall.

Northen, H. (1995). *Clinical social work* (2nd ed.). New York: Columbia University Press.

Orlinsky, D., Grawe, K., and Parks, B. (1994). Process and outcome in psychotherapy-noch einmal. In A. Bergen and S. Garfield (Eds.), *Handbook of psychotherapy and behavior change* (4th ed., pp. 270–376). New York: John Wiley.

Pincus, A., and Minahan, A. (1973). *Social work practice: Model and method.* Itasca, IL: F. E. Peacock Publishers, Inc.

Pinderhughes, E. (1983). Empowerment for our clients and for ourselves. *Social Casework, 64,* 331–338.

Pinderhughes, E. (1995). Direct practice overview. In R. Edwards (Ed.), *Encyclopedia of social work* (19th ed.). Silver Spring, MD: NASW Press.

Pray, J. (1991). Respecting the uniqueness of the individual: Social work practice within a reflective model. *Social Work, 36,* 80–85.

Prochaska, J. O., DiClemente, C. C., and Norcross, J. C. (1992). In search of how people change: Applications to addictive behaviors. *American Psychologist, 47,* 1102–1114.

Reeser, L. C., and Epstein, I. (1990). *Professionalism and activism in social work: The sixties, the eighties, and the future.* New York: Columbia University Press.

Rooney, R. H., (1992). *Strategies for work with involuntary clients.* New York: Columbia University Press.

Rothman, J., and Sager, J. S. (1998). *Case management: Integrating individual and community practice* (2nd ed.). Boston: Allyn and Bacon.

Rubin, H. J., and Rubin, I. S. (1992). *Community organizing and development* (2nd ed.). New York: Macmillan.

Russell, M. (1990). *Clinical social work: Research and practice.* Newbury Park, CA: Sage.

Saleebey, D. (2002). *The strengths perspective in social work practice* (3rd ed.). Boston: Allyn and Bacon.

Schroeder, H. E., and Black, M. J. (1985). Unassertiveness. In M. Hersen and A.S. Bellack (Eds.), *Handbook of clinical behavior therapy with adults* (pp. 509–530). New York: Plenum Press.

Shulman, L. (1999). *The skills of helping individuals, families, groups and organizations* (4th ed.). Itasca, IL: F. E. Peacock Publishers, Inc.

Specht, H. (1988). *New directions for social work.* Englewood Cliffs, NJ: Prentice-Hall.

Staples, L. (1990). Powerful ideas about empowerment. *Administration in Social Work, 14,* 29–42.

Thomas, N.D., (2000). Generalist practice with people of color. In J. Poulin, *Collaborative social work: Strengths-based generalist practice* (pp. 295–326). Itasca, IL: F.E. Peacock Publishers, Inc.

Weick, A., Rapp, C., Sullivan, W., and Kisthardt, S. (1989). A strengths perspective for social work practice. *Social Work, 34,* 350–354.

Weil, M. O., and Gamble, D. N. (1995). Community practice models. In R. Edwards (Ed.), *Encyclopedia of social work* (19th ed.). Silver Spring, MD: NASW Press.

Weissman, A. (1976). Industrial social service: Linkage technology, *Social Casework, 57,* 50–54.

Woodside, M., and McClam, T. (1998). *Generalist case management: A method of human service delivery.* Pacific Grove, CA: Brooks/Cole.

Yalom, I. D. (1995). *Theory and practice of group psychotherapy* (4th ed.). New York: Basic Books.

# THEORETICAL AND CONCEPTUAL FRAMEWORKS FOR GENERALIST PRACTICE

## CHAPTER 2

© Michael Newman/PhotoEdit

23

Karen L. was a first-year MSW student who had recently graduated from college. She had had no prior social work experience when she reported for her first day of field placement at a drug and alcohol treatment program. Karen was excited about beginning her social work career but nervous about working with clients.

The field instructor gave Karen a brief tour of the facility and introduced her to the staff. He then told her that the best way to begin was to "jump right in." He handed her three case files and copies of the agency's assessment form and told her that she was scheduled to conduct assessments of three new residents that morning. Karen felt stunned and overwhelmed as she went to meet her first client.

During the interviews, Karen felt completely lost. She was not sure how to proceed with the interviews. She was unfamiliar with many of the terms on the form. The form used open-ended questions. Karen had to ask clients about their ecosystems, target systems, system strengths and challenges, and factors that might influence their capacity to engage in a helping relationship. Karen did not see her field instructor again that day, and she left feeling discouraged and confused.

Karen's experience is every beginning social work student's worst nightmare. It raises a number of questions and issues. Generalist social workers deal with a wide range of problems in a variety of practice settings (Pinderhughes, 1995). Generalists define client issues, collect and assess data, and plan interventions. Once a problem has been identified and the intervention planned, the generalist selects and implements an appropriate course of action, monitors and evaluates outcomes, and plans termination (Baker, 1995).

This chapter begins with a review of the two major paradigms in social work. It continues with a discussion of the ecosystem and strengths perspectives. The chapter concludes with a review of social work values and ethics. By the end of this chapter, you should be able to help Karen

1. Summarize the differences between modern and postmodern approaches to social work practice
2. Describe the ecosystem perspective and its role in generalist social work practice
3. Interpret the major principles of strengths-based generalist social work practice and understand how strengths-based practice differs from the traditional problem-solving model of practice
4. Describe the core values of the social work profession
5. Assess and resolve any ethical dilemmas that occurred when Karen had to jump right in

All academic disciplines have philosophical and theoretical frameworks. Upon these frameworks are built practice models. The model of strengths-based generalist practice presented here integrates two very different conceptual frameworks: logical positivism and postmodernism.

# MODERN AND POSTMODERN PERSPECTIVES

"The social work profession is deeply rooted in the Enlightenment of the 18th century and its modernist frames of reference" (Irving and Young, 2002). Until recently, empiricism and the scientific approach have dominated the social work profession (Reid, 1994; Weick and Saleebey, 1995, 1998): "the history of the social work profession has been consistently marked by both its adherence to and its attempt to maximize its linkage to a scientific model of knowledge" (Weick, 1993, p. 15). Logical positivism calls for empiricism, objectivity, and neutrality (Allen, 1993). In this tradition, the social worker is an expert who helps clients resolve their problems. The social worker is expected to be a neutral, value-free participant, and the relationship is expected to be hierarchical. There is a power differential between the social worker and the client. Client assessment and diagnosis are based on the superior knowledge of the social worker:

> It was the social worker who determined what the problem was, giving rise to sophisticated and widely varied diagnostic catalogs. It was the social worker who orchestrated the course of treatment, presumably based on the diagnosis. The social worker took the role of actor and organizer; the client took the role of obedient recipient. (Weick, 1993, p. 16).

Social work's adherence to the scientific method began with the publication of Mary Richmond's *Social Diagnosis* in 1917. Richmond viewed "social diagnosis" as a scientific process of gathering facts and testing hypotheses about clients' social functioning. The psychoanalytic-oriented casework movement that began in the 1920s was also based on scientific principles of study, diagnosis, and treatment (Reid, 1994). The psychosocial and psychodynamic approaches that evolved out of the psychoanalytic tradition have dominated social work practice theory from the 1940s to the present.

In the 1960s, the **empirical practice movement** evolved (Reid, 1994). The empirical practice movement stresses the application of research methods to practice with individuals, families, and groups. The distinguishing characteristic of empirical social work is the use of the scientific method in assessing client situations, specifying goals, formulating solution-focused interventions, and evaluating effectiveness (Reid, 1994). Empirical social workers focus on the assessment of relevant facts, the specification of the problem in measurable terms, and the objective assessment of outcomes (Fischer, 1981; Hudson, 1982; Reid, 1994). **Logical positivism** and empirical practice

- Assume the existence of an objective reality that can be measured
- Emphasize the expertise of the helping professional and attribute less importance to the client's own knowledge and experience
- Place knowledge and power in the hands of the objective expert social worker
- Stress the application of research methods in practice
- Require clear specification of client problems

- Involve developing measurable goals and objectives
- Require measuring client progress and outcomes

"Although social work has been slow, even reluctant and resistant at times, to embrace the postmodern cultural surround, a considerable body of writing from the perspective of postmodernism has been accumulating" (Irving and Young, 2002). Thus, logical positivism's dominance in social work is being challenged (Dean, 1993; Greene and Blundo, 1999; Weick, 1987).

**Postmodernism** is based on the assumption that language is used to construct our perceptions of reality (Greene, Jensen, and Jones, 1996). "Constructivism is the belief that we cannot know an objective reality apart from our views of it. . . . Knowledge is not so much discovered as created" (Dean, 1993, p. 58). With postmodernism, the emphasis is on the experiences of individuals and their perceptions of experiences, as well as on the social aspects of knowing and the influence of cultural, historical, political, and economic conditions (Dean, 1993). The interpersonal and interactional aspects of an individual's experiences are stressed. Individuals' perceptions are influenced by their communities and social environment. The individual cannot be separated from his or her interactions with others.

In sharp contrast to logical positivists, postmodernists argue that it is impossible to distinguish facts from values. "Reality is invented, constructed largely out of meanings and values of the observer" (Allen, 1993, p. 32). The constructivist perspective is not value-free; rather, it is value-based (Murphy, 1989). Values, not objective facts, become the central issue of treatment (Allen, 1993; Dean, 1992). The values and attitudes of both the client and the social worker determine what facts are relevant and how they are interpreted. This perspective explicitly recognizes the importance of values in the helping process and encourages their exploration.

Social workers operating under the postmodernist perspective recognize that understanding comes through dialogue and communication with the client. The client is the expert who is most knowledgeable about his or her life situation. The social worker also recognizes that he or she is a coparticipant in the quest for meaning. Worker–client interactions are characterized as collaborative conversations designed to create mutual understanding of the client's life events and issues. "For clients, participating in a dialogue with workers can be both empowering and self-determining . . ." (Irving and Young, 2002). The exploration of each participant's values and beliefs and the process of hearing the client's story is the basis on which the worker–client relationship is developed. Postmodernism

- Highlights the importance of clients' subjective perceptions of their experiences
- Places clients in the role of expert about their life experiences and potential solutions
- Recognizes that clients' perceptions of their experiences are shaped by their culture and social environment

- Views the ongoing dialogue between the social worker and the client as fundamental to the change process
- Requires an open discussion of the social worker's and client's values and beliefs
- Recognizes that meaning is developed through the process of interaction between the worker and the client
- Stresses the collaborative aspects of the worker–client relationship

## ECOSYSTEMS PERSPECTIVE

The ecosystems perspective has been widely adopted as one of the primary conceptual bases of social work practice (Compton and Galaway, 1994; Meyer, 1988). Indeed, one could easily argue that it has been the dominant framework of social work practice since the mid-1970s. The ecosystems perspective fits in well with social work's long-standing mission to address the situational and environmental factors that negatively affect disadvantaged persons.

The heart of the ecosystems perspective is the **person-in-environment concept,** which views individuals and their environments as an interrelated whole (Germain and Gitterman, 1980). "Individuals are perceived as a system composed of biological, psychological (including cognitive), and emotional dimensions. Also, individuals are perceived as interacting with a variety of external systems, such as immediate family, extended family, peers, work or school, and community" (Jordan and Franklin, 1995, p. 5).

The person-in-environment perspective recognizes the interdependence of these various systems. The relationship between individuals and their social environment is reciprocal, with each component in the client's system affecting and being affected by the others. The social environment influences individuals' perceptions of themselves and their interactions with others. Individuals, in turn, influence their social environment (Sullivan, 1992).

In the ecosystems perspective, "understanding the nature of the ecological level of fit between a person's needs, capacities, and aspirations, on the one hand, and environmental resources and expectations, on the other, is the core task in assessing individuals' and collectives' life situations" (Gitterman, 1996, p. 475). The ecosystem perspective "helps the practitioner to see that all aspects of an individual's problem involve circular connections between the individual and environment, leading to a 'transactional focus' for practice that is consistent with social work's dual concern with person and environment" (Wakefield, 1996, p. 6).

A defining characteristic of social work practice, and one that sets it apart from most other helping professions, is the importance given to improving clients' person-in-environment transactions to facilitate their growth, health, and social functioning (Gordon, 1981):

> In attempting to understand a problem in social functioning, you cannot achieve understanding by adding together, as separate entities, the assessment

of the individual and the assessment of the environment. Rather you must strive for a full understanding of the complex interactions between client and all levels of social systems as well as the meaning the client assigns to these interactions. (Compton and Galaway, 1994, p. 118)

The ecosystems perspective recognizes the role of the worker in the client's environmental system (Germain and Gitterman, 1980). Worker–client transactions are viewed as a component of the client's ecological system (Figure 2.1). Interactions between the worker and the client and between the worker and the client's social environment become part of the client's dynamic person-in-environment system. Shulman (1991) portrayed the social worker as "in the middle," between the client and the systems he or she must negotiate. However, this puts the client in "a reactive, secondary role vis-à-vis the worker" (Petr, 1988, p. 624) and portrays the worker as intervening on behalf of the client and responsible for affecting change in the client. In this respect, mutuality and reciprocity do not characterize the worker–client relationship. The interaction is, instead, unidirectional, flowing from worker to client. This is *not* the case in strengths-based generalist practice.

## STRENGTHS PERSPECTIVE

The idea of building on clients' strengths received a lot of attention during the 1990s. It is still fashionable to claim adherence to "the strengths perspective." However, as Saleebey put it:

Many of these calls to attend to the capacities and competencies of clients are little more than professional cant. So let us be clear: The strengths perspective is a dramatic departure from conventional social work practice. Practicing from a strengths orientation means this—everything you do as a social worker will be predicated, in some way, on helping to discover and embellish, explore and exploit clients' strengths and resources. (2002, p. 1)

The strengths perspective is a dramatic departure from the traditional approach, which focuses primarily on client problems and history taking (Hepworth, Rooney and Larsen, 2002, p. 198). Social work has a long history of helping disadvantaged clients overcome individual problems and problem situations. Clients come to us with problems, and there is a natural tendency to attempt to resolve the problems and to view the clients from a deficit perspective. Maluccio (1979) found that social workers' perceptions were in stark contrast with their clients' self-perceptions. The clients viewed themselves as proactive, autonomous human beings who were using counseling services to enhance their functioning and competence. In contrast, social workers tended to underestimate clients' strengths, focusing on their problems, underlying weaknesses, and limited potential.

When social workers focus on problems, they tend to perceive clients in essentially negative terms, as a collection of problems and diagnostic labels. This negative perception may lower expectations for positive change. More

FIGURE 2.1 | PERSON-IN-ENVIRONMENT ASSESSMENT

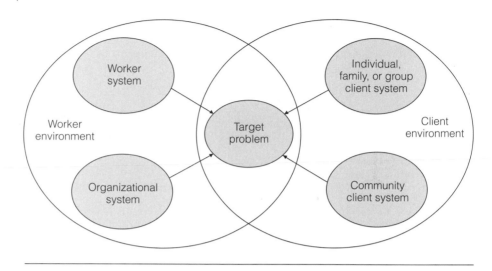

likely than not, clients are seen as diagnostic categories or their presenting problems, or both. These labels may create distance between clients and helpers (Saleebey, 2002, p. 5). They also create pessimism in both parties. Negative labels and expectations obscure the unique capabilities of clients. The social worker's ability to recognize and promote a client's potential for change is markedly reduced. The focus is on what is wrong and the client's inability to cope with his or her life situation. Saleebey (2002) suggests that instead of focusing on problems, we should focus on possibilities.

The pathologic problem approach searches the past for causes. How did the client get into this situation? Why is the client experiencing these difficulties? The search for causes and rational explanations assumes a direct link between cause, disease, and cure (Saleebey, 2002). Human experience is rarely that simple. More often than not, it is uncertain and tremendously complex. In addition, looking to the past diverts attention away from exploring the present. The shift from problems to strengths moves the focus from the past to the present and future. Strengths-oriented social workers seek to discover the resources clients currently have that can be used to change their futures. The past cannot be completely dismissed, because it provides a context for the present. However, in strengths-based practice the focus is on the present and the future.

Social work has a long tradition of dealing with problems as ordinary aspects of human life. The profession's early efforts in charity organizations and settlement houses developed "family-oriented and community-oriented strategies to help those who were caught in the tide of major social upheaval"

(Weick and Chamberlain, 1997, p. 40). However, during the 1940s, social problems and problems of everyday life were redefined as complex intrapsychic pathologic factors. "Psychological and psychiatric theories made human actions mysterious, complex, and rarely what they seemed" (Weick and Chamberlain, 1997, p. 41). Psychological definitions of problems and the focus on why a pathologic situation occurred have become the dominant perspective in social work, diverting attention from the "profession's historic commitment to working with people in the midst of their daily lives" (Weick and Chamberlain, 1997, p. 42).

Rather than focusing on why clients are having problems, social workers who have adopted a strengths perspective ask these questions:

> What do clients want? What do they need? How do they think they can get it? How do they see their situation—problems as well as possibilities? What values do they want to maximize? How have they managed to survive thus far? (Saleebey, 2002, p. 6)

These and similar questions will help you and your clients identify, use, build, and reinforce clients' strengths, resources, and abilities.

## Principles of Strengths-Based Practice

Six principles guide strengths-based generalist practice (Saleebey, 2002). They also link the strengths perspective to the core values of the profession. "Social work practice is not only about whether and how to intervene or about skills and techniques, but also about our entire attitude and stance toward the world, others, and human relations . . ." (Irving and Young, 2002).

**Principle 1: Every individual, group, family, and community has strengths.** Regardless of the situation, every person, family, and community possesses assets, resources, wisdom, and knowledge that you need to discover (Saleebey, 2002). To become aware of these strengths, you need to be genuinely interested in your clients and respectful of their perceptions of their own experiences:

> In the end, clients want to know that you actually care about them, that how they fare makes a difference to you, that you will listen to them, that you will respect them no matter what their history, and that you believe that they can build something of value with the resources within and around them. But most of all, clients want to know that you believe they can surmount adversity and begin the climb toward transformation and growth. (Saleebey, 2002, p. 14)*

The ultimate key to identifying client strengths is your belief in the client and his or her possibilities. Adopting a strengths perspective requires you to view your clients as underused sources of knowledge and untapped resources.

**Principle 2: Trauma, abuse, illness, and struggle may be injurious, but they may also be sources of challenge and opportunity.**   Dwelling on clients' pasts and hardships promotes "an image of themselves as helpless in the past, which then [becomes] the basis for fault-finding and continued helplessness in the present" (Wolin and Wolin, 1993, p. 14). Focusing on past hurts and deficits leads to discouragement, pessimism, and what Wolin and Wolin (1993) call the "victim trap." What is more extraordinary is that your clients have survived and that they are working with you to bring about changes in their lives. There is dignity and affirmation in having prevailed over trauma, abuse, illness, and other difficult situations. The strength of having survived and coped with numerous obstacles is often lost on clients who are struggling to meet life's daily challenges. A strengths approach recognizes clients' inherent competencies, resilience, and resourcefulness in having survived past difficulties as well as their current motivation for growth and development.

**Principle 3: Assume that you do not know the upper limits of the capacity to grow and change, and take individual, group, and community aspirations seriously.**  Simply put, this means that you should set high expectations for your clients and help expand their hopes, visions, and aspirations. The strengths perspective is the perspective of hope and possibilities. Believe in clients' capacities for change, growth, and self-actualization. If you do not believe in their abilities and motivation, you really do not believe in the possibility of change. Creating hope where there is little to hope for, strengthening belief when there is little to believe in, and creating aspirations where there are none is the essence of social work practice from a strengths perspective.

**Principle 4: We best serve clients by collaborating with them.**  The strengths perspective calls for a partnership characterized by reciprocity and mutual respect between you and your client. There should be a sharing of knowledge and resources. You are not the sole expert or the only one with specialized information; your client is the expert who knows more about coping with his or her situation than you do:

> A helper may best be defined as a collaborator or consultant: an individual clearly presumed, because of specialized education and experience, to know some things and to have some tools at the ready but definitely not the only one in the situation to have relevant, even esoteric, knowledge and understanding. (Saleebey, 2002, p. 16)

Take advantage of the wisdom, insights, and understanding your clients bring to the helping process by entering into a collaborative partnership with them. The strengths approach to social work practice requires it. Work with your clients in partnership. Do not presume to work *on* your clients or to do the work *for* them.

**Principle 5: Every environment is full of resources.**  No matter how deprived a client's community, neighborhood, or family system, each has an abundance of untapped resources. "In every environment, there are individuals, associations, groups, and institutions who have something to give, something that others may desperately need: knowledge, succor, an actual resource or talent, or simply time and place" (Saleebey, 2002, p. 17). Looking to these untapped resources does not negate our responsibility to work for social and economic justice, and it does not mean that we accept the notion that a disadvantaged person should assume sole responsibility for his or her situation and its amelioration. It does mean, however, that the possibilities for identifying and arranging needed resources for clients from within their own environment are more numerous than you would expect.

**Principle 6: Caring, caretaking, and context are important.**    Caring for others and being cared for is a basic human right. "Families must be permitted and assisted in caring for their members" (Saleebey, 2002, p. 17, citing Stone, 2000). Caring strengthens our social web, our interconnectedness. Social work is a caring profession, and the strengths perspective recognizes and embraces our dependence upon others for our well-being.

Case 2.1 illustrates how Dawn W., a first-year social work student, built on her client's strengths to further his treatment goals.

## SOCIAL WORK VALUES AND ETHICS

The practice of social work is based on a number of value positions and principles that guide the work with clients irrespective of the approach used, the presenting client problem, the client population, or the setting in which services are provided. These values and principles apply to all forms of social work practice.

## Core Social Work Values

Social work is a value-based profession (Reamer, 1990). Values provide the basis for professional social work practice (Loewenberg and Dolgoff, 1992). They guide the actions we take and our evaluations of what is "good" (DuBois and Miley, 1999). Values represent "a constellation of preferences concerning what merits doing and how it should be done" (Levy, 1976, p. 234).

Social work has a rich tradition of principles and beliefs. The heart of these is reflected in the 1997 National Association of Social Workers (NASW) Code of Ethics. The Code of Ethics identifies core social work values and associated ethical principles. Four of these values—service to others, social justice, dignity and worth of the person, and importance of human relationships—play a critical role in generalist practice.

**Service to Others**    The first ethical principle states that "social workers' primary goal is to help people in need and to address social problems" (NASW, 1996, p. 5). Service to others is placed above self-interest.

- Social work is a service profession dedicated to providing help to individuals, families, and groups in need and to improving community and

| CASE 2.1 | NO TIME FOR ME |

John R. is an 11-year-old boy with behavior management problems. He has attention deficit hyperactivity disorder and has a great deal of difficulty controlling his impulses. He is socially immature. His peers usually make fun of him and reject him. He usually plays with much younger children. In addition to his behavior problems, he has a very difficult family situation. His mother lives out of state. He lives with his father, stepmother, and 18-month-old stepsister. His stepmother resents his presence in the family and the difficulties he causes her.

John is a student at an alternative school, where he is in a special behavior modification program. Dawn W. is John's social worker at the school and is also assigned to work with the family. The behavior management program is working well, but John's relationship with his stepmother is undermining his progress at home. The stepmother refuses to follow the treatment plan and is very rejecting. In fact, she openly tells John that he is bad and that she does not want him anywhere near his stepsister. While at home, John is generally either being punished or is alone in his room.

One of the treatment goals is to improve the relationship between John and his stepmother. Dawn recognized that one of John's strengths is that he is very good with young children. He is thoughtful and caring and has a nice way of engaging them in play. Dawn suggests to John's stepmother that she allow him to take care of his little sister for one hour a day. The plan is to have Dawn supervise John for the first week or until the stepmother is comfortable with John's ability to care for his sister.

The intervention is successful. John takes care of his little sister well, and his appreciation of being allowed to play with and care for her is evident. His stepmother's confidence in and patience with him improves. John's self-esteem appears to improve, as does his overall relationship with his stepmother. By recognizing one of John's strengths and enlisting that strength in the case plan, Dawn ensures progress on a critical treatment goal.

---

social conditions. This commitment to service is reflected in the goals of the profession:

- To enhance social functioning of individuals, families, groups, organizations, and communities
- To link client systems with needed resources
- To improve the operation of social service programs and service delivery systems
- To promote social and economic justice through advocacy and policy development (DuBois and Miley, 1999, p. 11)

Inherent in each of these goals is service to others. All four goals focus on helping others directly by enhancing their capacities to resolve problems and indirectly by linking clients with resources, improving service delivery systems, and developing social programs and policies.

**Social Justice**   Social justice has long been valued in social work. Concern with social justice and inequality in the profession goes back to the advocacy efforts of Jane Addams and the settlement house movement of the early 1900s (Mickelson, 1995).

The Code of Ethics identifies social justice as a core social work value and states that challenging social injustice is an ethical principle of the profession:

Social workers pursue social change, particularly with and on behalf of vulnerable and oppressed individuals and groups of people. Social workers' social change efforts are focused primarily on issues of poverty, unemployment, discrimination and other forms of social injustice. . . . Social workers strive to ensure access to needed information, services, and resources; equality of opportunity; and meaningful participation in decision making for all people. (NASW, 1996, p. 5)

Beverly and McSweeney define "justice as fairness in the relationships between people as these relate to the possession and/or acquisition of resources" (1987, p. 6). Social workers traditionally work with people who are victims of discrimination and prejudice. Many of our clients are unemployed or underemployed, have limited access to resources, received inadequate education and training, and are among the most disadvantaged members of society. They often face prejudicial attitudes and are "identified as 'lesser'—less capable, less productive, and less normal" (DuBois and Miley, 1999, p. 148). Social injustice is manifested in discrimination on the basis of race, gender, social class, sexual orientation, age, and disability. Prejudicial attitudes provide justification for "social structures that provide fewer prospects—fewer opportunities, fewer possibilities, and fewer resources—for those with lower status" (DuBois and Miley, 1999, p. 148).

Social workers' commitment to social justice is based on concern about the negative effect of discrimination and prejudice on disadvantaged populations. We often work with clients who have been denied basic rights and opportunities. We are called on to challenge social injustice and to increase the opportunities, possibilities, and resources of our clients. We have an ethical responsibility to address the social, physical, and economic needs of our clients as well as their psychological needs.

**Human Dignity and Self-Worth**    A third core value is to treat our clients in a caring and respectful fashion, being mindful of individual differences and cultural and ethnic diversity. The underlying assumption of this value is that "all human beings have intrinsic worth, irrespective of their past or present behavior, beliefs, lifestyle, race, or status in life" (Hepworth, Rooney and Larsen, 2002, p. 59). As a social worker, you are expected to treat your clients with respect and dignity. They deserve respect by virtue of their humanness. This does not mean that you have to agree with your clients' life choices or decisions. It does mean that you should strive to affirm their dignity and self-worth. Not doing so can have profound negative effects on the helping process.

Hepworth, Rooney, and Larsen point out that "before people will risk sharing personal problems and expressing deep emotions, they must first feel fully accepted and experience the good-will and helpful intent of practitioners" (2002, p. 59). This attitude is more important when clients' problematic behaviors involve moral, social, or legal infractions. A client whose behavior has violated social and cultural norms is not likely to engage in a collaborative helping relationship with a professional who communicates disapproval and condemnation.

Closely associated with respect for the individual is a nonjudgmental attitude. The social worker must not blame the client in attitude or behavior (Biestek, 1957). You should focus on understanding clients and their difficulties and on helping them find solutions or alternative ways of behaving. If you blame them for their difficulties and assign pejorative labels, most will become defensive and unwilling to trust you. The more you understand the life experience of your clients, no matter how personally distressing their behavior or beliefs may be, the more likely it is that you will be able to accept them as human beings who may have "suffered various forms of deprivation and have themselves been victims of harsh, abusive, rejecting, or exploitative behavior" (Hepworth, Rooney, and Larsen, 2002, p. 60).

Many of our clients' behaviors conflict with our personal values and beliefs. More often than not, there will be a clash of values between you and your clients. These differences should be viewed as a normal part of generalist social work practice. Expect them and accept them. There are going to be differences, in fact, there are going to be major differences. If you focus on your values and assign blame to clients for adopting behaviors or attitudes with which you disagree, you will not be able to help them.

Adopting nonjudgmental attitudes is a prerequisite for developing effective working relationships (Perlman, 1979). The challenge is to maintain your own values without imposing them on others and without judging those whose behavior and beliefs are in conflict with your belief system. To accomplish this, you need to be open to others and treat everyone with respect and dignity. This is difficult when you have negative feelings about your client. You are human, and you will have negative feelings about some clients. Pretending that you do not have these feelings will not work; clients will sense insincerity and negative reactions. The best approach is to try to understand your client and communicate that understanding to him or her in a caring and nonjudgmental manner. Clients are not seeking your approval; they are seeking your help. They need to feel that they have been heard and that you understand them and their situations. They need to feel that you care and that you want to work with them. Communicating care and concern facilitates the helping process. If clients perceive you as judging and blaming them, they are not likely to accept help from you.

**Importance of Human Relationships**   A fourth core value of social work is the importance of human relationships. "Positive social exchanges may be the strongest elements shaping and enriching human life; adverse and coercive social exchanges are among the deepest sources of human pain" (Mattaini, 1997, p. 120). The Code of Ethics states that "social workers seek to strengthen relationships among people in a purposeful effort to promote, restore, maintain, and enhance the well-being of individuals, families, social groups, organizations, and communities" (NASW, 1996, p. 6). Focusing on the relationship issues of clients is common in generalist social work. Many clients need help in improving their human relationships and interpersonal interactions. "Deficits and excesses in social behavior often result in severe isolation (and loneliness), and many clients seen individually identify improvements in relationships among their most important goals" (Mattaini, 1997, p. 120).

Historically, the helping relationship has been given a central role in the helping process (Biestek, 1957; Perlman, 1979). The Code of Ethics states that "social workers engage people as partners in the helping process" (NASW, 1996, p. 6). **Relationship** implies that there is a reciprocal interactive process between two people. In social work, the helping relationship is a partnership. You and the client both have input and make decisions together. You are joint participants. Social workers do not solve problems for their clients; they work with clients and help them solve their own problems.

Beginning social workers often feel that unless they are doing something specific and concrete for their clients, they are not being helpful. You will be tempted to do things for clients, using your skills and abilities to get the task done and hand over the results to clients. It will make you feel useful and productive. Avoid the temptation, because it is a trap. More often than not, clients will not appreciate your generous efforts on their behalf. By doing work for them, you will put them in a dependent position, highlighting their inability to manage their lives. No one likes feeling incompetent and dependent. Rather than making your clients dependent on you, empower them. Help them help themselves. Help them do whatever they need to do to manage their own lives as best they can. Ultimately, your clients must become confident and learn to do tasks for themselves. The helping relationship in social work is a collaborative partnership. Social workers do not work *for* clients; rather they work *with* clients.

## Ethical Standards

The core social work values and ethical principles embody the ideals to which all social workers should aspire. The Code of Ethics sets specific standards and explains how the core values and principles influence the actions of professional social workers. "Values are concerned with what is good and desirable, while ethics deal with what is right and correct" (Loewenberg and Dolgoff, 1992, p. 21). The standards spell out social workers' ethical responsibilities to clients, to colleagues, in practice settings, as professionals, to the social work profession, and to the broader society (NASW, 1997, p. 7). They are detailed, comprehensive guidelines for professional conduct. For example, the standards for ethical responsibilities to clients cover sixteen areas, including commitment to clients, self-determination, informed consent, and competence (see Table 2.1). A detailed discussion of each ethical standard in the six professional practice areas may be found in the Code of Ethics.

The guidelines in the ethical standards section of the Code of Ethics provide a basis for formulating judgments regarding unethical behavior and help resolve value conflicts. It is your responsibility as a professional social worker to be familiar with the Code of Ethics and follow it in your professional practice.

TABLE 2.1 | OUTLINE OF ETHICAL STANDARDS

**Social workers' ethical responsibilities to clients**

| | | |
|---|---|---|
| Commitment to clients | Self-determination | Informed consent |
| Competence | Cultural competence | Conflicts of interest |
| Confidentiality | Access to records | Sexual relationships |
| Physical contact | Sexual harassment | Derogatory language |
| Payment for services | Decision-making capacity | Interruption of services |
| Termination of services | | |

**Social workers' ethical responsibilities to colleagues**

| | | |
|---|---|---|
| Respect | Confidentiality | Interdisciplinary collaboration |
| Disputes involving colleagues | Consultation | Referral for services |
| Sexual relationships | Sexual harassment | Impairment of colleagues |
| Incompetence of colleagues | Unethical conduct of colleagues | |

**Social workers' ethical responsibilities in practice settings**

| | | |
|---|---|---|
| Supervision and consultation | Education and training | Performance evaluation |
| Client records | Billing | Client transfer |
| Administration | Staff development | Commitments to employers |
| Labor–management disputes | | |

**Social workers' ethical responsibilities as professionals**

| | | |
|---|---|---|
| Competence | Discrimination | Private conduct |
| Dishonesty, fraud, and deception | Impairment | Misrepresentation |
| Solicitations | Acknowledging credit | |

**Social workers' ethical responsibilities to the social work profession**

Integrity of the profession, evaluation, and research

**Social workers' ethical responsibilities to the broader society**

| | |
|---|---|
| Social welfare | Public participation |
| Social and political action | Public emergencies |

## Ethical Dilemmas

Social workers frequently have ethical obligations to several parties at the same time. For example, we have ethical obligations to both our clients and our employing organizations. This creates the possibility of conflict, or ethical dilemmas. "An ethical dilemma occurs when you cannot simultaneously meet your obligations to two different parties in the role set without violating your ethical commitment to one or the other" (Compton and Galaway, 1994, p. 240). In these situations, you are forced to "choose between two apparent goods or to avoid two equally undesirable courses of action" (McGowan, 1995, p. 35). Because we have ethical responsibilities to our clients, our colleagues, our practice settings, the profession, and the broader society, value conflicts and ethical dilemmas occur often within and between the six areas of professional responsibilities outlined in Table 2.1.

Resolving ethical dilemmas is never easy or straightforward. Rarely is there a clear-cut right or wrong choice. The choice is between two seeming "rights"; the task is to determine which "right" is more so given the circumstances.

The first step in addressing ethical dilemmas is to refer to the Code of Ethics for clarification of the standards of practice. The Code, however, does not offer bases for choosing between two or more conflicting standards. A number of guidelines have been developed to help resolve ethical dilemmas. A hierarchy of value assumptions is the basis for decision making (Loewenberg and Dolgoff, 1992; Reamer, 1990; Rhodes, 1991). One such hierarchy is shown in Table 2.2.

The first guideline in Table 2.2 proposes that a person's right to health and well-being takes precedence over the right of confidentiality. If you had to choose between protecting a person's health and well-being and violating a client's confidentiality, you would choose health and well-being. For example, the right of neglected and abused children to protection takes precedence over their parents' rights to confidentiality.

The second guideline proposes that a person's right to health and well-being takes precedence over another person's right to privacy, freedom, or self-determination. When you must choose between protecting a person's freedom and protecting another person from harm, the choice is to protect the person from harm. For example, if a client reveals plans to seek physical revenge on his or her former spouse, you should warn the former spouse.

The third guideline states that a person's right to self-determination takes precedence over his or her own right to well-being. That is, an individual's self-determination supersedes that person's well-being. The principle promotes freedom to choose and possibly fail or make mistakes. It protects the right of people to carry out actions that do not appear to be in their own best interests, as long as they are competent to make informed and voluntary decisions. However, the first guideline takes precedence if the individual's decision might result in death or serious harm. For example, you must take action to protect a client who is at risk of committing suicide.

The final guideline proposes that the right to well-being may override agency policies and procedural rules. Social workers are obligated to follow the policies and procedures of social work agencies, voluntary associations, and organizations. When agency policy has a negative effect on a client's well-being, however, violating the policy or procedure may be justified. "It would be permissible, for example, for a social worker who is prohibited from treating clients outside of the agency to counsel a suicidal client who has called from home to request assistance" (Reamer, 1983, pp. 34–35).

The guidelines described above—or any other guidelines—will not provide "unambiguous and commonly accepted solutions to ethical dilemmas" (Reamer, 1983, p. 35). Guidelines prioritize values to help clarify your thinking about ethical issues. Resolving ethical dilemmas almost always entails making value judgments and subjective interpretations. For example, the third

TABLE 2.2 | ETHICAL GUIDELINES

1. The rights to life, health, well-being, and necessities of life are superordinal and take precedence over rights to confidentiality and opportunities for additive "goods" such as wealth, education, and recreation.
2. An individual's basic right to well-being takes precedence over another person's right to privacy, freedom, or self-determination.
3. People's right to self-determination takes precedence over their right to basic well-being providing they are competent to make informed and voluntary decisions with consideration of relevant knowledge and so long as the consequences of their decisions do not threaten the well-being of others.
4. Person's rights to well-being may override laws, policies, and arrangements of organizations. (Hepworth, Rooney and Larsen, 2002, pp. 77–78, based on Reamer, 1990).

guideline states that a person's right to self-determination takes precedence over his or her right to basic well-being, provided he or she is competent to make an informed decision. A social worker may have to apply this guideline to a person who is mentally ill and homeless, who prefers to remain on the street, and who has little or no interest in participating in a treatment program. Does this person have the right to refuse treatment as well as the right to live wherever he or she wants? The complicating factor in this situation is determining the person's competence and the degree of physical or mental harm that is likely to ensue. Can a person who is mentally ill, delusional, and exhibiting psychotic behavior make informed decisions? At what point does refusing shelter or treatment create a serious risk of physical and mental harm? Clearly, the answers to these questions are subjective and open to value judgments.

In attempting to resolve ethical dilemmas, always invoke the concept of shared responsibility and decision making. Do not make the decision on your own; enlist others in the process. Get your supervisor's or administrator's advice and approval before you take action on an ethical dilemma. Case 2.2 illustrates the difficult decisions involved in resolving ethical dilemmas.

Jill is faced with an ethical dilemma. She has been told by her supervisor to follow an agency policy that she believes is not in the best interests of her clients. What are Jill's options? Is it advisable for her to apply guideline four and disregard agency policy? What might be the consequences of such an action? How should she attempt to resolve her dilemma?

## SUMMARY

The ecosystems perspective is one of two primary frameworks guiding the model of generalist social work practice presented in this book. The heart of the ecosystems perspective is the person-in-environment concept. Clients are not viewed in isolation but rather within the context of their environments.

## CASE 2.2 | DON'T ROCK THE BOAT

Jill is a first-year MSW student who has been placed in an after-school program for emotionally disturbed children. The program is run by a comprehensive mental health agency that offers a wide range of services for children and adults. The agency is a subsidiary of a larger organization that owns and operates a large number of in-patient and out-patient mental health facilities. The after-school program has two full-time social workers, a case aide, a half-time supervisor, and a quarter-time program administrator. Approximately 20 children with emotional and behavioral problems are provided with on-site services five days a week and in-home services once a week.

Because of a technicality, the program lost its primary source of funding and was slated to close. Jill found out about the pending closing of the program from her supervisor. She was told not to tell the other staff or the children. The program administrator had decided that it was best for the children, their parents, and the staff not to know in advance about the closing.

Jill was concerned about the children's need to have enough time to deal with their feelings about leaving the program and about the parents' needs to have time to make other arrangements for the treatment and after-school care of their children. She also wondered how the lack of process about closing the program would affect the staff and their morale.

Jill believed that the well-being of the children was being subjugated to the perceived needs of the agency. She suspected that the agency administrator felt that telling the children and their parents would upset them and that the children would act out more than usual during the time remaining in the program. She also suspected that he wanted to avoid having the parents put pressure on the agency to continue the program. It appeared to her that the closing policy was designed to protect the agency from disruption at the expense of the children and their parents.

---

The focus is on the level of fit between the client system and the environment and on improving person-in-environment transactions to facilitate growth, empowerment, health, and social and economic justice.

The strengths perspective is the second framework or philosophical perspective guiding the model of generalist social work practice presented in this book. The strengths perspective provides a lens for viewing client situations that is very different from the traditional problem-focused approaches to social work practice. From the strengths perspective, the helping process emphasizes client strengths and resources as opposed to limitations and deficits. The client rather than the social worker is recognized as the expert. The focus of strengths-based generalist practice is on developing partnerships, empowerment, and collaboration.

The application of the ecosystem and strengths perspectives in generalist practice takes place with individual, family, small group, organization, and community client systems. Thus, generalist social workers are prepared to address both micro-level and macro-level concerns. In addition to working with client systems of various sizes generalist social workers often work with multiple client systems. Typically, generalist social workers work with a number of different client systems simultaneously. For example, generalist social work with individual clients often entails work with the family system as well as with organizations and community groups within the individual's environmental system. The target systems are persons or situations within the client's systems environment that are targeted for change or intervention.

Strengths-based generalist practice is consistent with the core values of social work. The social work profession and strengths-based generalist practice both emphasize service to others, social justice, human dignity and self-worth, and the importance of human relationships. Generalist social workers incorporate these core values into their work with clients and use the ethical principles described in the profession's Code of Ethics to help resolve issues related to clients, colleagues, agencies, the profession, and the broader society. Ethical dilemmas occur when an individual has to choose between two or more conflicting ethical standards. Ethical dilemmas can be resolved by using a hierarchical decision-making approach. This approach is useful when a social worker is faced with a choice between two apparent goods or two equally undesirable courses of action.

## CASE EXAMPLE

The final case in this chapter (Case 2.3) was written by Daniel Lafferty when he was a first-year MSW student. It describes one client with whom he worked in his field placement. The case illustrates the differences between a strengths-based approach and the traditional deficit approach.

---

## UNDER A CLOUD

BY DANIEL LAFFERTY

**Practice Setting**

The Parents and Children Together (PACT) program functions as a family preservation agency whose main mission is to support family well-being, prevent child abuse and neglect, and promote optimal child development. This mission is carried out via parenting skills training, family needs assessments, and assisting clients to assess needed resources. Clients are referred to the program through Children and Youth Services (CYS), the county public child welfare agency. The referral objectives are to prepare parents to be reunited with children that have been placed in foster care due to abuse or neglect or to prevent the removal of at-risk children from their homes by helping their parents to learn better parenting skills. PACT clients are expected to participate in agency-based parenting skills training every other week. In addition, home visits are scheduled for non-program weeks, so that clients can demonstrate learned parenting skills in the family's natural environment.

**Problem Situation**

Mr. J. is a 34-year-old single white man who works part time as a construction worker. He was referred to the PACT program by CYS following his daughter's placement in foster care due to neglect. Mr. J.'s daughter was three years old and living with her mother at the time of placement. Since then, Mr. J. has made it known that he intends to seek custody of his daughter. Mr. J. has been working with the staff at PACT, attending parenting classes and meeting with his daughter for one-hour supervised home visits every two weeks in preparation for this goal. Because Mr. J. was separated from his daughter during the years prior to her foster care placement, he is interested in building a father–daughter relationship with her that can result in his being awarded full custody of his daughter.

*(continued)*

CASE 2.3  |  *continued*

## History of Problem Situation

Mr. J. states that in 1992 he became involved in an intimate relationship. After a few months, his paramour informed him that she was pregnant. The couple continued to live together after their daughter was born. Three months after the birth of their daughter, Mr. J.'s paramour took their daughter and left to live with her parents because Mr. J. "refused to become a born-again Christian." Following this separation, Mr. J. had only sporadic involvement with his daughter. For the first three years of his daughter's life, the girl's mother reportedly denied him contact for religious reasons.

Mr. J. states that when he attempted to have contact with his daughter, he noticed that she was being neglected by her mother. He claims that on several occasions he made reports to CYS about his concerns, but none of the agency's investigations established a case of neglect until the last one, in February, 1997. At that time, his daughter was found to be extremely developmentally delayed and showed signs of emotional and medical neglect. Mr. J.'s daughter was placed in foster care as a result of these findings. Since that time, she has made remarkable progress. The mother is described as suffering from a serious mental illness. She has not made any attempts to regain custody of her daughter to date.

Following his daughter's placement in foster care, Mr. J. began working with CYS and the PACT program in an attempt to gain custody. Due to the early and lengthy separation between Mr. J. and his daughter, it was decided that they needed time to form a parent–child relationship before custody could be considered. Although progress has been made in this regard, Mr. J. believes the process has been slower than necessary because of restrictive handling of his case by CYS.

There are several reasons why the CYS staff appear to be reluctant about Mr. J. gaining custody of his daughter. Mr. J. has a significant substance abuse history (about 20 years of marijuana abuse), and questions have been raised about his mental health. Over six months ago, Mr. J. decided to seek treatment for his marijuana use. Recently, he completed a residential rehabilitation program and subsequent outpatient substance abuse treatment. He claims to have abstained from all substance abuse since entering rehab.

At the present time, questions about Mr. J.'s mental health status remain unanswered. Psychiatric assessments have been conflicting. Mr. J.'s substance use at the time of some of these evaluations may have contributed to the findings. The CYS worker assigned to the case has serious concerns about his mental health. The general opinion of the PACT staff is that Mr. J. does not suffer from a major mental disorder, although at times he does exhibit character traits consistent with a dependent personality disorder. The CYS worker is also concerned about his employment situation and his ability to provide full-time care for his daughter.

## Current Situation

Mr. J. has been consistent in visiting his daughter. He has attended all of the scheduled parent training classes and has met with his PACT social worker weekly. He is very motivated to establish a strong parent–child relationship and obtain custody of his daughter. He is looking for a full-time job, but the parenting classes and visitation schedule make it difficult for him to do so.

Mr. J.'s interactions with his daughter at the PACT program and during their visits are appropriate. His daughter appears to be comfortable with him, and their relationship is growing stronger. She seems to enjoy the visits and talks positively about going to live with her father.

The CYS worker continues to have concerns about Mr. J.'s suitability as a full-time parent and is very reluctant to increase his visitation privileges. The foster mother has become very attached to the daughter and has indicated that she wants to adopt her if possible. The foster mother does not seem to approve of having Mr. J. visit his daughter. She claims that it upsets the child and that she has no interest in visiting with her father. The foster mother frequently finds excuses to cancel the scheduled visits.

## Client System Obstacles and Strengths

The impact of certain obstacles is evident in the problem situation of this client. Mr. J.'s substance abuse history complicates the custody issues. If he relapses, the child may be at risk for further neglect. The extent of Mr. J.'s marijuana use appears to have created a negative impression of him among some of the staff in the child protection system. Another potential obstacle is the recent revelation that the foster mother may wish to adopt Mr. J.'s daughter. This has put a strain on the visits (she brings Mr. J.'s daughter to the visits), and it seems that she has the support of the CYS worker assigned to the case.

Mr. J.'s use of marijuana on an almost daily basis since he was 11 years old may have had serious implications for his developmental life stages. It is not surprising that he appears immature in certain life domains. Addressing this issue will be important

if Mr. J. is to gain insight into the source of some of his difficulties, especially with interpersonal relationships.

Mr. J.'s strengths include his decision to discontinue his substance use, the recent establishment of a healthier support system, weekly drug and alcohol and mental health counseling, having an AA/NA sponsor, PACT staff who are helping to increase the quality and number of visits with his daughter, and his supportive parents, who assist with these visits. In addition, Mr. J.'s expressed commitment to be reunited with his daughter is a real strength. He has been very cooperative with the demands that CYS has made on him in the interest of this goal.

## DISCUSSION QUESTIONS

1. Identify the various system levels associated with Mr. J.'s case. How does each system affect his attempts to obtain custody of his daughter?
2. What additional services or interventions might be appropriate for Mr. J.? To what extent has Dan been an advocate for Mr. J. in gaining custody of his daughter? How might Dan have strengthened his advocacy services? (For more information on social work advocacy, see Schneider and Lester, 2001).
3. Apply the six principles of strengths-based practice to Mr. J.'s case. How does viewing the case from a strengths perspective differ from the child protective worker's perspective?
4. What factors in Mr. J.'s background potentially influence his relationship with the PACT social worker? How might the social worker strengthen the helping relationship?
5. What additional information would you want to obtain if you were the social worker assigned to this case? What unanswered questions do you have about the case?
6. What social work values appear to have a bearing on this case? Are there any ethical dilemmas that you would want to address? If so, how would you resolve them?

## REFERENCES

Allen, J. A. (1993). The constructivist paradigm: Values and ethics. In Joan Laird (Ed.), *Revisioning social work education: A social constructionist approach* (pp. 31–54). New York: Haworth.

Baker, R. L. (1995). The social work dictionary (3rd ed.). Washington, DC: NASW Press.

Beverly, D. P., and McSweeney, E. A. (1987). *Social welfare and social justice.* Englewood Cliffs, NJ: Prentice-Hall.

Biestek, F. (1957). *The casework relationship.* Chicago: Loyola University Press.

Chambon, A., and Irving, A. (Eds.) (1994). *Essays on postmodernism and social work.* Toronto: Canadian Scholars' Press.

Compton, B. R., and Galaway, B. (1994). *Social work processes* (5th ed.). Pacific Grove, CA: Brooks/Cole.

Dean, R. G. (1992). Constructivism: An approach to clinical practice. *Smith College Studies in Social Work, 63,* 405–414.

Dean, R. G. (1993). Teaching a constructivist approach to clinical practice. In Joan Laird (Ed.), *Revisioning social work education: A social constructionist approach* (pp. 55–75). New York: Haworth.

DuBois, B., and Miley, K. K. (1999). *Social work: An empowering profession* (3rd ed.). Boston: Allyn and Bacon.

Fischer, J. (1981). The social work revolution. *Social Work, 26,* 199–207.

Germain, C. B., and Gitterman, A. (1980). *The life model of social work practice.* New York: Columbia University Press.

Gitterman, A. (1996). Ecological perspective: Response to Professor Jerry Wakefield. *Social Service Review, 70,* 472–476.

Gordon, W. E. (1981). A natural classification system for social work literature and knowledge. *Social Work, 26,* 134–136.

Greene, G. J., Jensen, C., and Jones, D. H. (1996). A constructivist perspective on clinical social work practice with ethnically diverse clients. *Social Work, 41,* 172–180.

Greene, R. R., and Blundo, R. (1999). Postmodern critique of systems theory in social work with the aged and their families. *Journal of Gerontological Social Work, 31,* 87–100.

Hepworth, D., Rooney, R., and Larsen, J. (2002). *Direct social work practice: Theory and skills* (6th ed.). Pacific Grove, CA: Brooks/Cole.

Hudson, W. (1982). Scientific imperatives in social work research and practice. *Social Service Review, 56,* 246–258.

Irving, A., and Young, T. (2002). Paradigm for pluralism: Mikhail Bakhtin and social work practice. *Social Work, 47,* 19–29.

Jordan, C., and Franklin, C. (1995). *Clinical assessment for social workers: Quantitative and qualitative methods.* Chicago: Lyceum.

Levy, C. (1976). *Social work ethics.* New York: Human Sciences Press.

Loewenberg, F. M., and Dolgoff, R. (1992). *Ethical decisions for social work practice* (4th ed.). Itasca, IL: F. E. Peacock Publishers, Inc.

Maluccio, A. (1979). Perspectives of social workers and clients on treatment outcome. *Social Casework, 60,* 394–401.

Mattaini, M. A. (1997). *Clinical practice with individuals.* Washington, DC: NASW Press.

McGowan, B. (1995). Values and ethics. In C. H. Meyer and M. A. Mattaini (Eds.), *The foundations of social work practice: A graduate text* (pp. 28–41). Washington, DC: NASW Press.

Meyer, C. H. (1988). The ecosystems perspective. In R. A. Dorfman (Ed.), *Paradigms of clinical social work* (pp. 275–294). New York: Brunner/Mazel.

Mickelson, J. S. (1995). Advocacy. *Encyclopedia of social work.* Washington, DC: NASW Press.

Murphy, J. W. (1989). Clinical intervention in the postmodern world. *International Journal of Adolescence and Youth, 2,* 61–69.

Murphy, J., and Pardeck, J. (1998). Renewing social work practice through a postmodern perspective. *Social Thought: Journal of Religion in the Social Services, 18*, 5–19.

National Association of Social Workers (1996). *Code of ethics.* Silver Spring, MD: National Association of Social Workers.

Perlman, H. (1979). *Relationship: The heart of helping people.* Chicago: University of Chicago Press.

Petr, C. (1988). The worker–client relationship: A general systems perspective. *Social Casework, 69,* 620–626.

Reamer, F. G. (1983). Ethical dilemmas in social work practice. *Social Work, 32,* 31–35.

Reamer, F. G. (1990). *Ethical dilemmas in social service* (2nd ed.). New York: Columbia University Press.

Reid, W. (1994). The empirical practice movement. *Social Service Review, 68,* 165–184.

Rhodes, M. L. (1991). *Ethical dilemmas in social work practice.* Milwaukee: Family Service America.

Richmond, M. (1917). *Social diagnosis.* New York: Russell Sage.

Saleebey, D. (2002). *The strengths perspective in social work practice* (3rd ed.). Boston: Allyn and Bacon.

Schneider, R. L., and Lester, L. (2001). *Social work advocacy: A new framework for action.* Pacific Grove, CA: Wadsworth.

Shulman, L. (1991). *Interactional social work practice: Toward an empirical theory.* Itasca, IL: F. E. Peacock Publishers, Inc.

Stone, D. (2000). Why we need a care movement. *The Nation, 270,* 13–15.

Sullivan, W. P. (1992). Reconsidering the environment as a helping resource. In D. Saleebey (Ed.), *The strengths perspective in social work practice* (pp. 148–157). New York: Longman.

Wakefield, J. C. (1996). Does social work need the ecosystems perspective? Part 1. Is the perspective clinically useful? *Social Service Review, 70,* 1–32.

Weick, A. (1987). Beyond empiricism: Toward a holistic conception of social work. *Social Thought, 13,* 36–46.

Weick, A. (1993). Reconstructing social work education. In Joan Laird (Ed.), *Revisioning social work education: A social constructionist approach* (pp. 11–30). New York: Haworth.

Weick, A., and Chamberlain, R. (1997). Putting problems in their place: Further explorations in the strengths perspective. In D. Saleebey (Ed.), *The strengths perspective in social work practice* (2nd ed., pp. 39–48). New York: Longman.

Weick, A., and Saleebey, D. (1995). A post modern approach to social work practice. The 1995 Richard Lodge Memorial Lecture, Adelphi University School of Social Work, Garden City, NY, October 20.

Weick, A., and Saleebey, D. (1998). Postmodern perspectives for social work. *Social Thought: Journal of Religion in the Social Services, 18,* 21–40.

Wolin, S. J., and Wolin, S. (1993). *The resilient self: How survivors of troubled families rise above adversity.* New York: Villard.

# THE COLLABORATIVE MODEL OF GENERALIST SOCIAL WORK PRACTICE

© Michelle D. Bridwell/PhotoEdit

Julie V. was a first-year MSW student placed in a unit of a drug and alcohol rehabilitation center. Her unit provided discharge planning for patients who were leaving the facility. Typically, Julie had one or two contacts with her clients before they were discharged.

Before she entered the MSW program, Julie worked for two years in a foster care agency that served children who were in long-term placement. She spent a lot of time with her clients, and she felt that she got to know them and developed strong helping relationships with them. In contrast, her work at the rehabilitation center was fast paced and short-term. She had to complete the assessment and discharge plans after one or two brief client contacts.

By the end of her first week of placement, Julie was concerned about the effectiveness of her work. She felt that her approach was too task-focused and that she was not making any connection with her clients. Instead, she was getting information as quickly as possible, filling out a form, and telling the clients about the plan. It felt rote and dehumanizing to her. She wondered what she could do to make the experience more positive for her clients and for herself. Was it possible, desirable, and important for her to engage her clients in the discharge planning process? Was it realistic to expect a positive helping relationship to develop in one or two brief contacts? How would the helping relationship in a short-term setting differ from one that developed over a longer period of time?

It is through the helping relationship and associated practice principles that social workers provide help and facilitate the change process. The helping relationship is the mechanism through which the client and the worker address the client's identified concerns. The helping relationship supports and structures clients' efforts to change. This chapter presents a model of generalist practice that focuses on the helping relationship. It begins with a review of the assumption of the collaborative model and its practice principles. The chapter concludes with a presentation of the phases, tasks, inputs, skills, and outputs of the model, followed by a review of the Helping Relationship Inventory, a rapid assessment instrument that measures the strength of the helping relationship.

By the end of this chapter, you should be able to help Julie

1. Conceptualize the helping relationship
2. Understand the importance of the helping relationship in the helping process
3. Describe what is entailed in a collaborative approach to generalist practice
4. Identify ways to empower clients
5. Conceptualize the role of evaluation in the helping process
6. Develop a rationale for using the Helping Relationship Inventory in work with clients

# THEORETICAL PROPOSITIONS

The collaborative model of social work practice presented here is built upon three theoretical propositions and three practice principles. The propositions are:

1. Disadvantaged and oppressed clients often mistrust helping professionals
2. Client change occurs through a collaborative helping relationship
3. Relationships are build upon trust

**Proposition 1: Disadvantaged and oppressed (reluctant) clients often mistrust helping professionals.** Alienation theory (Guillaumin, 1995; LaFromboise, Coleman, and Gerton, 1993) provides an explanation for the reluctance of oppressed and disadvantaged clients to fully engage in a helping relationship with social work professionals. People that are stigmatized and discriminated against on a continuous and systematic basis feel devalued by people who have power and occupy positions of authority in society (Fordham, 1996; LaFromboise and Dixon, 1981). A natural response to feelings of powerlessness, oppression, and devaluation is to distance oneself physically and emotionally from the oppressors. This sense of separateness or alienation can be viewed as a normal response or as a coping mechanism that helps protect the oppressed. Therefore, people who have experienced racism, discrimination, and other forms of oppression are unlikely to be willing to engage in an open and trusting relationship with a helping professional who, by virtue of her authority, has power and influence over their lives and well-being.

Most social work clients from disadvantaged communities have a long history of negative experiences with helping professionals and people in authority. They have learned to cope with "the system" by adopting a complying but noninvested style of interacting with it. At best, they become *reluctant* clients. Their experiences have conditioned them to be guarded with social work professionals and to approach them with mistrust. Marginalized people have no reason to trust social workers and other helping professionals. Overcoming **mistrust** is the primary obstacle faced by social workers working with marginalized client populations.

**Proposition 2: Client change occurs through a collaborative helping relationship.** The helping relationship is the heart of the helping process. Several studies have examined the correlation between the client's ratings of the relationship and the outcome of therapy. In a meta-analysis of 24 of these studies, Horvath and Symonds (1991) found that client ratings were positively associated with positive therapeutic outcomes. Others have verified that this correlation occurs with at least three types of therapy: behavioral, cognitive-behavioral, and interpersonal (Dore and Alexander, 1996; Marziali and Alexander, 1991). A large study funded by the National Institute of Mental Health found strong correlations between relationship and outcome, regardless of the type of treatment provided (Krupnick et al., 1996). Thus, social work and psychology research consistently and convincingly support the association between development of a positive helping relationship and successful treatment outcomes.

Historically, the profession of social work has recognized that the success of the helping process is dependent on the quality of the worker–client relationship (Biestek, 1957; Hollis, 1970; Perlman, 1979; Richmond, 1917). Biestek (1954) characterized the helping relationship as the "soul" of the helping process, a dynamic interaction of feelings and attitudes between the worker and the client. Perlman (1979) defined the professional helping relationship as a supportive, compassionate working alliance between the worker and client. Drawing on Rogers' (1957) work, Perlman named five worker attributes necessary for the development of a therapeutic relationship: warmth, acceptance, empathy, caring-concern, and genuineness. Clients who experience their interactions with social workers as caring, empathic, nonjudgmental, and genuine are more likely to engage in the helping process and to develop a sense of trust than those who do not.

Perlman's worker attributes have been widely accepted by the social work profession, and the importance of the worker–client relationship is a common assumption of social work practice. As with all assumptions, the importance of the helping relationship has been seen as a given rather than critically examined (Perlman, 1979). As early as 1979, Perlman noted that less and less attention was being paid to the helping relationship in social work research and practice literature. More recently, Coady observed "the continued neglect of relationship factors" in social work research (1993, p. 292). Although social work theory has consistently accorded the relationship between worker and client a central role in treatment, "the precise nature of this relationship and the manner in which it contributes to treatment has not been spelled out" (Proctor, 1982, p. 430).

Instead, social work research has for the most part focused on developing and testing models of intervention and on measuring outcomes (Reid, 1994). Much of the research conducted between 1970 and 1988 attempted to establish a scientific basis for clinical social work interventions (Russell, 1990). Social work practice research has consisted of outcome-oriented investigations that test the efficacy of structured interventions. There have been few direct studies of the helping relationship.

Most conceptual work and research on the helping relationship during the past 20 years has been done in the field of psychology (Dore and Alexander, 1996). It has been stimulated by the seminal ideas of Bordin (1979), who defined the construct of a therapeutic or working alliance. In social work, the focus has tended to be on the feeling dimension and on worker characteristics that promote positive feelings. In clinical psychology, on the other hand, the concept of the helping relationship has been expanded to include treatment goals and tasks (Hartley and Strupp, 1983; Horvath and Greenberg, 1986; Luborsky et al., 1983). These investigators view "the working alliance as a collaboration between the client and the therapist on the work of therapy" (Tichenor and Hill, 1989, p. 196). The relationship between therapist and client includes the specification of goals and agreed-on tasks for both the therapist and client, as well as the emotional bond between them.

In the collaborative model of generalist practice, the helping process has two components, which influence each other: a structural component and an interpersonal component (Poulin and Young, 1997). The **structural component** encompasses the purposeful activities or tasks undertaken to address the target concern or problem. The **interpersonal component** is the bond or mutual attraction that develops between the worker and the client. Both the structural and interpersonal need to develop for the helping relationship to be effective. The two components tend to develop concurrently. The process of collaborating on the structural activities builds and strengthens the interpersonal connection or psychological bond between the worker and the client. It takes time and the sharing of experiences to develop a strong interpersonal connection. The structural activities provide the interactions on which the interpersonal relationship is built. Through verbal and nonverbal interactions and collaborative efforts, the client experiences the worker as motivating and supportive.

As workers carry out structural activities, they should engage clients in an empowering collaborative process that is client centered. For example, during the initial sessions, the primary structural task is identifying concerns and strengths. The way the worker interacts with the client during this process profoundly influences the development of their interpersonal relationship. The worker should strive to motivate and support clients as they tell their stories. If the worker communicates understanding of the client's concerns and difficulties, provides comfort and calming strength, and pays attention to the client as a whole person, the client will probably experience the worker as supportive. This will in turn strengthen the client's interpersonal connection with the worker. Similarly, if the worker helps the client expand his or her self-understanding, strengthen his or her self-belief, and find hope and inspiration, the client will probably experience the worker as motivating. These experiences will also strengthen the psychological bond between the worker and the client.

**Proposition 3: Relationships are built on trust.** As noted above, developing a strong positive helping relationship is a process. Relationships are built over time. A key factor in developing a strong helping relationship is having shared experiences. In a professional relationship this occurs by undertaking the activities or tasks of the helping process, such as identifying client strengths and concerns and developing goals and a plan of action. Engaging in these purposeful activities helps build trust. Trust, in turn, helps strengthen the interpersonal connection or worker–client bond, which strengthens the client's motivation to engage in the structural activities.

Figure 3.1 illustrates the interrelationships between the structural and interpersonal components and the effects that positive interactions have on client trust and motivation.

A key to developing a strong positive collaborative relationship is establishing some level of trust. The client must be able to trust the social worker. Relationships cannot be built in the absence of trust. A certain degree of trust must be established between the client and the social worker for the client to engage in a collaborative helping process.

FIGURE 3.1 | THE HELPING RELATIONSHIP PROCESS

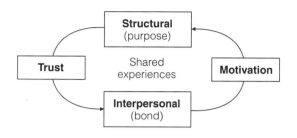

Trust is essential for relationships to develop and grow between social workers and their clients. To build strong collaborative relationships, the social worker must *reduce* the client's fear, suspicion, and mistrust at the same time as the worker *promotes* feelings of acceptance, support, and affirmation.

Building trust with reluctant clients is an interactional process. Trust cannot be built in the absence of interpersonal interactions between the client and the social worker. It is built upon a sequence of trusting and trustworthy interactions. The client must act in a trusting manner and the social worker must respond with trustworthy actions.

Within each interaction three conditions are required for trust to develop in a helping relationship. First, the client must **take a risk** (make a choice) where the potential harmful consequences outweigh the potential benefits associated with the risk. Second, the client must realize that the beneficial or harmful consequences associated with the risk **depend upon the worker's actions** (response) as the helping professional. Third, the client must **experience the worker's actions as beneficial** (Fong and Cox, 1983). All three conditions must be present for the interaction to contribute to the trust-building process. Figure 3.2 illustrates a trust-building interaction.

The bond of trust is built over time, through a series of trusting actions (risks) and trustworthy responses (confirmations). Although it takes time for trust to be established with reluctant clients, it can be destroyed through a single client **risk** and worker **disconfirmation** (nontrustworthy) response (Fong and Cox, 1983).

The critical element in developing trust is **risk.** Collaborative social work requires the client to actively participate in the helping process. The client is an active partner in the search for understanding and solutions. This cannot happen if the client is unable to take a risk by being open and honest with the social worker. Clients have to be willing to share their wants, desires, dreams, goals, skills, abilities, talents, and competencies as well as fears and concerns with a social worker. Reluctant clients usually have no reason whatsoever to be open with helping professionals. Why take a risk with someone in authority? Why risk exposing the real me to someone who can cause me harm or

FIGURE 3.2 | TRUST-BUILDING INTERACTIONS

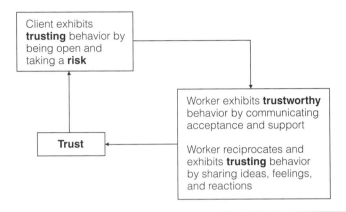

make my life difficult? The primary task for the social worker in working with reluctant clients is to facilitate risk taking. Trust cannot be built in the absence of risk.

Clients vary in their willingness to take risks with a helping professional. Figure 3.3 shows five levels of the worker–client risk continuum. At risk level I, the client is completely closed and unwilling to share even factual information. This type of client is often described as hostile or resistant. For people who have experienced a lifetime of oppression, prejudice, and discrimination, being unwilling to expose oneself to a stranger and authority figure is a normal and healthy coping mechanism. As one moves up the risk continuum, the client's willingness to share feeling and thoughts increases. At risk level V, the client is willing to be open about sensitive personal matters that place him or her in a potentially negative light. This level of risk requires a high level of trust and is usually reached over time through a series of lower-level risk-taking and confirming interactions with the social worker.

The three theoretical propositions discussed above are the underlying assumptions of the collaborative model of social work practice. These assumptions guide practice expectations. The following three practice principles provide additional guidance in using the collaborative model of practice.

## PRACTICE PRINCIPLES

The basic assumptions of the collaborative model of practice are (1) disadvantaged and oppressed clients often mistrust helping professionals; (2) client change occurs through a collaborative helping relationship, and (3) helping relationships are built upon trust. In light of these assumptions, the collaborative model is designed to build trust with clients whose life experiences have

FIGURE 3.3 | CLIENT RISK-TAKING CONTINUUM

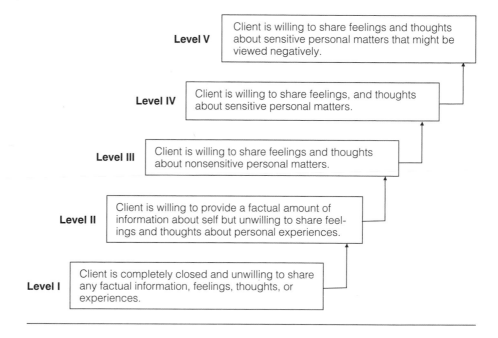

Level V — Client is willing to share feelings and thoughts about sensitive personal matters that might be viewed negatively.

Level IV — Client is willing to share feelings, and thoughts about sensitive personal matters.

Level III — Client is willing to share feelings and thoughts about nonsensitive personal matters.

Level II — Client is willing to provide a factual amount of information about self but unwilling to share feelings and thoughts about personal experiences.

Level I — Client is completely closed and unwilling to share any factual information, feelings, thoughts, or experiences.

given them very little reason to trust social workers and people in authority. This is accomplished by adopting a strengths perspective, by maximizing client collaboration and empowerment, and by adopting a system of ongoing feedback and evaluation.

**Practice Principle 1: Focus on client strengths.** The basic principles of the strengths perspective are discussed in Chapter 2. The focus here will be on reviewing the application of the strengths perspective in social work practice with disadvantaged clients. The strengths perspective focuses on inherent client strengths, resources, and coping abilities (Saleebey, 2002). Clients are viewed as capable of change and as active participants in the change process. Rather than the social worker being the problem solver, the client becomes the problem solver. The social worker's primary function is to help the client recognize, strengthen, and marshal his or her inherent strengths and abilities (Weick et al., 1989).

This "requires helpers to be open to negotiation, to appreciate the authenticity of the views and aspirations of those with whom they collaborate, and to be willing to subdue their own voices in the interest of bespeaking those of their clients" (Saleebey, 1992, p. 12). The worker and the client form a partnership to help the client resolve his or her own problems or concerns. Social workers cannot promote collaboration or foster client self-determination if they see their role as reforming or changing clients. Similarly, collaboration and client self-determination are not achieved if the social worker tries to fix the problem *for* the client. Social work is based on the premise that clients must ultimately help themselves. Self-determination requires workers and clients to collaborate in all decisions and aspects of their work together.

Strengths-based generalist practice places the client in the role of expert regarding his or her life situation. The worker's role is to help clients identify what is best for them. In this paradigm, the emphasis is on the collaborative process between the worker and the client. Engaging clients in a collaborative helping relationship, a relationship that recognizes the client as "expert," actually increases clients' ownership of their decisions and ultimately their level of self-determination. In a collaborative partnership, the worker helps the client expand his or her repertoire of choices and behaviors. Ideally, this involves helping the client identify the range of alternatives and the pros and cons associated with each possible choice. With this approach, the worker finds it easier to balance the offering of expert help with respect for the client's autonomy.

Collaboration—a partnership between the client and the worker—has been a pivotal practice ideal since the beginning of the social work profession (Richmond, 1917). Collaboration is closely tied to self-determination (Weick et al., 1989). The NASW Code of Ethics states that "the social worker should make every effort to foster maximum self-determination on the part of clients" (NASW, 1997, p. 3). Self-determination is achieved when "the client is fully involved and participating in all of the decisions and the social worker is working with the client rather than doing things to the client" (Compton and Galaway, 1994, p. 11). Self-determination is fostered by client participation in the decision-making process.

Self-determination is, for the most part, a "grand illusion" in actual practice (Perlman, 1965, p. 410). Achieving it is difficult at best. "The challenge for every practicing social worker is that of balancing the act of offering expert help while respecting the client's autonomy" (Bisman, 1994, p. 49). Problems arise when a client makes choices that are self-destructive or inconsistent with prevailing societal norms. In these situations, the dilemma for the social worker is how to resolve the conflict between his or her values and the value choices of the client while continuing to honor client self-determination. Levy (1972) suggests that the worker and the client openly discuss the value conflicts. Differences in value positions should be aired and the right to have different views respected.

Strengths-based generalist practice is based on the belief that clients are the experts and that they ultimately know what is best for themselves. The emphasis is on the collaborative process between the worker and the client. Engaging clients in a collaborative helping relationship increases clients' ownership of their decisions and ultimately their level of self-determination.

**Practice Principle 2: Put clients in charge of the helping process.** Collaboration requires the social worker to relinquish power, expertise, and control to the client. This does not mean that the worker has no expertise or role in the helping process. It does mean, however, that the balance of power and authority is distributed more equitably between the social worker and the client.

The use of empowerment in social work has grown out of the work of Solomon (1976), Rappaport (1981), and Pinderhughes (1983) and from feminist theory (Donovan, 1990; Ferree and Hess, 1985). "Feminism, like the civil rights, black power, and self-help movements, rapidly expanded the conceptual, methodological, and relational universe of empowerment-based social work of the 1970s and 1980s" (Simon, 1994). It has evolved as a method for working with women, people of color, and other oppressed groups (Gutiérrez and Nurius, 1994). **Empowerment** is defined as the "process of increasing personal, interpersonal or political power so that individuals can take action to improve their life situations" (Gutiérrez, 1990, p. 149). The process of empowerment emphasizes the acquisition of power, which is "the capacity to influence the forces which affect one's life space for one's own benefit" (Pinderhughes, 1983, p. 332).

The focus of social work practice with individuals should be on the "reduction of the power imbalance between workers and clients—specifically on increasing the client's power resources" (Hasenfeld, 1987, p. 478). The balance of power between the social worker and the client is inherently unequal. Theories of social work practice do not adequately address this power differential and tend to understate the effect of power on the helping relationship (Hasenfeld, 1987).

Social workers have three types of power: **expertise power** derived from their access to and command of specialized knowledge; **referent power** or persuasion, derived from their interpersonal skills; and **legitimate power** derived from their sanctioned position. In other words, social workers derive power from their expertise, their interpersonal skills, and the fact that they control resources needed by the client (Hasenfeld, 1987). Strengths-based generalist practice requires social workers to recognize the power they bring to the helping relationship and to engage clients in an open discussion of the various sources of power in their relationship. Acknowledging the inherent power differential is the first step in shifting the balance of power to the client. Although they rarely mention it, clients are acutely aware of the power differential between themselves and their social workers. Opening up the topic for discussion is in itself empowering (Gutiérrez, 1990). It gives the social worker and the client an opportunity to evaluate the resources available to address the client's areas of concern. The client is given a voice in defining the resources and determining how they will be used. As Hasenfeld states: "If we view social work practice as an exchange of resources, social work effectiveness, then, is predicated on the reduction of the power imbalance between workers and clients—specifically on increasing the client's power resources" (1987, p. 478).

Although strengths-based generalist practice acknowledges the client's expertise regarding his or her life situation, the social worker does not ignore his or her access to and command of specialized knowledge. This knowledge can help the client. But the social worker's view of the situation is not imposed on the client. The client is empowered by increasing his or her feelings of self-efficacy (Evans, 1992).

The helping relationship is the basis of empowerment (Gutiérrez, 1990; Weick and Pope, 1988). The helping relationship begins with an open discussion of each participant's interpersonal styles, preferences, and abilities. Giving clients a voice in determining what works for them is empowering. The social worker communicates a willingness to be responsive to the client's interpersonal preferences. Involving the client in the definition and evaluation of the relationship empowers the client and shifts the balance of power toward the client. The social worker's referent power becomes a resource that the client controls to some extent.

Empowerment also entails an analysis of the agency resources controlled by the social worker and an analysis of the client's resources (Hasenfeld, 1987). In discussing agency resources, the worker needs to describe the options available and the steps for obtaining them. The worker and client explore the possibilities and costs associated with each option. The client is empowered by being involved in the analysis and by being an active participant in the decision-making process.

The worker and client should also analyze the client's potential resources. Gutiérrez suggests that part of assessing the client's potential resources or strengths "involves analyzing how conditions of powerlessness are affecting the client's situation" (1990, p. 152). After exploring the factors that might contribute to the client's perception of powerlessness, the worker and client can examine the client's potential sources of power: "Clients and workers should be encouraged to think creatively about sources of potential power, such as forgotten skills, personal qualities that could increase social influence, members of past social support networks, and organizations in their communities" (Gutiérrez, 1990, p. 152).

The worker has to adopt an empowering mind-set, which involves giving up control and essentially abandoning the role of expert diagnostician and provider of expert advice. The worker has to become a team member with the client. The client must be willing to take responsibility for all aspects of the work together. The social worker can help the client take responsibility by believing in the client's right to self-determination, by expecting the client to assume responsibility for himself or herself and the planned interventions, and by giving up the need to be in control of the helping process. The social worker can also empower the client by listening. Being listened to and heard validates the client's perceptions of his or her life experiences (Irving and Young, 2002).

The client is unlikely to immediately move from a position of powerlessness to one of power. Individual empowerment is a process and should be viewed as a long-term goal of the helping relationship. Strengths-based generalist practice recognizes the shared responsibilities of the worker and the client. Ultimately, the success of the helping process depends on the client's ability to assume responsibility. "Clients who do not feel responsible for their problems may not invest their efforts in developing solutions unless they assume some personal responsibility for future change" (Gutiérrez, 1990, p. 150).

**Practice Principle 3: Continually evaluate your work and the client's progress.** In strengths-based generalist social work practice, evaluation means ongoing assessment throughout the helping relationship. This involves specifying problems and goals in measurable terms, developing solution-focused interventions, and using "evaluation methods in practice" (Reid, 1994, p. 176). Evaluation involves informal feedback from the client as well as the use of standardized measures and rating scales. It is a joint and collaborative effort. Both the worker and the client are involved in all aspects of evaluation.

**Informal evaluation** is one way of assessing the worker–client process. In keeping with the principles of collaboration and empowerment, in which the client is the expert about his or her progress, subjective assessments play a prominent role in strengths-based generalist practice. Clients' subjective assessments of their situations are the primary basis for evaluating the effectiveness of the helping process. The critical factor is whether the issues or concerns for which they are seeking help have improved.

Informal evaluation is an ongoing process. The client and worker begin by exploring the client's person-in-environment system and life experiences in order to identify concerns and factors that potentially affect them. During this and later stages, the social worker makes sure that his or her interpretations of the client's experiences are consistent with the client's perceptions. Strengths-based generalist practice emphasizes listening to the client's story and understanding the client's perceptions of experiences. The worker needs to continually evaluate the extent to which his or her understanding of the client's experiences is consistent with the client's.

As work continues, informal evaluation techniques identical to the process described above play a role. The social worker has to make a conscious effort to ensure that there is agreement about the identified goals and specifics of the helping contract. The worker and client need to evaluate the client's commitment to the plan. Is it genuine? How strong is it? What can the social worker do to help the client maintain or strengthen his or her commitment to change? Strengths-based generalist practice assumes client commitment to the helping process and stresses client responsibility. Unfortunately, clients are not always committed to addressing their concerns. A client's commitment should not be taken for granted or assumed. To address this, strengths-based generalist practice emphasizes an open dialogue between the worker and the client about commitment and responsibility.

**Formal evaluation** refers to the development of measurable goals and objectives and the use of standardized measures and single-item rating scales to evaluate progress on the goals. In recent years, the number of rapid assessment instruments appropriate for social work practice has increased. Such instruments are readily available and easily accessible (Fischer and Corcoran, 1994), and the range of problem areas covered is extensive. Thus, it is often possible to find a standardized scale that measures the problem area being addressed.

**Standardized measures** are an excellent way in which to evaluate progress. They are easily incorporated into generalist practice. Reviewing the results of standardized measures provides opportunities for the worker and client to discuss the identified area of concern. The standardized measures are first administered as part of the goal and contracting process and are read-ministered periodically as the helping relationship continues. They provide the worker and client with evaluative information on client progress and open the door for a discussion of why progress is or is not being made.

**Individual rating scales** are the second type of formal evaluation measures used in strengths-based generalist practice. The worker and client easily construct these scales. Their purpose is to assess the worker's and client's perception of progress on the identified areas of concern. Incorporating rating scales into the helping process is a way to evaluate progress and to obtain information on the client's perceptions of the effectiveness of the work. The primary value of this type of evaluation is that it provides a basis for a discussion of progress or the lack of it. It helps keep the work focused on the identified goals and opens up an opportunity to reevaluate priorities.

## THE COLLABORATIVE MODEL

As noted earlier, the basic assumption of the collaborative model is that because of prior negative life experiences and experiences with helping professionals, disadvantaged and oppressed clients are often mistrustful of helping professionals. Consequently, they are often reluctant to engage in a collaborative helping relationship. Each component of the model has been designed to build trust and promote the development of a strong helping relationship. Table 3.1 summarizes the model's phases, tasks, inputs, skills, and outputs. The collaborative model presented below can be used with individual, family, small group, organizational, and community client systems. The model is defined as time-limited. However, some client systems will need more contact and others less. The length of the helping relationship is determined by the problem situation being addressed and a host of interpersonal, environmental, and organizational factors.

### Phases

The beginning phase of the collaborative model is the **pre-engagement phase.** At this point, the client is in either the precontemplation or contemplation stages (Prochaska, DiClemente, and Norcross, 1992). The client has not yet made a decision to engage in a helping relationship. This is a critical period in the helping process. It is the time at which clients are most likely to drop out by simply not returning for the next session. The pre-engagement phase usually takes place during sessions one to three.

The **engagement phase** is the period in which clients are in preparation or action stage (Prochaska, DiClemente, and Norcross, 1992). Clients at this phase have acknowledged their commitment to make changes and are taking the necessary steps to achieve their identified goals. The engagement phase typically takes place during sessions four through eight.

**TABLE 3.1** | THE COLLABORATIVE MODEL

| Phase | Task | Input | Skills | Output |
|---|---|---|---|---|
| **Pre-engagement**<br>Sessions 1–3 | **Studying**<br>Population<br>   Culture<br>   Values and beliefs<br>   Experiences<br>   Life styles<br>Environment<br>   Resources<br>   Community<br>   Organizations | Understanding<br>Sensitivity | Information retrieval<br>   skills<br>     Database searches<br>     Internet searches<br>Resource identification<br>   skills<br>     Networking | Increased<br>   Knowledge<br>   Competence |
| | **Asking**<br>Obtain client's story<br>   Experiences<br>   Beliefs<br>   Expectations<br>   Strengths<br>   Coping abilities | Respect<br>Acceptance | Elaboration skills<br>   Open-ended question<br>   Minimal prompts<br>   Seeking concreteness<br>   Summarizing<br>   Containment<br>   Exploring silences<br>   Reframing | Identifying<br>   Needs<br>   Concerns<br>   Strengths<br>   Coping skills |
| | **Listening**<br>Tune in to client's<br>   Meaning<br>   Feelings<br>   Clues | Understanding<br>Empathy | Empathy skills<br>   Focused listening<br>   Reflective empathy<br>   Additive empathy | Identifying<br>   Feeling content<br>Validation |
| | **Clarifying**<br>Explore roles,<br>expectations, and<br>the helping process | Cooperative<br>Intentions | Elaboration skills<br>Empathy skills | Mutual under-<br>   standing<br>Collaboration |
| **Engagement**<br>Sessions 4–8 | **Articulating**<br>Develop an action<br>   plan | Hopefulness<br>Partnership | Contracting skills<br>   Partializing<br>   Identifying options<br>   Seeking consensus<br>   Sharing data | Change goals<br>Action plan<br>Evaluation plan |
| | **Persevering**<br>Persistent<br>   follow-through | Support<br>Commitment | Intervention skills<br>   Challenging<br>   Maintaining focus<br>   Checking for<br>     ambivalence<br>   Rehearsal | Client change |
| **Disengagement**<br>Sessions 9–10 | **Solidifying**<br>Gains made | Confidence | Ending skills<br>   Generalizing<br>   Identifying the next<br>     steps | Evaluation<br>Generalization<br>Aftercare plan |

The **disengagement phase** is the final phase of the collaborative model. This is comparable to the maintenance stage described by Prochaska, DiClemente, and Norcross (1992). The focus is on preventing relapse and consolidating the gains achieved. In a ten-session intervention, the last two or three weeks are devoted to the disengagement phase.

**Tasks**  The heart of the collaborative model is its seven tasks: study, ask, listen, clarify, articulate, persevere, and solidify.[1] These tasks are interrelated and overlapping. Although there is a logical way to implement the model, it should not be approached in a linear or step-wise fashion. All of the components overlap, and the process, more often than not, is cyclical rather than linear.

The **study task** begins before the initial contact with the client and lasts throughout the helping process. The **ask, listen,** and **clarify tasks** are begun during the pre-engagement phase and continue throughout the helping relationship. The **articulate** and **persevere tasks** take place during the engagement phase. The **solidify task** takes place during the disengagement phase.

## Inputs

Input, as used here, refers to what the social worker communicates both directly and indirectly to the client during their interactions together. Worker input is often not directly observable. It may be an attitude or expectation. For example, respect is an input. A social worker can communicate respect to clients in a number of different ways. Often, it is communicated indirectly through tone of voice, choice of words, and general attitude toward a person. Inputs are delivered through the worker's use of self in his or her interactions with the client. The various inputs identified in Table 3.1 are critical to the development of strong, positive helping relationships. For example, workers who are perceived as understanding, empathetic, comforting, and respectful tend to develop stronger relationships with their clients than those who are not (Poulin and Young, 1997). Effectively communicating the model's inputs helps strengthen the psychological bond between workers and clients, which in turn helps motivate both to engage in a helping relationship.

## Skills

The practice skills listed in Table 3.1 are those that are compatible with the strengths perspective and are client empowering. Although the various skills are linked to the different phases and components of the model, they are used throughout the helping process. The identified practice skills are important components of the social worker's use of self. They are the primary tools used

---

[1]The model's first six tasks were identified and named by Sarah Kulp, Aurelius Cousar, Laurie Bluhm, Christiana Drescher, Louann Kenefick, and Pat Mullen as part of a class exercise in their first-year MSW practice course.

to build trust, develop the helping relationship, and help clients negotiate the seven components of the model.

## Outputs

Outputs refer to the expected outcomes or results obtained from the worker inputs. At each stage of the model there are identified outcomes. These outcomes specify what the social worker should strive for during each component of the model. They help the social worker and client evaluate their process on a session-by-session basis.

## Assessing the Helping Relationship

The Helping Relationship Inventory (HRI) is a rapid assessment instrument designed to assess the strength of the structural and interpersonal components of the helping relationship (Poulin and Young, 1997). There are client (HRI:C) and worker (HRI:W) versions that are sensitive to important differences in client and worker concerns (Poulin and Young, 1997). Both are reliable and valid measures of the helping relationship.

The client version, HRI:C, measures the strength of the helping relationship in social work practice from the perspective of the client (Table 3.2). It is composed of ten structural and ten interpersonal items that capture those aspects of the helping relationship that are most important to clients. The worker version, HRI:W, measures the relationship from the perspective of the worker (Table 3.3). It is composed of ten structural and ten interpersonal items that capture those aspects of the helping relationship that are most important to workers providing help.

The worker and client versions of the HRI complement and strengthen social work practice with a variety of client populations. They evolved from a conception of social work practice that focuses on a collaborative process of assessment, goal specification, intervention, and evaluation within which the social worker motivates and supports the client's efforts to achieve his or her goals. Thus, the HRI:C and HRI:W are compatible with the collaborative model and are useful tools that support the model's practice principles.

## Scoring the HRI

The worker and client versions of the HRI both contain ten structural and ten interpersonal items. Each is rated on a five-point Likert-type scale. Scores for the structural component are calculated by summing items 1 through 10, and for the interpersonal component by summing items 11 through 20. The total HRI score is the sum of the structural and interpersonal scores.

Because the reliability and validity estimates of the structural and interpersonal subscales of the HRI are strong, social workers and their clients should calculate scores both subscales as well as the total score. Although scoring

TABLE 3.2 | HELPING RELATIONSHIP INVENTORY: CLIENT HRI:C[1]

1. How much input have *you* had in determining how the two of you will work together?
2. How much have you and your social worker discussed the specific problem(s) with which you want help?
3. How much input have you had in determining the specific problem(s) you are addressing in your work together?
4. To what extent have you and your social worker discussed the specific goal(s) you hope to accomplish in your work together?
5. How much input have you had in determining the goals you are working on?
6. To what extent have you and your social worker discussed the specific actions *you* will take to address your difficulties?
7. To what extent have you and your social worker discussed the specific actions *your* social worker will take to address your difficulties?
8. How much have you and your social worker discussed how your progress is going to be assessed?
9. How much input do you have in determining how you and your social worker will assess your progress?
10. To what extent have you and your social worker discussed your progress?
11. Do you feel your social worker pays attention to you?
12. Is your social worker's understanding of your difficulties similar to your own?
13. Does talking with your social worker help you get more organized about resolving your difficulties?
14. Does talking with your social worker have a calming, soothing effect on you?
15. Does talking with your social worker give you hope?
16. Does your social worker help you think more clearly about your difficulties?
17. Does talking with your social worker help you to believe more in yourself?
18. In general, do you feel you and your social worker see things in similar ways?
19. Does your social worker help you think more clearly about yourself?
20. Do you feel that you and your social worker are alike in some ways?

[1]All of the items are measured with Likert-type scales ranging from (1) Not at all to (5) A great deal. The HRI:C structural index has a reliability coefficient of .91, and the interpersonal index has a reliability coefficient of .96. Overall, the HRI:C has a reliability coefficient of .96. It demonstrates concurrent and discriminant validity. Originally published in "Development of a helping relationship for social work practice," by J. Poulin and T. Young, 1997, *Research on Social Work Practice, 7,* pp. 463–489. Reprinted by permission of Sage Publications, Inc.

norms have not been developed for the HRI, a score of 30 or lower on either component indicates a problematic relationship. If either the worker or client rates the structural or interpersonal component of their work together at or below this level, there is a strong likelihood that a satisfactory relationship is not developing or that there has been a rupture in the relationship. Workers and clients should compare both sets of scores to identify the areas of difficulty or disagreement and discuss ways to strengthen the relationship.

The scores are rough benchmarks the worker can use to assess the need to address relationship issues with the client. There are no clinically established cut-off scores. For example, a combined score of 61 should not auto-

**TABLE 3.3** | HELPING RELATIONSHIP INVENTORY: WORKER HRI:W[1]

1. How much input does your client have in determining how your work together will be approached?
2. How much have you and your client discussed the specific problem(s) with which he/she wants help?
3. How clear are you about the specific problem(s) that you and your client are addressing?
4. To what extent have you and your client discussed the specific goal(s) you hope to accomplish in your work together?
5. How much input does your client have in determining the goals he/she is working on?
6. How clear are you about your client's goals?

7. To what extent have you and your client discussed the specific actions *he/she* will take to address his/her difficulties?
8. How clear are you about the actions you are taking?
9. How much input does your client have in determining how you and your client will assess his/her progress?

10. How clear are you about how you and your client are assessing his/her progress?

11. Do you explain to your client your understanding of his/her difficulties?
12. Is your client's understanding of his/her difficulties similar to your own?
13. Is your client more organized about resolving his/her difficulties as a result of talking to you?
14. Does talking with you have a calming, soothing effect on your client?
15. Does talking with you give your client hope?
16. Are you able to handle the emotional aspects of your client's difficulties?
17. Do you enjoy meeting and talking with your client?
18. In general, do you feel you and your client see things in similar ways?
19. Do you help your client think more clearly about himself/herself?
20. Do you feel that you and your client are alike in some ways?

[1]All of the items are measured with Likert-type scales ranging from (1) Not at all to (5) A great deal. The HRI:W structural index has a reliability coefficient of .86, and the interpersonal index has a reliability coefficient of .91. Overall, the HRI:W has a reliability coefficient of .93. It demonstrates concurrent and discriminant validity. Originally published in "Development of a helping relationship for social work practice," by J. Poulin and T. Young, 1997, *Research on Social Work Practice, 7*, pp. 463–489. Reprinted by permission of Sage Publications, Inc.

matically be viewed as problem-free or a score of 59 as problematic. Worker and client scores on the HRI have to be viewed within the context of the helping relationship and the unique circumstances of the case.

## Applications of the HRI for Social Work Practice

The HRI is designed to help social workers and clients examine their perceptions of the helping relationship. Early in the helping process—no later than after the third session—the worker and client should complete the HRI and compare and discuss the results. Comparing the worker and client ratings of the individual items can lead to fruitful discussions about working together and what does and does not work in the helping relationship (Young and Poulin, 1998). Comparing the worker and client versions of the HRI facilitates the important process of collaboration and empowerment of the client early in the helping process.

Using the HRI:C and HRI:W as part of the helping process can provide both worker and client with important information on key elements of their work together. Clients and workers often have significantly different perceptions of the helping relationship (Horvath and Greenberg, 1994). For social workers to assume that clients share their view of their work together is risky and could impede progress.

The relationship between the worker and the client is the strongest predictor of both client change and client satisfaction (Horvath and Symonds, 1991). A solid helping relationship is a prerequisite for successful outcomes. Given the demonstrated differences in perceptions of shared experiences and the importance of the helping relationship in the change process, early and ongoing examinations of the client's and worker's perceptions of the relationship are critical.

If the client and worker do not develop a strong collaborative relationship that the client perceives as helpful, the client most likely will stop seeing the worker. Failure to develop a helping relationship is a common reason for termination (Levine and Herron, 1990). Using the HRI early in the helping process might increase client collaboration and reduce the likelihood that the client will discontinue treatment prematurely. Administering the HRI and discussing the adequacy of the relationship will in itself strengthen the helping relationship.

The HRI should be administered periodically throughout the helping process to obtain feedback on the strength of the relationship as the work evolves. This is particularly critical if clients or workers become discouraged about the possibilities of meaningful change or frustrated over what needs to be done to bring about change. Administering the HRI during the middle phase of treatment can provide the worker and client with important information on the strength of the relationship and open discussion about what they are working on and how they are doing so together.

Finally, the HRI should be administered as part of the planned termination of work. An important aspect of termination is reviewing the helping relationship. This review helps clients become better consumers of social work services. It helps them articulate what has and has not worked for them, how they have changed themselves or their situation, and how they brought about change. Reviewing the structural and interpersonal components of the HRI draws attention to specific aspects of the helping relationship. It can enhance the worker's and client's review of how they worked together. Completing the HRI during termination also allows the worker and client to compare their ratings with ratings made earlier in the process. This provides a basis for a review of progress and experiences.

# SUMMARY

The collaborative model of generalist social work practice assumes that most disadvantaged and oppressed clients are at best reluctant to engage in a helping relationship and that the development of a helping relationship is the key to client change. The importance of the helping relationship cannot be overemphasized. The helping relationship is composed of a structural and an interpersonal dimension, and its development is contingent upon the development of trust between the worker and the client. The structural component of the helping relationship focuses on tasks or purposeful activities, while the interpersonal component focuses on the psychological bond between the client and the worker. For the work to proceed, both dimensions of the helping relationship must be developed.

Three practice principles contribute to the effective implementation of the collaborative model. The first emphasizes client strengths. Clients are viewed as experts about their situations; they ultimately know what is best for them and they have the strengths needed to overcome the challenges in their lives.

The second practice principle focuses on client empowerment. Empowerment is the process of increasing personal, interpersonal, or political power, so that individuals can take action to improve their life situations. In the collaborative model, social workers do not control the helping process. Workers actively shift control and power to their clients. Clients are encouraged to take an active role in defining resources and in determining how they will use the helping relationship. Ultimately, the success of the helping process depends on how well the client assuming responsibility and control.

The third practice principle focuses on evaluation and feedback. Evaluation means ongoing assessment throughout the helping relationship. It involves informal feedback from clients as well as the use of formal standardized measures and rating scales. Evaluation is a joint and collaborative effort. The worker and the client take active roles in evaluating progress and the helping process.

The collaborative model is composed of phases, tasks, inputs, skills, and outputs. All aspects of the model are interrelated and support the three theoretical propositions and practice principles. The model has been designed to maximize client engagement and promote client strengths and empowerment.

The HRI is a tool for both the worker and the client to assess progress in the development of the helping relationship. The HRI measures the strength of the structural and interpersonal components of the helping relationship from the client's and worker's perspectives. Because the helping relationship is vital to the helping process, social workers should make a conscious effort to evaluate its development. Doing so can provide important information on differences between worker and client perceptions of how things are progressing as well as validation of what is working well. In addition to providing important feedback on the helping relationship, use of the HRI helps promote client empowerment and the development of a collaborative approach to the helping process.

# CASE EXAMPLE

Denise Bubel wrote the final case example in this chapter when she was a first-year MSW student. It is based on her work with a client at her field placement in a partial hospitalization program for elderly persons with serious and persistent mental illness. The case illustrates the importance of developing both the structural and interpersonal aspects of the helping relationship. It also is an excellent example of how listening to clients empowers them and promotes the development of the helping relationship.

---

## CASE 3.1 | NO ONE EVER ASKED BEFORE

BY DENISE BUBEL

### Practice Setting

Terra Firma, a partial hospitalization program for elderly mentally ill clients, serves as a temporary oasis to aid transition from crisis to regaining maximum function. The agency employs specialists to enable the clients to benefit from cognitive, behavioral, individual, group, and family therapy. A client experiences an intense structured program of five therapy sessions daily, from three to five days a week, until the treatment team agrees on the proper time of discharge.

### Problem Situation

Alfred C. is a 59-year-old African-American male who lives with his 80-year-old mother. Two weeks ago, his mother brought him to the emergency crisis center at the hospital. She was concerned that he was extremely depressed and that he had secluded himself inside the house. She reported to the doctor that he was not taking care of his personal hygiene and general health and that his condition was declining.

At the crisis center, Mr. C. told the doctor that he had a poor appetite and that he had lost approximately 50 pounds over the last 6 months. He talked about being unable to sleep and his feeling of being watched, which forced him to stay secluded in his house. Mr. C. also complained to the doctor about chronic auditory hallucinations. He denied having a history of substance abuse. Mr. C. was admitted to the locked psychiatric unit at the hospital.

The doctor reported that Mr. C. was "preoccupied, dysphoric, and was a relatively limited historian. He complained of depression and was ruminating about finances and appeared preoccupied and somewhat psychotic. He was very thin, disheveled, and pacing." When the doctor left the room, the client apparently had an episode of an undetermined cause that was either a seizure or a syncope. When the doctor returned, the client was "unresponsive and his pulse was not palpable and his breathing was shallow. At that point, a CODE was called and the client was brought into the medical part of the hospital." The doctor reported that the client "came around nicely." Medications were prescribed, and Mr. C. was returned to the psychiatric unit after a few days. The results of the tests to determine the nature of the seizure or syncope were not available at the time of the initial interview for admittance to the partial program.

### Initial Contact

As a social work intern, I was assigned to be Mr. C.'s case manager. When I first sat down to talk with him, he would not talk or make eye contact with me. He stared at one spot and seemed preoccupied with his thoughts or hallucinations. I felt very uncomfortable at first. I understood that I should not be aggressive, offer help, or be overly intrusive. Since I had a brief history from the initial intake, I decided that I would just focus on trying to establish some sort of connection with Mr. C.

I introduced myself in a quiet voice and sat a comfortable distance away from the client. I explained to Mr. C. that I was going to ask him some questions so I would be able to better assess his situation. Then he and I would make some goals for him to reach while he was in the program. I asked him if that was okay, and he did not respond. I gave it a few minutes and asked again. He looked at me and said, "Okay." I asked him questions about his circumstances and his situation. During the first 15 minutes, I collected very little information about his life. He was basically unresponsive to my inquiries.

I asked him about his delusions and hallucinations and gave him ample time to respond. He opened up and said that he was not able to tell if the voices were male or female, adult or child. He told me that many voices were whispering to him today, and that they had been yelling at him on the days before he was admitted to the hospital. He went on to explain that the voices upset his stomach so he could not eat, and it made him depressed. The voices told him not to let the doctor look at the lump in his side, to stay in the house, to stay away from others, and not to go near any steps. The voices were telling him to leave Terra Firma and go home.

I told Mr. C. that he did well and that we were happy to have him aboard. I told him that he did not have to participate in any activities, that he was safe and secure, and that no one would bother him. I felt I was able to convey empathy without being intrusive. Lastly, I asked him what he wanted to change in his life that Terra Firma could help him work toward. I was floored when he unexpectedly responded, "Get people to like me and get me to talk to people."

### Second Contact
During our second meeting, Mr. C. opened up to me, and I was able to collect some pertinent information about his life. Five years prior, as a result of mental illness, Mr. C. moved back in with his mother after he had lost his job packing goods at a dairy. Approximately 10 months prior to this episode, he lost his job as a janitor at a bus station as a result of his mental illness. He was divorced 20 years ago and has one adult son and one adult daughter with whom he has no contact. He denied any past or present history of physical, sexual, emotional, or substance abuse. Mr. C. reported that he is still hearing voices, but not as often as before he came to the hospital.

During the session, I tried to focus all my attention on Mr. C. Rather than thinking about asking the questions, I concentrated on listening to his answers. It seemed to work. He told me about his life and his experiences. It was a very satisfying experience for

both of us. I believe that he felt he was heard and that I was interested in him and what he had to say.

### Third Contact
I was able to collect extensive information from Mr. C. during the third interview. He seems to be stabilizing, which I attribute to his compliance with his medication, specifically the injection of Haldol Decanoate. He showed a major difference in his cognitive abilities. Mr. C.'s mood and affect still remain blunted and depressed, but he is less withdrawn and internalized.

During this session, Mr. C. did most of the talking. I tried to appear to be empathic and supportive. I told him I was happy with his progress and the strides he had made. I also told him how pleased I was with how well we seemed to get along and that I enjoyed working with him. He seemed to respond favorably to my comments.

### Current Situation
After three weeks, Mr. C. continues to show marked improvement. He has recovered from the hernia repair without incident. He is compliant about taking his medication and attends the Terra Firma program as scheduled. The client has not missed a day or been late since he began the program. He approaches me on the days I am there, says "Good morning," and is willing to hold extensive conversations with me and with the other clients attending the program. His spirits are up, and he appears to be adjusting well. The client has not yet attended any activities outside his home or returned to church. He has implemented a walking program in his neighborhood, but is not yet socializing with his neighbors. He has not yet made contact with his son or daughter. At this time, returning to work has not been suggested until further improvement is made.

### Client System Obstacles and Strengths
The client is a very likable and cooperative person. He is willing to try to improve his life situation. He is hindered by his mental illness and needs to stay on his medication and visit his doctor regularly so that the medicine can be monitored. This client is preoccupied with finances and needs to return to work to alleviate the major stress of this concern. Even though the

*(continued)*

## CASE 3.1 | *continued*

client does not have a formal education, he has been able to hold down jobs. The biggest obstacle to employment is the employer's lack of understanding of the client's mental illness.

The client needs to work on interpersonal skills to be able to communicate his concerns and disagreements with others. In the active phase of his illness, he becomes withdrawn and internalized, shutting out the world. The client has the will to achieve a self-sufficient status. He reports that he wants to be liked and to be able to communicate with others.

Though the client cannot drive, he is able to get a ride if needed. Also, he will eventually be able to take public transportation once he comes out of the active phase of his illness.

Even though he lacks relationships, friendships, and acquaintances, his mother and neighbor offer him support. Mr. C. needs to successfully return to a functioning capacity and return to work. He lives in an area close to public transportation and is in an area where he is able to find employment.

A major obstacle in his environment are the people who do not understand his mental illness. With some understanding and minimal accommodations, this client can function in society and be productive.

## DISCUSSION QUESTIONS

1. What contributed to the development of a helping relationship between Denise and Mr. C.? What did Denise do to facilitate the development of a relationship? What would you have done differently?

2. The case example focused only on Mr. C. and the services he was receiving from Denise and the day program. What other services or interventions could help Mr. C. maintain his independence in the community? How might Mr. C. benefit from participation in a "Club House" type of program? (For information on the Club House model for people with serious and persistent mental illness, see Flannery and Glickman (1996) and Rapp (1998).

3. Discuss the interrelationship between the structural and interpersonal components of the helping relationship. How is the process of developing a helping relationship with a client different than and similar to that of developing a relationship with a peer?

4. Contrast the collaborative approach to social work practice with the traditional diagnostic model of practice. Describe the approach used in your field placement agency. How might you adopt a more collaborative approach in a setting that adheres to the diagnostic model?

5. Brainstorm about all the possible ways a social worker could promote client empowerment. Examine a specific case from an empowerment perspective. What needs to happen in the helping relationship for client empowerment to occur? What do social workers need to do to empower clients?

6. How does informal evaluation differ from formal evaluation in generalist social work practice? How do you currently evaluate progress with your clients? What are the reasons for and against the use of informal and formal evaluation?

7. Discuss the use of the HRI in your practice. How might it enhance or inhibit the helping process? How would your clients react to being asked to evaluate the helping relationship? How would you feel about having your clients rate your relationship?
8. How do the concepts of collaboration, empowerment, and evaluation apply to working with people with serious and persistent mental illness? In what ways is developing a helping relationship different with this client population? In what ways is it the same?

# REFERENCES

Biestek, F. (1954). An analysis of the casework relationship. *Social Casework, 35,* 57–61.

Biestek, F. (1957). *The casework relationship.* Chicago: Loyola University Press.

Bisman, C. (1994). *Social work practice: Cases and principles.* Pacific Grove, CA: Brooks/Cole.

Bordin, E. (1979). The generalizability of the psychoanalytic concept of the working alliance. *Psychotherapy: Theory, Research, and Practice, 16,* 252–260.

Coady, N. (1993). The worker–client relationship revisited. *Families in Society, 74,* 291–300.

Compton, B., and Galaway, B. (1994). *Social work processes* (5th ed.). Pacific Grove, CA: Brooks/Cole.

Donovan, J. (1990). *Feminist theory: The intellectual traditions of American feminism.* New York: Continuum.

Dore, M., and Alexander, L. (1996). Preserving families at risk of child abuse and neglect: The role of the helping alliance. *Child Abuse and Neglect, 20,* 349–361.

Evans, E. (1992). Liberation theology, empowerment theory and social work practice with the oppressed. *International Social Work, 35,* 135–147.

Ferree, M., and Hess, B. (1985). *Controversy and coalition: The new feminist movement.* Boston: Twayne.

Fischer, J., and Corcoran, K. (1994). *Measures for clinical practice: A source-*book (Vols. 1–2, 2nd ed.). New York: Free Press.

Flannery, M., and Glickman, M. (1996). *Fountain house: Portraits of lives reclaimed from mental illness.* Center City, MN: Health Communications, Inc.

Fong, M. L., and Cox, B. G. (1983). Trust as an underlying dynamic in a counseling process: How clients test trust. *Personal and Guidance Journal, 62,* 163–166.

Fordham, S. (1996). *Blacked out: Dilemmas of race, identity, and success at Capital High.* Chicago: University of Chicago Press.

Guillaumin, C. (1995). *Racism, sexism, power and ideology.* London: Routledge.

Gutiérrez, L. (1990). Working with women of color: An empowerment perspective. *Social Work, 35,* 149–153.

Gutiérrez, L., and Nurius, P. (1994). Education and research for empowerment practice (Monograph No. 7). Seattle: University of Washington, School of Social Work, Center for Policy and Practice Research.

Hartley, D., and Strupp, H. (1983). The therapeutic alliance: Its relationship to outcome in brief psychotherapy. In J. Masling (Ed.), *Empirical studies of psychoanalytic theories* (Vol. 1, pp. 1–38). Hillsdale, NJ: Analytical Press.

Hasenfeld, Y. (1987). Power in social work practice. *Social Service Review, 61,* 469–483. Chicago: University of Chicago Press.

Hollis, F. (1970). The psychosocial approach to the practice of casework. In R. Roberts and R. Nee (Eds.), *Theories of social casework* (pp. 33–76). Chicago: University of Chicago Press.

Horvath, A., and Greenberg, L. (1986). The development of the working alliance inventory. In L. Greenberg and W. Pinsof (Eds.), *The psychotherapeutic process: A research handbook* (pp. 529–556). New York: Guilford.

Horvath, A., and Greenberg, L. (Eds.). (1994). *The working alliance: Theory, research, and practice.* New York: Wiley.

Horvath, A., and Symonds, B. (1991). Relation between working alliance and outcome in psychotherapy: A meta-analysis. *Journal of Counseling Psychology, 38,* 139–149.

Irving, A., and Young, T. (2002). Paradigm for pluralism: Mikhail Bakhtin and social work practice. *Social Work, 47,* 19–29.

Krupnick, J., Sotsky, S., Simmens, S., Moyer, J., Elkin, I., Watkins, J., and Pilkonis, P. (1996). The role of the therapeutic alliance in psychotherapy and pharmacotherapy outcome: Findings in the National Institute of Mental Health treatment of depression collaborative research program. *Journal of Consulting and Clinical Psychology, 64,* 532–539.

LaFromboise, T., Coleman, H. L. K., and Gerton, J. (1993). Psychological impact of biculturalism: Evidence and theory. *Psychological Bulletin, 114,* 395–412.

LaFromboise, T., and Dixon, D. N. (1981). American Indian perception of trustworthiness in a counseling interview. *Journal of Counseling Psychology, 28,* 135–139.

Levine, S., and Herron, W. (1990). Changes during the course of the psychotherapeutic relationship. *Psychological Reports, 66,* 883–897.

Levy, C. (1972). Values and planned change. *Social Casework, 53*(8), 488–493.

Luborsky, L., Crits-Christoph, P., Alexander, L., Margolis, M., and Cohen, M. (1983). Two helping alliance methods for predicting outcome of psychotherapy. *Journal of Nervous and Mental Disease, 171,* 480–91.

Marziali, E., and Alexander, L. (1991). The power of the therapeutic relationship. *American Journal of Orthopsychiatry, 61,* 383–391.

National Association of Social Workers (1997). *Code of Ethics.* Washington, DC.

Perlman, H. (1965). Self-determination: Reality or illusion? Social Service Review, 39(4), 410–421.

Perlman, H. (1979). *Relationship: The heart of helping people.* Chicago: University of Chicago Press.

Pinderhughes, E. (1983). Empowerment for our clients and for ourselves. *Social Casework, 64,* 331–338.

Poulin, J., and Young, T. (1997). Development of a helping relationship for social work practice. *Research on Social Work Practice, 7,* 463–489.

Prochaska, J. O., DiClemente, C. C., and Norcross, J. C. (1992). In search of how people change: Applications to addictive behaviors. *American Psychologist, 47,* 1102–1114.

Proctor, E. (1982). Defining the worker–client relationship. *Social Work, 27,* 430–435.

Rapp, C. (1998). *The strengths model.* New York: Oxford University Press.

Rappaport, J. (1981). In praise of paradox: A social policy of empowerment over prevention. *American Journal of Community Psychology, 9,* 1–15.

Reid, W. (1994). The empirical practice movement. *Social Service Review, 68,* 165–84.

Richmond, M. (1917). *Social diagnosis.* New York: Russell Sage.

Rogers, C. (1957). The necessary and sufficient conditions of therapeutic personality change. *Journal of Consulting Psychology, 21,* 95–103.

Russell, M. (1990). *Clinical social work: Research and practice.* Newbury Park, CA: Sage.

Saleebey, D. (1992). *The strengths perspective in social work practice.* New York: Longman.

Saleebey, D. (2002). *The strengths perspective in social work practice* (3rd ed.). Boston: Allyn and Bacon.

Simon, B. L. (1994). *The empowerment tradition in American social work history.* New York: Columbia University Press.

Solomon, B. (1976). *Black empowerment.* New York: Columbia University Press.

Tichenor, V., and Hill, C. (1989). A comparison of six measures of working alliance. *Psychotherapy, 26,* 195–199.

Weick, A., and Pope, L. (1988). Knowing what's best: A new look at self-determination. *Social Casework, 69,* 10–16.

Weick, A., Rapp, C., Sullivan, W., and Kisthardt, S. (1989). A strengths perspective for social work practice. *Social Work, 34,* 350–354.

Young, T., and Poulin, J. (1998). The helping relationship inventory: A clinical appraisal. *Families in Society, 79,* 123–133.

# 4

# COLLABORATIVE SOCIAL WORK

*The Pre-Engagement Phase*

© Mark Richards/PhotoEdit

Tom B. was a first-year MSW student placed in an in-patient psychiatric unit of a metropolitan hospital. The unit was designed to provide short-term treatment to stabilize patients who were experiencing mental health crises, conduct comprehensive assessments, and develop care plans for discharge.

The unit followed the traditional medical model of patient care. The treatment team placed a great deal of emphasis and time on diagnosing and identifying the patients' particular mental illnesses. There was a heavy emphasis on psychopharmacology and on fine-tuning patients' medications. The treatment team set the patients' goals and treatment objectives and developed the discharge care plans. Tom was impressed by the professionalism of the staff and by how much they seemed to know about various mental illnesses. Everyone seemed very committed to their jobs and worked hard to make diagnoses and complete their parts of the treatment and discharge plans.

Over the course of the semester, Tom noticed that a high percentage of the patients had been placed in the unit on previous occasions. Most had had multiple in-patient psychiatric hospitalizations. Tom began to question the effectiveness of the approach used to treat mental illness. Why didn't the patients have any voice in the treatment process? What was the value of diagnosis beyond affixing a label to the patient? How did focusing on patients' problems help them develop effective coping strategies after they were discharged? Why weren't patients' families involved in the assessment process and discharge care planning?

**Assessment** is the exploration and analysis of the client's situation. In collaborative social work, it is a process in which you and the client explore the client's perceptions and experiences. Major goals of the assessment process are to help the client identify and clarify problem areas and begin to understand characteristics of the client and the environment that influence the identified problems. It is from this understanding that plans to address the client's concerns are formulated. Assessment is the key to effective social work practice (Jordan and Franklin, 1995; Meyer, 1993).

This chapter begins with a general discussion of strengths-based assessment and then reviews the pre-engagement phase tasks: studying, asking, listening, and clarifying. The associated inputs, practice skills, and outputs associated with each pre-engagement task are also reviewed. By the end of the chapter, you should be able to help Tom

1. Understand the various tasks associated with the pre-engagement phase and role that diagnosis plays in the assessment process
2. Conduct a strengths-based assessment
3. Plot personal and environmental client systems strengths and obstacles
4. Describe the inputs and outputs associated with the pre-engagement phase of the helping process
5. Use a wide range of practice skills in working with disadvantaged and oppressed clients

# STRENGTHS-BASED ASSESSMENT

## Assessment versus Diagnosis

A strengths-based assessment is more than diagnosing the client's presenting symptoms and coming up with a diagnostic label. Indeed, the diagnosis often required for insurance purposes, which is based on the *Diagnostic and Statistical Manual of Mental Disorders (DSM-IV-TR)* (American Psychiatric Association, 2000), is antithetical to the principles and concepts of collaborative social work.

The *DSM-IV-TR* is useful in eliciting descriptions of symptoms from the client and talking about symptoms with others on the treatment team. The diagnostic labels themselves do not tell you everything about the unique circumstances of your clients. They may tell you something about how prescribed medications are working or not working, what type of medication is needed, or whether the client needs to be referred to a physician.

Diagnostic labeling can have negative consequences (Gambrill, 1997; Kinney, Haapala, and Booth, 1991; Kirk and Kutchins, 1992; Levy, 1972). Psychiatric labels tend to create negative expectations. They focus attention on deficits and away from the potential for change. "Labeling makes it harder for us to be warm and supportive, if we're thinking about coping with the negative traits we've assigned to our clients" (Kinney, Haapala, and Booth, 1991, p. 84).

Another negative consequence of labeling is that it reduces feelings of hopefulness. Labeling is all-inclusive (e.g., a client is psychotic or has a personality disorder). Labels imply that what clients are is what they will always be (Kinney, Haapala, and Booth, 1991). These negative expectations discourage a sense of hopefulness, reduce client motivation, and minimize possibilities for change (Rapp, 1998).

Many beginning social workers like to use the *DSM-IV-TR*. Referring to clients by diagnostic labels makes a new social worker feel and sound professional and gives him or her the illusion of being understanding and having expertise. Avoid the temptation and the trap. Most labels create negative expectations for both you and the client, focus on a condition or trait rather than the context in which a problem occurs, and offer little help in understanding the unique circumstances of the client. They do not provide any information about how to resolve a problem.

## Assessing Client Strengths

Focusing on pathologic labels promotes homogenization (Rapp, 1998). Clients are viewed as a collection of generalized problems that are finite and shared by many other clients. This results in a generic case plan that sees all clients as exhibiting the same groups of symptoms. Clients are not seen as unique individuals with unique circumstances and problem situations.

Strengths-based assessments enhance the individualization of clients. The focus is on what is unique about each client in terms of interests, abilities, and how they have coped with their problem situation. "The work should focus on what the client has achieved so far, what resources have been or are currently available to the client, what the client knows and talents possessed, and what aspirations and dreams the client may hold" (Rapp, 1998, p. 45). Cowger created these guidelines for a strengths assessment:

1. Give preeminence to the client's understanding of the facts.
2. Believe the client.
3. Discover what the client wants.
4. Move the assessment toward personal and environmental strengths.
5. Make the assessment of strengths multidimensional.
6. Use the assessment to discover uniqueness.
7. Use language the client can understand.
8. Make the assessment a joint activity between worker and client.
9. Reach a mutual agreement on the assessment.
10. Avoid blame and blaming.
11. Assess, do not diagnose. (1997, pp. 63–66)

Adherence to these guidelines will ensure that your assessment interviews are collaborative and that the process will identify client strengths. The tendency to focus on pathologic symptoms and dysfunction will be minimized.

Identifying client strengths is not always easy. Clients are often unable to name specific strengths they have used in coping with a problem situation. They often indicate that they do not have any strengths, or they respond in very general terms, such as "I am a nice person" (McQuaide and Ehrenreich, 1997). The challenge is to help clients recognize how they have "taken steps, summoned up resources, and coped" (Saleebey, 1997, p. 239). However, "whether a given client's characteristic represents a strength or a weakness depends on subtleties of personal history, the immediate social environment, the larger societal matrix, the mix of client characteristics, challenges, and the meanings the client ascribes to his or her experience and situation" (McQuaide and Ehrenreich, 1997, p. 211).

Using a strengths perspective does not negate the very real problems clients face. The problems that cause clients to seek professional help cannot be disregarded or ignored. The assessment process must attend to both the obstacles and the strengths that potentially affect the resolution of the problem and the helping process. Much of the assessment that takes place in social work is focused on client problems and deficits (Saleebey, 2002). The strengths approach seeks to provide a balance between client obstacles and strengths.

Cowger (1997) proposed an **assessment axis** to help attain this balance (Figure 4.1). It has two coordinates: an **environmental–personal continuum** and a **strengths–obstacles continuum.** There are four quadrants: environmental strengths, personal strengths, environmental obstacles, and personal obstacles. The quadrants for personal strengths and obstacles include both

FIGURE 4.1    │    ASSESSMENT AXIS

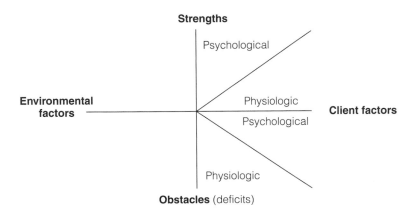

C. Cowger. In Saleebey, Dennis (Ed.). "Assessing client strengths," in *Strengths perspective in social work practice*, 3rd ed. Published by Allyn and Bacon, Boston MA. Copyright © 2002 by Pearson Education. Reprinted by permission of the publisher.

psychological and physiologic components. Attention to all four quadrants helps ensure a comprehensive assessment that is balanced in terms of individual and environmental strengths and obstacles.

## Identifying and Analyzing Person-in-Environment Factors

A major component of a strengths-based assessment is exploring and assessing the four quadrants in the assessment axis. Figure 4.2 shows the potential effect the worker, organization, community, and client systems have on a target problem. It also shows the influence the worker has on the client's environmental system. Worker–client transactions are viewed as a component of the client's ecological system (Germain and Gitterman, 1980). Interactions between the worker and the client and between the worker and the client's social environment become part of the client's dynamic person-in-environment system. In this respect, mutuality and reciprocity characterize the worker–client relationship. The conceptualization recognizes the mutual effect that worker and client have on one another and on the helping relationship (Petr, 1988).

The interrelationships of the systems shown in Figure 4.2 differ from the traditional ecological systems model, in which the worker is seen as a mediator operating between the individual and his or her environment. In the conceptualization presented here, the social worker is a major component of the client's person-in-environment system—a component that affects the system and is affected by the other system components.

This model also emphasizes the worker's role as a partner in the helping process. The critical issue for social workers and their clients is how the vari-

FIGURE 4.2 | PERSON-IN-ENVIRONMENT ASSESSMENT

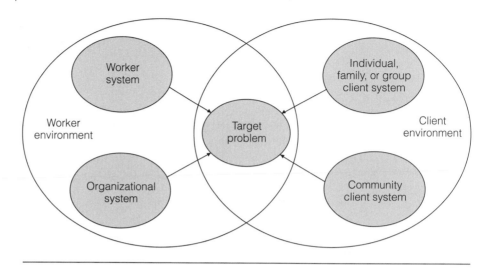

ous systems in the client's person-in-environment system affect the concerns the client is attempting to resolve. Factors that affect the client system but do not affect the helping relationship system are not relevant to their work together.

Social workers need to understand clients by "tapping into their unique perspective and personal realities" (Jordan and Franklin, 1995, p. 98). In exploring the client's reality, it is important for social workers to be aware of their own biases and beliefs, which may influence their clinical perceptions. Social workers need to be able to differentiate between their interpretations and those of the client (Gilgun, Daly, and Handel, 1992). They also need to recognize that by exploring a client's subjective reality, they become part of that reality. On entering into a helping relationship, the worker becomes part of the client's person-in-environment system. Thus, the worker can influence a client's subjective perceptions of self and of experiences. Care must be taken to allow the client's subjective reality to emerge. The social worker's job is to understand the client's experiences and perceptions and to engage the client in a discussion of how those experiences influence their work together. The worker needs to incorporate his or her understanding of the client's experiences into the helping process.

Conducting a person-in-environment assessment is immensely complex and difficult. It is, however, critical to the success of the work. Assessment is an ongoing task in the helping process and should not be limited to the beginning assessment phase. It requires mutual exploration and evaluation of the client's person-in-environment system throughout the helping relationship.

## Assessing Individual Client Systems

An individual client system consists of four major subsystems: demographic characteristics, ethnicity and culture, personal characteristics, and life experiences. These four subsystems and the specific characteristics associated with each of them are shown in Table 4.1.

## Demographic Characteristics

Demographic characteristics, such as gender, race, age, and socioeconomic status, potentially affect the helping relationship and the identified target problem. Although demographic characteristics might directly influence the helping relationship, their primary influence is through transactions with the worker system. Workers and clients need to explore the effects of clients' demographic characteristics on their work together. For example, there are often significant age discrepancies between workers and their clients. Social workers who are significantly younger than their clients should raise the issue of age for discussion. If it is not a concern for the client, no harm has been done, and it opens the door for a discussion of other factors. If it is a concern, it can be addressed.

Another sensitive demographic factor is race. In the United States, race is a highly charged issue for most people. Race may be an issue when there are racial differences between workers and clients. It may also be an issue when the worker and client both have minority status. Being willing to explore the potential effect of race on the helping relationship communicates sensitivity and a willingness to enter into a partnership.

## Ethnicity and Culture

The second category of client characteristics that affects the helping relationship is ethnicity and culture. This broad category includes personal ideologies and cultural values and beliefs. Assessment of this group of factors requires introspection. You have to understand your value system and how values influence your perceptions of yourself and others. Only after developing an awareness of your own value system can you explore value differences with clients.

You need to be sensitive to areas of disagreement and agreement when exploring personal beliefs, cultural traditions, and value positions with clients. It is important to explicitly recognize both. Identifying differences in values and beliefs allows recognition and acceptance of the differences and development of strategies for dealing with them. Identifying areas of agreement strengthens the connection between you and the client. It is important to limit mutual exploration of values and beliefs to areas that potentially affect the helping relationship and your work together. It is not possible or appropriate to explore all aspects of the belief systems of you and your client. However, the more that each understands what the other holds dear, the more likely it is that a strong helping relationship will develop.

TABLE 4.1 | INDIVIDUAL CLIENT SYSTEMS: SUBSYSTEMS FOR ASSESSMENT

| Demographics | Personal characteristics |
|---|---|
| Gender | Responsibility |
| Race | Commitment |
| Age | Motivation |
| Socioeconomic status | Coping skills |
| | Resoucefulness |
| **Ethnicity and culture** | **Life experiences** |
| Values and beliefs | Relationships |
| Spirituality and religion | Support networks |
| | Life cycle stage |
| | Mental health status |
| | Health status |

## Personal Characteristics

Three primary characteristics influence a client's ability to benefit from a helping relationship: responsibility, commitment, and motivation. A number of factors influence a person's ability or willingness to make a commitment and assume responsibility for creating change. Responsibility and commitment profoundly affect the helping relationship and are critical to the success of the helping process. Social workers help clients help themselves. Success requires a commitment to the change process.

It is unrealistic to expect all clients to assume responsibility for change and to be committed to the helping process at the outset. Clients need to develop commitment to the helping process and self-help through the ongoing helping relationship.

Many clients seeking social work services have difficulty taking responsibility for their actions and sustaining their commitment to improve their life situations. Thus, the interaction between you and the client is critical. You must use your interpersonal qualities and clinical skills to address the client's level of commitment and responsibility. You and the client need to explore experiences and feelings related to taking responsibility and making a commitment to change. You have to motivate clients to take responsibility for their actions and support their commitment to the process.

Two additional personal characteristics that should be assessed are the client's coping skills and resourcefulness. Identifying past ways of coping with problem situations is an important aspect of the assessment. The strengths perspective emphasizes client capacity and previous success in coping with the target problem. Clients often are unaware of their resourcefulness and past successes. Exploring past experiences and providing ideas about additional ways of coping empowers the client and enhances the helping relationship.

## Life Experiences

The broad category of life experiences refers to the client's history, including experiences with family and interpersonal relationships, support networks, developmental life stages, and mental health and health status. These are the traditional topics of biopsychosocial assessment. You need to explore the client's life story. You need to understand the client's self-perceptions, worldview, and prior experiences, and the way these experiences may potentially influence the helping relationship.

## PRE-ENGAGEMENT PHASE OF COLLABORATIVE SOCIAL WORK

As noted in Chapter 3, there are four major tasks associated with the pre-engagement phase of collaborative social work: studying, asking, listening, and clarifying. Each task is described here and also how the task contributes to the development of client trust, the practice skills associated with it, and the expected outcomes.

The four pre-engagement tasks are highly interrelated. In actual practice, they would be used in conjunction with one another. They are components of a single process and are used together within the context of the helping relationship. However, for the purposes of description, each task is discussed separately.

## Task 1: Studying Your Client's Culture, Values, Beliefs, and Environment

**Studying** refers to educating oneself about the client population with whom one is working. The study phase begins before you have your initial contact with the client and continues throughout the helping process. Before your initial meeting, you should become familiar with the cultural traditions, values, beliefs, and lifestyles of your client's population group. You should also try to find out as much as you can about the specific life experiences of your individual client. In addition to educating yourself about the client population and your client, you should educate yourself about the community, local service network, and resources available.

**Inputs: Understanding and sensitivity**    Figure 4.3 shows how the study task affects your ability to build trust with reluctant clients. Being knowledgeable about your client's culture, values and beliefs, experiences, life stage, and community increases your cultural competence and communicates (inputs) to your client **understanding** and **sensitivity**. Clients who feel understood and experience you as being aware of and sensitive to their situation, life experience, culture, traditions, and belief systems are more likely to be open and take appropriate risks than those who experience you as culturally unaware and insensitive. Cultural competence in itself does not guarantee a client's willingness to take risks. However, being culturally incompetent and insensitive does guar-

FIGURE 4.3    |    PRE-ENGAGEMENT TASK: STUDYING

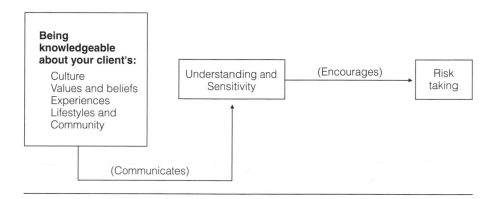

antee mistrust and risk aversion, especially if clients come from ethnic or racial backgrounds that differ from your own.

**Practice Skills: Information Retrieval and Resource Identification**    Table 4.2 lists the practice skills associated with the study task. These skills enable social workers to do research on client populations and become knowledgeable about their cultures, customs, values, beliefs, and person-in-environment situations as well as help them in identifying needed resources.

*Information Retrieval Skills*    Computer technologies and the emergence of the Internet have changed the ways social workers do research and obtain information. Understanding how to conduct literature searches with computerized databases is now a critical social work practice skill. The amount of information available on an array of topics related to social work is enormous. The challenge is finding the information.

Currently, there are a number of searchable databases that contain summaries or abstracts of published journal articles in social work, psychology, education, social science, nursing, and other related disciplines. The major one in social work is *Social Work Abstracts,* and in psychology, *PsyLit.* Most libraries subscribe to a number of electronic databases. They can be searched using key words, authors, or titles. The search usually leads to article summaries or abstracts. The full text of articles of interest can then be reviewed in the library if available or a copy can be requested through an interlibrary loan.

The Internet has become an excellent source of information on a variety of social work topics. There are a number of search engines that are free and easy to use. Most hosting Web sites have search functions. One of the more powerful ones is Google. Searches are conducted the same way as with electronic databases, and usually lead to a list of "hits" with links to the identified Web sites. There are also a number of social work Web sites maintained

TABLE 4.2 | STUDYING: PRACTICE SKILLS

> **Information retrieval skills**
> Database searches
> Internet searches
>
> **Resource identification skills**
> Networking

by professional organizations and schools of social work that have links pages with addresses of Web sites of particular interest to social workers.

Caution, however, must be used with information obtained from the Internet because there is no oversight or quality control. Anyone can post whatever he or she wants. Care must be taken to verify the legitimacy of the Web site, qualifications of the author, and validity of the information. Nevertheless, there is a wealth of information relevant to social workers on the Web, and the number of full text professional journals available online has increased dramatically during the past few years—a trend that will probably continue.

*Resource Identification Skills*    Identifying and obtaining needed resources and services are other important generalist practice skills, especially for those working with disadvantaged and oppressed client populations. Resource mobilization and client advocacy are fundamental components of generalist social work practice. **Networking** is the key to effective resource mobilization and client advocacy. Networking is the process of developing relationships with other professionals and service providers in the community. It is the process of building relationships and of becoming informed about available resources and services. Personal contact gets things accomplished. Formal requests for services and assistance are not as effective as presenting your case to someone you know and with whom you have a reciprocal relationship. Generalist social workers need to actively develop relationships with other professionals, and, as with any other relationships, they need to actively maintain them.

Developing a network begins by identifying relevant existing programs and services in the community and region. Most communities have published resource directories of human service organizations as well as blue page listings in the telephone directory. Identify key agencies, and contact a social worker at each one to learn more about their programs and services and develop a relationship with a contact person at that organization.

Another networking strategy is to attend and join community coalitions and task forces related to your service area. Become an active member of community-wide efforts to address issues related to your professional work. Working with others builds relationships and expands your professional network. Strengthening your network increases your ability to effectively serve your clients.

**Outputs: Increased Knowledge and Competence**   Knowledge and competence are the outcomes associated with the studying task. Knowledge about your client's culture, values, beliefs, experiences, and worldview as well as available resources and services is the anticipated outcome. Knowledge and competence go hand in hand. Doing research on background information of your client population, identifying existing resources, and building a strong professional network increase your competence in working with disadvantaged and oppressed clients.

## Task 2: Asking Your Client to Tell His or Her Story

**Asking** refers to the process of asking your client to tell his or her story, including experiences, beliefs, expectations, concerns, strengths, coping abilities, and most importantly, hopes and dreams. The asking approach contrasts sharply with the telling approach that most disadvantaged clients have experienced in their prior interactions with helping professionals and other people in authority. Being asked about your hopes and concerns is empowering. Being told what your problem is and what you need to do is disempowering.

The collaborative model places a great deal of emphasis on allowing the client to be in charge of the helping process. This begins when the worker simply asks the client to tell her or his story. You should approach this task from a position of curiosity or "not knowing" (Dejong and Berg, 1998). Show an interest in hearing what your client has to say. Do not make assumptions about the client's situation and perceptions. Be open and encourage exploration. This is accomplished through the use of **elaboration skills.** Use open-ended questions and minimal prompts to encourage elaboration. Ask for specifics, explore the meaning of silences, summarize when appropriate, reframe, and, most importantly, contain yourself. Containing oneself is critical at this point in the helping relationship. The focus must be on having clients tell their story and not on the worker talking about ideas, insights, expectations, or solutions. Rushing in with solutions before clients have had a chance to tell their story has more to do with the worker feeling good about herself or himself and her or his abilities than with helping a client.

**Inputs: Respect and Acceptance**   Figure 4.4 illustrates how the asking task builds trust with reluctant clients. Asking clients to tell their story communicates **respect** and **acceptance.** Collaborative social work is based on the premise that the client is the expert and the best source of information regarding his or her life situation. Proceeding from this assumption and asking clients about their experiences, beliefs, concerns, and strengths communicates respect to the client. Above all we want our clients to feel respected as people. Communicating respect is critical to building trust. Few would be willing to make themselves vulnerable and take risks in an atmosphere of disrespect.

FIGURE 4.4  |  PRE-ENGAGEMENT TASK: ASKING

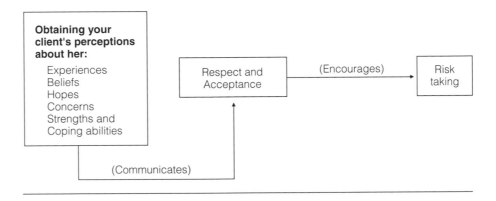

Eliciting the client's story is the first half of the asking task. The second half is accepting the story as reality for that person. This requires receiving the message in a nonjudgmental manner. If the client perceives the worker as both respectful and accepting, the client is encouraged to take risks that will help build trust and the helping relationship. There are a number of practice skills that can be employed to help the worker communicate respect and acceptance. They are referred to as elaboration skills (Shulman, 1999) or verbal following skills (Hepworth, Rooney, and Larsen, 2002).

**Elaboration Practice Skills**   Elaboration skills are micro-intervention techniques that encourage clients to tell their stories in detail. These techniques can be used with individual, family, small group, organizational, and community client systems. To understand a client's situation and perspective, we need to have their stories told in detail. The power of the story is in the specifics. Most people tend to avoid specifics and begin discussing their situation in very general terms. The social worker's job is to help the client tell a detailed story rich in facts and feelings. The seven elaboration skills, shown in Table 4.3, are using open-ended questions, using minimal prompts, seeking concreteness, summarizing, containment, exploring silences, and reframing.

*Using Open-Ended Questions*   There are basically two types of questions: those with predefined responses and those without predefined responses. The former are usually referred to as closed-ended questions. They do not encourage a detailed and elaborate response, and generally should be avoided. An example of a closed-ended question is, "Do you get along well with the other kids at school?" If the client responds at all, the answer will be yes or no. This is the only answer called for. Not much information is obtained from this type of question.

Alternatively, one should ask open-ended questions that elicit more information from the client. For example, the social worker could ask, "How do you

TABLE 4.3 | ASKING: PRACTICE SKILLS

**Elaboration skills**
Open-ended questions
Minimal prompts
Seeking concreteness
Summarizing
Containment
Exploring silences
Reframing

get along with the other kids at school?" This cannot be answered with just a yes or no response. The client has to formulate a more detailed or elaborate response to answer the question. Although the questions are similar, the open-ended one encourages elaboration, whereas the closed-ended one does not.

Open-ended questions are a simple and easy way to get clients to tell their stories. They give clients opportunities to tell their stories in more depth than do closed-ended questions (Kadushin and Kadushin, 1997). Limit your use of closed-ended questions. If a question is warranted, ask an open-ended one.

*Using Minimal Prompts*   As the term implies, minimal prompts are brief nonverbal or verbal indications of encouragement. Nonverbal minimal prompts include "nodding the head, using facial expressions, or employing gestures that convey receptivity, interest, and commitment to understanding" (Hepworth, Rooney, and Larsen, 2002, p. 140). These nonverbal prompts can be very effective in encouraging elaboration. They communicate in an attentive and nonintrusive way that you would like the client to tell you more and that you are interested in hearing her story.

Verbal minimal prompts are brief utterances such as "Mm-mmm" or "Ah-ha" or other short phrases such as "Tell me more" or "I see." As with the nonverbal prompts, the verbal ones encourage the client to go on without interrupting or asking a series of questions.

Another type of minimal prompt is an **accent response** in which the worker repeats a client's word or short phrase in the form of a question. The word or phrase selected should be the core component of the client's message. For example, if the client says, "I just hate all the kids at school," the social worker might say "Hate?" or "The kids?" to prompt the client to give more information about the client's feelings about the kids at school. Accent responses are easy to use, do not interrupt the flow of communication, and are very effective in getting clients to explore their feelings and concerns in depth.

*Seeking Concreteness*   As noted earlier, clients tend to introduce their concerns and describe their experiences in vague, general terms. Beginning social workers often do not probe for specifics and may allow clients to keep the conversation at a general level. Hepworth, Rooney, and Larsen (2002) point out that communicating one's feelings and experiences requires specificity. They call the process of helping clients to respond in specific terms "seeking concreteness"; others refer to it as "clarification" (Cormier and Cormier, 1991) or "moving from the general to the specific" (Shulman, 1999).

Often clients begin their stories in general terms because they have never put their feelings and experiences into words. They need help in exploring their feelings and experiences. Asking for specifics helps clients articulate their stories. Thus, seeking concreteness not only deepens your understanding of clients' stories but also helps clients understand and articulate their feelings and experiences.

Seeking concreteness is easy to do. The key is to recognize and respond to vague and overly general comments. For example, a community member might say, "The neighborhood is falling apart. It is just not the same any more." This is a fairly vague statement. At this point, the social worker really does not know what is causing the frustration. The worker could seek more concrete information by asking an open-ended follow-up question, such as, "How has it changed?" or by "What do you mean by falling apart?" Both responses invite the client to elaborate on her concerns.

Asking for specific information deepens the worker's and client's understanding of the topic. The technique of seeking concreteness has the added benefit of contributing to the natural flow of the conversation. It helps the worker stay on the topic introduced by the client. Seeking clarification helps the worker avoid jumping from topic to topic, a common mistake made by beginning social workers. It also communicates to the client interest in hearing her story.

*Summarizing*   Summarizing is a basic interviewing skill that is often used to highlight key points in a conversation with a client. When used this way, summarizing can help the client and worker make the transition to a different topic. Summarizing, however, can also be used as an elaboration technique. This entails making connections between relevant aspects of a client's story (Hepworth, Rooney, and Larsen, 2002). Summarizing can help clients explore in depth feelings and experiences that they might not recognize as being connected. This can be a powerful tool in helping them gain insight and understanding.

Summarizing is a more difficult skill to use than the other elaborating skills discussed above. It is a filtering and feedback process. It requires the ability to identify the key components of the story, pull them together, and repeat them back to the client in a combination statement—question form. The statement—question form prevents the social worker from taking the position of knowing or presuming to know that the different points are connected for the client.

Typically, a summary statement is concluded with a question to see if the worker's perception or summary is consistent with the client's view of the situation. Summarizing is used as an elaboration skill in this example:

COMMITTEE MEMBER: Well, I just don't know. The agency caseloads have risen to the point we cannot provide effective services to our clients, and the paperwork is totally getting out of control. The demands on the case-workers seem to be increasing, and the turnover problem is getting worse.

WORKER: Sounds like the working conditions here are making it hard for you to do your job, and you don't see any relief in sight. Is that right?

The worker has summarized the committee member's main points and invited her to explore the connection. In this way, summarizing is used as a practice skill to promote elaboration.

*Using Containment*   Shulman (1999) defines **containment** as the skill of "not acting" (p. 148). Many beginning social workers, in their desire to be helpful, rush in with solutions before the client has told his or her story. Containment is the ability to hold back on this impulse. It also is an important skill for those who have a tendency to finish a client's sentences or to focus on identified outcomes very early in the helping process. The following response by the social worker to the committee member illustrates a *lack* of containment:

WORKER: Yes, I agree. This place is falling apart, and the agency administrators really don't care about the caseworkers and the pressures they are feeling. We need to organize ourselves to put pressure on management to improve working conditions.

The worker failed to contain himself and immediately rushed in with a solution to the committee member's expressed concerns. The lack of containment shifts the focus and interrupts the exploration of the situation. The worker has single-handedly chosen the target problem and intervention. A worker skilled in containment would have continued to encourage the committee member to explore her feelings and tell her story.

*Exploring Silences*   Shulman (1999) calls this skill "reaching into silences" and describes it as attempting to explore the meaning of the silence. "The difficulty with silences is that it is often hard to understand exactly what the client is 'saying'" (Shulman, 1999, p. 152). The client might be processing a thought, struggling with powerful emotions, feeling bored, or any number of things. Beginning social workers are often uncomfortable with silence and rush in to fill it up. Doing so ensures that the meaning of the silence will be lost as the worker moves on to something else. The social worker needs to actively explore the silence. A clue to its meaning is the worker's own feelings (Shulman, 1999). Understanding one's own feelings at a particular moment helps one to make an educated guess about the meaning of the client's silence. Shulman's phrase "reach inside of silences" suggests that the worker should actively explore the meaning of silence.

The first strategy for dealing with silence is containment. Give the client some time, and stay with the silence. A simple probing question, such as,

"You are quiet right now. What's going on?" is often sufficient to get the client to open up. You have acknowledged the silence and encouraged the client to elaborate. If your feelings suggest that the client is feeling *(hurt)* then you could ask an open-ended question, such as, "Are you struggling with the *(hurt)* you feel?" The client needs to be encouraged to let the worker know if the guess is wrong. Even if the worker is off base, there is little harm done. The client can correct the misperception. Either way, the silence has been acknowledged and its meaning explored. Rather than feeling uncomfortable during periods of silence, view them as opportunities to better understand your client and her story.

*Reframing*    Reframing is a technique that is used often in family therapy (Janzen and Harris, 1997). It is sometimes referred to as relabeling. Reframing is the process of giving a positive interpretation to what the client sees as a negative or concern. It is reframing a negative into a positive. In collaborative social work, this is an important technique. It provides the worker with a way to highlight positives and help clients view their concerns from a different, more positive, perspective. It helps the identification of strengths and coping abilities. Reframing is an elaboration skill in that it invites clients to explore their stories from a different perspective. The following is an example of reframing:

GROUP MEMBER: My wife gets very upset when I have a couple of drinks and drive. It is ridiculous. Even if I only have one beer, she is on my case.

WORKER: Sounds like your wife really cares about you and your safety.

**Outputs: Identification of Needs, Concerns, Strengths, and Coping Skills**
The major outputs of the asking task are the identifications of client needs, concerns, strengths, and coping skills. Having the client tell her story provides the worker with the information needed to begin the assessment process. The conversation is purposeful. The client's natural focus is on needs and concerns. The worker adds to this the identification of strengths and coping skills. All four are the desired outcomes of asking the client to tell her story.

## Task 3: Listening for Meaning and Feelings

Asking and listening are obviously two interrelated tasks. When a social worker asks a question, clients assume that the worker will listen to their answer. The focus here is on listening for the meaning and feeling behind the client's words. It is more about *hearing* the message than listening to the words.

What are the areas of concern? How does the client perceive the problem situation? What are the indications or manifestations of the problem? Where, when, and how often does the problem occur? How severe is the problem? How does it affect the client? What are the client's emotional reactions to the problem? What other systems within the client's environment affect the problem situation? How has the client coped with the problem? Answers to these questions provide an understanding of the problem situation from the client's perspective. The way you go about developing this understanding is as critical as the answers themselves.

Ideally the answers will emerge as the client tells his or her story. Focus on listening and on communicating your understanding of the story. Be curious. Your goal is to obtain a detailed picture of the client's concerns. The client's perception of feeling heard is going to motivate him or her to open up to you and engage in a helping process. It will set a solid foundation for the development of the helping relationship. If your client does not feel heard, your work together will probably not continue.

Asking a battery of questions without really listening to the client's responses puts the focus on you, the worker, rather than where it needs to be, on the client. A common mistake by beginning social workers is to assume that their job is to ask brilliant questions. Many are preoccupied with their own responses to the client, with saying the right thing. Rather than focusing on what you are going to say or on the questions you need to ask, you should focus on what the client is saying. Do you understand what he or she is attempting to communicate? Are you listening to the client? Are you hearing what he or she is saying? Have you communicated your understanding back to the client? If you focus on listening and ask questions that help you understand what the client is saying, the information will be forthcoming.

**Inputs: Understanding and Empathy**   Figure 4.5 illustrates how the listening task builds trust with reluctant clients. Listening for the meaning behind your client's words and for feeling content and picking up on your client's indirect clues communicates **understanding** and **empathy**. Clients who perceive their social workers as being understanding and empathic are more likely to share feelings and thoughts about sensitive matters than those who perceive their social workers as not understanding them and their situation. Sharing feelings and thoughts helps build trust and strengthens the helping relationship. Communicating understanding and empathy is critical to the development of a collaborative helping process. The key to communicating understanding and empathy is the ability to respond to the feeling content in the client's story. Practice skills that are effective in doing just that are referred to as empathic skills (Shulman, 1999). Others refer to these as skills as empathic responding (Hepworth, Rooney, and Larsen, 2002) or reflecting feelings (Sevel, Cummins, and Madrigal 1999). Table 4.4 lists three empathic skills that are related to the listening task in collaborative social work.

**Empathic Skills**

*Focused Listening*   Focused listening (Shulman, 1999) or active listening (Chang and Scott, 1999) is the process of concentrating on a specific part of the client's message. The worker tries to identify the primary themes in the client's story and be sensitive to clues the client may give regarding the underlying feeling content of the message. The worker also tries to understand what the message means to the client (Chang and Scott, 1999). What is the client really saying, and what meaning does it have for the client?

FIGURE 4.5   |   PRE-ENGAGEMENT: LISTENING

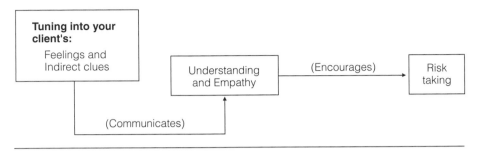

Focused listening requires the social worker to tune in to the meaning behind the client's words. This involves listening to the client's words, non-verbal communication, and affect as well as what is not being said. Listening and understanding the client's message is the first component of empathy. The second component is communicating back to the client your understanding.

*Reflective Empathy*    Conveying empathy and understanding is vital in developing a helping relationship. Clients need to feel understood. Those who feel that their social workers do not really understand them and their situations are unlikely to share personal thoughts and feelings. Why risk vulnerability with someone who does not understand you? Disadvantaged and oppressed clients' experiences of discrimination, abuse, or exploitation have left many feeling profoundly misunderstood (Cournoyer, 2000). The ability to respond empathetically is a critical social work practice skill, particularly when one has to overcome mistrust and reluctance.

In its simplest form, empathic responding is "reflecting" back to clients their message. At this level, the empathic response accurately captures the factual content and feelings expressed by the client. The response communicates an equivalent message. Reflective empathy is more effective if you paraphrase the client's words rather than just "parrot back" the same words.

The use of empathetic responding is vital to the development of trust and the building of a strong helping relationship. In practice, I do not believe that empathy can be overused. Respond empathetically whenever your client is dealing with or expressing affective content. If there is an emotional component in the message, either on the surface or below it, an empathic response is needed. The power of the relationship is in helping clients deal with and manage feelings. Understanding the facts is important, but understanding the feelings is essential. Doing so will communicate that you are listening, that you care about the client, and that you understand or, at the very least, are trying to understand.

Responding to the affective component is beneficial even if you have incorrectly described the client's feelings or their intensity. An incorrect empa-

TABLE 4.4 | LISTING: PRACTICE SKILLS

> **Empathic skills**
> Focused listening
> Reflective empathy
> Additive empathy

thetic response gives clients an opportunity to clarify their feelings. The example illustrates a reflective empathic response.

INDIVIDUAL: My parents are jerks. They are always on my back about something. I can never do anything right. My sister is the perfect one. She gets better grades, is more popular, and is always "little miss perfect." It's not fair. She isn't perfect, but my parents don't know that.

WORKER: Sounds like your parents are always on you and that they think your sister is perfect. It doesn't seem fair, and it makes you kind of angry. Is that what you are saying?

The social worker's response summarizes the facts and puts the client's surface feelings into words. Depending upon the client's tone of voice and emphasis, the surface feeling is most likely anger, but it could also be disappointment or something else. Identifying feelings underneath the surface feelings helps clients to better understand their own emotions (Hepworth, Rooney, and Larsen, 2002).

*Additive Empathy*   This level of empathetic responding occurs when the social worker accurately identifies **implicit underlying feelings.** "The response illuminates subtle or veiled facets of the client's message, enabling the client to get in touch with somewhat deeper feelings and unexplored meanings and purposes of behavior" (Hepworth, Rooney, and Larsen, 2002, p. 102). Not only does the social worker respond to the surface and underlying feelings, but the response connects the message to other themes of feelings expressed by the client. The use of additive empathy communicates a deeper level of understanding than the more basic reflective empathy. Both require the social worker to "risk" responding to the affective component of the client's message. Many beginning social workers shy away from dealing with clients' feelings directly. It is easier to stick to the facts and ignore the feelings. If one wants to build trust, then responding to the feeling content is necessary. This example is an additive empathetic response to the individual's statement in the example above. In this response, the worker tries to reach for the client's underlying feelings.

WORKER: Sounds like your parents are always on you and that they think your sister is perfect. I sense that this really hurts your feelings and makes you wonder if they love you as much as they love your sister. Does that capture it?

**Outputs: Identification of Feeling Content and Validation**    The major outputs of the listening task are (1) the identification of the client's feelings and the affective component of her story, and (2) validation. These two outputs are interrelated. If you are successful in identifying clients' feelings and can demonstrate that understanding, then clients feel validated. Feeling understood is validating. Having someone recognize and acknowledge one's feelings legitimizes them. Feelings are powerful emotions and having them acknowledged is even more powerful. This is particularly important when working with clients who have experienced discrimination and oppression in their lives.

## Task 4: Clarify How You and the Client Will Work Together

Please keep in mind the interrelated nature of the tasks associated with the pre-engagement phase. All are engaged in over the course of one to three sessions. At some point during the pre-engagement phase, you and your client need to discuss his or her expectations of the helping process as well as how you hope your work together will proceed. Clarifying expectations and agreeing on general guidelines about what will take place during the helping relationship set the framework for a collaborative process. Clients often have little understanding of the helping process, and their perceptions may differ widely from yours. Perlman (1968) found that fewer clients dropped out during intake when client expectations were clarified and worker–client discrepancies addressed. Zwick and Atkinson (1985) found similar results for clients who viewed an orientation video prior to psychological counseling.

Hepworth, Rooney, and Larsen (2002) suggest that you should determine what your client's expectations are and briefly explain the nature of the helping process when you begin working together. Unacknowledged discrepancies between your and your client's expectations about what is going to happen and how it is going to happen may jeopardize the helping process.

Clients may make it very clear what they expect you to do or what they think will happen. If they have not, ask them at an appropriate time during the pre-engagement phase. This applies to both voluntary and nonvoluntary clients. For nonvoluntary clients, review the mandated aspects of service provision, and then ask what they hope to get out of the experience. What would they like to have happen? How would they like the work to proceed?

The second component of clarifying the helping process is communicating your expectations about what you will and will not do, as well as what you expect your client to do and not do. Your job as social worker is to structure the helping process and help support and motivate the client throughout the process. The client's job is to make a commitment to engage in the helping process, to be the decision maker about choices that emerge as the process unfolds, and to follow through on those choices. Be respectful of the client's expectations, especially if they are at variance with yours. Acknowledge the client's expectations even if they are unrealistic. Be empathic regarding his or her feelings. Clients typically want help and answers to problems that they have struggled with and have been unable to resolve on their own. They are looking to you to provide expert advice and guidance. Acknowledge these feelings while emphasizing your partnership and how you will work together to address concerns. The helping relationship is a collaborative process.

It is also helpful to discuss the kind of relationship you hope to develop. A truly collaborative relationship requires openness. Your client has to be willing to share feelings, and you have to be willing to communicate openly. This requires the development of trust. Trust is built on actions and shared experiences. It is not created through words alone, and it does not happen instantaneously. You need to communicate concern, understanding, and empathy, both verbally and nonverbally, to provide opportunities for trust to develop. Share your feelings about the kind of open and collaborative relationship you hope to have with your client, and acknowledge that you must earn his or her trust. An open discussion of your feelings will model for your client the types of interactions you hope to have and will be an example of the reciprocal nature of the helping relationship and your client's role as a partner.

**Inputs: Cooperative Intentions**   Figure 4.6 illustrates how the clarification task builds trust with reluctant clients. Exploring with your client your respective roles, expectations, and how your work together will proceed communicates **cooperative intentions**. It is important for the client to have a voice in this conversation. The collaborative model emphasizes client empowerment. Telling the client "how it is going to be" is not in keeping with the philosophy of the model. Nevertheless, the approach requires client participation and involvement in all aspects of the helping process. This needs to be communicated to the client in a way that gives the client a choice in the matter. Be flexible and give the client as much say in how you work together as you can, within the framework of the model. You need to communicate your willingness to engage in a collaborative helping process and let your client know that he or she will have a strong voice in the process. This is accomplished by using the elaboration and empathy skills discussed earlier.

**Outputs: Mutual Understanding and Collaboration**   The expected output of the clarifying task is mutual understanding of the helping process and how the client and social worker will work together. A related output is the establishment of a collaborative partnership. Both of these intermediate outputs are critical to the success of the helping relationship.

The clarifying task is especially important in work with disadvantaged and oppressed client populations. Typically, as noted before, their experiences with helping professionals have not been collaborative. More likely than not they have been told what their problem is and what they need to do to remedy it. Often sanctions are employed if the remedy is not achieved or followed.

FIGURE 4.6 | PRE-ENGAGEMENT TASK: CLARIFYING

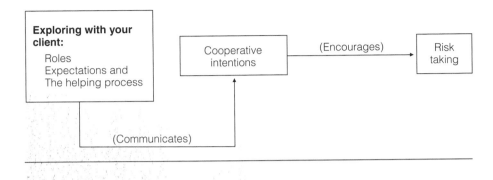

This is very different from the experience one would have with a social worker using the collaborative model. A successful outcome depends on clarifying roles, expectations, and the helping process.

## SUMMARY

Diagnosis is only a small part of the assessment process. It is useful in communicating symptom types. However, diagnostic labels do not tell you anything about the unique circumstances of clients or how to approach your work together. Psychiatric labels tend to create negative expectations and focus attention on client deficits. They focus on the condition or trait rather than on the context in which difficulties occur. They also offer little in the way of understanding the unique circumstances of the client, and they do not provide any information about how to resolve the problem.

Strengths-based assessments enhance the individualization of clients. They focus on what is unique about each client in terms of interests, abilities, and coping strategies they have used with their problem situation. Clients often need help in identifying their strengths. The challenge is to help them recognize how they have taken steps to resolve problem situations and how they have managed to cope with difficult circumstances.

The assessment process must take into account the challenges and the strengths that will affect the resolution of problems and the development of the helping process. A strengths-based approach tries to balance client obstacles and clients strengths. Cowger's assessment axis can help you maintain a balanced assessment by identifying personal and environmental strengths and obstacles.

An individual client system consists of four subsystems: demographic characteristics, ethnicity and culture, personal characteristics, and life experiences. These subsystems affect the helping process and the work on the target problem. The assessment process must explore with the client the ways these subsystems interact with the worker, community, and organizational systems in the client's environment.

The pre-engagement phase of the collaborative process usually lasts through sessions one to three. During this phase, the worker engages in four primary tasks: studying, asking, listening, and clarifying. The successful completion of these tasks communicates to the client understanding, sensitivity, respect, acceptance, empathy, and cooperative intentions.

The major practice skills employed during the pre-engagement phase are information retrieval, resource identification, elaboration, and empathy. These skills facilitate the collaborative helping process and intermediate session outputs. The outputs associated with the pre-engagement phase are increased knowledge; increased competence; identification of needs, concerns, strengths, and coping skills; identification of feeling content; validation; mutual understanding; and establishment of a collaborative partnership.

## CASE EXAMPLE

Susan Getty wrote the final case example in this chapter when she was a first-year MSW student in field placement at an alternative school for emotionally troubled children and adolescents. This assessment of a teenage client is an excellent example of the value of a comprehensive strengths-based assessment. In addition to providing both Susan and her client with a better understanding of the situation and the client's strengths and challenges, the assessment process strengthened their relationship, enabling Susan and her client to develop meaningful goals for their work together.

---

### CASE 4.1 | AT LEAST I CAN FIGHT
BY SUSAN GETTY

Erica W. is a 12-year-old African-American female. She was referred to the Community School for assessment and, ultimately, placement because of severe behavioral problems she exhibited in her district school. She continually got into fights with other students; she was both physically and verbally aggressive. Recently, she had to go to court concerning a fight she had been in. When she is questioned about the cause of these fights, she blames the other children for starting them. Erica reports that the other children pick on her and that she has a reputation for being a fighter. She has said that she likes it when children she doesn't know come up to her to talk about fights she has been in.

It is reported by her aunt that the fights started when other children were teasing her about her weight. Erica is quite overweight, and this is definitely a sensitive issue for her. Her weight concerned her primary care physician, who recommended that she be evaluated for an eating disorder. It appears to me, though, that her obesity stems from poor nutrition and bad eating habits of the family. Her aunt is also very overweight, and Erica doesn't appear to exhibit the signs of a true eating disorder.

She does seem to have very low self-esteem, as evidenced by several comments she has made, her intense wish for approval from others, and her inability to discuss positive aspects of herself. I see her pride in her ability to fight as another sign of low self-esteem. She sees fighting as a positive quality,

*(continued)*

## CASE 4.1 | *continued*

and she uses it to gain approval and attention. She feels that the way for her to gain acceptance and respect from her peers is to fight them—that she is not worthy otherwise.

In addition to the immediate problem of fighting in school, this client has academic difficulties. These difficulties are partly a result of the problem behaviors that continually got her in trouble, but prior reports indicate that there is a suspicion of a learning disability of some sort. Erica has trouble understanding much of her schoolwork, and this is a source of frustration for her. She repeated fifth grade because of poor academic performance.

Another aspect of this client's problem situation is that she has a stressful family life. For the past two years, she has lived in her aunt's and uncle's home with her mother, younger sister, and two older cousins. Erica's father is uninvolved with her and her sister; he reportedly promises to spend time with them, but he never shows up. Erica claims that this does not bother her in the least, but I believe it is a source of great disappointment to her. She has made remarks to her teacher that her father doesn't come to see her because he is upset about her performance in school. This is very telling with regard to her self-esteem because she has, in fact, been doing very well at Community School. The fact that she feels she isn't doing well enough for him, although she has been earning almost all of her points (behavior points on the system that the school uses), is indicative of how much value she places on his opinion.

Her relationship with her mother seems to be very up and down. She doesn't discuss it much, but from all indications, her aunt is the primary caretaker. Her aunt is the one who came in for intake, and her aunt is the one who takes all phone calls about Erica. The mother has custody, though. Recently, the mother disappeared for several days, and no one knew where she was. This was having an obvious effect on Erica's behavior; she became very irritable and wouldn't talk about what was bothering her. I had to call the aunt to discover what was wrong. Erica maintains that this wasn't what was bothering her at all—that she was perfectly fine, and everyone was assuming that her mother's disappearance was upsetting her. She told me that it was "no big deal," that her mother did this a lot, and that she always came back (she came back this time as well, the day after I called the aunt).

Even though her relationship with her mother has obvious problems, it is equally obvious that Erica craves her mother's attention. For example, she was so happy and proud a few weeks ago when her mother braided her hair for her. She basked in the compliments everyone gave her, and she was eager to say that her mother had done it for her.

Erica's relationship with her younger sister is problematic. She has reported that they fight all the time. I think this may be a result of normal sibling arguments. However, I have heard hints (from my supervisor) that the younger sister is the "perfect" child of the family, so maybe some jealousy is underlying the fighting between the sisters.

To summarize, my client's problem situation, on the surface, centers on the physical and verbal aggression that she uses to deal with her peers' teasing. When we look a bit deeper, though, we find a young girl struggling with poor self-esteem stemming from a weight problem, a rough family life, and a potential learning disability. This client knows no other way of dealing with her anger and frustration than fighting.

Erica has many strengths. First of all, she has begun to establish a relationship with me. She is starting to feel more comfortable talking to me and seems to look forward to our individual sessions. This is an important step; she needs to be able to talk about her concerns and have someone she trusts to help support her as she develops and works on goals. She also has the support of her aunt. She seems to have a good relationship with her aunt, and her aunt seems to be a very caring person who will help Erica as she tries to change. Another strength that I haven't delved into much yet is her religious affiliation. Erica told me that she is a Jehovah's Witness. I am not sure how much she identifies with this aspect of herself, but it could be another source of support for her. Also, her religious affiliation may help her see how important it is to try to change. A final source of support is the Community School environment. Erica's behavior has definitely been less severe since she has been attending our program. This is an indication that she feels more comfortable here (a fact she has expressed to me) and that the supportive environment is helpful to her.

Other strengths I see in Erica are that she is intellectually capable of making changes in her behavior, has no major physical or mental health issues impeding her progress, and has several friends from her district school who may be a source of support for her. These friends could just as easily be a problem, though. They could perpetuate her old behaviors by egging her on in fight situations. On the positive side, my client is definitely capable of making friends, and she could always make new ones.

Some strong obstacles face Erica in trying to work on her goals. As I have already mentioned, she is fix-ated on fighting as a solution to problems; she is proud of her fighting capabilities and sees fighting as necessary. A factor tied into this may be stereotypes of African Americans: she may feel that she is expected to be "tough" because that is the image she sees of African Americans.

An additional obstacle is her weight problem. She may need some help setting up an appropriate dieting plan, or if it turns out to be a true eating disorder, she may need extra counseling. This is not only an issue for her self-esteem; it is a health issue as well.

Another major obstacle is that Erica has problems with family support. Although she does have the support of her aunt, she craves the attention, recognition, and love of her mother and father. This could really affect her work on goals. She may feel that she has no reason to try to change if the people she wants to notice her most don't pay attention.

## DISCUSSION QUESTIONS

1. Erica W., the client in the final case study, has been diagnosed as having oppositional defiant disorder, dysthymic disorder, and an eating disorder. Compare the image of Erica you obtain from the strengths assessment with the image you obtain from the diagnostic categories. How are the two images alike, and how are they different? Are there differences in your expectations for Erica? What do you gain from the diagnosis? How does the diagnosis influence how you would proceed with the case?

2. What other services or interventions might be appropriate for Erica? Would she be a good candidate for an anger management group? (For information on anger management interventions, see Eggert, 1994, and Goldstein, 1987.)

3. What effect did the worker system have on the helping process with Erica? What are the advantages of assessing the transactions between the worker and client systems? What are the disadvantages?

4. Describe the process of conducting a strengths-based assessment. How is it different from the assessments made at your field placement? How is it similar? Which of the strengths guidelines are followed in your field placement agency?

5. Describe the individual subsystems that can potentially affect the helping relationship and a target problem. How would a social worker use a strengths-based approach to assess these subsystems?

# REFERENCES

American Psychiatric Association (2000). *Diagnostic and statistical manual of mental disorders: DSM-IV-TR* (4th ed.). Washington, DC: American Psychiatric Association.

Chang, V. N., and Scott, S. T. (1999). *Basic interviewing skills: A workbook for practitioners.* Chicago: Nelson-Hall.

Cormier, W., and Cormier, S. (1991). *Interviewing strategies for helpers* (3rd ed.). Pacific Grove, CA: Brooks/Cole.

Cournoyer, B. (2000). *The social work skills workbook.* Pacific Grove, CA: Brooks/Cole.

Cowger, C. (1997). Assessing client strengths: Assessment for client empowerment. In D. Saleebey (Ed.), *The strengths perspective in social work practice* (2nd ed., pp. 59–73). New York: Longman.

Cowger, C., and Snively, C. A. (2002). Assessing client strengths: Individual, family, and community empowerment. In D. Saleebey (Ed.), *The strengths perspective in social work practice* (3rd ed., pp. 106–123). Boston: Allyn and Bacon.

Dejong, P., and Berg, I. K. (1998). *Interviewing for solutions.* Pacific Grove, CA: Brooks/Cole.

Eggert, L. (1994). *Anger management for youth: Stemming aggression and violence.* Bloomington, IN: National Educational Service.

Gambrill, E. (1997). *Social work practice: A critical thinker's guide.* New York: Osford University Press.

Germain, C. B., and Gitterman, A. (1980). *The life model of social work practice.* New York: Columbia University Press.

Gilgun, J., Daly, D., and Handel, G. (Eds.). (1992). *Qualitative methods in family research.* Newbury Park, CA: Sage.

Goldstein, A. P. (1987). *Aggression replacement training: A comprehensive intervention for aggressive youth.* Champaign, IL: Research Press.

Hepworth, D., Rooney, R., and Larsen, J. (2002). *Direct social work practice: Theory and skills* (6th ed.). Pacific Grove, CA: Brooks/Cole.

Janzen, C., and Harris, O. (1997). *Family treatment in social work practice* (3rd ed.). Itasca, IL: F. E. Peacock Publishing, Inc.

Jordan, C., and Franklin, C. (1995). *Clinical assessment for social workers: Quantitative and qualitative methods.* Chicago: Lyceum.

Kadushin, A., and Kadushin, G. (1997). *The social work interview* (4th ed.). New York: Columbia University Press.

Kinney, J., Haapala, D., and Booth, C. (1991). *Keeping families together: The homebuilders model.* New York: Aldine de Gruyter.

Kirk, S., and Kutchins, H. (1992). *The selling of DSM: The rhetoric of science in psychiatry.* New York: Aldine de Gruyter.

Levy, C. (1972). Values and planned change. *Social Casework, 53,* 488–493.

Lewis, J., Beavers, W., Gossett, J., and Phillips, V. (1976). *No single thread: Psychological health in family systems.* New York: Brunner/Mazel.

McQuaide, S., and Ehrenreich, J. (1997). Assessing client strengths. *Families in Society: The Journal of Contemporary Human Services, 78,* 201–212.

Meyer, C. (1993). *Assessment in social work practice.* New York: Columbia University Press.

Perlman, H. (1968). *Persona: Social role and responsibility.* Chicago: University of Chicago Press.

Petr, C. (1988). The worker–client relationship: A general systems perspective. *Social Casework, 69,* 620–626.

Rapp, C. (1998). *The strengths model: Case management with people suffering from severe and persistent mental illness.* New York: Oxford University Press.

Saleebey, D. (1997). The strengths perspective: Possibilities and problems. In D. Saleebey (Ed.), *The strengths perspective in social work practice* (2nd ed., pp. 231–245). New York: Longman.

Saleebey, D. (2002). *The strengths perspective in social work practice* (3rd ed.). Boston: Allyn and Bacon.

Sevel, J., Cummins, L., and Madrigal, C. (1999). *Social work skills demonstrated: Beginning direct practice demonstration CD-ROM.* Boston: Allyn and Bacon.

Shulman, L. (1999). *The skills of helping: Individuals, families, groups, and communities* (4th ed.). Itasca, IL: F. E. Peacock Publishing, Inc.

Zwick, R., and Atkinson, C. (1985). Effectiveness of a client pretherapy orientation videotape. *Journal of Counseling Psychology, 32,* 514–524.

# PRE-ENGAGEMENT PHASE

*Families, Small Groups, Organizations, and Communities*

© Michael Newman/PhotoEdit

Karen A. is a first-year MSW student with a field placement at a private social service agency. The agency runs a life-skills and parenting program for teenage mothers and their children. Karen and Krystal W., a recent MSW who works at the agency, cofacilitate the weekly group session for the teenage mothers in the program. Karen is Caucasian and Krystal is African-American, as are most of the women in the program. Both Karen and Krystal are in their early twenties, and neither has children of her own.

Karen and Krystal had difficulty getting the young women to participate in the group sessions. During the first three sessions, most of them looked bored and rarely said anything. As a group, they were unresponsive and did not seem to be interested in the information that Karen and Krystal were presenting. Karen began to feel discouraged and a bit resentful about their lack of interest in child development and parenting skills. Karen and Krystal were unsure why the group was so unresponsive and what they should do to correct the situation. The one thing they were sure about was that what they were doing was not working.

Collaboration, client strengths, empowerment, and the helping relationship apply to working with families and groups as well as to individual clients. Using the collaborative model with families and small groups requires you to be sensitive to each individual member as well as to the ongoing dynamics of the family or group as a whole (Shulman, 1999; Reid, 1997). The assessment process involves individual assessments of each member's functioning as well as an assessment of the overall functioning of the group. "This requires an awareness of each member and an awareness of the themes and patterns of the group" (Reid, 1997, p. 14).

Working with families and groups has a long tradition in social work, dating back to the early charity organization societies and the settlement house movement (Popple and Leighninger, 1993). Social work practice with families and groups has increased in recent years. The use of groups has dramatically increased, in part because of managed care and cost containment incentives (Magen, 1995). Today, family practice and group work are major components of generalist social work practice.

This chapter presents information on the pre-engagement phase of collaborative social work with families, small groups, organizations, and communities. The chapter begins with information on assessing families and family dynamics. This is followed by information on small groups, group dynamics, and assessing group functioning. The chapter concludes with discussions of organization and community assessment.

By the end of the chapter, you should be able to help Karen and Krystal

1. Understand family systems and family dynamics
2. Classify the type of group they are running
3. Assess the functioning of a group and identify problem areas
4. Assess organizational and community functioning

# COLLABORATIVE SOCIAL WORK PRACTICE WITH FAMILIES

Generalist social workers often provide services to families. Social work has a long tradition of viewing individual functioning within the context of families. Janzen and Harris point out that even though "family treatment as a mode of practice was formally introduced in the 1950s, some of the underlying ideas and observations that support this process appeared in the social work literature as early as the first quarter of the century" (1997, p. 4). An individual's problems and concerns usually include difficulties with transactions with others. Because the family is the primary social unit for most people, assessment of an individual's person-in-environment system often results in the identification of the family as a target system in the helping process. Generalist social workers need to understand family functioning and become skilled in conducting family assessments.

The collaborative model of social work practice presented in Chapter 3 can be used in working with families. The phases, tasks, inputs, skills, and outputs of the model are all applicable to work with families as well as individual clients. The major challenge in working with families is helping the families view their concerns as family system problems rather than as problems with individual members of the family. Often the family seeks professional assistance to help resolve problems created by one person that makes life in the family difficult. The "identified patient" is seen as the problem, and the family comes in to have the identified patient fixed.

During the pre-engagement phase the social worker needs to listen to, study, and ask about the feelings and perceptions of the problem of each member of the family. Giving all members of the family a voice in the process promotes interactions among the members. The clarifying task in collaborative social work with families focuses on a cyclical process of helping the family view themselves as a system in which each member plays several roles. Reframing is a critical skill in this process. The family members need to recognize that their concerns are family system concerns, in order for the work to proceed. If this is not accomplished and the social worker and family members focus on the identified patient, then the client system and focus of the work is on the scapegoated individual in the family and not the family system. The following presents information on the pre-engagement phase with families. The focus is not on the components of the model but rather on content related to understanding family functioning and assessing family dynamics in a circular rather than linear way.

## Family Systems Problems

It is important to help the family view a problem as a family systems issue and not just the result of the behavior of the identified patient (Freeman, 1981). The worker needs to encourage the family to adopt a different way of viewing the problem situation (Watzlawick, Weakland, and Fisch, 1974). Often a single member of a family is considered to be the problem. This individual is the identified patient (Shulman, 1999). For example, a difficult child may be the identified patient, and the family seeks help in controlling the child. The worker will encourage the family to redefine the situation as a family system problem, not one caused simply by the child's difficult behavior. The task is to delabel the identified patient and help family members assume ownership for the roles they play in the problem (Hepworth, Rooney, and Larsen, 2002).

Hepworth, Rooney, and Larsen outline two strategies for delabeling the identified patient. One strategy is to "explore relationships between family members in lieu of focusing on the behavior of individual members" (1997, p. 485). For example, you may first focus on the interactions between the mother and the difficult child, then the father and the child, then the mother and the father, and finally among all three together. Your goal is to help family members see that the difficulties with the child do not take place in isolation and that the problems are in the functioning of the family system. This takes the blame off the identified patient and allows the problem to be viewed as belonging to the family.

The second strategy is to "focus initially on the role of blamers (or plaintiffs) in the difficulties about which they complain" (Hepworth, Rooney, and Larsen, 1997, p. 485). Instead of focusing on the difficult child, focus on the mother's or father's role (or both) in the problem behaviors exhibited by the child. Doing so shifts the family away from blaming to focusing on interactions between the parents and the child. It also helps family members take responsibility for changing their own behavior to improve family functioning. As Hepworth, Rooney, and Larsen point out, "it is critical to emphasize that members cannot change each other and that each individual can alleviate problems only by concentrating on changing his or her own behavior" (1997, p. 486).

Helping families change the way they view problem situations is not easy. More likely than not, you are asking them to give up long-held beliefs. They are likely to resist assuming responsibility for a difficult and painful situation. It is more comfortable to hold on to the belief that the problem belongs to the identified patient.

You need to be sensitive about how difficult it is for other family members to change their view of the problem. Avoid blaming as you explore the interactions among family members. Reframe problematic interactions. For example, if a mother is controlling and the child rebels, you might reframe the mother's controlling behavior as a positive expression of concern for the child's well-being that is not achieving the desired result. Empathize with the mother about how difficult the problem situation has been for her and the whole family. She is more likely to be receptive to this message than to one that blames her for being too controlling.

Despite your efforts, some family members may persist in blaming the identified patient. Your task is to support the entire family, not collude with some members in labeling the problem-bearer (Hepworth, Rooney, and Larsen, 1997). You must continue to try to help the family view itself as a system in which all members influence one another and all interactions are reciprocal. Ask family members to identify ways they might be contributing

TABLE 5.1 | FAMILY CLIENT SYSTEM: ASSESSMENT SUBSYSTEMS

| Structure | Emotional climate | Boundaries |
|---|---|---|
| Number of people | Affect | Open/closed |
| Ages of family members | Range of feelings | Rigid/diffuse |
| Relationship subsystems | Closeness | Enmeshed/detached |
| | Conflict | |
| **Ethnicity and culture** | **Communication patterns** | **Life-cycle stage** |
| Values and beliefs | Verbal | Developmental stage |
| Rules | Nonverbal | Transitions |
| Myths | Contextual | |

to the problem situation. What could they do to improve? How do their reactions affect the situation? What would they like to change to help cope with the problem situation?

## Family-in-Environment Assessment

The major family assessment subsystems are structure, life-cycle stage, emotional climate, communication patterns, boundaries, and ethnicity and culture. These subsystems for understanding and assessing families are highly interrelated (Table 5.1). It is difficult and may be misleading to separate them because they are so intertwined. Taken as a whole, they provide a comprehensive picture of the internal structure and functioning of a family system. For a thorough assessment, it is important to develop an overall picture of how the family relates and functions as a unit. This goal can be accomplished by using the family characteristics as a general frame of reference to guide the assessment process.

Structure    Family structure is the way family members organize themselves into interactional patterns (Minuchin and Fishman, 1982). "Repeated transactions establish patterns of how, when, and to whom to relate and these patterns underpin the system" (Minuchin, 1974, p. 51). Closely associated with the interaction patterns are the rules that govern them (Janzen and Harris, 1997). Families develop informal rules about family behavior and interactions. Issues of authority and power as well as other areas of family life are defined by those informal rules. Assessment of family systems requires an exploration and understanding of the unique rules that govern family interactions.

Another structural aspect of families is the subsystems in which they are organized (Aponte and Van Duesen, 1981). Most families have couple, parental, sibling, and parent–child subsystems (Janzen and Harris, 1997). Each subsystem needs to be evaluated. Figure 5.1 displays the four primary

FIGURE 5.1 | FAMILY SUBSYSTEMS AND NORMATIVE ROLES

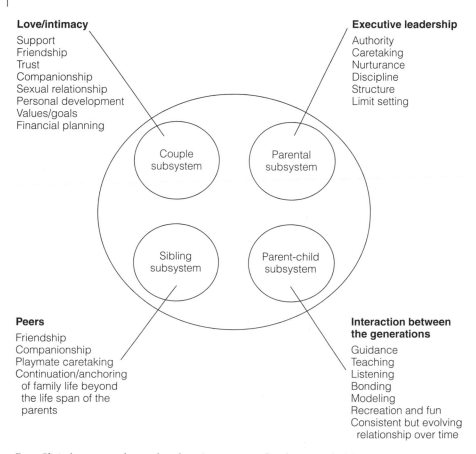

**Love/intimacy**
Support
Friendship
Trust
Companionship
Sexual relationship
Personal development
Values/goals
Financial planning

**Executive leadership**
Authority
Caretaking
Nurturance
Discipline
Structure
Limit setting

Couple subsystem

Parental subsystem

Sibling subsystem

Parent-child subsystem

**Peers**
Friendship
Companionship
Playmate caretaking
Continuation/anchoring
  of family life beyond
  the life span of the
  parents

**Interaction between the generations**
Guidance
Teaching
Listening
Bonding
Modeling
Recreation and fun
Consistent but evolving
  relationship over time

From *Clinical assessment for social workers: Quantitative and qualitative methods* by C. Jordan and C. Franklin. Copyright © 1995, Lyceum Books. Reprinted with permission.

subsystems and some of the important roles they fulfill (Jordan and Franklin, 1995). Understanding how the various subsystems interact and the roles they play is critical to understanding the overall functioning of the family and the effect of family structure on the target problem.

**Life-Cycle Stages**   Families pass through developmental life-cycle stages in much the same way as individuals. Carter and McGoldrick (1989) developed a conceptual life-cycle framework that characterizes the developmental stages of the traditional two-parent family with children (Table 5.2). Each stage has tasks that need to be accomplished for the family to make a successful transition to the next developmental stage (Jordan and Franklin, 1995). Although

**TABLE 5.2** | FAMILY LIFE-CYCLE STAGES
AND ASSOCIATED DEVELOPMENTAL TASKS

**Leaving home: single young adults**
Differentiating self in relation to family of origin
Developing intimate peer relationships
Establishing self through work and financial independence

**The joining of families through marriage: the new couple**
Forming marital system
Realigning relationships with extended families and friends to include spouse

**Families with young children**
Adjusting marital system to make space for child(ren)
Joining in child-rearing, financial, and household tasks
Realigning relationships with extended family to include parenting and grandparenting roles

**Families with adolescents**
Shifting parent–child relationships to permit adolescent to move in and out of system
Refocusing on mid-life marital and career issues
Beginning shift toward joint caring for older generation

**Launching children and moving on**
Renegotiating marital system as a dyad
Developing adult-to-adult relationships between grown children and their parents
Realigning relationships to include in-laws and grandchildren
Dealing with disabilities and death of great-grandparents

**Families in later life**
Maintaining own and couple functioning and interests in face of psychological decline
Supporting a more central role of middle generation
Making room in the system for the wisdom and experience of the elderly, supporting the older generation
without overfunctioning for them
Dealing with loss of spouse, siblings, and peers, and preparation for own death; life review and integration

From B. Carter and M. McGoldrick (Eds.) *The changing family life cycle: A framework for family therapy* (2nd ed.). Published by Allyn
and Bacon, Boston, MA. Copyright © 1993 by Pearson Education. Reprinted by permission of the publisher.

Carter and McGoldrick's family life-cycle stages have been widely accepted,
their conceptualization is based on a middle-class American family model. As
such it "has important weaknesses, especially when the family is not a 'traditional' family, has no children, or is in some other way different from the view
of the family as composed of a married couple and their children" (Garvin
and Seabury, 1997, p. 218).

Family life-cycle stages all involve additions or losses to family membership (Janzen and Harris, 1997). They require adapting to change, and they
necessitate changes in family roles and rules. The transitions between stages
often cause family difficulties and are the points at which families are most

likely to be in need of help (Janzen and Harris, 1997; Jordan and Franklin, 1995). A comprehensive assessment requires attention to important life-cycle transitions and the family's adjustment to them.

Carter and McGoldrick's family life-cycle stages provide a framework for identifying the stage and appropriate developmental tasks of a traditional two-parent family. The first step is to identify the family's stage of development. If you are working with a nontraditional family and the life-cycle stages do not appear to fit, the first task is to identify any transitions the family may be experiencing. Are there additions or losses to family membership? The second step is to assess family members' adaptation to the transition from one stage to another. Are there specific tasks that are more problematic than others? How are the various family members adjusting to their new roles and responsibilities? Are family members mourning the loss of tasks associated with the prior life-cycle stage?

**Emotional Climate**   Like individuals, families exhibit emotions. "When people are in close interaction (as in families or groups), the emotions of some individuals tend to be 'contagious,' and others begin to express similar feelings" (Garvin and Seabury, 1997, p. 218). Although the expression of individual affect within the family may vary, family patterns of emotions develop (Lewis, Beavers, Gossett, and Phillips, 1976).

An affect dimension and an involvement dimension influence a family's emotional climate. The affect dimension is the mode tone of the family system. Some family environments are hostile, tense, and conflicted, whereas others are more relaxed and peaceful, characterized by love, warmth, and harmony.

The second dimension of the family emotional climate is the extent to which the family members are involved with one another. This dimension encompasses the concepts of enmeshment and disengagement (Minuchin, 1974). In families that are disengaged, members have little emotional involvement with each other. In enmeshed families, on the other hand, members are overly involved with one another. There is "excessive closeness in which family members think and feel alike; there is little opportunity for independent functioning and what happens to one family member immediately affects others" (Gambrill, 1997, p. 575). The disengagement–enmeshment dimension has also been referred to as family cohesion (Olson, Sprenkle, and Russel, 1979). Families that fall at the extremes of this continuum are at risk of dysfunction. Those that fall between the extremes are considered to have a more balanced emotional climate and less risk of family dysfunction (Thomas and Olson, 1993). Members in more balanced families are supportive, help one another, and are committed to each other, but not to the extent that the individuality of the members is lost or subsumed by the family system.

The interaction between the affect and involvement dimensions of the family emotional climate is shown in Figure 5.2. Families with healthy emotional climates (+) are those in which the family mode tone is rated more toward the positive side of the affect dimension (love, relaxed, peace) and in the middle of the involvement dimension. Families with dysfunctional emotional

FIGURE 5.2 | FAMILY EMOTIONAL CLIMATE MATRIX

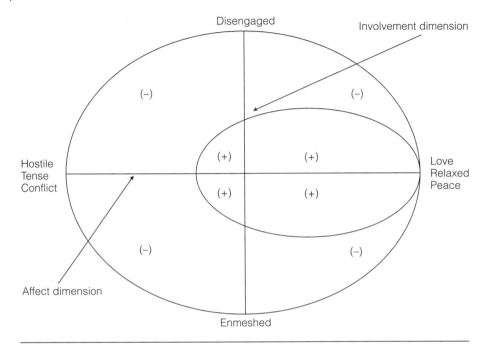

climates (–) are those rated on the negative side of the affect dimension (hostile, tense, conflict) and at the top or bottom of the involvement dimension (disengaged, enmeshed).

The inner circle of Figure 5.2 represents a healthy or acceptable range of the affective and involvement dimensions within families. It is assumed that within normal families there will be some conflict, tension, and hostility and that a normal family will fall approximately in the middle of the disengagement–enmeshment continuum. It is also assumed that there cannot be too much love within a family as long as the family is centered on the involvement dimension. Problems occur for families that are characterized by the extremes of the two dimensions.

**Communication Patterns**   A family's ability to communicate effectively and to deal with problems in communication can enhance its relationship and problem-solving ability (Satir, 1983). "Communication is important to competent functioning of family systems. For communication to be effective between family members, it must be open, direct, clear and congruent at different levels, such as one's tone and the content of the message" (Jordan and Franklin, 1995, p. 209). Communication problems are common when family members are having difficulty getting along and in families that show other signs of dysfunction (Satir, 1983). Janzen and Harris point out that communication modes and problems are intertwined with family structure and role divisions: "Family rules and structure are evident in the freedom or lack of it in expressing doubt or difference, and in who can say what to whom and when. Communication conveys how much each family member is valued and who has power in the system" (1997, p. 15).

Cultural beliefs and norms can influence family communication style and the degree of openness. Many cultural groups discourage the open expression of feelings (Ho, 1987). In assessing family communication patterns, be aware of possible cultural differences, and respect the communication styles practiced within the family's cultural system. Do not assume that open, direct, and honest communication is desirable for ethnically and culturally diverse families.

There are three basic levels of communication: verbal, nonverbal, and contextual (Satir, 1983). **Verbal communication** refers to the words and the content of the message. **Nonverbal communication** refers to the body language that accompanies the verbal message, including gestures, facial expressions, posture, and eye contact. **Contextual communication** refers to the context or situation in which the message is delivered, such as the tone of voice, the timing of the message, and the circumstances in which the message is delivered. Nonverbal and contextual levels of communication can reinforce or contradict the verbal message.

Effective communication requires **congruency** among the three levels of communication, and in dysfunctional families congruency is often lacking. Thus, an important aspect in assessing family communication patterns is to determine "the extent to which there is congruence between the verbal, nonverbal, and contextual levels of messages on the part of individuals in a family system" (Hepworth, Rooney, and Larsen, 1997, p. 311). Is there congruence among the three levels of communication? Is the verbal message supported by nonverbal messages and the situation in which the messages are delivered?

In addition to problems related to the congruence of messages, problems may be related to **sender skills,** such as expressing and owning feelings, or **receiver skills,** such as openness to hearing feelings, listening, and validating (Gambrill, 1997). Hepworth, Rooney, and Larsen point out that when comparing processes of optimally functioning families with those of troubled families, it becomes evident that the former possess several categories of verbal and nonverbal responses that are noticeably absent in the latter. Included in these responses are messages that convey understanding, demonstrate respect for the uniqueness of the sender's experience, and invite further expression and exploration (1997, p. 313).

In assessing sender and receiver skills of family members, ask how receptive or open they appear to be to the thoughts and feelings of other family members. Do they listen to each other? Do they acknowledge the sender's message? Do they encourage the sharing of feelings and the expression of thoughts? How open are the individual members to sharing their thoughts and feelings? Do they express how they are feeling or what they think? Do they take responsibility for their own feelings and thoughts? Are the messages expressed as "I statements" or as "you statements"?

**Boundaries**    Family system boundaries are the demarcations that define the subsystems within a family (internal) and its interactions with larger systems (external). Nichols (1984) defined boundaries as invisible barriers between individual family members, family subsystems, and larger systems that regulate interactions. "The function of boundaries is to safeguard the differentiation and autonomy of the family and its subsystems" (Janzen and Harris, 1997, p. 37). Boundaries can be rigid or diffuse (Minuchin, 1974). Rigid boundaries allow little interaction between systems, while diffuse boundaries are loose and blurred, providing little differentiation between the family subsystems or the family and other systems.

Families are part of larger systems, such as neighborhoods and communities. They interact with these other systems on a daily basis. "They differ widely, however, in the degree to which they are open to transactions with other systems and in the flexibility of their outer boundaries" (Hepworth, Rooney, and Larsen, 1997, p. 291). The extent to which people who are not family members are allowed to interact with the family varies. Kantor and Lehr (1975) identified three family boundary types: open, closed, and random.

**Open family systems** are those in which the family has a great deal of interaction with people outside the family. Members of open families have friends over frequently, are active in the community, and participate in outside activities. **Closed family systems,** on the other hand, are characterized by a lack of interaction with the external environment. The family restricts and limits involvement with others. Guests are not welcomed; family members are not involved in outside activities; and transactions with others are guarded. **Random family systems** have no boundary patterns. Each member of the family develops his or her own type of interaction pattern with the external environment.

Knowledge of the three boundary patterns can help you assess how a family interacts with its external environment. The patterns are prototypes, and any family's boundary pattern will probably include characteristics of all three. There are benefits and liabilities associated with each boundary type. Your task is to identify the boundary transactions of the family and, in collaboration with family members, assess how these transactions affect the identified target problem. This includes an assessment of strengths as well as obstacles associated with the family's external transactions.

**Internal family boundaries** relate to the transactions among the various subsystems within the family. As with external boundaries, internal boundaries can be characterized as rigid or diffuse. Families with rigid internal boundaries have a disengaged emotional climate, and those with loose or diffuse boundaries have an enmeshed climate, as discussed earlier in this chapter. Disengagement and enmeshment are not always problematic. "According to Minuchin, every family experiences some enmeshment or disengagement in its subsystems as a family goes through developmental phases" (Hepworth, Rooney, and Larsen, 1997, p. 294). Most families fall somewhere between the extremes. Assessment of internal boundaries requires an understanding of the developmental phase of the family, a description of the various interaction styles among the family's subsystems, and identification of the benefits as well as liabilities of the internal boundary patterns in relation to the identified target problem. It is also important to keep in mind cultural variations in family relationships. Family interactions and boundaries should be assessed from the perspective of the family's ethnic and cultural background.

**Ethnicity and Culture**   Families possess sets of beliefs that are drawn from their ethnic and cultural heritage. A family's cultural beliefs affect all aspects of family functioning and need to be taken into consideration when assessing structure, life-cycle stages, emotional climate, communication patterns, and boundaries. Assessment of the family's rules of behavior also needs to be culturally based. "Families have rules about who can do what to whom and what may or may not be discussed by whom in what context" (Gambrill, 1997, p. 574). Some rules are explicit and clearly stated (children do not talk back to parents), and others are implicit and not openly verbalized (be careful not to hurt mother's feelings). Implicit rules must be inferred from the interactions of family members; they are unwritten and unspoken and may be beyond family members' conscious level of awareness. Explicit and implicit family rules govern family members' behavior toward one another. The rules that emerge in families are influenced by the family's values and beliefs. "Although rules govern the processes of families from any cultural origin, they differ drastically from one culture to another" (Hepworth, Rooney, and Larsen, 1997, p. 279).

In considering family rules, you need to understand and respect the values and beliefs of the family. Understanding the cultural basis of the norms governing family members' behavior provides the context for assessing the effect of family rules on the identified target problem. Family rules can potentially have positive or negative effects on family functioning. The cultural context of a rule determines whether it enhances functioning or contributes to dysfunction. Assessment of ethnicity and culture takes into consideration values and beliefs and how they affect the functioning of the family system.

## Assessment and Family Strengths

Creating an empowering assessment process with families is similar to creating the process with individual clients. The main difference and the biggest challenge is to focus your attention and efforts on both the family as a whole and on each individual member. Assessment must be a collaborative process in which concerns are heard, strengths are recognized, and understanding, empathy, and hope are communicated. Together the worker and family explore the family members' perceptions of the problem situation.

Assessment emphasizes the identification of family strengths as well as strengths of each individual family member. "Social workers should help families build on their strengths, gain access to resources, learn how to negotiate the many systems their members contact (school, neighborhood, social services), and overcome problems that affect healthy family development" (Hodges, Burwell, and Ortega, 1998, p. 146). Families have power from within to bring about positive change. The strengths perspective, however, must come from you. Although all families have strengths, family members may not always recognize or be aware of them. By adopting the attitude that strengths exist and can be used to help the family resolve the problem situation, you can help the family recognize their individual and collective strengths. Focus on strengths. Look for the ways family members have coped with problem situations and concerns. Help them recognize past successes as well as resources and abilities they can draw on in the helping process.

A collaborative approach to family assessment empowers families by allowing their expertise in functioning and their concerns to emerge. Strive to empower the family as well as each individual member. The perceptions of the problem situation by the family and its members are where you should begin. Do not force on them your analysis and assessment of their problems, interpersonal relationships, or individual dysfunction, even if you believe that numerous problems exist. Engage in a collaborative exchange, sharing your insights and perceptions and exploring those of family members. "To engage in a truly collaborative relationship, each party must stay open to discussing and resolving differences in an honest and respectful manner" (Hodges, Burwell, and Ortega, 1998, p. 150). Become a partner with the family by sharing responsibilities and making decisions.

Assessment is the key to the helping process. To be able to effectively help clients, you need to understand their concerns, strengths, potential resources, and the challenges they face. The assessment process provides an opportunity for clients to tell their stories. It is more about listening than asking questions. Strengths-based assessments focus on clients' perceptions rather than on diagnostic labels. A comprehensive assessment takes into consideration the effect of clients' environments on problem situations. The strengths and challenges associated with all relevant systems are reviewed with clients. Ideally, the process should empower the client and create a sense of hopefulness. Focusing on strengths rather than deficits helps create expectations about possibilities for change.

## COLLABORATIVE SOCIAL WORK WITH SMALL GROUPS

As a generalist social worker, you may be involved in creating and implementing a new group. More often than not, however, you will be assigned to work with an existing group. Many social service agencies have established, ongoing groups. Regardless of whether you help design and implement a new group or join an existing group, at some point you will need to assess the functioning of the group in relation to a problem or concern.

The collaborative model of social work practice presented in Chapter 3 can be used with groups. The phases, tasks, inputs, skills, and outputs of the model are all applicable to groups as well as individuals and families. The major challenge in working with groups is having two clients: the individual group members and the group as a whole (Shulman, 1999). The social worker has to be attentive to the needs of individual members and their participation in the group and to the functioning of the overall group. The worker uses elaboration and empathy skills to bring individual concerns back to the group and to help the group develop trust and build cohesion. In the discussion of the pre-engagement phase with groups, the focus is not on components of the model but rather on understanding group functioning and assessing group dynamics.

## Types of Groups

Generalist social workers are involved with many different types of groups. At the broadest level, there are two categories of groups: treatment groups and task groups (Toseland and Rivas, 1995). Within these two categories, there are several subtypes. Toseland and Rivas (1995) have identified four types of treatment groups: educational, growth, remedial, and socialization groups. Garvin and Seabury (1997) have identified five types of individual change groups (therapy, support, self-help, educational, and peer groups) and four types of task groups (community professional, community resident, agency task, and policy groups). Others have developed similar classifications (Corey and Corey, 1997; Jacobs, Harvill, and Masson, 1994).

The primary purposes of treatment groups are to increase members' coping abilities and help them resolve sociopsychological needs. The primary purposes of task groups, on the other hand, are to accomplish a specific undertaking, produce a product, or carry out a mandate (Hepworth, Rooney, and Larsen, 1997). The distinction between treatment and task groups, however, "should be used loosely rather than rigidly" (Garvin and Seabury, 1997, p. 231). In actual practice, groups often overlap in terms of function and objectives (Toseland and Rivas, 1995). For example, individuals who belong to a treatment group for substance abuse problems may become involved in a community education task group aimed at informing teenagers about the dangers of substance abuse.

Groups can also be categorized by client systems level. Generalist social workers typically work with client groups, agency groups, and community groups. These may be formed or natural groups. "**Formed groups** are established through some outside influence, such as an agency, and are convened for a particular purpose. . . ." **Natural groups,** on the other hand, are those that develop in a spontaneous manner on the basis of friendship, location, or some naturally occurring event" (Reid, 1997, p. 10). Another way of classifying groups is by leadership. Some groups have a professional leader or group facilitator, whereas others are led by group members.

Table 5.3 lists the types of groups that are common in generalist social work practice. The classification does not include self-help groups or natural groups, since they usually do not have a professional leader. Social work, however, has a tradition of involvement with these types of groups (Reid, 1997). As a generalist social worker, you may have the opportunity to help develop a self-help group or assist a natural group. The assessment skills and concepts used with formed, professionally led client, agency, and community groups can also be applied to these groups.

TABLE 5.3 | TYPES OF DIRECT PRACTICE GROUPS

**Client groups**

| | |
|---|---|
| **Therapy** | Groups that focus on the remediation or rehabilitation of members' intrapsychic or interpersonal problems, such as groups for depression, anger management, and substance abuse |
| **Support** | Groups established to provide support to members and help them cope with an issue that is common to all the members of the group, such as a parent bereavement group |
| **Educational** | Groups that have an educational objective and use educational techniques, such as parent training groups and teen leadership groups |
| **Growth** | Groups that focus on self-improvement and personal growth of the members, such as consciousness-raising groups and empowerment groups |

As with other classifications, the categories of groups are not mutually exclusive. In practice, few groups are purely one type or another. Most have more than one purpose or function. Furthermore, there is a great deal of variety within each category. The range of possibilities for groups is extensive. It is limited only by client, agency, and community need.

## Group-in-Environment Assessment

Concerns about group functioning may arise from the group, or you may raise them. In this respect, group assessment is different from individual and family system assessment. Individuals and families usually seek professional help for a problem they are aware of and want to correct. Problems in group functioning, however, are not always apparent to individual members or to the group as a whole, and groups usually do not seek professional help. An important part of your job as the group leader is to identify potential issues and concerns and to bring them to the attention of the group.

As shown in Table 5.4, there are six major subsystems within the group-in-environment system that have potential relevance for the assessment process: purpose, structure, life-cycle stage, culture, alliances, and tasks. Like family subsystems, group subsystems are highly interrelated. Taken as a whole, they provide a comprehensive picture of the internal structure and functioning of a group system. An ecosystems assessment requires the social worker and the group to mutually and continually assess the effect the various subsystems have on one another and on the functioning of the group.

**Purpose**    Every formed group has a purpose. The purpose varies according to the type of group. Because in many respects, the type defines a group's purpose, assessment of purpose is an excellent first step in assessing group functioning. "The failure of many groups can be attributed to the lack of a consensus on the purpose of the group" (Magen, 1995, p. 162). The group's pur-

| TABLE 5.4 | GROUP CLIENT SYSTEMS |
|---|---|

| | |
|---|---|
| **Purpose (type)**<br>Therapy<br>Support<br>Education<br>Growth<br>Project<br>Administrative<br>Professional<br>Citizen | **Culture**<br>Traditions<br>Values<br>Norms |
| | **Alliances**<br>Communication patterns<br>Interpersonal attraction<br>Power<br>Leadership |
| **Structure**<br>Membership composition<br>Size<br>Duration<br>Open/closed | **Tasks**<br>Performance<br>Decision making |
| **Life-cycle stage**<br>Developmental stage | |

pose should be clearly stated and agreed on by group members. It is from the purpose that all other aspects of a group evolve. Is the identified problem or concern related to confusion or disagreement about the purpose of the group? Is the purpose clear and unambiguous? Is there agreement about the purpose of the group? Does the group have more than one purpose? If so, are the different purposes in conflict?

**Structure**    Structure is the composition of the group, its size, whether the group is time limited or ongoing, and whether the group is open to new members or closed. Problems in group functioning can often be traced back to structural issues. Examination of a group's structure and the effect that the four structural dimensions are having on the area of concern is an important aspect of group assessment.

**Composition**    Group composition refers to who is included in the group and who is excluded. It pertains to the vital issue of homogeneity versus heterogeneity (Hepworth, Rooney, and Larsen, 1997). There are a number of issues associated with group composition, including gender, age, education, socioeconomic status, and racial composition (Garvin, 1997). Another consideration is the socioemotional capacity and intellectual functioning of the members (Levine, 1991).

"Conventional wisdom suggests that for a group to be viable, it should be both homogeneous and heterogeneous" (Reid, 1997, p. 176). There are advantages to highly homogeneous groups (e.g., increased identification and group cohesion) and also disadvantages that stem from the lack of diversity, just as there are advantages (different points of view or perspectives) and disadvantages (difficulty in relating, less bonding, more time needed to develop trust) associated with highly heterogeneous groups (Flapan and Fenchel, 1987). "The challenge is to attain a workable balance between homogeneity and heterogeneity" (Hepworth, Rooney, and Larsen, 1997, p. 323).

Issues associated with group composition are numerous and complex. What is ideal for one group is less so for another. There is no single correct prescription. The composition depends, among other things, on the purpose of the group, the unique characteristics of its members, the leader's style and personality, and the prior experiences of the members and the group. In assessing composition, ask whether something about the composition is contributing to the target problem. Is gender, age, race, or another factor contributing to the identified concern? Is the homogeneity or heterogeneity of the group a contributing factor? What are the strengths of the group's composition? What are the weaknesses or obstacles associated with it?

*Size*    Whether a group is too small, too large, or just right is relative (Reid, 1997). It depends on the group's purpose, the characteristics of the members, and the leader's level of comfort, among other factors. Generally, smaller groups of 8–12 members allow everyone to participate and form close relationships. A group of 2–4 members often ceases to function as a group because it lacks the "critical mass" needed for sustained interaction among members (Yalom, 1995). "Interaction among members diminishes, and the practitioner finds himself or herself engaged in individual therapy within a group situation" (Reid, 1997, p. 180). At the other end of the continuum, groups of 13 or more are generally recommended when the purpose is to convey information and a high level of interaction among the participants is not expected.

Although group size is most directly related to purpose and expected level of participation, it can contribute to a number of other issues related to functioning. Does the size of the group have an effect on the identified problem situation? Is the group too large or too small to accomplish its purposes? What are the benefits of the group's size? What are the negatives associated with the number of participants in the group?

*Duration*    Duration refers to how long the group stays together. Some groups meet for a fixed number of sessions. One advantage of **time-limited groups** is that having a fixed termination point encourages productive work (Magen, 1995; Reid, 1997). "The primary disadvantage of a time-limited group is that time allotted for the group may not be enough for the group to reach its goals" (Reid, 1997, p. 181).

There is no fixed rule regarding the optimal number of meetings for a time-limited group. It depends on the group's purpose and the participants. Reid (1997) suggests that 20 sessions are ideal for therapy groups. Corey (1995) suggests that there should be enough sessions for cohesion and trust to develop and the work to be productive, but not so many that the group seems to drag on forever.

**Open-ended groups** have no fixed ending point (Magen, 1995). These groups continue meeting as long as the members desire. The primary advantage of an ongoing group is that members have adequate time to accomplish the tasks at hand. Clients need varying amounts of time to achieve change. On the negative side, open-ended groups foster dependency and are often less productive (Reid, 1997).

The decision regarding the duration of the group should be directly related to the group's purpose. However, duration can also affect a number of other issues associated with group functioning. What are the advantages and disadvantages associated with the number of sessions or meetings? Could limiting the number of meetings cause a problem? Has the group gone on for too long?

*Open or Closed Group*   Groups may be open or closed to new members. The membership of closed groups is fixed at the first meeting, and no new members are allowed to join once the group gets under way. The advantages of closed groups are greater cohesion, bonding, and identification among members (Reid, 1997). There is also a greater likelihood that trust and support will develop. A disadvantage of closed groups is the possibility that the group will terminate because of member attrition.

Reid (1997) identified three types of open groups: drop-in, replacement, and re-formed groups. The **drop-in group** is very flexible in terms of membership. Entry criteria are broad, and members may continue with the group as long as they wish. The **replacement group** usually has a fixed upper limit of members. As members drop out, they are replaced with new members, so that the size of the group remains relatively constant. In a **re-formed group,** members contract for a set time period. During this time period, no new members are added. At the end of the contracted time, the group is reconstituted. The new group contains some original members and some new members (Reid, 1997).

The advantages of an open group are a constant flow of members into the group and the flexibility it allows members in joining, participating, and dropping out. The primary disadvantage of an open group is that changing membership hinders the development of group cohesion and bonding among members. In addition, frequent changes of membership disrupt the work of the group.

Open and closed group membership is most directly associated with the purpose, setting, and population (Hepworth, Rooney, and Larsen, 1997). It also can be associated with a number of other issues related to group functioning. Group client system assessment should include an exploration of the effect of the membership format on an identified target problem. Is the target problem due in part to the group's having open or closed membership? Would a different membership policy improve the problem situation? What are the advantages and disadvantages of an open or closed membership for the group?

*Culture*   The traditions, beliefs, and norms developed by the group constitute the cultural components of group functioning. Traditions, beliefs, and norms are highly interrelated. An examination of a group's culture and the effect it has on an identified area of concern is an important aspect of group assessment.

All groups develop **traditions,** which are ritualized activities, such as ceremonies, prayers, and songs, that are incorporated into group meetings. A group's traditions are influenced by members' ethnic, racial, and cultural backgrounds (Garvin and Seabury, 1997). They are important symbols for group members, strengthening group identification and helping members feel closer to the group. They also help define the uniqueness of a group. Members who violate group traditions are not viewed favorably by fellow members. Violations can lead to reprimand and rejection by the group. To avoid this, "workers who begin to work with groups after their formation should learn their traditions as quickly as possible" (Garvin and Seabury, 1997, p. 242).

Group **norms** are the understandings group members have about behaviors. They define what members should and should not do within the group (Garvin and Seabury, 1997; Hepworth, Rooney, and Larsen, 1997). All groups develop unwritten rules that govern the behavior of the members. Norms may have a positive or negative influence on group functioning. Regular attendance at meetings, treating one another with respect, and communicating concerns directly to the group are examples of norms that have a positive effect on groups. Norms that have a negative or dysfunctional effect on the group include encouraging discussion of topics not related to the purpose of the meeting, letting a few members dominate the group, and avoiding talking about group problems.

Group norms are not explicitly expressed. They are implicit rules of behavior. Norms are discerned by observing the behavior of members and reactions to it. Sanctions and social disapproval are given for violating a norm; praise and social approval are given for compliance (Toseland and Rivas, 1995).

Groups also develop **values** or beliefs that are held in common by all or most group members (Toseland and Rivas, 1995). Values are what group members believe to be true. They are the shared belief system of the members. The values held by a group can have a positive or negative influence on group functioning. As with norms, values can only be inferred through observation. They are not written down, nor are they usually stated explicitly.

Assessment of a group's culture is an important function of the group leader. Cultural influences can have positive or negative effects on a concern or problem. To be able to effectively assess a group's culture you need to be aware of the traditions, values, and norms that have developed. This is an ongoing process. How does group culture affect the target problem? What are its positive influences? What are its negative influences?

*Alliances*    There are four dimensions of alliance: communication patterns, interpersonal attractions, power, and leadership. These four dimensions are highly interrelated. Taken together, they provide a comprehensive overview of the alliance component of group functioning.

**Communication patterns** involve who talks to whom and about what (Garvin and Seabury, 1997). It is the structure of the interactions among members. An analysis of communication patterns indicates who dominates group discussions, whether some members are isolated, and who the informal leaders are. It also provides insight into subgroup formation and the effect of the various subgroups on the functioning of the group (Hartford, 1971). Subgroups do not necessarily adversely affect a group. In fact, the formation of subgroups helps members form closer attachments to other members and to the group as a whole. Subgroups negatively affect the group when they become exclusive or when power struggles between subgroups interfere with member support for the larger group (Hepworth, Rooney, and Larsen, 1997).

Closely associated with communication patterns and subgroup formation is **interpersonal attraction** of members. As members get better acquainted, some members are attracted to others and some are not. Interpersonal attraction is influenced by race, culture, and gender as well as physical appearance, personality, and interests, among other factors (Garvin and Seabury, 1997). Members with similar backgrounds and interests are more likely to be attracted to each other than those who are very different from one another.

**Power** is the ability of one individual to influence another in a specific way. There are five types of power:

1. **Reward power** is the ability to influence others by providing them something that they value. A group member may offer friendship, support, praise, or other goods and services.
2. **Coercive power** is the ability to influence others by the use of punishment. A group member may use coercive power by criticizing, insulting, or physically threatening another group member.
3. **Legitimate power** is the ability to influence others by virtue of one's position in the group. The social work leader may exercise legitimate power based upon his or her assigned role.
4. **Referent power** is the ability to influence others by being liked or respected. A group member may have referent power based upon his or her personality or attractiveness.
5. **Expert power** is the ability to influence others because of specialized knowledge or skills. A member may exercise expert power by virtue of his or her special training. (Garvin and Seabury, 1997, p. 235; based on French and Raven, 1959.)

Both the sources of power and the locus of power within the group may vary. Power does not itself negatively affect group functioning. Problems arise when there are power struggles within the group. "Groups, in fact, are sometimes torn apart and meet their demise because of unresolved power issues that prevent the group from meeting the needs of some members" (Hepworth, Rooney, and Larsen, 1997, p. 338). The issue in group assessment is not so much who has the power but rather the group's ability to share power and to find resolutions to power conflicts that do not result in some members feeling that they have been forced to give up too much.

**Leadership** is more difficult to define than power. In simple terms, it is the capacity to mobilize group members into action. Garvin and Seabury (1997) view leadership as a process that grows out of interactions among group members related to the attainment of goals. They further break leadership into two types of group processes: task and social-emotional. "**Task leadership** occurs when the individual helps the group move toward defining and achieving group goals. **Social-emotional leadership** occurs when the member positively affects the interaction among group members by such things as reducing conflicts and facilitating the expression of positive feelings" (Garvin and Seabury, 1997, p. 239).

The alliance component has powerful influences on group functioning. A comprehensive assessment needs to carefully evaluate the effect of these processes on an identified problem area or concern. As the social worker involved with the group, part of your leadership task is to become aware of the alliance structure of the group. This requires ongoing observation of group behavior. Before you can assess the effect the processes have on the group, you need to understand how the group functions. Once you have a clear understanding of communication patterns, interpersonal alliances, power, and leadership within the group, you can assess their effect on a specific area of concern.

**Life-Cycle Stages**    This aspect of group functioning deals with group development. Groups go through a number of developmental stages. They change and evolve as they mature. Like humans, groups have a pattern of development. "While theorists and clinicians agree that groups go through various stages, there is no agreement as to how many stages exist and what the stages actually look like" (Reid, 1997, p. 56). Magen (1995) reports that the various typologies of group development range from three stages (Schwartz, 1986) to nine (Beck, 1983) and that there is considerable overlap in the labels applied to the stages and in their conceptualization. One widely used conceptualization is Tuckman's (1965) four-stage model of group development: forming, storming, norming, and performing. Magen (1995) added a fifth stage, adjourning, to Tuckman's model. Tuckman's model as modified by Magen provides the framework for the following discussion of group development.

Group development is not as tidy a process as the various conceptualizations suggest. Reid points out that

> Groups do not move along in an orderly sequence;
> Groups may revert to earlier stages;
> Stages cannot be thought of in any pure form but in various blends and combinations; and
> A group's life span and development can and will be influenced by the worker and by the members. (1997, p. 58)

*Forming*    The initial stage of the group, forming, is when members come together for the first time. In most groups, especially client groups, this is an exciting and anxious time for both the members and the leader. "Group members generally experience anxiety about the new situation and what will be expected of them" (Reid, 1997, p. 63). They are anxious about what will happen, what their experience in the group will be, and how they will perform. At this point, the group is a collection of individuals with individual concerns. "Excessive dependency on the worker is common in the initial session" (Reid, 1997, p. 64). Group members look to the leader for answers to questions about "expectations, about rules, roles, limits, and about how the sessions will run" (Reid, 1997, p. 64). Interactions among members are superficial and guarded. Members do not have a strong commitment to the group and have not developed an identification with the group as a whole.

The length of the forming stage varies. "Open-ended groups with frequent and excessive turnover of members would not be expected to move beyond the 'forming' stage of group development" (Magen, 1995, p. 166). Closed groups that meet on a fairly frequent basis might move to the next stage after a few sessions. Other groups never get beyond the initial stage and may terminate prematurely.

*Storming*    The second developmental stage, labeled storming by Tuckman (1965), is characterized by conflict among the members and with the leader. The emotional climate is characterized by tension. Members exhibit hostility toward one another and frustration with the group. The worker's leadership is challenged, and the purpose, structure, and operation of the group is often questioned. "Until this stage of development, the group has been the worker's group" (Reid, 1997, p. 68). Conflict is an expression of the group's emerging identity and group members' efforts to obtain power and control of the group. "Resistance may be directed at the subject matter, the group, or the leader, and may take the form of withdrawal, absence from the group, attacking others, or questioning the purpose of the group" (George and Dustin, 1988). Through this process, the group begins to develop a collective identity and a sense of togetherness.

Although this stage of group development is difficult for the worker, it presents an opportunity to model behavior for the group. In the face of often unpleasant challenges, you need to stay calm, nondefensive, and open to criticism, and you should demonstrate a willingness to share power and control with the group.

*Norming*    The third stage, norming, is the period during which group identity is solidified and the various roles, norms, and boundaries of the group emerge. Guidelines for group functioning are agreed on during this stage of development; they are the product of the group's coming together and developing a sense of itself. Guidelines are not just the leader's vision of what the group should do and how they should do it; they are the group's guidelines. At this point, the group has established ownership, and a collective sense of purpose and expected behavior has emerged.

*Performing*    This is the action phase of the group's life cycle, the time when the group has worked out its leadership issues, structural concerns, and behavioral expectations. The performing stage is characterized by solidarity, cohesion, and commitment (Reid, 1997). Patterns of communication have become more predictable, and the members are more comfortable with one another. Exchanges are open and honest, and differences are less likely to lead to conflict. The group has worked out mechanisms for managing and resolving conflict. There is a sense of cohesiveness among the members. They are now a group, and they are ready to work on and accomplish the tasks at hand.

One potential problem during this stage is unwillingness of members to challenge one another. There is a fear of upsetting the feeling of closeness the group has achieved, and members may be unwilling to do anything that might jeopardize that closeness (George and Dustin, 1988).

*Adjourning*    This is the ending phase or termination stage of the group's development. A wide range of feelings among the members often characterizes it. If the group has developed a sense of closeness characteristic of the performing stage, the adjourning phase can be difficult for group members and the leader. Feelings of loss and abandonment are common. There is often regression on the part of some members. They revert to earlier stages in an attempt to keep the group going. Reasons for continuing are put forth. Groups may go through a grieving process similar to that of individuals: denial, rage and anger, bargaining, depression, and acceptance (Kubler-Ross, 1969). "Because the ending of a group may trigger so many different responses—including flight, denial, repression, clinging together, and anger—the worker needs to help each member examine his or her responses" (Reid, 1997, p. 72).

Assessment of the group's stage of development is an important aspect of understanding group functioning. Groups develop at different rates and progress in their development differently. What might seem like a problem in group functioning may be a normal stage of the group's development. To what extent is the behavior being exhibited by group members related to the group's developmental stage? How far has the group progressed developmentally?

**Task Performance**    This subsystem is "related to the ways the group defines and carries out its purposes through enacting tasks" (Garvin and Seabury, 1997, p. 237). It is composed of two related dimensions: performance and decision making. Assessment of this subsystem provides information on how group processes are affecting the accomplishment of identified group tasks.

*Performance*    Performance is the way group members carry out tasks to accomplish group purposes. Drawing on McGrath's (1984) typology of group tasks, Garvin and Seabury (1997) saw performance as composed of four categories of tasks: generating, choosing, negotiating, and executing tasks. Each category is further divided into two subcategories (see Table 5.5).

If a group fails to accomplish the tasks at hand, the task performance classification helps determine the stage in the process the group is failing to accomplish. Once the problem is defined and located, solutions can be identified.

| TABLE 5.5 | GROUP PERFORMANCE TASKS |
|---|---|

**Generating tasks**
Planning tasks: Generating plans for how the group will undertake some activity
Creativity tasks: Generating ideas, "brainstorming"

**Choosing tasks**
Intellective tasks: Solving problems in which there exists an answer whose "correctness" will be clearly evident
Decision-making tasks: Solving problems about which some ambiguity exists about how members will agree upon the "correctness" of the answer

**Negotiating tasks**
Cognitive-conflict tasks: Resolving conflicts of viewpoints; that is, members disagree on the definition of the issue to be resolved
Mixed-motive tasks: Members have a conflict of interests; that is, gains may be made by some members at the expense of others as the task is carried out

**Executing tasks**
Contests/battles: Activities in which members are pitted against one another as in competitive sports
Performances: Psychomotor tasks performed against objective or absolute standards of excellence, such as producing a painting or a dance step

From *Groups: Interaction and performance* by J. McGrath. Copyright © 1984, Prentice-Hall. Adapted with permission of Pearson Education, Inc., Upper Saddle River, NJ.

---

*Decision Making*   "Effective deliberations and decision making are critical in determining the productivity and success of a group" (Hepworth, Rooney, and Larsen, 1997, p. 326). The way a group makes decisions is as important as the actual decisions made. Some groups allow a few members to make decisions. This excludes members from the decision-making process and can create conflict, unrest, and dissatisfaction. A common method of decision making in client groups is to adopt a decision-by-consensus approach. Everyone in the group is empowered and given an equal vote. The group encourages all members to express their opinions and to contribute to the deliberations.

Another factor in the decision-making process is the willingness of the group to make a decision. Some groups work hard to avoid making decisions. Groups with problems in making decisions find a variety of excuses not to make a decision. There are numerous legitimate reasons for not being ready to make a decision. But if it happens frequently or on a regular basis, it is probably a symptom of some other problem in the group.

Assessment of group functioning should include an assessment of the group's performance in relation to its purpose as well as an assessment of the group's decision making. Dysfunction in these areas can be related to problems in many other areas of group functioning. Is the target problem in part caused by the group's decision-making style and effectiveness? What role does the group's task performance play in the occurrence of the problem area? What are the strengths and weaknesses of the group's performance and decision making?

## STRENGTHS-BASED GROUP ASSESSMENT

Group assessment is a collaborative process that the leader and members of the group undertake to change conditions that impede the group from achieving its purpose or improving its functioning. An empowering approach to group assessment involves the members in the analysis of group functioning and the problem situation. You may raise an issue or concern, but the entire group explores it and its effect on the group. The group decides whether it is a problem, what contributes to the concern, and what should be done to help correct the situation. The group and its members are the experts. Your starting point is their perceptions of the problem situation. Do not force your analysis and assessment of the group's problems, interpersonal relationships, or individual dysfunctions on the group. Engage in a collaborative exchange with the group, share your insights and perceptions, and explore the perceptions of the members. You guide the assessment process, but the group members actually conduct the assessment. Ensure that each member's perception of the situation is acknowledged and validated. There is no single correct view. There are always multiple perceptions of reality. Each member's perception of the situation is accurate from his or her perspective. Seek consensus about the target problem. If that is not possible, seek agreement about the need to address the concern. The group has the power to set the agenda. It has ownership of the problem as well as the potential solutions.

A strengths-based assessment emphasizes the identification of group strengths as well as strengths of each individual member. Group members have individual and collective power to bring about positive change. Incorporating a strengths perspective in the assessment process, however, is the professional leader's responsibility. Regardless of the type of group, emphasizing strengths requires a conscious effort on your part. All groups, regardless of the level of functioning of individual members, have strengths. Do not expect group members to recognize or be aware of their individual and collective strengths. Adopt the attitude that strengths exist and that they can be used to help the group resolve the problem situation.

## COLLABORATIVE SOCIAL WORK PRACTICE WITH ORGANIZATIONS

As noted in Chapter 1, generalist social workers tend to work in human service organizations and, consequently, must follow the NASW Code of Ethics. They must work toward improving human service organizations and their services as well as promoting the development of new services to meet client and community needs. Generalist social workers seeking these objectives tend to promote organizational change by working with and influencing organizational decision makers or decision-making structures, such as agency task forces and committees. The pre-engagement phase of the collaborative model of generalist practice emphasizes organizational assessment.

## Organizational Assessment

The worker's organizational system is the agency or program through which services are provided to the client. As shown in Table 5.6, this organizational client system has three major subsystems: organizational policies, organizational resources, and organizational culture. Assessing an organization's functioning is an important aspect of generalist social work practice. Social workers need to assess the effect of the organizational climate on their work with clients. A negative organizational climate can have serious indirect negative effects on clients and the quality of the services they receive. Awareness of how these intangible factors affect job satisfaction and feelings of burnout helps social workers deal with potentially negative effects on the helping relationship.

**Organizational Policies**    Organizational policies include external and internal policies and procedures. Both external and internal policies can profoundly influence the helping relationship. Agency-based social workers function within an organizational context. The types of services provided, the length of service, and the kinds of clients served are but a few of the agency influences that can affect the helping relationship. Agency policies have a strong influence on the worker, on the client, and on the helping relationship. The influence of the worker and client on the agency is most likely weaker. Nevertheless, all social workers have a responsibility to work to improve agency policies and procedures and the efficiency and effectiveness of service delivery.

**Organizational Resources**    This subsystem encompasses your workload and the adequacy of support staff and professional staff. These organizational factors tend to be interrelated and strongly affect your work with client systems. Underfunded agencies often are understaffed, and social workers have large caseloads and workloads that negatively affect their energy, commitment, and capacity to develop strong helping relationships with their clients. Numerous research studies have found significant associations between adequacy of organizational resources and social worker job satisfaction and burnout (Poulin, 1994; Poulin and Walter, 1993a; Silver, Poulin, and Manning, 1997).

Social workers need to assess the effect of organizational resources on their work with clients. A realistic assessment of organizational resources will enable the worker and client to develop an understanding of the constraints facing the worker and how these constraints influence their work together. This assessment can also provide the worker with information that can be used to advocate for organizational change.

**Organizational Culture**    The organizational culture subsystem deals with less tangible components of the agency environment. These factors have a

TABLE 5.6 | SUBSYSTEMS OF ORGANIZATIONAL CLIENT SYSTEMS

**Organizational policies**
Internal policies and procedures
External policies and procedures

**Organizational resources**
Professional staffing patterns
Support staffing patterns
Workload

**Organizational culture**
Support
Autonomy
Trust

profound effect on the provision of services and the helping relationship. For example, studies have consistently found that the level of supervisor support is positively associated with a social worker's job satisfaction (Glisson and Durick, 1988; Poulin and Walter, 1992; Poulin and Walter, 1993b; Silver, Poulin, and Manning, 1997). Social workers who feel supported by their supervisors have significantly higher levels of job satisfaction and lower burnout rates than those who do not feel supported. Similarly, job autonomy and levels of trust among the professional, supervisory, and administrative staff are strongly associated with social worker job satisfaction and negatively asociated with burnout (Poulin, 1994; Poulin and Walter, 1993a; Poulin and Walter, 1993b). These and other aspects of organizational culture have indirect effects on the helping relationship and the services provided to clients.

# COLLABORATIVE SOCIAL WORK PRACTICE WITH COMMUNITIES

As noted earlier, generalist social workers engaged in community practice tend to work with professional task forces, community coalitions, and neighborhood or community citizens' groups. Often the purpose of community practice is to improve community or neighborhood conditions, empower residents, develop resources, increase community awareness of social and economic problems, and mobilize the community to advocate for needed resources and changes. The pre-engagement phase of the collaborative model of generalist practice focuses on community assessment.

## Community Assessment

As shown in Table 5.7, the community system has three major subsystems: ethnicity and culture, community conditions, and community resources.

**TABLE 5.7** | SUBSYSTEMS OF COMMUNITY CLIENT SYSTEMS

**Ethnicity and culture**
Values
Beliefs

**Community conditions**
Employment
Housing
Transportation
Education
Recreation
Crime and safety

**Community services and resources**
Social services
Community groups
Religious organizations

These subsystems are highly interrelated. An assessment of these subsystems provides a comprehensive picture of how community factors affect the identified target problem.

**Ethnicity and Culture**   This subsystem is composed of the community's values and beliefs. Cultural beliefs shape a community's value system the same way they shape an individual's value system. Community values play a major role in the helping relationship. They influence the client's and worker's values and beliefs. They also affect the agency's organizational policies and procedures. In assessing the client's concerns, you and your clients need to take prevailing community values and beliefs into account. If there is a value clash between the client and the community values, the implications of the clash need to be explored from the worker's, the client's, the agency's, and the community's perspectives. Often, value positions are taken for granted and not directly addressed in the assessment process.

A problem may arise if the client's perceptions or actions are viewed as unlawful, unethical, or inappropriate by the prevailing community values and beliefs. Mutual exploration of values and beliefs does not mean value consensus or agreement. It does mean, however, that the client's and worker's beliefs are articulated. The emphasis should be on understanding the client and the client's perceptions. Working out differences is part of the helping process. It requires mutual understanding and recognition of the value positions of everyone involved. As Compton and Galaway put it: "when the values of a person conflict with the rights of others or get in the way of the client achieving agreed-upon goals, the values themselves become a topic for discussion and for consideration as an appropriate target of change" (1994, p. 232).

**Community Conditions**    Community conditions can have a significant effect on clients and on the helping relationship. Employment opportunities, housing quality and availability, accessibility and affordability of transportation, quality of the educational system, availability of leisure activities, and other conditions can profoundly affect clients, their life situations, and the helping relationship. You and your clients need to assess all the potential environmental factors that might influence the client's ability to resolve the identified target problem. Many interpersonal or social functioning problems have environmental components. The helping relationship might focus on environmental change or on overcoming the difficulties associated with the environmental problem (Young, 1994). In other instances, simply increasing awareness of environmental conditions helps you and the client understand the client's subjective reality.

**Community Services and Resources**    Community services and resources can also affect the helping relationship system. Community resources include social service organizations, community groups, and religious organizations. You and your client need to review the client's past and current history with social service and community groups. This review can identify important sources of assistance in the client's life as well as the client's nonuse of available community services. It is also important to understand clients' perceptions of their experiences with other helping professionals and community groups. Helping clients think through and articulate what they liked and disliked about their previous interactions with helping professionals provides important clues about how to productively work together. The process also helps the client put this helping relationship into a perspective that differentiates it from previous experiences. If the client has not used other social or community services, you and the client need to explore the reasons the client did not use these available resources.

## Understanding Community Functioning

Generalist social workers need to be skilled in community assessment. Understanding community functioning is vital to the provision of services to individuals, families, and groups as well as to the development of interventions aimed at community change. The ethnicity and culture, social and economic conditions, and services and resources of communities vary widely. Ignoring the effect of these factors on client systems results in an unbalanced assessment. Environmental conditions and concerns have a tremendous effect on everyday lives, especially the lives of those living in impoverished and disadvantaged communities. As members of a profession committed to social and economic justice, generalist social workers must make efforts to strengthen and empower disadvantaged communities and their residents.

# SUMMARY

Collaborative social work with families often involves helping the family view their concerns as a function of the family system and not identified problem family members. The pre-engagement phase in working with families is similar to that with individuals. The content of the assessment, however, is different. The assessment of family systems involves examination of a number of subsystems. The major family subsystems are structure, life-cycle stage, emotional climate, communication patterns, boundaries, and ethnicity and culture. The assessment process is an exploration of the ways these subsystems affect and interact with the target problem.

Generalist social workers are involved with many types of groups. Types of client groups include therapy, support, educational, and growth groups. Social workers also are frequently involved with agency or organizational groups. Some agency groups are formed to deal with specific projects, and others are established groups or committees within the organization. Generalist social workers often come into contact with two types of community groups: professional task forces and citizen groups. Both tend to focus on community conditions or issues.

Assessment of small groups is an important part of the social worker's job as group leader. It is your responsibility to identify potential issues and concerns and to bring them to the attention of the group. A number of subsystems related to group functioning need to be assessed. The primary subsystems are purpose, structure, culture, alliances, life-cycle stage, and tasks. These subsystems are interrelated and together provide a comprehensive assessment of the functioning of the group system.

Organizational assessment is also an important aspect of generalist social work practice. The functioning of the organization has an effect on the work that is carried out within the organization as well as on the workers. The three major organizational subsystems that have the greatest effect on service delivery are organizational policies, resources, and culture. Assessment of organizational policies focuses on both internal and external policies and procedures. Organizational resources of particular relevance to the delivery of services are adequacy of professional staffing, support staff, and workload. The organizational climate subsystem focuses on support, autonomy, and trust issues within the organization, among the social workers, and between the workers and administrators.

Generalist social workers also need to be skilled in community assessment. Understanding community functioning is vital to the provision of services to individuals, families, and groups as well as to the development of interventions aimed at community change. Community systems have three major subsystems of particular relevance for generalist social work: ethnicity and culture, community conditions, and community resources.

## CASE EXAMPLE

The final case example in this chapter is based on the experience of a first-year MSW student who was placed in a setting that provided individual and group treatment for elderly persons by means of a partial hospitalization program. The case example illustrates the process of assessing problematic group functioning.

---

## CASE 5.1 | COMING TOGETHER

Danielle A. was in the second semester of her first year as an MSW student when she was placed at Springton, a partial-day hospitalization program for elderly persons with mental health problems. As part of her placement responsibilities, Danielle was coleader of an insight group for about one month. After a month, Danielle asked Anne Z., her field instructor and coleader, to let her take the lead in running the group. Danielle had observed Anne running a similar group during the first semester, and she was eager to try her hand at running the group under Anne's supervision.

Insight groups at Springton have a therapeutic focus and are designed to help the members deal with interpersonal and intrapersonal issues associated with their mental health problems. Membership in the insight groups is relatively fixed, with 6–10 clients assigned to each group. The groups meet once a week for 15 weeks, which is the usual length of time clients remain in the partial hospitalization program. Members occasionally leave the group early if they are discharged from the program, and every so often a new group member is added to a group after it has been formed. Insight groups are kept semiclosed in terms of membership so that the members can become comfortable enough with the social worker and with one another to share their personal stories and struggles.

Danielle was concerned that her group was not developing a sufficient level of trust. Discussions continued to be superficial even after one month of being together. She felt that the members were not using the group to truly work on their issues. Members seemed to enjoy the group and one another, but a level of openness and willingness to use the

group to help deal with common problems had not developed. Danielle discussed her concerns with Anne and agreed to conduct a preliminary assessment of the group's functioning that they could go over during their next supervisory session. The plan was to assess the situation and develop a strategy to try to get the group on track.

Danielle decided to assess the group's purpose, structure, life-cycle stage, and culture. She concluded that the group's therapeutic purpose was clearly defined and appropriate for the participants. However, she was not sure that all members of the group were clear about the purpose of the group. She also concluded that having 8 members in the group was ideal and that having it structured as a semiclosed group that met once a week for 15 weeks was appropriate given its purpose.

Danielle placed the group at the forming stage in terms of its developmental life cycle. Superficial and guarded interactions among members are characteristic of the beginning stage of group development, as are member's lack of strong commitment to the group and lack of identification with the group as a whole. Danielle concluded that the group seemed to be stuck at the forming stage or, at the very least, had not progressed to the storming or norming stage.

Also related to the group's developmental stage was the absence of group norms. Danielle felt that the group had not developed appropriate norms regarding member behavior. The only norms appeared to be politeness and superficial discussion. Norms regarding behavior appropriate to the therapeutic purpose of the group were absent.

In assessing the group's communication patterns, Danielle realized that interactions were for the most part directed toward her. The group was a wheel, and she was the hub. When anyone spoke, they seemed to direct their comments to her, and Danielle likewise tended to direct her comments to individual members. There was very little member-to-member interaction. Communication was rarely expressed to the group as a whole.

Danielle shared her preliminary assessment with Anne. Anne concurred with the assessment, and together they identified lack of understanding about the group's purpose and the communication pattern as problem areas that could be contributing to the lack of appropriate norms and the developmental-stage problem. Anne also pointed out to Danielle that she might be exercising too much control over the group and its interactions. She recommended that Danielle try to give the members a greater voice in shaping group experiences. Anne encouraged Danielle to view her role more as facilitator than leader. Danielle agreed to try to change her style and to address her concerns with the group at their next meeting.

Danielle was anxious about the meeting and was not sure how the elderly participants were going to react. She wanted to be honest with the group. She decided that the best approach was to share her concerns, to express her feelings, hopes, and fears, and to see how the group responded. Since the prevailing norm was politeness, she figured that the worst that could happen was that she would be met with indifference.

At the next meeting of the group, Danielle began talking about her concerns. She said that the purpose of the group was clear to her, but she was afraid that it might not be clear to everyone else. At this point, her natural instinct was to explain what the purpose was supposed to be. However, she resisted and instead focused on finding out what the group members thought the purpose should be. It was not easy, but after a while some of the members opened up and expressed what they would like to have happen in the group. By the end of the session, almost everyone was participating, and a common understanding of the purpose had been reached. They agreed that the following week they would talk more about the purpose of the group and what they would like to have happen in the group.

Although the agreed-on purpose was not exactly what Danielle had in mind for the group, it was close enough. The important thing was that the purpose was stated in members' words and that members started to feel ownership of the group. Although they had not talked specifically about any of the members' issues, Danielle felt that the meeting had been productive. It felt like a good beginning. She was hopeful that the group might turn out all right after all.

## DISCUSSION QUESTIONS

1. Critique Danielle's assessment of the insight group. What additional factors could have contributed to group functioning? In what other ways could Danielle have intervened with the group to build trust and cohesion? (For more information on intervention techniques with small groups, see Corey et al., 2004.)

2. Discuss Danielle's use of the strengths perspective and empowerment with the group. In what ways did she empower group members? Are there other ways she might have empowered them? What would have happened to the group if she had not changed her approach?

3. Describe the types of client, organizational, and community groups in your field placement agency. In what ways are they similar? How are they different?

4. Using your class as a group, assess its life-cycle stage and development, the culture of the group, and alliance patterns. How do the dynamics of the

group affect its functioning? What could be done to improve the functioning of the group?

5.  Critique your field placement agency in terms of its organizational functioning. In what ways do internal and external policies and procedures affect your work with clients? Are the agency's organizational resources adequate? How do they affect service delivery? Describe the organizational climate of the agency and its effect on the professional staff? How does the organizational climate affect service delivery?

6.  Create a hypothetical client who lives close to your school. Assess the client's community and its effect on his or her problem or concern. How does the ethnicity and culture of the community affect your client? What about community conditions and the availability of community services and resources? What do you need to know about the community to be able to understand your client's situation?

# REFERENCES

Aponte, H., and Van Duesen, J. (1981). Structural family therapy. In A. S. Gurman and D. P, Knirsken (Eds.), *Handbook of family therapy* (pp. 45–72). New York: Brunner/Mazel.

Beck, A. (1983). A process analysis of group development. *Group, 7,* 19–28.

Carter, B., and McGoldrick, M. (1989). *The changing family life cycle: A framework for family therapy* (2nd ed.). Boston: Allyn and Bacon.

Compton, B. R., and Galaway, B. (1994). *Social work processes* (5th ed.). Pacific Grove, CA: Brooks/Cole.

Corey, G. (1995). *Theory and practice of group counseling* (4th ed.). Pacific Grove, CA: Brooks/Cole.

Corey, G., Corey, M. S., Callanan, P., and Russel, J. M. (2004). *Group techniques* (3rd. ed.). Pacific Grove, CA: Brooks/Cole.

Corey, M., and Corey, G. (1997). *Groups: Process and practice* (5th ed.). Pacific Grove, CA: Brooks/Cole.

Flapan, D., and Fenchel, G. (1987). *The developing ego and the emerging self in group therapy*. Northvale, NJ: Aronson.

Freeman, D. (1981). *Techniques of family therapy*. New York: Aronson.

French, J., and Raven, B. (1959). The bases of social power. In D. Cartwright (Ed.), *Studies in social power* (pp. 150–167). Ann Arbor, MI: Institute for Social Research.

Gambrill, E. (1997). *Social work practice: A critical thinker's guide*. New York: Oxford University Press.

Garvin, C. (1997). *Contemporary group work* (3rd ed.). Boston: Allyn and Bacon.

Garvin, C., and Seabury, B. (1997). *Interpersonal practice in social work: Promoting competence and social justice* (2nd ed.). Boston: Allyn and Bacon.

George, R., and Dustin, D. (1988). *Group counseling: Theory and practice*. Englewood Cliffs, NJ: Prentice Hall.

Glisson, C., and Durick, M. (1988). Predictor of job satisfaction and organizational commitment in human service organizations. *Administrative Science Quarterly, 33,* 61–81.

Hartford, M. (1971). *Groups in social work*. New York: Columbia University Press.

Hepworth, D., Rooney, R., and Larsen, J. (1997). *Direct social work practice: Theory and skills* (5th ed.). Pacific Grove, CA: Brooks/Cole.

Hepworth, D., Rooney, R., and Larsen, J. (2002). *Direct social work practice: Theory and skills* (6th ed.). Pacific Grove, CA: Brooks/Cole.

Ho, M. (1987). *Family therapy with ethnic minorities*. Newbury Park, CA: Sage.

Hodges, V., Burwell, Y., and Ortega, D. (1998). Empowering families. In L. Gutiurrez, R. Parsons, and E. Cox (Eds.), *Empowerment in social work practice* (pp. 146–162). Pacific Grove, CA: Brooks/Cole.

Jacobs, E., Harvill, R., and Masson, R. (1994). *Group counseling: Strategies and skills*. Pacific Grove, CA: Brooks/Cole.

Janzen, C., and Harris, O. (1997). *Family treatment in social work practice* (3rd ed.). Itasca, IL: F. E. Peacock Publishing, Inc.

Jordan, C., and Franklin, C. (1995). *Clinical assessment for social workers: Quantitative and qualitative methods*. Chicago: Lyceum.

Kantor, D., and Lehr, W. (1975). *Inside the family: Toward a theory of family process*. San Francisco: Jossey-Bass.

Kubler-Ross, E. (1969). *On death and dying*. New York: Macmillan.

Levine, B. (1991). *Group psychotherapy*. Prospect Heights, IL: Waveland Press.

Lewis, J., Beavers, W., Gossett, J., and Phillips, V. (1976). *No single thread: Psychological health in family systems*. New York: Brunner/Mazel.

Magen, R. (1995). Practice with groups. In C. Meyer and M. Mattaini (Eds.), *The foundations of social work practice* (pp. 156–175). Washington, DC: NASW Press.

McGrath, J. (1984). *Groups: Interaction and performance*. Englewood Cliffs, NJ: Prentice-Hall.

Minuchin, S. (1974). *Families and family therapy*. Cambridge: Harvard University Press.

Minuchin, S., and Fishman, H. (1982). *Family therapy techniques*. Cambridge: Harvard University Press.

Nichols, M. (1984). *Family therapy: Concepts and methods*. New York: Gardner.

Olson, D., Sprenkle, D., and Russel, C. (1979). Circumplex model of marital and family systems: Cohesion and adaptability dimensions, family types and clinical applications. *Family Process, 18*, 3–28.

Popple, P., and Leighninger, L. (1993). *Social work, social welfare, and American history*. Boston: Allyn and Bacon.

Poulin, J. (1994). Job task and organizational predictors of social worker job satisfaction change: A panel study. *Administration in Social Work, 18*, 21–38.

Poulin, J., and Walter, C. (1992). Retention plans and job satisfaction of gerontological social workers. *Journal of Gerontological Social Work, 19*, 99–114.

Poulin, J., and Walter, C. (1993a). Social worker burnout: A longitudinal study. *Social Work Research and Abstracts, 29*, 5–11.

Poulin, J., and Walter, C. (1993b). Burnout in gerontological social work. *Social Work, 38*, 305–316.

Reid, K. (1997). *Social work practice with groups: A clinical perspective*. Pacific Grove, CA: Brooks/Cole.

Satir, V. (1983). *Conjoint family therapy* (2nd ed.). Palo Alto, CA: Science and Behavior Books.

Schwartz, W. (1986). The group work tradition and social work practice. *Social Work with Groups, 8*, 7–27.

Shulman, L. (1999). *The skills of helping: Individuals, families, groups, and communities* (4th ed.). Itasca, IL: F. E. Peacock Publishing, Inc.

Silver, P., Poulin, J., and Manning, R. (1997). Surviving the bureaucracy: Predictors of job satisfaction of direct service supervisors in public human services. *The Clinical Supervisor, 15*, 1–20.

Thomas, V., and Olson, D. (1993). Problem families and the circumplex model: Observational assessment using the clinical rating scale (CRS). *Journal of Marital and Family Therapy, 19,* 159–175.

Toseland, R., and Rivas, R. (1995). *An introduction to group work practice* (2nd ed.). Boston: Allyn and Bacon.

Tuckman, B. (1965). Developmental sequence in small groups. *Psychological Bulletin, 63,* 384–399.

Watzlawick, P., Weakland, J., and Fisch, R. (1974). *Change: Principles of problem formulation and problem resolution.* New York: Norton.

Yalom, I. (1995). *The theory and practice of group psychotherapy* (4th ed.). New York: Basic Books.

Young, T. (1994). Environmental modification in clinical social work: A self-psychological perspective. *Social Service Review, 68,* 202–218.

# ASSESSMENT TOOLS

Following completion of her BSW degree, Korrie A. took her first social work job with a small community-based program that helps teenage mothers obtain their GEDs and enter the job market. Korrie was hired to provide case management and supportive services for the program participants.

Korrie asked about the policies and procedures she should follow. The program coordinator told her that none had been developed for the social work position. All the intake and program functions focused on the participant's educational achievement and job readiness.

Korrie realized that, to effectively provide supportive services, she would need to have some basic psychosocial information about each participant as well as some understanding of her unique circumstances. She decided that her first project would be to design an assessment form. Korrie was not sure what to include on the assessment form or how to proceed.

The use of assessment instruments is a means to an end, not the end itself. Assessment is a process in which you and your client articulate the target problem and analyze the relevant factors in the client's person-in-environment system that may affect it. Assessment tools can help you and the client identify and organize information.

Obtaining the necessary information to complete assessment instruments requires sensitivity, compassion, caring–concern, and curiosity. Keep the focus on listening and understanding rather than on obtaining answers to the questions on the assessment tools. Attention to the interpersonal aspects of the helping relationship are extremely critical during the initial assessment phase. Let the information flow from the interview; focus on the client's story and concerns. If the client does not feel heard or understood, he or she will probably not return to complete the assessment, or in the case of a nonvoluntary client, he or she will not engage in a collaborative helping relationship.

In recent years, a number of instruments have been developed to measure client problems and assess client functioning (Fischer and Corcoran, 1994; Nurius and Hudson, 1993; Reid, 1994). Most of the work in this area has focused on developing measurements of specific client problems, such as self-esteem, anxiety, and marital satisfaction. These types of measurements are important in the evaluation process. Quantitative measurement tools designed to assess client outcomes are not presented here. The tools presented in this chapter aid in the collection and organization of assessment data, incorporate the ecosystems perspective, are relevant to generalist social work practice, and are easy to use.

A number of instruments can be used to collect and organize assessment data. Tools can help assess individual, family, group, organizational, and community client systems. This chapter presents strengths-based and traditional assessment forms and four graphic-type assessment tools. By the end of the chapter, you should be able to help Korrie

1. Develop a strengths-based assessment form
2. Construct a traditional biopsychosocial assessment form
3. Review the use of plot forms, ecomaps, and genograms in the assessment process

4. Evaluate the appropriateness of using a mental status examination with teenage mothers

## ASSESSMENT FORMS

Generalist social workers practice in a multitude of settings. The types of assessment tools they use are as varied as the settings. Agencies adopt or develop assessment procedures based on the kinds of information they need and the types of services they provide. Most assessment tools are variations of the generic biopsychosocial assessment that has been taught in schools of social work for many years. Typically, these instruments are used to collect information on client problems and past behaviors and experiences. Little or no attention is given to client strengths. Tools that focus on client strengths are now emerging, and strengths-based assessments are beginning to be incorporated into agency-based practice.

## Strengths-Based Assessment Worksheets

Strengths-based worksheets were developed to help social workers and clients identify clients' strengths as well as the obstacles they face in resolving problem situations. The strengths and obstacles worksheet helps social workers and clients

- Summarize areas of concern and priorities
- Identify client strengths and obstacles
- Analyze the effects of the obstacles and strengths on the target problem

The strengths and obstacles worksheet is Form 6.1 at the end of this chapter.

Complete as much of the worksheet as possible between your first and second meetings with the client. During the second meeting, review your initial assessment findings and then, with the client, revise and finish the worksheet. Not all content areas will be related to the target problem. Explore only those areas that appear to have a major effect on the client's concerns. At this point in the helping relationship, your primary objectives are to

- Help your client select a priority area on which to focus
- Identify strengths that can be employed to help the client resolve the target problem
- Identify obstacles that will impede progress

## Biopsychosocial Assessment Form

Strengths-based worksheets integrate ecosystems and strengths perspectives. They focus on the present, on the here and now. To complete the picture, some understanding of past experiences is also needed (Sheafor, Horejsi, and Horejsi, 1997). Biopsychosocial assessments incorporate an ecosystems perspective and are widely used in agency settings (Jordan and Franklin, 1995). Typically, these assessments focus on the biologic, psychological, and social functioning and the histories of individual clients. They often include a psychiatric diagnosis from the *Diagnostic and Statistical Manual of Mental Disorders,* fourth edition, text revision (*DSM-IV-TR*). A comprehensive assessment requires an examination of these factors as well as the strengths and obstacles outlined on strengths-based worksheets. Form 6.2 is a generic biopsychosocial assessment form.

Denise Bubel wrote the biopsychosocial assessment in Case 6.1 when she was a first-year MSW student, placed in an adult partial hospitalization program.

## MENTAL STATUS EVALUATION

Another type of assessment frequently used in mental health and family service agencies is a mental status evaluation (Lukas, 1993). This examination is designed to be used with individual clients. "The purpose of the mental status examination is to assess the quality and range of perception, thinking, feeling, and psychomotor activity so that the practitioner can understand how behavior is or is not symptomatic of mental disorders" (Jordan and Franklin, 1995, p. 180). The examination is usually organized around different categories of client functioning, including appearance, attitude, speech, emotions, thought process, sensory perceptions, and mental capacities (see Form 6.3).

### Appearance

The individual's physical appearance includes dress, posture, body movements, and attitude. What is the overall impression of the client's appearance? Are there any unusual aspects of the client's appearance, posture, movements, or demeanor? Is the "client overly flamboyant, meticulous, bizarre, exceedingly sloppy and dirty?" (Jordan and Franklin, 1995, p. 180).

### Speech

Is there anything unusual about individual's speech? Does he or she speak unusually fast or slow? Is the volume appropriate? How is the tone and pattern of the client's speech? Are there any noticeable speech problems?

### Emotions

Emotions or feelings encompass two dimensions: affect and mood. **Affect** "refers to the way the client shows his emotions while he is with you, and it may or may not coincide with the internal state the client describes himself as feeling over time" (Lukas, 1993, p. 19). Is the client's affect flat or blunted,

## CASE 6.1 | BIOPSYCHOSOCIAL ASSESSMENT
### BY DENISE BUBEL

### Identifying Information
Theodore J. is an 82-year-old Caucasian. He is married and lives with his 80-year-old wife in their own home in a suburban community.

### Problem Situation
Mr. J. has been diagnosed with irreversible dementia. He suffers from memory loss and cognitive decline, and he feels a great deal of frustration and anxiety. Mr. J. has become depressed over his continuing physical decline and agreed to come to the partial hospitalization program for help with his depression and memory loss. He also stated that he wanted to work on issues of shame and embarrassment that result from his medical condition. Mr. J. indicated that his wife has become "stressed out" from having to care for him and that he is worried about her ability to cope with his condition.

### Background
In early January, Mr. J. was admitted to the hospital because he was severely dehydrated and was not complying with his medication regimen. Apparently he was being treated for dementia and major depression with psychosis prior to being admitted to this hospital. Because Mr. J.'s original psychiatrist left his practice abruptly, previous mental health records are unavailable and only the diagnosis could be obtained. Therefore, the psychosis could not be further defined. The admitting psychiatrist reported that Mr. J.'s psychiatric history was limited to his wife's recollections, and she could not account for the "psychosis." However, the admitting psychiatrist stated that medical records revealed that Mr. J. was originally referred to a psychiatrist because of "vegetative symptoms of depression." Those symptoms were not described, nor were their duration or intensity.

The admitting psychiatrist reported a "complete remission of psychotic symptoms." He reported that Mr. J. denied any suicidal or homicidal ideation. The admitting psychiatrist noted that Mr. J.'s "thought process was impoverished with mild thought blocking" and that "there are definite problems with his memory." The admitting psychiatrist's report on

Mr. J.'s initial assessment and evaluation was brief and limited:

### Initial Diagnosis:
Axis I    Major depression with psychosis
Axis II   Deferred
Axis III  Dementia not otherwise specified and coronary artery disease
Axis IV   None reported
Axis V    None reported

### Medical and Psychiatric History
Approximately three years ago, Mr. J.'s prostate gland was removed, and he still experiences incontinence. Approximately two years ago, he had coronary artery bypass surgery. He suffers from exhaustion at times. Approximately one year ago, he had a bowel resection and suffers from continuing intermittent constipation and diarrhea as well as fear of embarrassment.

Apparently, while Mr. J. was hospitalized for the bowel resection, he threw a fire extinguisher at a window in the hallway. His wife reported that he was hollering at the nurses and going "mad" and that he needed to be restrained and medicated. Mr. J. was put on the antidepressant drug Venlafaxine, and the antipsychotic drug Risperidone while in the hospital. After discharge from the hospital, he began follow-up treatment with a psychiatrist. Mr. J. remained on the medication for six months. His wife reported, "Within a month after he came home from the hospital, he began to decay and would just sit around the house like a zombie."

Six months ago, Mr. J. had to give up his license as a pilot because of the decline in his memory and eyesight. At that point, he abruptly stopped taking the Effexor and Risperdol. He said, "I know the medicine was making me like a zombie and making me forget things. I couldn't get an appointment with the psychiatrist, he only saw me once after the surgery, so I just stopped taking it." Following this, Mr. J. began to become severely depressed and stated, "I just couldn't drink anything, I stopped drinking, I just stopped drinking fluids." This resulted in

*(continued)*

## CASE 6.1 | *continued*

his admission to the hospital two months ago for dehydration. This was the only change noted in his appetite and nutrition history. Prior to hospitalization in January, his weight had not fluctuated in many years.

### Additional History

Mr. J. denied any past or present substance abuse and any past psychiatric problems other than those mentioned. He said he noticed that his memory has been declining for the past three years, and his wife reported the same. He denied any family history of psychiatric or physical problems, any past or present physical, sexual, or emotional abuse, and any suicidal or homicidal ideation. No paranoid ideation was reported. He denied allergies to any medications or foods and denied any weight loss or gain other than a "few pounds" prior to admission to the hospital for dehydration. He denied any problems with sleep, any problems growing up, and any history of trauma.

### Family Situation and History

Mr. J. lives with his wife of sixty-two years in a large house in an upper-class suburban neighborhood. The couple is financially well off. The couple has two daughters, 39 and 45 years of age, who both live in a different part of the country. Both daughters sell real estate, and Mr. J. said that they are "very successful." He stated that the family is "very close." Before his medical problems began, he and his wife would visit their daughters four times a year for two weeks at a time. He has been avoiding social functions and travel because of the shame and embarrassment of having to wear adult incontinence protection. Also, he fears losing bladder and bowel control and not being able to "find a bathroom in time."

Mr. J.'s only brother passed away eleven years ago. Mr. J. stated that since his medical problems began, all his "friends have disappeared." He has no nieces or nephews, and the only support comes from his wife.

Mr. J. depends on his wife for everything, and this is how it has been for all sixty-two years of their marriage. She handles all the finances, shopping, and appointments and remembers all the birthdays and important dates. She picks out all his clothes, dis-

penses his medication, and takes care of all his "physical and emotional needs." He stated that he is concerned for his wife, and he feels all his problems have become an "enormous stressful burden" to her.

### Education History

Mr. J. stated that he stopped attending school at the end of ninth grade.

### Employment History

Mr. J. owned and operated his own printing business for "fifty very successful years." He said he was a typesetter, which required great precision and detail. He stated that he was very "eye-hand coordinated" and was proud of his work. He began working in a print shop after he dropped out of high school. "I would go to the corner print shop and help out with odd jobs. In a short time, I learned the business, and when the owner retired, he helped me get started with my own business."

### Current Diagnosis

After reviewing the intake assessment, the consulting psychiatrist evaluated Mr. J. Copies of lab work and other tests from admission were reviewed. Reversible causes for dementia were ruled out. The follow-up diagnosis was:

Axis I    290.43 vascular dementia with depressed mood
Axis II   Deferred
Axis III  Cerebrovascular disease, prostate cancer s/p resection of prostate, bowel symptoms of unclear cause
Axis IV   Moderate stress of chronic illness
Axis V    Global Assessment of Functioning Scale: 37 with difficulties with memory and confusion at times

The psychiatrist planned and recommended retrieval of all medical records, a discussion with the admitting psychiatrist, strict medication monitoring, consideration of an anti-Alzheimer agent, a family meeting, a discussion with the primary physician, and five days of group therapy to help Mr. J. cope with memory loss.

**Summary**

After reviewing the initial assessment with the psychiatrist, it is clear that Mr. J.'s dementia is irreversible. It is organic, resulting in symptoms of memory loss, depression, and cognitive decline. The psychosis was isolated to a one-time occurrence in the hospital, a superimposed delirium. The medication prescribed in the hospital was the origin of the vegetative symptoms of depression.

**Current Medication**

Venlafaxine (antidepressant), 75 mg at lunchtime
nitroglycerin patch (heart), on in the morning and off in the evening
Colchicine (bowels), 100 mg at 9:00 PM
Multivitamin (supplement to diet), one tablet in the morning
Mineral oil (bowels), 1 ounce in the evening

---

expressing little emotion? Does the client experience rapid shift in affect? Is the affect appropriate given the subject matter?

**Mood** refers to how the client is feeling most of the time (Lukas, 1993, p. 8). Is the client happy, sad, or angry? Do the client's feelings appear to be appropriate given his or her situation? Are they understandable given the topic and the context?

## Thought Process

This refers to the client's judgment about the content of speech and thought (Jordan and Franklin, 1995). **Process** concerns how the client thinks. Is there a logical flow? Are the client's thoughts all jumbled together? Is there a coherent flow of ideas? Does the client have difficulty getting to the point in responding to your questions? Does the client keep repeating certain words or phases? Does the client have difficulty connecting ideas?

**Content** refers to what the client says. Do the client's thoughts appear to be delusional? Does the client have thoughts that he or she believes to be true that you know absolutely to be untrue? Does the client have reoccurring thoughts that have an obsessive or compulsive quality?

## Sensory Perceptions

Sensory perceptions concern indications of illusions or hallucinations. "**Illusions** refer to normal sensory events that are misperceived" (Lukas, 1993, p. 25). **Hallucinations** are sensory experiences unrelated to external stimuli (Lukas, 1993). Are there clear distortions in the client's view of reality? If so, when and under what conditions do they occur?

## Mental Capacities

**Mental capacity** refers to orientation, intelligence, concentration, and memory. **Orientation** concerns time, place, and person. Does the client know the

| CASE 6.2 | MENTAL STATUS EVALUATION |
| --- | --- |
| | BY DENISE BUBEL |

Theodore J. is an 82-year-old Caucasian male. He was well groomed and very well dressed in appropriate, immaculate, casual attire that had been carefully coordinated. He sat in a slouched position, legs crossed, leaning to the left of his chair. He had swollen eyes and a washed-out complexion. His attitude was one of concern, and he appeared to be worried as exhibited by his facial expression and verbal presentation.

The volume of Mr. J.'s speech was low. His pace of speech was slow, and he presented slight psychomotor retardation. Mr. J. had difficulty recalling words to finish his thoughts and sentences but was able to formulate complete sentences.

Mr. J. was engaging but appeared to lack a positive self-image. His mood and affect were depressed. His perception of his problem, content of thought, and associations were appropriate.

The patient denied any hearing deficits, and none were noted. He denied having visual or auditory hallucinations. His eyesight had significantly declined over the last two years, and this appeared to be of major concern to him. He wore glasses.

Mr. J. was oriented to person but could not recall the name of the program he was in, the floor he was on, or the date. There were apparent deficits in his immediate memory. He appeared to be of average intelligence and had the ability to concentrate on the subject being discussed. However, he was not able to count backward by threes. Mr. J.'s short-term memory appeared somewhat intact in relation to recent events. He was able to recall facts from his past, but he was not able to recall or trace a timeline. He remembered that he had had surgery, but he could not remember if it was two or three years ago. His insight and judgment did not appear to be impaired.

Although depressed, Mr. J. was polite and cooperative. He was easy to relate to and appeared capable of developing a helping relationship. Mr. J. appeared motivated to participate in the partial hospitalization program and to get help with his depression and memory loss.

---

approximate time of day, day of the week, and year? Does the client know where he or she is and what his or her name is?

What is the client's overall level of intelligence? Does the client appear to possess average, above average, or below average intelligence (Lukas, 1993)? Can the client concentrate and focus on what you are discussing? Is the client easily distracted? Is the client able to remember recent events? How is the client's long-term memory? Can the client remember events from his or her past?

## Attitude

What kind of attitude does the client project toward his or her problem, the interview, and you? Is the client cooperative and forthcoming or uncooperative and withholding? Is the client overly aggressive or submissive? "If disturbed, how aware is the individual of his or her disturbance?" (Jordan and Franklin, 1995, p. 181).

Denise Bubel wrote the mental status evaluation of Mr. J. in Case 6.2 at the same time she wrote the biopsychosocial assessment presented earlier in this chapter.

# INPUT AND OUTPUT CHECKLIST

An input and output checklist is completed by the social worker following each client session and is reviewed before each session (Form 6.4). Its purpose is to provide an easy-to-use way to note worker inputs and client outputs of the collaborative model. Following each session the worker subjectively assesses progress in communicating the various inputs as well as client progress in achieving expected outputs. The checklist is then reviewed just before the next session as a reminder of what has been accomplished and what still needs to be accomplished.

# GRAPHIC DISPLAYS

Four types of graphic tools display information in a picture or graphic format. They condense what would be a long verbal description into a single image. Graphic displays are an effective way to summarize assessment information and present it so it is readily understandable to a wide range of clients. The four graphic displays presented here are plot forms, ecomaps, genograms, and sociograms.

## Strengths and Obstacles Plot Form

The strengths and obstacles plot form shown in Figure 6.1 is a modified version of the assessment axis developed by Cowger (1994). It is used in conjunction with the strengths and obstacles worksheet. Brief descriptions of the strengths and obstacles identified on the worksheets are written in the appropriate quadrants of the plot form. The completed form graphically summarizes the strengths and obstacles associated with the target problem. The value of this tool is that it succinctly summarizes all the identified strengths and obstacles on a single sheet of paper. It highlights in a concrete manner client strengths as well as obstacles that need to be overcome to resolve the identified target problem.

## Ecomaps

Ecomaps graphically display the person-in-environment perspective. They show the ecologic context of the client system (Hartman, 1995; Mattaini, 1993). Ecomaps focus on the relationships between the client and the major systems in the client's environment. The major systems vary by client. Typically, they include kin and friendship relationships; work, school, community, and neighborhood organizations; and the social worker, agency, and other social service and health care organizations. An ecomap shows the relevant systems, whether the relationships are positive or negative and strong or

FIGURE 6.1 | STRENGTHS AND OBSTACLES PLOT FORM

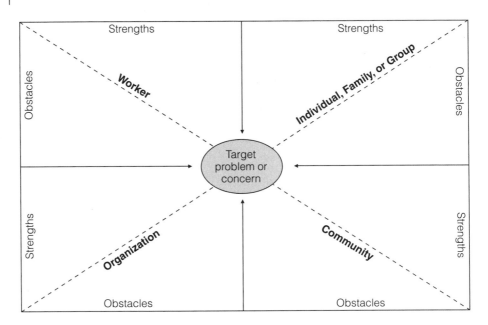

weak, and the direction or flow of energy and resources between the client and the systems (Hartman, 1995). As shown in Figure 6.2, a dashed arrow indicates a weak relationship, a solid arrow indicates a strong relationship, and a dashed line indicates the absence of a relationship between the client and the subsystem. A plus sign (+) or minus sign (-) indicates whether the relationship is positive or negative. The direction of the arrowhead indicates the direction of the energy or resource flow.

Ecomaps are constructed in collaboration with the client. The worker begins by placing the client in the middle of the ecomap, and then identifies the various personal and environmental systems with which the client interacts. The social worker reviews the relationships with the client using open-ended questions and elaboration techniques. Together, the worker and client complete the ecomap. The worker and client review and analyze the completed ecomap. This process encourages collaboration in the worker–client relationship (Hartman and Laird, 1983). Ecomaps can be very useful tools in helping clients understand their person-in-environment systems and the effects the various relationships or absence of relationships have on the presenting problem. They also help the worker and client identify areas of strength and resources.

Figure 6.2 is a completed ecomap for one client. The client is a 55-year-old African-American male named Harry M. He is divorced, has two adult children, lives alone, and is currently unemployed. He attends a partial hospitalization program for adults with mental health problems.

FIGURE 6.2 | ECOMAP OF AN INDIVIDUAL CLIENT SYSTEM

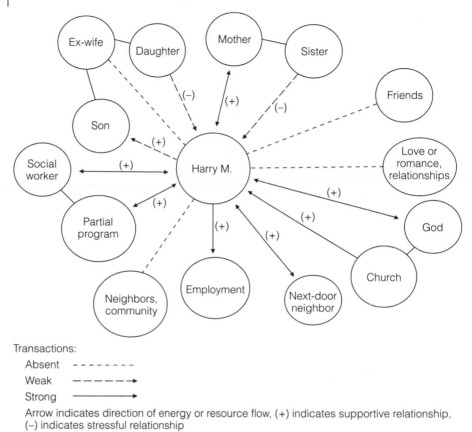

Transactions:

Absent  - - - - - - - -

Weak  - - - - - ⟶

Strong  ⟶

Arrow indicates direction of energy or resource flow, (+) indicates supportive relationship, (–) indicates stressful relationship

The ecomap indicates that Mr. M. has strong, mutually supportive relationships with the partial program, the social worker, his mother, and his next-door neighbor. He also receives support from his church and his belief in God, and from his job. Mr. M. has a weak but supportive relationship with his son and weak stressful relationships with his sister and daughter. His relationship with his ex-wife is completely dissolved. He does not have any romantic or friendship relationships or other connections with neighbors or the community.

Overall, Mr. M.'s person-in-environment assessment reveals a number of strengths and sources of support. He receives a great deal of support from formal associations, such as the partial program, his social worker, and his church. His informal support network appears to be limited to his mother and a next-door neighbor. His relationship with his ex-wife, children, sister, friends, and lovers are either weak or nonexistent.

FIGURE 6.3 | ECOMAP OF FAMILY CLIENT SYSTEM

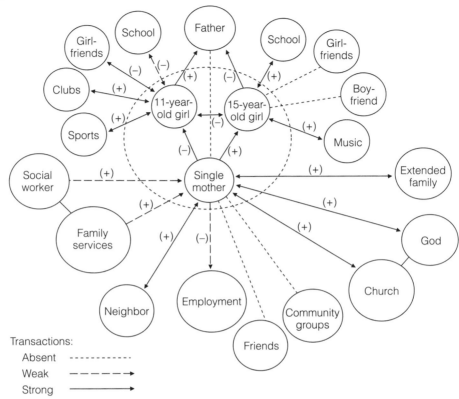

Transactions:

Absent    ------------

Weak      -- -- -- →

Strong    ————————→

Arrow indicates direction of energy or resource flow, (+) indicates supportive relationship, (−) indicates stressful relationship

Ecomaps can also be used with family client systems. A family ecomap portrays the relevant systems within the family's environmental system. Like an individual ecomap, it indicates whether the relationships are positive or negative and strong or weak as well as the direction or flow of energy and resources between the family and other systems. A family system ecomap is constructed the same way as an individual ecomap. The only difference is that the center of the map portrays the members of the family instead of an individual client.

Figure 6.3 is a completed ecomap for a family client system. The family consists of a single mother and her two daughters, ages 11 and 15. The mother has requested help from a family service agency for problems she is having with the 11-year-old daughter. She reports that the younger daughter is having problems in school and is acting out at home by not obeying her. She is disrespectful and defiant.

The ecomap shows that the mother has a stressful relationship with her younger daughter and a positive relationship with her older daughter, and that the two girls have a conflicted relationship. The father does not live with the family. He and the mother have no contact or ongoing relationship. The older daughter has a stressful relationship with her father, and the younger daughter feels close to him.

The identified patient is the 11-year-old daughter. She is having problems in school and in her relationships with her mother and sister. Her mother is also concerned about the girl's friends. She feels that they are a negative influence on her daughter. On the positive side, the daughter is active in clubs and sports. She has a supportive relationship with her father.

The older sister is close to her mother, does well in school, and gets a great deal of satisfaction from her musical pursuits. On the negative side, she does not have any close friends, and her relationships with her father and sister are strained.

The mother has a supportive extended family network and derives a great deal of support from church-related activities. She also has a neighbor who is a source of support. Other than her neighbor, she does not have close friends, nor is she involved in the community beyond her church activities. Her relationship with the social worker and the family service agency at the time of the interview was weak but supportive, while her job was viewed as moderately stressful.

## Genograms

Genograms use symbols to graphically display information about family members of at least three generations (McGoldrick and Gerson, 1985). They are commonly used in assessments of family client systems. Basic types of information included in genograms are births, gender, marriages, offspring, deaths, and household composition. "By highlighting contextual information, genograms aid our understanding of relationship patterns, transitional issues, and life cycle changes" (Miley, O'Melia, and DuBois, 1998, p. 242). Genograms are used to highlight cultural information about a family (Hardy and Laszloffy, 1995; McGill, 1992) and patterns of family strengths (Kuehle, 1995).

Genograms should be constructed in collaboration with family members. McGoldrick and Gerson (1985) recommend that gathering family information and constructing the genogram be part of the more general task of joining and helping the family. The social worker must explain to the family the meaning of each symbol as well as the relationships among them. Squares, circles, lines, crossed lines, and dashed lines have specific meanings. It is important for family members to understand the meanings clearly, so any suspicions they may have are minimized. When gathering family information for a genogram, McGoldrick and Gerson (1985) suggest casting the "information net" into wider and wider circles, moving from

- The presenting problem to the larger context of the problem
- The immediate household to the extended family and broader social systems
- The present family situation to a historical chronology of family events

FIGURE 6.4 | GENOGRAM

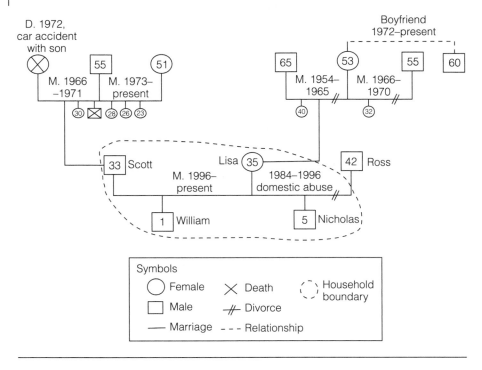

- Easy, nonthreatening inquiries to difficult, anxiety-provoking questions
- Obvious facts to judgments about functioning
- Relationships to hypothesized family patterns

The genogram in Figure 6.4 shows a family client system composed of a husband and wife and two children. It is the second marriage for the wife, who has a 5-year-old son from her first marriage. That marriage ended in divorce because of domestic abuse. The couple have a 1-year-old son.

The wife's mother divorced her first and second husbands and is currently in a long-standing relationship. The husband's mother and younger brother died in a car accident. His father remarried and had three daughters with his second wife.

## Sociograms

A group sociogram is similar to an ecomap. The ecomap describes a person-in-environment system, whereas a sociogram describes the relationships among members of a group. Hartford's (1971) approach to sociogram construction examines attraction and repulsion between members of the group. It is a graphic representation of the alliances within a group. Usually, a worker constructs a sociogram based on observations of the group interactions, including those

FIGURE 6.5 | GROUP SOCIOGRAM

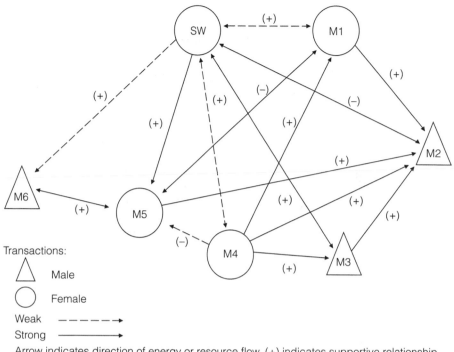

Transactions:

△  Male

○  Female

Weak    – – – – – →
Strong  ————————→

Arrow indicates direction of energy or resource flow, (+) indicates supportive relationship, (–) indicates stressful relationship

between the worker and group members. Doing so recognizes that the worker is part of the group-in-environment system and forces him or her to objectively analyze relationships with each member of the group. Garvin and Seabury (1997) point out that discussion of alliances within groups creates anxiety and concerns about rejection. Therefore, sharing a sociogram with the group should be approached with caution. However, a sociogram can be an effective tool for helping group members understand the dynamics of the group and the effect of group alliances on a problem area or concern.

The group shown in Figure 6.5 consists of six members, three males and three females, and the social worker. The sociogram shows that the social worker has strong positive relationships with members 3 and 5, weak positive relationships with members 1, 4, and 6, and a strong negative relationship with member 2. Members 3 and 6 are somewhat isolated. Each has a strong relationship with only one other member. Member 2 appears to be the informal leader of the group. She has strong positive relationships with members 1, 5, 3, and 4. She also appears to compete for leadership with the social worker, with whom she has a strong negative relationship.

# SUMMARY

This chapter presented a number of tools that can be used to assess client systems. Whereas traditional assessment tools focus on deficits and past history, most of the assessment tools presented here incorporate a strengths perspective. They are designed to help you and your clients organize relevant information in a way that promotes its integration and understanding. They are not designed as interview schedules in which the social worker asks structured questions. They complement the interview and data-gathering process. The focus must remain on the client's telling of his or her story, with the worker listening. Filling out the forms should never be the focus of the assessment process.

The tools allow for a comprehensive assessment. The strengths-based assessment worksheets can be used to assess the strengths and obstacles of individual, family, group, organizational, and community client systems. The traditional biopsychosocial assessment form and mental status examination can be used for individual clients. Using a strengths-based approach in combination with a traditional biopsychosocial assessment provides a comprehensive picture of individual and family client systems.

The graphic tools can enhance the assessment process. Ecomaps and genograms are useful in obtaining information as well as in conveying the information back to clients in a form that is readily understandable. The plot form is an excellent tool for summarizing client system strengths and challenges from an ecosystems perspective. Finally, the sociogram is useful for assessing group communication problems and other aspects of group functioning.

# CASE EXAMPLE

Jennifer Francella wrote the following case example when she was a first-year MSW student. Jennifer met with the family twice before completing the assessment. Together they completed the individual/family client systems–strengths-based assessment worksheet and the strengths and obstacles plot form. The case example illustrates a strengths-based family assessment.

---

## CASE 6.3 | ADJUSTING TO LIFE WITHOUT MOM
### BY JENNIFER FRANCELLA

The K. family consists of the father, Bob, and three children, Sharon, Chad, and Jason. Ellen, Bob's wife and the children's mother, passed away eight months ago as a result of injuries she sustained in an automobile accident. Bob is 45 years of age, Caucasian, and works in the banking industry. Sharon is 18 years old and a senior in high school.

Chad is 17 years of age and is currently a junior in high school. Jason is 15 years of age and in the ninth grade. Chad has taken the death of his mother especially hard. This past year, he has been receiving failing grades in school and has been involved in numerous fights. He also has begun to experiment with drugs and alcohol. Ellen had been a constant source of support for Chad and the other children. However, the children describe Bob as not being supportive of them, and as having an especially stressful relationship with Chad.

In addition to the above problems, the family seems to not have allowed outsiders, even extended family members, help them deal with their grief and loss. Family traditions ended with Ellen's death, as did involvement with the church and other organizations. The family's emotional climate has become tense, and the family's communication patterns have been greatly altered since Ellen's death.

Bob and the children all recognize that, first and foremost, they need to deal with the sudden death of Ellen. They also acknowledge the need to deal with the strained relationship between Chad and his father and to strengthen Sharon's and Jason's relationships with their father. Chad has also agreed to receive help for his academic and behavioral problems at school.

The greatest obstacle facing the K. family is Ellen's absence. It is clear that she maintained the closest relationships with the children, led family traditions, was the mediator between Bob and the children, kept communication open, and allowed family boundaries to remain open to the outside world. Ellen was involved with the schools her children attended, the church she and the rest of the family attended weekly, and numerous community-wide events. Ellen also kept the lines of communication open between extended family members, including Bob's mother, siblings, and cousins.

Upon Ellen's death, the K. family seemed to completely "shut down." Although Sharon's and Jason's performance at school has not changed as drastically as Chad's, the two children report not feeling as good about themselves as they once did and also

report not wanting to continue participating in extracurricular activities.

Chad's sudden change in behavior and school performance is directly related to the death of his mother. His recent experimentation with drugs and alcohol is related to his mother's death and to the fact that alcoholism is prevalent in Ellen's family history. Ellen's father and brother are both recovering alcoholics. Chad, like the rest of his family, is dealing with Ellen's death in an unhealthy manner.

The weak relationships between Bob and his children had an effect before Ellen's death and now greatly affect the family's identified problem situation. Another obstacle the family faces is the fact that Bob never learned effective coping or parenting skills.

However, the K. family does have several strengths. All family members realize that there are definite obstacles and that no one has been dealing with Ellen's death in a healthy fashion. Chad appears to want to stop using drugs and alcohol and to change his recent behavior patterns at school. The children have expressed interest in maintaining strong and supportive relationships with their father. Bob has admitted that he never had a strong relationship with any of his children— or with his own father.

Another major strength is that the family wants to return to family traditions, change their emotional climate, open communication patterns, reset the family's boundaries, and use family resources. In addition, the children seem to have strong and supportive relationships among themselves, and extended family members have expressed an interest in being active participants in the lives of Bob, Sharon, Chad, and Jason. External strengths include a sincere desire by all family members to again become a part of their church, the community, and other associations.

## DISCUSSION QUESTIONS

1. Critique the family assessment of the K. family (Case 6.3). What are the strengths of the assessment? Does it provide an adequate picture of the family situation? Is it comprehensive? Is there enough detail? What areas need to be strengthened? Is any critical information missing?

2. Based upon the family assessment completed by the social worker what interventions would be appropriate for the family system in Case 6.3?

Would having the family attend a bereavement group be warranted? (For more information on family bereavement groups, see Birnbaum (1991); Goldstein, Alter, and Axelrod (1996); and Hopmeyer and Werk, 1994.)

3. Discuss the use of ecomaps and genograms in the assessment process. In what ways can graphic tools facilitate the process? How might they hinder the process? How do assessment forms and graphic tools complement each other?

4. Review the family client system of the single mother and her two daughters portrayed in the sample ecomap (Figure 6.3). Develop at least two scenarios that describe the family dynamics of the case. Identify additional information that you need to complete the assessment. List specific questions about the case that you would like to have answered.

5. Critique the sample biopsychosocial assessment of Mr. J. (Case 6.1). What are its strengths? Does it provide an adequate picture of the case situation? Is it comprehensive? Is there enough detail? What areas need to be strengthened? Is there any critical information missing? What are the relevant client systems in this case? If you were assigned the case, what would you focus on? How would you proceed with the case?

# REFERENCES

Birnbaum, B. (1991). Haven hugs and bugs: An innovative multiple-family weekend intervention for bereaved children, adolescents, and adults. *American Journal of Hospice and Palliative Care.* 8(5), 23–9.

Cowger, C. (1994). Assessing client strengths: Clinical assessment for client empowerment. *Social Work, 39,* 262–267.

Fischer, J., and Corcoran, K. (1994). *Measures for clinical practice: A sourcebook* (Vols. 1–2, 2nd ed.). New York: Free Press.

Garvin, C., and Seabury, B. (1997). *Interpersonal practice in social work: Promoting competence and social justice* (2nd ed.). Boston: Allyn and Bacon.

Goldstein, J., Alter, C. L., and Axelrod, R. A. (1996). Psychoeducational bereavement support group for families provided in an out-patient cancer center. *Journal of Cancer Education, 11*(4), 233–237.

Hardy, K., and Laszloffy, T. (1995). The cultural genogram: Key to training culturally competent family therapists. *Journal of Marriage and Family Therapy, 21,* 227–237.

Hartford, M. (1971). *Groups in social work.* New York: Columbia University Press.

Hartman, A. (1995). Diagrammatic assessment of family relationships. *Families in Society, 76,* 111–112.

Hartman, A., and Laird, J. (1983). *Family-centered social work practice.* New York: Free Press.

Hopmeyer, E., and Werk, A. (1994). A comparative study of family bereavement groups. *Death Studies, 18*(3) 243–6.

Jordan, C., and Franklin, C. (1995). *Clinical assessment for social workers: Quantitative and qualitative methods.* Chicago: Lyceum.

Kuehle, B. (1995). The solution-oriented genogram: A collaborative approach. *Journal of Marital and Family Therapy, 21,* 239–250.

Lukas, S. (1993). *Where to start and what to ask: An assessment handbook.* New York: Norton.

Mattaini, M. (1993). *More than a thousand words: Graphics for clinical practice.* Washington, DC: NASW Press.

McGill, D. (1992). The cultural story in multicultural family therapy. *Families in Society, 73,* 339–349.

McGoldrick, M., and Gerson, R. (1985). *Genograms in family assessment.* New York: Norton.

Miley, K., O'Melia, M., and DuBois, B. (1998). *Generalist social work practice: An empowering approach* (2nd ed.). Boston: Allyn and Bacon.

Nurius, P., and Hudson, W. (1993). *Human service practice, evaluation, and computers.* Pacific Grove, CA: Brooks/Cole.

Reid, W. (1994). The empirical practice movement. *Social Service Review, 68,* 165–184.

Sheafor, B., Horejsi, C., and Horejsi, G. (1997). *Techniques and guidelines for social work practice* (4th ed.). Boston: Allyn and Bacon.

# Individual/Family Client Systems— Strengths-Based Assessment Worksheet

Client: _____   Worker: _____   Date: _____

---

**Instructions:** Briefly describe to the best of your knowledge as many items on the worksheet as possible. Base your assessment on information you have obtained directly from your client, indirectly by your observations, case records, contacts with collaterals, and any other sources of information. The first page focuses on a description of the clients' concern/problem situation. The remaining pages comprise an assessment of personal, family and environmental factors. For each relevant factor describe potential obstacles, strengths, and its impact on the problem situation.

---

## Concerns/Problem Situation

Briefly summarize client concerns and/or problems that the client wants to address.

List concerns/problems in order of priority from highest to lowest.

# Individual Factors

| Subsystem | Obstacles | Strengths | Impact on Problem Situation |
|-----------|-----------|-----------|------------------------------|
| Motivation and Commitment | | | |
| Coping and Resourcefulness | | | |
| Values and Beliefs | | | |
| Developmental Life Stage | | | |

## Individual Factors

| Subsystem | Obstacles | Strengths | Impact on Problem Situation |
|---|---|---|---|
| Mental Health Status | | | |
| Health Status | | | |
| Employment/ Economic Status | | | |
| Interpersonal Relationships | | | |

# Family Factors

| Subsystem | Obstacles | Strengths | Impact on Problem Situation |
|---|---|---|---|
| Structure & Subsystems | | | |
| Power & Authority | | | |
| Family Life Cycle Stage | | | |
| Family Values & Beliefs | | | |
| Family Rules & Myths | | | |

## Family Factors

| Subsystem | Obstacles | Strengths | Impact on Problem Situation |
|---|---|---|---|
| Emotional Climate | | | |
| Communication Patterns | | | |
| Boundaries | | | |

## Environmental Factors

| Subsystem | Obstacles | Strengths | Impact on Problem Situation |
|---|---|---|---|
| Work/School | | | |

# Environmental Factors

| Subsystem | Obstacles | Strengths | Impact on Problem Situation |
|-----------|-----------|-----------|----------------------------|
| Clubs, Churches and Associations | | | |
| Community/ Neighborhood | | | |
| Service Organization | | | |
| Other Formal Services and Programs | | | |
| Other Factors and Considerations | | | |

# Biopsychosocial Assessment Form

Client: _____   Worker: _____   Date: _____

(Indicate NA if problem does not exist or apply)

---

**Problem Situation** (Client's perception of the problem situation)

---

**History Problem Situation** (Duration, intensity, stressors, coping methods, change)

---

**Mental Health History** (Sequence and description of past symptoms and treatment)

---

**Substance Abuse History** (Age of onset, specific drugs, extent of abuse, family history, treatment)

**Physical Health and Developmental History** (Current and prior medical problems, family history)

**Current Medications** (List medications, dosage, schedule, reason, and length of time)

**Nutrition/Appetite** (Weight gain or loss, appetite, changes)

**Current or Prior History of Physical, Sexual and/or Emotional Abuse**

**Family Situation and History** (Current living situation, family relationships)

**Employment History**

**Education History** (Level completed, academic and behavioral functioning)

**Diagnosis**

# Mental Status Form

Client: _____    Worker: _____    Date: _____

(Be specific; indicate NA if problem does not exist or apply)

_____

**Appearance** (dress, posture, body movement, attitude)

_____

**Speech** (speed, volume, pattern, tone)

_____

**Emotions** (affect, mood)

_____

**Thought Process** (content, perception, associations)

_____

**Sensory Perceptions** (hearing, sight, hallucinations)

_____

**Orientation** (person, place, time)

_____

**Intellectual Functioning** (intelligence, concentration, insight, judgment, memory)

# Input and Output Checklist

| Phase | Input | | Output | |
|---|---|---|---|---|
| **Pre-Engagement (Sessions 1–3)** | | | | |
| Studying | Understanding | _____ | Knowledge | _____ |
| Asking | Sensitivity | _____ | Competence | _____ |
| Listening | Respect | _____ | Needs | _____ |
| Clarifying | Acceptance | _____ | Concerns | _____ |
| | Empathy | _____ | Strengths | _____ |
| | Cooperation | _____ | Coping Skills | _____ |
| | | | Feeling Content | _____ |
| | | | Validation | _____ |
| | | | Understanding | _____ |
| | | | Collaboration | _____ |
| **Engagement (Sessions 4–8)** | | | | |
| Articulating | Hopefulness | _____ | Change Goals | _____ |
| Persevering | Support | _____ | Evaluation Plan | _____ |
| | Agreement | _____ | Action Plan | _____ |
| | Commitment | _____ | Client Change | _____ |
| **Disengagement (Sessions 9–10)** | | | | |
| Solidifying | Partnership | _____ | Evaluation | _____ |
| | Confidence | _____ | Generalization | _____ |

# COLLABORATIVE SOCIAL WORK

*The Engagement and Disengagement Phases*

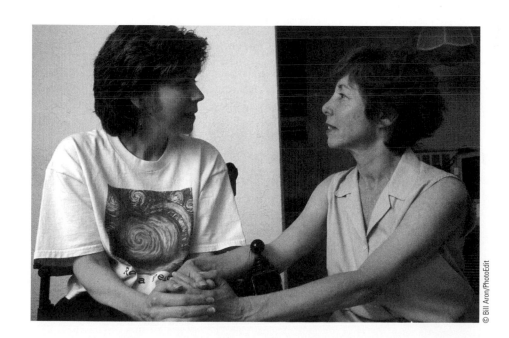

Vincent J. is a first-year MSW student with a field placement at a community health clinic in an economically disadvantaged urban community. The clinic has a large HIV/AIDS patient population of infected drug users. Vincent provides case management and supportive counseling services to individual clinic patients who have tested positive for HIV and to patients with AIDS. Vincent also runs a support group for persons with AIDS and is involved in a community education program about the disease and its prevention.

Vincent's prior knowledge of AIDS and HIV was limited. His social work classes had not really spent much time discussing working with AIDS/HIV clients. Early in his field placement he realized that he needed to understand the disease and its process as well as how it socially and psychologically affects individuals and families. What was the prognosis for his clients? Would he be able to focus on strengths with clients who are dying? How receptive would his clients be to developing an action plan? Could he really help his clients? Was he prepared to handle the emotional stress of ending with individuals suffering from AIDS?

This chapter begins with a general discussion of goals and objectives followed by a description of the engagement and disengagement phases of collaborative social work. The process of developing an action and evaluation plan is discussed as well as the collaborative tasks of articulating, persevering, and solidifying. The inputs, practice skills, and outputs associated with these tasks are also reviewed. By the end of the chapter, you should be able to help Vincent

1. Write measurable goals and objectives
2. Understand how communicating hopefulness, support, commitment, and partnership builds trust with reluctant clients
3. Use a variety of contracting and intervention skills with his clients
4. Describe the purpose of the disengagement phase
5. Understand the role of termination in the helping process

# DETERMINING GOALS

Client goals are derived directly from client problems and concerns. The assessment process focuses on identifying the areas of concern that clients want to address in the helping process. It also identifies client system strengths and resources. The contracting process follows this up by focusing on what the client system hopes to accomplish. Problems are negative statements about the client's current situation, whereas goals are positive statements about what the client's situation will be after the identified problem has been resolved or ameliorated (Bloom, Fischer, and Orme, 1995, p. 74).

## Purpose of Goals

Goals serve multiple purposes. Reid (1970) found that social workers who set overly general goals were less effective than those who set clear and specific goals. When goals were vague and very general, work was characterized by frequent shifts in direction and focus. Thus, one of the major purposes of goals is to set the direction for the work.

Specifying goals ensures that the client and the worker are in agreement about what is expected. Without specific goals, the client and worker may have different expectations about what needs to be accomplished.

Goals help facilitate the development of the intervention and evaluation plan. They help determine appropriate tasks and activities that will be undertaken to address the identified target problems and concerns. Goals provide benchmarks for monitoring client progress and criteria for assessing outcomes. Without clear and specific goals, it is impossible for the worker or the client to determine whether progress is being made and whether a desired end has been attained. Without goals, you do not know where you are going, and consequently you cannot tell when or whether you have gotten there. "Goals provide the standard or frame of reference for evaluating whether or not the client is moving, and whether or not the destination is met" (Bloom, Fischer, and Orme, 1995, p. 74). In summary, goals

- Provide direction for the helping process
- Ensure agreement between the client and the worker about the desired end state of the helping process
- Facilitate the development of the intervention and evaluation plan
- Provide benchmarks for judging progress
- Provide outcome criteria for evaluating the effectiveness of the intervention and the helping process

## Goals and Objectives

**Goals** are positive statements about desired ends. In fairly broad terms they describe the hoped-for end result of the helping process. They represent the client system's ultimate outcome for the resolution of the identified target problem. Goals have also been called "ultimate goals" (Rosen, 1993) and "long-term goals" (Goldstein, 1973; Jongsma and Peterson, 1995).

Goal statements do not need to be measurable (Jongsma and Peterson, 1995), but can be global statements of a desired positive outcome. Table 7.1 provides examples of target problems and related goal statements for various client systems.

It is usually not possible to go directly from a problem to its solution when the solution, or goal, is broadly worded (Bloom, Fischer, and Orme, 1995). Instead, clients often must move through a series of measurable steps in order to reach the goal (Sheafor, Horejsi, and Horejsi, 1994). These intermediate steps are commonly referred to as objectives (Kirst-Ashman and Hull, 1993). **Objectives** are subgoals that lead to the achievement of the long-term goal. They are the steps the client must take to arrive at the desired outcome or problem resolution. Well-written objectives answer the following questions:

1. Who?
2. Will do what?

TABLE 7.1 | SAMPLE GOAL STATEMENTS

| Client System | Target Problem | Goal |
| --- | --- | --- |
| Individual | I lose my temper with my teenage son | To be able to control my temper when dealing with my teenage son |
| Family | Family discussions always turn into shouting matches and arguments | To improve the family's ability to communicate without resorting to shouting and screaming |
| Group | Members of the support group do not trust one another | To have members of the support group develop a sense of trust |
| Organization | School system is unable to help children deal with family problems that affect school performance | To improve the school system's ability to help children with family problems |
| Community | Community and neighborhood groups are unwilling to work together to address community problems | To have community and neighborhood groups join together in addressing community problems |

3. To what extent?
4. Under what conditions?
5. By when? (From B. W. Sheafor, C. R. Horejsi, and G. A. Horejsi, *Techniques and guidelines for social work practice,* 3rd ed. Published by Allyn and Bacon, MA. Copyright © 1994 by Pearson Education. Reprinted by permission of the publisher.)

Objectives are specific and measurable. They describe in very concrete terms exactly what will be accomplished. Table 7.2 presents examples of objectives that answer the above five questions. The examples illustrate the relationship between goals and objectives as well as their differences. The relationship between target problems, goals, and objectives is illustrated in Figure 7.1.

## Selecting and Defining Objectives

Several factors should be kept in mind when selecting and formulating objectives (Hepworth, Rooney, and Larsen, 2002; Siporin, 1975). First and foremost, objectives should be steps toward goals, and progress should be incremental. Objectives are the intermediate steps that clients need to accomplish to ultimately reach their goals.

Objectives also need to be feasible. Try to help clients set objectives that are realistic given the available resources and abilities. Make sure the objectives are obtainable.

Whenever possible, write objectives in positive language. State what will be accomplished rather than what will be eliminated (Bloom, Fischer, and

TABLE 7.2 | SAMPLE OBJECTIVES

**Individual Client System Goal:**
*To be able to control my temper when dealing with my teenage son*

Objective 1: I (who) will wait ten seconds and take three deep breaths (what) 80 percent of the time (to what extent) that I have a conversation with my son that I find upsetting (under what conditions) by August 30 (by when).

Objective 2: I (who) will express my feelings to my son (what) 80 percent of the time (to what extent) that I find our conversation upsetting (under what conditions) by August 30 (by when).

**Community Client System Goal:**
*To have community and neighborhood groups join together in addressing community problems*

Objective 1: Representatives of the West End Neighborhood Association, the Community Action Association, the United Neighbors Block Club, and the Community Residents Coalition (who) will meet (what) at least twice (to what extent) to discuss the possibility of forming a Community Coordinating Council (under what conditions) before November 10 (by when).

Objective 2: Representatives of the West End Neighborhood Association, the Community Action Association, the United Neighbors Block Club, and the Community Residents Coalition (who) will create a Community Coordinating Council (what) that will hold monthly community meetings (to what extent) devoted to sharing information and coordinating community improvement efforts (under what conditions) by February 28 (by when).

---

Orme, 1995). Use words that describe specific behaviors. Describe what the client will actually do (or think or feel) to achieve the objective.

The activities should be measurable and, if possible, observable. In Table 7.2, all the objectives describe behaviors that are measurable and observable. For example, in objective 1 for the individual client system, the father will wait ten seconds and take three deep breaths before responding to his son. This behavior is both observable and measurable. It would be relatively easy to measure the extent to which the father has been successful in achieving this objective.

Another consideration in constructing objectives is to avoid confusing input with outcome (Sheafor, Horejsi, and Horejsi, 1994). A common mistake is to state objectives, especially direct service objectives, in terms of what the client will be receiving rather than a desired outcome. For example, stating that "the father will obtain counseling to help him deal with his temper problem" is both observable and measurable. However, the objective is not stated in performance terms and says nothing about the desired outcome. It is possible that the father could attend counseling and show no improvement in his temper problem. Or, on the other hand, he may make tremendous progress. However, the objective would not provide any basis for evaluating his

FIGURE 7.1 | RELATIONSHIP BETWEEN TARGET
PROBLEM, GOALS, AND OBJECTIVES

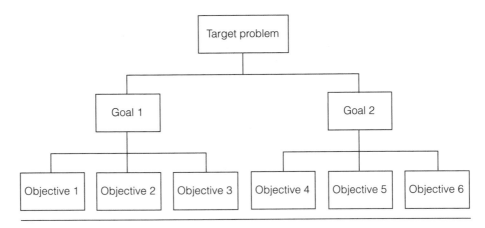

progress. In this situation, obtaining counseling is a means to an end. It is not the desired end in itself. A desired outcome of the counseling needs to be specified for the objective to be used to help evaluate the father's progress in controlling his temper.

Another important consideration is for the objectives to be in accordance with your knowledge and skill level. "Certain problems and goals require higher levels of expertise that you may not yet have attained, and it is your responsibility to clients, the profession, and yourself not to undertake interventions for which you lack competence" (Hepworth, Rooney, and Larsen, 1997, pp. 348–349). Recognize your limitations, and when appropriate help your clients obtain the specialized services needed to address the identified target problems or concerns.

The final consideration concerns the mission and function of your agency. The objectives you and your clients develop should be consistent with the functions of your agency. Are the client's service needs beyond the scope of activities and services provided by the agency? If so, referral to another agency or service provider for those services is the appropriate course of action.

In summary, effective objectives should be

1. Steps toward goals
2. Realistic and attainable
3. Observable and measurable
4. Stated in positive terms that emphasize outcomes
5. Acceptable to both clients and workers
6. In accordance with the knowledge and skill of the practitioner
7. Consistent with the functions of the agency

## Goals, Objectives, and the Helping Relationship

Developing goals and objectives is a collaborative process. It is an extension of the assessment process. The first step is to help your client identify areas of concern that need to be addressed. A comprehensive assessment will identify a number of potential target problems. Review the list of concerns that you developed earlier with your client, and set priorities according to which concerns are most pressing and most important to the client. Together determine which concern or problem has the highest priority. Bloom, Fischer, and Orme suggest negotiating with the client so as to work first on the problem that meets as many of the following criteria as possible. The problem is one that:

- The client prefers to start with;
- The client has the greatest concern about;
- Has the greatest likelihood of being changed;
- Is relatively concrete and specific;
- Can be readily worked on given the available resources;
- Has the greatest chance of producing the most negative consequences if not handled;
- Has to be handled before other problems can be tackled; and
- Will result in tangible, observable changes for those involved, thereby perhaps increasing the participant's motivation to work on other problems. (1995, p. 68)

It is critical to select only one or two problems on which to work. Failure to limit the focus of the work to one or two manageable areas is a common mistake (Bloom, Fischer, and Orme, 1995). The client needs to divide problems into component sections and to begin addressing the concerns one step at a time. It can be frustrating, discouraging, and disheartening to take on a number of problems at once or one vaguely defined large problem. Either situation can make the client feel that the task is unmanageable.

Once the priority target problem has been selected, the next step is to write down at least one goal for each problem. Use the client's words, no matter how vague they are (Mager, 1972). It is important for the client to have ownership of the goals. The goal statements should reflect the client's expectations about the desired changes in the client's own words.

After one or two goals have been developed for each target problem, specific objectives should be constructed for each goal. Every effort should be made to construct objectives that satisfy the seven criteria presented earlier. Mager (1972) suggests brainstorming with the client and writing down all the things that the client could say or do to attain the goal. This process allows the client to contribute to the identification of possible solutions. Ideally, the client will identify the activities. Encourage your clients to put forth ideas. Give them the opportunity to express their opinions. Your job is to help them identify solutions; you should not provide the solutions. At the very least, finding solutions should be a joint activity. At this point, you are focusing on the "what" component of the objective. Review all the possibilities. Is the potential solution realistic and obtainable? Is it observable and measurable? Is it a step toward the broader goal? Select the two or three activities that seem most promising and satisfy the criteria.

The next task is to determine a level of performance for each activity. This is the "to what extent" component of the objective. The client should determine the level of performance. What does the client consider a reasonable level of success? What level of progress is satisfactory? Do not set the performance standards so high that achieving them seems unrealistic and improbable. It is better to have modest successes and take small steps toward the desired result than to aim too high and fail.

After determining the performance level for each activity, discuss the timetable (by when) and the situations in which the changes are expected to occur (under what conditions). Make sure conditions are clear and specific. Are you and your client in agreement about the conditions under which the changes will take place? Are the specified conditions related to the target problem or concern? Is the timetable realistic?

You are now ready to craft specific objectives. Under each goal, write the objectives related to that goal. Use the client's words as much as possible. Make sure each objective states who will do what, to what extent, under what conditions, and by when. Review each objective. Revise as needed until both you and the client are comfortable with the objective and in complete agreement about what is expected.

## THE ENGAGEMENT PHASE OF COLLABORATIVE SOCIAL WORK

As shown in Table 3.1 in Chapter 3, the engagement phase of the collaborative model has two major tasks: articulating and persevering. The **articulating** task focuses on developing a contract or action plan to address the target problem and concerns identified in the pre-engagement phase. This chapter provides information on this process. The **persevering** task focuses on the implementation of the action plan. This is the work phase (Shulman, 1999) in the helping process.

### Task 5: Articulate Your Focus and Plan of Action

**Articulation** refers to the process of taking all the information you and your client gathered during the pre-engagement phase and using it to identify priorities and develop measurable goals and a plan of action. The action plan specifies a timetable and the steps that will be taken as well as how progress will be evaluated. At this point in the collaborative model you are **engaging** the client in a helping relationship. Prior to this, during the pre-engagement phase, you were setting the stage for client engagement. But it is not until your client agrees to a plan of action and makes a beginning commitment to change that he or she actually engages in a helping relationship. Prochaska, DiClemente, and Norcross (1992) refer to this as the "preparation" stage. The work that was done during the pre-engagement phase is a prerequisite to engagement. Moving to articulation without completing the tasks of pre-engagement usually results in a premature and superficial commitment to change. Most likely, the client will drop out and not return for the next session or will merely be "going through the motions" of engagement. The pre-engagement tasks must be undertaken if your client is going to truly engage in a helping relationship.

Typically, the articulation of priorities, goals, and the action plan takes place around session 3 or 4, depending on how long the pre-engagement tasks take. After the worker has a clear sense of the client's needs, concerns, strengths, and coping abilities, he or she needs to help the client move into the engagement phase. This action must be initiated by the social worker. It needs to be presented to the client as the next step in the helping process.

Many beginning social workers have trouble initiating the articulation task. They end up staying in the pre-engagement phase for a prolonged period of time. The client keeps telling his or her story, and the worker keeps listening. Although this is important, a helping relationship is purposeful. The worker and client must agree upon what it is they are going to do together. It might turn out that the agreement is to listen to the client and provide support, or a more elaborate plan of action might emerge. Either way, for the relationship to be purposeful, both parties must agree to what they want to accomplish as well as how they will accomplish it.

**Developing the Intervention and Evaluation Plan**    The intervention and evaluation plan specifies what will be done by whom to achieve the identified goals as well as how progress on the goals will be evaluated. Both the social worker and the client will work on the objectives of each goal as well as how each will be measured. It is the plan of action for the helping relationship. This action plan is essentially a contract between you and the client about how you will collaboratively work toward the identified goals. The contract is connected with the "goal-setting process because goals without commitment and action plans are more difficult to realize" (Locke, Garrison, and Winship, 1998, p. 169).

Several considerations are involved in developing the intervention and evaluation plan. The contract is an evolving entity (Miley, O'Melia, and DuBois, 1998). "Contracting continues throughout the entire course of the helping venture" (Hepworth, Rooney, and Larsen, 1997, p. 360). The intervention and evaluation plan should not be viewed as fixed once it is developed. The nature of social work practice is such that priorities, goals, and plans change and are modified as the helping process unfolds. Consequently, the contract evolves and is modified to reflect the changing nature of the work.

The social worker and the client decide whether the contract will be verbal or written (Locke, Garrison, and Winship, 1998). The disadvantage of verbal contracts is that they rely on memory. It becomes increasingly difficult to keep the specifics of the contract clear and in focus as time passes. Another disadvantage of a verbal contract is that there is a greater chance of miscommunication and misunderstanding between you and the client. Because of these potential problems, a written contract should be used whenever possible. The act of putting words on paper forces you and the client to come to terms with the specifics of the contract. A written contract helps ensure agreement, and it can be easily retrieved and reviewed at a later time.

The contracting process should also clarify the roles of the participants involved in the helping relationship. At a minimum, you and the client should review your respective roles, expectations, and preferences. Clearing up possible misperceptions about the nature of the work and the way you will work together is critical to the development of a strong collaborative helping relationship and positive change of the identified target problem.

The intervention and evaluation plan developed by the social worker and the client is the integrated plan of action. Development is a collaborative undertaking. Your task as the social worker is to provide guidance and technical support. Your client's task is to create the substance of the plan. Obviously, some clients can do this more easily than others. Regardless of the client's level of functioning, it is imperative that the client participate in creating the action plan. The plan should belong to the client, not to the worker or anyone else.

The intervention and evaluation plan should specify who will do what within what time frame to achieve each of the identified goals. For each goal, specify the tasks and activities that will be undertaken. This includes intervention as well as evaluation activities. The time frame for accomplishing each task also should be specified in the plan.

Form 7.1, a sample action plan and outcome evaluation form, can be found at the end of this chapter. The form contains space for listing the desired outcomes and the action steps needed to reach the desired change goals. There is also space for rating the progress on each stated change goal and to summarize the case disposition.

**Inputs: Hopefulness and Partnership**    Figure 7.2 shows how the articulating task influences the trust-building process. This is a vulnerable time for clients who have not experienced a great deal of success in their lives. People from disadvantaged and oppressed backgrounds usually have a lifetime of setbacks and disappointments. Making a commitment to bring about changes in one's life, changes that are not easily made, is a difficult process. It is scary. Clients from disadvantaged and oppressed backgrounds ask: Is this possible? Will this person stick with me if I run into difficulty? Can I do this?

The worker can help the client take these risks by communicating **hopefulness**. The client needs to be assured that it *can* be done. Inputting a sense

FIGURE 7.2 | ENGAGEMENT TASK: ARTICULATING

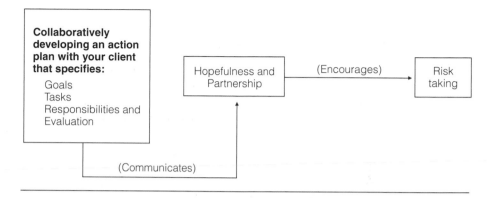

of hopefulness is very important at this stage of the helping relationship. The worker needs to clearly communicate through words, voice tone, and attitude that together the change can be made, that help is possible.

Along with communicating hopefulness, the worker needs to communicate a sense of **partnership** to the client. Stressing the collaborative aspect of their work together and the fact that both are making a commitment to the change process promotes feelings of partnership and collaboration. The challenge of making difficult changes and taking on responsibility for one's actions are substantial risks. They are major risks for people who have had to face discrimination and oppression and who in all probability continue to face discrimination and oppression in their everyday lives. The worker can help these clients take these risks by creating a sense of hopefulness and partnership. These two inputs are critical to the development of a purposeful helping relationship.

**Contracting Skills**   Table 7.2 lists the practice skills associated with the articulating task. These skills help facilitate the contracting process. They are purposeful in that they all contribute to the process of specifying priorities, goals, action steps, and evaluation procedures.

*Partializing*   Breaking complex problems down into component parts that can be addressed one at a time is the skill of partializing client concerns (Shulman, 1999). Often the process of telling the story results in a large number of interconnected problems. The prospect of tackling so many problems is discouraging and intimidating. Clients often feel helpless and overwhelmed about the prospect of change. The worker can help the client move forward by breaking down the problems into smaller, more manageable ones that can be addressed one at a time. The following example illustrates the skill of partializing client concerns.

TABLE 7.2 | ARTICULATING: PRACTICE SKILLS

**Contracting skills**
    Partializing
    Identifying options
    Sharing data
    Seeking consensus

GROUP MEMBER: My probation officer says that I have to look for work. I can't do that because I go to "meetings" every morning and I don't have a car. It is hard for me to use public transportation because of my bad leg. I just can't walk very far or stand for any length of time. I also don't want to miss my meetings because I am really trying to stay clean. I want to reconnect with my daughter but she won't have anything to do with me unless I get my life straightened out. I'm afraid if I don't get a job my probation officer will send me back. I don't want to go back.

WORKER: That's a lot to deal with. It kind of feels overwhelming. Maybe if we look at one thing at a time we can come up with some ideas. Let's see. You need to make a good-faith effort to find a job. You want to continue attending meetings. Transportation is an issue, and reconnecting with your daughter is a concern. And you are having problems with your leg. Where should we start?

Breaking down complex and interrelated problems into more manageable parts helps the client move forward and helps set the agenda for developing a contract or action plan. Specifying the issues of concern in manageable terms helps overcome client discouragement and creates hopefulness. Change does seem possible when the focus is on small intermediate steps instead of the larger overwhelming problem.

*Identifying Options*   Another skill that comes into play during the articulating task is that of helping the client identify options. Identifying options helps clients think about the various goals they might wish to address and helps them explore various solutions. A collaborative way of identifying options is to engage the client in **brainstorming.** Together create a list of all the possible options. Encourage your client to be creative and to come up with as many options as possible. In brainstorming, all ideas are correct and put down. Ultimately the client will decide upon the goals as well as the possible action steps. Brainstorming begins the process of making those decisions by exploring the full range of possibilities.

    Identifying options or alternatives is a helpful way to begin the process of setting priorities. Most disadvantaged and oppressed clients have a whole host of concerns that need attention. Taking on everything at once is not generally recommended. Establishing priorities provides you and the client with guidelines about the order of the work. It helps identify a small list of issues that will be the starting point of your work together. The worker should start prioritizing by beginning with the problem that the client initially presented during the pre-engagement phase. Beginning here will make the most sense to the client (Pillari, 2002). After brainstorming and listing the options, ask the client to rank them from least to most important. Setting priorities helps establish a clear focus for the beginning work together. It is a critical step in selecting the goals (outcomes) that are sought as well as the specific actions that will be taken (Epstein, 1988).

*Sharing Data*    This skill refers to having the social worker share facts, ideas, values, and beliefs with the client (Shulman, 1999). The collaborative model emphasizes partnerships and relationships. Relationships are, by definition, reciprocal. They have a give and take quality. They are not unidirectional. Clients need and look for input from their social workers. Sharing information, feelings, and opinions is the input they need and offering it has the added benefit of strengthening the helping relationship.

Shulman (1999) points out that in sharing data there are two key requirements: the data must be related to the work at hand, and it must be needed by the client for the immediate work (p. 186). Both conditions must be satisfied. They are the only two conditions under which social workers share their knowledge and beliefs with clients. Before sharing data, ask yourself: Is what I am about to share relevant to our work together, and is it immediately needed? If the answer is yes to both questions, share your observations. But make sure doing so is relevant and needed immediately. Bringing up information or ideas that might have relevance at some future date is not helpful and, in fact, is probably harmful to the helping relationship if the client does not see the connection to the work at hand.

Even if sharing information is clearly called for, caution must be taken in how the information is shared. First and foremost it must be presented as something for the client to consider and not as what should be done. It is important to give the client a clear sense that what you are offering is one perspective and not *the* perspective. Given the unequal power differential in a helping relationship, the worker has to be extra careful in sharing observations and opinions. Although the client is looking for your suggestions and thoughts, the emphasis and locus of control must remain with the client. Make it clear that you are offering your thoughts and that they are open to examination.

> The skill of sharing data in a way that is open for examination means that the worker must qualify statements in order to help the client sort out the difference between reality and the worker's sense of reality. Rather than being a salesperson for an idea, the worker should present it with all its limitations. (Shulman, 1999, p. 189)

The worker must encourage the client to question the ideas if they do not seem to fit his or her situation. The worker needs to explore any verbal or nonverbal signs that the client is not in agreement. It is hard for clients to dis-agree. Therefore, the worker needs to take the initiative in exploring the client's feelings about the information shared.

A second caution is to make sure you use brevity. Make your point, and turn the focus back to your client and his or her situation as quickly as possible. Carrying on about your thoughts and observations communicates that you are more interested in your story than your client's story. The purpose of sharing data at this point in the helping process is to help your client figure out priorities, goals, and the course of action to take. Your experiences can be helpful in this regard, but the client's experiences are most important here. Share your experiences only to the extent that you make your point and show the connection to your client's problem or concern. The following example illustrates appropriate sharing of data.

INDIVIDUAL: I am not sure how I feel. I want to reconnect with my daughter, but I am not sure how she will react if I contact her after all these years.

WORKER: I understand your reluctance. A close friend and I had a falling out. Neither one of us was willing to take the first step. As time went on, it got harder and harder. Finally, I called her on her birthday and she was glad to hear from me. I am not sure how your daughter will react, but in my situation I am glad I took the risk and called.

In the above example, the worker's sharing is related to the work at hand and deals with the immediate concern of the client. It also is fairly brief and qual-ified in terms of its applicability for the client.

*Seeking Consensus*    The fourth contracting skill is one that is used during the final phases of the articulating task. After you and the client have partialized and set priorities, identified options, and shared data, the skill of seeking con-sensus brings it all together in the form of a contract. In collaborative social work, both the client and the worker have to agree on the problems that are going to be addressed, the expected outcomes, and the steps that will be taken to bring about the change. There has to be agreement. Although the client has the final say in these matters, the worker has to have input and be in agree-ment. It makes little sense to engage in a helping relationship in which you dis-agree with what the client is attempting to change and the course of action chosen.

Seeking consensus requires open communication and a purposeful search for agreement. Often beginning social workers believe they are in agreement with their clients when, in fact, there is a breakdown in communication. It is imperative that you make sure you and your client agree on both the general and specific aspects of your work together. Writing it out and reviewing it together is a good way of making sure there is agreement. A verbal agreement is more prone to misinterpretation than a written one. In reviewing the specifics, if there are areas of disagreement actively explore alternatives until a consensus is reached. Both the client and the worker own the goals and plan of action when this occurs. The work becomes collaborative.

**Outputs: Change Goals, Action Plan and Evaluation Plan**   The outputs of the articulation task are very concrete. At the conclusion of this task the worker and client will have identified the specific goals that they will be addressing in the helping relationship and they will have specified their intervention and evaluation plan. Once the client and worker have accomplished these intermediate outputs, they become actively engaged in a professional helping relationship. The next task in the collaborative process is to persevere through the ups and downs of the helping process.

## Task 6: Persevere in Carrying Out Your Work Together

This phase of the helping process is called many things. Pillari (2002) refers to it as the intervention phase; Shulman (1999) calls it the work phase; Hepworth, Rooney, and Larsen (2002) call it implementation and goal attainment. No matter what it is called, this is the actual work phase of the helping relationship. During this period, usually session 4 and on, the action plan is implemented. During the articulation task, clients start to address their problems and are motivated to make the necessary changes (Prochaska, DiClemente, and Norcross, 1992). The objective is to help clients modify their behavior, experiences, or environment to overcome their problems. This is difficult for many clients. Making the needed changes is not easy. Changing long-standing behaviors or environments is extremely difficult. It is much easier to maintain the status quo than to make significant life changes.

Chapter 1 reviewed a number of system change activities (interventions) employed by generalist social workers. The action plans developed collaboratively by the worker and client specify the interventions that will be used to address the client's identified target problems and desired change goals. The specifics of the different types of interventions are not reviewed here. Rather, the focus is on the worker's use of self in helping the client follow through on the agreed-on action plan. The approach presented here is similar to Miller and Rollnick's (2002) motivational interviewing techniques. Their work focuses on the process of helping people overcome ambivalence and resistance to change.

**Inputs: Support and Commitment**   Figure 7.3 illustrates how the **persevering** task contributes to the trust-building process with reluctant clients. The key to helping clients make difficult changes is persistently and relentlessly following through on the action plan. Persistence is meeting often and regularly with your client. It is checking in with your client between meetings. It is regularly monitoring progress and exploring why or why not progress is being made. It is following up on missed appointments, and it is consistently completing your agreed-upon tasks on or before their due dates. Persevering is creating expectations for success and for making the identified changes. When this occurs the worker communicates to clients that he or she will support them in overcoming the challenge of making behavioral and environmental changes. It also communicates to clients your commitment to the change process and their success.

FIGURE 7.3 | ENGAGEMENT TASK: PERSEVERING

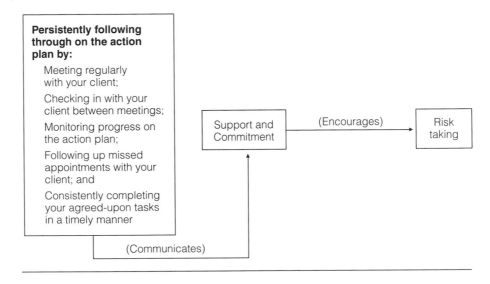

Inputting support and commitment encourages clients to take the risks associated with the change process. It helps solidify the trust that has developed, and it strengthens the helping relationship. These inputs are critical because the work phase requires a strong helping relationship. The relationship is tested most severely during this phase of the helping process. The focus is on client change, and this often requires confrontation and other types of intervention practice skills. Table 7.3 lists the intervention skills that are associated with the persevering task.

### Intervention Skills

*Challenging*    This is what Shulman (1999) refers to as "challenging the illusion of work." An illusion of work occurs when the client comes in and talks about making changes but never moves beyond the talking stage. The actual work is not being accomplished. The client gives the impression of being cooperative and engaged, but there is no action behind the words. The worker needs to challenge the lack of progress and the illusion. "For the illusion to take place, it is necessary to have two partners in the ritual" (Shulman, 1999, p. 175). Both the client and worker are "working," but in reality they are giving lip service to the situation. Goals have been written on paper, but there is no action other than lengthy social conversations. It is pure illusion.

Challenging the illusion is often difficult for beginning social workers. They want to be supportive and helpful. They are uncomfortable confronting or challenging clients. Many worry about negatively affecting their relationship when, in fact, challenging the illusion of work will probably strengthen the helping relationship.

TABLE 7.3 | PERSEVERING: PRACTICE SKILLS

**Intervention skills**
Challenging
Maintaining focus
Checking for ambivalence
Rehearsal

Challenging communicates that you care, that you really want the client to be successful. This strengthens the helping relationship. It communicates to clients that you care enough to risk confronting them. It demonstrates a caring concern and a seriousness about helping them make progress in realizing their goals. Letting the illusion continue unchallenged communicates the opposite. It tells the client you are more concerned about maintaining a comfort level than you are about helping the client make difficult changes.

Challenging is a skill that draws attention to discrepant aspects of the client's verbal and nonverbal behaviors (Egan, 1999). It is a skill that helps clients focus on aspects of their behavior or communication that are getting in the way of progress. It should only be used in relation to specific behaviors, and not to some vague generalization (Patterson and Welgel, 1994). It should also be directly relevant to the work at hand. This is best assured by connecting the challenge to the agreed-on action plan. Put the challenge in the context of your work together and progress toward goal attainment. Limit challenges to those connected to progress on the action plan. Make the challenge an invitation to examine and explore the discrepancies or illusions. Challenge in a way that encourages exploration rather than the marshalling of defenses. The purpose of the challenge is to point out the discrepancies so that the issue can be openly addressed. Blaming or attacking the client does not encourage exploration. The following example illustrates a worker's use of challenging.

WORKER: One of the goals we agreed to work on is establishing a relationship with your daughter, and for the past two weeks we have been talking about your contacting her and how much that means to you. I believe this is really important for you, and I'm concerned that it gets put off each week. Something is holding you back. Any ideas?

In the above example, the worker ties the challenge to the action plan and invites the client to explore the discrepancy between the client's words and behaviors in a fairly nonthreatening manner. Doing so puts the issue on the table and allows the worker and client to explore the client's reluctance. It may be that the client needs more time and that contacting the daughter at this time is premature. Or it might be something else altogether. Nevertheless, the challenge helps move the work along, whereas allowing the illusion of work to continue would have stalled progress. In this situation the worker invited the client to explore the discrepancy. In the next example the worker challenges the client while also demonstrating empathy.

WORKER: We have been talking about getting back in touch with your daughter for quite some time now. You say you want to contact her but keep finding excuses not to. I know making the first move is scary. Are you worried about being hurt or rejected? Is that what is holding you back?

In this example the worker has linked the challenge to the work, has pointed out the discrepancy, and has used additive empathy to try to help the client identify the underlying feelings. This helps the client feel understood and at the same time encourages an exploration of the discrepancy between the client's actions and words.

*Maintaining Focus*   The persevering task focuses on helping the client make changes and progress toward goal attainment. A critical skill in this regard is helping clients maintain their focus on the identified action plan and desired outcomes. Clients from disadvantaged backgrounds face a number of enormous challenges on a daily basis. Small obstacles, such as transportation or baby-sitting, often turn into crisis situations. It is easy for the worker to spend all his or her time with a client going from one crisis situation to another. In this respect the work becomes reactive rather than purposeful.

Some concerns need immediate attention, and others do not. The worker needs to help clients sort through the various issues as they arise and put them within the framework of their action plan. Using the action plan as the frame of reference helps the worker and client maintain the focus of their work together. The specifics of the work may shift during the helping process, but they should always be defined and articulated in a plan of action. The skill of maintaining focus is bringing the work back to the plan of action and keeping the framework of the contract in focus.

Shulman (1999) points out that sometimes "moving from concern to concern can be an evasion of work—that is, if the client won't stay with one issue, then he or she does not have to deal with the associated feelings" (p. 173). The worker maintains focus by bringing the work back to the issue the client is avoiding. This communicates a willingness to address the difficult issue and helps the client to stay focused on the issue instead of allowing the client to jump from concern to concern. The following example illustrates the skill of maintaining focus with a client who is jumping from issue to issue.

WORKER: So far today we have talked about some issues you are having with your landlord, problems with child care, and your concerns about the safety of your neighborhood. Before we get into those topics, can we spend some time on the concern that brought you here—the difficulty you are having with your teenage son?

Beginning social workers often have difficulty maintaining focus because of a desire to go "where the client wants to go." It is important to be flexible and respond to the client's immediate agenda. If the client has an issue that needs to be dealt with, then it would be inappropriate for the worker to insist on sticking to the original agenda or action plan. The key is to assess the urgency of the situation and respond accordingly. The trap is to jump from one issue to another without considering how the issues fit into the purpose of your work together.

*Checking for Ambivalence*   One of the obstacles many clients face in making behavioral or environmental changes is their mixed feelings about the proposed change. Most have some degree of ambivalence. "One of the dangers in a helping situation is that the client may choose to go along with the worker, expressing an artificial consensus or agreement, while really feeling very ambivalent about a point of view or decision to take the next step" (Shulman, 1999, p. 174). Ambivalence is manifested most often during the engagement phase of the helping process. It is during this period that work involves making decisions and following through on action steps.

Social workers should assume that the client has some degree of ambivalence and incorporate checking out this ambivalence into their practice repertoire. Ambivalence is a normal reaction to change and the change process. Exploring your client's ambivalence gives him or her the opportunity to work through mixed feelings. Talking about the feelings "diminishes the power of the negative feelings" (Shulman, 1999, p. 174). The following example illustrates the skill of checking for ambivalence.

WORKER: I think we have made excellent progress in deciding on our plan of action. Before we move forward, I just want to make sure you are comfortable and ready to begin. I'm not sure, but I have a hunch that you have some second thoughts or concerns about family therapy.

Some beginning social workers are reluctant to explore their client's mixed feelings. They are worried about questioning their agreed-upon decisions for fear that the client might change his or her mind. If ambivalence is not explored, however, it often results in an "illusion of work" or the client dropping out. Expect your clients to be ambivalent, look for it, and help them express it.

*Rehearsal*   A theme of this chapter is that making changes is generally not easy. Indeed, if making changes were easy, clients would not need the help of social workers. Rehearsing ahead of time what they will say or do is an effective way to support clients' change efforts. Role-play what your clients will say and do in carrying out the activities identified in their action plan. Role-playing helps clients find the words they need to sum up the real situation. The worker plays the role of the other person and gives the client feedback on their interaction. The client plays himself or herself and practices what he or she will say until feeling comfortable enough to proceed.

Another benefit of rehearsal is that it helps the worker and client identify ambivalence and other obstacles holding the client back from moving forward on the action plan. The role-play provides the client with an experience similar to what he or she would have in real life. The client experiences his or her reactions to the interaction or exchange. The role-play's affective component helps the client identify underlying feelings. It helps bring feelings out into the open so that they can be addressed.

**Output: Client Change**   The major output of the persevering task is **client change.** This is the phase of the helping process where the attention is focused on helping clients make the identified changes in their lives. Keeping clients engaged in the helping process during this difficult period is the key to realizing the desired output of client change. Communicating support and strong commitment to the change process helps strengthen the helping relationship. Use of the intervention skills of challenging, maintaining focus, checking for ambivalence, and rehearsal helps clients achieve their identified goals.

# THE DISENGAGEMENT PHASE OF COLLABORATIVE SOCIAL WORK

The disengagement phase of the collaborative model usually takes place during sessions 9 and 10. The major task to be accomplished, at this point, is solidifying the changes that have been accomplished during the engagement phase. Before reviewing the inputs, skills, and outputs of disengagement, we will review in more general terms the termination process.

In many respects, how you end with your clients is as important as how you begin. During the disengagement phase, you and your client review, evaluate, and consolidate the work; process feelings and experiences; and plan ways to maintain the beneficial changes that have occurred (Fortune, 1987; Fortune, 1995; Fortune, Pearlingi, and Rochelle, 1992; Garvin and Seabury, 1997).

## Types of Termination

There are six common reasons for ending the helping relationship: planned ending, time-limited service, ending open-ended service by mutual agreement, ending open-ended service for unanticipated reasons, transfer to another social worker, and dropping out (Fortune, 1995). Regardless of the reason, appropriate termination helps clients solidify the gains made and prepares them for the ending of the helping relationship.

**Planned Endings**   There are two types of planned endings. The first is the ending that was planned from the beginning of the service and that takes place after a specified amount of time. Managed-care companies typically require fixed time limits on social work services. As managed care becomes the norm, the occurrence of planned endings with time-limited services will increase. Because the ending is determined at the beginning of the service, the process is usually easier than in open-ended service (Fortune, 1995).

The second type of planned ending occurs when the service contract is open ended (i.e., there are no fixed time limits) and the social worker and client agree that the helping relationship does not need to continue. This usually occurs when the client has achieved the identified goals or has made sufficient progress on them and feels that other areas of concern can be handled outside the helping relationship.

In collaborative generalist practice, the client determines when to terminate the helping relationship. If the client feels ready to proceed without the help of a social worker, he or she should be given the opportunity to do so even if the social worker believes otherwise. Support the client's judgment and desire to function independently, but provide the option of returning if the need arises.

The ultimate goal of collaborative generalist social work practice is to empower clients and encourage their independent functioning. Long-term reliance on a helping relationship fosters dependency. If a client does not want to end a relationship that you believe should end, you need to communicate this to the client. One possible way of handling the situation is to revise the intervention and evaluation plan to set time limits and to identify goals related to termination. This way, the client is given a voice in the termination process and a set time frame for a successful, mutually agreed-on ending.

Another important reason to end the helping relationship is lack of success (Fortune, Pearlingi, and Rochelle, 1992). If progress is not being made, or if you agree that the chances of making progress are minimal, it is in your client's best interest to terminate service. Of course, this should be done only after an open and honest evaluation of your relationship and the reasons for the lack of success. If you have continually monitored progress and have adjusted the interventions in response to the lack of progress, a consideration of termination is warranted.

**Unanticipated Endings**   There are a multitude of reasons for unplanned endings. A common type of unanticipated ending is transfer to another social worker. The social worker must terminate the helping relationship because he or she is leaving the agency, or the client has been reassigned to another worker or to another service agency. Termination under these conditions is difficult because the client has a continuing need for service and has to establish a relationship with the new worker. The primary tasks associated with this type of ending are to process the client's feelings about the change of workers and help the client prepare to transfer to the new worker or agency.

Another form of unanticipated ending, one that unfortunately is all too common in the human service field, is dropping out. The client simply does not return and does not inform the social worker. The primary drawback is that clients who drop out do not have opportunities to access the helping process, make plans to maintain gains achieved, or plan for continued growth.

Between 40 and 60 percent of cases end because of situational factors (DeBerry and Baskin, 1989; Fortune, 1995; Hynan, 1990). Thus, for approximately half of all clients, service ends without achieving the desired goals or without mutual agreement. The probability of achieving positive outcomes in these situations is small. Additionally, clients might experience disappointment, frustration, or anger over the disruption of service.

## Clients' Reactions to Termination

Separation is inherent in ending a helping relationship. It is common to have mixed feelings about any type of separation. The intensity of feelings about termination vary depending on the amount of success achieved, the strength of the relationship, the type of termination, and the client's previous experiences with terminating professional and personal relationships.

Several factors influence clients' reactions to termination. The most important is the reason for termination. Planned, agreed-on terminations tend to be viewed as positive experiences. Unexpected terminations are more likely to result in negative feelings. Feelings of anger, disappointment, and a sense of unfinished business are common reactions to an unplanned termination (Fortune, 1995).

Not long ago, research on termination characterized the process in primarily negative terms. The emphasis was on sadness, loss, denial, depression, and other negative reactions (Fortune, 1995; Hepworth, Rooney, and Larsen, 2002). Recent research findings indicate that most clients react to termination in a more positive than negative way (Fortune, 1987; Fortune, Pearlingi, and Rochelle, 1992). The benefits gained from a positive helping relationship outweigh the loss associated with ending (Hepworth, Rooney, and Larsen, 2002). Positive feelings of accomplishment, positive feelings about the helping relationship, and increased self-worth are usually associated with planned terminations (Gutheil, 1993).

Although positive reactions appear to outweigh negative reactions, mixed feelings are the norm. Most clients experience some negative feelings about ending. Fortune (1987) found that negative reactions to termination occur more frequently in open-ended, psychosocial treatment. A common negative reaction to termination is to cling to therapy and the practitioner (Hepworth, Rooney, and Larsen, 2002). Some clients use the helping process as a substitute for interpersonal relationships. In these situations, giving up a long and meaningful relationship with the social worker is especially hard. In a sense, the client has become dependent on the relationship with the social worker. Hepworth, Rooney, and Larsen (2002) point out that it is important to stress the goal of independence within the shortest possible time frame throughout the helping relationship. If most of your clients have great difficulty ending the relationship, it is important to examine the extent to which you are fostering dependency by emphasizing weaknesses, deficiencies, and pathologic factors rather than strengths and opportunities for growth (Hepworth, Rooney, and Larsen, 2002).

Another common negative reaction to termination is reporting the recurrence of old problems (Hepworth, Rooney, and Larsen, 2002). This is sometimes referred to as regression. The client feels anxious about ending the relationship and wants to keep it going, so old problems reappear as areas of concern. A variation of regression is when the client shows deterioration in terms of current problems or concerns. Instead of getting better and maintaining improvement, the client appears to be getting worse. Hepworth, Rooney, and

Larsen (2002) suggest that when this occurs, it is important to focus on the client's fears about termination and the ending process rather than on the problems that have reappeared.

Sometimes new problems are introduced as the termination date draws near. This is often a ploy to continue the relationship. Although you have to be sensitive to the possibility of real problems that require attention, it is important to explore the client's feelings about termination before turning to these new issues (Hepworth, Rooney, and Larsen, 2002). Often, the new issues disappear once an open discussion about the fears and uncertainty of termination has taken place.

## Task 7: Solidifying the Changes Achieved

Solidifying or maintaining the gains made through the helping relationship is another task that needs to be addressed during the disengagement phase. "Workers cannot assume that beneficial changes the clients have attained will continue" (Garvin and Seabury, 1997, p. 428). One common reason is that the client's environment may not be supportive of the changes. The client may not have a support network that will bolster his or her new ways of coping. The kind of support the client received in the helping relationship may not be available. In fact, the client's environment may undermine the gains made.

Some researchers view ending as an intervention (Fortune, 1995), and others view it as a component of the helping process or as the final stage of the helping relationship (Hess and Hess, 1994). According to Fortune (1995), the ending process should

- Assess client progress and treatment process
- Generalize gains to other settings and situations
- Develop skills and strategies to maintain gains
- Assist in the transition to no service or to another service
- Deal with emotional reactions to ending treatment

Others have developed similar conceptualizations of the tasks that need to be completed during the disengagement phase (Garvin and Seabury, 1997; Miley, O'Melia, and DuBois, 1998). Regardless of the conceptualization of the specific activities, the primary objective is to solidify the client changes that have been achieved. Solidification entails maintaining the gains achieved and preventing relapse.

**Input: Confidence**   Figure 7.4 illustrates how the solidifying task builds trust. Reviewing progress with your clients during the disengagement phase is a critical step in the termination process. It is important for clients to hear about and acknowledge accomplishments as well as setbacks. This review sets the stage for helping the client examine ways in which your work together can be used outside of the helping relationship. It also sets the stage for identifying the next steps and an aftercare plan following the termination of the helping relationship. Engaging the client in this process helps create an expectation for success

FIGURE 7.4 | DISENGAGEMENT TASK: SOLIDIFYING

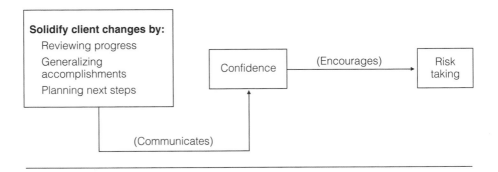

and communicates to the client confidence in her ability to maintain the gains made and continue creating positive life changes.

**Ending Skills**    The two primary practice skills that are somewhat unique to the ending process are generalizing and identifying the next steps. Both of these skills help clients prepare for the termination of the helping relationship.

*Generalizing*    This skill entails helping clients generalize the learning from one experience to other similar experiences. "This is a key skill of living, since it equips the client to continue without the worker and to use the newfound skills to deal with novel and unexpected experiences" (Shulman, 1999, p. 193). The first step in helping clients generalize is to evaluate progress related to the identified concerns and challenges. Evaluation is a process that continues throughout the engagement phase. Deciding to terminate the helping relationship is an evaluative act. In planned terminations, you and the client have agreed to end the helping relationship. A comprehensive review of progress during the termination phase is needed.

A comprehensive review can confirm or disconfirm the decision to terminate (Fortune, 1995). Is termination appropriate? Is the helping relationship no longer needed? Is the client ready to move on without service or move to a new service? Based on the outcome criteria you and your client established earlier, has sufficient progress been made? What issues have been resolved? What still needs to be done?

Reviewing progress during termination provides the opportunity to acknowledge the client's work, effort, and strengths. Termination brings mixed feelings. The client usually feels some degree of apprehension. Emphasizing client strengths and achievement is especially important when the client is feeling anxious and vulnerable. At this stage, one of your key tasks is to support the client and foster belief in himself or herself. Helping clients see how much they have accomplished and how they have successfully coped with their problems and challenges is critical.

| | |
|---|---|
| TABLE 7.4 | SOLIDIFYING: PRACTICE SKILLS |

**Ending skills**
   Generalizing
   Identifying the next steps

Reviewing the helping relationship can also help in generalizing gains. The helping relationship is the heart of collaborative generalist social work practice. It is through the helping relationship that clients address their concerns and challenges. During termination, it is critical for you and the client to explore each others' experiences and perceptions about your work together. This helps clients articulate what they liked and disliked in the helping relationship. Being aware of their feelings will make them better consumers of future relationships with helping professionals. In a concrete sense, an open and candid discussion of your helping relationship will begin preparing clients for possible future service episodes.

Reviewing your helping relationship will also give you and the client an opportunity to share feelings about working together. It is critical in a collaborative relationship for both you and the client to share what the relationship has meant to you and the joys and frustrations of working together. This is not a one-way street; both you and the client are expected to be open about the relationship.

In addition, the review provides an opportunity to explore the client's feelings about ending. Clients will have mixed feelings about terminating the helping relationship. There will be feelings of joy, excitement, and pride about accomplishments as well as feelings of anticipation, sadness, and loss. The intensity of clients' reactions to ending is influenced in part by their prior experiences with separation and ending relationships and in part by the type of termination and the progress they have made. Acknowledging the mixed feelings helps make them acceptable, validates the client's experiences, and allows a discussion to occur (Fortune, 1995). Clients with strong negative reactions will need more time to process their feelings about ending. They may be experiencing intense mourning and grief reactions and should have an opportunity to work through the grieving process as they would with any other significant loss.

At the other extreme are clients who deny having any feelings about ending. One possibility is that the client is responding as if there will be no ending (Garvin and Seabury, 1997). This may occur even if the client has agreed to termination. The client may have cognitively accepted the appropriateness of ending the helping relationship but has not accepted it emotionally. In this situation, sharing your feelings about ending may help the client become aware of his or her own feelings and confront and accept the impending separation (Hess and Hess, 1994).

Use the Helping Relationship Inventory (HRI) presented in Chapter 3 as a starting point for your review of your work together. It covers the major components of the helping relationship. Comparing your responses with the client's responses is instructive. It will help you ensure that you engage in a comprehensive review of the structural and interpersonal aspects of the helping relationship.

*Identifying the Next Steps*    The second ending skill is helping your clients plan for the future. Making future plans helps the client make the transition to no service or to another service and solidify the gains made during the helping relationship. Fortune (1995) suggests that increasing the sense of mastery through realistic praise and highlighting the client's role in creating and maintaining change will help ensure gains after service ends.

Whether the client is ending the process or being transferred to another service, the social worker needs to ease the transition by making the new situation real (Fortune, 1995). Events that are distant, unspecified, and abstract are less real than events that are close at hand, specific, and concrete. Your task is to make the pending change in circumstances as concrete as possible. Be specific about the future. Have the client visualize what his or her life will be like outside the helping relationship or what will need to be done to begin a new helping relationship. If the client is being transferred elsewhere, link the client with the new service, visit the new agency, and engage in other activities that promote the connection so as to help smooth the transition. If service is ending, link the client to a support network and engage in activities that will support the transition to nonservice. In both situations, explore the client's feelings and expectations and make plans for following up and checking back.

During termination, the client and worker must develop a plan that specifies how change will be maintained. This aftercare plan should lay out strategies that the client can use to avoid future difficulties and respond to challenging situations as well as proactive strategies and activities aimed at preventing the reccurrence of problems. Strategies that can be used for these purposes are overlearning, problem solving, and network interventions (Garvin and Seabury, 1997).

**Overlearning** focuses on helping clients practice new ways of coping after the initial learning. The key is to have the client practice the new skill or coping strategy in as many different situations as possible. Through role-playing and discussion, the client prepares to respond appropriately to a variety of anticipated challenging situations.

The second strategy is to help the client strengthen his or her **problem-solving skills.** Help your client predict problems that might be encountered in his or her environment, and brainstorm ways to effectively respond to each problem situation. Role-play with the client different strategies and approaches. The goal is to have the client develop problem-solving skills directly related to potential environmental challenges following termination.

The third strategy is **network intervention.** This entails strengthening the client's support network. The plan is to intervene in the client's environment, based on the premise that others in the environment may also require profes-sional help (Garvin and Seabury, 1997). Network intervention requires the participation of members of the client's social support system and environ-ment. They have to agree to support the client and to become involved in the change effort. Involvement of the support network should begin prior to the termination phase and increase as the client moves closer to ending.

**Outputs: Evaluation, Generalization, and Aftercare**   The major outputs associated with the solidifying task and disengagement are (1) completing a thorough evaluation of client progress; (2) helping your client generalize your experiences together to other experiences outside the helping relationship; and (3) developing an aftercare plan. These three outputs are critical to the main-tenance of the gains made and the prevention of relapse.

## SUMMARY

This chapter reviewed the process of developing goals and objectives that flow out of the client assessment. Goals are positive statements about what the client hopes to achieve. Objectives are measurable indicators of the identified goals. Together they specify the purpose of the helping relationship. All gen-eralist social work practice should be purposeful, with clearly articulated goals and objectives. Strengths-based practice is client centered and client directed. Consequently, goals and objectives are based on the client's percep-tions of need, not the social worker's.

Developing goals and objectives is a collaborative process. A comprehen-sive assessment will identify a number of potential target problems. Together you and the client determine one or two concerns that have the highest prior-ity. The identified problem areas are then converted into statements that reflect the client's broad expectations about desired changes.

Objectives are steps toward goals. They are the intermediate steps that clients need to accomplish to reach their goals. Well-written objectives are specific and measurable. They specify who will do what, to what extent, under what conditions, and by when.

The engagement phase of the helping process focuses on developing a contract or plan of action and implementing the plan. The two major tasks are articulating and persevering. Contracting skills are used to help clients articulate their action plan. The skills of partializing, identifying options, seeking consensus, and sharing data all help facilitate the development of the change goals and the action and evaluation plans. Intervention skills are used to help the client follow through in implementing the action and evaluation plans. The skills of challenging, maintaining focus, checking for ambivalence, and rehearsal help the client persevere in implementing the action plan and achieving the desired changes.

In the disengagement phase, the gains made during the intervention phase are solidified and future plans for maintaining the gains are developed. The worker helps solidify these changes by communicating confidence and an expectation that the changes will be maintained. The ending skills of generalizing and identifying next steps help clients complete an evaluation of their progress, generalize their experiences, and develop an aftercare plan. To simply end without attention to the outputs of disengagement is a disservice to clients.

# CASE EXAMPLE

The following case example is representative of some of the complexities involved in working with people infected with HIV or AIDS and their families. It depicts specific aspects of the helping relationship as well as multiple levels of care and collaborative efforts.

---

## EMOTIONAL EXPRESSION AND HIV
### BY BRENT SATTERLY

Rob W. was referred for individual therapy as a result of his case manager's recommendation to work on "some of his emotional issues." His presenting problems consisted of major depression, an inability to express emotion, and familial conflicts.

### Assessment
Rob is a 31-year-old, gay Caucasian who was infected with HIV in the mid-1980s. He reportedly engaged in high-risk sexual behavior as a maladaptive means of coping when a relationship ended. Rob's life was very secretive because of his fear of familial rejection over his sexuality. When he was 24, he left Pennsylvania and moved to Washington to flee such fears. He moved back to his family's home in Pennsylvania when he became too ill to care for himself.

Rob came out to his family as gay at the age of 28 when he disclosed his HIV status. This multiple disclosure shocked his family. They had little opportunity to process their feelings, however, because Rob's rapidly failing health meant that he needed care.

Rob's strengths were numerous. He was bright and insightful and was able to benefit from his insights. Rob had worked as a clerk in law offices in Pennsylvania and Washington. He had hoped to seek further education and possibly enter law school. His social support system was extensive and spanned the country. His family rallied around him emotionally, physically, and financially. His many friends from

Washington often traveled to his home to visit him, as did some of his local school friends. Their visits provided him with a sense of community and hope outside of his overwhelmed immediate family. In addition, his sense of spirituality was powerful.

### Intervention and Evaluation
Rob spoke of "emotional numbness" or a "block." Therapy focused on examining how to express his emotional wants and needs, as well as how to cope with the slow loss of the use of his left arm. He reported that therapy and case management helped him develop an internal resolve that he had not experienced previously. His willingness and motivation to actively participate in treatment contributed to this level of acceptance.

Rob attended therapy until his health deteriorated and mobility became problematic. The social worker began conducting in-home visits. Rob began feeling and expressing grief about his situation. A hospice nurse began to help with Rob's care. When Rob questioned her, this nurse disclosed her role as a hospice nurse and explained that hospice care is pain-management care given to those who are dying. Apparently, three months before, when Rob was in the hospital, he was diagnosed with progressive multifocal leukoencephalopathy (PML), a neurologic infection. The diagnosis explained the increasing weakness of his limbs. He had approximately six months to live. Reportedly, this was not discussed with Rob or the family, nor did he or the family ask what the diagnosis meant. So when the hospice nurse casually disclosed her role, it communicated to Rob for the first time that he was dying. He had a panic attack as a result and quickly contacted his social worker.

The social worker collaborated with Rob's case manager, case management assistant, and a social work colleague to provide additional social and professional supports and services to him and his family in the home. Rob's mother and father began seeing another social worker in outpatient treatment for issues of grief, loss, and anger. The case manager provided in-home social supports and delivery of services to Rob. The case manager and the social worker designed a family intervention where Rob could express his wishes for his memorial services and his grief and loss over his pending death. Unfortunately, Rob's throat swelled significantly due to a side effect of medication, making breathing difficult, so Rob,

who had struggled to express his emotions because of psychological blocks, was now physically blocked from having a good cry. The family session allowed everyone to express pain and grief, while individual work focused on helping Rob express grief in different ways than potent crying spells.

### Termination

Paradoxically, the tragic way Rob discovered his prognosis allowed for a significant emotional and spiritual breakthrough. While discussing the family session, he disclosed to the social worker that he "never really felt like I belonged on this planet." He described a sense of "not fitting in" here and needing to "move on." He reported a spiritual sense of peace around death. More than a dozen social service staff attended the funeral to mourn the loss of this courageous young man. Aftercare services are still in place for the family for bereavement counseling and support.

## DISCUSSION QUESTIONS

1. How might you develop a helping relationship with Rob and his family (Case 7.1)?
2. What other areas of intervention might have been effective for Rob and his family? Would crisis intervention services have been appropriate for Rob's family? (For information on crisis intervention, see Kanel, 2003, and James and Gilliland, 2001.)
3. What feelings or emotions might be raised by working with Rob? How would you care for yourself as a worker in this case?
4. How might you use strengths to help a person affected by HIV or AIDS?

## REFERENCES

Bloom, M., Fischer, J., and Orme, J. (1995). *Evaluating practice: Guidelines for the accountable professional* (2nd ed.). Boston: Allyn and Bacon.

DeBerry, S., and Baskin, D. (1989). Termination criteria in psychotherapy: A comparison of private and public practice. *American Journal of Psychotherapy, 43*, 43–53.

Egan, G. (1999). *The skilled helper* (4th ed.). Pacific Grove: CA: Brooks/Cole.

Epstein, L. (1988). *The task-centered approach*. Columbus, OH: Merrill.

Fortune, A. E. (1987). Grief only? Client and social work reactions to termination. *Clinical Social Work Journal, 15,* 159–171.

Fortune, A. E. (1995). Termination in direct practice. In R. Edwards (Ed.), *Encyclopedia of social work* (19th ed.). Silver Spring, MD: NASW Press.

Fortune, A. E., Pearlingi, B., and Rochelle, C. (1992). Reactions to termination of individual treatment. *Social Work, 37,* 171–178.

Garvin, C. D., and Seabury, B. A. (1997). *Interpersonal practice in social work: Promoting competence and social justice* (2nd ed.). Boston: Allyn and Bacon.

Goldstein, H. (1973). *Social work practice: A unitary approach.* Columbia, SC: University of South Carolina Press.

Gutheil, I. A. (1993). Rituals and termination procedures. *Smith College Studies in Social Work, 63,* 163–176.

Hepworth, D., Rooney, R., and Larsen, J. (1997). *Direct social work practice: Theory and skills* (5th ed.). Pacific Grove, CA: Brooks/Cole.

Hepworth, D., Rooney, R., and Larsen, J. (2002). *Direct social work practice: Theory and skills* (6th ed.). Pacific Grove, CA: Brooks/Cole.

Hess, H., and Hess, P. M. (1994). Termination in context. In B. R. Compton and B. Galaway, *Social work processes* (2nd. ed., pp. 529–539). Pacific Grove, CA: Brooks/Cole.

Hynan, D. J. (1990). Client reasons and experiences in treatment that influence termination of psychotherapy. *Journal of Clinical Psychology, 46,* 891–895.

James, R. K., and Gilliland, B. E. (2001). *Crisis intervention strategies* (4th ed.). Pacific Grove, CA: Brooks/Cole.

Jongsma, A., and Peterson, L. M. (1995). *The complete psychotherapy treatment planner.* New York: Wiley.

Kanel, K. (2003). *A guide to crisis intervention* (2nd ed.). Pacific Grove, CA: Wadsworth.

Kirst-Ashman, K., and Hull, G. (1993). *Understanding generalist practice.* Chicago: Nelson-Hall.

Locke, B., Garrison, R., and Winship, J. (1998). *Generalist social work practice: Context, story, and partnerships.* Pacific Grove, CA: Brooks/Cole.

Mager, R. (1972). *Goal analysis.* Belmont, CA: Fearon.

Miley, K., O'Melia, M., and DuBois, B. L. (1998). *Generalist social work practice: An empowering approach* (2nd ed.). Boston: Allyn and Bacon.

Miller, W. R., and Rollnick, S. (2002). *Motivational interviewing: Preparing people for change* (2nd ed.). New York: Guilford Press.

Patterson, L. E., and Welgel, E. R. (1994). *The counseling process* (4th ed.). Pacific Grove, CA: Brooks/Cole.

Pillari, V. (2002). *Social work practice: Theories and skills.* Boston: Allyn and Bacon.

Prochaska, J. O., DiClemente, C. C., and Norcross, J. C. (1992). In search of how people change: Applications to addictive behaviors. *American Psychologist, 47,* 1102–1114.

Reid, W. (1970). Implications of research for the goals of casework. *Smith College Studies in Social Work, 40,* 140–154.

Rosen, A. (1993). Systematic planned practice. *Social Service Review, 67,* 84–100.

Sheafor, B., Horejsi, C., and Horejsi, G. (1994). *Techniques and guidelines for social work practice* (5th ed.). Boston: Allyn and Bacon.

Shulman, L. (1999). *The skills of helping individuals, families, groups and organizations* (4th ed.). Itasca, IL: F. E. Peacock Publishing, Inc.

Siporin, M. (1975). *Introduction to social work practice.* New York: Macmillan.

# Action Plan and Outcome Evaluation

Client: _____   Social Worker: _____   Date: _____

Desired Outcomes: (List agreed-on change goals)

1. _____

2. _____

3. _____

4. _____

| Action Steps | Responsibility | Due Date | Completed |
|---|---|---|---|
| 1. _____ | | | |
| 2. _____ | | | |
| 3. _____ | | | |
| 4. _____ | | | |
| 5. _____ | | | |
| 6. _____ | | | |
| 7. _____ | | | |
| 8. _____ | | | |
| 9. _____ | | | |
| 10. _____ | | | |
| 11. _____ | | | |
| 12. _____ | | | |
| 13. _____ | | | |
| 14. _____ | | | |
| 15. _____ | | | |
| 16. _____ | | | |

Contracted Number of Sessions: _____

Number of Sessions per Week: _____

Contract Period:   from ___/___/_____ to ___/___/_____

Signatures:

Client: _____   Social Worker: _____

Outcome Evaluation Ratings (List change goals and rate progress on each goal)

1. _____

| 1 | 2 | 3 | 4 | 5 |
|---|---|---|---|---|
| No Progress | | Moderate Progress | | Optimal Progress |

2. _____

| 1 | 2 | 3 | 4 | 5 |
|---|---|---|---|---|
| No Progress | | Moderate Progress | | Optimal Progress |

3. _____

| 1 | 2 | 3 | 4 | 5 |
|---|---|---|---|---|
| No Progress | | Moderate Progress | | Optimal Progress |

4. _____

| 1 | 2 | 3 | 4 | 5 |
|---|---|---|---|---|
| No Progress | | Moderate Progress | | Optimal Progress |

---

Disposition (Circle appropriate disposition category)

1. Agreed-on Termination of Service

2. Client Terminated Service

3. Worker Terminated Client for Nonparticipation

4. Worker Referred Client to Another Service Provider

Case Disposition Summary

_____

_____

_____

_____

_____

_____

# GENERALIST PRACTICE
# INTERVENTIONS

Norma D. is an MSW student with a second-year placement in a family service agency in an urban community. Norma provides case management and supportive services to a primarily minority elderly client population. She enjoys working with the elderly and hearing their stories.

During her second month of placement, rains from a hurricane that hit North Carolina flooded the river that runs through the community. The rains were unusually heavy, and the river flooded for the first time in recent memory. The flood damage was limited to the streets relatively close to the river. Nevertheless, for those affected, the damage was extensive. Homes were flooded, cars floated down the street, and approximately 2000 people were displaced from their homes.

All agency personnel were dispatched to help the people affected by the flood. Norma was not prepared for the effect that the physical destruction of people's homes and their distress would have on her. By natural disaster standards the flood was a relatively small scale event, but Norma was overwhelmed by the magnitude of the damage and the suffering. She felt a sense of powerlessness in much the same way her clients did. Norma couldn't understand why her agency sent her out so completely unprepared. She also wondered why social work courses had not covered anything like what she was encountering.

The purpose of this chapter is to provide more detailed information on a range of micro and macro generalist interventions. By the end of this chapter, you should be able to help Norma

1.  Identify a number of micro-level interventions that she can undertake with her clients
2.  Identify a number of organizational interventions that she can undertake to improve services for her clients
3.  Identify a number of community interventions that she can undertake to improve community conditions

## MICRO-LEVEL INTERVENTIONS

As noted earlier, there are two major categories of intervention tasks: micro and macro. Most interventions are usually done in collaboration with the client system, or the social worker does them on behalf of the client system. Interventions represent the work phase of the action plan. The two micro interventions usually undertaken by generalist social workers are counseling and case management. Within each of these broad categories there are a number of more specific intervention tasks and activities. The following describes a number of micro interventions used by generalist social workers in their work with individuals, families, and small groups. The ones selected for inclusion here represent the more common generalist interventions. They do not represent the full range of intervention strategies and approaches.

## CASE 8.1 | SUPPORTIVE COUNSELING INTERVENTION

Jim L. is a fifteen-year-old sophomore previously diagnosed as having a moderate learning disability. He takes regular college preparation courses and has managed to maintain a "B" average. He receives tutoring in math and science and uses the writing center at the school to help him write all of his papers. Although he struggles academically, he has been relatively successful in school.

Jim has no close friends and very few friendly acquaintances. His peers view him as odd and as a "loser." His attempts to fit in and make friends have met with rejection and ridicule, and he has withdrawn socially and makes no attempt to interact with classmates. Jim spends all of his free time at home watching television and playing computer games.

While at home, Jim appears to take out his frustration on his family. He is very demanding of his parents and causes many disturbances within the family. He gets angry quickly and lashes out at his parents over little things. He constantly picks on his younger sister, puts her down in front of her friends, criticizes her looks and abilities, and treats her with general disrespect. When Jim gets into "one of his moods" or is "on the warpath," the tension in the family gets very high. During these times, everyone seems to be mad at everyone else. His parents start fighting, and the general mood in the family is tense and hostile.

Jim's parents are concerned about his lack of peer relationships and his behavior at home. They contacted the school social worker to inquire about help for their son. To his family's surprise, Jim agreed to meet regularly with the school social worker, and together they developed an intervention plan.

## Counseling

Supportive counseling and education and training are two traditional direct service interventions (Pinderhughes, 1995) that are frequently employed by generalist social workers. They are both counseling-type interventions.

**Supportive Counseling**   In supportive counseling, the social worker takes the enabler role in the helping relationship (Hepworth, Rooney, and Larsen, 2002). The social worker and client agree to meet for a specified time period and engage in a collaborative therapeutic or counseling process. The purpose of the intervention is to help the client resolve concerns and challenges, enhance coping, and improve functioning.

The example in Case 8.1 illustrates a supportive counseling intervention. In this case example, supportive counseling was one of the agreed-on interventions. Jim recognized his difficulties with peer and family relationships, and he wanted to do something to improve the situation. Jim and the school social worker met once a week to help him improve his relationships. The social worker provided supportive counseling to help Jim gain insight into the problem and to help him develop coping strategies that would increase his effectiveness with peers and family members. Jim also used the counseling sessions to deal with his feelings of low self-worth and the hurt and anger he felt toward his classmates.

Within the supportive counseling framework the worker and client can engage in a variety of specific therapeutic modalities. The choice of a specific modality is determined, in part, by the focus of the work and the identified concerns. Two intervention modalities often used in conjunction with supportive counseling are cognitive restructuring (CR) and problem-solving therapy (PST).

*Cognitive Restructuring*   Cognitive restructuring (CR) is a technique of cognitive therapy that enables one to identify negative, irrational beliefs and replace them with truthful, rational statements. For example, the statement "I am a worthless, unlovable person. No one likes me." would be replaced with "I am a worthy and lovable person." Cognitive restructuring revises the way clients think about the problems by rewriting their "internal script." The focus is on changing a negative perception to a neutral or positive one, making it less stressful. The approach is based on the belief that cognition affects one's mood and behavior (Beck, 1976; Ellis, 1962, 1977). A basic assumption of all cognitive approaches "is that a person's thoughts and beliefs can contribute to maladaptive behavior. Another is that maladaptive behaviors can be altered by dealing directly with a person's beliefs, attitudes, or thoughts" (Cormier and Nurius, 2003, p. 391).

Cognitive restructuring is the primary method of Beck's (1976) **cognitive therapy** (CT) and Ellis's (1962) **rational emotive therapy (RET)** (Cormier and Nurius, 2003; Maguire, 2002). Over the years it has been adopted as a major treatment modality in social work (Hepworth, Rooney, and Larsen, 2002) and has been used extensively to help resolve a wide variety of problems, such as depression (Beck, 1996; Beck et al., 1979; Dulmus and Wodarski, 1998); anger management (Whiteman, Fanshel, and Grundy, 1987); spouse abuse (Eisikovits and Edleson, 1989); anxiety (Carter, Marin, and Murrell, 1999); self-esteem (Horan, 1996); and career indecision (Mitchel and Krumboltz, 1987). Hepworth, Rooney, and Larsen (2002) point out that "cognitive restructuring techniques are particularly relevant for problems associated with low self-esteem, distorted perceptions in interpersonal relationships; unrealistic expectations of self, others, and life in general; irrational fears, anxiety, and depression; inadequate control of anger and other impulses; and lack of assertiveness" (p. 388).

The process of cognitive restructuring can be divided into four phases: awareness, reappraisal of the situation, adoption and substitution, and assessment and reinforcement. **Awareness** entails having your client identify feelings and emotions, the triggering situations and stimuli, the client's unproductive behaviors, and the negative thoughts that precede the behaviors. **Reappraisal** entails having your client question the rationality and productiveness of her feelings, behaviors, and thoughts and identifying new, more constructive beliefs and thoughts. **Adoption and substitution** is the process of replacing the negative thoughts with neutral or positive ones. **Assessment** is the process of reviewing with your client the effectiveness of her cognitive restructuring efforts in terms of feelings and behaviors.

Hepworth, Rooney, and Larsen (2002) have identified four practice guidelines for implementing cognitive restructuring with clients (pp. 389–397). The four guidelines outline the process of helping clients make changes in their cognitions, moods, and behavior.

**Guideline 1:** *Assist clients in accepting that their self-statements, assumptions, and beliefs largely mediate (i.e., determine or govern) their emotional reactions to life* (p. 389). One of the crucial first steps in using cognitive restructuring with your clients is to educate them about the connections between cognitions, moods, and behaviors. Clients must understand and accept the underlying assumptions of the model, and they must commit themselves to the process if the intervention is to be effective.

Give the client examples of how cognitive restructuring works. The more relevant the examples are to the client's situation and life experiences, the better. Before introducing the idea of using cognitive restructuring in your work together, reflect upon your client's life experiences, problem situation, culture, and values and beliefs in order to come up with examples of the approach that will have meaning for your client. Prepare the example ahead of time and plan how you will present the idea to your client. Make sure your client understands and is genuinely willing to work with you and the process.

**Guideline 2:** *Assist clients in identifying dysfunctional beliefs and patterns of thought that underlie their problems* (p. 390). After your client accepts the premises of cognitive restructuring, the next step is to examine the link between her thoughts, moods, and behaviors. Hepworth, Rooney, and Larsen (2002) suggest that "you begin the process of exploration by focusing on problematic events that occurred during the preceding week or events surrounding a problem the client has targeted for change" (p. 390). The key is to seek concreteness and help the client be specific about her behaviors, the situation, and her feelings. Your objective is to help your client identify the cognitive sets (thoughts) that are associated with the negative feelings and behaviors that created the problematic event. Have your client verbalize the self-statements that were going through her mind before, during, and after the event. Collaboratively review the rationality of the self-statements and the validity of your client's thoughts. "Clients, however, may not acknowledge the irrationality of certain beliefs . . ." (Hepworth, Rooney, and Larsen, 2002, p. 392). If this occurs, you must "be prepared to challenge or dispute such irrational beliefs and to persist in assisting clients to recognize the costs or disadvantages associated with not relinquishing these beliefs" (Hepworth, Rooney, and Larsen, 2002, p. 392). Asking the following questions can help you challenge a client's irrational thoughts:

1.   What is the evidence against the belief?
2.   What are alternative interpretations of the situation?
3.   What are the real implications if the belief is correct?

**Guideline 3:** *Assist clients in identifying situations that engender dysfunctional cognitions* (p. 394). This guideline focuses on helping your client to identify the situations that trigger the negative thoughts, feelings, and behaviors. As you review the specifics of the negative cognitions, also look for patterns in terms of where the stressful situations take place and if there are any key persons or types of persons associated with the events.

**Guideline 4:** *Assist clients in substituting functional self-statements in place of self-defeating cognitions* (p. 394). As clients become aware of their negative thoughts, feelings, and behaviors, they need help in creating alternative thoughts and beliefs. The social worker helps her clients create realistic, affirming self-statements. Self-statements are internal thoughts that the client thinks to herself when trigger situations arise. The new positive self-statements need to be realistic and recognize the difficulty of the situation or the struggle involved. For example, a client dealing with anxiety might say, "These meetings always make me anxious. That is to be expected. I will go anyway and listen to what the others have to say." In this example, the client recognizes the struggle and sets a realistic expectation.

It is important to fully explain self-statements to your clients and to demonstrate how they would be used. It is also helpful to role-play different scenarios with your client to help her practice their use. Role-playing also helps the client increase her awareness of trigger situations and coping strategies. The process of "substituting coping self-statements for self-defeating thoughts or misconceptions is the heart of cognitive restructuring" (Hepworth, Rooney, and Larsen, 2002, p. 396).

**Problem-Solving Therapy**    Problem-solving therapy (PST) is a cognitive-behavioral approach used to help clients identify effective coping strategies to deal with problems encountered in daily living (D'Zurilla and Nezu, 1999). It is structured, actively involves the client, and focuses on the present, by addressing current problems and generating solutions. The PST process entails analyzing problems, discovering new approaches, implementing the new strategies, and assessing their effectiveness in real world situations (Rose and LeCory, 1991). Cormier and Nurius (2003) report that PST has been effective with a wide range of client populations and problem situations.

*Stages of Problem-Solving Therapy*    A number of conceptualizations of the stages of PST have been proposed (Cormier and Nurius, 2003; D'Zurilla, 1986; Jacobson and Margolin, 1979; Janis and Mann, 1977). The basic elements of the various models are very similar. Hepworth, Rooney, and Larsen's (2002) steps for problem solving are presented here because of their simplicity and applicability for strengths-based generalist practice.

- Acknowledge the problem
- Analyze the problem and identify the needs of the participants
- Employ brainstorming to generate possible solutions
- Evaluate each option, considering the needs of the participants
- Implement the option selected
- Evaluate the outcome of problem-solving efforts (p. 409).

The first step in PST is to help your client recognize that a problem exists and that it needs to be addressed. Often people have difficulty in accepting the reality of their situation and rationalize their problems away. At this stage, you also need to focus on strengthening your client's belief that problem solving can help her cope with the problem and improve her functioning. Thus, as the worker you need to explore with your client the specifics of the problem situation and help her acknowledge that the problem has negative consequences and that PST has the potential to help.

The next step is to help your client analyze the problem situation and her needs that are not being met. Do not seek to identify the root causes of problems or solutions. Instead help your client discover factors that produce the difficulties and identify the needs that must be met in order to solve the problem (Hepworth, Rooney, and Larsen, 2002). The focus should be on what needs to change versus how one brings the change about. The social worker uses elaboration skills to help the client tell her story and containment to focus on listening to the client's story. The goal is to have an agreed-on description of the problem situation as well as a mutual understanding of client needs that are not being met.

After the problem and unmet needs are clearly defined, the next step is to brainstorm for possible solutions. Remember that the client is the expert and the best source of ideas for possible solutions. Remind the client that all her ideas are important and that the purpose of the brainstorming is to generate as many solutions as possible.

After writing down the ideas generated, collaboratively evaluate each option to try to identify the best possible solution. Explore the pros and cons as well as the feasibility and consequences of each proposed solution. The goal is to empower your client by having her make the decision as to which solution to select. The client must make the choice. It has to be her decision and not a decision you make for her. Your job is to help your client think through the options. You can provide input, challenge distortions, and share your feelings, but do so in a way that gives your client the power to disagree. The client must have ownership of the solution selected.

Hepworth, Rooney, and Larsen (2002) suggest that after the option has been selected the next step is to "implement it with enthusiasm and confidence" (p. 414). Your task is to help build your client's confidence in her ability to try out the problem-solving alternative she has selected. Role-play different scenarios and practice until your client is comfortable in using the selected solution. At the same time that you are helping to build your client's confidence, you also need to help inspire hope and optimism about the possibility of change.

The final step in the PST process is to collaboratively evaluate the effectiveness of the chosen solution. Engage your client in an open discussion about how it went. Help her honestly assess her effort in implementing the solution, her feelings at the time, and her reactions to the alternative approach. The evaluation needs to assess the process and the effort as well as the outcome. This ongoing conversation is critical in helping your client sustain her change effort and in maintaining her motivation and enthusiasm. If the solution has not achieved the desired results, then you and your client need to revisit your identified options and begin the process of selecting another possible solution.

*Guidelines for Using Problem-Solving Therapy*    Hepworth, Rooney, and Larsen (2002) and Cormier and Nuris (2003) provide guidelines for implementing problem-solving therapy. The first authors' guidelines are generic, and the second authors' focus on diversity. Hepworth, Rooney, and Larsen (2002) suggest that social workers using PST:

- Be specific in relating problems
- Focus on the present problem rather than on past difficulties
- Focus on only one problem at a time
- Suspend judgment about the validity of the client's concerns
- Be nonjudgmental and avoid blaming the client

Cormier and Nuris (2003) focus on guidelines for applying PST with diverse client populations. They recommend that PST "be adapted for client characteristics such as age, gender, race, and ethnic affiliation to make problem solving both developmentally appropriate and culturally relevant" (p. 412). They also recommend that PST for clients from diverse backgrounds be conducted in a culturally sensitive manner. The rituals and traditions of the client's culture must be respected. PST must also be sensitive to the client's cultural and socioeconomic status, and to other issues that may affect oppressed and disenfranchised populations.

**Education and Training**    Education and training is a micro intervention used frequently by generalist social workers (DuBois and Miley, 1999). It involves helping individuals, families, and groups learn new concepts and skills. Many clients do not have the skills needed to meet the demands and expectations of their environment (Garvin and Seabury, 1997). Generalist social workers empower their clients through an exchange of information. This occurs as a normal part of most social work interventions. However, when it is a primary goal of the interaction, it becomes an intervention.

When functioning as an educator or trainer with any client, especially with a disadvantaged and oppressed client, it is important to be mindful of the discrepancy in power between you and your client. You have the knowledge and power, and it is easy to assume the role of expert. Minimize the power differential by taking an empowering strengths-based approach, and begin with the capacities of your clients (Freud, 1987). Have them share their knowledge of the topic. Create a learning partnership in which you and the client are colearners (DuBois and Miley, 1999). Engage in an educational dialogue as opposed to a one-way conveying of information (Freire, 1990).

An educational intervention may involve helping clients learn new skills, such as parenting, disciplining children, lifecare, budgeting, time management, and shopping. Skills training can take place with individual clients and families or in group settings. Groups that have an educational function are common in social work (Middleman and Wood, 1990). The example in Case 8.2 illustrates an educational intervention.

| CASE 8.2 | EDUCATIONAL INTERVENTION |

Time Out for Tots is a parenting program for teenage mothers. There are 15 2-hour sessions. The young mothers attend a weekly mother-only group session, during which information on child development and parenting is presented by the social worker. Group members also share their personal experiences and challenges. The second component of the program involves both the mothers and the children in a weekly group play session. During these sessions, the social worker models appropriate parent–child interactions and supports the mothers' use of the concepts and techniques covered in the group sessions.

## Case Management

There are a number of micro generalist interventions that fall within the broad category of case management. Typically, a social worker provides one or more of the following case management interventions: service linkage, service coordination, service negotiation, resource mobilization, and advocacy.

**Service Linkage**    Service linkage is another traditional direct service function performed by social workers (Garvin and Seabury, 1997). The social worker takes the broker role in the helping relationship (Hepworth, Rooney, and Larsen, 2002), referring a client to another agency for service. The process is more than just making a referral; service linkage creates a new link between the client system and an existing service. This is a major function of generalist social workers, especially because many clients who are referred to agencies for service do not follow through on the referral or, if they do, are not accepted for service (Lantz and Lenahan, 1976).

"One important aspect of successful referrals is the worker's ability to develop contacts and cultivate relationships with other workers and professionals in community resources" (Garvin and Seabury, 1997, p. 318). Having relationships with key contact people throughout the professional community will help you get your client accepted for service. Often, the client does not exactly fit the eligibility criteria, or there may be a limited number of service slots available. In these situations, your relationship with the agency contact person can help smooth the way so that the client is accepted for service (Garvin and Seabury, 1997). The importance of knowing someone in the system cannot be overstated. Becoming familiar with existing services within the community as well as developing relationships with professional colleagues is an important aspect of the broker role in generalist social work practice.

You also need to make an effort to support and strengthen the linkage. Weissman (1976) identified five strategies to help ensure a successful referral: checkback, haunting, sandwiching, alternating, and individualizing. Collectively, they are referred to as **cementing strategies.** The first four strategies involve following up with the client. The **checkback** strategy requires the client to call the worker to report on how the referral went. In **haunting,** the worker assumes responsibility for the follow-up contact. **Sandwiching** is scheduling a follow-up interview with the client to review the referral process and develop other linkage strategies as needed. **Alternating** involves planning a series of interviews following each contact with the referral source. The fifth strategy, **individualizing,** refers to the worker's efforts to improve the match between client needs and agency requirements (Garvin and Seabury, 1997). Thus, service linkage involves a concentrated and sustained collaborative effort to help the client make a successful connection with a needed resource.

In the case example of Jim L. (Case 8.1), service linkage was one of the agreed-on interventions. Jim and his social worker, in consultation with Jim's parents, decided that a referral to an agency that provides family treatment was appropriate. The school social worker acknowledged that she had limited training and experience in family therapy and that family relationship problems could be more effectively addressed by a social worker that specialized in family treatment. The social worker also referred Jim to the social worker at the neighborhood teen center in an effort to get him involved in after-school activities with other teenagers. Both referrals and her follow-up efforts were part of a service linkage intervention.

**Service Coordination**    Service coordination is the **coordinator role** in the helping relationship (Woodside and McClam, 1998). Clients have multiple problems and often need more than one service. In service coordination, the social worker coordinates the various services and professionals to ensure that they are integrated and working toward common goals. This involves monitoring the current status of the client, the services delivered, and the client's progress (Woodside and McClam, 1998).

Service coordination is sometimes referred to as case management (Dorfman, 1996). However, case management generally involves a broader set of roles and responsibilities than service coordination (Moxley, 1997; Rothman and Sager, 1998; Woodside and McClam, 1998).

In the case of Jim L. (Case 8.1), a service coordination intervention was not employed. Although the social worker stayed in contact with the social worker providing family therapy and the worker at the teen center, she did not coordinate the unrelated services. No effort was made to ensure that the services were integrated. If Jim's social worker and the family therapist had developed an integrated treatment plan for Jim and the family, and if Jim's social worker had assumed responsibility for coordinating their efforts, a service coordination type of intervention would have taken place.

**Service Negotiation**    Service negotiation involves helping individuals and families overcome difficulties they have encountered with service delivery systems. This function is also referred to as **mediation** (Garvin and Seabury, 1997) and the **expediter role** (Woodside and McClam, 1998). Service negotiation focuses on helping the client resolve problems and difficulties with existing service linkages. The social worker takes a position between the client and the service provider to improve linkage and resolve conflicts. The worker helps the client negotiate with system providers to address duplication of service, ineligibility, and poor service quality (Woodside and McClam, 1998). The worker's primary task is to facilitate communication between the client and service representatives so that they can reach an agreement (Garvin and Seabury, 1997). The social worker does not advocate for the client directly: instead, he or she helps mediate conflicts.

Service negotiation was not used in Jim L.'s case (Case 8.1). However, later in her work with Jim, the social worker helped the family negotiate with the school system. Jim's parents asked the school to run a full battery of psychological and diagnostic tests to assess Jim's learning difficulties. The school system's first response was that he could not be tested until the start of the following school year, a delay of more than nine months. Jim's parents asked the school social worker to intervene. She helped the family negotiate a much earlier testing date by assisting them in presenting relevant information on Jim's functioning at home and his social isolation at school at a meeting she set up with the school psychologist. Thus the school social worker provided a service negotiation intervention for the family by facilitating better communication between the school psychologist and the family.

Case 8.3, written by Kathleen McCabe when she was a first-year MSW student, illustrates the use of service negotiation in working with a dialysis patient.

**Resource Mobilization**   Resource mobilization involves helping the client obtain needed resources, such as housing, clothing, food, furniture, financial support, or health care (Hepworth, Rooney, and Larsen, 2002). The distinction between resource mobilization and service linkage is minimal. Resource mobilization is the acquisition of needed services, while service linkage is helping clients obtain such services. Both are concerned with helping the client system gain access to needed services; both require knowledge of service networks; and both involve a referral process. The difference lies in the type of service. Resource mobilization focuses on helping clients obtain resources needed to meet basic human needs. Service linkage, on the other hand, focuses on obtaining social, psychological, and health care services. The case in Case 8.4 illustrates a resource mobilization type of intervention by a generalist social worker.

*Client Advocacy*   "Advocacy is speaking on behalf of clients when they are unable to do so, or when they speak and no one listens" (Woodside and McClam, 1998, p. 63). There are two types of client advocacy: case advocacy and class advocacy. In **case advocacy,** the client system is an individual, family, or group (Garvin and Seabury, 1997; Rothman and Sager, 1998). In **class advocacy,** the client system is a large collective or group of people defined by some demographic characteristic (Barber, 1995). Class advocacy is also referred to as **cause advocacy** (Miley, O'Melia, and DuBois, 1998).

**Advocacy** has a long tradition in social work and is defined as a professional responsibility of social workers (NASW, 1996). Ezell (1994) found that

## CASE 8.3 | MY DOCTORS ARE NOT TALKING TO EACH OTHER
BY KATHLEEN MCCABE

Jerome E. is a 45-year-old African-American male diagnosed with end-stage renal disease. He has been coming to the dialysis unit for hemodialysis for less than a year. Both of his kidneys were removed due to the onset of cancer, which makes him ineligible to be evaluated for a kidney transplant for two years. Mr. E. also has hypertension that is kept under control with medication.

Mr. E.'s medical condition has challenged him to adjust to a different lifestyle. He can no longer perform the physical activities he performed prior to his operation for cancer. Personal relationships with the opposite sex are no longer a priority for him at this time. Mr. E. pays child support to two former wives for three children with the Social Security disability income he receives. He has frequent contact with two daughters from his first marriage, and has a good relationship with them and with his first wife. He has not seen much of his third child, a son from his second marriage, because his second wife, with whom he has a strained relationship, will not allow him to visit. She feels he is not paying enough child support. Mr. E. would like to develop a relationship with his son. He is not sure how to approach the issue, and he is concerned about having to go to court because of his financial situation.

As a result of his medical condition, Mr. E. lost his last job as a corrections officer at a prison and has been unable to seek alternative employment. He can no longer perform physical activities that he could prior to his diagnosis. His blood pressure fluctuates, which leaves him feeling weak and light-headed at times. The doctors have not found the right combination of blood pressure medication and fluid removal during dialysis. Mr. E. is concerned that his renal doctor and the doctor who is treating his blood pressure seem to be unable to coordinate treatments or even to communicate with each other. They seem to dislike each other and have some sort of personal conflict. Mr. E. feels that his well-being is at risk because of his doctors' inability to communicate.

When Mr. E.'s treatments are correctly adjusted, he would like to find a part-time job. His treatment schedule complicates this. Dialysis treatments take up about six hours three times a week, and they leave him feeling tired and weak. The challenge is to find a part-time job with flexible hours in a work environment that is not physically demanding.

Mr. E. is also troubled and concerned about not being able to see his young son. He feels he is missing out on the quality time that is important to have with a child. He very much wants to resume visiting his son. Mr. E. realizes that for this to happen, he must reconcile his differences with his ex-wife.

### Goals
Mr. E. agreed to the following goals:
1. To have his renal and blood pressure doctors coordinate his medical care
2. To jave regular visits with his son
3. To find flexible part-time job that is not too physically demanding

### Intervention
With Mr. E.'s permission and in consultation with my supervisor, I spoke to each of his doctors about the possible communication problem. I felt that it was my ethical responsibility to try to make sure my client received the best medical care possible. Neither doctor appeared receptive to what I had to say, and each indicated that it was not a problem. Mr. E. and I also role-played his speaking to the doctors about their apparent lack of communication and coordination. He did not need to confront the doctors; their communication problem disappeared before he had a chance to put his role-play into action.

Mr. E. and I also discussed possible ways to pursue the second goal, that of regular visits with his son. Mr. E. was tired of contacting his ex-wife, and he felt that their history of disagreements would interfere with their ability to communicate. I offered to meet with his ex-wife and explain the current situation to her. He agreed, and I set up an appointment. Mr. E.'s ex-wife was somewhat sympathetic and agreed to a trial visitation period of three weeks.

To help Mr. E. find an appropriate part-time job, I met with him to discuss his options and identify the type of work he would like to pursue. I helped Mr. E. decide that he was not ready to take on part-time work. We agreed to put the job goal on hold until Mr. E.'s treatments were better coordinated and he felt better physically.

| CASE 8.4 | RESOURCE MOBILIZATION INTERVENTION |

Joanne R. is a first-year MSW student with a field placement at Catholic Social Services (CSS), where she is assigned to a case management unit that works primarily with low-income mothers who receive public assistance. One of her clients is a 20-year-old mother, Nicole B., who was referred to CSS by her welfare caseworker. Nicole had been evicted from her apartment and had no food for her two children, no money, and very few clothes for herself and her children suitable for the approaching winter. Joanne met with her client to assess her needs. Together they developed a list of Nicole's short-term and long-term resource needs.

Joanne helped her client locate an emergency shelter in which she could live until she found an apartment, obtained clothing from the Salvation Army, and secured a one-time emergency cash payment of $100 from her own agency. Joanne continued to work with Nicole during her stay in the shelter. Together they found a one-bedroom apartment, modestly furnished it, and filled the pantry with nonperishable food. After Nicole moved into the apartment, Joanne helped her learn to budget, learn more about child development and parenting, and enroll in a GED program.

---

90 percent of the social workers surveyed did case advocacy on a regular basis. Unlike the interventions described earlier, client advocacy requires the social worker to take a strong position on behalf of the client system (Garvin and Seabury, 1997).

Empowering practice involves the client system in the advocacy process. It is generally better to work with clients to advocate for rights, services, or resources than to advocate on their behalf without their participation in the process. Client advocacy involves educating clients about their rights, teaching advocacy skills to clients, and applying pressure to make agencies and resources respond to client needs. Case 8.5 illustrates the use of client advocacy.

## MACRO-LEVEL INTERVENTIONS

As noted earlier, three macro interventions that generalist social workers often undertake with organization and community client systems are education and training, program planning, and community development. The purposes of macro-level interventions at the organizational level are to improve the functioning of organizations, improve the delivery of existing services, and develop new services. Their purposes at the community level are to improve community conditions, empower residents, develop community resources, increase citizen awareness of community issues, and mobilize citizens to work for change.

### Education and Training

Education and training are major functions of macro generalist practice. At the organizational level, they occur primarily through staff development and continuing education workshops aimed at improving the quality of services and service delivery to clients.

## CASE 8.5 | CLIENT ADVOCACY

Tracy D. is the social worker at the Mission House, a shelter for homeless families. One of her primary tasks is to help families make successful linkages with social service agencies in the community. Families use the shelter for short-term emergency housing and must begin developing alternative arrangements on entering the shelter. Most of the families need a wide range of social services beyond housing. Tracy helps shelter residents identify needs and develop action plans to improve their situations.

Elaine T. is 36 years old and has two children, ages 10 and 12. Her husband had deserted the family four years earlier, and she had a job with a cleaning service to support her family. Two years ago, she lost her job and was unable to secure another that paid enough to cover her modest living expenses. She managed on welfare payments until she was terminated in October. Unable to pay her rent, she was evicted in December. She entered the shelter with no money, few possessions, and little hope.

Tracy referred Mrs. T. to the community action agency for enrollment in a job-training program that taught basic computer skills. But Mrs. T. was not accepted into the job-training program, because she did not have a high school diploma. The worker at the community action agency recommended that Mrs. T. enroll in their GED program. Mrs. T. was not in favor of this option, since completing the GED would take a fairly long time and on completion she still would not be prepared for a specific job.

Tracy and Mrs. T. decided to appeal the negative decision by the community action agency. First they worked together to compose a letter to the program coordinator requesting a reversal of the decision and indicating that if a reversal was not granted, she would appeal the decision. Tracy also worked with Mrs. T. to teach her how to approach her appeal and how to present herself in the meeting. Together they outlined several reasons why Mrs. T. should be allowed to participate in the job-training program. They role-played the appeal interview to help Mrs. T. become comfortable with the formal nature of the process. Tracy also called the job-training coordinator and argued Mrs. T.'s case. Tracy accompanied Mrs. T. to the appeal meeting and spoke on her behalf.

The appeal was turned down. Tracy and Mrs. T. began searching for alternative job-training programs and other employment opportunities within the community.

---

The macro practice task of conducting staff development training or an educational workshop can be broken down into seven steps. The amount of time needed to complete the various steps depends upon the scope of the training. A single 2-hour workshop for 15 people will obviously be much quicker to plan and carry out than a training program that consists of a series of workshops for a large number of participants. The steps described below pick up the process after the social worker or training team has been asked to conduct the training or workshop. The steps are:

1. Meet with decision makers to assess needs and interests
2. Meet with participants to assess needs and interests
3. Brainstorm with the team to plan the program
4. Meet with decision makers for program approval and implementation planning
5. Do research assignments and prepare program materials
6. Rehearse and finalize program
7. Deliver workshop and obtain feedback

**Step 1:** *Meet with decision makers.* Organizations have various ways of selecting topics for staff development training or workshops. In some organizations the chief executive or a management team makes the decision. In others there is a management–staff committee charged with developing the staff development program. Regardless of the locus of the decision making, you need to meet with the decision makers to assess the needs of the organization and staff in terms of the proposed workshop. This assessment meeting is critical in making sure you are clear about the purpose and focus of the workshop. The meeting also provides you with an opportunity to obtain additional information and insights about the organizational climate, service needs, staff morale and other factors that might affect the training.

**Step 2:** *Meet with training participants.* It is important to schedule a meeting with members of the target audience. The purpose of this meeting is to get their input about what they perceive as their training needs and interests. It also provides you with an opportunity to better understand their job pressures and the specifics of their work requirements in order to tailor the workshop to meet the staff's training needs.

After meeting with the staff, if there are discrepancies between what the decision makers envision and what the staff would like, a follow-up meeting with the decision makers is warranted. You need to find a focus for the workshop that meets the needs of both groups of stakeholders. Doing so is critical if there is a wide disparity between what management wants and what the staff feels would be helpful.

**Step 3:** *Brainstorm and plan the program.* After the general focus of the workshop has been agreed on, the next step is to brainstorm the structure and content of the workshop. Participants usually respond better to workshops that are well organized, participatory, draw upon their knowledge and expertise, have experiential components, summarize the content information in handouts, and provide materials they can take home. At this point, you need to outline the program and identify logistic considerations that will need to be addressed. Generally in this planning session, the trainer identifies (1) an opening groundbreaker exercise and the session introductions, (2) the structure and content of the program, (3) how the workshop will be evaluated, (4) the supplies needed, (5) refreshment needs, (6) and room and equipment needs. If a team is conducting the training, specific tasks and responsibilities are assigned.

**Step 4:** *Program approval and implementation planning.* In most cases, it is probably a good idea to tell the decision makers about the finalized program and get the official go-ahead for the workshop. Doing so gives you an opportunity to make any last minute changes as well as strengthen the decision makers' commitment to the training.

This meeting can also be used to plan the specifics of implementing the workshop. The details of promotion, staff attendance, room selection and availability, equipment requirements, and other details related to running the workshop need to be addressed.

**Step 5:** *Do research assignments and prepare program materials.* At this stage you and your team need to do research on your specific assignments to begin the process of putting together the information and content that will be delivered in the workshop. This includes preparing handouts, presentation materials, and experiential exercises. Each member of the team should also practice his or her part of the presentation and make sure it fits within the allotted time frame. A common mistake is to overestimate the amount of information that can be covered in a given amount of time. It always takes longer than you think, especially if the audience members are active participants and have been encouraged to ask questions and share their ideas and experiences.

**Step 6:** *Program review and finalization.* If there is more than one trainer, the team needs to have at least one additional meeting to rehearse the workshop. This gives the team an opportunity to fine tune the program and give feedback and suggestions to each other. It is also a check to make sure all the pieces of the program fit together, get a sense of the flow, and see how much time is needed.

**Step 7:** *Implement the program and obtain participant feedback.* The final step in this process is to deliver the training workshop and obtain feedback from the participants. If you have prepared well, it should go smoothly. However, it rarely goes exactly as planned. The participants' level of involvement, interest, and receptiveness is unknown and can vary from one workshop to the next. Expect the unexpected, and be willing to make adjustments as the need arises. Do not become overly tied to your plan. Some things might take longer than you expected, or your participants might be interested in pursuing one topic more than the others. Use your group assessment and intervention skills to engage the participants in the learning process.

Solicit feedback from the participants at the conclusion of the program. Simple self-constructed feedback questionnaires are used most often. Typically, participants are asked to comment or rate the extent to which the program met their needs, level of information, coverage of the materials, adequacy of the facilities, pace of the workshop, and other aspects of the program. They are also often asked to describe what they liked best, what needs to be changed, and what they would recommend for future workshops. Getting this feedback empowers the participants and provides the trainers with useful information for developing and delivering future workshops or trainings.

Case 8.6 illustrates the beginning steps in developing a staff workshop. This example illustrates the importance of getting input from members of the target group before implementing a training program. The probation officers' perceptions of what they were interested in were very different from their director's perceptions. The workshop turned out to be a success and was well received by the probation officers even though it was not exactly what the director originally envisioned. If the training team had proceeded without any

| CASE 8.6 | EARLY STEPS IN STAFF WORKSHOP DEVELOPMENT |
|----------|---------------------------|

Christiana D., Laurie B., and Pat M. all were graduate social work students doing their second-year field placements at Social Work Consultation Services (SWCS). SWCS provided generalist social work learning experiences for student interns and social work and capacity-building services for residents and organizations of an economically disadvantaged community. The Director of Adult Probation in the county contacted SWCS about conducting a staff development workshop for her probation officers. Christiana, Laurie, and Pat took on the project under the supervision of a school faculty member.

The training team scheduled a meeting with the Director of Adult Probation to get a better understanding of the agency's needs and her expectations about the purpose and objectives of the workshop. The director felt that her staff could benefit from a workshop on relationship-building skills and on how to engage reluctant, resistant, or hostile clients in a collaborative working relationship. She felt that many of the probation officers were showing signs of burnout and a lot of frustration with their clients and the legal system. Many seemed to have given up trying to make a difference in their clients' lives and were not making any efforts to connect with them. The team left the meeting with a clear understanding of what the director wanted. They felt it was something that they would be able to put together and deliver effectively.

With the approval of the director, the training team scheduled a preworkshop meeting with the probation officers who would be attending the workshop. The purpose of the meeting was to get an understanding of their training needs and interests. The meeting did not go as expected. The probation officers had absolutely no interest in learning "soft" relationship skills and were totally against the idea of having to attend a workshop on how to connect with reluctant or hostile clients. They felt that such training would be a total waste of time. They used the meeting to vent their feelings about the system and working with clients who lied and were manipulative.

The team struggled to find some common ground between the director's and staff's perceived needs. Because the probation officers were so clear about the frustrations of their job, Pat asked if they would be interested in a workshop that focused on coping strategies and burnout prevention. This, too, was rejected as a waste of time. Most of the group members claimed not to have any problems in that area and said they could take care of themselves just fine.

Having struck out making suggestions to this group, Christiana asked them what would be helpful. After quite a bit of back and forth discussion among the probation officers, it was decided that a workshop on the link between mental health and substance abuse would be helpful. All of their clients were substance abusers, and the workers felt that for many, mental health issues compounded their difficulties with substance abuse and the law. The team agreed to the proposed focus, pending approval by the probation officers' director.

---

input from the participants it would most likely have been less well received. The workshop would have been a trying experience for both the training team and the participants.

Education and training at the community level tends to focus on increasing community awareness and understanding of social issues and community problems (Miley, O'Melia, and DuBois, 1998). Generalist social workers make formal presentations at community meetings, serve as panelists at public forums, and conduct community workshops and seminars. Examples 1 and 2 in Case 8.7 illustrate how generalist social workers may use education and training as a macro-level practice intervention.

| CASE 8.7 | EDUCATION AND TRAINING INTERVENTIONS |

**Example 1**

Sam W. is the social worker with the Community Prevention Coalition (CPC), a grant-funded drug and alcohol prevention program. CPC is a community-based program that seeks to empower the residents of an economically disadvantaged community that has high rates of poverty, crime, substance use, and other social ills.

One of the objectives of the program is to increase awareness about social problems in the community. Education is the primary intervention Sam uses to achieve this objective. He began by organizing a series of presentations for all the churches in the community. His talks focused on the magnitude of the drug and alcohol problem in the community and the long-term effects it has on quality of life. Sam also spoke about the possibilities of change and how the community can take positive actions to improve conditions and address the various social problems.

**Example 2**

Dianna P., as part of her first-year field placement with Social Work Consultation Services (SWCS), worked with a community Wellness Center on a teen pregnancy prevention campaign. The local community had the highest teen pregnancy rate in the state. A community-wide effort was being undertaken by a coalition of agency professionals and citizen groups. The coalition members decided that one component of the campaign would be to target middle school youth in hopes of reducing pregnancy rates in these students when they become teenagers.

Dianna and a staff member from the Wellness Center developed an educational presentation aimed at middle school youth. The presentation focused on self-esteem issues, peer pressure, and the consequences of teen pregnancy. It had a lecture and discussion format with small breakout sessions for the participants. Dianna and her cofacilitator give their presentation to each middle school classroom in the district during the course of the year.

## Program Planning and Development

Program planning, which is also known as **social planning** (Kurzman, 1985; Lauffer, 1978), is the development, expansion, and coordination of social services and social policies (Lauffer, 1981). It involves activities that "address the development and coordination of community agencies and services to meet community functions and responsibilities and to provide for its members" (Hardcastle, Wenocur, and Powers, 1997, p. 2). Program planning can be conducted at the individual agency level, by a consortium of human service agencies, or by regional or state human service planning agencies (Weil and Gamble, 1995). Generalist social workers typically become involved in program planning activities that seek to improve the operation of existing services and programs and to develop new services and programs at the agency and community level by working with agency task forces, professional task forces, or community coalitions.

As part of the planning process, generalist social workers may evaluate existing programs and services, conduct needs assessments, identify funding sources, prepare grant proposals, or engage in public relations activities to build program support. To be effective in carrying out these tasks, the generalist social worker needs to be skilled in social work research methods and have well-developed writing and presentation skills.

As noted above, generalist social workers are often involved in developing new programs and services for their clients. Program development is a complex undertaking with a number of interrelated components. Some of the macropractice activities involved in the development process include establishing need, identifying funding sources, identifying program inputs, activities, and outputs, designing the program evaluation, and preparing the grant proposal. These generalist social work practice macrointervention activities are described below.

**Needs Assessments**   Needs assessments focus on identifying social problems as well as appropriate responses (Marlow, 2001). Assessing need is one of the first steps in developing a new service or program. Before grants or contracts are awarded for new programs or services, funders often require the presentation of a reliable and comprehensive needs assessment (Ginsberg, 2001). Needs assessments can be used to:

1. Determine if an intervention exists in a community
2. Determine if there are enough clients with a particular problem to justify creating a new program
3. Determine if existing interventions are known or recognized by potential clients
4. Determine what barriers prevent clients from accessing existing services
5. Document the existence of an ongoing or exacerbating social problem (Royse et al., 2001, p. 53).

Regardless of how the needs assessment will be used, the process entails the identification and documentation of needs.

*Needs Identification*   Needs may be organization, community, or client based. A first step in developing a new program or service is obtaining a clear understanding of the unmet service needs of the organization, service providers, community, or clients. Excellent sources of information about the adequacy of existing services and about unmet needs are those most directly involved in service delivery: service providers and consumers. Help on identifying need areas can be obtained from:

- Agency administrators
- Direct line staff
- Consumers or clients
- Representatives of other agencies and organizations
- The social worker's own experiences

Agency administrators and direct line staff are excellent sources of information on the adequacy of the services they offer and on the unmet needs of their clients. In the course of their work they are often confronted on a daily basis with the reality of how well the existing programs and services meet their clients' needs. They know firsthand how well the programs work or do not work. Open-ended interviews with administrators, other social workers, and current clients in conjunction with your own experiences and insights should provide you with enough information to identify service gaps and unmet client needs and possible solutions for these problems. If there is a fairly high level of agreement about needs, then you are ready to begin the process of documentation.

*Needs Documentation*    In developing new programs and services it is critical to demonstrate that the need being addressed is significant and that proposed solutions will alleviate the problem. Most needs assessments draw on multiple sources of information. The four major sources of information are:

- Research literature on the problem and proposed solutions
- Surveys of key informants, community members, or clients
- Focus groups
- Secondary data analysis

RESEARCH LITERATURE    Effective needs assessments must be grounded in the research literature. What do we know about the causes and consequences of the problem? What is the magnitude and scope of the problem? What has worked? What has not worked? How does the target community or population vary from those reported in the literature? Answers to these and other questions place your needs assessment within a context and provide a basis for comparing the significance of the problem being studied and the relevance of the proposed solution with the problem in general and in other communities. The information and retrieval skills discussed in Chapter 4 will help facilitate your literature search and the identification of existing research studies on your topic. In Royse et al. (2001), the chapter on writing an evaluation report has an excellent discussion on conducting a literature review and putting together an evaluation report (pp. 374–396).

SURVEYS    Often documentation of a local need will require a new data collection effort. Survey research methods can be used to collect need data. It is beyond the scope of this chapter to discuss the specifics of questionnaire design, measurement, sampling, and other survey research topics. Excellent descriptions of these methods can be found in *Social Work Research and Evaluation: Quantitative And Qualitative Approaches* by Grinnell (2001) or *Research Methods for Social Work* by Rubin and Babbie (2001). Three types of surveys frequently used to document local needs are key informant, community, and client satisfaction surveys. They are described briefly here.

*KEY INFORMANT SURVEYS*    "**Key informants** are those persons who are informed about a given problem because of training or work experience— usually because they are involved in some sort of service with that population" (Royse et al., 2001, p. 64). Typically, they are the social work administrators, social workers, and other service providers in your community who work with the client population whose need is being assessed. **"Snowball"**

**sampling techniques** are often used to generate a list of key informants. One begins with a few key informants and asks them to identify other professionals knowledgeable about the problem or population being studied. Depending on the size of the key informant list, the key informants can be interviewed by telephone, in person, or by a mailed questionnaire. The interview or questionnaire obtains their perceptions of the problem being studied as well as information about possible solutions. Survey research methods would be used to construct the questionnaire and to conduct the data analysis. Key informant surveys are a relatively inexpensive and convenient way to obtain subjective (expert opinion) needs assessment data.

*COMMUNITY SURVEYS*   A survey of households or community residents is another approach for assessing needs. Typically these types of surveys are more expensive and require a high level of survey research expertise to carry out. Community surveys can provide information on residents' perceptions of their needs and community conditions as well as empirical data that can be extrapolated to the community or population being investigated. The benefit of a well-executed community survey is that the findings are representative and can be generalized with a specified degree of confidence to the community or population being studied. The down side is cost and difficulties in carrying them out.

*CLIENT SATISFACTION STUDIES*   These types of surveys are similar to community surveys except that current or past recipients of a service or program are queried instead of community residents in general. Obtaining a sample of former or current clients tends to be easier than community surveys because the study population is known, defined, and more limited. Client satisfaction studies can provide useful information for needs assessments. Clients are in a unique position to provide feedback on how well the service or program is meeting their needs, additional unmet needs, and the operation of the service or program.

FOCUS GROUPS   Another approach to documenting needs is to conduct focus groups with key informants, community members, or clients. The sources of information are the same as for surveys. The difference is in the method used to collect the information. "Generally, focus groups are discussions guided by an interviewer that have a small number (6 to 12) of participants" (Ginsberg, 2001, p. 139). The social worker facilitating the focus group uses open-ended questioning and elaboration skills to obtain in-depth information on the topic under investigation. Focus group participants are selected based on their knowledge of the problem as well as how representative they are of the population group. They are not scientifically selected. Often convenience sampling is used. People are selected based on their perceived knowledge of the subject matter and on the extent that they appear to accurately represent the target population.

Focus groups usually last one to two hours and are run as discussion groups. The facilitator's role is to encourage discussion and elaboration. Prior to the group meeting the facilitator identifies broad topic areas to be covered during the meeting. Using a series of specific closed-ended questions would not be appropriate for focus groups. The goal is to help "participants build upon each other's contributions . . ." (Ginsberg, 2001, p. 139). The benefits of using focus groups for needs assessments are convenience, ease of administration, low cost, and depth of information obtained. The biggest negative is that there is no way to assess the validity of the findings obtained from focus groups. They may or may not be representative of the target population.

*Secondary Data*   The final major source of information available for needs assessments is data from a census, public document, or other government and private sources (Royse et al., 2001). Census data are available online at *www.census.gov.* Census data can be broken down by state, county, municipality, and census track. A wealth of population and neighborhood data are contained within the census data. Other types of government data from over 70 federal government agencies can be accessed on the World Wide Web at *www.fedstats.gov.*

In addition to federal data, "every state maintains a wealth of useful data for planners and evaluators" (Royse et al., 2001, p. 59). Most states have databases of crime and arrest statistics, health indicators, teen pregnancy rates, educational statistics, and many other kinds of information that can be helpful in conducting needs assessments.

Data from published reports and from private foundations can also be used to document need. Secondary data sources are excellent resources for needs assessments. They are available, are relatively cheap to access, and provide a wealth of quantitative data on many social and community problems.

Case 8.8 illustrates the role a generalist social worker played in a community-wide needs assessment process.

**Identify Funding Sources**   Obtaining funding for programs and services is an ongoing process for most nonprofit organizations. If the new program under development is responding to a **request for proposal (RFP)** or **solicited contract request,** identifying funding sources for the new program is not an issue. However, if your agency is taking the initiative in trying to develop a new program or service to meet client needs, identifying potential funding for the program is a critical step in the development process.

Your objective, at this point, is to do research on potential funding sources to develop a short list of sources that are appropriate for your program. This can be accomplished by:

- Consulting with agency administrators about internal funding of the program
- Networking with other professionals who work in an area related to your project

| CASE 8.8 | COMMUNITY NEEDS ASSESSMENT |
| --- | --- |

In his role as a generalist social worker with the Community Prevention Coalition, Sam W. was assigned to represent the agency on a professional task force organized by the local United Way. The task force was composed of professional representatives from most of the community's human service agencies as well as from several community and neighborhood groups. The task force was charged with identifying community needs and developing appropriate programs and services to address the needs.

At the initial organizational meeting, the members of the task force were assigned to various subcommittees, each of which was to assess needs relat-

ed to a specific community problem or service area. Sam volunteered for the substance abuse subcommittee. Sam and the other subcommittee members designed and carried out a needs assessment focusing on the community's drug and alcohol problem, services and resources that were available, and the need for additional services and resources. Subcommittee members designed questionnaires, interviewed a sample of community residents and service professionals, and conducted focus groups with key informants. They presented the task force with a comprehensive report describing their findings and preliminary recommendations.

---

- Brainstorming with colleagues and collaborators
- Contacting legislators and public officials about potential federal, state, or county grants
- Doing research in the *Federal Register* for RFPs that appear appropriate for your program
- Doing research on private foundations

At this stage, you need to determine if there are any reasonable matches between your proposed program and the mission, goals, and objectives of public or private funding sources. The fit between your proposed program and the mission of the funding source is critical. Eliminate funding sources if the fit between what you hope to accomplish and what they want to support and promote is not clear and unambiguous. Do not waste your time or the funders' time with grant requests that are not consistent with the stated purposes and objectives of the funding sources.

Much research on potential funding sources can be done on the World Wide Web. Some useful Internet sites are listed in Table 8.1.

**Program Inputs, Activities, and Outputs**   This program planning task focuses on the conceptualization of your proposed program. Many human service organizations follow the **United Way model** (United Way of America, 1996) that was designed to help their affiliates and other nonprofits measure program outcomes (Ginsburg, 2001). The model breaks programs into three major component parts: inputs, activities, and outputs.

**Inputs** are the resources provided to or consumed by the program. They include both financial and human resources, such as money, staff, supplies, equipment, and facilities.

TABLE 8.1 | ONLINE SOURCES OF FUNDING INFORMATION

| Name and Web Site Address | Description |
| --- | --- |
| Catalog of Federal Domestic Assistance (http://www.cfda.gov) | Government-wide compendium of federal programs, projects, services, and activities that provide assistance or benefits to the American public |
| Notices of Funding Availability (NOFAs) | Announcements that appear in the *Federal Register,* printed each business day by the U.S. government, inviting applications for federal grant programs |
| Commerce Business Daily (http://cbdnet.access.gpo.gov) | Daily listing of federal government solicitations for research, development, and training contracts |
| TRAM Research Funding Opportunities and Administration (http://tram.east.asu.edu) | Search engine for locating funding opportunities from many different agencies; updated daily; contains sets of applications and other useful grant information |
| SchoolGrants (http://www.schoolgrants.org) | Lists K–12 grant opportunities |
| GrantsWeb (http://www.srainternational .org/newweb/grantsweb/index.cfm) | Identifies government resources, general resources, policy information and regulations, and private funding sources |
| Federal Government Resources (http://lib.umich.edu/govdocs/fedgt.html) | Lists federal grants, contracts, and auctions |
| Foundation Finder (http://lnp.fdncenter.org/finder.html) | Allows searches by name for basic information about foundations within a universe of more than 61,000 private and community foundations in the United States |

**Activities** are what the program does to accomplish its mission or purpose, such as computer literacy training, counseling, case management, job training, or education.

**Outputs** are the expected products of the program activities, such as number of clients that have participated, number of sessions, and number of hours. Outputs are not the results of the program. They are not measures of program outcomes but rather measures of program efforts (Kettner, Moroney, and Martin, 1999).

In Chart 8.1, a program is broken down into some of its inputs, activities, and outputs.

**Program Evaluation**   Program evaluation is an area of social work research that is fairly broad. There are a number of excellent books on the topic, such as *Social Work Evaluation* by Ginsberg (2001), and *Program Evaluation: An Introduction* by Royse et al. (2001). The discussion of program evaluation presented here is limited to a four-step model developed by Linney and Wanderman (1991). The model focuses on the basics of program evaluation, which are the components that are particularly relevant for program planning

CHART 8.1 | INPUTS, ACTIVITIES, AND OUTPUT

Computer Literacy and After School Services (CLASS) is a program that was developed by Social Work Consultation Services (SWCS) for families living in public housing in a low-income urban community. The program was designed to increase parents' involvement in their children's education and to strengthen their capacity to provide educational support to their children. It is also designed to improve the children's computer, study, and time management skills to foster academic success and promote positive attitudes toward learning. Some of the CLASS program's inputs, activities, and outputs are:

| Inputs | Activities | Outputs |
| --- | --- | --- |
| Program coordinator | Parent support group | 20 parents completed the program |
| 3 MSW interns | Parent computer training | 45 children completed the program |
| Program assistant | Children's computer training | 24 support groups held |
| Computer lab instructor | Children's study skills and homework sessions | 48 computer sessions held |
| Computer lab assistant | Individual counseling and case management | 24 study skills and homework sessions held |
| Computer lab | Graduation ceremony | 25 individual counseling and case management sessions held |
| 2 classrooms | | 20 families received a new computer system for meeting attendance goals |
| Food and lunch supplies | | 65 CLASS book bags given to participants |
| Participant book bags | | 40 $15 gift certificates awarded for attendance goals |
| Participation gift certificates | | |
| Participation computer systems | | |

and program development by generalist social workers. The four steps of the program evaluation model are: identifying goals and desired outcomes, conducting a process evaluation, conducting an outcome evaluation, and conducting an impact evaluation (Wandersman, 2001). The four-stage model can be used to evaluate an existing program or to design the evaluation component of a new program. The discussion here focuses on the second use.

Step 1: *Identifying Goals and Desired Outcomes.* Developing goals and objectives was discussed in Chapter 7. The process is the same in developing program goals and objectives as it is in developing case goals and objectives. **Goals** describe what the program is striving for, and **objectives** specify measurable indicators of the desired outcomes. The following goals and objectives (Table 8.2) were developed for the CLASS program discussed in Chart 8.2.

Step 2: *Process Evaluation.* Process evaluations are also referred to as **formative evaluations** (Royse et al., 2001). Process evaluations examine the

TABLE 8.2 | GOALS AND OBJECTIVES FOR THE CLASS PROGRAM

| Goals | | Objectives | |
|---|---|---|---|
| 1. | To increase the parents' computer skills and their capacity to support their children's learning | 1.1 | The parents will complete 80% of their computer assignments |
| | | 1.2 | The parents will successfully conduct research on a school topic using the Internet |
| 2. | To strengthen the children's school attendance record | 2.1 | The children's school attendance record will increase an average of 20% during the program period |
| 3. | To strengthen the children's study skills | 3.1 | The children will create a weekly time/task schedule 8 out of the 12 program weeks |
| | | 3.2 | The children will develop a weekly task priority list 8 out of the 12 program weeks |
| 4. | To increase the parents' involvement in their children's education | 4.1 | The parents will help their children with homework and school assignments an average of 3 days a week |
| | | 4.2 | The parents will talk to their children about their homework and school assignments an average of 5 days a week |
| 5. | To involve former CLASS participants in the planning and implementation of the CLASS program | 5.1 | Recruit a 10-member CLASS Advisory Board |
| | | 5.2 | Recruit and train 8 former CLASS participants (4 youth and 4 adults) to be mentors in the CLASS program |

planning, development, and implementation of a program (Marlow, 2001). "A process evaluation centers on two related questions: What were the intended and actual activities of the program? After it was implemented, what did program planners and staff learn from their experiences?" (Wandersman, 2001, p. 186). Answers to these questions can provide valuable information that can be used to inform program development and planning. Process evaluations focus on documenting program activities and effort. They can be used to identify obstacles and barriers that were encountered during the implementation of the program as well as the strategies that were implemented to overcome the obstacles. They can also be used to assess the adequacy of program inputs and planned activities.

Clients, staff, administrators, and other stakeholders involved in the delivery of the program as well as program records and statistics are the sources of information typically used for process evaluations. Surveys, personal interviews, document analysis, and focus groups are the methods most often used to conduct process evaluations.

**Step 3:** *Outcome Evaluation.* Outcome evaluations assess the immediate effects of a program (Wandersman, 2001). Most outcome evaluations focus on the extent to which the program achieved its specified objectives. If the program goals and objectives were specified in measurable terms, the outcome evaluation is relatively straightforward. The program developer, as part of the development process, designs the outcome evaluation and the measurement of the program objectives. This includes identifying standardized measures or indices and developing measures specifically for the program outcome assessment. A well-designed outcome evaluation specifies exactly how each objective will be measured as well as the criteria that will be used to judge success.

**Step 4:** *Impact Evaluation.* Impact evaluations are concerned with the ultimate, long-term effects of the program. Impact evaluations are follow-up evaluations that occur after the program has been completed and tend to assess the overall program's impact on the targeted social problem. Impact evaluations assess the extent to which the program has achieved its stated goals. The key in designing impact evaluations is identifying indicators of goal progress and obtaining baseline measures on the indicators. There has to be a comparison in order to judge the impact of the program. Collecting data on the impact measures before and after their implementation is one way of obtaining a comparison. If this is not possible, impact data from the program can be compared with data on comparable populations or communities, if the data are available. Possible impact measures for the CLASS program could be school dropout rates, graduation rates, arrest rates, and other indicators of school success, parenting, or healthy development.

*Grant Proposals*   After establishing need; identifying a funding source; conceptualizing program inputs, activities, and expected outputs; and designing the program evaluation, it is time to put it all together in a program grant proposal. For more information on preparing a grant proposal, see *Grantseeker's Toolkit: A Comprehensive Guide to Funding* by New (1998); *Grant Writing for Dummies* by Browning (2001); or *Practical Grant Writing and Program Evaluation* by Yuen and Terao (2003). In preparing a grant proposal it is critical that you follow the exact format specified by the funding source. Chart 8.2 outlines the basic components of a generic grant proposal.

## Community Development

Community development refers to interventions aimed at improving community conditions and empowering residents to seek community change. Community development also has a social action component, which is activities aimed at challenging inequalities, confronting decision makers, and empowering people to change unjust conditions (Rubin and Rubin, 1992). Social action focuses on social, political, and economic justice for the disadvantaged and disenfranchised (Weil and Gamble, 1995). Thus, community practice is the "development, redistribution, and control of community statuses and resources, including social power, and the alteration of community relations and behavior patterns to promote the development or redistribution of community resources" (Hardcastle, Wenocur, and Powers, 1997, p. 2).

CHART 8.2 | GENERIC GRANT PROPOSAL APPLICATION

**Cover sheet**
    Date of application
    Name of organization to which grant would be paid
    Purpose of grant (one sentence)
    Address of organization
    Telephone number
    E-mail address
    Executive director's name
    Contact person and title (put your name here and make up a title)
    Amount of grant request

**Proposal summary** (half page, maximum)

**Qualifications of applicant** (1–2 pages)
    Brief summary of organization's history, mission, and goals
    Brief description of organization's current programs, activities, service statistics, and strengths and accomplishments

**Problem statement or needs assessment** (3–4 pages)
Objectively address specific situation, opportunity, problem, issue, need, and community your proposal addresses. Support your statement with qualified third-party research or evidence to justify the need or problem. Clearly and concisely demonstrate that a relevant, compelling problem or need exists.

**Program goals and objectives** (1–2 pages)
Describe the desired outcomes of the grant in measurable terms, with a succinct description of the proposed project outcome and accomplishment, including your overall goal(s); specific objectives or ways in which you will meet the goal(s), including:

    A minimum of one goal for each problem or need in the problem or statement

    At least one measurable outcome objective for each identified goal (outcome objectives should specify criteria for success and a time frame)

**Program description** (4+ pages)
Describe program inputs, activities, and expected outputs that will be used to achieve program outcomes, including:

    A restatement of problems and objectives
    A clear description and explanation of program or project scope and activities
    The sequence of activities, staffing, clients, and client selection
    A time line of activities

**Evaluation** (1–2 pages)
Your evaluation plan should include:

    At a minimum, a description of the evaluation plan for assessing process and outcomes
    A description of measures and instruments to be used in the program evaluation

**Budget** (1 page)
Clearly delineate administrative and program costs. Delineate personnel salaries and fringe benefits. Specify facility operating expenses (rent or mortgage, utilities, maintenance, taxes), and travel, postage, equipment, and supply costs.

**Long-term funding** (half page)
Present a brief, concise description of how the program will be funded over the long term

**References** (1 page)
List references cited in the proposal in APA style

**Appendices**
Put attachments in sequentially numbered appendices

---

Community development is used as an intervention strategy when disadvantaged populations have been excluded from the decision-making process and when the prevailing power structure does not appear to be responsive to the community as a whole or its representatives (Staples, 1990). Community development strategies seek to improve community conditions, empower residents, develop resources, and mobilize citizen groups. To achieve these purposes, the generalist social worker organizes constituent groups, builds com-

## CASE 8.9 | COMMUNITY DEVELOPMENT INTERVENTION

Steve K. is a social worker in an economically disadvantaged city of about 50,000 people. The majority of the population is minority, with a large proportion on public assistance. The community is located in a county that is composed primarily of affluent suburban communities. The county government funds most of the services that are provided to the residents of the city. The community action agency has been seeking additional monies from the county to fund community-based programs, but their funding requests have regularly been turned down.

The residents of the city believe that their needs are being neglected by the county commissioners, who are predominately white and from the more affluent communities in the county. City dwellers feel that the level of funding is far below what is needed given the magnitude of the problems they are facing.

For years, the various community groups in the city have been distrustful of one another and have refused to unite to seek funding. To address this problem, Steve began to meet with various neighborhood and community groups. His expressed purpose was to explore the possibility of creating a coalition of community groups. He convened a series of meetings in which the indigenous leaders of the various groups discussed the advantages and disadvantages of working together to improve community conditions. Steve's role in the process was to organize and mobilize citizen support for the coalition, to facilitate communication among participants, to provide information about the planning process, and to help the group prepare formal requests for community development projects.

munity coalitions, conducts community needs assessments, lobbies political and government leaders, and advocates on behalf of constituent groups.

Social workers involved in organizing constituent groups often take responsibility for convening and facilitating meetings. They do the planning and the legwork to get participants to attend. This requires skill in managing groups and conducting meetings. An empowering approach to the process focuses on having community residents assume control and leadership of the development effort. The social worker helps get the process going, but ultimate responsibility for the effort rests with participants and indigenous leadership.

**Coalition-building** occurs when representatives of diverse community groups join forces to influence external institutions on one or more issues affecting their constituencies (Mizrahi and Rosenthal, 1993). The goal is to build a power base sufficient to influence decision making and the allocation of resources (Weil and Gamble, 1995). Often, there is inherent tension between the coalition members' interest in maintaining the autonomy and power of their constituent groups and the need to share power and resources to make the coalition successful. Social workers need well-developed mediation and negotiation skills to effectively build coalitions, as well as skills in interorganizational relations and planning (Weil and Gamble, 1995).

**Class advocacy** involves organizing oppressed and disadvantaged groups to exercise their influence to correct inequality. This requires the active participation of citizens who are vulnerable or disenfranchised (Miley, O'Melia, and DuBois, 1998), and it provides an opportunity for whole groups of people to assume responsible participation in the social or public realm (Lewis, 1991). The social worker's role involves informing groups of disadvantaged people of their rights and entitlements, mobilizing citizen groups, and bringing pressure to bear on organizational decision makers, government officials, and political leaders. Case 8.9 illustrates a community development intervention.

# SUMMARY

Generalist social workers must be skilled in the delivery of a wide range of both micro and macro interventions. At the micro level, generalist social workers engage in supportive counseling, service linkage, service coordination, resource mobilization, client advocacy, and education and training activities. More specialized counseling-type interventions often used by generalist social workers include cognitive restructuring and problem-solving therapy.

At the macro level, generalist social workers engage in education and training, program planning, and community development-type interventions. The purposes of these macro-level interventions at the organizational level are to improve the functioning of organizations, to improve the delivery of existing services, and to develop new services. Their purposes at the community level are to improve community conditions, empower residents, develop community resources, increase citizen awareness of community issues, and mobilize citizens to work for change.

# CASE EXAMPLE

The final case example in this chapter illustrates the application of strengths-based generalist social work practice with survivors of a natural disaster (Case 8.10). It is an excellent example of how supportive counseling and case management interventions go hand in hand in the delivery of social work services to people in crisis.

---

## CASE 8.10 | WE LOST EVERYTHING
### BY HUSSEIN SOLIMAN

The W. family was on the FEMA list of people to visit, and when my supervisor asked me to visit Gloria W., I drove to the community and discovered that the W. home was surrounded by water. A community resident took me there in his boat.

Gloria W. told me that she and her husband had not evacuated because her husband would not leave the home. He was staying in his room and refused to go to the city. In the four days since the flood began, Gloria had gone to the city two times with her son-in-law. She bought food and registered with FEMA. She told me that the water covered their small motel

next door and that most of the furniture was destroyed.

The couple owns 10 acres of land, and Henry W. plants crops. He rents motel rooms to people who come during hunting seasons every year. Gloria mentioned that Henry had just finished renovating the eight-room motel three weeks before. She indicated that her greatest concern was that they would not receive compensation from FEMA because they did not have flood insurance.

Gloria told me that she wanted to leave the house and move to the city camp like everybody else, but she didn't want to leave her husband alone. Since the flood, she had not seen her only sister, who lived nearby and had moved to live with her son in Georgia after the water ruined her small house. Her only daughter moved with her husband and two children to an apartment complex, and FEMA paid their rent. Her only son called some friends who were able to get his message to her. Gloria stated, "I know that my son will leave everything and come to see me." She worried because her son just started a new job in New York, and she didn't want him to risk losing it.

Gloria was extremely worried about her husband. He wasn't sleeping or eating. She thought he might be suicidal. "I sometimes want to go and apply for loans or emergency assistance like everybody else, but I'm also afraid that if I leave him he would hurt himself. I told him that we can't stay here by ourselves because we don't have a boat, and it does not seem that the water will go away soon." When I asked about her immediate need, she said, "I know we need food and stuff, but the most important thing is to leave and go where everybody is."

She felt that her husband was traumatized by the experience. He had fought in Vietnam and still had dreams about the war. Since the flood, he had refused to take his blood pressure medicine, and she saw him crying the other day. She added, "We had a similar experience in the sixties, but the water didn't destroy everything. We helped each other, and the water receded three days after the flood." When I asked her what she thought would help her this time, she said, "I know we live in a floodplain area. We didn't buy insurance because the county decided to withdraw from the plan, but we have our will and many people are helping us. The thing that is difficult to accept is the flood and try to work with the difficult circumstances, but my husband has a difficult time accepting that."

### Assessment

Mr. and Mrs. W. had different perceptions of the situation. Henry was traumatized by the loss. Water covered their house, farm, and business. Henry felt isolated from his neighbors and immediate family. Gloria understood that living in a floodplain meant a high probability of flooding. She accepted the fact that the flood happened. Although she did not accept victimization, she struggled with their losses.

When I asked Gloria to assess the family's needs, she indicated that the most important thing was to move to temporary housing with the other survivors. She wanted to apply for assistance, communicate with people, and find out what resources were available. She also wanted to establish contact with her daughter, her son, and her sister. She asked for help in convincing her husband to leave and in getting him medical and professional assistance to help him deal with his feelings of loss and depression. By the end of the first interview, Gloria and I agreed on the following needs:

- Help Gloria convince her husband to move to a new place (she suggested asking Tom J., an old friend of her husband, to help convince Henry)
- Obtain information on possible places to move
- Obtain copies of and review the application procedures of emergency relief programs and loans
- Arrange for Henry to visit their family doctor
- Make arrangements with someone who has a boat to take Gloria grocery shopping

Gloria seemed highly motivated and willing to pursue solutions.

### Intervention and Service Provision

I visited the W. family the next day. Prior to the visit, I had contacted Tom J., who agreed to go with me to see Henry. Tom said, "I know that Henry W. loves his place so much, but I think I will be able to talk with him and convince him to move. We have 3 apartments in this building, and it is only 15 miles away from our community." I also spoke with two families who agreed to visit the W. family once a day to help them.

Gloria was pleased when she saw Tom. Tom went straight to Henry's room, and in 15 minutes, Tom and Henry came out and joined the discussion.

I gave Gloria the application forms for compensation and emergency funds. Tom mentioned the difficulty that the survivors from this community are having with FEMA. Because the community had withdrawn from the flood insurance plan, residents were not eligible to receive compensation for their damaged homes. I told them that I would be meeting with a FEMA representative in three days and would share the results with them. Gloria was happy when

*(continued)*

## CASE 8.10 | *continued*

I told her I had arranged a doctor's appointment for Henry and that Bob P., her old neighbor, would take them to the appointment in his boat.

I talked about applications for emergency assistance and loans. Tom thought that some of the assistance applied to their situation, but that the compensation from FEMA wouldn't apply because of the insurance problem. By the end of the visit, Henry stated that he would like to move to where Tom lived. He also agreed to meet me in the emergency center to fill out the forms and applications.

When I met the couple at the center the next day, Henry looked better and engaged in conversation. I helped them fill out applications for small loans. I drove them to look at the apartment and visit with their daughter. Henry's spirit got a boost from visiting his daughter and seeing his grandchildren. The process of moving to the new place was easier than they thought it would be. Gloria was glad that the temporary apartment was close to her daughter's apartment.

Four days later, Gloria called me from their new apartment. She asked me to refer Henry to the community mental health center for help with his depression. I did so, and Henry had his first counseling session with a mental health therapist the following week. The W.'s support network began to take shape. Their son came from New York and spent four days with his parents. Neighbors and friends surrounded the family. They began to attend church services.

I worked with FEMA, the county administrator, state emergency officials, and a state representative to set up a community meeting at which residents expressed their anger and frustration with the local community leaders who had withdrawn from the National Flood Insurance Program three years before. Following a heated discussion, a FEMA representative announced that FEMA would meet with survivors to discuss their requests for assistance.

Some of the needs were for food and furniture. I contacted the local church and helped open a food pantry there. I also found a way to transport food and supplies that were donated by people in other states.

### Follow-Up

After six months in the temporary apartment, Henry and Gloria W. were able to move back to their house. The loan from FEMA helped them refurnish their small motel. Local volunteer groups painted their house and did construction work. Like other families, they experienced difficulty preparing their land for farming. The flood left more than three feet of sand on the land. The state provided a public assistance fund to remove the sand and prepare for planting.

## DISCUSSION QUESTIONS

1. Describe the various interventions the social worker used in working with the W. family and the community (Case 8.11). What additional macro interventions could have been employed? What additional micro interventions could have been used? Would brief treatment be appropriate in helping Mr. W. deal with the trauma he suffered and his symptoms of depression? (For more information on brief treatment models, see Maguire, 2002, and Corwin, 2002.)

2. Identify Mr. and Mrs. W.'s strengths. What were the primary challenges they faced? In what ways did the social worker adopt a strengths perspective? In what ways did he adopt a deficits perspective?

3. Discuss the appropriateness of using cognitive restructuring or problem-solving therapy with the W. family. Which would you choose and why? How would you implement the intervention?

4. How does social work practice in disaster relief differ from generalist practice with other client populations? How is it the same?

# REFERENCES

Barber, J. G. (1995). Politcally progressive casework. *Families in Society, 76,* 30–37.

Beck, A. T. (1976). *Cognitive therapy and the emotional disorders.* New York: International University Press.

Beck, A. T. (1996). *Depression: Causes and treatments.* Philadelphia: University of Pennsylvania Press.

Beck, A., Rush, A., Shaw, B., and Emery, G. (1979). *Cognitive therapy of depression.* New York: Guilford Press.

Browning, B. A. (2001). *Grant writing for dummies.* Foster City, CA: IDG Books Worldwide.

Carter, M. M., Marin, N. W., and Murrell, K. L. (1999). The efficacy of habitation in decreasing subjective distress among high anxiety–sensitivity college students. *Journal of Anxiety Disorders, 13,* 575–589.

Cormier, S., and Nurius, P. S. (2003). *Interviewing and change strategies for helpers: Fundamental skills and cognitive behavioral interventions* (5th ed.). Pacific Grove, CA: Brooks/Cole.

Corwin, M. D. (2002). *Brief treatment in clinical social work practice.* Pacific Grove, CA: Brooks/Cole.

Dorfman, R. (1996). *Clinical social work: Definition, practice, and vision.* New York: Brunner/Mazel.

DuBois, B., and Miley, K. K. (1999). *Social work: An empowering profession* (3rd ed.). Boston: Allyn and Bacon.

Dulmus, C. N., and Wodarski, J. S. (1998). Major depressive disorder and dysthymic disorder. In B. A. Thyer and J. S. Wodarski (Eds.), *Handbook of empirical social work practice: Vol. 1: Mental disorders* (pp. 273–285). New York: John Wiley and Sons.

D'Zurilla, T. J. (1986). *Problem-solving therapy: A social competence approach to clinical intervention.* New York: Springer.

D'Zurilla, T. J., and Nezu, A. M. (1999). *Problem-solving therapy: A social competence approach to clinical intervention* (2nd ed.). New York: Springer.

Eisikovits, Z. C., and Edleson, J. L. (1989). Intervening with men who batter: A critical review of the literature. *Social Services Review, 63*(3), 384–414.

Ellis, A. (1962). *Reason and emotion in psychotherapy.* New York: Lyle Stuart.

Ellis, A. (1977). The basic clinical theory of rational-emotive therapy. In A. Ellis and R. Grieger (Eds.), *Handbook of rational-emotive therapy.* New York: Springer.

Ezell, M. (1994). Advocacy practice of social workers. *Families in Society, 75,* 36–46.

Freire, P. (1990). *Pedagogy of the oppressed.* New York: Continuum.

Freud, S. (1987). Social workers as community educators: A new identity for the profession. *Journal of Teaching in Social Work, 1,* 111–126.

Garvin, C. D., and Seabury, B. A. (1997). *Interpersonal practice in social work: Promoting competence and social justice* (2nd ed.). Boston: Allyn and Bacon.

Ginsberg, L. H. (2001). *Social work evaluation: Principles and methods.* Boston: Allyn and Bacon.

Greenberg, J. S. (1996). *Comprehensive stress management.* Madison, WI: Brown and Benchmark.

Grinnell, R. M. (2001). *Social work research and evaluation: Quantitative and qualitative approaches* (6th ed.). Pacific Grove, CA: Brooks/Cole.

Hardcastle, D. A., Wenocur, S., and Powers, P. R. (1997). *Community practice theories and skills for social workers.* New York: Oxford University Press.

Hepworth, D. H., Rooney, R. H., and Larsen, J. A. (2002). *Direct social work practice: Theory and skills* (6th ed.). Pacific Grove, CA: Brooks/Cole.

Horan, J. (1996). Effects of computer-based cognitive restructuring on rationally mediated self-esteem. *Journal of Counseling Psychology, 43,* 371–375.

Jacobson, N., and Margolin, G. (1979). *Marital therapy.* New York: Brunner/Mazel.

Janis, I., and Mann, L. (1977). *Decision making: A psychosocial analysis of conflict, choice, and commitment.* New York: Free Press.

Kettner, P. M., Moroney, R. M., and Martin, L. L. (1999). *Designing and managing programs: An effectiveness-based approach* (2nd ed.). Thousand Oaks, CA: Sage Publications.

Kurzman, P. (1985). Program development and service coordination as components of community practice. In S. H. Taylor and R. W. Robers (Eds.), *Theory and practice of community social work* (pp. 59–94). New York: Columbia University Press.

Lantz, J., and Lenahan, B. (1976). Referral fatigue therapy. *Social Work, 12,* 239–240.

Lauffer, A. (1978). *Social planning at the community level.* Englewood Cliffs, NJ: Prentice Hall.

Lauffer, A. (1981). The practice of social planning. In N. Gilbert and H. Specht (Eds.), *Handbook of the social services* (pp. 583–597). Englewood Cliffs, NJ: Prentice Hall.

Lewis, E. (1991). Social change and citizen action: A philosophical exploration for modern social group work. *Social Work with Groups, 14,* 23–34.

Linney, J. A, and Wandersman, A. (1991). *Prevention Plus III: Assessing alcohol and other drug prevention programs at the school and community level: A four-step guide for useful program assessment.* Rockville, MD: U.S. Department of Health and Human Services, Office of Substance Abuse Prevention.

Maguire, L. (2002). *Clinical social work: Beyond generalist practice with individuals, groups, and families.* Pacific Grove, CA: Brooks/Cole.

Marlow, C. (2001). *Research methods for generalist social work* (3rd ed.). Pacific Grove, CA: Brooks/Cole.

Middleman, R., and Wood, G. (1990). From social group work to social work with groups. *Social Work with Groups, 13,* 3–20.

Miley, K., O'Melia, M., and DuBois, B. L. (1998). *Generalist social work practice: An empowering approach* (2nd ed.). Boston: Allyn and Bacon.

Mitchel, L. K., and Krumboltz, J. D. (1987). The effects of cognitive restructuring and decision-making training on career indecision. *Journal of Counseling and Development, 66,* 171–174.

Mizrahi, T., and Rosenthal, B. (1993). Managing dynamic tensions in social change coalitions. In T. Mizrahi and J. D. Morrison (Eds.), *Community organization and social administration* (pp. 11–40). New York: Haworth.

Moxley, D. P. (1997). *Case management by design: Reflections on principles and practices.* Chicago: Nelson-Hall.

National Association of Social Workers (1996). *NASW code of ethics.* Silver Spring, MD: NASW Press.

New, C. C. (1998). *Grantseeker's toolkit: A comprehensive guide to finding funding.* New York: John Wiley and Sons.

Pinderhughes, E. (1995). Direct practice overview. In R. Edwards (Ed.),

*Encyclopedia of social work* (19th ed.). Silver Spring, MD: NASW Press.

Rose, S. D., and LeCroy, C. W. (1991). Group methods. In F. H. Kanfer and A. P. Goldstein (Eds.), *Helping people change* (pp. 422–453). New York: Pergamon.

Rothman, J., and Sager, J. S. (1998). *Case management: Intergrating individual and community practice* (2nd ed.). Boston: Allyn and Bacon.

Royse, D., Thyer, B. A., Padgett, D. K., and Logan, T. K. (2001). *Program evaluation: An introduction* (3rd ed.). Pacific Grove, CA: Brooks/Cole.

Rubin, A., and Babbie, E. (2001). *Research methods for social work* (3rd ed.). Pacific Grove, CA: Brooks/Cole.

Rubin, H. J., and Rubin, I. S. (1992). *Community organizing and development* (2nd ed.). New York: Macmillan.

Staples, L. (1990). Powerful ideas about empowerment. *Administration in Social Work, 14,* 29–42.

United Way of America. (1996). *Measuring program outcomes: A practice approach*. Alexandria, VA: United Way of America.

Wandersman, A. (2001). Program development, evaluation, and accountability. In L. H. Ginsberg (Ed.), *Social work evaluation: Principles and methods* (pp. 178–210). Boston: Allyn and Bacon.

Weil, M. O., and Gamble, D. N. (1995). Community practice models. In R. Edwards (Ed.-in-Chief), *Encyclopedia of Social Work* (19th ed.). Silver Spring, MD: NASW Press.

Weissman, A. (1976). Industrial social service: Linkage technology. *Social Casework, 57,* 50–54.

Whiteman, M., Fanshel, D., and Grundy, J. (1987). Cognitive-behavioral interventions aimed at anger of parents at risk of child abuse. *Social Work, 32*(6), 469–474.

Woodside, M., and McClam, T. (1998). *Generalist case management: A method of human service delivery*. Pacific Grove, CA: Brooks/Cole.

Yuen, F. O., and Terao, K. L. (2003). *Practical grant writing and program evaluation*. Pacific Grove, CA: Brooks/Cole.

# 9

# EVALUATING PROGRESS

Ron A., who is in his second year of a three-year part-time MSW program, has a work site field placement at an Area Agency on Aging. Ron had worked at the agency for three years before he began his graduate studies. He is a case manager for elderly clients. In this role, he oversees the delivery and coordination of the various services being provided to the clients. As part of his field placement duties, Ron visits the elderly person in his or her home and completes a comprehensive assessment, from which he develops a case management plan.

Ron met with his first field placement client twice and completed the agency assessment form. He obtained all the necessary information. He felt that he had a beginning relationship with his client and that he had a clear understanding of his client's concerns and service needs.

In his job as a case manager, Ron had worked with clients in implementing their case management plans, but he had never been involved in systematically evaluating client progress. He was unsure how to measure progress on the goals they had set up. He also was unsure how his clients would react to filling out forms and questionnaires. By the end of this chapter, you should be able to help Ron

1. Construct self-anchored rating scales and goal attainment scales
2. Use client logs and behavioral observation in measuring client system progress
3. Locate standardized measures that are appropriate for use with social work client systems
4. Interpret the reliability and validity of standardized measures
5. Design a single-system evaluation to monitor client system progress
6. Plot single-system evaluation data on a line graph
7. Interpret the clinical, visual, and statistical significance of single-system evaluation data

This chapter focuses on the task of evaluating progress. The chapter describes measurement guidelines, types of measures, single-system evaluation designs, and analyses of evaluation data. The concepts and methods for evaluating client system progress presented in this chapter are very relevant for generalist social work practice. They are widely used for evaluating the progress of individual, family, and group client systems. They are equally applicable for evaluating progress with organizational and community client systems. Thus, regardless of the size of the client system, the concepts and methods discussed here can be used to evaluate the effectiveness of your work and client system progress.

These evaluation methods are very compatible with the collaborative model of generalist practice presented in this book. The collaborative model uses a goal-directed approach to practice. The worker and client system specify the desired outcomes of their work together. A single-system design is ideally suited to evaluating progress on goals. The key is identifying measures or indicators of target problems. The same process is used for individual, family, small group, organization, or community target problems.

The ability to evaluate client system progress has become increasingly important in recent years (Franklin and Jordan, 1992). Funding sources such as managed care companies now require social workers and other helping professionals to document client problems and the effectiveness of services provided. Skill in measurement is needed to comply with this requirement. The practice environment in which generalist social workers currently find themselves requires a higher level of accountability than at any other time in our professional history. It is no longer acceptable to rely solely on professional judgment in determining client service needs and in evaluating client progress.

There are also compelling ethical reasons to measure client progress. Social workers have an ethical responsibility to provide the best services available to their clients. You are responsible for making sure the services you are providing are helping your clients. To assume that what you are doing is working without systematically evaluating effectiveness is unethical. If the client is not making progress, both of you need to know, so that you can address the lack of progress and, if appropriate, change the intervention (Berlin and Marsh, 1993).

Evaluation can also help motivate clients. If the client is making progress, concrete evidence of it can strengthen his or her resolve to make further gains. Conversely, evidence of lack of progress can be a wake-up call, a challenge to renew commitment to change. Measuring progress forces you and the client to take stock. Are we making progress? Are the interventions working? Do we need to try another approach?

A common concern about measurement is that clients will react negatively to it and that it will disrupt the helping relationship (Witkin, 1991). Research has determined that this is not the case. Campbell (1988, 1990) found that clients prefer to systematically evaluate the effectiveness of the services they receive instead of relying solely on practitioner opinion. Applegate (1992) also found that this concern was not justified. Indeed, Poulin and Young (1997) found that clients placed a higher value on evaluation procedures than did their social workers. Social workers tended to underestimate the importance clients placed on evaluating progress. They were much more interested in developing and implementing interventions than in evaluating effectiveness. Clients, on the other hand, were as interested in evaluating effectiveness as they were in developing and implementing interventions. A follow-up qualitative study obtained similar results (Young and Poulin, 1998), showing that clients are more concerned about evaluation than social workers. The message from these studies is clear: It is a mistake to assume that clients will resist measurement procedures and that they do not care about assessing and measuring progress. Clients of social work services, like other consumers, want to know that the services they are receiving are effective.

## MEASUREMENT GUIDELINES

Jordan and Franklin state that "competence in measurement will improve social work's status, power base, and the profession's ability to function autonomously" (1995, p. 40). It will also improve the effectiveness of your practice and strengthen the helping relationship (Young and Poulin, 1998).

Collaborative social work practice seeks to empower clients. Having clients involved in the development of the measurement plan and in constructing measures is empowering. For this reason, it is best to use measures that involve the client in the data collection process.

Drawing on the work of Barlow, Hayes, and Nelson (1984), Berlin and Marsh developed guidelines for collecting client data. They suggest that the data collection effort will be enhanced if you:

- Specify the client's problems and goals clearly
- Use multiple measures for each objective
- Collect information that is relevant rather than convenient
- Collect information early in the course of the work with the client
- Use good and accurate measures
- Organize the data
- Obtain the client's cooperation and consent (1993, p. 93)

**Step 1:** *Clearly specify problems and goals.* This guideline is fundamental to the measurement process. As noted earlier, client problems and expected outcomes must be specific and stated in clear, unambiguous terms. Measurable objectives related to each goal must be developed. Collecting client data is impossible without specific and observable indicators attached to each objective (Berlin and Marsh, 1993).

**Step 2:** *Use multiple measures.* The use of more than one measure to assess a single phenomenon is a basic research strategy referred to as **triangulation** (Royse and Thyer, 1996). The assumption behind this strategy is that all measures are to some extent flawed or imperfect. Because any one measure may not be accurate, it is necessary to use more than one measure to assess client progress. The logical assumption is that if two or more imperfect measures indicate change, there is more reason to be confident that change has occurred than if only one imperfect measure is used. Relying on a single measure of client progress is risky. The problems addressed by generalist social workers and their clients are too complex to be assessed with a single imperfect measure.

The inaccuracy of measurement strategies should not discourage you from using quantitative measures in your practice. Crude indicators of progress are preferable to no indicators. What is important is to be aware of the limitations of measurement tools. The data alone will not provide you and your clients with definitive answers. The data will, however, provide you and your clients with helpful information that can be incorporated into your work together. Analyzing the data with your clients will facilitate the helping process and provide a basis for ongoing assessment of your work together.

**Step 3:** *Collect relevant information.* Berlin and Marsh warn that "one of the most frequent mistakes that clinicians make is to track something that is not very important" (1993, p. 94). Typically, the client's problem is reconceptualized to fit an existing measure or instrument. The convenience factor is high, but the relevance factor is low. "If the clinician is to collect useful information, he or she must look beyond the enticements of easily acquired, but barely relevant, assessment indices and focus on whether the aspects of the problem targeted for change are really changing" (Berlin and Marsh, 1993,

p. 95). If you cannot specify the expected changes, the problem may not have been conceptualized accurately or the terms may not be specific enough. Relevant measures should flow directly from clearly conceptualized problems and objectives.

**Step 4:** *Collect information early.* There are a number of reasons to begin the process of collecting data early in the helping process. The first reason is that measuring the target problem or objective prior to implementing the intervention provides baseline data, which are a basis for future comparisons. Change must be evaluated comparatively. Without some sort of comparison, it is impossible to assess the extent to which the desired changes have occurred. Collecting assessment data early in the helping process will allow you to periodically evaluate the effectiveness of the work throughout the helping relationship.

A second reason to begin collecting data early in the helping process is to communicate to clients that you are interested in understanding their situation and that you are committed to helping them successfully address their concerns or problems. Measurement is an active and concrete process. Developing measures communicates that you take their concerns seriously and that their concerns are important enough to warrant the effort required to develop measures and collect data.

A third reason to start the measurement process early is that it engages the client in a collaborative activity. You and the client define the target problem, develop the objectives, and develop the measurement plan. You and your client may even develop many of the measures used. The client becomes an active participant in the process. This communicates expectations about how you will work together as well as the idea that the client is the expert on his or her situation.

**Step 5:** *Use good and accurate measures.* Every effort should be made to use the best measures available. According to Berlin and Marsh (1993), four criteria are useful in judging the adequacy of different measures: relevance, sensitivity to change, reliability, and validity.

**Relevance** refers to the extent the measure is directly related to the targeted outcomes. Is there a good fit between the measure and the expected changes? For example, in Chapter 7 one of the objectives for the father who was having trouble controlling his temper was to count to 10 and take 3 deep breaths before responding to his son. In this situation, a measure of how many times the father counted to 10 and took 3 deep breaths would be directly relevant and very appropriate. Measuring how often he refrained from yelling at his son might appear to be an appropriate measure, but it would in fact be less relevant given the change objective. If the treatment objective was to increase the father's self-control, then a self-control measure would be directly relevant. The relevance of any measure is a function of the identified target problem or the specific change objectives.

**Sensitivity to change** is the second criterion of a good measure. Not all measures are capable of capturing change. Some are more sensitive than others. It may be possible to use measures that have shown change in previous evaluations and have thus been proved useful. A measure's track record of detecting change is one of the best indicators of its sensitivity to change (Berlin and Marsh, 1993; Bloom, Fischer, and Orme, 1995). Often, however, information on a measure's sensitivity is not available.

It is not always possible to know in advance whether a measure will be sensitive to change (Bloom, Fischer, and Orme, 1995). Berlin and Marsh (1993) suggest that global measures are usually less sensitive to change than measures directly related to specific behaviors targeted for change. Bloom, Fischer, and Orme state that measures of behaviors that occur more frequently are more likely to be more sensitive than measures of behaviors that occur less frequently. "This is because a high-frequency behavior is likely to be more responsive to small changes and can both increase or decrease, while a low-frequency behavior can only increase and may be responsive only to major changes" (1995, p. 52).

**Reliability** refers to the consistency of measurements. "In testing for change, at least two and preferably more measurements are required" (Gabor, Unrau, and Grinnell, 1998, p. 165). When measuring client change, you want to be reasonably confident that the differences among the first measurement and subsequent ones relate to changes in the client and not to problems with the measure. "It is therefore important that a measuring instrument gives the same result with the same unchanged client every time it is administered. An instrument that can do this is said to be reliable" (Gabor, Unrau, and Grinnell, 1998, p. 165).

"Every type of measure involves some kind of error, and the measure is reliable to the extent that the error is minimal" (Berlin and Marsh, 1993, p. 97). The two most common ways of testing the reliability of a measure are to assess its internal consistency and test–retest characteristics. **Internal consistency reliability** is the extent to which the individual items that make up a scale or index are correlated with one another. **Test–retest reliability** refers to the extent to which the same result is obtained when the same measure is administered to the same client at two different points in time. Both types of reliability are important. However, in evaluating client change, test–retest reliability is critical. To the extent possible, use at least one measure that has been tested for reliability and has reliability coefficients of .80 or higher.

**Validity** refers to the extent to which an instrument measures what it is supposed to measure and not anything else (Kyte and Bostwick, 1997). For example, if you are assessing a client's self-confidence, the instrument should measure self-confidence, not a related concept such as self-esteem. "An instrument is said to be valid when it closely corresponds to the concept it was designed to measure" (Royse and Thyer, 1996, p. 188). Because concepts in social work tend to be complex, no measure will be entirely valid, only more or less so (Gabor, Unrau, and Grinnell, 1998).

There are various ways to determine the validity of an instrument. The least rigorous kind of validity is face validity. Does the instrument appear to measure the concept? A measure is said to have **face validity** if knowledgeable persons agree that it measures what it is intended to measure. "Do the items on the questionnaire appear to be 'getting at' what they should?" (Bloom, Fischer, and Orme, 1995, p. 187).

Another type of validity is **content validity.** This method also relies on expert opinion. In this case, "experts are asked to review it to see if the entire range of the concept is represented in the sample of items selected for the scale" (Royse and Thyer, 1996, p. 188). For example, a scale designed to measure stress should have items that represent the different components of stress, such as feeling tense, feeling pressured, having difficulty sleeping, and being short tempered.

"Neither content nor face validity is sufficient for establishing that a scale has **'true' validity**" (Royse and Thyer, 1996, p. 188). For this to occur, a measure must empirically demonstrate its validity. There are a number of methods to empirically demonstrate a measure's validity. "**Concurrent validity** is demonstrated by administering to the same subjects the new scale and another scale that has previously been determined (proven) to have validity" (Royse and Thyer, 1996, p. 188). If the two scales are highly correlated, at .80 or above, the new scale has demonstrated concurrent validity.

**Predictive validity** refers to the ability of a measure to predict future behavior or attitudes. "The simplest way to determine predictive validity would be to correlate results on a measure one time with the criterion information collected at a later time" (Bloom, Fischer, and Orme, 1995, p. 49). An example is correlating Scholastic Aptitude Test (SAT) scores with students' grade point averages.

**Construct validity** refers to the extent to which an instrument actually measures the concept in question. Construct validity is established by demonstrating convergent validity and discriminant validity. A measure is said to have **convergent validity** if it is correlated in a predicted manner with other measures with which it theoretically should correlate (Bloom, Fischer, and Orme, 1999). For example, a measure of the strength of a helping relationship should correlate positively with measures of trust and openness. Those who are more trusting and open are more likely to develop strong helping relationships with their social workers than those who are less trusting and open.

A measure's **discriminant validity** is demonstrated by a lack of correlation with measures with which it theoretically should not be correlated. This indicates that the measure can discriminate between concepts. For example, there is no theoretical basis for predicting how certain client problems will correlate with the development of a helping relationship with the social worker. Clients with high self-esteem are as likely to develop a strong helping relationship as those with low self-esteem. Similarly, a client's level of depression is not associated with the strength of the helping relationship.

Construct validity is demonstrated when a measure is correlated with other measures that it theoretically should be related to (convergent validity) and not correlated with measures with which it theoretically should not be correlated (discriminant validity). When selecting measures to evaluate client change, look for some evidence of the validity of the measure. At the very

FIGURE 9.1 | CLIENT'S WEEKLY SELF-ESTEEM SCORES

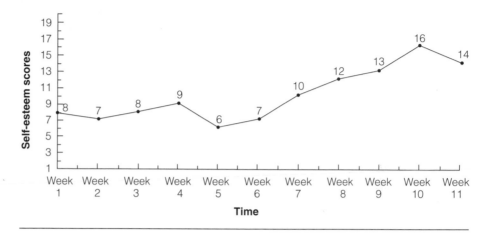

least, the measure should have face validity. Empirical verification of the measure's validity is preferable.

**Step 6:** *Organize the data.* For data to be useful, they have to be organized in some systematic way. It is difficult to interpret or draw meaning from unorganized raw data. Data need to be presented in a way that makes sense to both you and your client. Typically, data obtained to evaluate client change can be easily computed and presented in simple graphs.

The basic graphic presentation of change data is a **line graph** on which the client's scores are plotted over time. A visual inspection of the data points provides feedback on client progress. Time is plotted on the horizontal (*x*) axis, and scores measuring the target problem on the vertical (*y*) axis. The time dimension reflects the number of times the measure of the target problem is completed and the time period between measurements. The time unit selected depends on the nature of the target problem. Typically, measures of the target problem are completed on a daily or weekly basis. Figure 9.1 is a sample line graph on which a client's level of self-esteem is plotted over an 11-week period.

An important component of the helping process is reviewing the data on the graphic displays with clients. In collaborative social work, the clients are actively involved in inspecting the organized data and interpreting the patterns and results. Most clients are interested in examining graphs of their progress and in providing interpretations of what is happening. Involving clients in this process can be a powerful tool. It keeps your work focused on the change objectives, and it provides an opportunity for you and the client to review progress, tasks, and effort as well as the appropriateness of goals and objectives. If strides are being made, it can motivate further efforts. If progress is not forthcoming, you and the client can assess the situation and make adjustments as needed.

**Step 7:** *Obtain client cooperation and consent.* Naturally, the process of selecting and incorporating measurement strategies into generalist practice requires the full cooperation of clients. Collaborative social work is based on the assumption that clients are full partners in the helping process. Measuring client progress without their full cooperation is a waste of time. Clients need to have ownership of the measures and willingness to engage in a process of self-assessment. Their commitment to the data collection and evaluation process reflects their commitment to achieving the changes they are seeking.

## MEASUREMENT TOOLS

There are a number of measurement methods that involve clients, are easy to construct and implement, and are appropriate for generalist social work practice. The more frequently used methods are:

- Client logs
- Behavioral observations
- Rating scales
- Goal attainment scales
- Standardized measures

### Client Logs

Having clients prepare narrative accounts of their activities, thoughts, and feelings is an effective method of monitoring progress. Client logs or journals help clarify the nature of client problems and the circumstances that contribute to the problem situation. Clients often find that keeping a log helps them increase their understanding and awareness of the factors that contribute to the identified problem situation. It enables them to "track the antecedents and consequences, or the feelings and thoughts, surrounding the occurrence of a specific event" (Berlin and Marsh, 1993, p. 99). Client logs allow a client to systematically take notes on the occurrence of a target problem and the events surrounding each occurrence. Doing so prevents distortions and misperceptions caused by faulty memory (Bloom, Fischer, and Orme, 1999).

Client logs also are an excellent source of baseline data on the frequency of the target problem. Baseline data obtained from logs serve as clinical measurements of client thoughts, feelings, and behaviors. "These recordings help the client and the practitioner to gain appropriate insights into the client's functioning, aid in structuring treatment tasks, facilitate client change, and monitor clinical progress during treatment" (Jordan and Franklin, 1995, p. 41).

Client logs are easy to construct. Most are divided into columns, with the types of information the client should record listed at the top of each column (Figure 9.2). "At a minimum it involves recording whether some incident occurred, when it occurred, and how the client responded to it" (Bloom,

FIGURE 9.2 | CLIENT LOG

| Date | Time | Event | Before Problem | After Problem | Reaction |
|------|------|-------|----------------|---------------|----------|
|      |      |       |                |               |          |
|      |      |       |                |               |          |
|      |      |       |                |               |          |

From M. Bloom, J. Fischer, and J. Orme, *Evaluating practice: Guidelines for the accountable professional* (2nd ed.). Published by Allyn and Bacon, Boston, MA. Copyright © 1995 by Pearson Education. Reprinted with permission of the publisher.

Fischer, and Orme, 1995, p. 238). Information on circumstances just prior to and just after the problem event may also be included in client logs.

Two decisions need to be made regarding the completion of logs. The first is when to record the information, and the second is what to record. Clients can record at preset time periods or immediately following the occurrence of the target event. **Recording at preset time periods** works if you have narrowed down the occurrence of a target event to a specific period, that is, if you know in advance approximately when the target problem is likely to occur. For example, a family might complain about sibling fights after school and during dinner. The client log then might cover the time period of 3:00 P.M. to 7:00 P.M. in the evening. The client keeping the log would record all the sibling fights that occurred during this time period.

The second option is to use **open time categories.** This method is sometimes referred to as **critical incident recording** (Bloom, Fischer, and Orme, 1995). With this type of log, the client decides whether to record an event. The client decides if the event is related to the problem or target and then records it as soon as possible after it occurs. This method works best when you need information about events that are likely to be spread out over the entire day.

In addition to specifying when the recording will take place, you also need to clarify in advance what will be recorded. By design, client logs give the client control over the content. Clients choose which of the many thoughts, feelings, and behaviors they experience daily to include and exclude. They employ a great deal of subjective judgment in completing logs. Information recorded on the log should be limited to what the "client perceives as significantly related to the target" (Bloom, Fischer, and Orme, 1995, p. 240). Thus, you and the client need to be clear about what constitutes a critical incident. Discuss with the client the types of events that would be appropriate for inclusion in the log. In the beginning, encourage clients to be inclusive rather than exclusive in their recordings. Review the first logs together with an eye toward the appropriateness of the entries as well as events that the client did not record but should have.

## Behavioral Observations

"Behavioral observations represent one of the most direct and effective measures of client behavior" (Jordan and Franklin, 1995, p. 46). The frequency and duration of specific client behaviors can be observed and recorded (Bloom, Fischer, and Orme, 1995). Behavioral observation can provide detailed information on the occurrence of client behaviors and the context of those behaviors. It represents one of the most reliable and valid methods of measuring client change.

Typically, the first step in using behavioral observation is to operationally define the target behavior. An example would be specifying the types of disruptive behavior a child displays in the classroom, such as getting out of his or her seat or talking with classmates while the teacher is talking. The target problem must be clearly defined in behavioral terms and must be observable. Observation cannot be used to measure target problems that focus on feelings or thoughts. It is limited to measuring the frequency, duration, and context of behaviors.

The second step is to select the observer or observers. Often, the observers are significant others, family members, or other professionals who have access to the client's person-in-environment interactions. For example, a young child having a problem controlling his or her temper can be observed at home by a parent and at school by a teacher or teacher's aide.

Ideally, at least two people should observe the same events. This makes it possible to establish interobserver agreement and determine the reliability of the observations. "Eighty percent or higher agreement is believed to be acceptable for most clinical situations" (Jordan and Franklin, 1995, pp. 46–47). However, not all practice situations lend themselves to direct observation. If using two or more observers is impractical, you will have to settle for a single observer. "Behavioral observation using one observer lacks the scientific reliability of observation with two or more raters, but it remains an important measurement indicator in clinical assessments because it provides observations of the client's behavior in natural settings" (Jordan and Franklin, 1995, p. 47).

The third step is to train the observers. Observers must know in advance exactly what behavior to look for and how to recognize the behavior when it occurs (Jordan and Franklin, 1995). In addition, they have to be trained to conduct the observations. "Deciding how to sample the behaviors is the fundamental question in conducting a structured observation" (Berlin and Marsh, 1993, p. 107). You must decide whether to record all instances of the behavior or a sample. "Continuous recording involves recording every occurrence of a target behavior every time it occurs" (Bloom, Fischer, and Orme, 1995, p. 133). This requires the observer to be willing and available, and it works best when the target behavior does not occur with great frequency. Often, these conditions cannot be satisfied, and a sampling strategy is used. Figure 9.3 is a form for continuous recording.

FIGURE 9.3 | OBSERVATION FORM FOR CONTINUOUS RECORDING

Client's Name _____    Recorder's Name _____

Behavior to be Observed _____

_____

Date _____    Location _____

| Time | Description of Behavior and Context |
|------|-------------------------------------|
|      |                                     |
|      |                                     |
|      |                                     |
|      |                                     |

From M. Bloom, J. Fischer, and J. Orme, *Evaluating practice: Guidelines for the accountable professional* (2nd ed.). Published by Allyn and Bacon, Boston, MA. Copyright © 1995 by Pearson Education. Reprinted with permission of the publisher.

FIGURE 9.4 | OBSERVATION FORM FOR INTERVAL TIME SAMPLING RECORDING

Client's Name _____    Recorder's Name _____

Behavior to be Observed _____

_____

Date _____  Location _____  Time Period _____  Interval Length _____

| Interval | Behavioral Occurrence | Context | Comments |
|----------|----------------------|---------|----------|
| 1.       | Yes      No          |         |          |
| 2.       | Yes      No          |         |          |
| 3.       | Yes      No          |         |          |

From M. Bloom, J. Fischer, and J. Orme, *Evaluating practice: Guidelines for the accountable professional* (2nd ed.). Published by Allyn and Bacon, Boston, MA. Copyright © 1995 by Pearson Education. Reprinted with permission of the publisher.

FIGURE 9.5  |  OBSERVATION FORM FOR DISCRETE TIME SAMPLING RECORDING

Client's Name _____     Recorder's Name _____

Behavior to be Observed _____

_____

Time Period _____     Location _____

| Date | Number of Times Behavior Occurred | Comments |
|------|-----------------------------------|----------|
|      |                                   |          |
|      |                                   |          |
|      |                                   |          |

From M. Bloom, J. Fischer, and J. Orme, *Evaluating practice: Guidelines for the accountable professional* (2nd ed.). Published by Allyn and Bacon, Boston, MA. Copyright © 1995 by Pearson Education. Reprinted with permission of the publisher.

**Time sampling** is appropriate when events occur continuously or frequently. "Time sampling requires the selection of specific units of time, either intervals or discrete points, during which the occurrence or nonoccurrence of a specific behavior is recorded" (Berlin and Marsh, 1993, p. 107). The assumption is that the sample behavior would be the same if all occurrences of it were recorded (Haynes, 1978). There are two types of time sampling: interval and discrete. **Interval sampling** involves selecting a time period and dividing it into equal blocks of time. The observer records the occurrence or nonoccurrence of the behavior during each interval. The behavior is recorded once for each interval regardless of how many times it occurs (Bloom, Fischer, and Orme, 1995). Figure 9.4 shows a form for interval recording.

**Discrete time sampling** involves selecting specific time periods and recording all instances of the target behavior that occur during the selected periods. The key issue in this type of recording is to select periods that are representative in terms of the target behavior. If the behaviors occur often and regularly, you would need fewer periods to obtain a representative sample of them (Bloom, Fischer, and Orme, 1995). If the behaviors occur during certain time periods, for example, during meals, then the selected periods must correspond to the behavioral patterns of the client. Figure 9.5 shows a form for discrete time sampling recording.

Overall, direct observation is an excellent method for assessing client outcomes. It is one of the most effective tools we have for measuring behavior. When it is used with two or more observers, it can provide reliable and valid outcome data. It also has the potential to provide valuable clinical information on the context within which target problems occur. Direct observation should be seriously considered when a target problem is behavioral in nature, the situation allows for direct observation, and implementing direct observation is feasible.

## Rating Scales

**Individualized rating scales** are measures of client problems that are created by the client and the social worker together (Bloom, Fischer, and Orme, 1995). These types of measures are also referred to as **self-anchored rating scales** (Jordan and Franklin, 1995). The major advantage of an individualized rating scale is that it measures the specific problem or concern that you and your client have identified as the focus of intervention. Thus, a rating scale is directly linked to the feeling, thought, or event that is being addressed in the helping process.

Another advantage of individualized rating scales is that they are based on the client's unique experiences and perceptions. The anchor points of the scale are defined by the client. The low, middle, and high points of the scale are labeled with short, succinct terms. The labels (anchors) describe what the numbers represent (e.g., behaviors, thoughts, and feelings that the client would experience at various points along the scale). Having the client define the anchor points gives the measure great relevance for the client. It becomes a unique measure of the client's feelings, thoughts, or behaviors. It represents his or her perceptions and experiences.

Individualized rating scales usually have 5–10 points. Scales that have more than 10 points are difficult for clients to score and are therefore not recommended (Bloom, Fischer, and Orme, 1995). For example, if a self-esteem scale had 1 to 100 points, it would be very difficult to determine the difference between ratings of 70 and 75. Scales with seven points are considered ideal, allowing "for some deviations that capture the client's varying experiences, but not creating so many deviations that they lose meaning" (Jordan and Franklin, 1995, p. 43).

Individualized rating scales are easy to construct. Identify with the client the behavior, thought, or feeling that is targeted for change. A wide range of characteristics of the target can be rated: "For example, the seriousness, intensity, importance, or frequency of the target might be rated" (Bloom, Fischer, and Orme, 1995, p. 165). It is important for the target to be clearly articulated and for each rating scale to measure only one aspect or dimension of the target (Gingerich, 1979). Bloom, Fischer, and Orme warn against using different dimensions at each end of the scale, such as happy at one end and sad at the other. People often experience contradictory feelings and can feel happy and sad at the same time. It is preferable to develop two measures, a sadness scale and a happiness scale rather than one scale on which both dimensions are rated. They also recommend that the target and its measurement be worded "in a way that emphasizes that the client is working toward something positive rather than just trying to eliminate something undesirable" (1995, p. 166). For example, if the problem is feelings of sadness, the goal might be to increase feelings of happiness, and the rating scale would measure the level of happiness.

FIGURE 9.6 | INDIVIDUALIZED RATING SCALES

**Comfort in social situations**

| 1 | 2 | 3 | 4 | 5 | 6 | 7 | 8 | 9 |

Terrified, overwhelmed, completely unable to engage in conversation with strangers

Somewhat anxious, yet able to respond when spoken to

Relaxed, confident, able to initiate conversations with strangers

**Ability to control temper**

| 1 | 2 | 3 | 4 | 5 | 6 | 7 | 8 | 9 |

Out of control, completely unable to control temper, flying off the handle for the slightest reason

Somewhat able to control temper, only losing temper when provoked

In complete control, able to control temper even in the most trying conditions

The next step is to decide on the number of scale points and develop anchor descriptions for the two end points and possibly the middle point. Scales with seven or nine points are popular because they have a clear midpoint. The numbers on the scale represent gradations for the target problem from low to high. The higher the score, the more frequent, serious, important, or problematic the target problem. The end points of the scale are defined by the client, as are the descriptions or examples of the low, middle, and high numbers. These anchor descriptions define the meaning of the numbers on the rating scale. Begin by asking the client to describe what it would be like at one end of the scale for the given target problem. Repeat the process for the other end of the scale and for the midpoint. Anchors should describe the behaviors, thoughts, or feelings the client would experience along the continuum of the scale:

> The depressed client might characterize himself or herself as being most depressed (level 9 on the scale) when he or she can't sleep, can't work and has suicidal thoughts. Thus, when these conditions occur, the client would know to rate himself or herself at level 9. The depressed client may be least depressed, level 1, when he or she feels like going out, wants to eat a large meal, and really enjoys being with friends. (Bloom, Fischer, and Orme, 1995, p. 167)

After you and your client construct the scale, make sure that the anchors fit the client's perception of the situation and that both of you are clear about what constitutes a low or high score. This is best accomplished by practicing using the scale and asking the client to retrospectively complete a rating for different points in his or her life. This will increase the client's comfort in using the scale and provides an opportunity to determine whether the anchor points provide adequate differentiation of the target problem. Individualized rating scales are shown in Figure 9.6.

FIGURE 9.7 | GENERAL RATING SCALES

**Amount of anxiety**

| 1 | 2 | 3 | 4 | 5 | 6 | 7 | 8 | 9 |

Little or no anxiety          Moderate anxiety          Extreme anxiety

**Frequency of feeling lonely**

| 1 | 2 | 3 | 4 | 5 | 6 | 7 | 8 | 9 |

Never          Sometimes          All the time

An important point to keep in mind in constructing individualized rating scales is that they must be truly *individualized*. The anchors reflect images and pictures of what the situation is like for the client. Your job is to help the client put those images into words. Make sure the words are the client's, not yours or someone else's. The strength of individualized rating scales is that they are client defined and derived directly from the identified target problem.

An alternative to individually constructed anchors is **general anchor descriptions**. Rating scales with general anchors can be used for different client situations. For example, a general rating scale measuring feelings of connectedness could be used to measure a client's relationships with each member of his or her family. The disadvantage of general anchors is that they are more ambiguous and less precise than individually tailored anchors (Coulton and Solomon, 1977). Figure 9.7 shows general rating scales.

Individualized and general rating scales are excellent tools for measuring client progress and change on identified target problems. They have a high level of face validity because they are derived directly from client problems or concerns. There is some evidence that the validity of single-item rating scales is comparable to that of standardized measures (Nugent, 1992). However, the validity and reliability of individualized rating scales cannot be readily established, because they are designed for use with individual clients (Berlin and Marsh, 1993). In this sense, "these scales are not rigorous, scientifically valid, or reliable forms of measurement" (Jordan and Franklin, 1995, p. 46). Rating scales do, however, have a high level of clinical applicability and are excellent tools for measuring client target problems and assessing progress.

## Goal Attainment Scales

**Goal attainment scaling (GAS)** was developed in the field of mental health during the 1960s (Royse and Thyer, 1996). It has been used in a large number of settings and with a wide range of client populations. GAS is similar to individualized rating scales in that the client develops and defines the scale anchors or descriptors. The two methods differ, however, in that goal attainment scales are based directly on the client's goals rather than on behaviors, thoughts, or feelings. A strength of GAS is that it can be used to monitor client progress toward the identified treatment goals (Jordan and Franklin, 1995). Thus, GAS has been effective in assessing client change related to the identified goals (Corcoran, 1992).

To use GAS, you and your client need to have specified change goals. A question that arises is which goals or how many should be measured (Seaburg and Gillespie, 1977). In general, the number of goals measured should correspond to the number of goals being addressed in the helping relationship. The number of goals being addressed at any given time should be limited. As discussed earlier in this chapter, the goals selected should be those most significant to the client that intervention is most likely to change (Royse and Thyer, 1996).

In conjunction with the client, list each goal on a 5-point scale ranging from − 2 to + 2. The scale categories are:

(+ 2)  Most favorable outcome expected
(+ 1)  More than expected outcome
(0)     Expected outcome
(− 1)  Less than expected outcome
(− 2)  Most unfavorable outcome

Work with the client to develop anchors for each scale point. The anchors should represent potential outcomes related to each category and should be as specific as possible. Avoid vague, general outcome statements. Figure 9.8 shows a sample goal attainment scale that was developed with an 80-year-old woman who was caring for her 55-year-old mentally retarded son. The social worker was helping the women address her anxiety and concern about her son's future.

Instead of the − 2 to + 2 scoring system, the worker is using a modified format that is more intuitive and easier to explain to clients. It uses the following scale categories:

(4)  Optimal progress
(3)  Major progress
(2)  Moderate progress
(1)  Some progress
(0)  no progress

These categories focus on desired progress to a greater extent than the traditional GAS scoring format and thus reflect a more positive orientation. Figure 9.9 contains the same examples as Figure 9.8 but in the modified scoring format.

GAS is a client-focused method of measuring progress. It is a direct extension of the goal-oriented approach to practice and is easily incorporated into generalist social work practice with a diverse range of client populations. GAS also empowers clients by placing responsibility for defining and monitoring progress with them. The client is viewed as the expert on what constitutes progress and on determining the extent to which progress is being made. In

FIGURE 9.8 | GOAL ATTAINMENT SCALE

| Level | Goal 1: Increase Ability to Deal with Panic Attacks | Goal 2: Make Plans for Son's Future |
|---|---|---|
| Most unfavorable outcome (– 2) | Unable to calm myself down; unable to catch breath; heart racing, extreme anxiety | Unable to discuss with son his future needs and plans |
| Less than expected outcome (– 1) | Limited ability to calm myself down, some difficulty breathing, pacing the floor, moderate anxiety | Discussed son's future with other members of the family |
| Expected outcome (0) | Able to calm down using breathing/relaxation techniques, maintain composure, low anxiety | Discussed with son his future needs |
| More than expected outcome (+ 1) | Able to verbalize feelings, remain calm in stressful situations, almost no anxiety | Discussed with son his future needs and involved family and outside agencies in assessing son's needs |
| Most favorable outcome (+ 2) | Able to deal with stressful situations without experiencing panic attacks; very low anxiety; calm and relaxed | Working with son, family, and outside agencies and services to prepare son to care for himself in the future |

FIGURE 9.9 | MODIFIED GOAL ATTAINMENT SCALE

| Level | Goal 1: Increase Ability to Deal with Panic Attacks | Goal 2: Make Plans for Son's Future |
|---|---|---|
| No progress (0) | Unable to calm myself down; unable to catch breath; heart racing, extreme anxiety | Unable to discuss with son his future needs and plans |
| Some progress (1) | Limited ability to calm myself down, some difficulty breathing, pacing the floor, moderate anxiety | Discussed son's future with other members of the family |
| Moderate progress (2) | Able to calm down using breathing/relaxation techniques, maintain composure, low anxiety | Discussed with son his future needs |
| Major progress (3) | Able to verbalize feelings, remain calm in stressful situations, almost no anxiety | Discussed with son his future needs and involved family and outside agencies in assessing son's needs |
| Optimal progress (4) | Able to deal with stressful situations without experiencing panic attacks; very low anxiety; calm and relaxed | Working with son, family, and outside agencies and services to prepare son to care for himself in the future |

these respects, GAS is useful as a clinical measurement tool for engaging clients in the helping process.

## Standardized Measures

Standardized measures are instruments developed following empirical scale construction techniques with uniform administration and scoring procedures (Jordan and Franklin, 1995). Their reliability is known, and their validity has usually been empirically tested.

Standardized measures are available for a wide range of client behaviors, including marital satisfaction, self-esteem, anxiety, and family relations. Some standardized measures assess global behaviors, such as generalized contentment, while others assess specific behaviors and problems, such as fear, depression, and sexual satisfaction. Standardized measures are available in rapid assessment formats with up to 25 scale items, as well as in lengthy, comprehensive formats with hundreds of scale items. Rapid assessment instruments are easy to use and to incorporate into generalist social work practice. Figure 9.10 reproduces a rapid assessment instrument designed to measure argumentativeness.

"Standardized measures represent the most useful quantitative clinical measurement tools that are available to practitioners" (Jordan and Franklin, 1995, p. 53). There are numerous sources of standardized measures. *Measures for Clinical Practice* by Fischer and Corcoran (1994) is an excellent two-volume collection of rapid assessment instruments. Volume 1 contains measures for use with couples, families, and children, and Volume 2 contains instruments for individual adults. The two-volume set contains more than 300 different brief assessment instruments, with supporting information on each instrument's purpose, scoring, reliability, and validity. Another excellent source of rapid assessment instruments is *Measures of Personality and Social Psychological Attitudes* (1991) by Robinson, Shaver, and Wrightsman. In this book, measures are organized by clinical topic (e.g., self-esteem, depression, anxiety).

An excellent list of commercially available measures can be found in *Clinical Assessment for Social Workers* by Jordan and Franklin (1995). The WALMYR Publishing Company is an excellent source for commercially available measurement instruments designed specifically for use in social work practice. Walter Hudson, the founder of WALMYR, pioneered the use of rapid assessment instruments in social work practice (Hudson, 1982). WALMYR sells a number of individual and family adjustment scales as well as comprehensive multidimensional assessment instruments.

Standardized measures, especially the rapid assessment variety, are well suited for use in generalist social work practice. If you can locate one that closely corresponds to identified client problems or concerns, standardized

FIGURE 9.10 | ARGUMENTATIVENESS INDEX (ARG)*

**AUTHORS:** Dominic A. Infante and Andrew S. Rancer

**PURPOSE:** To measure argumentativeness.

**DESCRIPTION:** The ARG is a 20-item scale designed to measure the tendency to argue about controversial issues (or argumentativeness). Argumentativeness is viewed as a generally stable trait which predisposes the individual in communication situations to advocate positions on controversial issues and to attack verbally the positions other people take on those issues. Ten of the items indicate a tendency to approach argumentative situations and ten involve the tendency to avoid argumentative situations. The ARG is considered useful for examining communication and social conflict and dysfunctional communication. Both areas have implications for clinical practice in that high scores on the ARG may identify the incessant arguer whose behavior impairs interpersonal relations while very low scores may identify people who almost never dispute an issue and are compliant and/or easily manipulated. Thus, the ARG may prove useful particularly in couple and family counseling.

**NORMS:** A series of studies involving over 800 students in undergraduate communication courses formed the basis for much of the research on the ARG. No demographic data are reported nor are actual norms.

**SCORING:** Scores for each item ranging from I to 5 are totaled separately for the two dimensions. The total score for the tendency to avoid argumentative situations (items 1, 3, 5, 6, 8, 10, 12, 14, 16, 19) is subtracted from the total score for the tendency to approach argumentative situations (2, 4, 7, 9, 11, 13, 15, 17, 18, 20) to provide an overall score for the argumentativeness trait.

**RELIABILITY:** The ARG has good to excellent internal consistency, with the approach dimension (ARG ap) having a coefficient alpha of .91 and the avoidance dimension (ARG av) having an alpha of .86. The ARG also is a stable instrument with an overall ARG test–retest reliability (one week) of .91 and test–retest reliabilities of .87 for ARG ap and .86 for ARG av.

**VALIDITY:** The ARG has fairly good concurrent validity, correlating significantly and in the expected direction with three other measures of communication predispositions. In addition, the ARG significantly correlates with friends' ratings of argumentativeness. Further, the ARG has some degree of construct validity in accurately predicting a series of behavioral choices which should and should not correlate with argumentativeness.

**PRIMARY REFERENCE:** Infante, D. A. and Rancer, A. S. (1982). A conceptualization and measure of argumentativeness, *Journal of Personality Assessment, 46,* 72–80. Instrument reproduced with permission of Dominic A. Infante and the *Journal of Personality Assessment.*

**AVAILABILITY:** Journal article.

### ARG Index

This questionnaire contains statements about arguing controversial issues. Indicate how often each statement is true for you personally by placing the appropriate number in the blank to the left of the statement. If the statement is *almost never true* for you, place a "I" in the blank. If the statement is *rarely true* for you, place a "2" in the blank. If the statement is *occasionally true* for you, place a "3" in the blank. If the statement is *often true* for you, place a "4" in the blank. If the statement is *almost always true* for you, place a "5" in the blank.

*(continued)*

FIGURE 9.10 | *continued*

_____ 1. While in an argument, I worry that the person I am arguing with will form a negative impression of me.
_____ 2. Arguing over controversial issues improves my intelligence.
_____ 3. I enjoy avoiding arguments.
_____ 4. I am energetic and enthusiastic when I argue.
_____ 5. Once I finish an argument I promise myself that I will not get into another.
_____ 6. Arguing with a person creates more problems for me than it solves.
_____ 7. I have a pleasant, good feeling when I win a point in an argument.
_____ 8. When I finish arguing with someone I feel nervous and upset.
_____ 9. I enjoy a good argument over a controversial issue.
_____ 10. I get an unpleasant feeling when I realize I am about to get into an argument.
_____ 11. I enjoy defending my point of view on an issue.
_____ 12. I am happy when I keep an argument from happening.
_____ 13. I do not like to miss the opportunity to argue a controversial issue.
_____ 14. I prefer being with people who rarely disagree with me.
_____ 15. I consider an argument an exciting intellectual challenge.
_____ 16. I find myself unable to think of effective points during an argument.
_____ 17. I feel refreshed and satisfied after an argument on a controversial issue.
_____ 18. I have the ability to do well in an argument.
_____ 19. I try to avoid getting into arguments.
_____ 20. I feel excitement when I expect that a conversation I am in is leading to an argument.

From A conceptualization and measure of argumentativeness, by D. A. Infante and D. S. Rancer, 1982, *Journal of Personality Assessment, 46*, 72–80. Copyright © 1982 by Lawrence Erlbaum Associates, Inc. Reprinted by permission.

measures offer several advantages. They have known psychometric properties, that is, their reliability and validity have been established. They are also efficient, do not require extensive training, and are easy to administer and score (Fischer and Corcoran, 1994).

## DESIGNING THE EVALUATION

Having established measurable goals and selected measurement strategies, the next step is to determine how you are going to implement the evaluation process. The term *evaluation design* is often used to describe how practitioners plan to evaluate progress and case outcomes (Bloom, Fischer, and Orme, 1995). One of the most widely used ways to evaluate practice effectiveness in social work is the single-system design (Miley, O'Melia, and DuBois, 1998). *Single-system designs* are sometimes referred to as single-case designs, N = 1 designs, interrupted time–series designs, and subject-replication designs. "Whatever name is used, a formal case-level evaluation is a study of one entity—a single client, a single group, a single couple, a single family, a single organization, or a single community—involving repeated measurements over time in order to measure change" (Gabor, Unrau, and Grinnell, 1998, p. 175).

Single-system designs hold great promise for generalist social workers. The requirements for using them fit well with generalist practice principles. Single-system designs require clear specification of the target problem, development of measurable goals, selection and implementation of an intervention, and continued monitoring of the client's progress on the identified target problem. All these requirements are consistent with the requirements of sound generalist social work practice.

Bloom, Fischer, and Orme (1999) provide a comprehensive and detailed description of numerous types of single-system designs (see also Tripodi, 1994). However, as Berlin and Marsh point out, "the types of designs that are likely to be used in an ongoing way in practice are more limited" (1993, p. 120). The single-system design selected depends primarily on what questions you are attempting to answer (Berlin and Marsh, 1993). Two questions appropriate for generalist social work practice evaluations are: Is the intervention working? and Is the intervention causing the change?

More complex experimental designs provide information on the causal effect of the intervention. Did the client system improve because of the intervention? What aspects of the intervention are most important in causing the change? Answers to such questions contribute to social work knowledge. They help document the effectiveness of various interventions with different types of clients and target problems. However, answering questions about causality and implementing experiential type designs are beyond the level of evaluation expected for generalist social work practitioners. They are better addressed through research than through ongoing social work practice with clients.

As social workers, we have a responsibility to promote the well-being of our clients (NASW, 1997). This entails, in part, assessing the effectiveness of our interventions. Is the client making progress? Does the intervention appear to be working? Is the target problem improving, getting worse, or staying the same? This book focuses only on designs that provide information on client progress. Such designs best fit generalist social work practice. They are easy to implement with client systems, and they provide important information on the effectiveness of the work.

## Components of Single-System Designs

There are a number of single-system evaluation designs. Some components are common to all of them. The basic components of single-subject designs are

- Specifying the target problem
- Developing quantitative measures of the target problem
- Establishing baseline measures of the target problem before intervention
- Measuring the target problem repeatedly throughout the intervention
- Displaying the data on a graph
- Making comparisons across phases

Specifying the target problem, developing measures, and displaying data on graphs discussed earlier.

**Establishing Baselines**   The **baseline** is the measure of the target problem before the worker provides service. Repeated measurements prior to the intervention are necessary to establish a baseline. The baseline allows you to compare the client's target problem before and after the intervention (Marlow, 1998).

There are two types of baselines. For the **concurrent baseline,** data are collected while other assessment activities are taking place. Repeated measures of the target problem are collected before you implement an intervention with the client system. For the **retrospective baseline,** the client reconstructs measures of the target problem from an earlier time period, using his or her memory. In many situations, delaying the intervention while a concurrent baseline is obtained is unacceptable. For example, it would be unethical to delay providing counseling services to people who experienced a traumatic event, such as a school shooting, in order to obtain baseline information on the victims' level of traumatic stress. In such cases, using a retrospective baseline is an acceptable alternative.

A common question is how many data points or measurements are needed for the baseline. The answer is that it depends. For meaningful comparisons to be made between the preintervention (baseline) and the intervention phases, the baseline has to be stable. That is, there has to be an observable pattern of measurement scores during the baseline period. "A stable baseline is one that does not contain obvious cycles or wide fluctuations in the data" (Bloom, Fischer, and Orme, 1995, p. 333). Fluctuations are acceptable only if they occur with some regularity (Marlow, 1998). Thus, ideally, the baseline phase does not end until the baseline is stable. How long this takes is influenced, in part, by the amount of variation between the data points. The greater the variation (range of scores), the more data points needed to achieve stability. Conversely, if the variation between points on the baseline is relatively small (similar scores), fewer data points are needed to achieve stability.

Using an unstable baseline is problematic. If the measures of the target problem fluctuate widely and no pattern exists, it is difficult to determine what factors are affecting changes in the target problem and whether change has occurred once the intervention starts (Bloom, Fischer, and Orme, 1995). In other words, it is unclear whether changes between the baseline and the intervention phases are due to usual fluctuations in the target problem or if change has actually taken place.

**Making Comparisons**    Assessing change requires making some sort of comparison. In traditional experimental evaluation designs, a treatment group is compared with a control group that does not receive treatment. In case evaluations using single-system designs, the client provides the basis for comparison. In essence, the client serves as his or her own control group. Is the client better after getting help than before? Without comparisons, it is impossible to assess change.

Work with clients can be divided into phases (Gabor, Unrau, and Grinnell, 1998). During the first few contacts, baseline data on the target problem may be collected; this is the assessment phase. The second phase is the next series of sessions, in which an intervention is implemented. If the first intervention did not achieve the desired results, a second intervention may be tried; this would be the third phrase.

FIGURE 9.11 | SAMPLE AB DESIGN

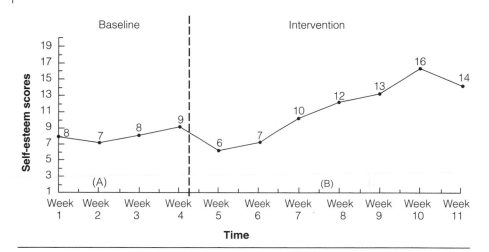

Single-system evaluations use letters to label the different phases. The letter *A* is used to designate the baseline phase. "Successive interventions are represented by successive letters: B for the first, C for the second, D for the third, and so on" (Gabor, Unrau, and Grinnell, 1998, p. 180). A single-system design that consists of a baseline phase followed by an intervention is called an **AB design.** An evaluation that does not have a baseline and only one intervention is called a **B design.** An **ABA design** is one in which a baseline (*A*) phase is followed by an intervention (*B*) phase and a second baseline (*A*) period. The various phases of a single-subject design are usually labeled on the line graph and represented by dashed vertical lines. Figure 9.11 is a line graph of an AB design.

The AB design is the most frequently used single-system design in service settings (Berlin and Marsh, 1993). In this design, repeated measurements of the target problem are taken during the baseline (*A*) and intervention (*B*) phases. Measures of the target problem are taken before the intervention is implemented and throughout the intervention. As with all single-system evaluations, the findings are analyzed by plotting the data points on a chart.

The advantage of the AB design is its simplicity (Marlow, 1998). One must merely identify or develop an appropriate measurement of the target problem and then take repeated measurements during the first baseline phase and the intervention phase. This design can easily be incorporated into generalist social work practice. It is consistent with normal practice procedures in that an assessment data-gathering phase is followed by an intervention phase (Berlin and Marsh, 1993). The design usually does not compromise or hinder the development of a helping relationship and the provision of service. It fits well into a collaborative model of generalist practice, and it provides evidence of whether the intervention is working.

The one area of potential difficulty with the AB design is obtaining a baseline. This is a problem with all single-system designs used to evaluate ongoing practice with client systems. Delaying the intervention while baseline data is collected is problematic when the situation warrants immediate attention. Obtaining measures of the target problem over a prolonged period of time often is not feasible or desirable. In these situations, developing a retrospective baseline is best. You and the client construct a baseline from the client's recollection of the target problem in the recent past. Although it is a compromise, a retrospective baseline provides a basis of comparison to answer the fundamental question: Is the intervention working?

The B design is the preferred option when it is necessary to intervene immediately, as in a crisis situation, without collecting baseline information or retrospective baseline information (Berlin and Marsh, 1993). The B design is often referred to as a **monitoring design** (Miley, O'Melia, and DuBois, 1998) or a **case study design** (Bloom, Fischer, and Orme, 1999). It consists solely of an intervention (B) phase. Repeated measures of the target problem are taken throughout the intervention. This design is weaker than the AB design because preintervention comparison data are not available. It does, however, provide information on client progress, whether the target problem is improving, and whether the goals of the intervention have been achieved.

A third design that can be used to evaluate client progress is the **ABC design,** or the **successive intervention design.** This design is an extension of the AB design. It entails the introduction of a second intervention (C) phase. If additional interventions are added beyond the second (C), they are labeled D, E, and so on. The ABC design is used when the first (B) intervention is modified or when the first intervention does not appear to be working. It does not provide information on which intervention caused change in the target problem, nor does it allow for separation of the effects of the successive interventions. It does, however, provide information on client progress.

## ANALYZING SINGLE-SYSTEM DATA

Single-system design data is plotted on line graphs similar to those in Figures 9.11 and 9.12. Three types of significance can be used to judge change in the target problem: clinical, visual, and statistical.

## Clinical Significance

Clinical significance, also known as **practical significance,** is based on the idea "that somebody—especially the client—believes that there has been meaningful change in the problem" (Bloom, Fischer, and Orme, 1999, p. 506). Clinical significance is achieved when the specified goal of the intervention has been reached (Marlow, 1998). Determining clinical significance is generally a subjective process that requires discussion and negotiation among the involved parties (Bloom, Fischer, and Orme, 1999). If everyone involved agrees that the target problem has been resolved, clinical significance has been achieved.

FIGURE 9.12 | THREE TYPES OF STEADY DATA TRENDS

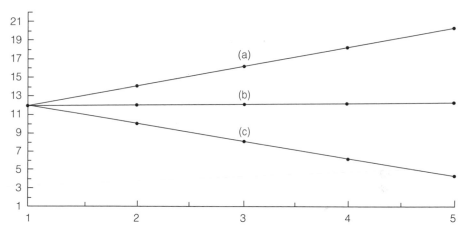

From *Fundamental approaches to single subject design and analysis* by C. H. Krishef. Copyright © 1991 by Krieger Publishing Company. Reprinted with permission.

Determining clinical significance when a goal has not been fully achieved is more difficult: How much change is clinically meaningful? There are no criteria for establishing the clinical significance of partial change in the target problem. Client change can be considered clinically significant if those involved in the helping process agree that meaningful change has occurred.

## Visual Significance

Visual analysis is used for data that has been collected over time. It focuses on the trend and direction of the data (Krishef, 1991). A **trend** occurs when data points move directionally in a relatively steady manner. Figure 9.12 shows three basic steady trends. "The 'a' line represents a steadily increasing pattern, the 'b' line displays steadiness of the data without either positive or negative direction, and the 'c' line depicts a steadily decreasing data pattern" (Krishef, 1991, p. 43).

Visual analysis also focuses on changes in the level of the data (Berlin and Marsh, 1993; Marlow, 1998). **Level** refers to the magnitude of the data. For example, a change in level occurs when scores that were at 2 or 3 in the baseline stage jump to 8 or 9 during the intervention stage. Figure 9.13 shows a line graph in which there is a change in the level of the data.

Data in which there are no discernible trends or patterns are considered **unstable.** Unstable data show wide fluctuations in the measurement of the target problem (Figure 9.14). The interpretation of unstable data is difficult. Little can be said beyond the fact that there is no pattern and the scores vary widely.

The visual analysis of single-system data is based primarily on a comparison of the baseline and intervention phases. For meaningful comparisons to

FIGURE 9.13 | CHANGE IN LEVEL OF DATA

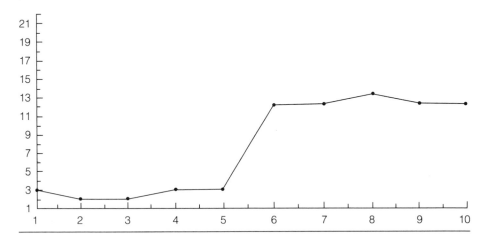

FIGURE 9.14 | UNSTABLE DATA

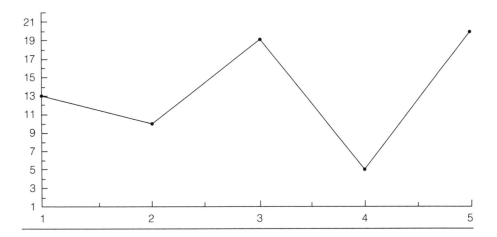

be made, the baseline data must be stable. If they are not, interpretation of the effect of the intervention is impossible. Interpretation is also difficult if the baseline data are moving steadily in a direction that would represent improvement on the target problem. For example, if a decrease in occurrence of the target problem represents client improvement and the baseline trend shows a steady decline on the measure, it would be difficult to attribute the improved scores to the effectiveness of the intervention, because the data were already moving in the desired direction (Krishef, 1991).

Figure 9.15 shows nine configurations of change in the baseline and intervention phases. Determining change is unequivocal when the baseline is stable

FIGURE 9.15 | POSSIBLE CONFIGURATIONS OF CHANGE
IN BASELINE AND INTERVENTION PHASES

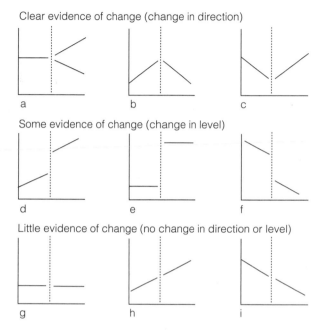

From S. Berlin and J. Marsh, *Informing practice decisions*. Copyright © 1993 by Allyn & Bacon. Reprinted by permission of the publisher.

and the intervention has a sharply increasing or decreasing trend, as in panel a in Figure 9.15, or when the trend at the intervention phase is in the opposite direction of the trend at baseline (panels b and c). The strongest change is when there is a shift in both trend and level in the improved direction (Berlin and Marsh, 1993). Figure 9.14 shows unstable data with no trends.

Calculating a celeration line helps visually determine a trend in the data (Bloom, Fischer, and Orme, 1999). A **celeration line** connects the midpoints of the first and second halves of the baseline phase and extends into the intervention phase (Figure 9.16). The basic idea is that the trend established during the baseline phase is an estimate of what would happen if the baseline pattern were to continue and there were no intervention.

The steps involved in calculating a celeration line are as follows:

1.   Plot the baseline and intervention data on a line graph.
2.   Divide the baseline section of the line graph in half, drawing a vertical line. If there are an even number of data points in the baseline, draw the line between the data points; if there are an odd number of points, draw the line through the midpoint number.

FIGURE 9.16  |  LINE GRAPH WITH CELERATION LINE

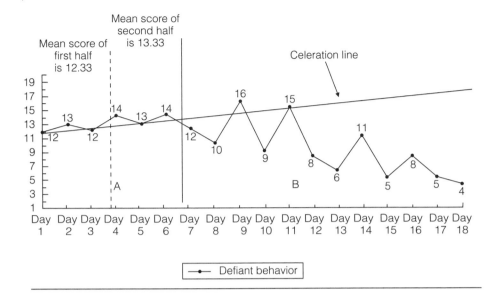

3. Divide each half into half by drawing dashed vertical lines on the chart.
4. Determine the mean score of the first half of the baseline by adding the scores in the half and dividing by the number of scores in the half. For baselines with an odd number of scores, omit the middle number.
5. Determine the mean score of the second half of the baseline by adding the scores in the half and dividing by the number of scores in the half. For baselines with an odd number of scores, omit the middle number.
6. Mark the dashed vertical line at the mean point for each half.
7. Draw a solid line connecting the two marks in the baseline, and extend the line through the intervention phase.

## Statistical Significance

Statistical analysis of single-system data has become an accepted practice (Berlin and Marsh, 1993). There are a number of methods for determining statistical significance of time-series data (see Bloom, Fischer, and Orme, 1999, for a detailed discussion). One straightforward method for calculating statistical significance of single-system data is the **two standard deviation approach.** This approach, as its name suggests, is based on the **standard deviation,** which measures the dispersion of scores around the mean.

The basic idea is that ± 2 standard deviations (SD) represents about 95 percent of the scores, and the likelihood that 2 scores would fall outside of ± 2 SD is less than 5 times in a hundred. Thus, if two or more scores fall out-

FIGURE 9.17 | LINE GRAPH WITH TWO STANDARD DEVIATION APPROACH

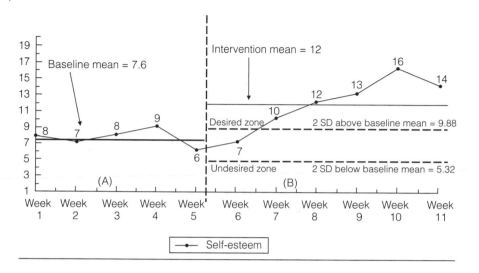

side the two standard deviation band, we assume that statistically significant change has occurred. The two standard deviation approach was developed by Shewart (1931) for industrial evaluation and was first used with single-system data by Gottman and Leiblum (1974). The approach offers many advantages: "The procedure can be completed easily with a hand calculator, it can be completed even with 'short' baselines (i.e., when there are fewer than ten points in the baseline)" (Berlin and Marsh, 1993, p. 135).

The steps involved in calculating the two standard deviation approach are shown in Case 9.1.

Interpretation of the two standard deviation approach is simple. Plot the bands representing 2 SD above and below the baseline mean on a line graph that contains baseline and intervention scores. If two consecutive data points in the intervention phase go beyond the 2 SD band, the results show change that is statistically significant at the .05 level. If two or more data points go beyond the band in the desired direction, the results show improvement that is statistically significant at the .05 level. If two or more data points go beyond the band in the undesired direction, the results show deterioration that is statistically significant at the .05 level (Bloom, Fischer, and Orme, 1999). Figure 9.17 is a line graph in which the two standard deviation approach is used.

Incorporating existing measures or developing your own instruments is a critical component of responsible generalist social work practice. In almost every practice setting, social workers are required to show effectiveness and to document client progress. Measurement and practice are becoming interdependent. No longer is an understanding of evaluation methods left to researchers. It is something that all social workers need to understand and master.

| CASE 9.1 | STEPS FOR COMPUTING TWO STANDARD DEVIATION BAND APPROACH* |

| Computational steps | Data |
| --- | --- |

1. Record baseline observations.

$$
\begin{array}{c}
x \\
\hline
6 \\
6 \\
5 \\
4 \\
3 \\
\end{array}
$$

2. Sum ($\Sigma$) these scores.

3. Calculate mean:
   divide sum by $n$ where $n$ is the
   number of scores in baseline phase.
   $$\left( \text{Mean} = \bar{x} = \frac{\Sigma x_i}{n} \right)$$

$$
\begin{array}{c}
4 \\
4 \\
5 \\
5 \\
4 \\
\hline
46 \; / \; 10 = 4.6 = \text{mean} = \bar{x}
\end{array}
$$

4. Calculate standard deviation:
   find $(x - \bar{x})$ for all scores, then $(x - \bar{x})^2$, then sum
   and divide by $(n - 1)$.
   Find the square root.
   $$\left( \text{Standard Deviation} = \sqrt{\frac{\Sigma(x - \bar{x})^2}{n - 1}} \right)$$

| $x$ | $(x - \bar{x})$ | $(x - \bar{x})^2$ |
| --- | --- | --- |
| 6 | 1.4 | 1.96 |
| 6 | 1.4 | 1.96 |
| 5 | .4 | .16 |
| 4 | − .6 | .36 |
| 3 | −1.6 | 2.56 |
| 4 | − .6 | .36 |
| 4 | − .6 | .36 |
| 5 | .4 | .16 |
| 5 | .4 | .16 |
| 4 | − .6 | .36 |
| 46 | 0 | 8.40 / 9 = .93 |

$$\sqrt{.93} = .96$$

5. Form the two standard deviation band by
   doubling the standard deviation, adding it to the
   mean for the upper band, and subtracting it from
   the mean for the lower band.

$2 \times .96 = 1.92$
$4.6 + 1.92 = 6.5$
$4.6 - 1.92 = 2.7$

6. Plot the upper and lower bands around the mean.

7. If two consecutive data points during the intervention phase drift outside the standard deviation line,
   there is evidence for a statistically significant shift.

*From S. Berlin and J. Marsh, *Informing practice decisions*. Published by Allyn and Bacon, Boston, MA. Copyright © 1993 by Pearson Education. Reprinted by permission of the publisher.

## SUMMARY

Evaluation is not separate from social work practice; it is an integrated part of generalist social work practice. The reasons for evaluating client progress are many. Social workers have an ethical responsibility to provide the best services available to their clients and to make sure that the services are helping. To assume that what you are doing is working without systematically evaluating effectiveness is unethical. If the client is not making progress, both of you need to know.

Guidelines for collecting evaluation data stress the importance of clearly specifying problems and goals. Multiple measures should be used to assess each goal; only relevant information should be collected; and measurement should begin as early as possible in the helping process. An important consideration in selecting measures is the reliability and validity of the instrument.

Five types of measures can easily be used in evaluating practice. Client logs help clients monitor their own behaviors, thoughts, or feelings. Logs can be a powerful tool not only in documenting the occurrence of specific behaviors but also in helping clients clarify the nature of problems and problem situations.

Behavioral observation is similar to client log recording, except that someone other than the client does the recording. The other person, who may be a parent or a teacher, observes the client and records the frequency of specified behaviors. Behavioral observation can provide detailed information on the occurrence of client behaviors and the context of those behaviors.

Rating scales are easy to construct and use. Individualized rating scales incorporate the client's own descriptions of the desired changes. The scale is the client's own personal measure of progress. General rating scales are also created by the worker and client to measure desired changes. They are "general" in that the client does not describe in specific terms the lower and upper points of the scale. More general descriptors are used.

Goal attainment scales are similar to individualized rating scales in that the client develops and defines the scale anchors. They differ in that goal attainment scales are based directly on the client's goals rather than on behaviors, thoughts, or feelings. Their strength is that they can be used to directly monitor progress on the identified goals.

Standardized measures are instruments that have been developed following empirical scale construction techniques. The advantage of standardized measures is that they have established reliability and validity. There may or may not be standardized measures available that fit the identified target problem. If standardized measures are available that closely correspond to the identified client concerns, their use in evaluation is recommended.

Three single-system evaluation designs are easily incorporated into generalist social work practice. The AB design is the most frequently used single-system design in social service settings. In this design, repeated measurements of the target problem are taken during the baseline and intervention phases. Baseline data may be collected concurrently or retrospectively. This design fits well with the collaborative model of generalist practice, and it provides evidence of client progress.

The case study, or B design, is the preferred option when it is necessary to intervene immediately without collecting baseline information or even retrospective baseline information. This design is weaker than the AB design because of the lack of preintervention comparison data. Nevertheless, it does provide information on client progress.

The ABC design can be used to evaluate additional interventions. This design is used when the first intervention is modified or does not appear to be working. A second intervention is added and monitored. Additional interventions are labeled *D, E,* and so forth.

Analysis of single-system design data is derived from an examination of the data on line graphs. The data points are plotted and can be examined visually and statistically. In both methods, the baseline data points are compared with the intervention data points. Visual significance occurs when there is a distinct change in the pattern of the data points between the baseline and intervention phases. Statistical significance can be determined by the two standard deviation method.

The intervention and evaluation plan specifies what will be done by whom to achieve the identified goals as well as how progress on the goals will be evaluated. It is the contract between the worker and the client regarding the helping process. It is the plan of action that the social worker and client lay out in response to the client's problems and concerns. However, it should not be viewed as fixed once it has been developed. Priorities, goals, and plans often change and are modified as the helping process unfolds.

## CASE EXAMPLE

The following case study consists of an intervention and evaluation plan for Theodore J., who was introduced in Chapter 5. Denise Bubel prepared it when she was a first-year MSW student placed in an adult partial hospitalization program.

---

 **CASE 9.2** | **THEODORE J.'S INTERVENTION AND EVALUATION PLAN**

**Problem Situation and Case Assessment Summary**

Mr. J. is an 82-year-old Caucasian who lives with his 80-year-old wife. He attends the adult partial hospitalization program five days a week. He has been diagnosed with irreversible dementia. He suffers from memory loss and cognitive decline, which cause him frustration and anxiety. He also has strong feelings of shame and embarrassment about his medical condition. Mrs. J. is very stressed and is having difficulty coping with the demands of his care and his deteriorating health.

**Change Goals:**

Goal 1: To have Mr. J. take more responsibility for himself.

Goal 2: To reduce Mr. J.'s feelings of shame and embarrassment about his incontinence.

Goal 3: To reduce Mrs. J.'s level of stress.

### Goal, Intervention, Evaluation Worksheet (1)

**Goal:** To have Mr. J take more responsibility for himself.

**Objective:** Mr. J. will review his daily "to do" list every day before each meal by December 1.

**Objective:** Mr. J. will take his medications every day at noon without being told to by his social worker or his wife by December 1.

**Intervention Activities:**

**Client:** Mr. J. will meet with his social worker at least once a day during the week to identify and discuss memory aid strategies.

**Worker:** Mr. J.'s social worker will meet with him daily to discuss memory aid strategies and to reinforce his taking responsibility for self-care.

The social worker will monitor Mr. J.'s compliance in reviewing his "to do" list before his breakfast and noon meals.

The social worker will monitor Mr. J.'s compliance in taking his medications before his noon meal.

The social worker will review with Mr. J. his progress at the end of each week.

**Others:** Mrs. J. will monitor Mr. J.'s compliance in reviewing his "to do" list before his meals on the weekends.

Mrs. J. will monitor Mr. J.'s compliance in taking his medications before his noon meal.

Mrs. J. will report Mr. J.'s weekend compliance to the social worker every Monday morning.

**Evaluation and Measurement:**

At the end of each week the social worker and Mr. J. will complete the two goal attainment scales.

**Goal Attainment Scales**

| Level | Objective 1: Review "to do" before each meal | Objective 2: Take noon meds every day |
|---|---|---|
| Most unfavorable – 2 | 0 to 20% of the time | Never |
| Less than expected – 1 | 21% to 40% of the time | Remembers 1–2 days |
| Expected 0 | 41% to 60% of the time | Remembers 3–4 days |
| More than expected + 1 | 61% to 80% of the time | Remembers 4–5 days |
| Most favorable + 2 | 81% to 100% of the time | Remembers 6–7 days |

### Goal, Intervention, Evaluation Worksheet (2)

**Goal:** To reduce Mr. J.'s feelings of shame and embarrassment about his incontinence.

**Objective:** Mr. J. will acknowledge his feelings of shame and embarrassment about his incontinence in his support group by October 1.

**Objective:** Mr. J. will feel comfortable going in public wearing undergarments designed for incontinence by November 1.

**Intervention Activities:**

**Client:** Mr. J. will attend his daily support group at the adult partial hospitalization program.

Mr. J. will meet with his social worker once a day to discuss his feelings about his incontinence.

**Worker:** The social worker will provide individual counseling to Mr. J. on a daily basis.

The social worker will monitor Mr. J.'s participation in his support group.

The social worker will review with Mr. J. his progress at the end of each week.

**Others:** Mrs. J. will encourage Mr. J. to wear adult undergarments when they go out in public.

**Evaluation and Measurement:**

The social worker will monitor Mr. J.'s participation in the support group and his willingness to discuss his concerns about his incontinence.

At the end of each week the social worker and Mr. J. will complete the public comfort rating scale.

Feelings of comfort in public
over incontinence issues

| I am not comfortable going in public | | | I am somewhat comfortable going in public | | | I am comfortable going in public | | |
|---|---|---|---|---|---|---|---|---|
| 1 | 2 | 3 | 4 | 5 | 6 | 7 | 8 | 9 |

### Goal, Intervention, Evaluation Worksheet (3)

**Goal:** To reduce Mrs. J.'s level of stress.

**Objective:** Mrs. J. will have a home health aide to help her care for her husband by October 1.

**Objective:** Mrs. J. will use relaxation techniques when she feels stressed by November 1.

**Intervention Activities:**

**Client:** Mrs. J. will apply for home health aide services.

*(continued)*

CASE 9.2 | *continued*

Mrs. J. will learn and practice relaxation techniques.
**Worker:** The social worker will provide Mrs. J. with a referral to the home health care agency.
The social worker will teach Mrs. J. relaxation techniques.
The social worker will meet with Mrs. J. once a month to review her situation.
**Others:**

**Evaluation and Measurement:**
The social worker will monitor Mrs. J.'s referral for home health care.
Once a month the social worker and Mrs. J. will meet to discuss the effectiveness of the relaxation techniques.
Once a month Mrs. J. will complete the Index of Clinical Stress (Hudson and Abell, 1992).

---

## DISCUSSION QUESTIONS

1. How realistic are the stated goals and objectives for Mr. and Mrs. J. (Case 9.2)? Does the measurement and evaluation plan appear to be appropriate? How else might one assess progress on the goals? How would you proceed in evaluating progress?

2. Mrs. J. is reported to be very stressed and is having difficulty coping with the demands of her husband's care and deteriorating health. What interventions would be appropriate to help Mrs. J. cope with her situation? Would a stress management approach be warranted? For information on stress management techniques and concepts, see Greenberg 2001.

3. Discuss the use of evaluation in your field placement. How is progress evaluated? What roles do clients play in the process? How could you strengthen the evaluative component of the social work services provided by your field placement agency?

4. Discuss the strengths and limitations of the five types of measures commonly used in single-system design evaluation. Under what conditions could you incorporate their use in your generalist practice? In what ways would you have difficulty using these types of measures in your practice?

5. Discuss possible ways of introducing clients to the idea of using a single-system evaluation design. List the major points you would cover, and identify possible concerns clients might have about measurement and graphing.

## REFERENCES

Applegate, J. (1992). The impact of subjective measures on nonbehavioral practice research: Outcome vs. process. *Families in Society, 73,* 100–109.

Barlow, D., Hayes, S., and Nelson, R. (1984). *The scientist practitioner.* New York: Pergamon Press.

Berlin, S., and Marsh, J. (1993). *Informing practice decisions.* New York: Macmillan.

Bloom, M., Fischer, J., and Orme, J. (1995). *Evaluating practice: Guidelines for the accountable professional* (2nd ed.). Boston: Allyn and Bacon.

Bloom, M., Fischer, J., and Orme, J. (1999). *Evaluating practice: Guidelines for the accountable professional* (3rd ed.). Boston: Allyn and Bacon.

Campbell, J. (1988). Client acceptance of single-system evaluation procedures. *Social Work Research and Abstracts, 24,* 21–22.

Campbell, J. (1990). Ability of practitioners to estimate client acceptance of single-system evaluation procedures. *Social Work, 35,* 9–14.

Corcoran, K. (1992). Practice evaluation: Setting goals, measuring and assessing change. In K. Corcoran (Ed.), *Structuring change: Effective practice for common client problems* (pp. 28–47). Chicago: Lyceum.

Coulton, C. J., and Solomon, P. L. (1977). Measuring outcomes of intervention. *Social Work Research and Abstracts, 13,* 3–9.

Fischer, J., and Corcoran, K. (1994). *Measures for clinical practice: A sourcebook* (Volumes 1 and 2, 2nd ed.). New York: Free Press.

Franklin, C., and Jordan, C. (1992). Teaching students to perform assessment. *The Journal of Social Work Education, 28,* 222–241.

Gabor, P. A., Unrau, Y. A., and Grinnell, R. M. (1998). *Evaluation for social workers: A quality improvement approach for the social services.* Boston: Allyn and Bacon.

Gingerich, W. (1979). Procedure for evaluating clinical practice. *Health and Social Work, 4,* 104–130.

Gottman, J. M., and Leiblum, S. R. (1974). *How to do psychotherapy and how to evaluate it.* New York: Holt, Rinehart and Winston.

Greenberg, J. S. (2001). *Comprehensive stress management* (7th ed.). New York: McGraw-Hill.

Haynes, S. N. (1978). *Principles of behavioral assessment.* New York: Gardner.

Hudson, W. (1982). *The clinical measurement package: A field manual.* Homewood, IL: Dorsey Press.

Hudson, W., and Abell, N. (1992). *Index of clinical stress (ICS).* Tallahassee, FL: WALMYR Publishing Co.

Infante, D. A., and Rancer, A. S. (1982). A conceptualization and measure of argumentativeness. *Journal of Personality Assessment, 46,* 72–80.

Jordan, C., and Franklin, C. (1995). *Clinical assessment for social workers: Quantitative and qualitative methods.* Chicago: Lyceum.

Krishef, C. H. (1991). *Fundamental approaches to single subject design and analysis.* Malabar, FL: Krieger Publishing Company.

Kyte, N. S., and Bostwick, G. (1997). Measuring variables. In R. M. Grinnell, Jr. (Ed.), *Social work research and evaluation: Quantitative and qualitative approaches* (5th ed., pp. 161–183). Itasca, IL: F. E. Peacock Publishing, Inc.

Maluccio, A., and Marlow, W. (1974). The case for contract. *Social Work, 19,* 28–35.

Marlow, C. (1998). *Research methods for generalist social work* (2nd ed.). Pacific Grove, CA: Brooks/Cole.

Miley, K. K., O'Melia, M., and DuBois, B. L. (1998). *Generalist social work practice: An empowering approach* (2nd ed.). Boston: Allyn and Bacon.

National Association of Social Workers (1997). *Code of ethics.* Washington, DC: NASW Press.

Nugent, W. R. (1992). Psychometric characteristics of self-anchored scales in clinical application. *Journal of Social Service Research, 3,* 137–152.

Poulin, J., and Young, T. (1997). Development of a helping relationship inventory for social work practice. *Research on Social Work Practice, 7,* 463–489.

Robinson, J. P., Shaver, P., and Wrightsman, L. S. (1991). *Measures of personality and social psychological atti-tudes.* San Diego, CA: Academic Press.

Royse, D., and Thyer, B. (1996). *Program evaluation: An introduction.* Chicago: Nelson-Hall.

Seaburg, J. R., and Gillespie, D. F. (1977). Goal attainment scaling: A critique. *Social Work Research and Abstracts, 13,* 43–56.

Seabury, B. (1976). The contract uses, abuses, and limitations. *Social Work, 21,* 16–21.

Shewart, W. A. (1931). *Economic control of quality of manufactured products.* New York: Van Nostrand Reinhold.

Tripodi, T. (1994). *A primer on single-system design for clinical social workers.* Washington, DC: NASW Press.

WALMYR Publishing Co., P.O. Box 12217, Tallahassee, FL 32317-12217, (850) 383-0045. Internet: www.syspac .com/~walmyr/wpchome.htm.

Witkin, S. (1991). Empirical clinical prac-tice: A critical analysis. *Social Work, 36,* 158–163.

Young, T., and Poulin, J. (1998). The helping relationship inventory: A clinical appraisal. *Families in Society, 79,* 123–133.

# GENERALIST PRACTICE WITH ECONOMICALLY DISADVANTAGED CLIENTS AND COMMUNITIES

*Stephen E. Kauffman*

Kelly K. is a first-year MSW student placed in a community-based program that provides consultation services to grassroots human service programs in an economically disadvantaged community with numerous social problems. The agency's mission is to increase the number of services available to community residents as well as to strengthen the capacities of the local service organizations. Kelly is developing a collaborative program with the local legal aid clinic. The clinic provides legal services to the low-income residents, many of whom also need social work and case management services. The objective is to develop a program that will provide social work and case management services to the legal aid clients.

Kelly is excited and overwhelmed about helping develop a new service for the residents that would also strengthen an existing community agency. She knows that her first step is to learn all she can about the community and the experiences of the low-income residents who will use the new program. What is it like to be a member of a disadvantaged community? What is it like to be poor? What kinds of services and assistance do the potential clients need? How is working with disadvantaged communities and citizens different than working with other client populations? In what ways is it similar? What professional and community groups need to be involved in the planning process?

Poverty is without question the most ubiquitous, complex, and intractable of all social problems. It is a worldwide issue of concern, and it affects individuals and families in rich and poor nations alike. Poverty is often associated with a wide variety of other social problems, including substance abuse, domestic violence, disease, and environmental degradation. As a result, understanding poverty and developing skills for working with the poor are critical elements of effective generalist social work practice.

Social work owes its existence to the problem of poverty. The very first social workers, the Charity Organization Society and the settlement house volunteers, were driven by a concern for the poor. From these two groups of early social workers evolved the basic micro and macro practice approaches that are the core of the profession today. Such contemporary practice methods as case management, advocacy, community organization, and policy development all are linked to the historical relationship between the profession and the problem of poverty.

Although social work practice areas today are often diverse and the populations that social workers serve demonstrate a range of problems and economic classes, the issue of poverty is as important as it was a hundred years ago. Many of the principles of social work practice and the values of the profession are defined by the relationship of the profession to the poor. The concept of empowerment, for example, comes in part from recognition that discrimination and oppression are among poverty's most important causes. Empowering individuals and communities is therefore a significant tool for remedying these problems. Similarly, much of the curriculum in social work education is oriented toward educating students to understand the problem of poverty and develop skills to work with the poor.

In light of the critical necessity for social workers to understand poverty, this chapter examines the issues associated with generalist practice with the poor. The goals of the chapter are to provide an understanding of poverty and to equip you with some essential tools for effective interventions with economically disadvantaged clients. The chapter discusses the size and scope of the problem, macro policy issues, micro and macro practice issues, including various theories about the causes of poverty, and issues related to human behavior and social environment, including the consequences of poverty for individuals, families, and communities. The chapter also examines practice issues for social workers that engage in generalist practice with economically distressed clients and communities. By the end of this chapter, you should be able to help Kelly

1. Describe and critique the way poverty is measured in the United States
2. Understand the individual and social causes of poverty
3. Examine the economic and political factors that contribute to community poverty
4. Describe the consequences of poverty for individuals, families, and communities
5. Articulate the various micro and macro strategies a generalist social worker would adopt in working with economically disadvantaged clients and communities

# THE PROBLEM OF POVERTY

Poverty knows no boundaries. Three billion people around the world live on less than $2 a day (Wolfensohn, 2002), and 1.2 billion live on less than $1 a day (United Nations Development Programme, 2003). Although such extreme poverty is rare in the United States, over 32 million individuals or about 11.7 percent of the U.S. population, are poor (Proctor and Dalaker, 2002). Certain subgroups in the United States, including children, African Americans, and Latinos, have substantially higher poverty rates (Proctor and Dalaker, 2002). Many others are near the poverty threshold. Nearly 42 percent of households either live in poverty or live in a household with no more than twice the income defined as "poverty" (DeNavas-Walt and Cleveland, 2002).

Poverty has a profound effect on the American economy. Public expenditures for social welfare comprised 20.9 percent of the gross domestic product (GDP) in 1997, and the total dollar cost for all public social welfare activities was $1.505 trillion (U.S. Department of Health and Human Services, 2001). These figures include all social welfare activities, including education, which is the largest single category of expenditure. Excluding education, more than $1.1 trillion in public funds were spent on aid to the poor in 1997 alone.

The number of individuals receiving public assistance is large. **Medicaid,** the primary governmental medical assistance program for the poor, served more than 40 million Americans in 1999 (U.S. Department of Health and

Human Services, Social Security Administration, 2001). **Social Security,** a collection of programs targeting the poor and also the many Americans who could easily slip into poverty, provided benefits to 46.4 million people in 2002 (U.S. Department of Health and Human Services, Social Security Administration, 2003). The largest income support program for the poor, known as **Temporary Assistance for Needy Families (TANF),** served more than 5 million recipients in fiscal 2002 (U.S. Department of Health and Human Services, 2003). Its annual program budget was more than $16 billion. Although there have been declines in state welfare caseloads in TANF in the past few years, there is uncertainty as to whether the change reflects an improvement in the poverty picture or is simply a consequence of new, more restrictive rules.

In terms of **indirect costs,** which are costs to the economy beyond dollars spent by federal, state, and local programs, the figures are equally staggering. Looking at childhood poverty alone, the Children's Defense Fund has estimated that for every year that 14.5 million American children continue to experience poverty, their lifetime contribution to the economy will decline by approximately $130 billion. This is because poor children grow up to be less educated and less productive workers (Children's Defense Fund, 1998).

Poverty may even be more pervasive than the official statistics suggest. The number of people classified as poor depends on the way poverty is defined. Although defining poverty may seem to be a simple task, it is in fact a complex one. Definitions differ according to what is being measured.

The official U.S. definition of **poverty** is an absolute income level based on family size that changes from year to year as a result of changes in the cost of living. This income figure was initially computed using the family spending patterns, food costs, and family size of the 1950s. It used an estimate of the cost of food an individual would need for short-term survival multiplied by three to account for other living expenses (Fisher, 1992, 1995). The underlying assumption was that spending patterns for all Americans were similar. The average American family of the 1950s spent about one-third of its income on food and two-thirds on other expenses. This pattern was assumed to also apply to the poor. Using this measure, the poverty level is currently $18,100 for a family of four, with $3,080 added for each additional person in the family. The poverty line changes from year to year, but only with amounts equaling inflation.

There are questions about the adequacy of this measure (Citro and Michael, 1995; Fisher, 1995). The measure, for example, does not take into account changes in average income created by noninflationary factors such as worker productivity, which is the output of a worker per unit of work. Increased worker productivity has resulted in wage increases over the past 40 years at a pace much greater than inflation. This means that the average poor person today is "poorer" relative to the average worker than a poor person 30 years ago. Nor has the official poverty measure been adjusted for changes in spending patterns over time. The cost of food is no longer as significant an expense as it was in the past. Generally, Americans now spend a lower percentage of their income on food and a higher percentage on housing and medical care than they did in the 1950s.

Moreover, wealth, assets, power, education, and other psychological and social quality-of-life variables are not addressed by the measure. Some of these other variables might be as important as income in determining an individual's status in the larger society. For example, there is evidence that the accumulation of wealth contributes to the development of behaviors and attitudes consistent with those of the dominant culture (Sherraden, 1991), and the effect of wealth might be more important on the development of these values and behaviors than income (Yamada and Sherraden, 1997). Although this perspective has been ignored in the measurement of poverty, it has had important policy implications, with a number of governmental programs now more supportive of assets accumulation than in years past.

Nevertheless, measures of wealth indicate vast differences between the poor and other groups in the society. Median household wealth in 1995 for the poorest 20 percent of all Americans was $5,000, which compares unfavorably to the average wealth of all American households, which was $40,200, or the richest 20 percent, which was $116,232 (U.S. Bureau of the Census, 2001). By focusing on income alone, the absolute measure of poverty misses important differences between the poor and the "typical" American.

Yet the absolute poverty measure has value. It sets the income thresholds for determining benefit eligibility for many government antipoverty programs. It allows us to identify trends over time and to identify groups in the population that might require special attention. It also highlights certain risk factors for poverty that are important in the assessment process. Using this measure, the poverty rate of children is 16.3 percent; of African Americans, 22.7 percent; of Latinos, 21.4 percent; of African-American children, 30.2%; and of households headed by women, 28.6 percent (Proctor and Dalaker, 2002).

## THE CAUSES AND CONSEQUENCES OF POVERTY

The large number of people who are poor and the costs to the economy associated with poverty result in significant attention by policymakers. Thousands of federal, state, and local policies have been enacted in the last century to deal with the problem of poverty. Why does the problem remain?

There are many differing opinions about what causes poverty and, therefore, how to address the problem. Poverty is associated with almost every component of the human condition, including employment, health, values, ideology, social relations, psychological factors, and social and economic justice. Even religions have affected thinking about poverty. Thus policymakers are confronted with an extremely complicated issue, and one that changes through time.

Of course, the importance of understanding the causes of poverty is the linkage between cause and solution. Among the many approaches to the problem of poverty that have been implemented are governmental employment programs, child-care assistance, cash assistance, tax-based approaches, education and training, entrepreneurship assistance, and asset development. Some argue that none of these approaches should be used, and, in fact, the central policy thrust of recent years has been to decrease policy efforts to eradicate poverty. Here, the idea has been to remove public assistance because of a belief that assistance itself may perpetuate poverty. This belief is ingrained in the current "welfare reform" approach.

## Theories of Causation on the Micro Level

The critical question affecting policy choices about poverty as well as the effectiveness of direct practice with the poor may be: What causes poverty? An important distinction has been drawn between those who are poor through no fault of their own, "the **deserving poor**," and those whose poverty is linked to some kind of failure of personal responsibility, "the **undeserving poor**" (Katz, 1989). The deserving poor usually includes children, the elderly, women with very young children, people who are sick, and people who are disabled. The capacity of these individuals to work is limited, and there is general agreement that the provision of assistance is both acceptable and necessary.

On the other hand, poverty among able-bodied men and women creates questions about the reasons for their poverty. Causality theories have been developed to explain poverty among these individuals. In general, there are three types of theories that attempt to explain poverty causation: theories that focus on individual deficits, theories that focus on social and structural causes, and theories that link the individual with the social environment. Although each model has serious limitations, they all have some value in defining poverty.

**Individual Deficits**    Theories of poverty that focus on individual deficits suggest that poverty results from one or more of a variety of biologic, behavioral, or psychological deficits. These models suggest that the poor are poor because of genetic tendencies, such as low intelligence levels, that limit their ability to function in a modern, competitive capitalistic economy, or because of a psychological or behavioral limitation, such as laziness (Goodwin, 1983; Handler and Hasenfeld, 1991; Katz, 1989).

There is little doubt that such personal attributes as problem-solving ability and personal efforts affect the capacity to earn a living. The principal weakness of these theoretical perspectives, however, is that they do not take into account the role of the environment. Biologic, behavioral, and psychological deficits may be caused by the environment or may result from the interaction of the environment and genetic factors. Inadequate nutrition, exposure to toxic substances such as lead, instability of social relationships, poor schools, few opportunities for steady employment, and many other similar factors have all been demonstrated to affect behavior, brain development, and learning capacity (Bower, 1994).

**Social and Structural Causes**   A second set of poverty theories focuses more on the consequences of social and environmental conditions than on individual deficits as the cause of poverty. According to these models, the larger society has failed to provide the opportunities necessary for personal success or has placed roadblocks in the way of the poor. Unjust occupational and merit structures, lack of power, the inaccessibility of high-wage employment (Danziger and Gottshalk, 1995; Wilson, 1987), poor schools and limited educational opportunities, and discrimination are all seen as social conditions that cause and perpetuate poverty.

There is evidence that, at least in the past, structural factors have created or reinforced poverty. Until very recently, women, African Americans, Latinos, and other minorities experienced legal, institutionalized discrimination that limited their opportunities to move out of poverty (Polenberg, 1980). Although almost all forms of legal discrimination have now been eliminated, the legacy continues. Unintentional discriminatory acts rooted in the value systems of the past and even intentional illegal discrimination still affect employment patterns and living and social conditions.

In employment, for example, the upward mobility of women and minorities is slowed by a "glass ceiling" through which few pass. As a consequence, these groups tend to remain in lower-paying jobs, earning significantly less on average than their white male colleagues. Moreover, because women are the primary caregivers for children, their special needs, such as child care or maternity leave, affect their employment patterns.

Another structuralist perspective suggests that the foundations of poverty are deeply rooted in the social and economic organization of society. There has never been a time when poverty did not exist, and it is unclear whether, under the best of circumstances, the American economy can produce enough jobs or enough income for welfare recipients to escape poverty (Poole, 1995, 1997). Poverty, at least in terms of relative deprivation, will probably exist as long as our economy is structured as it is now.

The argument supporting this position is based in part on the perception that poverty is useful to the affluent in American society (Gans, 1976). Further, poverty is embedded in the goals, processes, and assumptions that guide the marketplace. A primary goal of a capitalistic free-market economy is efficiency in the distribution of goods and services. **Efficiency** here refers to the optimal or best price, which takes into account the demand for the product or service, competition between producers, and the cost of production. One of the predominant elements of the cost of production and, in turn, the ability of a producer to compete is the price of labor. There will always be a desire on the part of producers to spend the least amount possible for labor. One way to ensure low labor costs is to have a ready pool of the unemployed who are willing to work at low wages—what Marx (1867) referred to as the "industrial reserve army."

This ready pool of the unemployed ensures low labor costs, but in so doing serves another function for the economy. It helps keep inflation low. If everyone were employed, employers would have a difficult time finding employees. Prospective employees would be able to demand higher wages, and employers would have little choice but to pay more or risk losing the employee. To ensure an adequate return on their investments, the employers would then have to charge higher prices to their customers. As all employers would presumably face the same wage pressures, the aggregate increase in costs would result in society-wide inflation. As the cost of everything increased, workers would see their spending power decrease. To keep up with the increased cost of living, workers would demand higher wages, causing even more cost and wage increases. Thus, a pool of the unemployed improves the capacity of a producer to compete and serves to keep inflation low.

Other factors are also involved. Improvements in productivity can improve the ability of a producer to compete and keep inflation low. But such improvements may also serve to reduce the need for new workers. In addition, the globalization of the economy means that low labor costs and an even larger pool of the unemployed are available outside the United States.

A second argument supports this assertion of inevitability. The central thesis is that as wealth accumulates, reasonable investments will generate new wealth. In other words, "the rich get richer." Those without a reserve supply of cash (wealth) may be forced into borrowing money for even small household emergencies, such as car repair or a minor illness. Significant debt can accrue, and catching up may not be possible: "the poor get poorer." Wealth has been moving from the poor to the rich in recent decades (Center on Budget and Policy Priorities, 1997). In the years between 1980 and 1999, the percentage of income earned by the poorest one-fifth of Americans has fallen from 5.3% to 4.3%, while the wealthiest one-fifth have seen income grow from 41.1% to 47.2% (U.S. Bureau of the Census, 2003a). This redistribution of wealth has been caused by changes in federal tax rates that have favored high-income individuals, even as many benefit programs targeting the poor have been reduced or eliminated. This trend appears likely to continue (DiNitto, 1996; Murdock and Michael, 1996).

Structuralist perspectives have limitations. The primary issue is that many of the preconditions of poverty have been addressed by the implementation of a variety of social policies. Most forms of discrimination, for example, were made illegal with such laws as the Civil Rights Act and Voting Rights Act of the early 1960s. Unemployment and higher educational access also have less effect because of legislative actions such as unemployment insurance and student aid programs. Further, focusing on social conditions ignores the fact that some individuals thrive and become wealthy under deplorable environmental constraints, and a substantial number of children who attend the poorest schools are able to escape poverty through personal efforts.

**Individual–Social Linkages**    A third set of theories examines the relationship between individual and social causes. Perhaps the best known of these theories are those collectively titled "culture of poverty" (Lewis, 1959, 1961, 1966).

According to these theories, people have historically suffered from social constraints such as low wages, legal discrimination, and limited educational opportunities. Individuals have adapted their behaviors to the conditions in order to survive. Socially questionable behaviors are such adaptations, with crime, drug dealing, and gambling adopted as means of making a living. As families and communities accept these behaviors as tools for survival, individuals develop a tolerance for the behaviors. The behaviors and tolerance of the behaviors are passed from one generation to the next, representing a change in what constitutes normative behavior (Banfield, 1968, 1974).

At this point, culture of poverty models diverge into a more conservative and a more liberal perspective. The more conservative perspective argues that the social conditions initially leading to the antisocial behaviors have been remedied by such social policies as the Civil Rights Act and unemployment compensation. At the same time, other social policies, such as Aid to Families with Dependent Children (AFDC) or programs put in place during the War on Poverty in the early 1960s, created another form of antisocial behavior: **welfare dependency.**

The argument is that welfare dependency becomes a barrier to mainstream American life because it destroys individual initiative and creativity (Bane and Ellwood, 1994; Mead, 1986, 1992): Why work or even dream of a better life when all your needs are being met? Thus, according to this perspective, the solution to poverty is to eliminate (or at least severely restrict) welfare assistance and antipoverty programs (Gilder, 1981; Murray, 1984). This perspective has recently come to prominence and fits nicely with what have been identified as historical American beliefs about hard work and individualism (Katz, 1989).

The more liberal culture of poverty perspective, on the other hand, does not agree that the barriers of discrimination and limited opportunities were removed by the policies of the last few decades (Wilson, 1987). Although legal discrimination has been dismantled and greater educational and employment opportunities have been created, say proponents, less overt forms of discrimination continue to exist. Likewise, available employment is generally limited to low-wage occupations. The social policies put in place to help the poor are often so full of restrictions and disincentives that they help only a small percentage of those who need assistance. The policy implications of this perspective are not focused on eliminating assistance but rather on expanding it to address ongoing barriers to mainstream life while vigorously attacking the continuing problems of subtle discrimination and a low-wage economy.

So what causes individual and family poverty? While the absence of money is the core problem, the reasons given for this deficit depend very much on the values and beliefs of the person asking the question. Clearly, poverty has both a personal and a social dimension. Individuals differ in their innate abilities, motivations, and physical capacities, all of which affect their income. But at the same time, the environment's ability to nurture and the capacity and will of the social, political, and economic systems to provide or limit opportunities also play a major role. Thus, effective social work practice with the poor requires careful attention to the attitudes, behaviors, and environmental situation of the client.

## The Consequences of Poverty for Individuals and Families

There are numerous consequences of poverty for individuals and families, and the consequences are interrelated. The interrelationships make effective practice and the selection of interventions with the economically disadvantaged somewhat problematic. The consequences of poverty are often as serious for an individual, family, or community as the lack of cash itself. Thus, it often makes sense to aim interventions at the secondary problem even if the root cause, poverty, continues unabated. For individuals and families, the consequences of poverty include hunger and poor nutrition, inadequate shelter, and other deprivations.

The United States, as an advanced capitalist country, allows the marketplace to make many of its decisions about the production, distribution, and consumption of goods and services. Such decisions are usually expressed by the exchange of cash or credit for goods or services. Most people do not directly trade a good or service for some other good or service, nor do most people have the skills to produce all of the products necessary for survival. Instead, our economic system requires people to exchange some skill or form of labor for cash, which is then exchanged for the items that people need or desire.

Cash is necessary in order to purchase many of the products that are necessary for simple survival. This includes almost all of the resources needed for adequate biologic functioning, such as food, water, clothing, and shelter. A lack of any of these resources can cause stress and can lead to illness and death. Hence, the most immediate consequence of poverty is its potential effect on the capacity of an individual to survive, let alone thrive. We exist within a fairly narrow set of biologic imperatives, and if sufficient resources are not available, the consequences may be catastrophic.

**Hunger and Nutrition**    The number of hungry people in the United States is open to some debate, but the number no matter who measures it is large. Officially, in 2001, 10.7 percent of U.S. households (11.5 million) were food insecure. Of these, about 3.5 million households experienced some degree of hunger during the year (Nord, Andrews, and Carlson, 2002). Using similar methods, the U.S. Department of Agriculture found that an average of 0.07 percent of households with children (275,000 households) experienced hunger at some point in 1998–1999 (Nord and Bikel, 2002). As many as 1 in 12 American children under the age of 12 suffers from hunger (Hunger Action Coalition, *n.d.*).

Another measure of the size of the hunger problem in America comes from examining the use of services. At the federal level, 15 food and nutrition programs administered by the U.S. Food and Nutrition Service assist 1 in 6 Americans. The largest federal food program, Food Stamps, was estimated to serve 19.1 million individuals in fiscal year 2002, at a cost of $20.6 billion (U.S. Department of Agriculture, 2003a). The federal Women, Infants, and Children (WIC) program, specifically designed to address nutritional deficits, served almost 7.5 million people in 2002 (U.S. Department of Agriculture, 2003b).

The consequences of hunger and inadequate nutrition are substantial and far reaching. Problems can range from inadequate physical and mental development to death. The problem is especially acute among children. The more severe the poverty a child experiences, the more likely nutritional deficits will exist (Brown and Pollitt, 1996). A list of the possible health consequences is presented in Table 10.1.

**Shelter**   Shelter is of equal importance to food and nutrition for survival. A steady income is necessary for adequate shelter, and the two most important variables are the availability of shelter and the quality of living conditions. Both may suffer when an adequate income is not available.

For most people, housing represents the largest ongoing expense. Although 67.9 percent of American householders own their homes (U.S. Bureau of the Census, 2003b), about 43 percent of families could not afford to purchase a moderately priced home in their community (Savage, 1999), because of the down payment and mortgage requirements. The median monthly housing cost is $653, $724 if maintenance is included (U.S. Bureau of the Census, 2002b). More than 5.3 million households report that housing costs consume more than half of their total income (U.S. Department of Health and Human Services, 1999). With such high costs associated with shelter, it is not surprising that an estimated 3.5 million people, 1.35 million of them children, experience homelessness each year (Urban Institute, 2000).

The living conditions are also problematic. Over 20 percent of American households have significant external problems, including damaged roofs, sagging walls, and broken windows. Additional problems include unsafe water supplies (8%), inadequate plumbing (2%), and a complete lack of kitchen facilities (4%) (U.S. Bureau of the Census, 2002b).

Among the more important problems facing those who live in older, substandard housing is **lead poisoning.** Lead was used extensively in the past in paints, plumbing fixtures, and gasoline. Thirty million homes in the United States contain lead-painted surfaces (Congressional Quarterly Weekly Reports, 1991), and more than 80 percent of all homes built before 1978 have lead-based paint in them (Centers for Disease Control and Prevention, *n.d.*). Lead poisoning can cause learning disabilities, behavioral problems, seizures, and death. As many as one child in six has toxic levels of lead in his or her blood. Over 890,000 children in America have elevated blood lead levels, and over 22 percent of African-American children who live in older homes have toxic levels of lead in their blood (Centers for Disease Control and Prevention, 2002).

Although the severity of lead poisoning is recognized in the larger public health community, one recent study suggests that few social workers have been trained to recognize or act on the symptoms (Silver, Kauffman, and

TABLE 10.1 | LIFE-CYCLE STAGE AND MALNUTRITION EFFECTS*

| Life-Cycle Stage | Malnutrition Effects |
| --- | --- |
| Prenatal and neonatal | Low birth weight |
| | Brain damage |
| | Neural tube defect |
| | Stillbirths |
| | Growth retardation |
| | Developmental retardation |
| | Brain damage |
| | Early anemia |
| | Continuing malnutrition |
| Young children and adolescents | Developmental retardation |
| | Increased risk of infection |
| | High risk of death |
| | Blindness |
| | Anemia |
| | Delayed growth spurt |
| | Stunted height |
| | Goiter |
| | Inadequate bone mineralization |
| Adults and the elderly | Thinness |
| | Lethargy |
| | Obesity |
| | Heart disease |
| | Diabetes |
| | Hypertension and stroke |
| | Anemia |
| | Spine and hip fractures and accidents |

*World Health Organization (n.d.).

Soliman, 1998). It is highly likely that a substantial number of children have behavioral problems that might best be addressed through lead treatment interventions.

**Other Consequences**    There are many other undesirable consequences associated with poverty. Forty-one million Americans, for example, lack health insurance (U.S. Bureau of the Census, 2002). Other consequences include

- Higher rates of diseases, including cancer
- Higher family stress levels (Brooks-Gunn et al., 1995)
- Greater childhood abuse rates (U.S. Department of Health and Human Services, 1996)

- Lower levels of educational attainment
- Higher levels of mental illness
- A greater likelihood of crime victimization (U.S. Department of Justice, Bureau of Justice Statistics, *n.d.*)
- Lower income and earning potential (Mizell, 1999)
- Lower self-esteem, occupational status, and educational attainment levels (Mizell, 1999)
- Reduced access to legal assistance and health insurance (U.S. Bureau of the Census, 1995b, 1996)

With such a vast array of problems, frustration and a form of learned helplessness may also appear. Most of these consequences are due to increased stresses on the individual and the family, which result from an ongoing attempt to adapt to their situation. The effect of these stresses and traumas may carry across generations (Cattell-Gordon, 1990).

## Theories of Causation on the Macro Level

The factors affecting **community poverty** are slightly better understood and less controversial than those affecting individuals and families. A variety of interrelated factors limit the capacity of the environment to nurture. At the community level, poverty can often be traced to the interplay of two issues: economics and political power.

**Economic Issues**   Just as individuals do, communities require an adequate supply of income to pay for the services they provide. These services usually include public safety, education, infrastructure, and governance. The quality and quantity of these services are dictated, at least in part, by the tax base, or the revenues generated by personal, property, and business taxes. Other revenue sources include fees charged by the community for various services, grants from the state or federal government, and credit obtained by public debt financing (i.e., loans to the community through financial instruments such as bond sales).

In a community populated by a large percentage of middle- and upper-income wage earners or characterized by a vibrant business and commercial sector, the taxes and fees generated will most likely be adequate to purchase and provide the desired services. Similarly, public debt financing is easier when the community is perceived as having adequate future revenues to make loan payments.

On the other hand, when a community is populated by a large percentage of low-income wage earners or characterized by a weak business sector, the taxes and fees generated may be inadequate. Under these conditions, very few options exist for the community, all of which will result in the same set of problems. First, the quality and quantity of needed services may be reduced in order to keep tax rates low. Second, the community may attempt to raise taxes or fees, but increased taxes often will drive taxpayers away to live or work in communities with lower tax rates. Third, the community will attempt to borrow money, but higher interest rates will be charged because the creditworthiness of the community is in question. This last option may lead to the need to raise taxes to pay the debt, or it may strap the community with a high future debt or reduced services (Karger, 1994), which may force the community to again raise taxes in the future. All three options almost inevitably result in service cutbacks, since they all depend on having a wage-earning or commercial population that can pay the taxes necessary to pay for the services.

Many communities lack a strong wage-earning or commercial sector for several reasons. One of the most important is that the American economy has undergone sweeping changes in the last 30 years. Many of the high-wage, low- to moderate-skill manufacturing jobs that were available from the 1940s to the 1970s have moved to areas where labor costs are much lower, such as Central America or Asia, in recent years. At the same time, job growth in this country has centered on two very different sets of skills. At one level, the high-technology and financial services sectors have expanded and have created a large number of high-paying jobs that require significant training and education. At another level, a large number of low-paying, low-skill jobs have been created in the service economy in areas such as retail commerce. Communities that have seen significant high-technology or finance job creation have done well in maintaining civic services, whereas communities that have not experienced such growth have suffered.

**Political Power**    To at least some degree, a community can overcome the lack of a strong tax base if community leaders can muster the political coordination to efficiently develop new resources, such as external grants or new businesses. Such efforts may succeed, but they often result in substantial tax giveaways by the community as incentives to business development. The degree to which these tax giveaways benefit the community and the poor is an open question (Vidal, 1995).

A far more common outcome is that communities are unable to muster sufficient political strength. Instead, political fragmentation and, occasionally, political corruption result. As a community begins to spiral downward, a form of competition emerges among various interests in the community to hold onto available resources. With mounting and diverse problems facing the community, interest groups may erect barriers to prohibit other interest groups from allocating scarce resources differently. In light of diminishing external resources, this trend could get worse (Bailey and Koney, 1997).

## The Consequences of Community Poverty

As a community spirals downward, a variety of social problems are likely to manifest themselves. These problems include increasing crime rates; higher rates of substance abuse; deterioration of schools, transportation, and the recreational infrastructure; and a decline in the accessibility of high-quality medical care. The community simply does not have the money to provide the services that may stop the spread of problems.

Moreover, as city services deteriorate and taxes increase, individuals and families who can afford to move from the community often do so. This not only reduces the tax base even further; it also removes other valuable assets from the community, including the political strengths and knowledge of those who move and their function as role models for children. It has been argued, for example, that one of the principal reasons for the development of what has been called the "underclass" was the departure of the middle class and professionals from inner-city communities (Wilson, 1987). Many of the social programs of the last four decades helped those who were most able to be helped, primarily the better-educated middle class. These individuals moved to the suburbs or other affluent communities, whereas the poor remained in areas characterized by inadequate services, high crime rates, and high unemployment.

Another consequence of poverty in poor and powerless communities, and one little recognized by the social work profession, is the problem of environmental justice. Because there is a desperate need for employment and because of the intentional targeting of certain communities for undesirable types of business (Kauffman, 1994; Rogge, 1993, 1994), poor communities are likely to be home to prisons, factories that discharge large amounts of pollutants, and waste management companies. The concentration of such businesses may result in a variety of negative social and health effects, ranging from lowered property values and disagreeable odors to increased rates of respiratory diseases and cancer. One community has even noted an increase in prostitution to serve the truckers who bring garbage into several recently built trash incinerators (Resident of Chester, PA, personal communication, May 1997)!

## GENERALIST PRACTICE WITH ECONOMICALLY DISADVANTAGED CLIENTS AND COMMUNITIES

The complex, multidimensional aspects of poverty demand flexibility from the generalist social work practitioner. Individuals and communities will almost inevitably present a range of different problems, each requiring different skills and knowledge. Because of the scope of the problem, this section will not attempt to address all of the practice issues with these client groups, but instead will focus on a set of generalist concepts as they apply to this rewarding area of practice. These concepts include the range of target problems and goal setting; the importance of research and planning; collaboration, coalition building, and the importance of relationships; and effective interventions.

### The Range of Target Problems and Goal Setting

The essential starting point in generalist social work practice with economically disadvantaged clients and communities is determining the desired outcomes of the intervention. At least three types of goals apply to this area of practice:

1. Goals that seek improvements in intangible concepts, such as the distribution of rights or psychological status

2. Goals that seek improvements in processes
3. Goals that seek specific, measurable, targeted outcomes

Table 10.2 links each goal to a partial list of potential target problems. This may serve to guide your thinking about where to focus your intervention. Specifically, after the identification of the target problem, the client, whether an individual, a family, or a community, may require assistance in determining where best to focus corrective efforts. Consider, for example, the problem of poor community planning. Here, the appropriate goal is improvement of the processes the city uses to make its decisions. This may then require interventions at the level of city government. On the other hand, violence within a family might be better addressed by direct practice with the family to improve its internal communication or problem-solving skills.

The process of selecting goals is as important as the goals themselves, if not more so. It is critical to work closely with the client system. You bring a level of expertise to the relationship, but it is the client who experiences the problems, and more often than not, it is the client who actually implements the intervention. This means, at the very least, that the client is ultimately responsible for the change.

The goal when addressing poverty is **empowerment.** It does not matter if the target of change is the individual, the family, or the community. In all cases, improvements in the quality of life will be achieved through the desire and efforts of individuals, either alone or in groups, to bring about change. You will seek to assist individuals and communities to work for and advocate on their own behalf. It is a collaborative process. Empowerment comes about by helping individuals, families, and communities "take action to improve their situation" (Guiterrez, 1994, p. 202) through the development of "organized responses to circumstances that affect their lives" (Nystrom, 1989, p. 161).

Empowerment of clients who have a long history of powerlessness is not a fast process. Education and support of the clients' own problem-solving abilities are effective empowerment strategies (DuBois and Miley, 1996). Beyond this, collaboration, use of a strengths perspective, and adopting a perspective that shows the client the relationship between personal problems and the social and structural causes of those problems all promote empowerment (Simon, 1994). Shared responsibility, mutual trust, and a track record of small successes are also important. Strategies that use community or small groups are also helpful as tools of empowerment (Breton, 1994; Guiterrez, 1994; Hirayama and Hirayama, 1987).

## The Importance of Assessment

The large number of varying consequences and the problems of unclear or different causality make practice with the economically disenfranchised both challenging and rewarding. Individuals, families, and communities differ in their unique circumstances. They also differ in the tools and resources available to them. Hence, a significant amount of time must be spent in assessing

TABLE 10.2 | POSSIBLE TARGET PROBLEMS AND GOAL TYPES

| Goals Which Seek Improvements in Intangible Concepts | | Goals Which Seek Improvements in Processes | | Goals Which Seek Specific, Measurable, Targeted Outcomes | |
|---|---|---|---|---|---|
| Microsystems | Macrosystems | Microsystems | Macrosystems | Microsystems | Macrosystems |
| Lack of empowerment | Environmental racism | Low political participation | Low political participation | Unemployment Family violence | Unemployment Crime rates |
| Lack of self-efficacy | Social injustice Discrimination | Poor family communication | Poor community planning | Substance abuse Mental illness | Family violence rates |
| Resident | Community isolation | | Service availability | Literacy Hunger | Substance abuse rates |
| | | | | | Population rates |
| | | | | | Cost and availability of housing |

individual as well as community needs. Effective practice requires getting to know the community and having various members of the community articulate their concerns as well as their strengths. Only a well-developed familiarity with the community will prepare you for work with this population.

The values, cultural standards, and past history of interventions with the community also must be examined. Some poor communities have experienced a kind of roller-coaster effect. The community has often been promised the moon by social workers and others. Great expectations arise, only to be shattered as the scope of the problems overwhelms the process. Or, more likely, funding priorities change and monies available for even a promising and successful project dry up before the community is back on its feet. This roller-coaster effect, moreover, is the basis for some of the powerlessness felt by residents in the community.

On the other hand, it is a mistake to focus only on the problems the community faces. Using the strengths perspective articulated in earlier chapters avoids the tendency to focus on deficits (Saleeby, 1992). The reasons for bringing a strengths perspective to the relationship are both practical and conceptual. The resources of the individual or the community will be the available tools for change. Thus, knowing what these tools are is critical. But, in a larger sense, keeping your attention on the problems or deficits is disempowering to the client (Hepworth, Rooney, and Larson, 1997). The residents already know what the problems are. Constantly reminding them of problems may bring up feelings of powerlessness from the past. Moreover, focusing on problems or deficits can result in a "blaming the victim" perspective. Thus, you need to keep the focus on the possibilities for change and the means to achieve the desired outcomes.

## Collaboration, Coalition Building, and the Importance of Relationships

A collaborative partnership approach is effective with economically disadvantaged clients. First, as discussed above, empowerment is a central goal for this type of practice, and working collaboratively with the client is essential for meeting this desired outcome. Second, there is strength in numbers. Only in a few instances can an individual or single agency bring all of the resources and expertise necessary for correcting complex, multidimensional problems for a single client or an entire community. Developing coalitions brings together expertise from a variety of different areas, which may expand resources, better integrate existing services, and increase the likelihood of reaching the identified change goals (Alter and Hage, 1993).

A range of skills are essential for practice with poor individuals and families. The worker may be required to provide different services at different times, including advocacy, counseling, linkages with other services, information, and referrals. Further, the client will need multiple services from multiple providers, and the social worker provides a vital coordination role. In this context, the whole realm of micro practice skills outlined in Chapter 7 come into play. In fact, it would be difficult to find a social work practice domain where the range of generalist practice skills is more necessary than with this client population. Any individual client, particularly a long-term welfare recipient, is likely to have a variety of different needs for a variety of different services. As a generalist social worker with low-income clients, you will see needs for employment, training, childcare, transportation, health services, life skills, substance abuse or mental health counseling, and legal assistance, all in a single day. As such, collaborative service networks with the social worker and the client at the center are inevitable and necessary.

Collaborations and coalitions are equally necessary when working with communities. The same argument about strength in numbers applies, and you will need even more resources and technical skills. Increasingly, funding sources such as foundations and governmental agencies are demanding collaborative components. They recognize that single-focus community programming is not as effective in bringing about change as are multifocus coalitions and partnerships. If community development activities do not voluntarily organize, efforts to bring about coalitions will be facilitated by the demands of resource providers (Bailey and Koney, 1997).

Residents should be participants in the coalitions. Partnerships should create a meaningful role for citizens in voluntary community associations and other institutions (Florin and Wandersman, 1990). Citizen participants are likely to improve outcomes (Bendrick and Egan, 1995; Mier, 1994), and intentional efforts to involve citizens in community coalitions lead to stronger communities (Unger and Wandersman, 1983; Woodson, 1981) and increased feelings of personal and political efficacy (Cole, 1974; Cole and Caputo, 1984; Florin and Wandersman, 1984; Zimmerman and Rappaport, 1988).

There is a downside to casting a wide net. Coalitions and the involvement of citizens may slow down processes in at least two ways. First, planning is substantially more complicated as the number of participants increases. Setting priorities is more difficult. Competition for scarce resources may overwhelm the planning process. Second, as individuals move in and out of the coalition, substantial time may have to be spent educating new members about the processes and decisions already made. Skillful group facilitation can minimize these problems. Over the long term, the time spent in planning and educational efforts will pay off through a more cohesive and committed coalition membership.

In almost any social work context, relationships are critical to the helping process. When working with economically disadvantaged clients, relationships are of particular importance. Past encounters with other outsiders may have eroded trust. Poor individuals and poor communities may have a long history of problematic relationships with social workers, government officials, or other authoritative figures and agencies.

Besides collaboration, the best way to build trust and a positive relationship is to

- Move slowly
- Avoid making promises you cannot keep
- Take time to educate clients about your actions
- Explain the limits of your programmatic efforts
- Avoid demanding more from clients than they can give

In addition, don't be disappointed if your ideas and suggestions are not initially carried out or if you feel you are being tested by the community (Guiterrez et al., 1997). Low-income clients face a variety of demands on their time and have scarce resources. To some degree, even with the best of intentions, social work interventions represent an imposition.

Research activities, for example, such as surveys or interviews, not only demand time but may also be perceived as a significant intrusion into the clients' personal lives. Some planning activities such as public meetings, or interventions such as social actions, may not be well attended, as people do not feel comfortable. The process of building trust and effective collaborative relationships take time.

## Generalist Interventions

Almost all generalist social work skills are potentially useful when working with economically disadvantaged clients. In a short time, you may see clients with problems as straightforward as needing assistance finding a job all the way to complex problematic familial and community relationships. It is important to be prepared for any and all eventualities.

It cannot be stressed enough that you must start where the client is. This means understanding the client's needs, strengths, and cultural perceptions. Most social workers do not work with people like themselves, and many of our assumptions are rooted in our cultural background. Avoid assuming that your client sees the world the same way you do. Assume that you are different, and find out the specifics of your differences. Keep up with the literature. The current welfare reform activities will soon begin to generate a large amount of research that will be useful for your practice. The more you know about current policies, practices, and your client population, the more effective you will be.

At the level of the community, a wide range of knowledge, skills, and activities are necessary and useful. These include the knowledge and practical application of different practice modes, such as locality development, which attempts to improve cooperative problem solving; social planning, which attempts to address concrete deficiencies; and social action, which attempts to force legislative or organizational change (Rothman, 1995). It also requires multicultural sensitivity (Guiterrez et al., 1997). More specifically, skills include group problem solving, group and collaborative facilitation, research and analysis (McNeely, 1996), resource development (Rubin and Rubin, 1992), planning and organizing, and skills in dealing with conflict, such as active listening and consensus building (Guiterrez et al., 1997).

As may be clear, practice work with economically disadvantaged clients and communities is complex and challenging. It demands a range of skills and knowledge perhaps greater than any other form of social work practice. The rewards are great. The opportunities to work with a large number of committed and concerned individuals present an experience rarely felt elsewhere. By engaging in this practice domain, you are working to correct the central problem of our society: poverty. Many, perhaps most, of our social problems are either caused by or closely connected to poverty. Finding solutions will improve the quality of life for many Americans.

In addition to the macro practice skills and knowledge areas discussed above, a variety of interventions, techniques, and skills may be needed in a given situation. Assuming that the needs assessment is complete and the goals and objectives of the intervention have been selected, the determination of the most appropriate course of action must be selected. One way to help conceptualize an appropriate course of action is to divide the process into two levels of planning: strategy (the big picture) and tactics (the day-to-day activities) (Kahn, 1991). A number of options exist within each level, and one of the true points of creativity for the social worker is the selection of the appropriate tools. Thus, the question that must be asked is: What is the most effective method of meeting our goals given the problems we face and the resources at our disposal? And of course, a complicating factor is that sometimes a strategy may be a tactic, or the other way around.

**Strategy** refers to the "big picture," the general plan used to bring about the desired change. The basic types of strategies have already been presented above, and include locality development, social planning, and social action. But beyond these labels, it might be appropriate, although a bit simplistic, to say that the difference between approaches is the degree to which they work within the system or outside and through confrontation with the system. Here, "in" the system refers to methods of policy or program changes that are enacted using established and legal governmental structures or organizations. Generally, locality development and social planning are strategies that tend to illustrate this approach because they typically use existing or new organizations and various governmental structures to bring about the desired end. Social action on the other hand, often implies a more confrontational approach, with the goal being change brought about by the demands of an active citizenry.

Sharp (1973) provides an extensive list of strategies that fall within this "social action" approach. These include nonviolent protest and persuasion, social noncooperation, economic noncooperation (boycotts; strikes), political noncooperation, and nonviolent intervention.

**Tactics** are the tools used in support of the strategy. Regardless of the strategy, there are certain types of tools that are available. It is here where many important macro practice skills must be developed. First, it is often the case that information is lacking among the policy makers, the general public, or those that have the capacity to influence change (Haynes and Mickelson, 1997). Thus, the social worker may need to expand his or her technical ability in public speaking and writing. It may be necessary to speak to large audiences; give testimony to policy makers; and write press releases, letters to the editor, testimonials, and even legislation. Similarly, the social worker may need to prepare and assist individuals of low literacy for these same purposes. The emotional impact of the testimony of a victim of a social injury is a powerful tool.

In addition to tactics that are informational in nature, there are many tactics that require the organization of individuals, many who may never have worked in a coordinated way before. Bringing people together for single events such as rallies is often difficult enough. But consider the problems in organizing people for sustained action (such as a boycott) or for forming an organization. These organizing skills are among the most important macro practice tools available. Remember, power comes from many sources, and while your clients may be poor and unable to exert the power that wealth and influence bring, they will be able to exert the power of the ballot box, the pocket book, and the attention of the larger public.

Finally, the effective macro practitioner will also want to use tactics associated with formal policy change. Being an effective policy advocate (Ezell, 2001) is one approach (and one that adopts many of the points in this section), as are program development and grant writing. While these tools have been discussed elsewhere in the book, it is important to remind the reader that policies are not only the legislative acts that come out of Washington, D.C. They are also produced in every social service agency every time that agency develops a new program. Policies are solutions to problems, maybe not always effective or permanent, but important tools nevertheless, and the effective macro practitioner will learn to use these tools.

# SUMMARY

Poverty is a worldwide problem. In the United States, more than 32 million people representing 11.7 percent of the population are poor (U.S. Bureau of the Census, 2001). The number of people classified as poor depends on the way poverty is defined. The accuracy and adequacy of the poverty threshold has been called into question.

Poverty has been a persistent social problem with multiple theories of causation and multiple consequences. Some theories focus on individual deficits, others attribute poverty to social and structural factors. A third set of theories examines the relationship between individual and social causes.

Factors affecting community poverty are better understood and less controversial. At the community level, poverty can often be traced to the interplay of economics and political power. Poor communities lack the economic base to pay for needed community services. These services include public safety, education, infrastructure, and governance. Most poor communities also lack political power. Political fragmentation and, occasionally, political corruption characterize poor communities. There often is competition for scarce resources, which further contributes to the downward spiral of economically disadvantaged communities.

The consequences of poverty for individuals and families are profound. The most immediate is its effect on an individual's capacity to survive. Hunger and poor nutrition are common. Inadequate housing, exposure to environmental risks, unsafe streets and neighborhoods, and increased health problems are all associated with poverty.

Generalist social work practice with this population focuses on individual and community empowerment. The goal is to empower the poor individually and collectively to improve the quality of life socially, physically, and economically. This entails developing collaborative helping relationships with individuals and families to facilitate and strengthen their capacities to cope with the challenges that come with being poor as well as building community-based coalitions that seek resources and solutions to the economic and political problems facing economically disadvantaged communities.

# CASE EXAMPLE

The case example in Case 10.1 illustrates generalist social work practice with a community client system. It describes the process the author went through in helping a low-income community develop and implement a community-based social service center.

| CASE 10.1 | THE CHESTER EXPERIENCE |
|-----------|------------------------|

Chester, Pennsylvania, presents a classic case of a distressed city in the United States. The city has a population of approximately 36,000 and is located one-half hour south of Philadelphia. Chester was once a thriving manufacturing center, producing ships, steel, iron, cloth, pottery, paper, and refined oil. But between the 1950s and the 1980s, the city lost 32 percent of its jobs, the economy collapsed, and much of the middle class moved away. The city's problems were compounded by several decades of corrupt political leadership.

### Assessment

Economic changes and political inefficacy have created a number of socioeconomic problems for the community. Needs assessments demonstrated that unemployment, crime, housing, substance abuse, environmental pollution, truancy, and low adult educational attainment rates are all serious problems in Chester. In addition, a number of barriers made services to residents inaccessible. These included a poor transportation network, service fragmentation, and a lack of awareness of the services that were available.

### Intervention

Recognizing the need for better coordination between services and the reduction of barriers to service, several agencies met in the summer of 1995 to discuss methods to overcome these problems. The meetings were called by an organization that had been contacted by the Ford Foundation about a new program initiative designed to develop collaborative relationships between service providers. I was invited to help develop the program proposal and to formulate a client assessment and program evaluation plan.

The Ford Foundation provided funds for a program in Chester in 1996. Endless hours were spent on the telephone with organizations such as the United Way and combing the telephone directory to generate an exhaustive list of agencies. Next, questions had to be resolved about which agencies should be members. Should the organization be open to social service agencies only, or should government agencies, church groups, and informal groups be invited as well? We decided to be as inclusive as possible, even inviting unaffiliated residents.

More than a hundred social service organizations banded together in a formal network. Their organization, which they named Communities That Care (CTC), began holding regular monthly meetings and planning new service initiatives. The focus of these meetings was to improve coordination, which, it was hoped, would not only improve client functioning, but would also facilitate dialogue among service providers and strengthen the process of community advocacy.

There were questions about how to organize the meetings. Should one agency take the lead in calling and coordinating the effort, or should the meetings be less structured and controlled? If one agency served as the leader, would other agencies be jealous and refuse to participate? We decided to use a formal structure, with the agency that had been approached by the Ford Foundation as the lead agency. The justification was that this agency would be the grant recipient and would therefore be accountable for the funding. Fortunately, our fears were unwarranted.

CTC meetings have since become forums for the exchange of information. Newsletters and information pamphlets inform clients and other providers of services offered at the various agencies. The meetings have also generated ideas that individual agencies and small groups of agencies have formalized into proposals or grants for new programs. In discussions at CTC meetings, for example, it was determined that a real need existed for some form of centralized social services facility in Chester. Centralized service provision could help ameliorate problems faced by clients in accessing services, such as transportation, lack of awareness about available services, and excessive time expenditures.

Fortunately, a facility became available immediately. One of Chester's two hospitals was acquired by the other, much larger hospital. The larger hospital was a member of CTC, and it decided to use the smaller hospital building for its social service programs, including inpatient and outpatient substance abuse and mental health treatment. Unused space

*(continued)*

**CASE 10.1** | *continued*

was made available to other providers at low or, in some cases, no cost. The new facility, called the One-Stop Shop (OSS), opened in mid-1998. More than 20 public and private social service agencies are now located in the facility. Services available include job training and placement, domestic and family mediation, childcare, counseling, computer skills training, and educational support. Because many clients failed to follow up on referrals from and to such public social services as Medical Assistance and Temporary Assistance for Needy Families, an on-site county assistance office was established at the OSS in the fall of 1998.

Another initiative of the CTC network has been the development and adoption of a standardized assessment and client service planning system to make practice and program evaluations easier. Prior to the implementation of this system, clients often underwent several different assessments by the different agencies helping them. At the request of several agencies, I formulated a plan to eliminate this burden on the clients, meeting frequently with the various providers to address issues of client confidentiality, agency needs, and the overall assessment process.

In addition, several initiatives focus on the development of community leadership skills. Several of the agencies using the One-Stop Shop are offering newly designed programs to strengthen client leadership skills and problem-solving capacity. These interventions not only empower clients to self-advocate; they also promote ownership of change efforts, thus avoiding the perception that change has been imposed by outsiders.

Finally, several of the agencies provide intensive case management to families and individuals. Case management enables service linkage and follow-up assistance. In two of the agencies, the case management system has undergone major expansion because of grants to enlarge their service scope.

**Evaluation**

Although Chester continues to face many problems, it appears that the CTC network and the One-Stop Shop are having a significant effect on the community. Several initiatives of the CTC network have been funded, although these successful initiatives have depended upon the hard work of a few extremely dedicated agency partners. It is unclear if these efforts would have been successful without these "go-getters." In addition, many agencies that would fit well with CTC either do not participate or remain on the fringe. The agencies operated by the city of Chester, for example, fall into these categories. Along this same line, there are starting to be a few "cliques" of organizations that are seeking funding to the exclusion of others. Also, only a few residents are members of CTC. As a result, the planning of activities is slowed because agencies must spend time to gather the support of the residents.

Finally, in an impoverished community like Chester, job development is critical, and the One-Stop Shop does not address this need. My hope is that reducing barriers to service will assist clients in their attempts to have their immediate needs met, and as their capacity to self-advocate improves, real change will take place with the community as the change agent. Empowering the residents is an important by-product of several of the programs of the One-Stop Shop, and in time, I believe this will be the most beneficial outcome.

## DISCUSSION QUESTIONS

1. What strategies could be used to address the multiple problems in a city like Chester (Case 10.1)? What role should the residents play? Would legislative or political lobbying be a possible strategy for addressing the community's problems? For more information on lobbying, see Haynes and Mickelson, 2003.

2. Why would a community like Chester be selected for the development of new, environmentally unfriendly businesses, such as hazardous waste incinerators?

3. Which, if any, social problems in the United States are caused by poverty? If a problem is caused by poverty, is it better to address that problem or to address poverty?

4. What is the role of the generalist social worker when working with a poor person and his or her family? In other words, assuming there are no other problems, such as substance abuse or domestic violence, what strategies would you use?

5. Is poverty the fault of the poor person? Is it the responsibility of the poor person to solve the problem?

# REFERENCES

Alter, C., and Hage, J. (1993). *Organizations working together.* Newbury Park, CA: Sage.

Bailey, D., and Koney, K. (1997). Interorganizational community-based collaboratives: A strategic response to shape the social work agenda. In P. Ewalt, E. Freeman, S. Kirk, and D. Poole (Eds.), *Social policy: Reform, research and practice* (pp. 72–83). Washington: NASW Press.

Bane, M. J., and Ellwood, D. T. (1994). *Welfare realities: From rhetoric to reform.* Cambridge, MA: Harvard University Press.

Banfield, E. (1968). *The unheavenly city.* Boston: Little, Brown.

Banfield, E. (1974). *The unheavenly city revisited.* Boston: Little, Brown.

Bendrick, M., and Egan, M. L. (1995). Worker ownership and participation enhances economic development in low-opportunity communities. *Journal of Community Practice, 2,* 61–85.

Bower, B. (1994). Growing up poor. *Science News, 46,* (July 9), 24–25.

Breton, M. (1994). On the meaning of empowerment and empowerment-oriented social work practice. *Social Work with Groups, 17*(3), 23–37.

Brooks-Gunn, J., Klebanov, P., Liaw, F., and Duncan, G. (1995). Toward an understanding of the effects of poverty upon children. In H. E. Fitzgerald, B. M. Lester, and B. Zuckerman (Eds.), *Children of poverty: Research, health,* *and policy issues* (pp. 3–41). New York: Garland.

Brown, L., and Pollitt, E. (1996). Malnutrition, poverty and intellectual development. *Scientific American, 274*(2), 38–43.

Cattell-Gordon, D. (1990). The Appalachian inheritance: A culturally transmitted traumatic stress syndrome. *Journal of Progressive Human Services, 1*(1), 41–57.

Center on Budget and Policy Priorities (1997). *Poverty rate fails to decline as income growth in 1996 favors the affluent: Child health coverage erodes as Medicaid for children contracts.* Washington, DC: Author.

Centers for Disease Control and Prevention (n.d.). *What every parent should know about lead poisoning in children.* Atlanta: Author.

Centers for Disease Control and Prevention (2002). Childhood lead poisoning. Atlanta: Author. Available Internet:http://www.cdc.gov/nceh/lead /factsheets/childhoodlead.htm.

Children's Defense Fund (1998). *Poverty matters: The cost of child poverty in America.* Washington, DC: Author.

Citro, C., and Michael, R. (1995). *Measuring poverty: A new approach.* Washington, DC: National Academy Press.

Cole, R. L. (1974). *Citizen participation and the urban policy process.* Lexington, MA: D. C. Health.

Cole, R. L., and Caputo, D. A. (1984). The public hearing as an effective citizen participation mechanism: A case study of the General Revenue Sharing Program. *American Political Science Review, 78,* 404–416.

Congressional Quarterly Weekly Reports (1991). Lead exposure bill stalls in markup. *Congressional Quarterly Weekly Reports, 49,* 3206.

Danziger, S., and Gottshalk, P. (1995). *America unequal.* Cambridge, MA: Russell Sage Foundation and Harvard University Press.

DeNavas-Walt, C., and Cleveland, R. (2002). *Current Population Reports, P60–218, Money Income in the United States: 2001.* Washington, DC: U.S. Government Printing Office.

DiNitto, D. (1996). The future of social welfare policy. In P. Raffoul and A. McNeece (Eds.), *Future issues for social work practice* (pp. 254–265). Boston: Allyn & Bacon.

DuBois, B., and Miley, K. K. (1996). *Social work: An empowering profession* (2nd ed.). Boston: Allyn & Bacon.

Ezell, M. (2001). *Being an effective policy advocate.* Pacific Grove, CA: Brooks/Cole.

Federal Register (1998). *Federal Register, 63*(36), 9235–9238.

Fisher, G. (1992). The development and history of the poverty thresholds. *Social Security Bulletin, 55*(4), 3–14.

Fisher, G. (1995). Is There Such a Thing as an Absolute Poverty Line Over Time? Evidence from the United States, Britain, Canada, and Australia on the Income Elasticity of the Poverty Line. Poverty measurement working papers. Washington, D.C.: U.S. Census Bureau. Available Internet: http://www.census.gov/hhes /poverty/povmeas/papers/elastap4.html.

Florin, P. R., and Wandersman, A. (1984). Cognitive social learning and participation in community development. *American Journal of Community Psychology, 12*(6), 689–708.

Florin, P. R., and Wandersman, A. (1990). An introduction to citizen participation, voluntary organizations, and community development: Insights for empowerment through research. *American Journal of Community Psychology, 18*(1), 41–54.

Gans, H. (1976). The positive functions of poverty. *American Journal of Sociology, 78*(2), 275–289.

Gilder, G. (1981). *Wealth and poverty.* New York: Basic Books.

Goodwin, L. (1983). *Causes and cures of welfare: New evidence on the social psychology of the poor.* Lexington, MA: Lexington Books.

Guiterrez, L. (1994). Beyond coping: An empowerment perspective on stressful life events. *Journal of Sociology and Social Welfare, 21*(3), 201–219.

Guiterrez, L., Alvarez, A., Nemon, H., and Lewis, E. (1997). Multicultural community organizing: A strategy for change. In P. Ewalt, E. Freeman, S. Kirk, and D. Poole (Eds.), *Social policy: Reform, research and practice* (pp. 62–71). Washington, DC: NASW Press.

Handler, J., and Hasenfeld, Y. (1991). *The moral construction of poverty: American welfare reform.* Newbury Park, CA: Sage.

Haynes, K., and Mickelson, J. (2003). *Affecting change: Social workers in the political arena* (5th ed.). New York: Longman.

Hepworth, D., Rooney, R., and Larson, J. (1997). *Direct social work practice: Theory and skills* (5th ed.). Pacific Grove, CA: Brooks/Cole.

Hirayama, H., and Hirayama, K. (1987). Empowerment through group participation: Process and goal. *American Journal of Community Psychology, 15,* 353–371.

Hunger Action Coalition (n.d). Factsheet. http://comnet.org/hacmi/facts.htm.

Kahn, S. (1991). *Organizing*. Washington, DC: National Association of Social Workers.

Karger, H. (1994). Toward redefining social development in the global economy: Free markets, privatization, and the development of a welfare state in Eastern Europe. *Social Development Issues, 16*(3), 32–44.

Katz, M. (1989). *The undeserving poor: From the war on poverty to the war on welfare*. New York: Pantheon.

Kauffman, S. (1994). Citizen participation in environmental decisions: Policy, reality, and considerations for community organizing. In M. D. Hoff and J. G. McNutt (Eds.), *The global environmental crisis: Implications for social welfare and social work* (pp. 219–239). Brookfield, MA: Avebury Press.

Lewis, O. (1959). *Five families; Mexican case studies in the culture of poverty*. New York: Basic Books.

Lewis, O. (1961). *The children of Sanchez*. New York: Random House.

Lewis, O. (1966). *La Vida: A Puerto Rican family in the culture of poverty*. New York: Basic Books.

Marx, K. (1867). Capital (S. Moore and E. Averly, Trans.). Available Internet: http://www.marxists.org/archive/marx/works/1867-c1/index.htm.

McNeely, J. B. (1996). Where have all the flowers gone? In R. Stone (Ed.), *Core issues in comprehensive community building initiatives* (pp. 86–88). Chicago: Chapin Hall for Children.

Mead, L. M. (1986). *Beyond entitlement*. New York: Free Press.

Mead, L. M. (1992). *The new politics of poverty: The working poor in America*. New York: Free Press.

Mier, R. (1994). *Social justice and local development policy*. Newbury Park, CA: Sage.

Mizell, C. (1999). Rising Above Poverty: The Consequences of Poverty Status and Individual Characteristics on Earnings. JCPR Working Paper 106, 09-01-1999. Chicago: Joint Center for Poverty Research, Northwestern University/University of Chicago.

Murdock, S., and Michael, M. (1996). Future demographic changes: The demand for social welfare services in the 21st century. In P. Raffoul and A. McNeece (Eds.), *Future issues for social work practice* (pp. 3–18). Boston: Allyn & Bacon.

Murray, C. (1984). *Loosing ground: American social policy, 1950–1980*. New York: Basic Books.

Nord, M., Andrews, M., and Carlson, S. (2002). *Household food security in the U.S., 2001*. Washington, D.C.: U.S. Department of Agriculture.

Nord, M., and Bikel, G. (2002). *Measuring children's food security in U.S. households, 1995–99*. Washington, D.C.: United States Department of Agriculture.

Nystrom, J. F. (1989). Empowerment model for delivery of social work services in public schools. *Journal of Social Work Education, 11*, 160–170.

Polenberg, R. (1980). *One nation divisible: Class, race, and ethnicity in the United States since 1938*. New York: Penguin.

Poole, D. (1995). Beyond the rhetoric: Shared responsibility versus the Contract with America. *Health and Social Work, 20*, 83–86.

Poole, D. (1997). *Welfare reform: The bad, the ugly, and the maybe not too awful*. In P. Ewalt, E. Freeman, S. Kirk, and D. Poole (Eds.), *Social policy: Reform, research and practice* (pp. 96–101). Washington: NASW Press.

Proctor, B., and Dalaker, J. (1999). *U.S. Census Bureau, Current Population Reports, P60–219, Poverty in the United States: 2001*. Washington, DC: U.S. Government Printing Office.

Rogge, M. (1993). Social work, disenfranchised communities, and the natural environment: Field education opportunities. *Journal of Social Work Education, 29*, 111–120.

Rogge, M. (1994). Environmental injustice: Social welfare and toxic waste. In M. D. Hoff and J. G. McNutt (Eds.), *The global environmental crisis: Implications for social welfare and social work* (pp. 53–74). Brookfield, MA: Avebury Press.

Rothman, J. (1995). Approaches to community organization. In J. Rothman, J. Erlich, and J. Tropman (Eds.), *Strategies of community intervention* (5th ed., pp. 23–63). Itasca, IL: F. E. Peacock Publishing, Inc.

Rubin, H. J., and Rubin, L. S. (1992). *Community organizing and development* (2nd ed.). New York: Macmillan.

Saleeby, A. C. (1992). *The strengths perspective in social work practice.* New York: Longman.

Savage, H. (1999). *Who could afford to buy a house in 1995?* Washington, DC: U.S. Bureau of the Census.

Sharp, G. (1973). *The methods of nonviolent action.* Boston: Porter Sargent.

Sherraden, M. (1991). *Assets and the poor: A new American welfare policy.* New York: M. E. Sharpe.

Silver, P., Kauffman, S., and Soliman, H. (1998). Environmental hazards: Social worker practices and attitudes. Unpublished manuscript.

Simon, B. L. (1994). *The empowerment tradition in American social work: A history.* New York: Columbia University Press.

Unger, D. G., and Wandersman, A. (1983). Neighboring and its role in block organizations: An exploratory report. *American Journal of Community Psychology, 11*, 291–300.

United Nations Development Program (2003). Millennium goals and the UNDP role. http://www.undp.org/dpa/publications/ffmdg.pdf.

U.S. Bureau of the Census (1995). *Health insurance coverage: 1995: Who goes without health insurance?* Washington, DC: Author.

U.S. Bureau of the Census (1996). *March 1996 current population survey.* Washington, DC: Author.

U.S. Bureau of the Census (1997a). *March 1997 current population survey.* Washington, DC: Author.

U.S. Bureau of the Census (1997b). *1993 American housing survey.* Washington, DC: Author.

U.S. Bureau of the Census (1999). Frequently asked questions. Available Internet: http://www.census.gov/hhes/housing/ahs/ahsfaq.html.

U.S. Bureau of the Census (2000). Who can afford to buy a house in 1995? Washington, DC: Author. Available Internet: http://www.census.gov/hhes/www/hsgaffrd.html.

U.S. Bureau of the Census (2001a). Household net worth and asset ownership, 1995. Washington, DC: Author. Available Internet: http://www.census.gov/prod/2001pubs/p70-71.pdf

U.S. Bureau of the Census (2001b). Nation's Household Income Stable in 2000, Poverty Rate Virtually Equals Record Low, Census Bureau Reports, Available Internet: http://www.census.gov/Press-Release/www/2001/cb01-158.html.

U.S. Bureau of the Census (2002a). Current population survey, March supplement. Washington, D.C.: Author. Available Internet: http://ferret.bls.census.gov/macro/032002/health/h01_000.htm

U.S. Bureau of the Census (2002b). American housing survey of the United States, 2001. Washington, DC: Author.

U.S. Bureau of the Census (2003a). 2001 Statistical abstract of the United States. Washington, D.C.: Author. Available

Internet: http://www.census.gov/prod/2002pubs/01statab/stat-ab01.html

U.S. Bureau of the Census (2003b). Housing vacancies and homeownership, Annual statistics: 2002. Washington, D.C.: Author. Available Internet: http://www.census.gov/hhes/www/housing/hvs/annual02/ann02ind.html.

U.S. Department of Agriculture (2003a). Food Stamp participation and costs. Washington, DC: Author. Available Internet: http://www.fns.usda.gov/pd/fssummar.htm

U.S. Department of Agriculture (2003b). Special supplemental nutrition program for women, infants and children (WIC). Data as January 29, 2003. Washington, DC: Author. Available Internet: http://www.fns.usda.gov/pd/WIC_Monthly.htm.

U.S. Department of Health and Human Services (1994). *Priority home! The federal plan to break the cycle of homelessness.* (HUD-1454-CPD). Washington, DC: Author.

U.S. Department of Health and Human Services (1999). *The state of the cities, 1999.* Washington, DC: Author.

U.S. Department of Health and Human Services, National Center on Child Abuse and Neglect (1996). *Third national incidence study of child abuse and neglect: Final report (NIS-3).* Washington, DC: Author.

U.S. Department of Health and Human Services, Social Security Administration (2001). Social security bulletin: Annual statistical supplement 2001. Washington, DC: Author. Available Internet: http://www.ssa.gov/statistics/Supplement/2001/

U.S. Department of Health and Human Services, Social Security Administration (2003). Benefits in Current Payment Status. Washington, DC: Author.

Available Internet: http://www.ssa.gov/cgi-bin/benICP.cgi.

U.S. Department of Health and Human Services (2003). TANF: Total Number of Recipients Fiscal Year 2002. Washington, DC: Author. Available Internet: http://www.acf.dhhs.gov/news/stats/2002tanfrecipients.htm/

U.S. Department of Justice, Bureau of Justice Statistics (n.d.). Victim characteristics. http://www.ojp.usdoj.gov/bjs/cvict_v.htm.

Urban Institute (2000). *A new look at homelessness in America.* Washington, D.C.: Author.

Vidal, A. (1995). *Reintegrating disadvantaged communities into the fabric of urban life: The role of community development.* Housing Policy Debate, 6, 169–230.

Wilson, W. J. (1987). *The truly disadvantaged: The inner city, the underclass and public polity.* Chicago: University of Chicago.

Wolfensohn, J D. (2002). Statement to the International Monetary and Financial Committee. Washington, D.C.: International Monetary Fund.

Woodson, R. L. (1981). *A summons to life: Mediating structures and prevention of youth crime.* Washington, DC: American Enterprise Institute.

Yamada, G., and Sherraden, M. (1997). Effects of assets on attitudes and behaviors: Advance test of a social policy proposal. In P. Ewalt, E. Freeman, S. Kirk, and D. Poole (Eds.), *Social policy: Reform, research and practice* (pp. 193–205). Washington, DC: NASW Press.

Zimmerman, M. A., and Rappaport, J. (1988). Citizen participation, perceived control, and psychological empowerment. *American Journal of Community Psychology, 16,* 725–750.

# GENERALIST PRACTICE WITH PEOPLE AFFECTED BY ADDICTIONS

*Allan E. Barsky*

Tyra is a 42-year-old MSW student in the foundation year of her 2-year MSW program. Tyra describes herself as "in recovery, having been abstinent from alcohol for 3 years after a 19-year bout with the disease of alcoholism." Her first field placement is with the local Drug Court, a program that serves people charged with drug-related offences and diverted from the regular criminal court for assessment, counseling, and therapeutic services. Tyra is excited about this placement because she believes that she can use her experience with alcoholism and recovery to help others overcome their addictions. Tyra is a firm believer in the twelve-step program of Alcoholics Anonymous (AA) (2003).

Tyra's first client is an African-American woman named Claudia.[1] Claudia was charged with theft and possession of cocaine. She agreed to diversion from regular court at the recommendation of her lawyer, so that she would not get a criminal record or risk being incarcerated. During the initial interview with Tyra, Claudia denies that she has a problem with cocaine. She says that she was just caught in the wrong place at the wrong time, and the police assumed she was up to no good because she was black. She argues that someone must have placed the coke in her bag without her knowing. Tyra, also African American, tries to identify with Claudia, but has trouble with where to begin. Tyra questions how can she help Claudia if she is in denial about her cocaine addiction. After all, the first step in recovery is admitting that one has a problem, that alcohol or other drugs (AODs) have control over your life. Tyra believes that if Claudia is not ready to admit this, there is not much Tyra can do. Tyra also wonders whether Claudia is telling the truth. Perhaps Claudia was the victim of racism and did not commit any crime. How, if at all, can Tyra develop a helping relationship with a client who says she has no cocaine problem? How can Tyra and her client jointly assess whether the client actually does have a cocaine problem? What types of help can Tyra offer when the client resists any suggestion that she has an AOD problem? What societal, legal, and systemic issues could Tyra address that would help clients with AOD problems engage in change processes more effectively?

For some people, the use of AODs is a means of relaxing, socializing, or having a brief escape from the stresses of work, family, or day-to-day life. For others, AOD use can lead to family violence, property crimes, trafficking, lost jobs, extreme risk-taking behavior, damage to the brain and other vital organs, depression, anomie,[2] or premature death. For Claudia, AOD use led to being charged with theft and possession of an illicit substance. The United States incurs over $245 billion per year in economic costs relating to AOD abuse, including health care, lost work productivity, criminal law enforcement and incarceration, and social welfare (National Institute on Drug Abuse, 2003). These costs do not take into account the full human toll, biologically,

---

[1]To help you remember which client uses which substance, the first letter of the person's name is the first letter of their substance of abuse; for example, Claudia uses cocaine, Albert uses alcohol, and Hank uses heroin.

[2]*Anomie* refers to a sense of meaninglessness in life. For example, life may seem to be disorganized and without purpose.

psychologically, socially, and spiritually. Still, it would be misleading to suggest that all AODs are evil or that there is no hope for people who use AODs. Many substances have important medical uses. Even illicit substances can be used to cope with various psychosocial issues. Given the pervasiveness of AOD use in society, social workers must learn how to recognize the various roles that AODs play in people's lives, how to help people at risk to avoid AOD problems, and how to help those with AOD-problems overcome these concerns.

The purpose of this chapter is to provide developing social workers with a generalist framework for assessing and intervening with individuals and families affected by AOD use and addictions. Upon completion of this chapter you should be able to help Tyra:

1. Understand the pharmacologic bases, causes, and effects of addictions, as well as terms such as *addiction, dependence, use, abuse, misuse,* and *categorization of AODs*
2. Describe the ways in which addictions have been viewed historically, and how these views have affected social policy, laws, and prevention and intervention programs
3. Understand ways of engaging clients at different stages of motivation toward change
4. Assess biological, psychological, social, and spiritual strengths; resiliencies; risks; and areas for help in relation to AOD use
5. Identify the range of services to which one can refer people affected by AODs
6. Articulate the following interventions for individuals, families, groups, and communities affected by AODs that build on client strengths and honor the social work principle of client self-determination: cognitive-behavioral therapy, twelve-step programs, harm reduction, motivational interviewing, and the transtheoretical model of change

## UNDERSTANDING THE PHARMACOLOGIC BASIS OF AODS AND ADDITIONS

Before exploring the pharmacologic bases of AODs and addictions, one must first come to an understanding of the meaning of addiction and how it is differentiated from related concepts. Although *addiction* is a term used in common parlance, there is no single agreed-upon definition in the professional literature. Addiction has been referred to variously as a disease, a bad habit, a personal choice, a coping mechanism, and a loss of control (van Wormer and Davis, 2003). As you will see from the historical discussion below, each definition of addiction has different implications for social policy and social work practice. For the purposes of this chapter, addiction is defined as a compulsive behavior. Focusing on the behavior as the problem, rather than labeling the individual with a pathologic disorder or weakness, fits with the strengths perspective and the social work principle of respect for all people.

Addiction is not restricted to compulsive use of substances. Addiction can also refer to compulsive gambling, eating patterns, exercising, sexual behaviors, shopping, computer use, or any number of other behaviors. There is an incredible breadth of issues related to each type of addiction. This chapter focuses on addiction to psychoactive substances (i.e., AODs that have significant effects on the mood or psychological experience of the person). Still, many of the interventions described below for substance addictions are applicable to other behavioral addictions. Further, social workers must help clients avoid substituting a substance addiction for another type of behavioral addiction.

Mental health professionals generally assess clients for "dependence" rather than addiction. *Alcohol* and *substance dependence* are defined in the *Diagnostic and Statistical Manual,* fourth edition, text revision (*DSM-IV-TR*), published by the American Psychiatric Association (2000), as maladaptive patterns of AOD use resulting in distress or clinically significant impairment and involving 3 or more of the following symptoms occurring within the same 12-month period:

- Tolerance to the effects of the substance
- Withdrawal effects upon cessation of use
- Using larger amounts or over a longer period than intended
- Persistent desire to cut down or control drinking
- Spending excessive amounts of time procuring the substance, using the substance, or recovering from its effects
- Reduced involvement in important social, occupational, or recreational activities
- Continued use despite the presence of recurrent physical or psychological problems caused or exacerbated by use (APA, 2000)

**Tolerance** refers to the relative effects that a person experiences when ingesting a specific dosage of a substance. For many substances, if an individual ingests a significant amount each day over a period of months or years, that person will develop increased tolerance, meaning that the person's body has adjusted to the substance. If Albert drinks four beers each day, Albert's tolerance is likely to increase over time so that he will experience more moderate effects of alcohol if he drinks the same quantities. To regain the desired effects of alcohol that he previously experienced, he will have to drink more beer or switch to another drink with a higher alcohol content.

**Withdrawal** refers to the negative physical and psychological reactions that a person who is dependent on substances experiences upon cessation of use. In other words, when a person uses certain substances over months or years, the body and mind adjust to the substance in a manner that results in withdrawal symptoms when the person ceases use for a period of hours or days. Withdrawal effects are specific to different substances. Withdrawal effects characteristic to alcohol dependence include nausea, anxiety, irritability, tremors, fever, rapid heartbeat, insomnia, and hallucinations. Some substances, including alcohol, heroin, and nicotine, have a high addictive liability, meaning that dependence develops quickly and withdrawal effects can be severe. Other substances have moderate addictive liability. Still other substances, such as LSD, produce no withdrawal effects.

**Physical dependence** refers specifically to how the body adjusts to prolonged and repeated exposure to a substance. Withdrawal essentially means that body tissues and organs are craving the substance to function normally. The withdrawal effects for physical dependence include both physical and psychological consequences. For example, the withdrawal effects for heroin include restlessness, muscle and bone pain, insomnia, diarrhea, vomiting, cold flashes with goose bumps ("cold turkey"), and kicking movements ("kicking the habit") (NIDA, 2003). Psychological dependence refers to how the mind adjusts to exposure to a substance. For example, if a substance produces effects that feel good (e.g., the exhilaration of a cocaine high), the theory of operant conditioning (from behavioral theory) tells us that this experience reinforces behavior and the person is more likely to repeat it. Likewise, the theory of classical conditioning (remember Pavlov's dog?) tells us that when one stimulus is matched with another stimulus, over time the person will associate the second stimulus with the response of the first stimulus. Consider a person who smokes cigarettes and feels relaxed as a result. If the person tends to smoke while drinking coffee, the person will eventually associate drinking coffee with smoking cigarettes and the relaxed feeling it provides. If the person tries to stop smoking, one of the hardest times to resist smoking will be while drinking coffee. In other words, coffee will act as a trigger for smoking. The person will crave cigarettes, finding it difficult to think, feel, and function normally (Fisher and Harrison, 2000). If the person does not give in to this craving and smoke, the person might experience withdrawal effects that include both physical consequences (e.g., shakes and increased heartbeat) and psychological consequences (e.g., irritability). Likewise, psychological dependence could occur through other psychological processes, such as modeling, cognitive learning, and psychodynamic means (e.g., sublimation of unconscious drives).

The **DSM-IV-TR** (2000) defines **substance abuse** as a maladaptive pattern or harmful use of a substance leading to significant impairment or distress. The harm could be physical, psychological, or social. Examples include overdosing; driving while intoxicated and having an accident; becoming depressed or suicidal; becoming unable to fulfill major role obligations at work, school, or home; breaking laws; and getting into arguments or physical fights. Some might view substance abuse as less severe than substance dependence because a person with substance abuse may not have developed tolerance or go through withdrawal. The effects of substance abuse, however, can be extreme, including family violence, accidental death, or suicide. Substance abuse may lead to substance dependence, although the majority of people who abuse substances do not become dependent on them.

The immediate physical and psychological effects of AOD use vary depending upon the specific type of substance (described below), dosage, history and frequency of use, personal expectations and social setting of use, personal level of tolerance (which is affected by genetic and physiological factors, including body size), and route of administration. Consider the following example: When you ask your client, Albert, to describe the effects of alcohol, he says that he experiences many different types of effects. When he drinks a glass of wine, he starts to feel giddy and energized. When he drinks larger quantities, he feels fatigued or mellow. If he is depressed prior to drinking, drinking makes him feel more depressed. If he goes to a bar expecting to pick up a woman, drinking tends to loosen his inhibitions. When he was younger, he had a low tolerance for alcohol, getting sick and vomiting after only three drinks. Now he can have eight drinks without feeling sick.

Albert's giddiness likely relates to the initial effects of smaller amounts of alcohol, whereas his fatigue relates to the dominant depressive effects of larger amounts of alcohol. Being depressed prior to use leads to even more extreme depression with alcohol use. Alcohol itself does not loosen a person's inhibitions, although it does affect thought processes. More importantly, if social norms allow a person to be less inhibited while drinking, then drinking gives a person permission to act in ways that he or she might not act without using alcohol. The fact that Albert can now have eight drinks without feeling sick indicates that prolonged use of alcohol has raised his tolerance for it.

The primary route of administration for alcohol is drinking. Other methods of administration for AODS include eating; inhaling nasally or orally; injecting intravenously, subcutaneously, or intramuscularly; or applying to mucous membranes around the nose, mouth, eyes, or anus (Lewis, Dana, and Blevins, 2002). Swallowing or eating an AOD tends to reduce its effects and slows down the time it takes for the person to start feeling the effects (e.g., 5–60 minutes). This is because the substance has to go through the digestive system, where it is metabolized and distributed to the central nervous system. During metabolism, some of the substance is eliminated through the urine. One advantage of swallowing a substance is that the effects tend to last longer. That is why doctors often prescribe medications as pills to swallow or liquids to drink. Inhaling fumes or smoke nasally or orally tends to produce the quickest, most intense highs. The difference between powder cocaine and crack cocaine is illustrative. Powder cocaine is administered to the inside of the nose, where it is absorbed through the mucous membranes. Its effects are less intense and take longer to feel than those of crack cocaine, partially because crack is inhaled and goes into the lungs and central nervous system much more quickly (within a few seconds). Crack is also purer and more potent than powder cocaine, which is cut with a base substance. If Claudia tells you that she used to inhale cocaine but she now smokes crack, this might indicate that her tolerance to cocaine has increased and she has switched to a more potent form. Most inexperienced users avoid injection drug use because of the pain, as well as the risk of infections and collapsed veins.

Although each person's specific experience of AODs is unique, the general effects of different substances can be understood according to their classification as depressants, opiates, stimulants, hallucinogens, cannabis, or

CHART 11.1 | EFFECTS OF DRUGS

| Class | Substance | Immediate Effects | Use with Pregnancy | Continued Heavy or Regular Use | Ways of Using |
|---|---|---|---|---|---|
| **Stimulants** | | | | | |
| | Tobacco | Lasts 15 minutes to 2 hours. Increased heart and pulse rate. | Harmful | Heart and lung disease, cancer, high blood pressure, bronchitis, and breathing difficulties | Smoking |
| | Caffeine | Lasts 2–4 hours. Increased alertness. Large doses can delay sleep. | Doctors advise < 4 cups of tea or coffee per day. | Restlessness, upset stomach. Can be harmful for people with heart problems. | Orally |
| | Amphetamine (speed) | Lasts 4–8 hours. Highly stimulating. Excitement, increased activity, and decreased appetite. Larger doses delay sleep. | Harmful | Inability to sleep, restlessness, headaches, aggression. Can cause severe mental or emotional disturbances. | Snorting Injecting Anally Orally |
| | Cocaine | Can last up to 4 hours. Feeling of self-confidence and power, increased energy, and decreased appetite. | Harmful | Loss of concentration and motivation. Dizziness, aggression, and mental disturbances. Can cause psychiatric complications. Snorting can lead to tearing of the nasal wall. | Snorting Injecting orally Anally |
| | MDMA (Ecstasy) | Can last up to 6 hours. Increased blood pressure. Increased confidence, feeling of closeness with others. Sensation of floating, anxiety, nausea, and paranoia can occur. | Harmful | Sensation of floating and other disturbed perceptions. Can cause convulsions, irrational behavior, insomnia, and depression. | Injecting orally Anally |
| **Depressants** | | | | | |
| | Alcohol | Slurred speech, loss of inhibitions, relaxation, feelings of happiness and well-being or depression. Large doses can cause unconsciousness or hangover. | Harmful | Can damage brain and nervous system, heart, pancreas, stomach, and liver. Death sometimes occurs. Withdrawal can produce sweating, tremors, convulsions, and delirium. | Orally |

| Drug | Effects | Rating | Risks / Long-term effects | Method of use |
|---|---|---|---|---|
| Minor tranquilizers (diazeparm [Valium], flunitrazepam [Rohypnol], oxazepam [Serepax]) | Lasts 12–24 hours. Relief of anxiety and tension, drowsiness (possible sleep), lack of muscle coordination, blurred vision. In some cases, excitability. | Harmful. Use only under medical supervision. | Depression, lack of muscle and speech coordination. Withdrawal symptoms such as anxiety, insomnia, tremor, and convulsions can also occur while on a stable dose. | Injecting orally Anally |
| Opioids (heroin, morphine, codeine, pethidine, methadone, opium) | Lasts 4–24 hours. Relief of pain and anxiety, feelings of well-being, decreased awareness of outside world. Vomiting, drowsiness, and sleep in some. High doses can cause unconsciousness and death. | Harmful. Use prescribed preparations only under medical supervision. | High risk of overdose; HIV and hepatitis if sharing needles. Withdrawal symptoms are anxiety, sweating, cramps, runny nose, vomiting, insomnia, pain. | Injecting orally Smoking Snorting |
| Cannabis (marijuana) | Can last up to 5 hours. Relaxation, laughter, increased appetite, slowing down of time, loss of concentration, decreased coordination, and blood-shot eyes. Can be hallucinogenic. | Long-term effects are still to be assessed. | Respiratory complications. Can decrease concentration and memory. Psychiatric problems possible if schizophrenic condition already exists. | Oral smoking |
| Inhalants and Solvents (petrol, glue, aerosol cans, butane gas) | Lasts 1–3 hours. Petrol sniffing effects can last up to 6 hours. Feelings of happiness, relaxation, and drowsiness. Large amounts can cause illness and sudden death. | Harmful | Liver, kidney, and brain damage can result. Suffocation caused by plastic bags, choking on vomit. | Inhaling |
| **Hallucinogens** Hallucinogens (LSD, magic mushrooms, trips) | Lasts 6–12 hours. Hallucinations (i.e., seeing, hearing, feeling, or thinking things that do not exist). Anxious feelings, panic, and nausea can occur. | Harmful | Can increase the risk of severe mental disturbances. Can cause "flashbacks" (where the drug experience can recur at any time). | Orally |
| Injecting | | | HIV and hepatitis B and C infection can occur if injecting equipment is shared. Injecting with dirty syringes can cause abscesses and blood poisoning. New injecting equipment should be used every time. | |

*Note:* Mixing drugs can sharply increase their effects (e.g., mixing alcohol with minor tranquilizers can markedly impair driving ability).

**Sources:** The Effects of Drugs chart was produced by CEIDA (Centre for Education and Information on Drugs and Alcohol) © CEIDA 1985, revised 1995. Reprinted with permission from the NSW Department of Health, Australia.

inhalants.[3] **Depressants** include alcohol, benzodiazepines (e.g., relaxants such as diazepam [Valium], and barbiturates (e.g., sleeping pills such as secobarbital [Seconal]). The primary effect of depressants is the slowing down of the central nervous system. Physically, they tend to reduce blood pressure, heart rate, breathing, reflexes, and motor coordination. Psychologically, they tend to produce feelings of relaxation, calmness, disinhibition, and reduced anxiety. Signs of recent depressant use include shallow breathing, depressed mood, slurred speech, and constricted pupils. If a person is physically dependent on depressants, cessation of use can be medically dangerous. Accordingly, if you are helping a client who is physically dependent stop using depressants, the client should go to a detoxification unit for the withdrawal period (typically, 7–10 days). The staff will monitor the client's withdrawal and dispense medication, where appropriate, to alleviate severe withdrawal effects. Depressants tend to produce both tolerance and dependence over time. Risks of long-term use include damage to the liver and brain (McNeece and DiNitto, 1998).

Although some experts categorize **opiates** as a subclass of depressants, others view opiates as a separate class of drugs because of their distinctive effects. Opiates vary in strength, from weaker substances such as codeine and morphine to stronger ones such as heroin, methadone, and oxycodone (OxyContin). Medically, opiates are used as analgesics (painkillers). Different opiates may be smoked, injected, or taken orally in the form of pills or liquids. Recreationally, the stronger opiates are used not only for their analgesic effects on mind and body but also for the initial "rush" or euphoria that they produce. This rush distinguishes them from other depressants. When a person injects heroin, for example, he or she will feel a surge of pleasurable sensation for several minutes, followed by several hours of drowsiness or fatigue (nodding off). A key risk of injection drug use is the spread of HIV or hepatitis if users are sharing needles. Opiates are highly addictive, both physically and psychologically. Withdrawal effects are very strong, making it difficult for a person to stop using heroin, although they are not generally as dangerous as those of alcohol and may not require medical detox (van Wormer and Davis, 2003).

**Stimulants** include amphetamines, crack cocaine, methylphenidate (Ritalin), caffeine, and nicotine. Most stimulants are used orally (liquid or pills), smoked, or applied to mucous membranes in the nose (especially cocaine), although they can also be injected. Initially, stimulants tend to elevate the central nervous system, raising the heartbeat, blood pressure, breathing rate, and level of physical energy, and depressing the appetite (e.g., diet pills are typically stimulants). Psychologically, stimulants tend to elevate the mood, producing feelings of euphoria, confidence, and excitement. After the initial high, the person experiences a "down," which is similar to the effects of depressants. To assess if Claudia has recently used cocaine, Tyra would need to look for signs and symptoms related to both the initial intoxication and the down side. If the substance is one of the more potent stimulants (e.g.,

---

[3]There are other classifications, such as antidepressants, antipsychotics, steroids, and antibiotics. The ones focused on in this chapter are the psychoactive substances that are most commonly abused.

methamphetamine or crack), the crash after the initial high can be severe. To avoid crashing, some AOD users continue to take successive hits or doses of the substance. Although caffeine is a weaker stimulant, coffee drinkers might note a similar pattern. In the morning, the person feels tired and irritable and has a headache. Coffee seems to relieve these symptoms. By coffee break time, the person is starting to feel tired again, but the next cup of coffee once again alleviates the fatigue. Although substances such as methylphenidate (used to treat attention deficit disorder) and nicotine are classified as stimulants, users of these substances will often report feeling relaxed or less anxious when using them. This is partially because their stimulant effects are not as strong and people become tolerant to them over time. Stronger stimulants such as cocaine and amphetamines are highly psychologically addictive because the strong euphoric effects tend to produce cravings. The withdrawal effects vary between stimulants, but generally include irritability, depressed mood, headaches, and anxiety. Going through withdrawal from stimulants is unpleasant but generally not medically dangerous, so that clients usually do not need to stay at a medically supervised detoxification facility. Severe depression ("crashing") and suicidal ideation may occur in clients withdrawing from cocaine or amphetamines, so support and monitoring are generally indicated for the first three or four days of withdrawal (Fisher and Harrison, 2000). Users of stimulants sometimes use depressants to help soften the effects of coming down (e.g., mixing cocaine and heroin is called a "speedball"). Combining substances can be medically risky because of the uncertain effects of mixing, and because an intoxicated user's thinking is impaired as he or she tries to make decisions about what combination and amount of each substance to use.

Whereas the primary effects of stimulants and depressants are to increase or decrease the functioning of the central nervous system, the primary effects of **hallucinogens** are perceptual. Hallucinogens such as D-lysergic acid diethylamide (LSD), mescaline (mushrooms), phencyclidine (angel dust), and ketamine (special K) distort and blend the person's visual, auditory, olfactory, or tactile senses and thought processes. Most hallucinogens are taken orally, although they can also be administered in other forms. The effects of LSD "trips" typically last 5–12 hours, although flashbacks can occur days, weeks, or months later. Use of hallucinogens does not lead to physical dependence. Although some users experience some psychological cravings to use, these are not as strong as for stimulants (McNeece and DiNitto, 1998). Risks of hallucinogen use include accidental death related to altered perceptions and cognitions (e.g., thinking one can fly and jumping off a balcony, or having a scary flashback while driving a car). Some hybrid substances, such as the club drug methylenedioxymethamphetamine (MDMA, Ecstasy), produce both stimulant and hallucinogenic effects (NIDA, 2003).

**Cannabis** includes marijuana, hash, and hash oil. Cannabis is typically smoked, brewed as a tea, or mixed with food items so that it can be eaten. Initial intoxication produces feelings of euphoria, increased heartbeat, and perceptual changes, such as intensifying of sounds and colors or slowing of the passage of time. Inexperienced users might feel anxious, giddy, panicky, or distrustful. More experienced users tend to feel more relaxed and sleepy following the initial euphoria. Risks of cannabis use include impairment of memory, coordination, and thinking, which might lead to other risky behaviors, such as driving while "high" or engaging in unsafe sex. Risks of long-term use include cancer, heart attack, lung infections, memory loss, and impairments of the immune system (NIDA, 2003).

**Inhalants** are volatile chemicals that can be sniffed or huffed, breathing in vapors through the mouth or nose. Children and youth often use inhalants because of ease of access. Many inhalants are substances that can be found commonly around the house, such as gasoline, aerosols, paint thinner, and glue. The user huffs fumes directly from the original container, a paper bag, or a cloth soaked with the fluid. The effects depend on the type of inhalant but can include delusions, hallucinations, dizziness, euphoria, impaired judgment, slurred speech, and sleepiness. People often report using inhalants as an escape or a way to dull emotional pain. Risks of use include loss of consciousness, paralysis, asphyxiation, and irreversible brain damage (McNeece and DiNitto, 1998).

Although social workers with clients affected by addictions need to understand the pharmacologic principles and immediate physical and psychological effects of various substances, this information is just one part of the equation. Addictions can be caused or maintained by a myriad of biological, psychological, social, and spiritual factors. Further, addictions can result in or aggravate problems in each of these spheres. The news about addictions is not all gloomy. Many people with addictions develop strengths that not only help them to overcome addictions but also help them in other areas of social functioning. The following section provides a historical overview of perspectives on addictions, demonstrating various ways that professionals and society generally have tried to make sense of the various interacting factors that affect people with addictions.

# HISTORICAL AND CURRENT PERSPECTIVES ON ADDICTIONS

Over time and across various cultures, addictions have been understood and treated from a range of different frameworks, including the moral model, medical model and disease concept, pharmacologic perspectives (described above), public health model, psychological perspectives, sociocultural perspectives (including family systems and ecosystems), and structural perspectives.

The **moral model** suggests that addictions are caused by the individual's moral weaknesses, such as being weak willed, self-indulgent, or sinful (McNeece and DiNitto, 1998). People who ascribe to the moral model generally do so out of religious and cultural attitudes that support the notions of self-responsibility and free will. There is no empirical research to support the connection between morality and addiction. In fact, many people with addictions have strong wills and a high sense of moral values. Still, the moral model has had a strong influence on public policy historically and currently.

Policies such as prohibition (beginning in 1919), which made the production and sale of alcohol illegal, are based on the moral model. They suggest that addiction, as an immoral behavior, ought to be punished through the criminal justice system. The "war on drugs" declared by Ronald Reagan in the 1980s also built on the moral model by seeking to eliminate drug trafficking and use through criminal law enforcement.

Stereotypes such as the skid-row alcoholic portrayed in movies and other media continue to propagate the connection between addiction and immorality. The stereotype of an addict as a strung-out, impoverished minority person with a substantial criminal record does not reflect the reality of persons affected by addictions. People from all socioeconomic and ethnocultural groups have addictions.

The medical model and disease concept are related but are nonetheless different concepts. The **medical model** suggests that addiction is a condition that should be diagnosed by an expert, who will prescribe a treatment for the cure or control of the condition. The **disease concept** suggests that addiction is a disease or medical illness. By viewing addiction as a disease, the individual is not stigmatized as having a moral defect.

Although the medical model suggests that the disease of addiction should be diagnosed and treated by an expert, **self-help groups** such as Alcoholics Anonymous (AA) and Narcotics Anonymous (NA) suggest that an individual can self-declare as having alcoholism or addiction and that the most effective form of help is self-help rather than professionally led treatment. AA and NA also believe that addiction can be controlled but not cured (similar to diseases such as epilepsy or diabetes). The disease concept was popularized through AA in the 1930s and remains prevalent among mental health professionals and self-help addiction groups to this day (Alcoholics Anonymous, 2003).

Research trying to prove that addiction is a disease has linked alcoholism and other addictions to genetic factors. Environmental factors also play a role in the development of addictions. For social workers, proving whether addiction is a disease is not as important as how the research affects societal perceptions of addiction. If society views addiction as a disease, addicts are less likely to be oppressed or discriminated against than if society views addiction as a moral defect. Some professionals do not refer to addiction as a physical or mental health disease but rather as a social "dis-ease," or a lack of ease within families, groups, or other social units.

The **public health model** suggests that addiction problems arise from interactions between the agent (AOD), the host (the potential AOD user), and the social environment. In order to promote health, prevention strategies can target any one, two, or three of these factors. For example, to reduce access to the agent, the state could levy taxes, control where the agent can be sold, and restrict who can purchase it to people over a certain age (e.g., the current policies regulating sales of cigarettes and alcohol).

Prevention strategies that target the host include education or persuasion to discourage the use of particular substances or unsafe practices, such as drinking and driving. Environmental prevention strategies include implementing policies at work and school and in the media that shape attitudes and discourage certain types of substance use (e.g., banning steroid use among football players) (Jung, 2001).

**Psychological perspectives** on addictions include trait, psychodynamic, cognitive-behavioral, and existential-spiritual theories. **Trait theories** suggest that people are born with certain personality characteristics, such as compulsiveness, that make them prone to addictions. These theories provide a negative view of individuals and have no empirical support. **Freudian psychodynamic theory** provides a range of possible explanations for addictive behavior. One is that addiction is related to having an overactive id (the pleasure center of the mind) or a malfunctioning ego (the rational center). Alternatively, addiction could be a response to a fixation at a specific psychosexual developmental phase (e.g., a person who drinks might be fixated at the oral stage) or an unresolved, unconscious conflict from childhood (e.g., anger at parents turned inward to self-destructive behavior, such as overeating). Once again, these theories do not have empirical support and are not broadly accepted among social workers in the field of addictions.

**Cognitive-behavioral theories** suggest that addictions can be explained by the connections between stimulants, behaviors, consequences, and the way that people think about these connections. As noted above, classical learning suggests that substance abuse can be triggered by certain conditions that the user associates with the positive effects of AODs. Similarly, if AOD use is reinforced with positive consequences (e.g., feelings of euphoria), the person is more likely to repeat those AOD behaviors. Because people have the capacities of awareness and thinking, AOD behaviors are not simply automatic responses. A person who feels immediate pleasure from snorting cocaine, for example, might decide not to use it if that person is aware of the long-term risks. AOD behaviors can also be learned through social learning or modeling after people who are important in their lives (e.g., parents, peers, or celebrities). Cognitive-behavioral theories have significant research support and are broadly used by AOD helping professionals (Fisher and Harrison, 2001).

**Existential-spiritual theories** suggest that addiction is related to lack of meaning or anomie within a person's life. Research does support the notion that having a strong spiritual or religious connection can act as a protective factor against addictions (van Wormer and Davis, 2003). Both professionally led treatment programs and self-help groups often include spirituality as part of the helping process.

**Sociocultural perspectives** look at the development and maintenance of addictions within social units such as family systems, communities, schools, religions, cultural groups, and other organizations. Addiction is not seen as an individual phenomenon but rather as a result of certain patterns of interaction (McNeece and DiNitto, 1998). Within a family, for instance, the mother might be coping with the stress of raising children by taking antianxiety medication and the father might support this behavior by praising her for how much more relaxed she seems since she has started to take this medication. Within a counterculture such as a street gang, peer pressure to use illicit drugs might be very strong. Sociocultural perspectives fit with the **ecological model** that is popular among social workers. In other words, addictions occur within the transactions between clients and their social environments, as a method of coping with stress or lack of goodness of fit. Although the ecological perspective takes the focus of addiction away from individual pathologic traits, many social workers view addiction as both a social problem and a disease that affects individuals, families, organizations, and communities.

A **structural perspective** on addiction views discrimination and oppression in the structures of society as the key causes. From this perspective, oppressive forces such as classism, patriarchy, sexism, heterosexism, religious chauvinism, ableism, and racism cause addiction. Large corporate purveyors of beer, for example, could be seen as fostering and profiting from an underclass in society that is addicted to alcohol. Similarly, in response to heterosexist laws and stereotypes, some gay men and lesbians turn to illicit substances as a form of escape. Marxist and radical feminist social workers tend to adopt a structural perspective on addictions (Fook, 1993).

Addiction is a complex phenomenon that cannot be reduced to a single theory of causation or intervention. Social workers must understand the range of explanations and theories, learning how to assess and intervene with clients from across this spectrum. In her own recovery, Tyra found AA and the disease concept to be very helpful.

When working with Claudia, however, Tyra must be careful not to impose these beliefs on her. Although it might be appropriate to introduce Claudia to AA perspectives, a generalist social work framework suggests exploring various understandings of addiction and various methods of dealing with it.

Social workers have served people with addictions in many roles: as advocates, assessors, community development workers, policy practitioners, and individual, family, and group counselors. The strengths, biopsychosocial, and ecological perspectives of social workers have sometimes been at odds with other perspectives in the addictions field, including self-help groups and mental health professionals who focus on addiction as a disease of the individual.

Further, some addiction programs suggest that the main prerequisite to being an effective addictions worker is having a background of addiction and recovery, rather than having professional training as a social worker or mental health professional. These tensions continue in the field. Research suggests that there are many ways to effect positive change (NIAAA, 2001c). Social workers can play a role not only in advancing their own perspectives but in helping to build bridges between professionals with different perspectives and in helping clients make self-determined choices based on knowledge of the range of helping processes available.

# CURRENT POLICY ISSUES REGARDING ALCOHOL AND OTHER DRUGS

Fundamental policy issues include the ethical appropriateness and cost-effectiveness of various public responses to substance use and addiction: criminal and health laws to control substance use, mandated treatment, education as prevention, and harm reduction approaches.

Current social policy on AODs reflects a hodge-podge of criminal laws, health regulations, prevention programs, and treatment services. Although the human and economic costs of addiction have been well documented and accepted, there is little consensus about how to prevent and remediate addiction problems. In terms of dollars spent, the largest social program for people affected by addictions is the criminal justice system. The United States spends over $24 billion per year on policing, adjudicating, and incarcerating people for AOD-related crimes (NIDA, 2003). When one considers that AOD treatment costs range from $1,800 to $6,800 per client compared to over $18,000 per person (annually) for incarceration, the need for prevention and treatment programs seems clear (NIDA, 2003).

The **Controlled Substances Act** (1970) classifies drugs into five different schedules. Each class has its own rules, regulations, and prohibitions, which are based on lawmakers' views of the risks of abuse and dependency associated with each substance. Schedule I drugs, including heroin, hallucinogens, and marijuana, are the most restricted drugs. Their production, sale, or use is prohibited under all circumstances. Schedule II, III, and IV drugs have medically accepted uses but must be prescribed by a physician and sold by a licensed pharmacist.

According to the laws, Schedule II drugs (including cocaine, methamphetamine, and opiates other than heroin) have high potential for abuse or dependence, so they are subject to strict regulation and penalties for illicit sales. The act suggests that Schedule III drugs (including anabolic steroids, codeine, and some barbiturates) have lower potential for abuse or dependence, and Schedule IV drugs (including diazepam [Valium], alprazolam [Xanax], and other benzodiazepines) have a low potential for abuse and limited risk of dependence. Schedule V drugs include over-the-counter medications that can be purchased without a physician's prescription.

The relative strictness of regulation of various substances and corresponding penalties for offenses are topics of much debate. Why are substances such as marijuana and heroin prohibited outright and their mere possession a cause for criminal prosecution, whereas substances such as morphine and amphetamines are allowed to be used for medicinal purposes? Should marijuana be available for medical uses, such as the relief of pain and nausea in cancer patients? Does imposing a criminal record on users of illicit substances do more harm than good by creating a stigma and preventing employment for people affected by addictions? Would decriminalization of offenses have sufficient deterrent effect if people who committed AOD offenses were fined but not incarcerated or given a criminal record? Is legalization of harmful substances really the answer, given that two legalized drugs, nicotine and alcohol, actually cause the greatest costs to society in terms of health problems, family violence, and substance-related death?

Claudia's drug of choice is cocaine. Although she was charged with possession of cocaine, she was diverted from criminal proceedings by a program that recognizes that criminal prosecution and incarceration are costly and generally ineffective in treating people with addiction problems. In fact, many people who leave the prison system emerge with a more severe addiction problem than the one that led to their incarceration.

A related policy issue concerns whether or not involuntary treatment, particularly referrals through the criminal court and child protection systems, is effective and appropriate (van Wormer and Davis, 2003). If someone like Claudia is not ready for help, does the social work ethic of self-determination mean that she should not be coerced into treatment, or are there overriding societal values that justify mandatory treatment? Some treatment programs and self-help groups (e.g., AA) were built upon the premise that an individual must self-declare as having an addiction problem and that a person cannot be forced into this first step in the recovery process.

Other programs and models, including the transtheoretical model described below, have been developed specifically for clients who are not currently expressing a desire to change their substance use behavior.

According to cliché, an ounce of prevention is worth a pound of intervention. From a more critical perspective, some addiction prevention programs are cost-effective, but not all. One study, for instance, found that high-threat messages presented to male college students were associated with higher levels of beer consumption in comparison to low-threat messages (Jung, 2001).

Although large sums of resources have been placed into generic drug education messages, such as the "Just Say No" campaign, the most effective prevention programs are ones geared to particular risk and protective factors for a specific group (Kumpfer, 2002). If a group of young people is at risk because their parents lack certain parenting skills, then providing parenting skills programs would redress this risk factor.

"Protective factors" are personal and social attributes that help people avoid developing AOD problems in the face of risks such as growing up in a family affected by alcoholism or mental illness. Examples of protective factors include having a sense of humor, problem-solving skills, success in school performance, and a positive relationship with at least one adult.

Prevention programs can focus efforts on individuals or groups at risk by helping people develop these protective factors, for example, by providing problem-solving skills training or mentoring programs (e.g., Big Brothers or Big Sisters). This fits with the strengths perspective of social work, by focusing on strengths rather than risks, pathologic problems, or deficits.

Ethnoculturally specific prevention programs also fit with social work's emphasis on respecting and accommodating people from diverse backgrounds.

Providing information is only effective prevention if the problem is related to lack of information. Teaching someone who has been dependent on alcohol for 20 years about the risks of alcohol addiction is not likely to change the person's behavior, as the person already knows very well about the effects of alcohol.

If a new and dangerous form of heroin emerges on the streets, it would be useful to provide potential users with information about the dangers. This will enable heroin users to stay with safer forms of heroin. At a community level, prevention of problems is related to attitudinal change rather than simply change in beliefs or information.

Before the 1980s, drinking alcohol and driving was socially acceptable in many segments of American society. A combined and prolonged effort to change attitudes toward drinking and driving, including advertising, school-based education, and targeted criminal law enforcement, has led to changes in attitudes. Bartenders and hosts of parties now take more responsibility to ensure that their customers and guests get home safely, and people who plan on drinking prepare to have safe drivers or use public transportation.

Programs focusing on the effects that alcohol and cigarettes can have on the health of a fetus have caused many women to avoid or reduce drinking and smoking during pregnancy. Changing attitudes toward certain patterns of substance use can take a generation to effect. Unfortunately, government leaders tend to look for "quick-fix" solutions, so they can appear to be effective before their two- or four-year term is up and they face reelection.

**Harm-reduction approaches** focus on prevention of harm rather than use of a substance. This approach fits with the ethical principles of "self-determination" and "promoting safety," although there is much debate about the effectiveness and ethical appropriateness of this approach. Examples of harm-reduction approaches include providing intravenous-drug users with clean needles or bleach kits to reduce HIV and hepatitis transmission, providing methadone to heroin users to reduce risks related to impurities in street drugs and involvement in criminal activity, and providing information on how to use substances more safely (e.g., someone dependent on alcohol might be advised to take Vitamin D supplements) (Johnson, 2004).

In general, opponents of harm reduction suggest that these approaches condone substance abuse and actually contribute to more problems in the long term. These opponents suggest that policymakers and addiction specialists must provide clear messages that people should not use dangerous substances, particularly those which society has deemed illicit.

Proponents of harm reduction tend to be grounded in a public health model of addiction, whereas detractors tend to be grounded in a moral model or disease concept of addiction and believe that abstinence is the best policy (Harm Reduction Coalition, 2003). Ultimately, each harm-reduction program should be evaluated on its own merits and risks rather than on assumptions or a steadfast insistence on a single ideology.

Communities often respond to high-profile cases involving AODs, for instance, a promising high school student who accidentally falls off a balcony at a rock concert while high on LSD, a police officer who is killed during a drug-bust operation, or a child who is born addicted to crack. These cases can mobilize grassroots and political forces to promote change through public policy.

Social workers can play a valuable role in educating the public about the effectiveness of certain types of prevention programs, as well as the pitfalls of overly simplistic, quick-fix educational programs or knee-jerk reactions that promote fear of or disgust toward people with addictions rather than empathy, supportive guidance, and empowerment.

## GENERALIST PRACTICE WITH PEOPLE AFFECTED BY ADDICTIONS

Helping individuals and families affected by addictions is complicated not only by the fact that there are many theories of addiction and models of practice, but also by the complex range of service delivery systems and how they are administered. Services providing care for people affected by addictions include the following:

1. Assessment and referral services: These services provide specialized biopsychosocial assessments for people affected by addictions, helping clients understand the nature of their issues, providing information about various treatment options, identifying whether clients qualify for certain types of programs, and linking clients to programs that best suit their current needs. Some clients are ordered by a criminal court or child protection court to be assessed. It is particularly difficult to assess a client who might not want help and fears that any problems identified will be used against him or her in any further proceedings.

2. Self-help groups: These groups are facilitated by and for people with addiction problems. They usually meet once a week. People can attend many different self-help groups in different locations on different days of the week. These programs are usually free. Donations may be requested to pay for room rental and refreshments.

3. Hospital emergency units: Emergency units are often the first point of entry for people who are in a crisis state related to their AOD use, for example, people who are actively suicidal, have recently overdosed on AODs, or have been involved in a serious physical accident as a result of AOD use. Emergency units should be used only for true emergencies. Other medical issues should be treated by family physicians or detoxification units, as described below.

4. Detoxification units: Detoxification units provide a safe place for people to physically withdraw from substances such as alcohol or barbiturates, where medical monitoring and intervention are required to ensure that the person does not have a heart attack or other severe response during the

withdrawal process. Family or other supports in the community can generally monitor withdrawal from other substances.

5. Outpatient services: These counseling services provide individual or group work once a week for people who continue to live in the community during the helping process.

6. Day treatment programs: These programs offer intensive group therapy and counseling to clients who live at home but come to the program at least five days a week (e.g., from 9:00 A.M. to 5 P.M.). They are more expensive and intrusive than outpatient services, but less expensive and intrusive than institutional services.

7. Institutional services: These are hospital-like facilities that provide intensive inpatient counseling and therapy, typically for 21–28 days.

8. Residential or community-based rehabilitation: These programs provide longer-term support and counseling services (three months to a year) in a facility that resembles a home more than a hospital. Some programs start with an intensive phase that requires clients to participate in eight hours of programming per day. In later phases, the amount of programming is reduced and the person is encouraged to go back to work, school, or job training, as part of the process of reintegration into the community.

9. Pharmacotherapy services: These refer to clinics that offer medications to help clients remain abstinent or avoid withdrawal effects. Methadone, for example, allows people to stop using heroin without going through immediate withdrawal. Clients can be maintained on methadone on an indefinite basis or there can be a plan for strategic detoxification within a few weeks. Antabuse helps people who have stopped using alcohol to remain abstinent. Antabuse causes a negative reaction if the person consumes any alcohol, thus creating a strong incentive not to use. Pharmacotherapy requires medical supervision, as well as psychosocial counseling. Medications are not "magic pills" that cure all problems, but they are part of a possible combination of interventions.

10. Half-way house: Not to be confused with criminal half-way houses, addiction half-way houses are residential facilities that help people move from more intensive treatment programs back to the community. They offer support and a safe home environment but not intensive treatment.

11. Aftercare or relapse prevention: These are typically groups that offer supportive counseling for people who have achieved initial sobriety and want to prevent relapse. They recognize that addiction problems are not simply cured out of existence, but can re-emerge at any time.

12. Collateral services: These are services that are not addiction-specific ones, but part of the overall mental health and social service delivery system. People with addiction problems are much more likely to present in these types of programs than in substance-abuse specific programs. Whether the presenting problem is brain injury, depression, marital conflict, loss of a job, or any other biopsychosocial problem, social workers and other helping professionals need to assess for and provide help for AOD problems. (Barsky, forthcoming)

Ideally, help for people affected by addictions would be accessible, individualized, comprehensive, and strategic. In terms of accessibility, services should be affordable, available within reasonable timeframes, geographically handy, and without barriers for people with disabilities, special needs, and dual diagnoses. In reality, there are many barriers to access. Although health insurance covers some types of programs, it does not cover others, particularly programs lasting longer than 28 days. For those without health insurance coverage, publicly funded services are available, but often have waiting lists and vary in their quality. Specialized and intensive programs are only available in larger cities, making access for people in rural and remote regions difficult. As advocates, educators, and brokers of resources, generalist social workers play a key role in ensuring accessibility to AOD services.

**Group counseling** is the intervention of choice in many programs, particularly day treatment, institutional, and residential programs. The advantages of group work include cost efficiency (with one worker for many clients), as well as the following factors:

1.  A group context provides a safe yet realistic place for clients to learn new social skills through modeling, rehearsal, and feedback
2.  Groups can offer instillation of hope, education, and realization that the client is not alone with his or her addiction problems
3.  Feedback and peer pressure from others affected by addictions allow clients to observe and confront denial systems in themselves and others in ways that could not be provided by a professional
4.  Groups can offer clients a new and positive support system (Johnson, 2004)

Heavy reliance on group work may detract from individualizing treatment services for clients with special needs, for example, clients who are deaf or have learning disabilities, clients who are not fluent in English, and clients with a burden of secrets that they may not be able to share in group treatment programs (e.g., a lesbian client who is "in the closet," a survivor of childhood sexual abuse, or someone who has perpetrated a heinous crime). When helping clients determine the best venues for help with addictions, social workers need to take these issues into account, as well as other aspects of client diversity (e.g., culture, ethnicity, socioeconomic status, spirituality). Consider, for example, how Claudia would feel as the only African-American woman or as the only evangelical Christian at a treatment program whose main demographic group consisted of secular white men.

Research on the effectiveness of addictions treatment has explored whether matching certain clients with particular interventions or combinations of interventions could raise the level of success in treatment. An eight-year study conducted by the National Institute on Alcohol Abuse and Alcoholism randomly assigned clients to one of three treatment modalities: twelve-step facilitation, cognitive-behavioral coping skills, or motivational enhancement therapy (NIAAA, 2001c). This study used individual counseling for all three modalities, though the twelve-step approach also encouraged clients to participate in AA group meetings. Individual counseling using the twelve-step approach facilitates the client's active participation in AA, supporting tenets such as:

- Clients must accept that alcoholism is a chronic progressive illness, which if not arrested, will lead to insanity or death
- There is hope for recovery (sustained sobriety) but only through accepting the reality of loss of control and having faith that a higher power can help the individual whose willpower has been defeated by alcoholism
- Recovery and abstinence occur one day at a time
- Participation in the fellowship of AA groups, sponsors (mentoring), and steps toward recovery that have helped millions of alcoholics (NIAAA, 2001d)

In the case example, Tyra could ask Claudia what she knows about Narcotics Anonymous and offer to provide information about it. Tyra could also offer to escort Claudia to an open meeting of NA just to "check it out" rather than asking her to agree to participate on an ongoing basis. Tyra might explain that she is "not into God or any of that religious ideal." Claudia could help Tyra understand how twelve-step programs are spiritual rather than religious and how Tyra could define her own higher power, perhaps as her inner self, as the group, or even as the chain that she is wearing around her neck as a symbol of strength.

Counseling that follows cognitive-behavioral coping skills helps clients by teaching them to identify situations where they are at higher likelihood of drinking (e.g., when the client feels depressed, experiences stress at work, or thinks that people are out to "get" him or her). The worker then teaches the client cognitive and behavioral skills to deal with these high-risk situations. For example, the worker can teach the client problem-solving skills, help the client with communication and interpersonal problems by rehearsing high-risk situations in role-plays, or help the client to reframe situations more positively or realistically (NIAAA, 2001a).

Claudia says that she uses cocaine whenever she is "hanging out in the 'hood.'" Tyra helps her explore the precise nature of the risk, whether the trigger is the neighborhood itself, access to cocaine, pressure from peers, or having nothing else to do. Claudia suggests that the main issue is that she associates the neighborhood with shooting cocaine. Tyra and Claudia work out a plan where Claudia will locate other communities where she can socialize, develop friendships, and find other interests.

The **motivational enhancement approach** attempts to mobilize the client's own change resources, leading the client to initiate, persist in, and comply with behavior change efforts because the change fits with the client's internal goals. The role of the worker is to listen empathically and support the client's sense of self-efficacy, offering encouragement and consultation. The worker avoids argumentation and rolls with resistance, meaning that the worker encourages new ways of thinking about problems but does not try to impose solutions or labels for the problems (Barsky and Coleman, 2001).

The worker can help the client tap into his or her own motivation by enhancing and focusing the client's attention on the discrepancies between "where the client is" and "where the client wants to be" (NIAAA, 2001b; Rollnick and Morgan, 1997). Clients are able to define their own goals, whether they are abstinence, controlled use, harm reduction, or goals that are not directly related to substance abuse or addiction (e.g., to improve a marital relationship).

Initially, Claudia is in the precontemplation stage. She is angry that she has been forced to see Tyra, saying there are no problems. Tyra does not contradict Claudia, but helps her explore whether there are any issues that she'd like to change. Claudia says that she'd like to make sure that she has no more problems with the law. This gives Tyra an opportunity to work on an issue that is of interest to Tyra. Once they agree to work together on "no more legal problems," Tyra starts by having Claudia share her stories about harassment by police. Tyra validates Claudia's feelings of frustration and anger. Claudia begins to trust Tyra.

Three sessions later, Claudia finally mentions cocaine use, asking whether people can control their use or whether it is an all or nothing choice. Tyra does not ask Claudia if she is talking about her own cocaine use. Tyra helps Claudia find information about cocaine and controlled use treatment without making any judgments for Claudia.

The findings of Project Match suggest that all three modalities lead to positive change, defined as decreases in drinking frequency, intensity, and total volume, as well as social functioning, subjective well-being, and service use (NIAAA, 2001c). This study did not isolate strong matching effects as originally had been hypothesized, although researchers continue to look for combinations of modalities and matching with different client characteristics in order to provide more guidance for evidence-based, effective practice. This research did confirm the value of having clearly prescribed models of practice (NIAAA, 2001a, b, d), well-trained practitioners, and a rigorous method for evaluation of success.

For generalist social workers, there are certainly many more models to consider, but these three models are among the more popular ones and they do fit with collaborative generalist practice. The twelve-step approach fits with the brokering role of social work, linking clients with social support systems, including self-help groups. Although the disease concept of AA might seem to conflict with the ecological perspective, the idea that addiction is a disease does not mean that it is only an individual one.

Ecologically minded social workers can reframe addiction as a disease that arises from both individual and social causes. Claudia, for instance, may have a genetic predisposition to substance abuse because she was born with a learning disability. Her cocaine addiction, however, developed as it did because she was raised in a neighborhood where cocaine was available and its use condoned, and because her school environment was not adequately supportive of her learning disability.

Cognitive-behavioral skill training fits with the generalist problem-solving approach. The social worker helps the client identify problems (here, risks for abusing substances) and then helps the client build skills to reduce these risks. Motivational enhancement counseling fits with many social work principles: honoring client self-determination by allowing the client to set goals; respecting the client by providing the client with validation and empathic understanding; and empowering the client to make informed decisions by helping the client think about possible discrepancies between what the client wants and what the client's current behavior is leading toward.

For most generalist social workers, clients will not typically come to them stating that they want to change their AOD behaviors. Family members, employers, school officials, child protection workers, or the criminal justice system often exert subtle or overt pressure on people with addictions to get professional help. While social workers might be quick to suggest that these reluctant or involuntary clients are "in denial," the transtheoretical model provides a more strengths-based perspective, suggesting that they are in either the precontemplation or contemplation stage of change (Prochaska, 1994).

In the precontemplation stage, the client is not aware of having a problem or is not thinking about the possibility of making a change in AOD behavior. The worker's role is to help the client gain awareness and begin to consider the possibility of change. The worker begins with the client, working on issues that the client is concerned about and helping the client develop insights about how AOD abuse or addiction might be interfering with the client's own goals.

Behavioral feedback from the worker as well as from family members and other support systems can help the client become aware of the possible need for change, but this feedback must be offered in a supportive manner rather than a confrontational or guilt-provoking manner. The worker paces the intervention with the client's stage of change, first helping the client move from precontemplation to contemplation.

In the contemplation stage, the client is considering the possibility of change. The worker helps the client think about the positive and negative effects of the AOD behavior, as well as the life goals that the client wants to achieve. The worker helps the client move toward making a determination by weighing the positives and negatives, including both short-term and long-term risks and potential benefits.

The worker also helps the client by building the client's sense of hope and possibility, building on the client's personal strengths and connecting the client with supports from the community, including people who have been successful in achieving the desired changes and treatment programs that the person could investigate as possible sources of help. The worker does not try to move the person to make AOD behavior changes until the client has moved to the next stage, a determination to change.

The determination to change could be a decision to control use, to reduce harm, or to become abstinent. Alternatively, the person might determine to go back to the precontemplation stage. When the client has decided to change, he or she moves into the action stage. Generalist social workers must consider whether they are in the best position to continue to offer support or whether they should facilitate referral to a professional or program that specializes in addictions work.

Sometimes, a generalist and specialist can work in combination, with the specialist focusing on addictions therapy and the generalist focusing on collateral aspects of rehabilitation, including relationships with family; peers; work, school, recreation, spiritual, and cultural communities; and other social systems.

Whereas many addictions programs focus upon change within the individual or family, generalist practitioners must also focus on change within larger systems (e.g., advocating with the employer for time away from work to participate in a treatment program; teaching teachers how to treat a student as a person with potential rather than stigmatizing the student as an addict or trouble-maker; or encouraging local businesses to limit sales of solvents to minors because of a history of solvent abuse in the community).

In Claudia's case, assume that she agrees to go to a 28-day institutional treatment program. After 28 days, Claudia has become abstinent and says she is ready to go back to her community. But has her environment changed? Fortunately, Tyra has helped Claudia plan for the return to the community prior to her admission to the treatment program: Claudia's partner agreed to go to a group for family members of people with addictions; Claudia has pre-registered in a job-upgrade program; and Tyra has worked with community police to help them eliminate racial harassment.

Once the client has initially achieved the goal that was established for the action stage, the client moves into the maintenance stage. The client is still at risk for returning to old patterns of behavior or substituting other addictive behaviors. During the maintenance stage, the worker provides the client with ongoing support, skills training for relapse prevention, and assistance with any lapses. Few people with chronic addictions are able to go through the stages of change without any lapses.

Social workers can help clients build on strengths by reframing lapses as part of the growth and learning processes. Claudia's worker might say, "The fact that you were able to remain cocaine-free for 8 months was a huge success for you. This was the longest period of sobriety you've had since you were 16. Look at what you've accomplished at work . . . Now, let's also look at what led to the lapse and what can be done to help you get back on track . . ."

Working with people affected by addictions can be challenging but also rewarding, even if clients terminate without achieving abstinence, controlled use, or harm reduction. Social workers might not see immediate change in clients, even though they are instrumental in helping clients over the long term simply by showing respect, planting seeds of hope, building self-efficacy, providing information about services, connecting people with support systems, and offering the client further help should the client decide to return for services.

# SUMMARY

Regardless of agency context, generalist social workers are likely to work with many clients affected by AODs and addictions. To be prepared, workers must be aware of their own attitudes and theoretical perspectives toward AODs and addictions. It is easy to say, "I am a competent professional and I respect all clients."

If a client enters your office looking disheveled, agitating from withdrawal, denying any AOD problems, and resenting being sent to see a social worker, good intentions are not sufficient. The worker's understanding of the nature of addictions, causes, and consequences is critical for developing a joint assessment with the client and determining an appropriate course of change.

Encouraging a client to go "cold turkey" could be dangerous if the person is physically dependent on a substance that has medically dangerous withdrawal symptoms. In such situations, abstinence must be monitored in a detoxification unit and there must be a plan for ongoing help and support.

Putting a client through withdrawal and then having him or her relapse because there is no follow-up professional support can amount to malpractice, even if the worker thinks encouraging the person to stop using AODs is a good thing to do. If a client has an addiction that is not familiar to the worker, the worker should seek supervision, explore the literature, and consult with a specialist about how to proceed with the client. There are also many self-help and professional addictions resources that can be accessed through the Internet (e.g., www.aa.org; www.samhsa.gov).

Starting with the client and building on strengths is vital for work with people affected by AODs. By understanding the stages of change, a worker can ensure that help is offered in a manner and at a pace that is appropriate to the client's present motivation. Helping strategies such as cognitive-behavioral, motivational enhancement, and twelve-steps counseling offer clients different ways of achieving change.

More important than the choice of intervention is the knowledge and skill that the worker uses to implement the change strategy. Workers must also be involved with various systems in the client's social environment, including school; work; and recreational, cultural, and criminal justice systems.

Often, substance-abuse specific programs focus on helping the individual or family. Generalist practitioners are vital in helping clients negotiate their way through various service systems, advocating removal of barriers to access to services, and assisting clients with a long-term strategy that includes ongoing support following more intensive services.

From a macro perspective, social workers must work with mental health professionals and public policy decision makers to establish a more comprehensive and research-based approach to addictions policies and programs. Prevention strategies should focus on particular populations at risk and target the underlying causes of addiction, for example, poverty, stress, history of violence, or norms condoning abuse of AODs. Public and privately funded programs need to ensure that people affected by addictions have access to appropriate, cost-effective professional help, rather than simply offering the least costly form of help under the guise of managed care.

---

**CASE 11.1** | SOCIAL WORKER INTERVENTION WITH CLIENT WITH HEROIN ADDICTION

Hank is a 66-year-old man of British-American descent. He is a minister of a Presbyterian church and has been married to his partner, Patricia, for 42 years. Patricia and Hank have one son, Steven, who is 39 years old. One day, Hank is driving to work and has an accident, causing severe injuries and requiring hospitalization.

About seven hours after his arrival at the hospital, physicians notice that he starts to vomit, perspire, and become very restless. On further examination, they notice he has tracks on his arms, indicative of intravenous (IV) drug use. Dr. F. asks Hank what types of drugs he has been using. Hank's face flushes and he becomes silent. Dr. F. says, in a matter-of-fact manner, "It looks as if you are withdrawing from heroin. We've had a number of patients recently who have been using heroin. We'd like to help you." Hank says, "I'll take morphine, methadone, naltrexone, anything you've got." Dr. F. conducts a medical history, orders blood tests, and agrees to prescribe clonidine to relieve the withdrawal symptoms (Gill, 1995). In turn, Hank agrees, reluctantly, to meet with a hospital social worker, Shauna, to help plan what he wants to do about his addiction.

The following day, Shauna comes to visit Hank. Hank says he is too sick to talk. Shauna acknowledges that he must feel miserable, both physically and emotionally, but that he should start to feel better soon. Shauna returns the next day and Hank agrees to talk with her. He acknowledges that he has used heroin but that it was not a problem. He says

he can take care of himself once he is released from hospital. Shauna decides to use motivational enhancement to guide her interaction with Hank. She avoids getting into a debate with Hank over whether he has a problem.

She notes that people who use heroin must be getting something from it or they would not use it. She invites him to talk about his reasons for using heroin. Hank seems leery of Shauna's intentions and asks her when she is going to start lecturing him about the evils of heroin. Shauna explains that some people view heroin as evil but that mental health professionals view addiction as a disease and do not view people who use heroin as immoral or weak willed.

She tries to tune into his anxiety, asking him if he is concerned about how his family or congregation will react to information about his heroin use. He begins to open up, explaining how he could lose his family, his job, everything. Hank seems overwhelmed, so Shauna screens for suicidal ideation. Although he has thought about suicide, he says it would go against his faith and he never seriously planned to act out his suicidal thoughts.

Shauna also screens for risk of HIV transmission via IV drug use. Hank reports he is well aware of this risk, and he has never shared needles with others. He has his own works and knows how to keep them clean.

Shauna returns to the topic of the positive effects that Hank receives from using heroin. Hank describes the feelings of intense pleasure that he feels

*(continued)*

## CASE 11.1 | *continued*

shortly after he shoots up. He has never felt anything as exhilarating. He speaks of heroin as a drug that takes care of him. As a pastor, he is always taking care of others. He is always dealing with their problems, loss of a loved one, family conflict, political infighting in the church, and just day-to-day problems. He also views himself as the primary emotional support for his wife and son. He says he does not feel that he can talk to anyone about his problems, that is, anyone except heroin. Heroin helps him relax and not be bothered by any problems, his own or those of others. Heroin does not judge him, either.

As they discuss these "positives" from heroin, Shauna gains an understanding of the function that heroin plays in Hank's life. She empathizes, "Sounds as if heroin is your closest friend, someone you can talk to, confide in, and depend on for relief from life's stresses." Hank nods in agreement.

Knowing that Hank is a minister, Shauna asks if he knows any parishioners who use heroin and how the Presbyterian Church views those people. Hank says the only people he knew who used heroin were two young men. Both had little to do with the church after everyone found out they were addicts. Hank said that the church teaches love for all people, but not everyone is so open minded. He says he never saw himself as an addict, "After all, I'm a minister of God's word, and people expect me to be a positive role model."

Shauna suspects that Hank is in the early contemplation stage in terms of dealing with his addiction. In fact, he would likely be in the precontemplation stage if he had not ended up in the hospital without easy access to heroin. Shauna believes it is far too early to move Hank toward action, deciding instead to focus on raising Hank's self-confidence and educating him about intervention options.

Shauna applauds Hank for talking to her about heroin and trusting her with this information. Shauna asks what he knows about methadone, detoxification, behavior modification, family therapy, and harm-reduction approaches. Shauna lends Hank a videotape on families affected by heroin, asking him to watch it so they can discuss it at the next meeting.

At the next meeting, Hank appears very distraught. He had just met with Patricia and Steven. He told them about his heroin addiction. They responded with shock and betrayal. They interrogated him about his "secret life." One of Patricia's first questions was whether he had AIDS. After allowing Hank to vent, Shauna asks, "Do you feel any sense of relief, or do you regret telling them?" Hank says that he feels a burden has been lifted from his shoulders, but feels he has put a new burden on Patricia's and Steven's shoulders.

They discuss where to go from here. Shauna inquires whether Hank knows of any self-help groups for family members of people with addictions. Hank says he does not. Shauna offers Hank a brochure about Families Anonymous and asks whether Hank thinks it would be a good idea to give this to Patricia and Steven. Hank agrees. He is not sure if they will go, but at least they will have this information and can make an informed choice. Shauna offers to have a family session. Hank says he does not think they would be ready to talk.

Shauna turns the discussion to Hank's impending discharge from the hospital. They discuss various options, including natural recovery (trying to control or abstain on his own), methadone maintenance, outpatient services, institutional programs, and long-term residential programs.

She educates him about the nature of each program, including the advantages and disadvantages of each. Hank's first response is that he is not sure if he is ready for any treatment program. Shauna says that she is not asking for any commitments to begin treatment, but if he did decide to begin, she wonders what type of program would best meet his needs. Hank suggests that a 28-day institutional program sounds good. It is not too long; his insurance will cover the costs; and it uses a multimodal approach to treatment. Shauna raises the possibility of follow-up groups, noting that 28 days is just the start of a recovery process.

Hank expresses concern that he could be fired once the church finds out he has been using heroin. Shauna explains that the Americans with Disabilities Act views addiction as a disease and that people cannot be fired because they have a disease. She provides him with a pamphlet on the act and they discuss ways he can present this information to people at the church, if the need arises. She also says she can give him the names of lawyers who specialize in this area.

Hank agrees to continue to work with Shauna following his discharge. He says he is not sure he will decide to give up heroin or go into an intensive treatment program, but he is willing to continue to explore these possibilities with her. Shauna believes that Hank would be a good candidate for an intensive treatment program, but she is careful to remain at his pace, offering support, information, and assistance with problem solving, focusing on issues that Hank is ready to work on. Ultimately, choices about abstinence, controlled use, or harm reduction will have to be made by Hank. When Shauna evaluates the success of her intervention, it will be in relation to whether she helped Hank achieve his own goals.

## DISCUSSION QUESTIONS

1. Identify Hank's strengths or protective factors, based on the information presented in Case 11.1. How could Shauna help Hank build on these strengths or protective factors to work on his problems with heroin?

2. Hank has advised Shauna that he has used heroin. Knowing that possession of heroin is illegal, what legal and ethical obligations, if any, does Shauna have to report Hank's heroin use to the police or to Hank's wife, as someone who might be affected by his heroin use if he had not agreed to tell her? What are the ethical justifications for either maintaining confidentiality or disclosing this information to specific authorities or individuals? Would Shauna's ethical and legal obligations be any different if she knew that Hank was trafficking heroin to either adults or minors?

3. What additional interventions would be appropriate with Hank? Would he be a good candidate for rational recovery treatment? (For more information on rational recovery, see Trimpey, 1996.)

4. Shauna decided not to conduct an in-depth psychosocial assessment with Hank, given her role at the hospital and Hank's being in the contemplation stage of change. At what point should she or another social worker conduct an in-depth assessment of Hank's heroin dependence? What is your rationale? Does the timing and emphasis on assessment depend on whether the worker is approaching help from a twelve-step, cognitive-behavioral, motivational enhancement, or other theoretical perspective?

5. How can a social worker incorporate spirituality in the helping process for a person affected by addictions, without imposing spiritual beliefs on a client?

6. Given that alcohol abuse is associated with many biopsychosocial problems (e.g., liver and brain damage, fetal alcohol syndrome, depression, suicide, family violence, car accidents, and lost work productivity), what types of social policies should social workers promote? Which models should these policies be based on, and why (consider both effectiveness and ethical appropriateness)?

7. What special considerations arise when a social worker is working with a teenager who admits to abusing substances? Consider, for example, a

teenager who is caught huffing glue and is sent by his teacher to talk to a school social worker. Should the worker involve family members? If so, how? What life-cycle issues need to be taken into account?

8. Describe how alcohol use and abuse is viewed in your culture and family. What are your family's and culture's beliefs about the cause of addiction? Does your family have any ritual or socially accepted uses for alcohol? How do people in your family know what is acceptable and unacceptable use of alcohol?

# REFERENCES

Alcoholics Anonymous. (Accessed March 17, 2003). Available online at www.aa.org

American Psychiatric Association. (2000). *Diagnostic and Statistical manual*, 4th ed., text revision.

Barsky, A. E. *Addictions: A professional development manual for social work and the human services*. Pacific Grove, CA: Brooks/Cole, forthcoming.

Barsky, A. E., and Coleman, H. (2001). Evaluating skills acquisition in motivational interviewing. *Journal of Drug Education, 31*(1), 69–82.

Controlled Substances Act (1970). Title 21, Chapter 13. Available online at http://www .fda.gov/opacom/laws/cntrlsub/ctlsbtoc.htm

Cox, G., Brown, L., Morgan, C., and Hansten, M. (2001). Drug court evaluation project: Final report. Seattle: Alcohol and Drug Abuse Institute. Available online at http://depts.washington.edu/adai/pubs/tr/ drugcourt/fullreport.pdf

Fisher, G. L., and Harrison T. C. (2000). Substance abuse: Information for school counselors, social workers, therapists, and counselors (2nd ed.). Boston: Allyn and Bacon.

Fook, J. (1993). *Radical casework: A theory of practice*. London: Allen and Unwin.

Gill, T. (1995). Heroin addiction. Center for Education and Information on Drugs and Alcohol. Available online at http://www.ceida .net.au/medical_practitioners/supplements/ Documents/supp8.pdf

Harm Reduction Coalition. (Accessed April 6, 2003). Available online at www .harmreduction.org

Johnson, J. (2004). *Fundamentals of substance abuse practice*. Pacific Grove, CA: Brooks/Cole.

Jung, J. (2000). Psychology of alcohol and other drugs. Thousand Oaks, CA: Sage.

Kumpfer, K. (2002). Identification of drug abuse prevention programs. Washington, DC: National Institute on Drug Abuse. Available online at http://www.drugabuse .gov/about/organization/hsr/da-pre/ Kumpfer LitReviewPartC.html#Ccomparison

Lewis, J. A., Dana, R. Q., and Blevins, G. A. (2002). *Substance abuse counseling* (3rd ed.). Pacific Grove, CA: Brooks/Cole.

McNeece, C. A., and DiNitto, D. M. (1998). *Chemical dependency: A systems approach* (2nd ed.). Needham Heights, MA: Allyn and Bacon.

National Institute on Alcoholism and Alcohol Abuse (NIAAA). (Accessed March 17, 2003). www.niaaa.nih.gov.

National Institute on Alcohol Abuse and Alcoholism (NIAAA). (2001a). *Cognitive-behavioral coping skills therapy manual: A clinical research guide for therapists treating individuals with alcohol abuse and dependence*. Washington, DC: NIAAA.

National Institute on Alcohol Abuse and Alcoholism (NIAAA). (2001b). *Motivational enhancement therapy manual: A clinical research guide for therapists treating individ-*

uals with alcohol abuse and dependence. Washington, DC: NIAAA.

National Institute on Alcohol Abuse and Alcoholism (NIAAA). (2001c). *Project MATCH hypotheses: Results and causal chain analyses.* Washington, DC: NIAAA.

National Institute on Alcohol Abuse and Alcoholism (NIAAA). (2001d). *Twelve-step facilitation therapy manual: A clinical research guide for therapists treating individuals with alcohol abuse and dependence.* Washington, DC: NIAAA.

National Institute on Drug Abuse (NIDA). (Accessed March 2003). NIDA Infofax. Available online at www.nida.nih.gov/Infofax/Infofaxindex.html

Prochaska, J. O. (1994). *Systems of psychotherapy: A transtheoretical analysis* (3rd ed.). Pacific Grove, CA: Brooks/Cole.

Rollnick, S., and Morgan, M. (1997). Motivational interviewing: Increasing readiness for change. In Washton, A. M. *Psychotherapy and substance abuse: A practitioner's handbook.* New York: Guildford.

Trimpey, J. (1996). *Rational recovery: The new cure for substance addiction.* New York: Pocket Books.

van Wormer, K., and Davis, D. R. (2003). *Addictions treatment: A strengths perspective.* Pacific Grove, CA: Brooks/Cole.

# GENERALIST PRACTICE WITH
# GAY AND LESBIAN CLIENTS

*Frann S. Anderson, LCSW, CADC*

Reuters/Jeff Christensen/Archive Photos

Nichole B. is a part-time MSW student in her second year of a three-year program. Her foundation field placement is with a high school located in a working-class community. In her placement, Nichole provides individual counseling services to teenagers who are having academic or social problems in the school. As a school social worker, Nichole is also expected to work with the students' families.

Tom H., a 16-year-old junior, dropped by Nichole's office just after the holiday break. Tom appeared nervous and was hesitant to tell Nichole what was on his mind. Finally, he told Nichole a story about a friend who was gay and who was struggling with the decision about coming out. The friend was worried about how his parents would react and about the lack of tolerance for minorities among his peers. Nichole asked Tom to return the next day so they could explore his friend's situation in more detail.

After Tom left, Nichole was uncomfortable about the interaction. She was not sure why. Was it how she had handled his unexpected visit? Did she really understand what Tom was telling her? Was it the seriousness of the decision to come out? Was it her level of comfort with the topic? Was it her feelings of being over her head and not really knowing much about gays and lesbians or the coming-out process? Was it Tom? Was it the topic? Was it her?

This chapter examines the current cultural roadblocks to providing social work services to gay and lesbian clients. It covers the dynamics of homophobia and heterosexism as they relate to the perpetuation of stereotypes about gays and lesbians and the way these stereotypes affect the helping relationship. The chapter presents real experiences of gay men, lesbian women, and gay and lesbian youth and explains how to tailor social work practice to meet the special needs of this minority. Macropractice issues related to current civil rights issues are presented and discussed in terms of the responsibilities generalist social workers encounter as advocates for sexual minorities. By the end of the chapter, you should be able to help Nichole

1.  Describe the social and psychological ramifications of homophobic and heterosexist attitudes on gay men and lesbian women
2.  Identify the major policy issues affecting the gay and lesbian community
3.  Understand the complexity of the coming-out process for gay and lesbian clients
4.  Understand the role of the social worker in helping gay and lesbian clients through the coming-out process
5.  Describe the special needs of gay and lesbian teenagers and elderly persons
6.  Describe the special needs of children with gay and lesbian parents

# GAYS AND LESBIANS AS A SPECIAL POPULATION

Until as recently as 1973, "homosexuality" was widely accepted as an Axis I mental illness in the *Diagnostic and Statistical Manual (DSM)* (Maylon, 1981). It was also, and in many cases still is, condemned by many religious groups as an evil perversion. (For information on specific religious groups, see

Hellman et al., 1981; Hetrick and Martin, 1987; Jonsen and Stryker, 1993; Lauritsen, 1993; Panem, 1988; Pierce and VanDeVeer, 1988.) Social stigma, vernacular stereotypes and myths, and religious condemnation of gays and lesbians continue to permeate society (Maylon, 1981). Bigotry and discrimination against gays and lesbians present the generalist social worker with many personal and cultural challenges.

For some time, the gay and lesbian population has been a hidden minority, and little attention has been paid to their needs in the community (Fassinger, 1991). However, gay men and lesbian women living in the United States are becoming more and more visible, and it is likely that more will seek the services of social workers or other mental health practitioners. When working with gay and lesbian clients, it is important to understand the effect of homophobia on their lives. Even more important is the need for the practitioner to understand his or her own attitudes toward gays and lesbians so as not to add to their problems by unconscious homophobic responses (Mackelprang, Ray, and Hernandez-Peck, 1996). If social workers approach the helping relationship with homophobic attitudes, inaccurate beliefs and stereotypes, and limited knowledge about the special needs of their gay and lesbian clients, they run the risk of alienating gay and lesbian clients and intensifying their clients' internalized homophobic response.

## Homophobia

**Homophobia** has been defined as "dread of being in close quarters with homosexuals" (Weinberg, 1972, p. 4), "explicit hostility or prejudice toward gay men and lesbian women" (Herek, 1986, p. 563), and "a negative or fearful reaction to homosexuals" (Neisen, 1990, p. 22). Homophobia has been attributed to people's attempts to deny same sex attraction within the heterosexual community (Maier, 1984) and to the effort to "keep men within the boundaries of traditional sex roles" (Neisen, 1990, p. 23). The latter belief suggests that all men, gay and straight, are victims of homophobic stereotyping that forces them to conform to particular sex roles.

It was once believed that homophobia was more common among heterosexual men than heterosexual women (Ernulf and Innala, 1987; Millham, San Miguel, and Kellog, 1976; Mosher and O'Grady, 1979; Weinberg, 1972). However, studies conducted in the 1990s suggest that there is no significant gender difference in homophobic responses to gays and lesbians (Simon, 1995; Van de Ven, 1994; Van de Ven, Bornholt, and Baily, 1996). Although the general public's opinions about gay and lesbian relationships are starting to take a more positive turn, large numbers of men and women are still homophobic.

The manifestations of homophobia range from less destructive acts, such as name-calling (Zastrow and Kirst-Ashman, 1990), to more violent acts, such as assault and murder (Bohn, 1984; Britton, 1990; Clift, 1988; Herek, 1989; Herek and Berrill, 1990; Lance, 1987; Stevenson, 1988). Homophobia permeates our culture and influences not only how heterosexual individuals perceive other sexual minorities but also how gays and lesbians perceive themselves (Neisen, 1990, 1993; Sophie, 1987; Zastrow and Kirst-Ashman, 1990). Negative and destructive behaviors directed at gays and lesbians can result in damaging internalized messages about their self-worth, self-acceptance, and overall value as human beings. Gays and lesbians are susceptible to internalized homophobia: "an internalization of negative attitudes and assumptions . . . expressed by others in the individual's environment, from her immediate friends and family to the institutions of the church, school, and mass media" (Sophie, 1987, pp. 53–54).

Internalized homophobia can complicate the therapeutic relationship when therapists do not understand the genesis of homophobia or their own homophobic beliefs. Therapists who have not confronted their own negative belief system about gays and lesbians or have not educated themselves on how homophobia damages the self-esteem of gay and lesbian clients may fall into the trap of focusing on the negative introjects that the client brings to the therapeutic relationship. This can lead to therapists unknowingly reinforcing the shame and guilt that many gay and lesbian clients struggle with when coming to terms with their sexual orientation.

## Heterosexism

Homophobia is not the only force that leads to internalized, negative messages about sexual orientation. The oppression of sexual minorities is perpetuated by basic societal beliefs that heterosexuals (or "straight people") are better than gay and lesbian people and that heterosexuality is the only acceptable form of sexual expression (Neisen, 1990, 1993; Spaulding, 1993). The term *heterosexism* refers to the social construct that supports these beliefs and continues to fuel prejudice and discrimination toward sexual minorities.

Neisen likens heterosexism to racism and indicates that the same power structures that support discrimination based on race also support discrimination based on sexual orientation:

> Heterosexism manifests itself in subtle but not necessarily less obvious forms of exclusion or lack of acknowledgment of gay/lesbian/bisexual lifestyles. For example, heterosexism is manifest when individuals refuse to rent to gays/lesbians/bisexuals, when the military discharges or imprisons someone for homosexual behavior or mere suspicion of being homosexual, and when governments prohibit gays and lesbians to legally marry (1990, p. 25).

Other examples of heterosexism include gay bashing, gay or lesbian teenagers being thrown out of their homes when they reveal their sexual orientation, employers terminating gay and lesbian employees based on their sexual orientation, and parents forbidding their gay and lesbian children to bring their partners to family gatherings. Heterosexism is very much a part of the daily life of gay and lesbian individuals.

Women are victimized by heterosexist beliefs that define them "in terms of men, or not at all" (Spaulding, 1993, p. 233). Lesbian women are perceived

**TABLE 12.1** | EFFECTS OF SEXUAL AND PHYSICAL VICTIMIZATION COMPARED WITH EFFECTS OF CULTURAL VICTIMIZATION (HETEROSEXISM)

| Effects of Sexual and Physical Victimization | Effects of Heterosexism |
|---|---|
| Blame self for causing the abuse<br>"I deserve to be abused."<br>"It's my own fault." | Blame self for same sex attraction<br>"Maybe gay people are sick and I deserve to be put down, beat up, etc." |
| Shame or negative self-concept<br>"I'm dirty for participating in the sexual acts."<br>"I'm bad, otherwise I wouldn't have gotten hit."<br>"No one will love me because I'm damaged and used." | Shame or negative self-concept<br>"I'm going to hell for being gay."<br>"I'm bad for acting on my homosexual desires."<br>"No one will love me because I'm gay . . . especially my friends and family." |
| Anger directed toward self<br>"I'm going to kill myself."<br>"I'll drink or do drugs so I can forget what happened."<br>"I'm going to go out and do to someone else what happened to me." | Anger directed toward self<br>"I'm going to kill myself."<br>"I'll drink or do drugs to forget about being sexual with someone of the same sex."<br>"I'll drink or do drugs to cover up my thoughts about being gay and to cover up my attraction to other people of the same sex."<br>"I'm going to have as much sex as I can." |
| Victim mentality<br>"I feel helpless and powerless."<br>"Other people are in control of my body."<br>"I can't tell anyone what happened."<br>"I don't trust anyone."<br>"I'm going to protect myself by staying alone." | Victim mentality<br>"I feel helpless and powerless."<br>"I can't come out."<br>"I can't be what I am."<br>"There is no one I can tell I'm gay."<br>"I'm not going to let any of the neighbors know I have a lover . . . I'll just say he is my friend." |

Adapted with permission from "Healing from Cultural Victimization" by J. H. Neisen in *Journal of Gay and Lesbian Psychotherapy,* Vol. 2, No. 1. Copyright © 1993. The Haworth Press.

---

to be heterosexuals who are unable to have the "right" kind of sexual experience with men (Spaulding, 1993). Heterosexism also defines men according to rigid sex roles. Gay men are perceived to be heterosexual men who are unable to have the "right" kind of sexual experience with women. In other words, heterosexism defines the gay or lesbian love relationship in terms of failure to attract members of the opposite sex. For instance, in the heterosexual construct, lesbian women are believed to be women who hate men, rather than women who love women.

Heterosexism can damage the psyche of the gay and lesbian client. Internalized shame stunts emotional growth and contributes to a devaluing of self (Neisen, 1990). Like other victimized groups, gays and lesbians internalize a multitude of attitudes and beliefs that they incorrectly attribute to their sexual orientation, when in fact they are responses to the abusive nature of heterosexism. Table 12.1 illustrates how heterosexism causes the same sense of victimization as do sexual and physical abuse.

TABLE 12.2 | PROCESS OF HEALING FROM SEXUAL OR PHYSICAL VICTIMIZATION COMPARED WITH PROCESS OF HEALING FROM CULTURAL VICTIMIZATION (HETEROSEXISM)

| Recovery From Sexual or Physical Abuse | Recovery From Heterosexism |
| --- | --- |
| Breaking the silence | Breaking the silence |
| "I have been abused." | "Mom, I'm gay." |
|  | "Beth, I've really struggled with my sexual feelings and I think I'm lesbian." |
| Establishing perpetrator responsibility | Establishing perpetrator responsibility |
| "I didn't ask to be sexually abused." | "I didn't do anything to be harassed." |
| "I didn't deserve to be abused." | "I don't deserve to be harassed for being gay . . . |
| "(Name) abused me." | for being myself." |
|  | "(Name of individual or institution) abused me because of my homosexuality." |
| Reclaim personal power | Reclaim personal power |
| "I'm okay." | "I'm okay." |
| "I am lovable." | "I am lovable." |
| "I set my own boundaries regarding my sexual behavior and physical space." | "I am proud to be gay." |
| "I celebrate myself." | "My God loves and accepts me as a lesbian." |
|  | "I decide whom I come out to and how much about my personal life I will share." |

Adapted with permission from "Healing from Cultural Victimization" by J. H. Neisen in *Journal of Gay and Lesbian Psychotherapy*, Vol. 2, No. 1. Copyright © 1993. The Haworth Press.

In later stages of the coming-out process, it is helpful for gay and lesbian clients to understand shame as an introject of heterosexism in order to move to more self-affirming behaviors and internalized messages. Table 12.2 (p. 334) illustrates the recovery process for gays and lesbians as it parallels the recovery process for victims of abuse.

When conducting coming-out groups for lesbians, Morrow (1996) dedicates one session to discussing heterosexism and homophobia. She encourages group members to recall instances of both in their daily lives and to consider the influence of external forces on decisions about coming out. This helps group participants see how societal views about gays and lesbians directly influence their thoughts, feelings, and behaviors and contribute to the sense of oppression experienced by sexual minorities.

Heterosexism can invade relationships between heterosexual individuals and gay and lesbian individuals even when the heterosexual in the relationship does not consciously embrace the heterosexist construct. The example in Case 12.1 (p. 334) illustrates this point.

Mr. S.'s belief that all children are conceived through heterosexual sex and that all families are composed of a mother and father is an example of how heterosexism can make itself known when supportive heterosexual allies are unaware of their own heterosexist beliefs.

## CASE 12.1 | WHAT DID I SAY?

As a second-year MSW student, Melissa T. was "out" to most of the faculty and students at her school. It was common knowledge that Melissa and her partner of 10 years were lesbian mothers raising their 7-year-old daughter together and struggling openly with the challenges facing gays and lesbians in the late 1990s.

When Melissa began her second-year practice class, the students took turns introducing themselves and sharing important facts about themselves. Melissa once again shared her sexual minority status and her status as a lesbian mother. The instructor, Mr. S., was a licensed social worker who taught at the school as an adjunct faculty member. As a part-time faculty member, Mr. S. spent little time on campus and knew very few students. Mr. S. was impressed by Melissa's candor. He thanked her for

being so open about her minority status and noted that she would add a new dimension to class discussions about macro practice and social work with oppressed groups. Mr. S. and Melissa talked about the struggles facing gays and lesbians and about the special challenges for same sex families as the media drew more attention to gay and lesbian parenting.

Anyone eavesdropping on the conversation would have thought Mr. S. was open and accepting of gay and lesbian parents—that is, until his covert heterosexist beliefs emerged. "Tell me, Melissa," Mr. S. inquired, "what does your daughter's father think about your being lesbian?" To the heterosexual listener, this may have seemed like an innocent question. But to a lesbian mother whose child was conceived by donor insemination, the question reeked of heterosexism.

---

It is a common myth that, in gay and lesbian relationships, one member of the couple chooses a masculine, dominant role and the other a feminine, submissive role. This may be true of some gay and lesbian couples but is not the norm for the majority (Jay and Young, 1979; Peplau, 1981). Not all gay men behave in an effeminate manner (the queen), and not all lesbian women behave in a masculine manner (the dyke). A small number of gay men and lesbian women identify strongly with the opposite sex and dress accordingly, but the majority do not dress any differently than their heterosexual counterparts (Zastrow and Kirst-Ashman, 1990). Even gay and lesbian people who prefer to dress in attire typically associated with the sex opposite of their own ("drag" or "butch") are very certain about and embrace the fact that they are men or women. Social workers who approach the helping relationship with the notion that homosexual relationships are built around one member of the couple "playing the man" and the other "playing the woman" bring their own heterosexist beliefs. This can impede work because the social worker's heterosexual paradigm may force gay and lesbian clients to explore relationships according to opposite sex partnerships rather than same sex partnerships. Successful work with sexual minorities should focus on building healthy, meaningful relationships between same sex partners and exploring the challenges unique to these unions.

To better equip social work students for work with clients of various sexual orientations, the Council on Social Work Education (CSWE) included sexual minorities in their 1993 curriculum policy statement and mandated inclusion of educational material on diverse populations. With the inclusion of educational content on gays and lesbians in social work curricula, CSWE addressed sexual discrimination, oppression, and homophobia in institutions of social work education (Mackelprang, Ray, and Hernandez-Peck, 1996).

A study investigating attitudes toward gays and lesbians (Newman, Dannenfelser, and Benishek, 2002) found that a majority of beginning social work students expressed acceptance and openness toward the gay and lesbian community. These findings are hopeful and suggest that social workers in clinical practice may be a great source of support for gay and lesbian clients and the gay and lesbian community in general. Yet, the beginning social worker still has much to learn about this special population.

As with other special populations, education about culture, lifestyle, and community norms is paramount before one engages in a helping relationship. Beginning social workers may be tempted to take the "learn by doing" method, where they gather information about sexual minorities from clients they meet in their day-to-day practice. Clients can be a useful source of information; however, heterosexism gone unchecked can plague the therapeutic relationship with all sorts of negative transferential barriers before the therapeutic alliance has been successfully established. For example, Conley et al. (2001) discovered that certain common comments made by heterosexual individuals when they come into contact with gays and lesbians are offensive to gays and lesbians or cause them to have to "overlook" the ignorance of heterosexuals even when the comments make them uncomfortable. Making comments such as "I know a gay person," as if to reassure the client that "they're not the first one" or "I'm not prejudiced toward gay people; what you do in the privacy of your bedroom is your own business . . ."; asking prying questions about sexual practices; or ignoring gay issues as if they do not exist can make gay and lesbian clients uncomfortable and put them on guard in the therapeutic relationship. When a social worker makes these or similar comments or asks similar questions, his or her own discomfort with sexual minorities becomes apparent and takes priority in the early stages of the therapeutic relationship. Gay and lesbian clients who find that they must help the clinician work through his or her own heterosexism in the early stages of the relationship find that positive rapport in the relationship and the ability to trust the clinician are greatly diminished (Bernstein, 2000).

Gay and lesbian clients should not be responsible for educating practitioners about their lives. To prepare for their work with gay and lesbian clients, Bernstein (2000) suggests that practitioners do their homework ahead of time. Reading gay fiction, viewing gay films, reviewing the existing literature, and, when possible, talking with gay and lesbian colleagues about homosexual issues can prepare the beginning social worker for work with sexual minorities. The more work the beginning social worker does around heterosexist and homophobic attitudes before working with sexual minorities, the more likely workers and their gay and lesbian clients are to find the therapy helpful.

## Policy Issues

The civil rights of sexual minorities are regularly violated in the areas of housing, employment, and education. Gays and lesbians are legally prohibited from marrying their life partners. On the federal level, civil rights laws do not provide for the fair treatment of sexual minorities. The battle for state civil rights is being fought, one right at a time. Opponents attempt to overturn laws that protect the civil rights of sexual minorities as soon as they are passed. Although the civil rights of sexual minorities are better protected than in the past, the political arena remains a place of hostility and discouragement for gays, lesbians, and their families.

Gay men and lesbian women take responsibility for most of the organizing and political activism on behalf of sexual minorities. But the rights of minorities will not be realized until the majority seeks justice for oppressed groups as well. Social workers can lobby for civil rights issues when they are being voted on in state legislatures. Generalist social workers must remain up to date on legislative proceedings as they occur at the state and federal levels. This is true for all legislative activity that affects disenfranchised populations.

Many of the issues that prevent sexual minorities from realizing civil rights are directly related to homophobia and heterosexist ideologies. Educating heterosexual individuals about the real lives of gay men and lesbian women can diminish homophobic attitudes and broaden the heterosexual viewpoint to include same gender partnerships. Because social workers are found in diverse settings, the opportunity to educate diverse groups of people about sexual minorities is readily available. It is not only important to speak up for the rights of gays and lesbians; it is equally important to look for opportunities to educate clients, coworkers, and others about homophobia and heterosexism. The more that heterosexual individuals receive accurate information about sexual minorities, the more they will support gay and lesbian rights (Bohan, 1997; Bernstein, 2000). Social workers can fill the important role of educator in addressing discrimination against sexual minorities.

Many people continue to reject sexual minorities on the basis of religious convictions. In the study measuring attitudes of beginning social work students toward sexual minorities, the researchers discovered that those individuals who held conservative religious views were more likely to express negative attitudes toward gays and lesbians (Newman, Dannenfelser, and Benishek, 2002). Spiritual support and belonging to a religious group may be a very important part of a social worker's life, and working with sexual minorities may directly challenge religious beliefs and practices. Many religious denominations are struggling with the issue of sexual orientation and deciding whether and how to incorporate gays and lesbians into their church families, or whether to bar them. It is a difficult issue with no easy answers. However, the issue of civil rights for sexual minorities is justice for all. Religious diversity needs to be respected and revered, but civil rights issues cannot be determined according to one or all denominations or religious groups.

# MICROPRACTICE ISSUES

Traditionally, research on sexual minorities has been conducted with gay men rather than lesbian women, and the findings have been generalized to lesbian women (de Monteflores and Schultz, 1978; Kaplan, 1974; Klein and Wolf, 1985; Leiblum and Rosen, 1989; Masters and Johnson, 1970; Minton and McDonald, 1983–1984). Although gay men and lesbian women have many issues in common, gay men's experiences are very different from those of lesbian women (Behrendt and George, 1995; Buhrke, 1989; Cox and Gallois, 1996; de Monteflores and Schultz, 1978; Lipton, 1996).

## The Gay Male Experience

Society's stereotype of men as strong, unemotional, and competitive has led gay men to feel confusion and inner turmoil when they recognize that they are attracted to other men (Behrendt and George, 1995; Green, 1987; Herek, 1986; Zilbergeld, 1992). Men cannot show feminine traits lest they be considered "sissies." Although it can be endearing for a girl to be called a "tomboy," a sissy is ostracized and degraded (Green, 1987). Boys in our culture carry a greater burden to be "manly" than do girls to be "womanly," regardless of sexual orientation.

Because most gay men have been socialized in a heterosexist society, they, too, grow up believing in stereotypic gender roles. Gay men enter adulthood believing that being a man is directly related to mastering masculine behaviors (competition, emotional detachment, pursuit of female sex partners), rejecting feminine behaviors (being tender, seeking emotional support from others, submission to men), and, most importantly, never acknowledging same sex feelings or attractions (Behrendt and George, 1995; Herek, 1986; MacDonald, 1976; Morin and Garfinkle, 1978; Nungesser, 1983). The gay male who is beginning to become aware of his same sex attraction becomes anxious about his identity as a man. Gay men may also feel confused about who initiates relationships and sex (men are expected to be in control), what it means when one man allows another to initiate contact (only women are submissive), and how a relationship can thrive when both partners are expected to be emotionally distant (Behrendt and George, 1995). This affects not only gay male relationships but also how gay men perceive themselves. As products of a heterosexist society, many gay men question their value and, in turn, experience shame and guilt.

Helping relationships with gay men may mean addressing issues that are very different from or even foreign to social workers, especially when the social worker is heterosexual. Some issues that are common to gay men in helping relationships include loneliness, being "invisible," limited availability of partners, lack of knowledge about "dating," and reliance on sex to feel intimately connected with a partner (Sanders and Kroll, 2000). Helping interventions with gay men are best focused on working with individuals and couples to explore their feelings of isolation, being invisible (which is directly related to having to keep their sexual orientation a secret), and feeling rejection or perceived rejection when the weight of "their secret" becomes internalized. Being able to first acknowledge their own vulnerability and then express this to others (the therapist, a partner) allows for the opening of meaningful dialogue around internalized heterosexist and homophobic attitudes.

Work from this starting point can then move on to exploring heterosexist paradigms that conflict with the development of meaningful love relationships between men. For example, "dating rituals" among gay men are often nonexistent, because "dating" has traditionally been a heterosexual activity. Further complicating the situation is the fact that social settings in which gay men can meet other gay men, interact with gay couples that can be seen as "role models," and provide a supportive environment for men to "fall in love" are limited. The rules for being a gay man are not clearly delineated, and many gay men may find themselves "making them up" as they go along or acting in a manner they "think" is appropriate within the limits of the myths society has attributed to gays. The fact is that an educated helper can support gay clients to identify and verbalize their own value system around partnering, and help gay men to use these values as the blueprint for their own "dating ritual." To do this successfully, social work practitioners need to be aware of their own values around dating, sex, and long-term partnering and then be open to the possibility that their gay client's values may be vastly different but still "healthy" within the experiences of the gay community. Issues such as monogamy versus multiple partners need to be addressed by gay clients, not so much because one style of connecting is better than the other, but more to allow the gay client to understand his own value system and then pursue relationships with men who share similar values. This may not be easy for a social worker that buys into the myth that gay men are promiscuous and that this is unacceptable to a healthy, meaningful relationship. Gay men may engage in sex with multiple partners as a way of feeling connected and reducing their feelings of isolation or may prefer sexual experiences that are varied with multiple partners. Workers should discuss safe sex practices with gay clients who prefer multiple partners. However, the social work practitioner must remain open to the client's style of finding partners both in the short term and the long term without imposing his or her own personal beliefs about what it means to be in a "healthy relationship." This approach is paramount in the helping relationship.

**HIV/AIDS**    The social stigmatization of "gay love" has been firmly in place for many years. Attacks on gay men, however, have never been as blatant or malicious as they became in the early 1980s, when the AIDS epidemic and its initial connection to the gay community became known. It sparked an unnerving response from the government and from religious and right-wing political groups whose insistence that AIDS was unique to gays set back research and treatment by 10 years (Brandt, 1988; Jonsen and Stryker, 1993; Lauritsen, 1993; Panem, 1988; Patton, 1986; Peck and Bezold, 1992; Pierce and VanDeVeer, 1988; Shilts, 1987). The portrayal of AIDS as a disease contracted through immoral acts by immoral individuals strengthened bigotry and prejudice against gays (Shilts, 1987; Stine, 1993; Zastrow and Kirst-Ashman, 1990).

Stigmas about HIV and AIDS are now more broadly directed to substance abusers and, more specifically, substance abusers who use and share hypodermic needles. Still, attitudes about homosexuality are correlated with attitudes about AIDS (Price and Hsu, 1992). The legacy of public policy formation in the 1980s continues to be influenced by the perception of individuals with HIV and AIDS as living immoral lives, a belief that beckons from the past when HIV and AIDS were believed to be associated with immorality and the "gay lifestyle."

Because of the focus on AIDS as a gay man's disease, mental health programs for gay men have focused on AIDS rather than on mental health issues and other issues associated with their sexual orientation (Lipton, 1996). Programs that were formed during the early years of the epidemic have become less focused on issues facing gay men and more on issues specific to substance abusers, leaving few if any services available to gay men and their special concerns.

Fear of AIDS and HIV infection is a common concern of adult gay men seeking counseling related to their sexual orientation (Harowski, 1988; Lipton, 1996). Harowski uses the term "worried well" to describe members of the gay male community who are not infected with the HIV virus but have "increased general anxiety, some decrease in sexual desire, and over-concern with health and bodily functioning" (1988, p. 303). Adult gay men continue to struggle with fears of HIV/AIDS as they look for meaningful relationships with partners or seek satisfying sexual experiences with multiple sexual partners over time. Paradoxically, adolescent and young gay men associate HIV and AIDS with older gay men in their community. This misconception has led to a steady increase in the numbers of young gay men who have contracted HIV. Concern for this population diminished during the early 1990s as the numbers of infected gay men began to decline steadily. Through continued education and outreach to the gay community, social workers can reach adolescent and young gay men and dispel the beliefs that HIV and AIDS only affect older gay men.

Generalist social workers are likely to come into contact with gay men who are living with AIDS and who have a host of other problems or concerns. "Any social worker who works with an adult gay or lesbian client needs to be aware of the ramifications and emotional impacts AIDS has had . . . These include not only serious illness, but poverty when their resources have been depleted, social isolation, insurance and public assistance problems, and problems getting medication" (Zastrow and Kirst-Ashman, 1990, p. 559). To effectively advocate for the gay man with AIDS, it is important to know what services are available and how to obtain them. The social service system and medical system can be cumbersome, so it is necessary to be prepared to help clients navigate these systems when their energy and spirits are depleted.

Most adult gay males have personally experienced the effects of AIDS through the loss of a partner, lover, or friend. Many others are living with HIV or AIDS themselves or are offering support to partners, lovers, or friends who are HIV positive or living with AIDS. When young heterosexual adults were beginning relationships, careers, and families, most gay and lesbian adults were burying the young members of their community who had fallen to AIDS. People often experience death for the first time when elderly members of the family die (Germain, 1991), but AIDS has forced adult gay men to deal with the loss of loved ones much earlier in their lives than is normally expected. It is likely that issues of unresolved loss and grief will need to be addressed in the helping relationship with gay men.

In contrast, issues around sexual expression and safety may be the focus of the helping relationship with young gay men and gay adolescents. Because the fear of contracting HIV has waned among younger gay men, issues around safe sex and responsible sexual activity need to be examined and incorporated into sexual exploration among younger gays. As with adult gay men, the social worker needs to be comfortable discussing the sex lives of their gay clients in a meaningful way. Exploring the sex lives of clients in general can be a source of discomfort for many clinicians. Beginning practitioners must not only examine their own attitudes around sexual expression between heterosexual couples but also remember that sexual expression between gay men may not fall into a familiar heterosexual construct. Therefore, what may appear to be "promiscuous and irresponsible" to the practitioner may be acceptable and satisfying to the gay client or gay couple. Where HIV/AIDS is concerned, the worker should address safe sex practices, disclosure to sex partners of HIV-positive status, and education about the continued prevalence of HIV infection among young gay men. These issues should be addressed in a supportive, nonjudgmental way.

**Gay Men as Fathers**   In the heterosexual world, few people think of gay men as fathers. However, many gay men come to terms with their sexual orientation only after entering into a heterosexual relationship and fathering children. Approximately 25 percent or more of gay men have been heterosexually married (Dunne, 1988).

Gay men marry for many reasons. Some men do not acknowledge their same sex attractions until after engaging in a heterosexual relationship. Others marry to fit in and avoid the social ostracism associated with being gay. Some hope their same sex attraction will disappear once they engage in a heterosexual marriage. Others desire a family and want to father children (Coleman, 1981–1982; McDonald and Steinhorn, 1990).

Gay men perceive their sexual orientation as potentially harmful to their children and as having a potentially negative influence on the children's own development of sexual identity (Coleman, 1981–1982; Dunne, 1988; McDonald and Steinhorn, 1990). Because of this, gay men are more likely than lesbian women to keep their sexual orientation a secret from their children. Only 46 percent of gay fathers revealed their homosexuality to their children, compared to 94 percent of lesbian mothers (Wyers, 1987). This statistic suggests that gay fathers are greatly affected by internalized homophobia and the shame imposed by heterosexist beliefs. These dynamics coupled with a lack of support in the general population keeps internalized homophobia and shame alive even today.

Other gay fathers keep their orientation secret in order to gain custody and visitation rights after a divorce. The judicial system tends to grant custody rights to a heterosexual parent over a gay parent even when there is evidence that the heterosexual parent may not be the best caretaker (Germain, 1991).

Although the majority of gay fathers have children in heterosexual relationships, many are finding other ways to become parents. Gay men become fathers through adoption and foster parenting. Female friends or a partner's female family members act as surrogates and give birth to the biologic children of gay men. Others have fathered children with lesbian women who share the responsibilities of parenting much as heterosexual couples do who live apart. As the number of gay fathers increases, social workers will need to develop services and interventions that address the needs of families headed by gay men.

Information on helping relationships with gay fathers is limited. Whereas general studies about gay men were generalized to lesbians, information available about gay fathers is in large part generalized from studies specific to lesbian mothers (Ritter and Terndrup, 2002). Lynch (2000) studied lesbian and gay stepfamilies and found that although there are similar expectations among gay parents and heterosexual parents when families are blended (e.g., the misconception that once together, stepfamilies will fall into the same day-to-day rhythm of "normal family life"), gay-headed families face very different challenges. For instance, heterosexual couples approach stepparenting with a focus on the couple as a team and work together to help in the raising of the children. Children in the heterosexual stepfamily are expected to respect the stepparent as a "parent" and respect the relationship between their parent and his or her spouse. However, because of the stigma attached to being gay, two-father families tend to be more child focused in their approach to parenting (Lynch, 2000). This becomes apparent when gay parents must address the prejudices around gay issues and help their children work through their own issues of shame and guilt related to having a gay parent or issues around living in a sometimes hostile world where their family will be ostracized. In this way, the parenting style becomes more child centered than couple centered (Nelson, 1996). Likewise, gay couples do not have the legal ritual to establish them as important members of a stepfamily. Therefore, the gay stepparent must work diligently with his partner and their children to define their roles in the children's lives.

Despite various challenges to gay men parenting together, families with same sex parents develop strengths by actively addressing discrimination within the family. Gay-headed families show remarkable resilience, flexibility, and commitment to "family" as they look to each other for support and acceptance. Gay-headed families survive and children thrive without the outside support and recognition that mixed sex couples experience, which strengthens the bonds between family members and aids them in being flexible throughout family transitions (Lynch, 2000).

Family therapy with gay-headed families is new ground. Social work practitioners are in the position to take the lead in research and intervention. Focusing on the strengths of gay-headed families is a good start and can lead to a better understanding of how gay men are able to provide a loving, nurturing, and supportive environment in which their children can grow.

## The Lesbian Experience

Although gay men and lesbian women experience the same kinds of prejudice and discrimination by virtue of their sexual minority status, lesbian women must deal with additional societal pressures (Morgan, 1997; Simon, 1995; Smalley, 1988; Spaulding, 1993). Lesbians are forced by a heterosexist society to grapple not only with their status as a sexual minority, but also with their status as women in a male-dominated society (Morgan, 1997; Riddle and Sang, 1978; Spaulding, 1993).

Just as boys are socialized to engage in male-related behaviors, so too are girls socialized to engage in female behaviors. These gender roles generally begin to take shape during childhood (Riddle and Sang, 1978). When boys are learning to be competitive and emotionally distant, girls are learning to be sensitive, nurturing, supportive, and noncompetitive. Girls also learn that these traits rank them as subordinate, ineffectual, and less valued than males (Herek, 1986; Morgan, 1997; Riddle and Sang, 1978; Spaulding, 1993).

Like gay men, lesbians experience rejection, self-loathing, anxiety, worry, shame, and ostracism related to their status as a sexual minority. However, these issues tend to be entangled with equally damaging messages women receive about being female. Lesbians must deal with sexual harassment and unwanted sexual advances by men who believe that lesbians are waiting for men to "turn them straight." Gay men do not experience this aspect of heterosexism as frequently as lesbians do. It puts lesbians at risk for both physical and sexual violence, whereas gay men tend to be victims of physical violence only (Spaulding, 1993).

Women face discrimination in employment and are less likely than men to be granted career advancement. Heterosexual women benefit from their relationships with male spouses who receive financial and career advances with regularity. Because both partners in a lesbian relationship are likely to face discrimination on the job, lesbians tend to be disadvantaged financially compared to their gay male and heterosexual peers (Riddle and Sang, 1978). Further, the social pressures placed on lesbians to socialize with business acquaintances put them at a disadvantage when they feel that they must hide their sexual orientation and find male escorts to attend business functions.

Whereas gay men struggle to learn ways to be emotionally close, lesbian relationships are often emotionally intense because both partners have been socialized to be sensitive, nurturing caretakers. Lesbians encounter problems when a relationship becomes intensely close (Roth, 1985). Overcloseness, or "fusion," interferes with each person's ability to develop a separate sense of self and heightens the amount of stress the couple experiences. Typical behaviors include the following:

> one partner may begin to distance in an effort to establish separateness, or each partner may distance in an alternating fashion;
> conflicts may become open and intense, possibly leading to violence;
> one of the partners may involve a third element to reduce the intensity (a child, a romantic involvement); and
> the couple may engage in repeated cycles of fusion and unrelatedness. (Roth, 1985, p. 288)

To meet the needs of lesbian women, it is important to understand the realities of heterosexist oppression. Lesbian couples often need help sorting through relationship issues and discovering healthy ways to be in a relationship. The notion that emotional intensity in a lesbian couple is inherently pathologic must be put aside. The helping process entails educating lesbian partners about boundaries, autonomy, and healthy relationship formation (Roth, 1985; Smalley, 1988).

It is also important to offer affirmation to the lesbian couple and support the relationship as one that has been able to endure despite many obstacles, including the weight of oppression. Many heterosexual relationships would have difficulty withstanding the civil injustices and prejudices lesbian couples face on a daily basis. The strengths of such a union should be respected, acknowledged, and regarded as positive aspects of the relationship.

Because many lesbian women have been victimized by men, it is important to understand the dynamics of abuse and the complicated nature of being twice victimized—as a female and as a sexual minority. When addressing victimization with lesbian women, do not make the mistake of attempting to find the cause of a lesbian's attraction to women (Riddle and Sang, 1978). This can be tempting when a lesbian client is a survivor of sexual abuse. Lesbian identity development needs to be understood as separate from abuse experiences. Affirm a lesbian client's identity as a gay woman with a history of trauma, not as a woman who is gay because of a history of trauma.

**HIV/AIDS**    During the early years of the AIDS epidemic, the U.S. government turned a deaf ear to doctors who were treating gay men with AIDS, and there was a widespread belief that gay men deserved to die a horrid death because of their "immoral lifestyle" (Lauritsen, 1993; Patton, 1986; Shilts, 1987; Stine, 1993; Zastrow and Kirst-Ashman, 1990). When the government finally did respond, it was in the form of policy debates about mandatory testing, quarantining, tattooing, and other methods of branding persons suspected of having AIDS. Policies were being developed with gays and lesbians in mind, sometimes as a means of singling gays and lesbians out in visible ways (Pierce and VanDeVeer, 1988; Shilts, 1987). As a result, discrimination toward sexual minorities was being condoned and supported by the government, some of whose members were content to let the gay and lesbian population die off from this dreadful illness.

The general assumption in the United States was that being gay or lesbian made an individual susceptible to AIDS. Lesbians were included in attempts to limit the activities of gays, using AIDS as the rationale for differential treatment. The number of lesbian women who contracted the disease was much smaller than the number of gay men. In fact, lesbians were considered, at that time, to be one of the lowest-risk groups for HIV. This fact should have dispelled the idea that being gay or lesbian was a precursor to becoming infected with the AIDS virus. Nevertheless, discrimination against the gay and lesbian community intensified, and lesbian women bore the burden of hate directed toward all gays.

Before the AIDS crisis, gay men and lesbian women rarely socialized. Believing the heterosexist myths about gay men and women, lesbians assumed that gay men hated women, and gay men assumed that lesbians hated men. The two groups had little or no interest in each other. But by 1980, it was clear that the government had no interest in the health crisis that was sweeping through urban gay communities. Gay men and lesbians had no other choice but to tend to gay AIDS patients themselves. Gay and lesbian doctors, nurses, and social workers began to band together to offer services on a volunteer basis, since federal monies were being withheld. Grassroots organizations formed to offer gay men dying of AIDS a safe place to meet and receive the few available services. Lesbian women nursed dying gay men and offered companionship and support to those who were HIV-positive. In the midst of death, discrimination, and homophobic panic, lesbian women and gay men embraced each other as family.

Like gay men, lesbian women have had to deal with loss and grief as they nursed and buried young friends dying of the disease. With great compassion, lesbian women working with gay men established comprehensive social services programs for people living with AIDS. Acknowledgment of their contribution is long overdue.

**Lesbian-Headed Families**   Lesbian women become parents in various ways. Like gay fathers, a small number of women marry and have children within the context of a heterosexual relationship (Kirkpatrick, 1988). Other lesbian women adopt children or become foster mothers. More and more lesbian women are turning to donor insemination to conceive and give birth to their own biologic children. Because women tend to win custody of their children more frequently than men, some lesbian women become mothers when they meet and commit to a partner who is rearing children (Pies, 1988).

Perhaps the biggest issue facing lesbian mothers is the homophobic belief that lesbians are unfit mothers and that a female-headed household will damage the child (Faria, 1994; Fraser, Fish, and Mackenzie, 1995; Hare, 1994; Levy, 1992; Zastrow and Kirst-Ashman, 1990). Because of this stigma, some lesbian mothers may attempt to pass as heterosexual to avoid losing a job or housing (Zastrow and Kirst-Ashman, 1990). Women who have had children in heterosexual relationships may hide their sexual orientation because they fear they will lose custody of their children if it is discovered that they are lesbian. Lesbian mothers who are open about their sexual orientation tend to

## CASE 12.2 | I'M HER PARENT, TOO!

Mary A. and Emily L. have been together as a couple for eight years. Early in their relationship, they decided they wanted to have children. Because Emily had medical problems that prohibited her from carrying a child, Mary became pregnant through anonymous donor insemination and bore two children. When their daughter was four and their son two, Emily decided to become a "stay-at-home mom" so that the couple could save on day-care expenses. Because the children called Emily "Mama," Emily's status as their mother was never questioned.

When Mary and Emily's daughter, Alexis, was hit by a car and rushed to the hospital, Emily sat with her in the ambulance and held her hand. At the hospital, the medical team discovered that Alexis's wrist and hand were fractured. Halfway through the examination, a nurse in the emergency room noticed that

Emily's last name was different than Alexis's. She asked Emily why the two did not share the same name. Without giving it much thought, Emily explained that she was Alexis's nonbiologic mother and that her partner was Alexis's birth mother. The hospital staff then questioned Emily's authority to give permission to treat Alexis and insisted that she contact Mary before they would proceed. Because Alexis's injuries were not life-threatening, the hospital staff would not provide further treatment until Mary gave legal consent to give Alexis something to relieve the pain. Since Emily had contacted Mary immediately when Alexis had been injured, Mary was on her way to the hospital and could not be reached. Emily helplessly held the little girl's hand while Alexis pleaded with her to stop the pain. They waited for 30 agonizing minutes for Mary to arrive at the hospital.

---

form supportive relationships with other gay-headed or lesbian-headed families, or gay-friendly heterosexual couples. Thus, they find support within their own community (Levy, 1992; Pies, 1988).

Many lesbian women lack the traditional support systems that are available to heterosexual women, and those who hide their sexual orientation to protect their families may be adding further stress to internal family functioning as the weight of the secret takes its toll (Hare, 1994). Lesbian women may obtain less support from their birth families than heterosexual women (Levy, 1992). Consequently, they create support systems with other lesbian mothers or lesbian friends to help cope with the stresses of parenting.

When lesbian mothers decide to parent together, complicated issues can arise. In many states, only one mother can claim legal custody of a child. The nonbiologic mother may participate equally in the daily care of the child, but cannot legally claim the child as her own. Society may not acknowledge the nonbiologic mother as a parent and therefore withholds recognition (Pies, 1988). The case example in Case 12.2 illustrates how nonbiologic mothers are disregarded by social systems.

This is one example of how nonbiologic lesbian mothers are disregarded by various systems in society. Other institutions that need to serve nonbiologic mothers and their children include schools, churches, scout troops, and sports teams. Disregard can add more stress to emotionally overburdened relationships and can affect the couple's relationship with each other and their children. Yet, like gay-headed families, lesbian-headed households emerge with incredible strength, and flexibility in dealing with day-to-day family transitions.

# GENERALIST PRACTICE WITH GAY AND LESBIAN CLIENTS

The term *coming out,* or *coming out of the closet,* describes the process in which gay men and lesbian women acknowledge and come to terms with their sexual orientation. The process has been described in different ways (Coleman, 1981–1982; de Monteflores and Schultz, 1978; Hanley-Hackenbruck, 1989; McDonald and Steinhorn, 1990; Morrow, 1996; Moses and Hawkins, 1982; Sophie, 1986), but it has three specific phases: the awareness phase, the acceptance phase, and the integration phase.

During the awareness phase, gay and lesbian individuals begin to acknowledge for the first time that they are experiencing romantic feelings for members of the same sex. These feelings may be as simple as a thought or a fantasy (Coleman, 1981–1982). During this stage, gay and lesbian individuals begin to realize that there is something different about them compared to the heterosexual individuals they identified with (Cass, 1979). This first realization of same sex attraction or this awareness of difference often manifests itself as confusion, isolation, and anxiety as the gay or lesbian person becomes consciously aware that his or her feelings are in direct conflict with prevailing societal expectations.

During the acceptance phase of coming out, individuals begin to grapple with their identity as gay or lesbian people. Acceptance means the person's acceptance of sexual orientation, not that the person becomes settled with this identity. In this phase, gay men and lesbian individuals begin to explore their feelings by experimenting with same sex relationships (Coleman, 1981–1982) or associating with other gay and lesbian individuals or groups. The person begins to identify himself or herself as gay or lesbian rather than heterosexual (Moses and Hawkins, 1982). The person may also disclose sexual minority status to family members and friends. This can be the most difficult phase in the coming-out process. The gay or lesbian person will generally experience the most severe attacks to self-esteem and self-identity as others voice their disdain of gays and lesbians in direct ways (de Monteflores and Schultz, 1978). Because of rejection, persons in this phase may oscillate between heterosexual and same sex relationships as they attempt to resolve their own internalized homophobia and heterosexism (Moses and Hawkins, 1982).

In the integration phase of coming out, gay and lesbian individuals begin to integrate more positive beliefs about themselves and embrace their sexual orientation (Cass, 1979; Coleman, 1981–1982; de Monteflores and Schultz, 1978; Hanley-Hackenbruck, 1989; Moses and Hawkins, 1982). They are able to acknowledge their status as a sexual minority and experience a sense of pride and connectedness to the gay and lesbian community. Once an individual has entered the integration stage, she or he may be more likely to publicly acknowledge her or his status as a lesbian woman or gay man (Moses and Hawkins, 1982) and no longer feel compelled to keep feelings and relationships a secret.

These phases may seem fairly straightforward and appear to progress in a linear fashion. However, the process of coming out is fraught with complicated issues that must be negotiated by gay and lesbian persons and those engaged in a helping relationship with them. Not every gay or lesbian person will come out of the closet. Many people become stuck in the earlier stage of awareness and invest their energies in denial of their same sex attractions. Others may acknowledge their status as gay men or lesbian women during the acceptance stage, but continue to live double lives, posing as heterosexuals in public and engaging in same sex relationships in private. A gay or lesbian parent may choose to remain in the closet in order to protect his or her rights to children. Because of the social stigma that is still associated with homosexuality, coming out is not always a safe choice, depending on family, employment, and community circumstances.

There has been a great deal of debate about the necessity of coming out. One camp supports an individual's right to choose whether to come out of the closet, citing discrimination and victimization as real concerns. The other camp takes the position that living in secrecy and denying one's true self can be psychologically damaging (Zastrow and Kirst-Ashman, 1990). Gay and lesbian clients may seek professional help to address the decision to come out. There are no easy answers. Information on the positive and negative aspects will help gay and lesbian clients weigh the advantages and disadvantages within the context of their own lives and make choices that best support their personal development.

While the successful integration of a gay or lesbian identity may seem like the final stage of the coming-out process, even after successful integration occurs, coming out is a life-long process. Gay and lesbian people who are out are faced with decisions about whether to disclose their sexual minority status on a daily basis. Each new situation, such as meeting new employers, coworkers, neighbors, business associates, classmates, or teachers means making another decision about whether to come out.

The decision is complicated by the fact that the federal government does not offer legal protections to sexual minorities. Discrimination against gay men and lesbians is legal and widely practiced. This is a unique stress that heterosexual individuals do not experience. Do not underestimate the effect of discrimination on gay and lesbian clients.

The helping process for gay men and lesbian women should incorporate work around externalizing introjected shame and guilt. In order for the work to be beneficial, you need to be aware of your own heterosexist beliefs and remain open to accepting the diverse experiences of gay men and lesbians without imposing personal opinions (Lipton, 1996).

Lesbian mothers need support with coming-out issues, addressing both internalized and societal homophobia and self-esteem (Levy, 1992). Support for lesbian mothers and gay fathers must extend beyond emotional support. To fully meet the needs of gay and lesbian parents, you need to understand such legal issues as power of attorney, joint custody of minor children, and partnership agreements.

## Families of Origin

Heterosexist and homophobic beliefs about gays and lesbians abound in the families of sexual minorities. When a child comes out of the closet, parents often experience the same kind of shame and guilt that gays and lesbians experience as a result of internalized heterosexism and homophobia (Beeler and DiProva, 1999). While some parents of gay and lesbian children are accepting of their children, many experience guilt related to their own beliefs that they "did something wrong" in rearing their children and therefore "caused" their sexual orientation (Laird, 1998). Family members of gay and lesbian individuals may also begin to question whether or not they will continue to be accepted in their own circle of friends, by colleagues, or by society in general if it is discovered that their family member is gay or lesbian. These dilemmas and others present the social worker with very specific issues to resolve when working with the families of gays and lesbians.

Ritter and Terndrup (2002) identify four styles of relationships between homosexual children and their families once they have come out. **Loving open parents** had loving and open relationships with their children before the disclosure and continued to have similar relationships with their children after the disclosure. These parents were also more likely to disclose their children's sexual orientation to friends, family, and others that they may have come into contact with. **Loving denial parents** continued to have loving relationships with their children but were unable or unwilling to disclose their children's sexual orientation to other family members or friends. The family (including the gay or lesbian child) conducted their family affairs with the agreement (spoken or unspoken) that the gay or lesbian child would not call attention to their sexual orientation in any way and that open expressions or discussions about their sexual orientation were not acceptable. Parents who engaged in relationships with their children with **resentful denial** avoided regular contact with their gay or lesbian child and remained "in the closet" about having a gay or lesbian child. These parents made their disapproval known to their children and avoided discussing their children's sexual orientation. A final group of parents responded to their gay and lesbian children with **hostile recognition.** In contrast to the loving open family interactions, these families usually were plagued by difficult family relationships before the disclosure. Parent–child relationships were strained or estranged and rejection of the gay or lesbian child was often absolute (Ritter and Terndrup, 2002, p. 301).

Perhaps the most common emotions shared by the parents of gay and lesbian children are grief and loss (Beeler and DiProva, 1999; Ritter and Terndrup, 2002). More specifically, parents grapple with the reality that their gay and lesbian children will never marry, making the possibility of grandchildren seem unlikely. Grief and loss may be related to the actual loss of the gay or lesbian family member if the family rejects the gay or lesbian child or if the gay or lesbian family member decides to distance themselves from the family for the sake of self-preservation. Some families are able to work through their disappointment and grief and accept and support their gay or lesbian family member. Some families remain frozen in their anger, guilt, and shame and are unable to accept their family member once they disclose their sexual orientation.

The first step to helping families accept gay and lesbian children is to assist parents and other family members to resolve their grief (Beeler and DiProva, 1999; Sanders and Kroll, 2000; Ritter and Terndrup, 2002). A stage model of grieving, such as the one proposed by Kübler-Ross (1969), can be useful in helping family members to identify their feelings, accept them as part of a natural grieving process, and allow resolution of the grief.

Dispelling the myths about gays and lesbians and addressing homophobia and heterosexism also allows families to integrate new knowledge about their gay and lesbian children into their evolving identity as families. This includes letting go of the fantasy that gay and lesbian children will participate in the rites and rituals afforded heterosexual couples. Laird (1993) acknowledges that the typical rituals and rites of passage available to heterosexual couples are not available to gay and lesbian couples. Not only do gays and lesbians have to create their own meaningful rituals, family members must also create a new family identity that allows for the acceptance of the partners of gay and lesbian children and the gay and lesbian child's children. This may become less cumbersome when families are able to share their own experiences with integrating their gay and lesbian family members into their lives with other families of gays and lesbians (Beeler and DiProva, 1999). Support groups such as **Parents, Families, and Friends of Lesbians and Gays (PFLAG)** provide a safe environment for parents and family members of gays and lesbians to talk about their shared experiences and offer support and understanding.

The struggle for many families is painful. Many choose not to embark on the journey and reject or distance themselves from their gay and lesbian children. Gay and lesbian adults have adapted to this rejection by forming families of choice that include supportive friends and communities that accept them unconditionally. Yet, the hope for most gay and lesbian individuals is that eventually their parents and other family members will be able to come to terms with their status as the family member of a gay or lesbian person. Social workers in generalist practice can help make this transition more manageable if and when it presents itself by understanding beforehand the process of grief and how to help the family re-create their notion of "family" to include gay and lesbian members.

## Gay and Lesbian Adolescents

Adolescence can be a trying time. Developmentally, it is a period of separation and individuation from the family and establishment of membership and connection with peer groups (Newman and Newman, 1995). Because of the conflict between individuality and group membership, teens ask themselves "Who am I?" and "Where do I fit in?" A teen who answers the first question "Gay or lesbian" soon discovers that the answer to the second question is "Nowhere."

Gay and lesbian teens are victims of the same homophobic and hetero-sexist biases as their adult counterparts. The fragile nature of the adolescent ego makes adolescent children even more vulnerable to stigmatization. As mentioned previously, the cultural ethos that perpetuates hate toward same sex love also erodes the gay or lesbian adolescent's main source of support, role modeling, and sense of identity—the family (Cates, 1987; Herdt and Boxer, 1993; Hetrick and Martin, 1987; Maylon, 1981; Morrow, 1993; Saltzburg, 1996; Telljohann and Price, 1993; Unks, 1995). Indoctrinated into heterosexist, stigmatizing beliefs about gay men and lesbian women, the par-ents of gay and lesbian youth often feel the same fear, hate, and disgust as the general culture (Telljohann and Price, 1993). Unlike their adult counterparts, gay and lesbian adolescents find themselves having to live day to day with their parents' anger and rejection as they continue to remain dependent on their parents to meet their basic needs.

Gay and lesbian youth face social discrimination as they attempt to assim-ilate themselves into a minority group that is foreign even to their parents. However, gay and lesbian youth must face the stark reality that their families may not be able to offer the same support or guidance as parents of other minority children because they do not understand the experience of being gay or lesbian. This dynamic often intensifies the homophobic response that the gay or lesbian teen experiences in the family.

A common coping strategy is for the family to reject the gay or lesbian child's sexuality and, very often, the child as well. This can make existence for a gay or lesbian adolescent uncomfortable at best, and violent and abusive at worse (Herdt and Boxer, 1993; Kruks, 1991; Maylon, 1981; Telljohann and Price, 1993; Unks, 1995). The gay or lesbian teen may be faced with a deci-sion about whether to remain in a hostile family environment or leave home for a life on the streets.

It is estimated that gay and lesbian youth make up approximately one-quarter of all homeless youth in the United States (Unks, 1995). Gay children are at greater risk for being violently thrown out of their homes, whereas les-bian children are more likely to suffer physical, verbal, and sexual abuse at home (Hetrick and Martin, 1987). Homelessness and victimization related to their sexual orientation put gay and lesbian youth at greater risk for drug and alcohol dependence (Seattle Commission on Children and Youth, 1998). Substance abuse is a coping strategy gay and lesbian youth use to deal with feelings about being rejected by family and about their own homosexuality (Hetrick and Martin, 1987; Seattle Commission on Children and Youth, 1988).

The school setting plays a pivotal role in adolescent development. Within the context of peer relationships, teens experience the social pressures of con-forming to societal norms. Since adolescence is a time of group identification, the gay or lesbian teen experiences great stress related to rejection by peers and the education system as a whole. Many gay and lesbian teens drop out of school as a means of coping with homophobic harassment and violence directed toward them by peers (Morrow, 1993). Educational systems do little to address the harassment of gay and lesbian youth. The schools are not a source of support for gay and lesbian students (Morrow, 1993). Burdened by social stigma, many gay and lesbian youth take their own lives before they reach adulthood. The Department of Health and Human Services estimated that one-third of all successful teen suicides are committed by gay or lesbian youth (Unks, 1995).

When working with family members of gay and lesbian youth, the practitioner must understand that when a child chooses to come out of the closet, the family often goes into the closet. Saltzburg (1996) has had success working with the families of gay and lesbian youth in family therapy interventions. She has found that helping parents know and embrace the total identity of their gay or lesbian adolescent facilitates their acceptance of their child. Challenging stereotypes and teaching parents about the positive aspects of being gay or lesbian will ensure parental involvement in their children's lives into adulthood.

An important function of social work practice is "active advocacy and intervention on behalf of gay and lesbian adolescents" (Morrow, 1993, p. 659). Social workers can play a key role in introducing support groups for gay and lesbian teens and their families. Such youth groups as **Project 10** (Uribe, 1995), **Gay/Straight Alliance** (Blumenfeld, 1995), and **OutRight!** (Singerline, 1995) offer supportive and safe environments for gay and lesbian youth and their families. The group format can also be used to educate heterosexual youth about gays and lesbians, address homophobia, and dispel myths that stigmatize gay and lesbian youth.

Gay and lesbian teens need healthy role models to help acclimate them to the gay and lesbian community and validate their identities as sexual minorities. Heterosexual parents usually cannot provide this type of support. Therefore, it is important for gay and lesbian adults to offer guidance to the children in their community. Social workers can ask gay and lesbian adults to act as mentors to gay and lesbian youth and their families. By directly addressing the isolation that gay and lesbian youth experience because of their sexual minority status, social workers can help gay and lesbian teens feel less hopeless and prevent them from acting out their despair in self-destructive ways.

## Gay and Lesbian Elders

Research about elderly gays and lesbians is limited and is for the most part dominated by studies of gay males (Friend, 1988). These studies show that heterosexism continues to adversely affect gay men and lesbian women during the later stages of the life cycle (Friend, 1988).

Because same sex partners do not enjoy the legal protections of marriage, many gay and lesbian elders find themselves left out of important decisions made on behalf of a sick or dying partner (Berger, 1982a, 1982b). Grief over the loss of a spouse is often compounded by feelings of anger about being left out of important decisions about medical treatment and the estates of partners (Friend, 1988). The deceased partner's family, jeopardizing the financial security of the surviving partner, who may have owned property jointly with the spouse or established a joint bank account during their lives together, may call a will into question. Gay and lesbian couples can reduce the risk of being excluded from making important health or property decisions by taking legal action to protect their rights (e.g., wills that specifically identify their partner as their heir, powers of attorney). However, these protections are costly and, in some states, not guaranteed protection. A heterosexual spouse rarely faces these problems and inherits the estate and holds onto the possessions that were accumulated through the years.

Older lesbians and gay men are a diverse group with diverse lifestyles (McDonald and Steinhorn, 1990). Some are parents or grandparents; some live in committed relationships with life partners; and some remain single. Many older gay men and lesbian women are better equipped to deal with the stigma and problems of aging because they have dealt with the stigma and problems of being gay or lesbian (Friend, 1988; McDonald and Steinhorn, 1990; Moses and Hawkins, 1982).

Older gays and lesbians have been forced to look to their own resources as individuals; this is not true for older heterosexuals, who have most likely been able to look to their families of origin and their families of procreation for the support they need. When that support is lost to them, heterosexuals often do not have a supportive friendship network to fall back on, as lesbians and gay men do. Lesbians and gay men, who have not tended to form traditional family groups, have most often had to learn how to depend on themselves. This is an important attribute that is not always developed in our society, even though it may be given lip service (McDonald and Steinhorn, 1990, p. 110). In other words, heterosexual women have learned to rely on their husbands and families for a great deal of financial and emotional support and often find themselves in financial crisis when they are widowed or divorced and feel displaced when their children leave home. This is not true for older lesbians, who have most likely been on their own since coming out. Many heterosexual men have spent their lives being cared for by women, whereas their gay counterparts have spent most of their lives tending to their own needs, such as cooking, cleaning, doing laundry, shopping, and making social arrangements.

Older lesbians and gay men face the same life-cycle issues as older heterosexuals, that is, financial security, health, loss of friends and spouses, and acceptance (Germain, 1991). Because of the coping styles they were required to develop as sexual minorities, older lesbians and gay men seem to be better equipped to address old age. They continue to enjoy many of the same activities they participated in as younger men and women (Moses and Hawkins, 1982). In working with older lesbians and gay men, remember that life-cycle issues related to the loss of a spouse and financial security may be of greater concern to clients than the stigma of aging. Be careful not to impose your beliefs about ageism on older lesbians and gay men, but rather support the strengths that these individuals bring to the elderly community.

## Children of Gays and Lesbians

Heterosexual society has three fears about gay men and lesbians raising children:

1. That children raised in same sex households will be sexually abused by their gay or lesbian parent or their parent's partner
2. That the children of gay men and lesbians will be coaxed into a same sex sexual orientation by their fathers or mothers
3. That children of gay men and lesbians will be ostracized and humiliated by peers because of their parents' sexual orientation and therefore are likely to be psychologically damaged (Germain, 1991).

The myth that gay men and lesbians are child molesters continues to be perpetuated by society. Although a small percentage of child molesters are gay or lesbian, 80 percent to 97 percent of adults who sexually abuse children are heterosexual men who prey on young girls (Moses and Hawkins, 1982; Newton, 1978). There is no support for the notion that the children of gay men and lesbians are more likely than the children of heterosexual parents to be molested by their parents.

It is also a myth that their fathers or mothers will coax the children of gay men and lesbians into a same sex orientation. If it were true that parents determined their children's sexual orientation, all children raised in heterosexual households would be heterosexual. We know it is not true, because the majority of gay men and lesbians were raised in heterosexual families and nonetheless grew up to be gay men and lesbians (Golombok, Spence, and Rutter, 1983; Moses and Hawkins, 1982; Pies, 1988; Tasker and Golombok, 1995). The children of lesbians and gay men are no more likely to be gay or lesbian than the children of heterosexuals. It is interesting to note that children raised in gay and lesbian households who self-identify as gay or lesbian tend to make a better adjustment to their sexual minority status as teens or young adults. Gay and lesbian children raised in heterosexual households tend to keep their sexual orientation a secret longer and do not act on their feelings until adulthood (Tasker and Golombok, 1995).

The third fear, that children of gay men and lesbians will be ostracized and humiliated by peers and are more likely to be psychologically damaged, also turns out to be a myth. Children belonging to other minority groups, such as those with handicapped parents and those from other nontraditional family units, are also ostracized by peers. They find ways to cope with the unique aspects of their family, and there is no reason to expect that the children of gay men and lesbians will not do the same (Moses and Hawkins, 1982). Many children from lesbian households have been teased by peers and have not experienced this teasing as any different from, say, being teased about wearing glasses (Tasker and Golombok, 1995).

As children enter adolescence, they become less open about their parents' sexual orientation and may even feel embarrassed by it (Kirkpatrick, 1988;

Lewis, 1990; McDonald and Steinhorn, 1990). However, lesbian mothers and gay fathers have been able to help their children see themselves as separate from their parents and as having a sexual orientation of their own by allowing the children to express their anger and confusion about their parent's sexual orientation. When the children externalized their feelings about having a gay or lesbian parent, they became more accepting of their parent's sexual orientation (Lewis, 1990). It is important to note that studies have been conducted with children conceived within heterosexual relationships whose parents struggled with their own sexual orientation. Because there are few studies on children who have been raised from birth by gay men or lesbian women, these findings cannot be generalized to all children of gay men and lesbian women.

In school settings, the children of gay and lesbian parents go virtually unnoticed. Because of the general assumption that all children come from heterosexual relationships, children from same sex families seem invisible when units on family issues are presented. It must be stressful for the children of gay men and lesbians to spend their school years never having their unique and special families acknowledged. Nonetheless, children from same sex households tend to be as well-adjusted as children from heterosexual households (Hare, 1994; Kirkpatrick, 1988; Levy, 1992; McDonald and Steinhorn, 1990; Pies, 1988; Tasker and Golombok, 1995). This suggests that children of gay men and lesbians receive support and love from their families to help them negotiate larger heterosexist institutions such as schools.

Do not assume that the problems bringing the children of gay and lesbian parents to treatment are related to their parents' sexual orientation (Hare, 1994). Adults working in educational systems should acknowledge the partner of a child's parent as an adult living in the child's home who has the same responsibility for the child as its biologic parents. This will strengthen the child's sense of family and lessen the burden of having to keep a parent's relationship with a partner a secret.

The best way for social workers to help gay men, lesbians, and their children adjust in a heterosexual world is to make a commitment to educate the general public on issues related to homosexuality (Levy, 1992). When homophobia is diminished in society, gay men and lesbian parents can spend more of their time and energy tending to the needs of their children. This is the best support any family can receive.

## SUMMARY

The gay and lesbian population in the United States is much less a hidden minority than in the past. Gay men and lesbian women are becoming more visible, and it is likely that more will seek the services of social workers or other mental health practitioners. If social workers approach the helping relationship with homophobic attitudes, inaccurate beliefs and stereotypes, and limited knowledge about the special needs of gay and lesbian clients, they run the risk of alienating their clients and intensifying their clients' internalized homophobic response.

Homophobia is the dread of being in close quarters with gay or lesbian individuals. It is common among heterosexual men and women. Homophobia permeates our culture and influences not only how heterosexuals perceive gay people, but also how gay men and lesbians perceive themselves.

Heterosexism is the oppression of sexual minorities that is perpetuated by the societal beliefs that heterosexuals are better than gays and lesbians and that heterosexuality is the only form of sexual expression. It is a social construction that supports these beliefs and sustains prejudice and discrimination toward sexual minorities.

The civil rights of gays and lesbians are regularly violated in the areas of housing, employment, and education. Federal laws do not provide for the fair treatment of sexual minorities, and few states have laws protecting their rights. The lack of civil rights protection is directly related to homophobic and heterosexist ideologies.

Coming out is the process in which gay men and lesbian women acknowledge and come to terms with their sexual orientation. It consists of three phases: awareness, acceptance, and integration. Coming out is a complicated issue and complex process. Generalist social workers can aid this process by helping individuals weigh the positive and negative aspects of coming out within the context of their own life. The goal is to help gay and lesbian clients make choices that best support their personal development.

Families of gays and lesbians may need the assistance of the social work generalist to resolve grief and the sense of loss they experience when a gay or lesbian child comes out. Family members who are able to successfully resolve their grief and remain open to redefining their family to include gay and lesbian family members are able to continue loving relationships with their family members and the spouses and children of their gay or lesbian family member.

Gay and lesbian teens are victims of the same homophobic and heterosexist biases as their adult counterparts. However, the fragile nature of the adolescent ego makes adolescent children even more vulnerable to stigmatization and internalized negative self-perceptions. Rejection by family members and peers may force the gay or lesbian adolescent to leave home for a life on the streets. Social workers can work with families, schools, and other institutions that care for children to be more open and accepting of gay and lesbian teens at a time when fitting in is vital to the development of the adolescent.

Elderly gays and lesbians are a diverse group with diverse lifestyles. Many have learned to cope with the stigma of being gay or lesbian. Their concerns are similar to those of elderly heterosexuals. They tend to be more concerned about finances, partner relationships, loss of friends and partners, and health issues than about the stigma of aging or minority sexual orientation.

The children of gays and lesbians face special challenges and are also victims of homophobic prejudices and beliefs. Our heterosexual society views children being raised by gay or lesbian parents with trepidation. There is a fear that they will be sexually abused by the gay or lesbian parent or partner, that they will be converted to same sex sexual orientation, and that they will be psychologically damaged by social rejection by their peers.

There are many obstacles to providing good social services to sexual minorities. Homophobia, heterosexism, and ignorance about the lives of gay and lesbian people are just a few. As social workers, it is important to investigate our own biases and beliefs about this special population and take personal responsibility for working through our own misinformation about gays and lesbians. A good understanding of our own belief system and a willingness to accept our gay and lesbian clients as healthy, valuable members of society can make a vast difference in the helping relationship. Once we succeed in this endeavor, we can begin to tackle the daunting task of becoming advocates for this minority group as it struggles for justice.

## CASE EXAMPLE

The final case in this chapter illustrates the complexity of the coming-out process (Case 12.3). It highlights the difficulties gays and lesbians have with family and professional relationships. It also brings home the internal struggle gays and lesbians go through regarding their sexual identity.

---

### CASE 12.3 | I FEEL SHAME

Michael C. was a 26-year-old Caucasian male who sought help with issues related to his sexual orientation. Although he had dated women off and on since he was 16, he was concerned about his fantasies about being with men. He had never pursued a physical relationship with a man, but he believed that over the past several years he had been in love with at least two male friends.

#### Assessment

During the course of the assessment, Michael revealed that he had never discussed his sexual orientation with anyone. He was anxious about his feelings and experienced shame and guilt whenever he allowed himself to fantasize about men. He was raised with strong Christian morals and believed that being gay was dirty and sinful. He used alcohol to deal with his anxiety and often drank to excess to avoid intense self-loathing. Michael also reported bouts of depression during which he actively planned

his death. He admitted to two suicide attempts, one of which resulted in a two-week hospitalization. Both attempts involved overdoses of amphetamines and alcohol. The last attempt was six months prior to the assessment.

At the time he sought help, Michael reported increased bouts of depression that were interfering with his ability to perform his job. As a young attorney, he had demanding responsibilities. He wanted desperately to get rid of the feelings of hopelessness that intensified with each passing day and made it more and more difficult to concentrate on work. He hoped that discussing his feelings about his sexual orientation would end the depression once and for all.

In the early weeks of treatment, Michael discussed his fears about what it meant to be gay. He had worked hard to become involved in "masculine" activities so as not to be identified as a "queer" or "fag" by his friends and associates. He was goalie of a local ice hockey team, and he always accepted invitations to dinner when friends "fixed him up" with women. Michael feared that accepting himself as a gay man meant that he would have to become more feminine in order to be attractive to other gay men. Once this transformation occurred, he was fairly certain that he would lose his job and his family's love and support. The fear of contracting AIDS lay heavy on his mind. He associated gay sex with AIDS and seemed fairly certain that accepting himself as a gay man also meant accepting that he would die of AIDS. Addressing these fears became the starting point for Michael's treatment.

### Intervention

I began educating Michael on the damage that homophobia and heterosexism can cause to self-esteem. Once Michael understood that his fears were directly related to his own internalized homophobia and heterosexism, he was able to freely explore his desire to establish meaningful romantic relationships with men. With my support, Michael began to attend events sponsored by gay and lesbian organizations in neighboring cities. He socialized with other gay and lesbian people at "gay bingo" (bingo for gays and lesbians) and at coffeehouses where gay men and lesbians performed. Michael began to meet men who shared his interest in sports and began to develop a social network of gay men. He enjoyed their company and found that very few fit the stereotype of the "swish" he had feared he would become. As he became more acclimated to gay culture, his depression began to lift, and his alcohol abuse greatly decreased.

Four months into the helping process, Michael decided to come out to his brother and his best friend from college. Both had supported him during his bouts of depression and showed genuine concern for his well-being. Michael's college friend took the news better than his brother did. Michael asked his brother to join him in family sessions with me. Working together, Michael and I were able to lay his brother's homophobic and heterosexist beliefs aside. Michael was then able to reconnect with his brother. Once the secret of his sexuality was revealed, Michael's relationship with his brother and best friend grew closer.

Michael struggled with telling his parents. He was certain that coming out at work would cost him his job. He discussed this issue extensively in treatment and decided that he wanted to come out to his parents before becoming involved in a relationship. The work issue was more complicated. He knew that coming out could cost him his livelihood. In therapy sessions, Michael examined how the secret of his sexuality would require ongoing deception. Michael believed that he could not shed the shame he associated with his sexuality until he was able to bring his secret into the open. He decided to speak with his parents first, and then decide how to handle work and other relationships.

At my suggestion, Michael asked his brother to go with him for support when he told his parents that he was gay. They took the news badly and asked him to leave the house. Michael initially had difficulty with the rejection, but he was able to use the helping process to better understand his coming out as part of his individuation from his parents. Michael continued to keep in touch with his parents, giving them time to come to terms with his status as their adult gay son. He reasoned that it would take time for them to come to terms with something that took him years to accept.

### Evaluation and Termination

Eight months after beginning his work with me, Michael reported feeling less depressed and free of the feelings of shame and hopelessness that had consumed him. He became more confident in his identity as a gay man, and his anxiety about others discovering his sexuality was greatly reduced. Michael met two colleagues from work at a Gay Pride Parade, and they introduced him to a support group for gay and lesbian attorneys. Through this group, Michael began volunteering his legal services to the gay and lesbian community, working on civil rights legislation for sexual minorities. He began dating and occasionally introduced his gay dates and friends to his parents. He had also found a church that was affirming of sexual minorities and had begun to attend services regularly. Michael and I agreed that he had made significant progress during our eight months together and that Michael was ready to leave treatment. Michael left my office with the understanding that he should return whenever he felt the need to do so.

## DISCUSSION QUESTIONS

1.  Gay men and lesbian women may experience life-cycle issues differently than their heterosexual counterparts. In the case of Michael, coming out complicated his becoming autonomous from his family (Case 12.3). What other life-cycle issues can become complicated for gay men and lesbian women? Are there life-cycle issues that become complicated for the families of gays and lesbians? If so, what are they?

2.  If you were treating Michael's parents, how would you approach the treatment? What would be your goals in treatment? Do you think that the issues for Michael's parents would be vastly different from the issues that Michael addressed in treatment? What interventions would be appropriate for Michael's parents? Would providing them with information on PFLAG (Parents, Families, and Friends of Lesbians and Gays) and suggesting that they join a support group be appropriate? For more information on PFLAG go to the organization's Web site at www.pflag.org.

3.  What macroissues does the social work practitioner need to be aware of when treating gay and lesbian clients? Are there macroissues that affect the treatment on a micro level? Using the case example of Michael, discuss macroissues that affected him as an individual.

4.  Are you aware of any current legislative measures that directly affect gays and lesbians? If so, what are the issues? What is your stance on these issues? If not, are there current problems that directly affect gays and lesbians that you would consider taking to the legislature? If so, what issues? How would you present your case to the legislators?

5.  Do you think a gay or lesbian therapist can work more effectively with gay or lesbian clients? What might be issues for the heterosexual therapist working with gay and lesbian clients? What might be issues for the gay or lesbian therapist working with gay and lesbian clients?

6.  If you worked in a school setting, what kind of curriculum would you develop to educate staff and faculty about gay and lesbian families? How would you educate parents and students about this subject? How would you educate employers and employees in the work setting?

7.  What would you tell your child if she told you she was gay? What would you feel if your sister told you she was lesbian?

## REFERENCES

Beeler, J., and DiProva, V. (1999). Family adjustment following disclosure of homosexuality by a member: Themes discerned in narrative accounts. *Journal of Marital and Family Therapy, 25*(4) 443–459.

Behrendt, A. E., and George, K. (1995). Sex therapy for gay and bisexual men. In L. Diamant and R. D. McNaulty (Eds.), *The psychology of sexual orientation: Behavior and identity* (pp. 220–236). Connecticut: Greenwood.

Berger, R. M. (1982a). The unseen minority: Older gays and lesbians. *Social Work, 27*, 236–242.

Berger, R. M. (1982b). *Gay and gray.* Urbana, IL: University of Illinois Press.

Bernstein, A. C. (2000). Straight therapist working with lesbians and gays in family therapy. *Journal of Marital and Family Therapy 26*(4), 443–454.

Blumenfeld, W. J. (1995). Gay/straight alliance: Transforming pain to pride. In G. Unks (Ed.), *The gay teen* (pp. 211–224). New York: Routledge.

Bohan, J. S. (1997) Teaching on the edge: The psychology of sexual orientation. *Teaching of Psychology, 24*(1), 27–31.

Bohn, T. R. (1984). Homophobic violence: Implications for social work practice. *Journal of Social Work and Human Sexuality, 2*(2/3), 91–112.

Brandt, A. M. (1988). AIDS in historical perspective: Four lessons from the history of sexually transmitted diseases. *American Journal of Public Health, 78*, 367–371.

Britton, D. M. (1990). Homophobia and homosociality: An analysis of boundary maintenance. *Sociology Quarterly, 31*, 423–439.

Buhrke, R. A. (1989). Lesbian related issues in counseling supervision. *Women and Counseling, 8*(1/2), 195–206.

Cass, B. C. (1979). Homosexuality identity formation: A theoretical model. *Journal of Homosexuality, 4*, 219–235.

Cates, J. A. (1987). Adolescent sexuality: Gay and lesbian issues. *Child Welfare, 66*(4), 353–364.

Clift, S. M. (1988). Lesbian and gay issues in education: A study of the attitudes of first year students in a college of higher education. *British Education Research Journal, 14*, 31–50.

Coleman, E. (1981/1982). Developmental stages of the coming out process. *Journal of Homosexuality, 7*(2/3), 31–43.

Conley, T., Calhoun, C., Evett, S. R., and Devine, P. G. (2001). Mistakes that heterosexual people make when trying to appear non-prejudiced: The view from LGB people. Journal of *Homosexuality, 42*(2), 21–43.

Council on Social Work Education, Commission on Accreditation. (1993). *Handbook of accreditation standards and procedures.* Washington, DC: Author.

Cox, S., and Gallois, C. (1996). Gay and lesbian identity development: A social identity perspective. *Journal of Homosexuality, 30*(4), 1–30.

de Monteflores, C., and Schultz, S. J. (1978). Coming out: Similarities and differences for lesbians and gay men. *Journal of Social Issues, 34*(3), 59–72.

Dunne, E. (1988). Helping gay fathers come out to their children. In E. Coleman (Ed.), *Psychotherapy with homosexual men and women* (pp. 213–222). New York: Haworth.

Ernulf, K. E., and Innala, S. M. (1987). The relationship between affective and cognitive components of homophobic reactions. *Archives of Sexual Behavior, 16*, 501–509.

Faria, G. (1994). Training for family preservation practice with lesbian families. *Families in Society: The Journal of Contemporary Human Services, 75*(7), 416–422.

Fassinger, R. E. (1991). The hidden minority: Issues and challenges in working with lesbians and gay men. *The Counseling Psychologist, 19*, 157–176.

Fraser, I. H., Fish, T. A., and Mackenzie, T. M. (1995). Reactions to child custody decisions involving homosexual and heterosexual parents. *Canadian Journal of Behavioral Science, 27*(1), 52–63.

Friend, R. A. (1988). The individual and social psychology of aging: Clinical implications for lesbians and gay men. In

E. Coleman (Ed.), *Psychotherapy with homosexual men and women* (pp. 307–331). New York: Haworth.

Germain, C. B. (1991). *Human behavior in the social environment.* New York: Columbia University Press.

Golombok, S., Spence, A., and Rutter, M. (1983). Children in lesbian and single mother households: Psychosexual and psychiatric appraisal. *Journal of Child Psychology and Psychiatry, 24,* 551–572.

Green, R. (1987). *The "sissy boy syndrome" and the development of homosexuality.* New York: Yale University Press.

Hanley-Hackenbruck, P. (1989). Psychotherapy and the coming out process. *Journal of Gay and Lesbian Psychotherapy, 1,* 21–39.

Hare, J. (1994). Concerns and issues faced by families headed by a lesbian couple. *The Journal of Contemporary Human Services, 1,* 27–35.

Harowski, K. J. (1988). The worried well: Minimizing coping in the face of AIDS. In E. Coleman (Ed.), *Psychotherapy with homosexual men and women* (pp. 229–306). New York: Haworth.

Hellman, R. E., Green, R., Gray, J. L., and Williams, K. (1981). Childhood sexual identity, childhood religiosity and homophobia as influences in the development of transsexualism, homosexuality and heterosexuality. *Archives of General Psychiatry, 38,* 910–915.

*Herdt, G., and Boxer, A. (1993). Children of horizons.* Boston, MA: Beacon.

Herek, G. M. (1986). On heterosexual masculinity. *American Behavioral Scientist, 29*(5), 563–577.

Herek, G. M. (1989). Hate crimes against lesbians and gay men: Issues for research and policy. *American Psychologist, 44,* 948–955.

Herek, G. M., and Berrill, K. T. (1990). Anti-gay violence and mental health: Setting an agenda for research. *Journal of Interpersonal Violence, 5,* 414–423.

Hetrick, E. S., and Martin, A. D. (1987). Developmental issues and their resolution for gay and lesbian adolescents. *Journal of Homosexuality, 26*(1), 25–43.

Jay, K., and Young, A. (1979). *The gay report.* New York: Summit.

Jonsen, A. R., and Stryker, J. (Eds.). (1993). *The social impact of AIDS in the United States.* Washington, DC: National Academy Press.

Kaplan, H. S. (1974). *The new sex therapy: Active treatment of sexual dysfunction.* New York: Brunner/Mazel.

Kirkpatrick, M. (1988). Clinical implications of lesbian mothers studies. In E. Coleman (Ed.), *Psychotherapy with homosexual men and women* (pp. 201–211). New York: Haworth.

Klein, F., and Wolf, T. (1985). *Bisexualities: Theory and research.* New York: Haworth.

Kruks, G. (1991). Gay and lesbian homeless/street youth: Special issues and concerns. *Journal of Adolescent Health, 12,* 515–518.

Kubler-Ross, E. (1969). *On death and dying.* New York: Macmillan.

Laird, J. (1998). Invisible ties: lesbians and their families of origin. In C. J. Patterson and A. R. D'Augelli (Eds.), *Lesbian, gay, and bisexual identities in families: Psychological perspectives* (pp. 197–228).

Lance, L. M. (1987). The effects of interaction with gay persons on attitudes towards homosexuality. *Human Relations, 4,* 329–336.

Lauritsen, J. (1993). *The AIDS war.* New York: Asklepios.

Leiblum, S., and Rosen, R. (1989). *Principles and practice of sex therapy* (2nd ed.). New York: Guilford.

Levy, E. F. (1992). Strengthening the coping resources of lesbian families. *Journal* of Contemporary Human Services, 1, 23–31.

Lewis, K. (1990). Children of lesbians: Their point of view. Social Work, 25(3), 203–214.

Lipton, B. (1996). Opening doors: Responding to the mental health needs of gay and bisexual college students. Journal of Gay and Lesbian Social Services, 1(2), 7–24.

Lynch, J. M. (2000). Considerations of family structure and gender composition: the lesbian and gay stepfamily. Journal of Homosexuality, 40(2), 81–95.

MacDonald, A. (1976). Homophobia: Its roots and meanings. Homosexual Counseling Journal, 3(1), 23–33.

Mackelprang, R. W., Ray, J., and Hernandez-Peck, M. (1996). Social work education and sexual orientation: Faculty, student and curriculum issues. Journal of Gay and Lesbian Social Services, 5(4), 17–31.

Maier, R. A. (1984). Human sexuality in perspective. Chicago: Nelson Hall.

Masters, W. H., and Johnson, V. E. (1970). Human sexual inadequacy. Boston: Little, Brown.

Maylon, A. K. (1981). The homosexual adolescent: Developmental issues and social bias. Child Welfare, 60(5), 321–329.

McDonald, H. B., and Steinhorn, A. I. (1990). Homosexuality. New York: Continuum.

Millham, J., San Miguel, C. L., and Kellog, R. (1976). A factor analytic conceptualization of attitudes toward male and female homosexuals. Journal of Homosexuality, 2, 3–10.

Minton, H. L., and McDonald, G. J. (1983–1984). Homosexuality identity formation as a developmental process. Journal of Homosexuality, 9(2/3), 91–104.

Morgan, K. S. (1997). Why lesbians choose therapy: Presenting problems, attitudes and political concerns. Journal of Gay and Lesbian Social Services, 6(3), 57–75.

Morin, S., and Garfinkle, E. (1978). Male homophobia. Journal of Social Issues, 34(1), 29–47.

Morrow, D. F. (1993). Social work with gay and lesbian adolescents. Social Work, 38(5), 505–648.

Morrow, D. F. (1996). Coming-out issues for adult lesbians: A group intervention. Social Work, 41(6), 647–656.

Moses, A. E., and Hawkins, R. (1982). Counseling lesbian women and gay men: A life issues approach. St. Louis: Mosby.

Mosher, D. L., and O'Grady, K. E. (1979). Homosexual threat, negative attitudes toward masturbation, sex guilt, and males' sexual and affective reactions to explicit sexual films. Journal of Consulting and Clinical Psychology, 47(5), 860–873.

Neisen, J. H. (1990). "Heterosexism": Redefining homophobia for the 1990s. Journal of Gay and Lesbian Psychotherapy, 1(3), 21–35.

Neisen, J. H. (1993). Healing from cultural victimization: Recovery from shame due to heterosexism. Journal of Gay and Lesbian Psychotherapy, 2(1), 49–63.

Nelson, F. (1996). Lesbian mothers: An exploration of Canadian lesbian families. Toronto: University of Toronto Press.

Newman, B., Dannenfelser, P., and Benishek, L. (2002). Assessing beginning social work and counseling students' acceptance of lesbians and gays. Journal of Social Work Education, 38(2), 273–288.

Newman, B., and Newman, P. (1995). Development through life: A psychosocial approach. New York: Brooks/Cole.

Newton, D. E. (1978). Homosexual behavior and child molestation: A review of evidence. Adolescence, 13, 29–43.

Nungesser, L. (1983). Homosexual acts, and identities. New York: Praeger.

Panem, S. (1988). *The AIDS bureaucracy.* Cambridge, MA: Harvard University Press.

Patton, C. (1986). *Sex and germs: The politics of AIDS.* Buffalo, NY: Black Rose Books.

Peck, J., and Bezold, C. (1992, July). Health care and AIDS. *The Annals of the American Academy of Political and Social Science, 522,* 130–139.

Peplau, L. A. (1981). What homosexuals want in relationships. *Psychology Today, 15*(3), 28–38.

Pierce, C., and VanDeVeer, D. (1988). *AIDS: Ethics and public policy.* Belmont, CA: Wadsworth.

Pies, C. (1988). *Considering parenthood: A workbook for lesbians.* San Francisco: Spinster Ink.

Price, V., and Hsu, M. L. (1992). Public opinion about AIDS policies: The role of misinformation and attitudes toward homosexuals. *Public Opinion Quarterly, 56,* 29–52.

Riddle, D. I., and Sang, B. (1978). Psychotherapy with lesbians. *Journal of Social Issues, 34*(3), 84–100.

Ritter, K., and Terndrup, A. (2002). *Handbook of Affirmative Psychotherapy with Lesbians and Gay Men.* New York: The Guilford Press.

Roth, S. (1985). Psychotherapy with lesbian couples: Individual issues, female socialization and social context. *Journal of Marital and Family Therapy, 11*(3), 286–307.

Saltzburg, S. (1996). Family therapy and the disclosure of adolescent homosexuality. *Journal of Family Psychotherapy, 7*(4), 1–18.

Sanders, G. L., and Kroll, I. T. (2000). Generating stories of resilience: Helping gay and lesbian youth and their families. *Journal of Marital and Family Therapy, 20*(4), 433–442.

Seattle Commission on Children and Youth. (1988). *Report on gay and lesbian youth in Seattle.* Seattle: Author.

Shilts, R. (1987). *And the band played on.* New York: St. Martin's.

Simon, A. (1995). Some correlates of individuals' attitudes toward lesbians. *Journal of Homosexuality, 29*(1), 89–103.

Singerline, H. (1995). OutRight! Reflections on an out-of-school gay youth group. In G. Unks (Ed.), *The gay teen* (pp. 235–232). New York: Routledge.

Smalley, S. (1988). Dependency issues in lesbian relationships. In E. Coleman (Ed.), *Psychotherapy with homosexual men and women* (pp. 125–135). New York: Haworth.

Sophie, J. (1986). A critical examination of stage theories of lesbian identity-development. *Journal of Homosexuality, 12*(2), 39–51.

Sophie, J. (1987). Internalized homophobia and lesbian identity. *Journal of Homosexuality, 14*(1/2), 53–65.

Spaulding, E. C. (1993). Unconsciousness raising: Hidden dimensions of heterosexism in theory and practice with lesbians. *Smith College Studies in Social Work, 63*(3), 221–245.

Stevenson, M. R. (1988). Promoting tolerance of homosexuality: An evaluation of intervention strategies. *Journal of Sex Research, 25,* 500–511.

Stine, G. J. (1993). *Acquired immune deficiency syndrome: Biological, medical, social and legal issues.* New Jersey: Prentice-Hall.

Tasker, F., and Golombok, S. (1995). Adults raised as children in lesbian families. *American Journal of Orthopsychiatry, 65,* 203–215.

Telljohann, S. K., and Price, J. H. (1993). A qualitative examination of adolescent homosexuals' life experiences: Ramifications for secondary school personnel. *Journal of Homosexuality, 26*(1), 41–56.

Unks, G. (Ed.). (1995). *The gay teen.* New York: Routledge.

Uribe, V. (1995). Project 10: A school-based outreach to gay and lesbian youth. In G. Unks (Ed.), *The gay teen* (pp. 3–12). New York: Routledge.

Van de Ven, P. (1994). Challenging homophobia in schools. Unpublished doctoral thesis, University of Sydney.

Van de Ven, P., Bornholt, L., and Baily, M. (1996). Measuring cognitive, affective and behavioral components of homophobic reaction. *Archives of Sexual Behavior, 25*(2), 155–179.

Weinberg, G. (1972). *Society and the healthy homosexual.* New York: Doubleday Anchor.

Wells, J. W. (1991). The effects of homophobia and sexism on heterosexual sexual relationships. *Journal of Sex Education and Therapy, 17*(3), 185–195.

Wyers, N. L. (1987). Homosexuality in the family: Lesbian and gay spouses. *Social Work, 32*(2), 143–148.

Zastrow, C., and Kirst-Ashman, K. K. (1990). *Understanding human behavior and the social environment.* Chicago: Nelson Hall.

Zilbergeld, B. (1992). *The new male sexuality: The truth about me, sex and pleasure.* New York: Bantam.

## GAY AND LESBIAN RESOURCES

**Family Resources:**
Children of Gays and Lesbians Everywhere (COLAGE)
3543 18th Street, #1
San Francisco, CA 94110
Phone: 415.861.KIDS (5437)
Website: http://www.coloage.org
(COLAGE is a support and advocacy group for the children of gay, lesbian, bisexual and transgendered parents.)

Family Pride Coalition (FPC)
P.O. Box 34337
San Diego, CA 92163
Phone: 619.296.0199
Website: http://www.glpci.com
(FPC provides education and resource information to gay, lesbian, bisexual, and transgendered parents and their families.)

Parents, Families and Friends of Lesbians and Gays (PFLAG)
1726 M Street NW, Suite 400
Washington, DC 20036
Phone: 202.467.8180
Website: http://www.pflag.org
(PFLAG provides support and guidance to the family members and friends of sexual minorities.)

Partners Task Force for Gay and Lesbian Couples
P.O. Box 9685
Seattle, WA 98109
Phone: 206.935.1206
Website: http://www.buddybuddy.com
(Partners Task Force for Gay and Lesbian Couples provides resources and
    information on legal issues, creating rites and rituals, adoption, parenting,
    and much more for gay and lesbian couples.)

**Legal Organizations**
Gay and Lesbian Alliance Against Defamation (GLAAD)
Phone: 800.GAY.MEDIA
Website: http://www.glaad.org
(GLAAD's main focus is education and raising awareness of gay and lesbian
    issues in the media.)

Human Rights Campaign (HRC)
1640 Rhode Island Ave., N.W.
Washington, DC 20036
Phone: 202.628.4160
Website: http://www.hrc.org
(HRC is dedicated to addressing civil rights issues for sexual minorities
    through education, lobbying, and financial assistance.)

Lambda Defense and Education Fund (LLDEF)
National Headquarters
120 Wall Street, Suite 1500
New York, NY 10005
Phone: 212.809.8585
Website: http://www.lambdalegal.org
(LLDEF provides advocacy through combating discrimination and intoler-
    ance toward sexual minorities by addressing civil rights issues and nation-
    al policy.)

National Lesbian and Gay Law Association (NLGLA)
P.O. Box 180417
Boston, MA 02118
Phone: 508.982.8290
Website: http://ww.nlgla.org
(NLGLA is an affiliate of the American Bar Association and consists of gay,
    lesbian, bisexual, and transgendered lawyers, judges, law students, and
    other legal organizations.)

**School-Based Support and Education Groups**
Gay, Lesbian, and Straight Education Network (GLSEN)
121 West 27th Street, Suite 804
New York, NY 10001
Phone: 212.727.0135
Website: http://www.glsen.org
(GLSEN works nationally to educate school staff and students K–12 on sexual minority issues as a means of promoting acceptance and support to gay and lesbian youth and their families.)

Gay/Straight Alliance
Massachusetts Department of Education
350 Main Street
Malden, MA 02148
Phone 781.388.3000
Website: http://www.doe.mass.edu/lss/GSA
(Gay/Straight Alliance provides information and support to schools that want to advocate for sexual minorities and reduce the incidents of violence, harassment, and prejudice against gay and lesbian students.)

OUTRIGHT:
Central Maine OUTRIGHT
c/o Dayspring
One Weston Court
Augusta, ME
Phone: 202.621.6393
Website: http://www.outright.org
(OUTRIGHT is committed to creating a safe, positive environment for gay, lesbian, bisexual, and transgendered teens ages 22 and under.)

Project 10
115 West California Boulevard, #116
Pasadena, CA 91105
Phone: 626.577.4553
Website: http://www.project10.org
(Project 10 provides educational support services to gay, lesbian, bisexual, and transgendered youth in the school environment.)

# GENERALIST PRACTICE WITH OLDER PEOPLE

*Norma D. Thomas*

John L. is an MSW student in a first-year field placement with an Area Agency on Aging. As part of his placement duties, John makes home visits to his elderly clients to coordinate the various services they receive and to provide supportive counseling if needed. Prior to this field placement, John had little contact with elderly people.

John's first client was Mrs. P., an 80-year-old widow who lives alone in a dangerous part of the city. In the past, her son, who lives nearby and is a cocaine addict, abused her. John's field instructor asked John to assess the appropriateness of her living situation. Before meeting Mrs. P., John pictured her as a helpless old woman trapped in an unsafe neighborhood who needed help finding a safer place to live. What John found was a strong-willed woman who knew what she wanted and what she did not want and who had no intention of letting some young social worker tell her what was best for her. After his first meeting with Mrs. P., John realized that he was going to learn a lot from his elderly clients. He also wondered if they would all be so independent.

This chapter provides information on generalist practice with elderly clients. The chapter begins with a description of the demographic characteristics of the elderly. This is followed by a discussion of policy issues and micro- and macropractice issues. The chapter then covers developing helping relationships with older adults. By the end of the chapter, you should be able to help John

1. Appreciate the size and heterogeneity of the elderly population in the United States
2. Understand the major social and economic policy issues affecting the elderly and the delivery of services to elderly clients
3. Identify interview techniques that are appropriate for professional interactions with elderly clients
4. Identify content areas that should be included in a social work assessment of elderly clients
5. Describe the major generalist practice issues that need to be taken into consideration in working with older individuals, families, and groups

The United States, like most of the developed world, is experiencing a dramatic increase in the numbers of people we call "senior citizens" (or "seasoned citizens," a term that is gaining in popularity). In 2000, there were 34.8 million Americans age 65 and older. By the year 2050, there will be 82 million, who will comprise 20 percent of the total population (U.S. Bureau of the Census, 2000). The fastest-growing population segment in this country is people age 85 and older. By the year 2050, there will be 19.4 million people over the age of 85 (U.S. Bureau of the Census, 2000). The need for generalist social workers to work with the elderly has never been greater, and it will continue to increase as the population of older adults increases.

The older adult population is not only increasing in numbers at a rapid pace but also in its racial and ethnic diversity. From 2000 to 2050, the 65 and

TABLE 13.1 | PROJECTED GROWTH OF THE POPULATION AGE 65 AND OLDER IN THE UNITED STATES*

| Year | Total Numbers (Millions) | Caucasian | | Nonwhite | |
|------|--------------------------|-----------|---------|----------|---------|
| | | Total Numbers (Millions) | Percent | Total Numbers (Millions) | Percent |
| 2000 | 34.8 | 29.1 | 84 | 5.7 | 16 |
| 2030 | 70.3 | 51.7 | 74 | 18.6 | 26 |
| 2050 | 82.0 | 52.7 | 64 | 29.3 | 36 |

*From United States Bureau of the Census (2000). *Projections of the Total Resident Population by 5-Year Age Groups, Race and Hispanic Origin with Special Age Categories—Middle Series 1999–2000; 2025–2045; 2052–2070; Reports NPT4A; NPT4F; NPT4G.* Washington, DC: Populations Projection Program, Population Division.

older population is projected to increase from 34.8 million to 82 million people (U.S. Bureau of the Census, 2000). As shown in Table 13.1, during that same period, the percentage of nonwhite elderly is expected to increase from 16 percent of the elderly population to 36 percent.

## THE DEMOGRAPHICS OF AGING

The average life expectancy from birth in 1998 was 79.5 years for women and 73.8 years for men with an overall life expectancy of 76.7 years (U. S. Bureau of the Census, 1996, 1998b, 2000). There are ethnic and racial variations in life expectancy. For example, African-American women have an average life expectancy of 74.5 years, compared to 65 years for African-American males (Administration on Aging, 1997). Life expectancy at birth for First Nations peoples is 65 years (National Institutes of Health, 2000).

Although women live longer, they do not necessarily live better. Women suffer disproportionately from chronic illnesses as they age. This is due in part to their living longer than men. Also, women tend to neglect their own health while caring for their families. Women make up the majority of residents in nursing homes that provide long-term care. They also experience higher rates of poverty. Nearly 13 percent of elderly women live in poverty, compared to 7 percent of men over the age of 65 (Hooyman and Kiyak, 2002).

In terms of income, 35 percent of First Nations elderly live in poverty, compared to 26.4 percent of African-American elderly, 21 percent of Latino elderly, 16 percent of Asian and Pacific Islander elderly, and 9 percent of Caucasian elderly (Federal Interagency Forum on Aging Related Statistics, 2000). Lower income contributes to other differences between minority and Caucasian elderly. Minority elderly have less formal education, diminished overall health, and decreased access to health and social services than their Caucasian peers.

There are so many myths about aging that it is impossible to explode them all in one brief section. One popular myth is that older people live in nursing homes. However, only about 4.3 percent of persons 65 and older are in long-term care facilities at any one time (U.S. Bureau of the Census, 1998). Similarly, it is not true that most old people have multiple chronic illnesses and are dependent on others for their care. The majority of older people live independently with some degree of chronic illness that may require some minimal assistance. Dependency does increase with age, and people age 85 and older need assistance with at least one activity of daily living. They also suffer disproportionately from Alzheimer's disease (Cox, 1993; Leon and Lair, 1990). Families provide 70–80 percent of care needed by older people with chronic illnesses (National Alliance for Caregiving and AARP, 1997).

Another set of myths is centered around mental and personality characteristics of older persons. For example, it is widely believed that older people cannot learn new things. In fact, older people do learn new things, even though the way they learn may change. Older people are constantly adapting and keeping up with societal changes along with everyone else. Older people are also said to be grouchy and set in their ways and to have no interest in sex. Personality does not change because of age, but rather because of some physical or psychological disorder. Sex and affection are important parts of life as people get older. What is often missing is a partner. Barring any physiologic or psychological disorder, older people can and do remain sexually active throughout life. Statistics are hard to come by. A negative statistic that documents sexual activity among older people is the rise in the rate of HIV infection and AIDS. The Centers for Disease Control has reported a 94 percent increase in the number of older men infected with HIV as a result of heterosexual sex and a 106 percent increase in the number of older women (CDC, 1998).

# POLICY ISSUES

With the exception of the Social Security Act of 1935, social policy as it pertains to older adults is a product of the decades that began with the 1960s. Up until this point in history, older people did not have the numbers or the political power to significantly effect social service provision.

## Ageism

American society values youth over old age. **Ageism,** the general collective stereotypes that depict older people as less productive, less attractive, resource draining, asexual, or mentally deficient, is pervasive in our culture (Comfort, 1976):

> Despite our increase in knowledge about aging, there is still a persistent belief that the aged are less capable—and less important—than other people. Ageism can be a barrier to obtaining quality services. If service providers believe that the aged are less valuable than other members of society, they

may render a lower quality of service. Beyond that, older people are well aware of the way others feel, so that the fact of ageism's existence has a negative effect on the mental and emotional health of older people. (Roff and Atherton, 1989, p. 94)

Ageism also has an enormous effect on income potential. While 62 percent of U.S. corporations encourage early retirement, only 4 percent offer retraining for persons who might want to return to the workforce (Hooyman and Kiyak, 1999; Ramirez, 1989). Despite the Age Discrimination in Employment Act of 1987, litigation because of alleged age discrimination is on the rise (Hooyman and Kiyak, 1999; Quadagno and Hardy, 1996).

Ageism also affects the provision of social services. For example, mental health care for senior citizens has always lagged behind the need. The 1995 White House Conference on Aging identified significant unmet needs for mental health services for seniors in nursing homes and in the community (Rosen and Persky, 1997). This is due in part to ageist beliefs that older people who exhibit psychiatric symptoms are suffering from organic disease rather than from a treatable mental health problem.

# Social Services

The first White House Conference on Aging in 1961 was the catalyst for the creation of a system to provide services for persons when they reach old age. The resultant policy, the **Older American's Act of 1965 (OAA),** called for the establishment of the **Administration on Aging** in the Department of Health and Human Services. The act provided funds for the development of Area Agencies on Aging to coordinate the delivery of services to older Americans. It also provided funding for an expanded research effort on the service needs of the elderly. The broad-range goals under Title I of the act were to ensure that all elderly had

- Adequate incomes
- The best possible physical and mental health care
- Suitable housing
- Full restorative services for those requiring care in an institution as well as comprehensive community-based long-term care services
- Opportunity for employment without age discrimination
- The ability to retire in health, honor, and dignity
- Opportunity to pursue meaningful activities
- Efficient community services when needed
- Immediate benefit from proven research knowledge
- Freedom, independence, and the free exercise of individual initiative (Butler, 1975; Gelfand, 1993)

The OAA established a continuum of services for the elderly. These include transportation for medical appointments and grocery shopping, home health and homemaker services, senior centers, home and congregate meal programs, educational opportunities, information and referral services, and adult day care.

In 1973, the minimum age for services was established as 60. Over time, the original goals of the OAA have been expanded and altered in response to the changing needs of the older population. Recent technologic advances, for example, have made it possible for many medical treatments to be provided in the home by skilled nursing professionals or, in some cases, by family members. Some medical tests, such as blood work and x-rays, can also be done in the older person's own home.

The current system is not adequate to keep up with the rapidly growing older population. This is especially true for those living in rural areas where medical care, community-based in-home services, and access services, such as transportation, are not available. Urban elderly who live in high-crime areas also find it difficult to access in-home services because care providers are afraid to go to their homes (Thomas, 1998). Thus, minority elderly, who tend to live in low-income urban areas, are less likely to have access to formal services than Caucasian elderly (National Association of Area Agencies on Aging, 1992).

The demands for aging services have increased in proportion to the increase in the number of older persons. Waiting lists for services are common. The shortage of services for the elderly is exacerbated by the increasing percentage of women in the work force who can no longer care for elderly parents. The increased mobility of children also contributes to the increased demand for services. More adult children no longer live near their parents. This creates additional demand for support services for the elderly.

In many areas of the country, clients can wait for months and years if their service needs are deemed a low priority. Persons with higher incomes are able to obtain services privately, but older people with lower and more moderate incomes must wait for assistance from the public sector. The service shortage also has a negative effect on care providers. Their inability to help clients obtain necessary resources and services contributes to burnout among geriatric social workers (Poulin and Thomas, 1998).

Concurrent with the service shortage has been a shift in the ideological stance toward older people in this country (Atchley, 1997). There is concern that older people are benefiting disproportionately from the government's social welfare system to the detriment of younger people. The Older Americans Act, as amended in 2000, provided for substantial increases in service delivery through the **Family Caregiver Support Services Program.** However, in 2003, the overall funding for aging services increased before an across-the-board cut was instituted in light of increased funding for education, drought relief, election overhaul activities, and Medicare physician payment increases. While home-delivered meals and the Family Caregiver Support Programs are projected to see increased dollars, funding for congregate meals and supportive services is expected to decrease (National Association of Area Agencies on Aging, 2003). Overall, however, there is a lack of policies for the elderly compared to other at-risk populations, such as children and families. This in combination with cuts in Medicare funding, decreases in prescription drug coverage, and proposed cuts in or privatization of Social Security will have very serious negative consequences for the health and well-being of older persons. The projected increase in the number of low-income and minority elderly persons will only serve to exacerbate the pending crisis.

## Economic Security

Economic security is more than income; it is the ability to command goods and services to meet one's needs. A number of factors, such as accessible and affordable health care, adequate housing, and formal and informal service assistance must be taken into consideration along with income levels to comprehensively assess economic security. In addition, economic security or its lack must be viewed from a life course perspective. During a lifetime, assets and resources are accumulated or lost, determining economic security in old age (Chen, 1991).

The **Social Security Act of 1935,** which established the Social Security program, provides a measure of income security to people who worked and contributed to the system. In 2000, 38 percent of the income of persons age 65 and older was from Social Security (U.S. Census Bureau, 2000). Dependence on Social Security has increased, whereas other resources such as pension and investment income have decreased. Given the current employment trend toward downsizing and the decreased time that employees stay in jobs, fewer retirees can be expected to have access to pension income. Social Security was never intended to provide the sole income of the elderly, but about 18 percent of people over the age of 65 rely exclusively on income from it (U.S. Census Bureau, 2000).

Since 1974, **Supplemental Security Income (SSI)** has been available to low-income individuals who need assistance because of age or disability. The amount of money varies from state to state, but generally it is at or near the poverty level. African-American elderly rely disproportionately on SSI; 13.2 percent of African Americans and 12.7 percent of Latinos, as compared to 4 percent of Caucasians, receive SSI (U.S. Bureau of the Census, 1992).

Older women who rely on Social Security as their primary source of income face diminished income security. Women live longer than men and often leave the workforce for long periods of time to care for young children and older relatives. Some of the issues affecting women are

- Equity and adequacy of spouse and survivor benefits
- Fairness of coverage of one-earner versus two-earner couples
- The nature of coverage for homemakers and divorced persons (Schulz, 1995)

Concerns about Social Security have reached crisis proportions because of fear that the aging of the baby boomers will bankrupt the system. Proposals to deal with the pending crisis range from increasing payroll taxes, to raising the age at which benefits can be collected, to privatizing the system. None of the proposals has widespread support. Americans generally resist tax increases. Raising the benefit age has potential adverse effects on women and minority group members. Privatizing the system would require financial sophistication on the part of American workers in order to guarantee adequate income on retirement. Practitioners need to pay strict attention to all proposals for modifying the Social Security system because of their possible effects on the elderly and on people of all ages.

People face increased out-of-pocket expenses for health care as they age. As an individual ages, the amount of money spent for community-based and long-term health care increases above available income (Atchley, 1997; Liu, Perozek, and Manton, 1993). In 1995, a person age 65 or above who lived in the community paid, on average, $2,750 annually in out-of-pocket expenses for health care costs (Wiener and Illston, 1996). The lack of universal health care forces many older people to choose between medicine and food.

Older people on Medicare are being pressured into signing up for such managed care options as health maintenance organizations (HMOs). Many do not understand HMO restrictions, such as controlled access to physician and other services through a primary physician referral system. Medicare expenses are estimated to increase sixfold in the last year of a beneficiary's life because of the increased rate of chronic disease (Kronenfeld, 1993). Since older people cost HMOs more money than younger people, some observers expect premiums to increase for the elderly and for elderly people to be dropped from plans because of profit issues.

Media coverage of the debate over welfare reform has focused on younger recipients. However, numerous seniors, especially those who are not citizens, have lost benefits. The **Personal Responsibility and Work Opportunity Reconciliation Act of 1996 (PRWOR)** barred immigrant seniors arriving in this country from receiving food stamps, Medicaid, SSI, and other services. It also stopped benefits for many legal immigrants already here. Original estimates were that PRWOR would save more than $54.2 billion, of which 44 percent ($23.8 billion) would result from cuts to legal immigrant benefits (Friedland and Pankaj, 1998). Although adjustments in 1997 restored SSI benefits to people who received them prior to PRWOR, the restoration of food stamps has been left to individual states. Confusion over this law has resulted in loss of benefits for many older legal immigrants. In 1997, 400,000 legal immigrants lost benefits, including 65,000 residents of nursing homes who relied on Medicaid as payment (Keigher, 1997).

## Housing

As the size of the older population increases, there will be a greater need for additional housing units as well as for creative housing options. Living with children or other relatives is not a viable alternative for many older persons who wish to remain independent and not be a burden to their children. Often, their children do not live nearby. Consequently, substantial numbers of older people "age in place": they stay in their own homes or apartments as they grow older. This can be positive if the home can safely accommodate the physical changes and functional ability of the older person and if the person has enough income to maintain the home. But for others, this phenomenon has been referred to as "stuck in place" because the older person is unable to relocate (Skinner, 1992). Elderly African Americans and other minority elders often have few housing options because of lifelong disadvantages (Skinner, 1992). Approximately 80 percent of those considered elderly own their own homes. The median age of the dwelling in which the elderly reside is 39 years old (U.S. Bureau of the Census, 2001). Gillespie and Sloan (1990) reported that 244,000 older homeowners and 506,000 elderly renters are living in residences that have two or more structural deficiencies.

For many seniors, making a home safe requires taking an environmental inventory. Removing throw rugs, increasing the lighting, moving electrical cords, and installing handrails and grab bars around the tub to help decrease the incidence of falls are safety modifications that can be easily made. Converting a room on the first floor to a bedroom and putting in a first-floor bathroom or using a portable commode will decrease the need to climb the stairs. If the stairway will accommodate modification, a chair glide could be installed. Emergency response systems placed in the home allow the older person to contact someone in case of an emergency. Occupational therapists can instruct older people and their families in the use of adaptive devices that increase the likelihood that they can remain at home in the community.

There are a number of housing alternatives for older people who do not need the skilled or intermediate-level supervision of a nursing home. Shared housing is an option in which an older person invites someone into his or her home or moves into the home of another. The other person can be unrelated or a family member. Multigenerational families living under the same roof are more common among minority groups. This is rooted in differences in value systems, the need to share resources, and blocked access to other housing options.

The board and care or personal care home, a form of assisted living, is one option used by the low-income elderly. Many individuals in these homes require greater supervision because of mental or physical challenges. Residents usually share their bedroom space. The quality of the activities, services, and supervision varies from facility to facility.

Assisted-living developments, which cater to seniors in the higher-income brackets, have become increasingly popular. Generally, an individual receives some help with instrumental activities of daily living, such as group dining or minimal housekeeping. Most residents of more upscale assisted-living facilities are fairly independent in activities of daily living (bathing, dressing, eating, mobility, and medication management).

Retirement communities, which offer a continuum of care services, give an older person the security of levels of increased care in the same community. Generally, retirement communities are an option only for older people with very high incomes.

For older people who cannot remain in their own homes and who require the most medical care and supervision, there are nursing homes. Although nursing homes are highly regulated, the quality varies greatly. Social workers assisting families in finding a nursing home need to consider the following factors:

- Appearance isn't everything, but it is important. Is the facility clean and free of odors? Is the atmosphere like a home or a hospital?
- How are visitors greeted? Are family members encouraged to stay involved with the older resident? Does the facility have programs to support the caregivers? How are the residents addressed by the staff?
- Are residents involved in activities or are they just sitting in the hallway? Are large numbers of them in bed?
- Does the facility appear to respect and acknowledge cultural differences among the residents?
- Are the patient's and family's rights clearly spelled out?

Contact the state's Department of Health to verify the current licensure status of the facility. Also, ask questions about the medical staff in order to feel comfortable about the quality of medical care provided (Smith, 1992).

Unfortunately, many decisions about nursing home placement are made as a result of hospital policies and the availability of space. Often, the elderly person is placed in the first nursing home that has an available bed. Deciding to move an elderly person to a nursing home should be done only after careful consideration, and the older person and the family should be involved in the decision so as to reduce trauma and loss.

Economics are a prime consideration. Nursing home care is expensive. Even older people with considerable resources may run out of money within approximately two years. After they have exhausted their resources, and for those without assets or income, Medicaid pays for nursing home care. For economic reasons, most nursing homes prefer private-pay patients. There are fewer beds available for Medicaid patients. It is more difficult to find a nursing home for an elderly person with limited resources. For both economic and cultural reasons, minority group members are underrepresented in nursing homes. Collectively, they make up only about 12 percent of the nursing home population (Strahan, 1997).

There is a clear need for housing alternatives for older persons, especially those of low to moderate means, who cannot remain in their own residences. Unfortunately, the number of seniors who find themselves homeless is increasing. At any point in time, approximately 100,000 elders are homeless (Atchley, 1997). Deinstitutionalization, poverty, and inadequate housing options all contribute to the increase in homelessness among the elderly (Tully and Jacobson, 1994).

# GENERAL PRACTICE WITH OLDER ADULT CLIENTS

In order to successfully engage with older people and develop positive helping relationships, social workers must overcome institutionalized ageism as well as face issues related to their own aging, family members' aging, and their own mortality (Greene, 1986; Poulin and Thomas, 1998; Schneider and Kropf, 1992). The negative image of aging in this country influences the choices that students entering social work school make in terms of placement experiences as well as course work. Many practitioners see aging as synonymous with death and dying, forgetting that all people ultimately die. Successful practice in this field requires a reversal of thinking so that we can help people live with the complications of aging.

Social work practice with older adult clients encompasses a variety of target problems. Much of the work with this population centers on connecting clients to needed formal resources and helping them develop and maintain informal support systems in order to prolong their ability to remain in the community with the highest possible quality of life. Social workers provide therapeutic interventions with persons who have mental health problems, such as depression. Generalist social workers also provide supportive counseling to elderly persons who have experienced multiple losses and help those needing assistance and support in caring for their grandchildren. Older people and their support systems may have the same problems as younger people. The major difference is that the elderly have had a longer time to accumulate them.

Holosko and Feit (1991) cite five **intervention activities** for social workers serving elderly clients identified by Tobin and Gustafson (1987):

1. **Touch** was used frequently with the elderly and reflected an active approach to meeting their needs (touch activity demonstrates caring and reassurance and is readily understandable, whereas other techniques used by social workers may not be as easily understood by the older person).
2. **Activities** typically include providing more concrete assistance, more reaching out to families, and more talking by the worker in sessions.
3. **Reminiscence** or the use of the past, helps clients to develop ego strength (by noting past coping) and adaptation capabilities, as well as recapturing and reaffirming the current self.
4. **Transference** referring projections onto the worker of meaning, wishes, and thoughts that are redirected from other persons.
5. **Countertransference** is specific concerns evoked by the worker to the client (e.g., dependency, helplessness, and death). (Holosko and Feit, 1991, p. 25)

Informality is an American trait that often extends into interactions with clients. Beginning social workers mistakenly think that addressing someone with an air of familiarity is the key to building a relationship. But for most ethnocultural groups, formality is the expectation. Older people, especially, prefer formality because veneration of elders is a key component of their value systems (Randall-David, 1989). In addition, older people believe that they have earned the right to be respected by those who come to provide them with assistance. The following **communication guidelines** are recommended for working with elderly clients, especially those who are members of racial and ethnic minority groups:

- Never address older people by their first names unless you have been given permission to do so. Do not ask them if it is all right to call them by their first names; because you are an authority figure, they will more than likely tell you it is fine even when they are offended. If people want to be addressed by their first names, they will tell you. Using surnames connotes respect.
- Older people usually enter service delivery systems because someone else suggested it; typically they are not self-referred. Understand that there is a great reluctance to enter helping relationships, and be willing to take the time in an initial visit to ease the discomfort of the potential client and the client system (Watt and Soifer, 1991).
- Much of the community-based service provided to older people is done in their homes. Food, which is important to many ethnocultural groups and may be the only thing someone has to offer in exchange for assistance, is very important to seniors when welcoming someone into their home. Do not offend the person offering the gift. In other words, be careful how you turn a gift down.
- Older people have lived a long time and have a story to tell. They resent attempts to structure their information into categories. Start conversations on less threatening subjects, and guide the older person into telling his or her own story. You will get all the information you need, but using a narrative approach will enhance the interaction.
- Nonverbal communication is critical in obtaining the trust of the elderly. Physical space, eye contact, greetings, and hand gestures, including shaking hands, have to be measured by culture as well as circumstance (NAAAA, 1992, p. 34).

## Assessment

Assessment of older people requires a comprehensive, broad-based ecological approach. Psychological, biological, and sociological factors become more complex and intertwined as people age (Kropf and Hutchison, 1992). Often, a physical disease may be the cause of serious psychiatric symptoms. Depression can result from later-life issues, such as grief over the loss of family members and friends, diminished physical capacity, or rapid role changes, or it may be a symptom of an underlying medical condition (Watt and Soifer, 1991). Social work practice with older people requires knowledge of pharmacologic and disease processes and how they affect client functioning. In addition, you must be able to differentiate psychiatric problems that are treatable from problems that originate from an organic disease. Many factors must be included in a comprehensive assessment of an older person.

**Depression**   The psychiatric problems that affect younger people are also present in older age groups. There is a high prevalence of depression among the elderly. Approximately 15 percent to 22 percent of elderly community residents report symptoms of depression, with 10 percent to 15 percent requiring clinical intervention (Blazer and Williams, 1980). Even more nursing home residents suffer from depression. Between 12 percent and 25 percent of the aged living in institutional settings meet the diagnostic criteria for major depression (LaRue, 1992).

Symptoms of depression among the elderly include

- Prolonged sadness
- Insomnia or excessive sleeping
- Loss of interest in things normally enjoyed
- Fatigue or constant tiredness
- Psychomotor retardation
- Significant weight gain or loss
- Guilt
- Anxiety
- Self-blame
- Helplessness and hopelessness
- Sexual dysfunction
- Agitation
- Real or perceived cognitive deficit
- Persistent pain, headache, or chest pain
- Thoughts about death
- Feeling that they want to die (Philadelphia Corporation for Aging, 1995)

Because all of these symptoms could signal physical problems, it is important for older people to receive a comprehensive assessment by a multidisciplinary team in order to determine causation.

Associated with the high rate of depression among the elderly is a high rate of suicide. For persons 65 and over, the rate of suicide is 21.4 per 100 people, nearly double that of younger age groups (Turk-Charles, Rose, and Gatz, 1996). The oldest age group, those over 85, have the highest suicide rates. The elderly are more successful at committing suicide than their younger counterparts. If an older person talks about suicide, he or she must be taken seriously. Questions to ask elderly clients who are at risk of attempting suicide include:

- Do you ever feel that life is not worth living?
- Do you feel that your situation is hopeless?
- Have you ever thought of really hurting yourself?
- Have you been thinking about killing yourself?
- Have you planned how you would do that?
- What do you think you would do?
- Do you have the means (pills, weapon, etc.) to carry out your plan? (PCA, 1995, p. 9)

CASE 13.1    |    WHAT IS MOTHER TRYING TO DO?

Senora R., a 78-year-old Latina, was referred to a local Area Agency on Aging because her daughter, Maria, was worried. Maria had recently visited her mother and found that she had lost 30 pounds in the last 2 months, was not taking her medication properly, rarely left the house, and seemed to have no interest in anything. Senora R. does have chronic illnesses: diabetes, high blood pressure, and an unspecified heart condition. Maria thought her mother was deliberately not eating or taking her medication in an attempt to end her life.

Rachel J., a social worker, scheduled an appointment the next day and talked to Senora R. The client described several losses in the past year, including her husband, two sisters, her best friend, and a neighbor. In addition, the neighborhood was changing around her. Drugs were being sold openly on the corners, and her house was next to one that had been abandoned. She did not want to move but was fearful of venturing out of her home even to buy groceries. She didn't want to carry much money, so she brought home only small quantities of food at a time. She had no one who would regularly go to the pharmacy for her, so she tried to stretch her medication, cutting down on the dosage. She was fully aware of the negative results that poor nutrition and medication mismanagement could produce, but she stated that she did not care.

"What is there really to live for? I am still here but everyone around me has gone," she stated.

Rachel expressed to her the concern that Senora R. was not eating and not taking her medicine as a benign way to end her life. Senora R. did not confirm this, but she asked if the worker and daughter blamed her if it was true? Instead of trying to convince Senora R. of all she had to live for, Rachel asked her to describe what her life was like before all the losses occurred. She was devoted to her house and the care of her husband. She had not worked outside of the home but did volunteer for her church and at the children's school when they were young. Senora R. was a pianist and had taught local students.

With the assistance of Maria, Rachel convinced Senora R. to visit the local senior center. The staff members were all bilingual and bicultural, and most of the participants were Latino. The activity coordinator talked to Senora R. about help she could provide to the center, for example, she could assist with the choir and the intergenerational programs. The center had shopping assistance as well as an on-site nurse who could monitor Senora R.'s health and assist in obtaining prescriptions. The housing situation would need to be worked on over time. Senora R. did not want to give up her independence by moving in with her daughter, which would be another loss, but the neighborhood did pose a threat to her safety.

**Memory**   If you are 30 and forget where you put your keys, it is assumed that you have too much to remember, are stressed, or are just absent-minded. If you are 80 and do the same thing, you are assumed to have Alzheimer's disease. Decreasing ability to remember becomes a source of worry to people as they age and to those who care for them. As with symptoms of depression, memory problems require a comprehensive assessment to rule out causes that can be treated, such as a disease process, psychiatric disorder, nutritional deficiency, or medication problem.

For most people, both long-term and short-term memory are well preserved into advanced old age (Albert, 1988). However, forgetting names or recent events is common and can be a source of frustration. It would seem logical that the longer one lives, the more information there is to remember and recall. Therefore, some of it will be lost or take longer to retrieve when an individual gets older. Providing cues, or other forms of recognition assistance, such as pictures, helps to improve recall (Albert, 1988). Using lists, having a consistent place for keys and purse or wallet, writing down telephone numbers, and using message pads, voice recorders, and medication organizers all aid memory and help the elderly keep information straight.

Some diseases produce irreversible declines in memory and physical functioning. These diseases are classified under the heading of **dementia**. Strokes account for 10 percent to 20 percent and Alzheimer's disease 50 percent to 60 percent of irreversible dementia cases (PCA, 1995). From 20 percent to 50 percent of people age 85 and older have Alzheimer's disease (Evans, Funkenstein, and Albert, 1989; National Institute on Aging, 1996; Pennsylvania Care Management Institute, 1990).

**Alzheimer's disease** is marked by a slow decline in mental and physical ability over a period of 2–20 years (National Institute on Aging, 1996). The person progresses from not remembering how to do simple things to a total inability to even feed himself or herself. This disease places a tremendous burden on caregivers and is one of the leading reasons for placement of an older person in a nursing facility.

The Alzheimer's Association provides a list of 10 warning signs that should prompt older persons and their families or caregivers to seek an evaluation:

1. Recent memory loss that affects job skills
2. Difficulty performing familiar tasks
3. Problems with language
4. Disorientation of time and place
5. Poor or decreased judgment
6. Problems with abstract thinking
7. Misplacing things
8. Changes in mood or behavior
9. Changes in personality
10. Loss of initiative (Alzheimer's Association, *n.d.*)

There is still no cure for Alzheimer's disease. Environmental (Harvard Medical School, 1992) and genetic links (Mayeux et al., 1991) are under intense study to determine predictors of the disease. Treatment often involves medication to control behavior problems, a change in the environment to reduce overstimulating the person, a routine that is followed every day, behavioral management exercises, and reminiscence therapy that seeks to retrieve long-term memory. Drug therapies that have received recent FDA approval are aimed at improving or slowing the decline of cognitive functioning. These drugs have had mixed results (Youngjohn and Crook, 1996).

**Capacity**    The term *capacity* refers to the ability of an older person to make reasonable decisions and to understand the consequences of those decisions. All of us, regardless of age, have used poor judgment at one time or another. Older people are presumed to have the capacity to make decisions for themselves until it is demonstrated that their actions endanger themselves or others.

| CASE 13.2 | CATS, CATS, AND MORE CATS |

Mr. M., a Caucasian, is an 84-year-old former teacher. He was referred to a local Area Agency on Aging because the neighbors were complaining about odors coming from his home. His wife had died early in the marriage, and there were no children. Mr. M. never remarried and was estranged from his siblings. On investigation, the social worker, June P., discovered a gracious man who lived alone except for a large number of cats that freely roamed inside and outside a large split-level home.

Mr. M. did not receive Social Security because he never applied for it. He was from a well-known family in the area. Neighbors and his estranged family believed that he had sufficient assets to take care of his needs. He drove his car to the bank daily, and he regularly visited a niece, Sara G., who lived one hour from his residence. It was clear that his cognition and judgment were impaired. As a simple test, June asked him for directions to his niece's home, but he could not provide them. She also asked him to add simple figures; he was also unable to do that.

Mr. M. refused to allow the SPCA to take the cats, which were his only companions. When June called the SPCA, she learned they had previously removed the cats from the home, and Mr. M. retrieved them and paid all associated fees.

The home was filled with antiques, which had been ruined by cat urine, droppings, and scratches. The client, however, was in good physical health, which was verified by a nursing assessment. He shopped for food for himself and the cats, and all his bills had been paid at the time of the initial visits. The neighbors reported that the situation had been deteriorating for years and described him as "eccentric."

Mr. M. consented to and underwent a complete physical and psychological assessment, which found him to be in good physical health with severe cognitive deficits, probably of the Alzheimer's type. The task of all agencies now involved was to visit frequently and watch for signs that this fragile situation was changing for the worse.

A neighbor took it upon himself to disable Mr. M.'s car by removing the distributor cap, since the local and state police would not stop him from driving. Since Mr. M. then stopped visiting his niece, Sara visited him. She was appalled at his living conditions and vowed to take a more active role in planning for her uncle's care.

Mr. M. began to deteriorate. Although he could still get food delivered to the home for himself and the cats, he began to neglect the cats. It was then possible for the Humane Society, in cooperation with the SPCA, to remove the cats from the home. They removed around 80 cats. His physical condition eventually required hospitalization. Sara pursued legal guardianship in order to have his affairs taken care of, since he did have a vast estate. Mr. M. was eventually placed in a nursing home (Thomas, 1997 p. 50).

---

The question of competency often arises in cases that are referred for older adult protective services, especially when the referral is for self-neglect. In states that have an elder abuse law, the highest percentages of protective service referrals are for self-neglect (Salend et al., 1984). The question often raised is whether the protective service agency is violating an individual's right to live the way he or she wishes to live. Intervention is justified if the person no longer has the ability to make informed decisions and the quality of life deteriorates. An assessment of an elderly person's capacity or competence should include:

- Evaluating the patient's orientation to person, place, time and situation
- Testing of recent and remote memory and logical sequencing
- Assessing intellectual capacity, including the ability to comprehend abstract ideas and to make a reasoned judgment based on that ability

## CASE 13.3 | ALZHEIMER'S DISEASE

Ms. B. was 69 and lived in a small apartment. A referral to the Protective Service Agency was made by the landlord, who liked the resident but considered evicting her because her apartment was cluttered with trash and infested with bugs, and the neighbors were complaining. Since Ms. B. lived in a first-floor apartment, which opened to the trash area, no one could understand why she was so "lazy" that she would not even throw the trash into the bins.

A social history revealed that, until approximately two years before the referral, Ms. B. had worked and was meticulous. After a comprehensive assessment was completed, Ms. B. was diagnosed with Alzheimer's disease and eventually moved to a long-term care facility. Unfortunately, Ms. B. received this evaluation only after she was hospitalized through an involuntary commitment. She was not willing to voluntarily receive treatment, and the landlord served her with an eviction notice, to which she reacted so violently that commitment to a psychiatric facility for evaluation was necessary (Thomas, 1997, p. 52).

---

- Assessing mood and affect, noting any suicidal ideations
- Examining the content of thought and perception for delusions, illusions, and hallucinations
- Inspecting visible behavior, noting agitation and anxiety as well as appetite, eating habits, and sleeping patterns
- Reviewing past history for evidence of psychiatric disturbance that might affect the patient's current judgment (Knapp, 1996, p. 183)

Courts are often called upon to declare an older person incompetent if he or she will not accept assistance on a voluntary basis. Social workers who handle issues of guardianship often find themselves in the uncomfortable role of advocating against the client's wishes in order to have someone appointed to safeguard the client's interests.

**Addiction**    Social workers often bypass discussions of addiction when doing assessments of the elderly. It is hard to believe that someone's grandmother or grandfather could possibly have an addiction to prescription or nonprescription drugs or to alcohol. The extent of alcohol and drug abuse among the elderly is difficult to measure. Estimates range from around 5 percent (Maddox, 1988) to 10 percent (Pennsylvania Care Management Institute, 1990). Approximately 20 percent of admissions of elderly people to hospitals are related to the abuse of alcohol (Pennsylvania Care Management Institute, 1990).

Older people turn to alcohol to handle the many losses in their lives. They use alcohol to mask the pain of day-to-day existence. This includes isolation due to loss of family and friends and, for some, chronic physical pain. The use of alcohol in combination with prescription drugs taken by older persons can have deadly consequences. Do not be afraid to ask questions about alcohol use, including

- Do you drink alcohol?
- How much do you drink at one time?

- When do you drink?
- What kind of alcohol do you drink?

These questions must be asked if a person is having blackouts, frequent falls, or memory loss. Treatment interventions that work for younger people are also appropriate for older people.

**Other Considerations**   Assessment is complicated by the fact that older people are not socialized to accept assistance from social workers and formal social service agencies:

> Elderly persons often believe that problem solving is a matter of honor, something one does on one's own; and the concept of asking strangers for help is viewed as an abrogation of responsibility by many. Similarly, the elderly commonly view professionals as possessing authoritative knowledge—"the truth"—and thus may feel obligated to follow the "prescription" even if the options presented are not viewed as necessary or desirable. Self-determination, a cherished social work value, can easily be set-aside in such situations. (Watt and Soifer, 1991, p. 38)

Before data gathering and assessment take place, establish the reason that the client or the client's support system is requesting assistance, and overcome any discrepancies between the two. Most older people are not self-referred, and it is not uncommon for clients to deny that they need assistance. Your first contact is a critical point at which trust may or may not begin to be established.

A holistic assessment should be based on the client's self-report, so long as the older person has capacity, as well as from information from significant others in the person's network and professional service providers. Collect information on the level of service being provided by the support network, both formal and informal, along with information on unmet social, psychological, and environmental challenges and strengths. This information will provide the basis for a comprehensive assessment and the development of an intervention plan (Kropf and Hutchison, 1992).

## Intervention

Generalist social workers in the field of gerontology work in a variety of settings with a variety of client systems that deal with a variety of micro- and macropractice issues. This area of generalist social work requires a range of practice skills as well as the ability to understand and function on an interdisciplinary team. Social workers need to recognize that differences in culture, history, geographical location, gender, religion, sexual identity, and age all affect the helping process with this population.

Generalist social work with older people is an exciting and dynamic field of practice. Where else can one provide assistance and at the same time learn from people who have a wealth of experience? Given the dramatic increase in the number of people over the age of 60, many who enter social work in other areas of practice will eventually find that their employment includes service to senior citizens. Our goal should be to advocate for the increased quality of life of senior citizens in the hope that, if we live long enough, we personally will benefit from those efforts.

**Care Management**    Care management is the model of practice most often used with senior citizens and their families (Morrow-Howell, 1992; Soares and Rose, 1994). Most of the services available to older people are funded by the Older Americans Act and provided through the national system of Area Agencies on Aging (AAA), usually through a care management model. Care management encompasses assessing the strengths and needs of older clients from an ecological systems perspective and linking the client to those services, formal or informal, that can meet the person's needs (Frankel and Gelman, 1998). Care managers sometimes monitor the cost of service provision as well as service quantity (Frankel and Gelman, 1998; Moxley, 1997). Clients needing care management usually have complex multifaceted needs that cannot be met by simple information and referral programs.

Care management requires workers to develop high-level skills in collaborating with professionals from other disciplines. Care managers should take an interdisciplinary approach to providing services to elderly clients and coordinate the intervention with formal and informal service providers. It is necessary to learn the language of medical practitioners, mental health professionals, financial planners, managed care counselors, religious leaders, and informal gatekeepers. The case example in Case 13.4 illustrates why social workers and people from other disciplines—in this case, financial planners—must work together to develop the best possible care plan.

The care manager approached the situation in Case 13.4 by completing a comprehensive biopsychosocial assessment with Mrs. G. As part of the assessment process, Mrs. G. discussed her future plans with her son. This was done even though she is currently exhibiting cognitive impairment. Finances, which are part of the overall assessment, were evaluated in terms of the options available to the family. The financial planner assumed that, despite what the client and family may want, it is the resources that dictate Mrs. G.'s options. The financial planner felt that the client should sign a durable power of attorney, a living will, and a will while she has the capacity. In addition, the financial planner recommended maximizing Mrs. G.'s current assets in order to provide for her during her projected life span (Tacchino and Thomas, 1997).

A cooperative, interdisciplinary approach ensures that all aspects of a client's life are handled by the people who have the most expertise in each area. Instead of adversarial relationships, practitioners can cooperate if they understand the basic values of their respective professions, understand each other's professional language, and are willing to listen and respect each other's expertise.

**Issues in Working with Older Individuals**    Generalist social work practice with older individuals necessitates recognizing each person as a unique indi-

| A PLACE OF MY OWN

Lenora G., age 78, is a retired teacher. A few years before she retired at age 63, she sold her home and moved into a rent-controlled apartment. About 10 years after she retired, she had a mild heart attack, and she moved to New Mexico to live with her son.

For the past five years, Mrs. G. has lived a moderately active and fairly independent life. She has what amounts to a small apartment in her son's home, with her own bedroom, bathroom, kitchenette, and entrance. Her rooms adjoin the family room, so she is integrated into the household but also perceives herself as independent. Her son is 54 years old and unmarried. He is a sales representative for a middle-sized computer hardware manufacturer and has responsibility for the Southwest region of the United States. Although he has some control over his travel schedule, he often has to be away from home for days at a time.

Mrs. G.'s daughter, a housewife, lives in Texas with her husband, a policeman, and their two college-age children. Mrs. G. and her daughter are estranged and have not spoken to each other in more than 14 years. Mrs. G. receives $16,000 annually from her teacher's retirement fund, but this pension does not include cost-of-living adjustments. She receives $8,000 a year from Social Security. In addition, she has financial assets of about $130,000, which are invested conservatively. She is a member of a health maintenance organization and is covered by Medicare, but she has no long-term care insurance.

Mrs. G. complains a lot about being sick, although her physical health is reasonably good. In addition to her cardiac history, her chronic problems include high blood pressure and late-onset diabetes. All of these problems were controlled by a complex pharmaceutical regimen until recently. For the past two years, Mrs. G. has exhibited symptoms of depression. Five times in the last six months, she completely confused her medication schedule and had to be taken to the emergency room by ambulance. Her son thought her complaints about depression and her failure to properly comply with her pharmaceutical schedule were a ploy for attention because of his difficult travel schedule, but it has become increasingly apparent that Mrs. G.'s memory and cognitive capacities are declining rapidly (Tacchino and Thomas, 1997, pp. 41–42).

---

vidual and not part of a homogeneous group of people. Unless they are hampered by some form of dementia, seniors can take an active role in determining their treatment plan goals and objectives. Someone who is over the age of 60 has the right to make decisions, even if a social worker does not always agree with the decisions.

Giving older people the time to tell their stories is not only the best way to gather necessary information for an assessment; it is also a form of intervention that works well with older people. Reminiscent approaches to practice have been associated with Robert Butler's research and development of life review therapy, which in essence allows people to reevaluate, resolve, and ultimately integrate the past with the present (Butler, 1980–1981). From a strengths-based perspective, reminiscence encourages people to apply coping strategies that worked previously to current situations. It also allows people to gain satisfaction from successes, as well as to resolve past difficulties in order to live better in the present (Silver, 1995).

Allowing older people to tell their many stories helps them develop a positive identity. Their life and their experiences are validated. A narrative approach provides the elderly with guidance and helps them create order out of chaos in their day-to-day existence. It also gives the storyteller a sense of power that he or she might not normally feel (Viney, 1993).

Practical issues must be taken into consideration when working with older people. For example, hearing loss is a significant problem as one ages. Around 30 percent of persons 65–74 years of age and 50 percent of people 75 years of age and older have some hearing loss (Roff and Atherton, 1989). If interviews take place in hospital rooms, in office cubicles, or in a home where there are loud noises and other distractions, the older person may have difficulty understanding what you are saying. Medication, illness, stress, and exhaustion also affect an older person's ability to hear and understand verbal communication.

Guidelines for working with hearing-impaired elderly include the following:

- Face the hearing-impaired person directly and on the same level whenever possible
- Remember that your speech will be hard to understand if you are eating, chewing, or smoking while talking
- Keep your hands away from your face when talking
- Get the person's attention before you begin speaking
- Don't talk with your back turned or attempt to talk from another room
- Reduce background noise, such as the radio, stereo, or television
- Don't shout; speak in a normal fashion
- Find different media for communicating if the older person does not understand you, such as writing out the message (Kropf and Hutchison, 1992; Schneider and Kropf, 1987)

The American Association for Retired Persons reported in 1999 that 67 percent of persons 65 years of age and older had completed high school and 15 percent had college degrees (AARP, 1999). This figure varies based on gender, race, ethnicity, and region of the country. Bear this in mind when giving printed information to older clients. Do not assume that a client can read and understand consent forms, medical instructions, medication regimens, special diets, or other written communications. You should also avoid using professional jargon when interviewing older adults. One way to ensure that a client understands your intended communication is to have him or her repeat it.

**Issues in Working with Older Families**    Because people are living longer, there are more people age 85 and older who are living with or receiving care from children who are themselves senior citizens. They in turn may still have responsibility for their children or their grandchildren. Daughters provide 70 percent of the care to chronically ill elders (Pavalko and Artis, 1997). This responsibility, combined with the need to interrupt employment and the stress that this produces, may have future health and economic implications for women and their families (Robison, Moen, and Dempster-McClain, 1995). Caregivers rarely receive any outside support:

## CASE 13.5 | EVERYTHING HAS CHANGED

Mr. Z. is a 76-year-old first-generation Italian man who lives alone in an inner-city neighborhood. His wife died several years ago, and his children no longer live in the same city. He was recently hospitalized due to complications related to diabetes. His vision and hearing are both impaired, but he refuses to wear glasses or a hearing aid, saying that they will make him "look old."

The hospital social worker, Amy L., was asked to talk to Mr. Z. about the need to follow his diet and medication regimen and the complications that could result if he does not. She was also asked to determine what other supports could help Mr. Z. comply with his medical program. The attending physician had also ordered a psychiatric consult in order to see if the noncompliance was related to a cognitive impairment.

Amy introduced herself to Mr. Z. and explained why she was asked to meet with him. She asked him how long he had been in United States, what type of work he did, and about his family. His command of English was limited even though he had been in this country for more than 60 years. He had always lived and worked in the same close-knit Italian-speaking neighborhood and had not needed to learn English. It was evident that Mr. Z. did not understand the written instructions provided by his physicians and home health nurse. Mr. Z. was a man of great pride and would not ask for assistance in reading the material.

Amy also discussed with Mr. Z. his refusal to wear glasses and use a hearing aid. The issues were his self-image and lack of information about hearing aids that were virtually undetectable and glasses that were attractive. The worker found someone in the hospital who could write out instructions in Italian and arrange for hearing and vision evaluations on Mr. Z.'s return to the community. The social worker found no evidence of cognitive impairment.

---

One-third of the caregivers of the frail are themselves over sixty-five. As might be anticipated, husbands are the oldest group, and half of these male caregivers receive no informal or formal assistance in their caregiving tasks. Twenty percent of caregivers have children at home, and almost half of the adult daughters providing care are employed full time. With the needs that these families and their frail relatives are likely to have, it is startling to note that less than 10 percent receive assistance from any formal services. (Cox, 1993, p. 108)

Multigenerational households are more common for African-American, Asian and Pacific Islander, Latino, and First Nations families. The living arrangements of these ethnocultural groups reflect cultural values that emphasize concern for the collective as well as veneration of elders. This does not mean, however, that such living arrangements come without stress. Indeed, caring for an elderly family member places strain on the time, resources, and privacy of the caregiver and family.

The phenomenon of second-time-around parenting is increasing in this country. Approximately 3.7 million children live with their grandparents, and the number of grandparents with permanent custody of their grandchildren has doubled in the last decade (Hooyman and Kiyak, 1999). It has always been common for African-American grandparents to take care of their grandchildren or other people's children (Hill, 1981; Kennedy, 1978). The difference now is the permanency of the arrangements. Because of AIDS, addiction

## CASE 13.6 | I CAN'T TAKE CARE OF MOM, TOO

When she was 53 and recuperating from injuries and other side effects of an automobile accident, Ms. J., an African American, was called on to care for her 72-year-old mother, Mrs. P., who had had a stroke. Ms. J. was already caring for two grandchildren whose mother, a drug addict, had died the previous year from AIDS. The children were eight and nine. Ms. J.'s mother moved into her home.

Until the accident, Ms. J. worked full time. Eventually, her own health problems, the demands of caretaking, and the strain on the family income contributed to Ms. J.'s having a heart attack. She was hospitalized, and Mrs. P. was placed in a nursing home for a temporary stay; she died shortly after admission. Ms. J. is slowly recovering, but she feels guilty and blames herself for her mother's death. She is having difficulty coping with the care of the grandchildren, and her employer is pressuring her to return to work.

---

problems, unemployment, and the young age of many parents, grandparents are taking on roles that have traditionally been assumed by much younger people. Parenting grandchildren produces physical, emotional, and economic stress. It is important to provide support and education to older people who are trying to cope with generational differences and their own needs as well.

Ms. J. could benefit from a host of support and therapeutic groups for grief and loss issues, second-time-around parenthood, and her own physical problems and chronic illness. The children also need support; they have their own issues of grief and loss, fear of abandonment, and stresses in this household. It is important to take a holistic approach when there is an older person in the family. While the older person may be the focus, everyone has to be included. In the family in Case 13.6, even when the older person is no longer there, there is still a great deal of work that needs to be done. This family, like so many, could have used intervention much sooner. It may have prevented some of the stresses that were allowed to build to the breaking point.

Resist the current practice of working only with the older person and not the whole family. In most service delivery systems, one worker may deal with the person over 60, someone else with the children, another will find a support group for the caretaker, and someone else may help with health and disability issues. In order to empower older people and their families, recognize that multiple systems are involved and be able to work in a collaborative, interagency, and interdisciplinary environment.

Josephine was successful in developing a tight, coordinated plan of care and took the responsibility to follow up with all those involved, keeping everyone informed. She was able to work with legal aid to resolve the most pressing crisis, which was the eviction. Through the relationship she developed with Mrs. H., Josephine was able to get a clear picture of all the formal and informal assistance received by the family in order to help the family help themselves.

## CASE 13.7 | ARE WE IN THIS TOGETHER?

The H. family is the classic example of too many social workers trying to deal with all the issues of one family. Muriel H. is 65 and bedridden but is alert. She was referred to the social work agency because the family was being evicted for nonpayment of rent. Mrs. H. received home-delivered meals and personal care service, and a nurse visited weekly.

When the worker, Josephine S., went to the home for the assessment, she found a daughter, Lisa H., and her two children, John and Carrie, living there. Lisa and her children were involved with the local child protection agency because of allegations of neglect. The house was dirty and infested with vermin. The school social worker was also involved because of the children's poor attendance and poor grades at school.

On investigation, it was learned that John and Carrie were required to stay home to help care for Mrs. H. if Lisa had to leave the home for any reason. Lisa, who was the primary caretaker for the young children and the older woman, had a caseworker from public assistance who was pushing her toward employment. Legal aid was involved in order to stop the eviction, as were a host of other social service agencies that Josephine would find out about when she would bump into them going to or coming from the home. Mrs. H. was skillful in negotiating the system and had a wide variety of formal and informal resources. She was mistrustful of formal agencies and only reluctantly gave out information.

Josephine called a meeting of all the social workers she knew of in this case, to review the various goals and objectives for this family, to determine where resources could best be consolidated, to eliminate duplication, and to fill in the gaps. In frustration, she exclaimed that if all the money that was being spent on all the social workers was just given to the family, they could probably solve their own problems.

---

**Issues in Group Work with Older Adults**    Support groups, education, advocacy, and therapeutic groups are all beneficial to people as they age. Working with a frail elderly population, however, requires different practice approaches. A sensory orientation group can be very beneficial to persons with cognitive deficits (Bowlby, 1993; Burnside and Schmidt, 1994; Corey and Corey, 1997; Ott, 1993; Thomas and Coleman, 1998). Such groups are used in settings where some sensory deprivation can occur, such as long-term care facilities. They concentrate on increasing cognition by stimulating the senses. These groups not only help increase the elderly person's awareness of person, place, and time; they can also assist with the development of peer relationships, provide emotional support and much needed stimulation (especially in institutional settings), and help in identifying formation and in maintaining whatever level of social functioning the person has remaining (Rice, 1997; Thomas and Coleman, 1998; Toseland, 1995). A recent study found that sensory orientation groups helped residents of a skilled care unit maintain their level of cognitive functioning, especially if the level had not deteriorated too much (Thomas and Coleman, 1998).

Group activity provides an outlet for older persons who may have lost their natural support network and need to develop new relationships to avoid being isolated. You can be instrumental in helping older persons begin to relearn socialization and relationship-building skills. Group activities provide older people with the opportunity to practice having meaningful conversations with people they do not know. "Get to know you" group exercises can be used in senior citizen centers or similar settings. In these exercises the group is divided into dyads. Each person asks the other questions and listens to and records the responses in order to report to a larger group. "Get to know you" questions include:

- Where was the best place you ever lived? What made that place so special?
- What is your favorite season of the year, and why?
- Name and describe one of the most beautiful things you have ever seen.
- Where is the farthest place you have ever visited?
- What is the most exiting thing you have ever done? Why was it so exciting?
- What do you think was good about the "good old days"?
- What is good about the time in which we live now?
- What is the best advice you ever gave anyone?
- Do you have a favorite quote (or Bible verse or other religious teaching)?
- What is your most prized possession?
- If you could have lunch with someone, living or deceased, who would that someone be?
- What is the secret to having a happy life?

These questions help older persons feel comfortable asking for information that elicits more than a yes or no response. It also allows them to practice listening skills. You and the members of the group will learn a great deal about one another. You will discover commonalities and begin to see others in a different light.

## SUMMARY

The elderly population in the United States is expanding rapidly. The most dramatic increases are in the number of people age 85 and older and in elderly members of minority groups. Social workers and policymakers must work together to effectively plan for the changing face of the older population.

Not only must there be increased community-based and long-term care services for people who need assistance, but better housing options and a plan to ensure future economic security are also needed. Issues surrounding health care are critical for the entire population. However, for older people on fixed incomes who must pay disproportionately for medical expenses, health care concerns have reached a crisis point.

In addition, older people have a wealth of knowledge, skills, and talent that is underused. Social workers can be instrumental in better using senior citizens as a resource.

Social work with older people requires continued training from a multidisciplinary perspective. Knowledge of the biological, psychological, and sociological aspects of aging is critical in holistic assessment and intervention with older people. This is a field of practice that allows the social worker to use a wide range of therapeutic approaches.

# CASE EXAMPLE

Case 13.8 illustrates the range of generalist practice skills that are required in working with elderly persons and their families or caretakers. The case is based on a client of a protective service worker I supervised at an Area Agency on Aging.

---

## CASE 13.8 | BEDRIDDEN AND ALONE

Mr. W., who is African American, age 62, was referred to the county Area Agency on Aging by an anonymous neighbor who was concerned that the client was often left alone in a basement apartment. In addition, the client was bed bound and would not be able to leave his apartment in an emergency.

The protective service social worker was asked to make an emergency home visit. Upon arrival, the social worker in fact discovered that the door was locked and the caregiver, the son, was not at home. The worker could observe and talk to the client through an open window with bars. Mr. W. stated adamantly that he was well taken care of, did not wish to leave the situation, and only wanted to remain with his son. He further stated that the son was running some errands and never left him alone for long periods of time. The social worker's assessment was that the client was alert to person, time, and place and knew the consequences of his decision. Therefore, he did not take the action of petitioning to have the client removed from the home against his wishes. Since this home had no telephone, the client was asked to inform the son that the worker would return in the morning.

The next day, the social worker did return and met with the son, who displayed hostility and demanded to know who had called the agency. The social worker let the caregiver vent his anger. Then he explained that the agency was concerned about the client's well-being. After the caregiver calmed down, he, the client, and the social worker were able to have a three-way conversation. The father was terminally ill with colorectal cancer. It turned out that the family was receiving assistance from a local nursing agency. The caregiver stated that they were in danger of being evicted because of nonpayment of rent. The apartment itself was filthy,

although the area around the client was kept clean. The worker knew that if he did not gain the trust of the son, he would not be able to improve the situation for the client. He therefore asked the caregiver and client how he could best help them. The most immediate problems they indicated were the eviction and transportation to medical appointments. In exchange for his assistance, the social worker asked the family's permission to list the client with the local police and fire station so that if a call came in from his address, emergency personnel would know that an incapacitated older person lived there. The son explained that he must sometimes leave the father alone in order to take care of errands, because there was no one else to assist. He also had to lock the doors because they lived in an high-crime urban area. The worker was able to determine through this initial interview that there were other children and several other siblings of the client who lived in the area. They would not, however, divulge names or contact information at this initial interview. In this situation, the social worker decided that the family was in need of ongoing, long-term assistance rather than emergency protective services.

### Intervention

The social worker contacted an agency that provides legal assistance to low-income families, to assist with delaying the eviction proceedings. He also contacted the local nursing agency. Their perception of the caregiver was that he was difficult to work with, often did not get the parent to medical appointments, and did not follow the prescribed medication regimen for their patient. They did have names and contact information for a few of the relatives and provided this information to the social worker.

*(continued)*

**CASE 13.8** | *continued*

During the next visit, the social worker decided to try and gain the trust of the caregiver by being empathetic. The worker tried to convey to the caregiver that he understood how difficult this role must be for him, especially without the assistance of the other relatives. A picture began to emerge that this caregiver, who was in his late 30s, was bitter about caring for his father but also felt obligated to do so. When the social worker shared some of the concerns from the nursing agency perspective, the caregiver and the father stated that they did not understand the regimen and what the medicine was supposed to do. Neither really trusted doctors and nurses and believed more in natural healing remedies. In addition, the nursing agency never helped the caregiver arrange for ambulance transportation to get the client to clinic appointments. He did not drive, and the father could not go in a regular van. This time the social worker was given permission to contact other family members. The social worker's hidden agenda was to make the family members feel guilty about not assisting the caregiver.

The social worker did determine that there were two other older children and nine brothers and sisters of the client, all living in the area. This family, although concerned about the client, did not like his choice of the son as the caregiver. The consensus was that the caregiver had a "difficult" personality, and

they were estranged from him because of his past lifestyle. It was easier to just stay away. They were unaware of the current living situation and of the terminal diagnosis and the pending eviction. It was clear to the worker that his own biases about how a family should respond had to be kept in check. The social worker organized a family meeting in order to enable this family to talk about their deep-rooted issues and come together to work on this immediate situation. As a result, the mutual decision was that the father would move to the home of an older sibling who had the space, resources, and supports to provide the care needed. The nursing agency that served this area continued to medically monitor the client and agreed to provide concrete reeducation about the medication regimen and to assist with better transportation arrangements.

**Termination**

Once the client was placed with the family member and the goals of the care plan were being met, the care manager terminated official involvement with the family. Through follow-up, he did learn that the son eventually was evicted from the home but was able to find his own apartment. The client died at home and thereby avoided his fear of going to a nursing home. This was his ultimate fear during this whole process.

## DISCUSSION QUESTIONS

1.  What would you have done on the initial visit to Mr. W.'s home (Case 13.8)? Discuss the pros and cons of the social worker leaving a bedridden client in a locked apartment.
2.  Mr. W. did not want to be placed in a nursing home and was willing to endure less than ideal conditions. What could the social worker have done to ease the client's fears? What other services might have been appropriate? Could Mr. W. have benefited from hospice care? (For more information on hospice care, see Davies et al., 1995.)
3.  Discuss some of the ethnocultural beliefs that might be part of the W. family dynamic. How are these beliefs a source of strength? How might they present obstacles?

4.  The social worker decided that the way to help Mr. W. was to gain the trust of his son, the caregiver. Would you have done anything differently? How might the situation have changed if the worker focused his initial attention on the client?
5.  From a strengths perspective, what are the positive attributes of this case situation?
6.  What effect will the predicted demographic changes in the elderly population have on the delivery of social services in the year 2050? How will the changing demographic profile in the United States affect the training of future social workers?
7.  What is the key to developing helping relationships with elderly clients? What practice guideline would you focus on in working with an elderly client?
8.  What makes assessment of elderly clients challenging? What special factors need to be taken into consideration? How would you conduct an assessment with an elderly client?

# REFERENCES

Administration On Aging. (1997). *Aging into the 21st century.* Washington, DC: Administration on Aging.

Albert, M. S. (1988). General issues in geriatric neuropsychology. In M. S. Albert and M. B. Moss (Eds.), *Geriatric neuropsychology* (pp. 3–10). New York: Guilford.

Alzheimer's Association *(n.d.). Is it Alzheimer's? Warning signs you should know.* Chicago, IL.

American Association of Retired Persons. *A profile of older Americans: 1999.* Washington, DC: AARP.

Atchley, R. C. (1997). *Social forces and aging: An introduction to social gerontology* (8th ed.). Belmont: Wadsworth.

Blazer, D., and Williams, C. (1980). Epidemiology of dysphoria and depression in an elderly population. *American Journal of Psychiatry, 137,* 430–444.

Bowlby, C. (1993). *Therapeutic activities with persons disabled by Alzheimer's disease and related disorders.* Gaithersburg, MD: Aspen.

Burnside, I., and Schmidt, M. (1994). *Working with older adults: Group processes and techniques.* Boston: Jones and Bartlette.

Butler, R. (1975). *Why survive? Being old in America.* New York: Harper and Row.

Butler, R. (1980–1981). The life review: An unrecognized bonanza. *International Journal of Aging and Human Development, 12,* 35–38.

Centers for Disease Control and Prevention. (1998, January 23). *Morbidity and mortality weekly report: AIDS among persons aged 50 years.* Rockville, MD: CDC National AIDS Clearinghouse.

Chen, Y. (1991). Improving the economic security of minority persons as they enter old age. In *The Gerontological Society of America, Minority elders: Longevity, economics, and health: Building a public policy base* (pp. 14–23). Washington, DC: The Gerontological Society of America.

Comfort, A. (1976). Age prejudice in America. *Social Policy 7* (3), 3–8.

Corey, M., and Corey, G. (1997). *Groups: Process and practice* (5th ed.). Pacific Grove, CA: Brooks/Cole.

Cox, C. (1993). *The frail elderly: Problems, needs, and community responses.* Westport, CT: Auburn House.

Davies, B., Reimer, J. C., Brown, P., and Martens, N. (1995). *Fading away: The experiences of transition in families with terminal illness.* Amityville, NY: Baywood Publishing Co.

Evans, D. A., Funkenstein, H. H., and Albert, M. S. (1989). Prevalence of Alzheimer's disease in a community population of older persons. *JAMA, 262,* 2551–2556.

Federal Interagency Forum on Aging Related Statistics (2000). *Older Americans 2000: Key indicators of well-being.* Appendix A: Detailed Tables. Washington, DC: Office of Management and Budget.

Frankel, A., and Gelman, S. (1998). *Care management: An introduction to concepts and skills.* Chicago: Lyceum.

Friedland, R. B., and Pankaj, V. (1998, January/February). Most-vulnerable older immigrants hit by welfare reform. *Aging Today,* p. 4.

Gelfand, D. E. (1993). *The aging network: Programs and services* (4th ed.). New York: Springer.

Gillespie, A. E., and Sloan, K. (1990). *Housing options and services for older adults: Choices and challenges.* Santa Barbara, CA: ABC-CLIO.

Greene, R. (1986). Countertransference issues in social work with the aged. *Journal of Gerontological Social Work, 9*(3), 79–88.

Harvard Medical School (1992, August). Alzheimer's disease part I. *The Harvard Mental Health Letter, 9*(2), 1–4.

Hill, R. B. (1981). *Economic policies and black progress: Myths and realities.* Washington, DC: National Urban League.

Holosko, M. J., and Feit, M. D. (1991). *Social work practice with the elderly.* Toronto: Canadian Scholars' Press.

Hooyman, N., and Kiyak, H. A. (1999). *Social gerontology: A multidisciplinary perspective* (5th ed.). Boston: Allyn and Bacon.

Hooyman, N., and Kiyak, H. A. (2002). *Social gerontology: A multidisciplinary perspective* (6th ed.). Boston: Allyn and Bacon.

Keigher, S. M. (1997). America's most cruel xenophobia. *Health and Social Work, 22*(3), 232–237.

Kennedy, C. E. (1978). *Human development: The adult years and aging.* New York: Macmillan.

Knapp, M. (1996). Assessment of competence to make medical decisions. In L. Carstensen, B. Edelstein, and L. Dornbrand (Eds.), *The practical handbook of clinical gerontology* (pp. 174–187). Thousand Oaks, CA: Sage.

Kronenfeld, J. J. (1993). *Controversial issues in health care policy.* Newbury Park, CA: Sage.

Kropf, N. P., and Hutchison, E. D. (1992). Effective practice with elderly clients. In R. L. Schneider and N. P. Kropf (Eds.), *Gerontological social work: Knowledge, service settings, and special populations* (pp. 3–28). Chicago: Nelson-Hall.

LaRue, A. (1992). *Aging and neuropsychological assessment.* New York: Plenum.

Leon, J., and Lair, T. (1990). *Functional status of the noninstitutionalized elderly: Estimates of ADL and IADL difficulties, research findings 4.* (DHHS Publication No. PHS 90-3462.) Rockville, MD: Public Health Service.

Liu, K., Perozek, M., and Manton, K. (1993). Catastrophic acute and long-term care costs: Risks faced by disabled elderly persons. *The Gerontologist 33*(3), 299–307.

Maddox, G. L. (1988). The future of gerontology in higher education: Continuing to open the American mind about aging. *The Gerontologist 28*(6), 748–752.

Mayeux, R., Sano, M., Chen, J., Tatemichi, T., and Stern, Y. (1991). Risk of dementia in first-degree relatives of patients with Alzheimer's disease and related disorders. *Archives of Neurology, 48*, 269–273.

Morrow-Howell, N. (1992). Clinical care management: The hallmark of gerontological social work. *Journal of Gerontological Social Work, 18*(3/4), 119–131.

Moxley, D. P. (1997). *Care management by design: Reflections on principles and practices.* Chicago: Nelson-Hall.

National Alliance for Caregiving and American Association of Retired Persons (1997, June). *Family caregiving in the U.S.: Findings from a national survey.* Washington, DC: Author.

National Association of Area Agencies on Aging (1992). *Choosing to meet the need: A guide to improve targeting of Title III services to low-income minority elderly* (Grant No. 90-AM-0392). Washington, DC: U.S. Administration on Aging, Department of Health and Human Services.

National Association of Area Agencies on Aging (Feb. 13, 2003). *Legislative Update: FY03 Final Omnibus measure includes modest overall increase to older Americans act programs.* Washington, DC.

National Institute on Aging (1996). *Progress report on Alzheimer's disease* Publication No. 96-4137). Washington, DC: U.S. Department of Health and Human Services.

National Institutes of Health (2000). *Women of color health data book.* Washington, DC: Office of Research on Women's Health.

Ott, R. L. (1993). Enhancing validation through milestoning with sensory reminiscence. *Journal of Gerontological Social Work, 20*(1/2), 147–159.

Pavalko, E. K., and Artis, J. E. (1997). Women's caregiving and paid work: Causal relationships in late midlife. *Journals of Gerontology, 52B*, S170–179.

Pennsylvania Care Management Institute (1990). *Care management orientation manual.* Philadelphia, PA: PCMI.

Philadelphia Corporation for Aging (1995). *Clinical protocol series for care managers in community based long-term care* (Grant #90-AM-0688). Washington, DC: Administration on Aging, Department of Health and Human Services.

Poulin, J., and Thomas, N. D. (1998). Burnout and the geriatric care manager. *Geriatric Care Management Journal, 8*(1), 25–29.

Quadagno, J., and Hardy, M. (1996). Work and retirement. In R. H. Binstock and L. K. George (Eds.), *Handbook of aging and the social sciences* (4th ed.), pp. 325–345). San Diego, CA: Academic Press.

Ramirez, A. (1989, January). Making better use of older workers. *Fortune*, pp. 179–182.

Randall-David, E. (1989). *Strategies for working with culturally diverse communities and clients.* Washington, DC: Association for the Care of Children's Health.

Rice, S. (1997). Group work with elderly persons. In G. G. Greif and P. H. Ephross (Eds.), *Group work with populations at risk* (pp. 105–120). New York: Oxford University Press.

Robison, J., Moen, P., and Dempster-McClain, D. (1995). Women's caregiving: Changing profiles and pathways. *Journals of Gerontology, 50B*, S362–373.

Roff, L. L., and Atherton, C. R. (1989). *Promoting successful aging.* Chicago: Nelson-Hall.

Rosen, A. L., and Persky, T. (1997). Meeting mental health needs of older people: Policy and practice issues for social work. *Journal of Gerontological Social Work, 27*(3), 45–54.

Salend, E., Kane, R. A., Satz, M., and Pynoos, J. (1984). Elder abuse reporting: Limitations of statutes. *The Gerontologist, 24*(1), 61–69.

Schneider, R. I., and Kropf, N. P. (1987). *Virginia ombudsman program: Professional certification curriculum.* Richmond: Virginia Department for the Aging.

Schneider, R. I., and Kropf, N. P. (Eds.). (1992). *Gerontological social work: Knowledge, service settings, and special populations.* Chicago: Nelson-Hall.

Schulz, J. H. (1995). Economic security policies. In R. H. Binstock and L. K. George (Eds.), *Handbook of aging and the social sciences* (4th ed.), pp. 410–426. San Diego, CA: Academic Press.

Silver, M. H. (1995). Memories and meaning: Life review in old age. *Journal of Geriatric Psychiatry, 28*(1), 57–74.

Skinner, J. H. (1992). Aging in place: The experience of African American and other minority elders. *Generations, 16*(2), 49–52.

Smith, L. (1992). *Right choices: Handle with care.* Lafayette, IN: Lynn Smith Enterprises.

Soares, H., and Rose, M. (1994). Clinical aspects of care management with the elderly. *Journal of Gerontological Social Work, 22*(3/4), 143–156.

Strahan, G. (1997). *An overview of nursing homes and their current residents: Data from the 1995 national nursing home survey.* Vital and Health Statistics. No. 280. Hyattsville, MD: National Center for Health Statistics.

Tacchino, K., and Thomas, N. (1997). Why financial practitioners and geriatric care managers must talk to each other. *Generations, 21*(2), 41–44.

Thomas, N. (1997). Hoarding: Eccentricity or pathology: When to intervene? *Journal of Gerontological Social Work, 29*(1), 45–55.

Thomas, N. (1998). Care management from urban and suburban perspectives. *Journal of Care Management, 7*(4), 139–146.

Thomas, N., and Coleman, S. (1998). Using the sensory orientation group with a frail elderly population. *Groupwork, 10*(2), 95–106.

Tobin, S., and Gustafson, J. (1987). What do we do differently with elderly clients? *Journal of Gerontological Social Work, 10*(3/4), 107–120.

Toseland, R. W. (1995). *Group work with the elderly and family caregivers.* New York: Springer.

Tully, C. T., and Jacobson, S. (1994). The homeless elderly: America's forgotten populations. *Journal of Gerontological Social Work, 22*(3/4), 61–81.

Turk-Charles, S., Rose, T., and Gatz, M. (1996). The significance of gender in the treatment of older adults. In L. Carstensen, B. Edelstein, and L. Dornbrand (Eds.), *The practical handbook of clinical gerontology* (pp. 107–128). Thousand Oaks, CA: Sage.

U.S. Bureau of the Census (1992). *Income sources of persons 65 and over, by race and Hispanic origin: United States.* Washington, DC: U.S. Government Printing Office.

U.S. Bureau of the Census. (1996). *Population projections of the U.S., by age, sex, race, and Hispanic origin data: 1995–2050. Current Population Reports* (P-25, No. 1130). Washington, DC: U.S. Government Printing Office.

U.S. Bureau of the Census. (1998a). *Household and family characteristics. Current Population Reports. Series P20–515.* Washington, DC: U.S. Government Printing Office.

U.S. Bureau of the Census. (1998b). *International brief: Gender and aging. IB/98-2.* Washington, DC: U.S. Department of Commerce.

U.S. Bureau of the Census. (2000). *Projections of the total resident population by 5-year age groups, and sex with special age categories: Middle Series 1999–2000; 2025–2045; 2050–2070 (NP-T4A, NPT4F, NPT4G).* Washington, DC: Populations Projection Program, Population Division.

U.S. Bureau of the Census. (2001). *American housing survey national tables.* Washington, DC: The Department of Housing and Urban Development.

U.S. Bureau of the Census. (2002). *Current population survey: Income supplement.* Washington, DC: Government Printing Office.

Viney, L. (1993). *Life stories: Personal construct therapy with the elderly.* New York: Wiley.

Watt, S., and Soifer, A. (1991). Conducting psycho-social assessments with the elderly. In M. J. Holosko and M. D. Feit (Eds.), *Social work practice with the elderly* (pp. 31–46). Toronto: Canadian Scholar's Press.

Wiener, J. M., and Illston, L. H. (1996). Financing and organization of health care. In R. H. Binstock and L. K. George (Eds.), *Handbook of aging and the social sciences* 4th ed. (pp. 427–445). San Diego, CA: Academic Press.

Youngjohn, J. R., and Crook, III, T. H. (1996). Dementia. In L. L. Carstensen, B. Edelstein, and L. Dornbrand (Eds.), *The practical handbook of clinical gerontology* (pp. 239–254). Thousand Oaks, CA: Sage.

# 14
CHAPTER

# GENERALIST PRACTICE
# WITH PEOPLE OF COLOR

*Norma D. Thomas*

© Spencer Grant/PhotoEdit

Donna J. is an MSW student with a first-year field placement at an inner-city Head Start program. The program serves predominantly low-income children of color. Donna is in her early twenties and comes from a middle-class suburban family. Prior to her field placement, Donna had had almost no contact with low-income inner-city people of color.

Donna enjoys her interactions with the children she works with in the program. Her contacts with the children's parents, however, have been less positive. She cannot understand why they seem either hostile or indifferent to her attempts to help them with their children's behavior at school and in the home. Donna wonders what she is doing wrong and why she is having such a difficult time developing trust with the children's parents.

This chapter describes various approaches and guidelines for working with people of color. It provides information on the major racial groups in this country in terms of differences in culture and communication style and explores value differences between majority workers and minority clients that, if not understood, can have a negative effect on relationship building. The chapter also presents a model for the assessment of people of color and their environment, and discusses the effect of racism on micro and macropractice. By the end of this chapter, you should be able to help Donna:

1. Summarize the social work profession's history in working with people of color
2. Describe the major macropolicy issues affecting people of color in this country
3. Identify the major micropractice issues in working with people of color
4. Describe differences in communication styles of various groups of people of color and the majority population
5. Describe the major values of the different groups of people of color and compare them with the values of the dominant society
6. Describe the major generalist practice issues that need to be taken into consideration in working with individuals, families, and groups of color

People of color are the second–fastest-growing population group in the United States, just behind the Latino/Hispanic population. In 2000, there were 34.7 million African Americans, 35.3 million Latinos/Hispanics, 10.6 million Asians and Pacific Islanders, and 2.5 million First Nations Peoples, including the Eskimo and Aleut, and 2.4 million persons reporting two or more races living in the United States (U.S. Bureau of the Census, 2002). By the year 2010, there will be 40 million African Americans, 44 million Latinos, 15 million Asians and Pacific Islanders, and 2.8 million First Nations peoples (U.S. Bureau of the Census, 2000).

Social work has traditionally served disadvantaged populations (Trattner, 1999). People of color are disproportionately represented among the nation's poor. In 2001, 22.7 percent of African Americans were living in poverty. Latino populations are also overrepresented among the poor, with 21.4 percent living in poverty. Asians and Pacific Islanders experience overall poverty rates of 10.2 percent. This is in comparison to an 11.7 percent overall rate of poverty, and a 9.9 percent poverty rate for Caucasians. (Proctor and Dalaker, 2002). Consequently, more and more clients will be people of color.

We will also find ourselves working with more people who do not speak English as their primary language. These clients will need assistance in creating a bridge between their native culture and U.S. culture. This is as true for people of color born in this country as it is for those born elsewhere. In addition, class differences between people of color and social workers can create barriers to building a working relationship.

Acquiring cross-cultural understanding requires us to go inside ourselves to explore what makes us unique and what has influenced our behavior. In other words, we need to discover how our culture has influenced who we are before we can understand why culture is so important to those to whom we are providing assistance (Devore and Schlesinger, 1999; Pinderhughes, 1989).

## HISTORY OF SOCIAL WORK WITH PEOPLE OF COLOR

Historically, the field of social work has responded to people of color by not acknowledging their cultural differences and by assuming that they are responsible for their own plight in life and are therefore undeserving. Social welfare was denied from the beginning:

> There was little social welfare for Native Americans during the colonial period—or later on, for that matter; most of those who survived were forced onto the nation's worst lands where, out of sight, they were either ignored despite their poor plight or placed on federal reservations administered by corrupt and uncaring officials.
>
> Then there were blacks, who were also viewed by most colonists as uncivilized and permanently inferior—children of Satan not entitled to the same rights as white people and hence excluded from the social welfare system. Black slaves were the responsibility of their masters and were prohibited from receiving aid under most of the poor laws; free blacks, for the most part, were simply denied assistance and forced to develop their own informal self-help mechanisms. (Trattner, 1999, pp. 23–24)

Because of their own cultural traditions and because they were excluded from majority institutions, members of racial and ethnic groups formed their own social welfare institutions. For example, Chinese immigrants brought their own systems of mutual aid, which included trade associations, formal lending institutions, and informal loan mechanisms (Day, 1989). This practice is still used by ethnocultural groups that cannot obtain loans from formal lending institutions.

Social work has often followed the policies espoused by the broader society and has therefore not been immune to discriminatory practices. Some workers in the early social work movement provided services to people of color and were instrumental in the development of social change organizations, such as the National Association for the Advancement of Colored People (NAACP). Nevertheless, racism among social workers is well documented (Trattner, 1999). *Social Work,* the journal of the National Association of Social Workers (NASW), had only two articles on the civil rights movement before 1963 (Ehrenreich, 1985). The National Association of Black Social Workers was formed in 1968 in response to the belief that the NASW was not addressing issues related to African Americans.

Social work students are often taught generic practice models that are supposed to fit all population groups. The result is misunderstanding and stereotyping (Pinderhughes, 1989). Even within ethnic and racial groups, one approach does not fit all (Hardy, 1989). Color-blind and culture-neutral approaches attempt to remove barriers from social work practice by pretending that no differences exist among peoples:

> [T]he system and its agencies provide services with the express philosophy of being unbiased. They function with the belief that color or culture makes no difference and that all people are the same. Culturally-blind agencies are characterized by the belief that helping approaches traditionally used by the dominant culture are universally applicable; if the system worked as it should, all people—regardless of race or culture—would be served with equal effectiveness. . . . The consequences of such a belief are to make services so ethnocentric as to render them virtually useless to all but the most assimilated people of color. (Cross et al., 1989, p. 15)

To develop competency in working with people of color, generalist social workers must first suspend the notion that everyone is the same. All people have the basic needs of food, clothing, and shelter and share most of the goals outlined in Maslow's hierarchy of needs (1968), but the way people achieve these goals may depend on their culture and history. Needs are also shaped by socioeconomic status, gender, sexual identity, physical and mental abilities, and religious factors (Harper and Lantz, 1996; Lum, 1996).

## MACROPOLICY ISSUES

Racism still wields the most negative impact on people of color and their communities, although some voices believe that class is most negative (Wilson, 1980). The legacy of slavery and the genocide of First Nations persons have left a permanent scar on the nation. For people of color, issues related to race have more of an effect than issues related to gender, sexual identity, and age (Lorde, 1995). People of color often do not believe majority workers who state that they do not see color when they look at them. The fact is that our society is very color conscious.

Race and racism are often conceptualized as a black and white issue. However, other groups also experience racism, as this discussion of the reluctance of Asian Americans to seek mental health services indicates:

> Cultural differences and minority group experiences must be jointly examined if one is to fully understand Asian Americans. The reluctance of Asian Americans to utilize mental health services may be due to different cultural

> values or attitudes toward mental health or toward services. Another plausi-
> ble explanation for this phenomenon is that some Asian Americans, experi-
> encing racial prejudice or discrimination, may avoid services because of dis-
> trust or suspiciousness. Minority group experiences do affect mental health.
> (Sue and Morishima, 1982, p. 8)

Racism is the root cause of generational poverty, diminished self-esteem that promotes community violence, self-medicating through drugs and alcohol, and disproportional involvement in the criminal justice system. Different groups have sought redress through the courts by seeking reparations for past injustices rooted in racism.

If social workers believe that everyone in America begins on an equal playing field and continue to blame the victims when they do not succeed, social work practice will be a frustrating experience (Ryan, 1976). It is diffi-cult to work with people who have been so beaten down by issues out of their control that they cannot put their lives together to get back up. Because many of us who enter the profession are of different races and social classes than the people with whom we work, it is hard for us to see the world from the view-point of those who have not had the benefits we take for granted.

Communities of color are currently facing a backlash in this country. Policymakers and much of the American public assume that people of color, especially African Americans, now have the same opportunities as white Americans. Programs directed toward correcting past injustices are viewed as reverse discrimination against the white majority, especially white males. These beliefs have fueled a push to dismantle procedures and policies that pro-mote affirmative action:

> Almost any set of data that is examined shows the subordinate position of
> women and of people of color in our economy. Wages, incomes, promotion
> rates, middle management, top management, number of contractors, number
> of independent manufacturing firms: The numbers all tell the same story.
> Women and minorities suffer their gender and their race severely. And yet there
> is a growing series of objections from white men who claim to have suffered
> because of affirmative action programs. (Axinn and Levin, 1997, p. 320)

The perception that white males are the victims of affirmative action is fairly widespread, even though reverse discrimination occurs infrequently. A survey conducted by the National Opinion Research Center found that 70 percent of the American public believed that whites were being hurt by affirmative action policies, but only 7 percent reported experience with reverse discrimination (Patterson, 1995).

The backlash against communities of color is also being manifested in leg-islation. In California, Proposition 187, passed in 1994, terminated all public social services to persons who could not document their legal status in this country, and Proposition 209, passed in 1996, prohibited preferences based on race and gender in public education, employment, and state contracting (Karger and Stoesz, 1998). In Texas in 1996, the Fifth Circuit Court of Appeals ruled in *Cheryl J. Hopwood v. State of Texas* that the University of

Texas Law School could use neither race nor ethnicity in admission decisions. The outcome of two cases before the United States Supreme Court concerning the admissions policies of the University of Michigan may have far-reaching effects in the area of affirmative action.

These laws and cases have led to the perception of a more hostile environment for persons from underrepresented minority groups. The Association of American Medical Colleges reported a 17 percent drop in minority applications to medical schools in 1997 in California, Texas, Louisiana, and Mississippi. There has also been a 27 percent decrease in the number of minority students accepted into medical schools (Hawkins, 1997). African-American, Latino, and First Nations freshmen enrollment declined the year after Proposition 209 was passed in California, and so too did enrollment of Caucasians and Asians. This is generally attributed to the increase in the number of students who refuse to list their race on college applications (Locke, 1998). California law and medical schools reported an increase in the enrollment of Blacks, Hispanics and First Nations persons in 2002, but the numbers are still below those reported during the period when affirmative action was in effect (Cox et al., 2002).

Although discrimination based on race is illegal, it is still prevalent, and it is the basis of all macroissues that negatively affect people of color. Social work practitioners must guard against perpetuating institutionalized practices of agencies that promote unequal treatment of communities of color. We can debate the merits of many programs that grew out of the civil rights movement, but the problems that they were attempting to rectify still exist.

# MICROPRACTICE ISSUES

Social work practitioners must investigate and use practice approaches that are suited to work with multicultural groups. Working effectively with people of color requires an approach that builds on the capacities of people to overcome difficulties:

> Focusing exclusively on problems, including racism, ethnocentrism, or classism, makes the problems more important than the [people]. Focusing exclusively on problems minimizes the celebration of what is human in those we serve, especially the resourceful, creative, joyful power of the human spirit. (Baker and Steiner, 1996, p. 302)

Strengths-based social work practice focuses on helping client systems tap into the strengths within them (Saleebey, 1992). Potential strengths include cultural values and traditions, resources, coping strategies, family, friends, and community support networks. Past successful experiences need to be linked to solving current problems (de Shazer, 1985, 1988). The client is the expert in identifying past success and in developing solutions based on past experiences. Focusing on concrete tasks and objectives (Reid, 1986; Reid and Epstein, 1972) works better for people of color than more abstract methods (Devore and Schlesinger, 1999; Freeman, 1990; See, 1998).

Strengths are identified during the interview process. One way of identifying strengths is to help clients and client systems reconnect with their cultural and geographic roots. This helps African Americans and other displaced people of color develop a sense of belonging (De Jong and Miller, 1995; Saleebey, 1992).

Reconnecting people with their cultural and geographic roots is a core tenet of Afrocentric social work practice. Afrocentric practice recognizes that African-American history began before Africans were brought to America as slaves and that the African experience must be included in understanding and working with African-American people (Asante, 1987; See, 1998). Afrocentric practice incorporates the concept of the collective, that is, the individual, the family, and the community, while acknowledging that African-American culture has connections to both African and Western cultures (Harvey, 1997). The term *Maafa*, a Swahili word meaning disaster, calamity, damage, injustice, or catastrophe, has been applied to the long-term effect of slavery on African people, the continuing psychological trauma, and the miracle of survival (Marimba, 1994; Roberson, 1995). Maafa-based practice focuses on helping practitioners and clients recognize their recent history, get in touch with their ancient cultural history, and use those strengths to cope with the present.

To help people of color determine the problem for which they seek social work intervention, whether at the micro or macrolevel, we must allow clients to tell their stories in their own way and to construct their own versions of reality (Saleebey, 1994). We must therefore be active listeners, use our skills to guide clients in telling their stories, and use techniques that help them construct their reality.

Storytelling, which is the way history was passed on by many peoples of color, especially those of African and First Nations descent, is a natural way to develop the helping relationship. It allows for the incorporation of cultural references because the story is told from the person's perspective. This is not a one-way interaction. You will need to also use a storytelling approach to interpret the story to the client and to relate it to current issues. Sometimes, you can use metaphor, which is a powerful tool for building relationships with people of color because it allows for the influence of culture to emerge (Baker and Steiner, 1996; Barker, 1985; Baynes, 1967; O'Hanlon and Weiner-Davis, 1989; Whan, 1979). A simple example of the use of metaphor is shown in Case 14.1.

The use of narrative allows clients to tell their stories from the beginning or to start with the end of the story and work backward. In telling their stories, clients' conceptions of self, relationships, and life experiences take shape and provide meaning and purpose (Goldstein, 1990). The case example in Case 14.2 illustrates the narrative approach.

This case did not necessitate a long assessment period for gathering scientific data, but rather the ability of the social worker to actively listen in a nonjudgmental way. The intervention also required some knowledge of how the religious practices of Haiti, influenced by African and European religions,

<table>
<tr><td>CASE 14.1</td><td>USE OF METAPHOR IN STORY-TELLING</td></tr>
</table>

An African-American woman in her fifties has come to a career-counseling center for assistance in finding a job. She was recently laid off from a factory where she had worked for a number of years, and she knew that the prospects of being rehired were bleak. Her self-esteem was at a low point.

The counselor could have asked her a series of set application questions to ascertain her skill level and employability. Instead, he asked her to talk about her early life before coming to work at this factory. He also asked her to describe obstacles she had overcome as well as opportunities she was given.

The woman described going to segregated schools in the rural South, working long, hard hours as part of a sharecropping family, and her eventual move to the North. She raised a large family, and all of her children were in college or had graduated from college. The counselor used her description of preparing the soil for seed, providing the young plants with the right amount of water, and harvesting the crops at the right moment as a metaphor for how she now had to begin again and prepare herself for a new career. The counselor was able to help her list her strengths and her skills from listening to her tell her story and to build on them to make a plan for additional education and training that would enable her to find new employment.

<table>
<tr><td>CASE 14.2</td><td>I'M NOT POSSESSED</td></tr>
</table>

Tamika C., a young teenager born in this country whose parents are from Haiti, was encouraged to talk to the school social worker by her teachers, who were concerned about Tamika's repeated crying episodes in the classroom. Tamika had not experienced previous emotional problems and was an exceptional student. She did not talk about these crying spells with her family, because she was convinced they would believe she was "possessed."

At the beginning of the session, Shirley W., the social worker, asked Tamika to describe the events that led up to these episodes. Tamika described seemingly disconnected recollections of various discussions with teachers or other students that made her sad and want to cry. Mrs. W. began to realize that these descriptions were metaphors. When Tamika was asked to talk about other times she had had these feelings, she described the death of her uncle, with whom she was close, six months earlier. Her family would not discuss the death; apparently there were mysteries surrounding it.

Being able to finally tell the story, to relate current experiences to a past one, and to have her feelings validated allowed Tamika to express her grief and begin the healing process. She was encouraged to talk to her family about their religious beliefs so that she could better understand their reasons for not wanting to discuss the death of her uncle. Her parents raised her as a Catholic and sent her to Catholic schools in order to promote her assimilation into American culture, but they themselves still held onto their culture and spiritual beliefs.

affected this young woman's reluctance to appear to be "possessed" (Bibb and Casimir, 1996; Brandon, 1997; Charles, 1986). Tamika struggled with the two cultures, and the social worker recognized her dilemma.

The concept of culture is key to effective practice with people of color. **Culture** is a set of unified values, ideas, beliefs, and standards of behavior shared by a group of people; it is the way a person accepts, orders, interprets, and understands experiences (Saleebey, 1994; Thomas and Hayman-El, 2000;

Velasquez, Vigil, and Benavides, 1994). Culture is also an unconscious phenomenon; people do not necessarily think about it even though it influences day-to-day behavior. It is transmitted from generation to generation, influenced by current conditions as well as history, and carried forth in unconscious group memories (Brandon, 1997; Roberts, 1964):

> Social groups help individuals remember. Society tests our memory for personal information, for cognitive data, and places demands on our skills, but it also provides help for us when we cannot recall something. Other people often help us reconstitute our own past experiences, and our own experience comes to encompass images of the experiences of other people which they have conveyed to us from their memories. Collective memory is part of a group's way of managing and storing its own information. The idea of an individual memory totally separate from social memory is an abstraction almost devoid of meaning. Individuals' memories exist and are maintained in a social and cultural context. Every recollection, however personal it may be, exists in relationship with the whole material and moral life of the societies of which we are part (or of which we have been part) and with ideas which many other people around us also hold. Through membership in a social group—particularly kinship, religious, and class affiliations—individuals are able to acquire, to localize and to recall their memories. (Brandon, 1997, p. 132)

The concept of **collective memory** is instrumental in understanding why culturally competent practice requires abandoning the notion that people of color will adapt to Eurocentric models of practice. Culture is an integral component of a healthy identity, a healthy family, and ultimately a healthy community. Understanding the cultures of the people to whom we provide service is mandatory.

Determining a client's level of **acculturation** is an important part of understanding their culture (Atkinson, Thomson, and Grant 1993; Pinderhughes, 1982, 1989). Standardized instruments that help determine the degree of acculturation are the Acculturation Rating Scale for Mexican Americans (Cuellar, Harris, and Jasso, 1980), the Suinn-Lew Asian Self-Identity Acculturation Scale (Suinn et al., 1987), and the Black Identification Scale (Whittler, Calantone, and Young, 1990).

An understanding of clients' culture can also be achieved through the interview process. The following open-ended questions can gather relevant information about the importance of culture in the life of the client and client system:

- Do you (or members of your immediate family) speak a language other than English?
- How would you describe your racial/cultural/ethnic heritage?
- To whom do you (or members of your immediate family) go when you are sick or in pain?
- Does your view of the world differ from that of the majority culture?
- What is your cultural heritage?
- Describe your religious/spiritual beliefs?

- Who makes the decisions in your household? (Thomas and Hayman-El, 2000)

Another set of questions helps clarify the importance of culture in the lives of the people with whom clients interact:

1. What values do you see as of great importance in your culture?
2. How are the values of the mainstream U.S. culture different from those of your own culture? Would you share conflicts or stress that this has caused you?
3. What is the relative importance of self and your family or other groups in decision making in your culture? Are decisions made on a collective or on an individual basis?
4. How important is the role of history in your culture and in your family?
5. When people in your culture have problems, where do they go for help?
6. What kind of help would they be looking for when they go for help?
7. What kind of personal qualities would the people of your culture expect in the person they go to for help?
8. How might religious beliefs influence the helping process in your culture?
9. How much is it of concern to your family if you go for help outside of the family?
10. Have you served as a helper in your culture? If so, describe what you did.
11. What other things do you think I need to know about your culture so that I can be a better helper? (Wehrly, 1995, p. 150)

# GENERALIST PRACTICE WITH PEOPLE OF COLOR

People of color have the same problems and concerns as Caucasians. Racism, oppression, and blocked opportunities compound their problems. People of color come to formal services reluctantly, often when they have exhausted all other family and community resources. Therefore, the first contact with a social worker not only determines whether an individual will engage in a helping relationship but also whether other members of the community will use that agency system. A first step in building relationships with people of color is understanding differences in communication and values.

## Communication Differences

Even when we are talking the same language, our perceptions of an interaction are culturally influenced (Samovar and Porter, 1994). Different groups of people translate nonverbal communication, such as spatial observance, handshaking, and eye contact, in different ways (Samovar and Porter, 1994; Sue and Sue, 1990). Mastering cross-cultural communication is the key to effective practice with individuals, families, groups, and communities of color. This requires sharpening observation and listening skills as well as learning about clients' cultural beliefs and traditions.

## CASE 14.3 | I DIDN'T MEAN TO BE DISRESPECTFUL

Dorothy M., a social worker, went to the home of an African-American family composed of a middle-aged woman, Mrs. L., who works full time, her terminally ill mother, Mrs. T., for whom she is primary caretaker, and her two small children, Terry and Tina. Dorothy, who correctly recognized the stress on Mrs. L., suggested to Mrs. T., without prior consultation with Mrs. L., that she should consider going to a nursing home to relieve her daughter of this stress. Although everyone was polite to Dorothy, after she left Mrs. L. called the agency to request that this worker never again return to her home. When asked to explain, Mrs. L. stated that the worker had talked to her mother alone about the option of a nursing home instead of discussing this with both of them. She had no intention of ever placing her mother in a nursing home because it was against everything in her experience. She had called the agency for assistance, not for someone to destroy her household. When Dorothy was told about this complaint, she could not remember anything in the tone of voice or the body language of Mrs. L. or Mrs. T. that would have indicated that they were offended by her suggestion.

Because social workers are seen as experts and authority figures and represent agencies from which clients must sometimes receive service involuntarily, clients and their networks are often reluctant to tell us that our service does not meet their needs. However, 50 percent of people of color quit therapy after the first interview, even if they come to treatment voluntarily (Ivey, 1981; see also Boyd-Franklin, 1989; Marin and Marin, 1991; Sue and Sue, 1990; Wilkinson and Spurlock, 1986; Yamamoto, 1986). Beginning social workers often make the mistake of taking everything that is said at face value. For example, metaphors, riddles, and proverbs are interspersed in the speech of First Nations persons (Sutton and Broken Nose, 1996) and African Americans (Weber, 1994). Their use can be very confusing to white Americans:

> Proverbial wisdom can be found on every socioeconomic level in the black community, and it is transmitted from generation to generation. Listening to speech that is peppered with proverbial sayings might seem strange to non-blacks. But, because proverbial sayings are generally accepted as "truths" because they are taught to children at a very early age, they effectively sum up events and predict outcome. (Weber, 1994, p. 224)

Being of the same race and ethnicity as the client can assist the worker in terms of relationship building, but it does not automatically eliminate barriers. Most schools of social work teach from a Eurocentric perspective. For example, the traditional problem-solving approach (Perlman, 1957) assumes that if a logical, rational progression is followed, the desired outcome will occur. Because ways of thinking are shaped by culture and experience, what is logical thinking to the worker may not be logical thinking to the client. In such cases, the client is considered to be the problem. The result is that clients and their support systems are negatively labeled based on cultural differences. The social worker can face negative labeling based on the past experiences of the client and client system. For example, a social worker may view the client as resistant and dysfunctional and the client may view the social worker as judgmental, remote, and unconcerned.

Minority and white clients sometimes feel that a worker of color is less effective than a white worker because they assume that the worker's training must have been inferior (Proctor and Davis, 1994). Therefore, minority workers often have to prove themselves to their clients:

> Social workers may wish that clients came to helping situations already accepting their competence. Yet workers may have to deliberately work toward a perception of their competence, particularly when perceptions are affected by societal based racial biases. (Proctor and Davis, 1994, p. 320)

Communication barriers are sometimes created because we are unaware of group differences in verbal and nonverbal communication. The following subsections provide illustrations of different communication patterns of people of color. These generalizations do not apply to all of the people all of the time, but rather illustrate some of the common patterns that are often labeled as "pathologic" rather than as cultural differences.

**African-American Communication Patterns**   This section specifically describes characteristics, values, and communication styles of African Americans and not all persons of African descent. Even though English is the spoken language of most African Americans, there are differences in use of words, meanings, pronunciation, interpretation, and thought processes between African Americans and white Americans. Since most African Americans are educated in Eurocentric schools, they tend to be bicultural. Most European Americans are not bicultural. They do not have to understand the African-American community or any other community of color unless they choose to do so.

The African-American communication style is based primarily on West African communication patterns. West Africa is where much of the slave trade originated. However, there are also influences from East Africa and other parts of the continent. Call and response (in which a speaker calls out to the audience, which responds in unison), the use of the verb *to be*, riddles, and expressive verbal and nonverbal language are typical (Asante, 1990; Kochman, 1981; Sue and Sue, 1990; Weber, 1994). Examples of expressive language are boasting, bragging, and "playing the dozens" (repeated teasing putdowns about family and heritage):

> That something of the African backgrounds of Black Americans survived in their speech is not difficult to argue despite the intense efforts to prove that Blacks were incapable of cultural retention because of slavery. However, no displaced people ever completely loses the forms of their previous culture.... It is in this sense that language in Afro-America is uniquely more African than European, other factors aside. (Asante, 1990, pp. 235–236)

African Americans often have trouble with work relationships because white workers feel threatened by their expressive manner of speech (Foreman and Pressley, 1987; Kochman, 1981). For example, an African-American male social worker was trying to get his point across to a white female supervisor. As his voice got louder and he increasingly used hand gestures to emphasize his point, the supervisor felt more threatened. Neither really heard the other. She ended up documenting the interaction to demonstrate the worker's instability. He ended up believing that his supervisor had not listened to him and had acted in a discriminatory manner because of his race. Differences in expression were interpreted as aggression rather than communication style. If differences are not understood between peers, they are unlikely to be understood between workers and clients.

African-American clients are often viewed as unresponsive if they do not look a worker directly in the eye when the worker is speaking. Even worse, clients are sometimes labeled as dishonest, deceitful, or having something to hide. The African-American style of eye contact conflicts with the Eurocentric expectation that people should look other people directly in the eye (Thomas and Hayman-El, 2000).

**Communication Patterns of First Nations Peoples (Native Americans, American Indians, Indians)**   Throughout this chapter the term *First Nations peoples* is used in discussing the indigenous population of the United States. The terms *Native American, American Indian,* and *Indian* are still commonly used, but for many they are deemed both inaccurate and oppressive (Yellow Bird, 1999) The First Nations population is very diverse, with more than 500 officially recognized tribes living on and off the reservations (Sutton and Broken Nose, 1996). Many of the members not living on reservations live in urban centers. Because there is so much diversity in terms of language, traditions, lifestyles, and treatment by the government, First Nations peoples are not really a single population group. However, there are a few communication characteristics that are common to most First Nations peoples.

The First Nations communication style is characterized by a more indirect, softer speech pattern than that of clients of European heritage. Individuals are less likely to use interjections or initiate conversation and tend to use longer periods of silence than most other population groups (Sue and Sue, 1990; Sutton and Broken Nose, 1996). They consider it impolite to look a speaker directly in the eye, especially an authority figure (Lewis and Ho, 1994).

Social workers are likely to seat themselves facing the client. They look a client straight in the eye and expect the client to look them in the eye. This can get in the way of developing a helping relationship:

> A Native American considers such behavior—covert or overt—to be rude and intimidating; contrary to the white man, he shows respect by not staring directly at others. Similarly, a worker who is excessively concerned with facilitating the display of inner feelings on the part of the client should be aware of another trait. A Native American client will not immediately wish to discuss other members of his family or talk about topics that he finds sensitive or distressing. . . the client—particularly the Native American—will test the

worker by bringing up peripheral matters. He does this in the hope of getting a better picture of how sincere, interested and trustworthy the worker actually is. (Lewis and Ho, 1994, p. 169)

Many of the questions social workers ask during initial interviews create barriers to developing helping relationships. First Nations peoples may be offended if questions about their personal lives are asked before a sense of trust has been established, and they may see the questioning as a sign of disrespect (Harper and Lantz, 1996). It is better to ease into interviews with general conversation and allow group members to construct their stories in their own way, rather than to ask direct questions.

**Latino-American and Hispanic Communication Patterns**    The term *Hispanic* generally is used to describe persons with Spanish ancestry, whereas *Latino* refers more to people who come from Latin American countries (Chong, 2002). Latino groups include Mexicans, Cubans, Puerto Ricans, Central and South Americans, Dominicans, and others. The communication styles of these various groups differ, and it is imperative to understand the unique attributes of each. Latino communication patterns are also influenced by whether the person was born in this country or migrated here from another country (Garcia-Preto, 1996).

In general, Latino groups approach interviews with social workers in a low-key manner, especially when dealing with authority figures. They are generally respectful of authority. They show this respect by not making eye contact, and they tend to respond to conversation rather than to initiate it (Sue and Sue, 1990). However, when speaking their first language in situations they find comfortable, they can appear quite animated (Morales and Sheafor, 1995)

The concept of personalismo, or interpersonal relationships, is important in Latino culture. **Personalismo** is a preference for face-to-face contact or a sense of personal attention. Latinos do not like feeling absorbed by bureaucratic institutions or being treated as cases or numbers (Chong, 2002; Rivera and Erlich, 1998).

This case points to the fact that we must be flexible in applying our training in cross-cultural situations. If something does not work in a particular situation, we must be willing to try something different and to follow the lead of the client and client system.

**Asian-American Communication Patterns**    This diverse group includes people who are Chinese, Japanese, Filipino, Pacific Islander, Vietnamese, Korean, Cambodian, Laotian, Hmong, Indian, Nepalese, and Tibetan, among many other nationalities. It is important to learn about the individual group with whom you are interacting.

The communication styles of Asian Americans are in many ways very similar to those of First Nations and Latino Americans (Sue and Sue, 1990). Often Asian Americans and Pacific Islanders are labeled "passive." Asian cultures emphasize the virtues of conforming, following rules, minimizing

## CASE 14.4 | THE NEW WORKER

When Ms. K. began working in a primarily Latino community center, she posted her hours of availability on the office door, had the information posted in the newsletter, and informed the center participants she met about her hours and the need to make appointments. She was annoyed when people stopped her in the hall, dropped by her office outside of the posted times, and expected her to be available to them. Although bilingual, Mrs. K. was not bicultural and did not understand that the concepts of time and personalismo were different for this population group. It took socialization and the patience of the center members before she was able to abandon her notions of proper client–worker interactions and boundaries, and build trust.

## CASE 14.5 | OUR WORST FEARS

Mr. N. is a 65-year-old Vietnamese refugee. He escaped with his wife and two oldest children through the jungle, avoided land mines, and made it to a refugee camp in Thailand at the end of the Vietnamese war. There, the family experienced brutal treatment. After six months, they were sent to the Philippines, where they were taught English by persons whose primary languages were Spanish and Filipino dialects. The family's education about the United States came from the media. This education gave them a distorted view of Americans, and African Americans in particular, who they learned to fear.

The family eventually came to the United States and settled in a black neighborhood in a southern city. They were assigned by the refugee resettlement agency to an African-American worker. The family could not understand the English spoken in this city and were afraid of the neighborhood and the caseworker.

Mr. S., the caseworker, approached this new situation with trepidation; he did not speak Vietnamese and knew nothing about the culture. In fact, he asked to be reassigned, but his request was not granted because the agency had no one who was any more knowledgeable than he. Before scheduling his first visit, Mr. S. found someone who could interpret the language and instruct him about acceptable behavior. The Vietnamese interpreter also connected the family with places to shop for Vietnamese food and a Buddhist Temple for worship. Mr. S. introduced the family to people in the neighborhood on whom they came to rely for many basic necessities.

Much later in the relationship, the younger family members shared with Mr. S. their fears of African Americans, the reasons for their difficulty in understanding the English that was being spoken around them, and their experience in coming to America. This helped the worker better understand the trauma that the family had faced and their resilience in being able to survive.

conflict, and promoting harmony (Morales and Sheafor (2002). Because problems are not discussed, this can cause the exclusion of Asian Americans from special programming because they are viewed as not needing assistance (Sue and Morishima, 1992).

Members of Asian and Pacific Island groups often view needing assistance as shameful (Sue and Morishima, 1992). It is important to understand the reluctance of this population to participate in the helping relationship. The worker must reframe issues in a positive way to help the client and family save "face" (Harper and Lantz, 1996).

# Value Differences

People of color have different values and belief systems than the majority population. In many ways, ethnocultural groups are more similar to each other than they are to the majority culture in the United States. Although people who are born and educated here learn Euro-American values, they also retain the values of their particular ethnic groups. Culture is ancient and lasting. Despite attempts at acculturation and assimilation, culture does not disappear. It adapts to fit the circumstances in which groups of people find themselves (Brandon, 1997). Table 14.1 compares the values of the majority culture with those of other ethnocultural groups. These are generalizations, and all group members do not necessarily espouse these beliefs.

Pinderhughes (1982) contrasted American and West African values. She noted sharp contrasts in beliefs about

- Individualism versus collectivity
- Ownership versus sharing
- Power versus obedience to authority
- Mastery of the environment versus spiritual communing with the environment
- Efficiency versus acceptance of fate
- Emphasis on youth, the future, and progress versus the past

Common values that hold Asian and Pacific Island groups together include group orientation encompassing family and family relationships, filial piety, respect for authority, self-control, and emphasis on educational achievement. Asian peoples also have a strong tradition of using shame to control behavior as well as a belief in the wisdom of the middle position (Chung, 1991; Min, 1995; Ross-Sheriff, 1991).

Latinos generally share a belief in fate, the importance of the family, and respect for age. They also show respect for socioeconomic position and authority and a preference for personalismo (Morales and Sheafor, 1995).

First Nations peoples are also oriented to the family and tribe. They value humility and modesty, have a nonmaterialistic view of the world, and hold values similar to those of Latinos concerning personal interaction (Attneave, 1969; Everett, Proctor, and Cartnell, 1983; Harper and Lantz, 1996; Jilek, 1982).

All of the different groups of color venerate elders. This contrasts sharply with the youth orientation of United States society. Respect is demonstrated through formal boundary systems. It is not acceptable to call adult clients by their first names unless given permission to do so. This is contrary to the American belief that being informal shows that one is friendly. For people of color, not using titles and surnames is a sign of disrespect. To call an African American only by his or her first name is viewed as a remnant of slavery.

**Spirituality**   The concept of spirituality goes beyond being religious or part of an organized religion, and even the belief in a higher being. It is a part of

TABLE 14.1 | VALUES COMPARISONS BETWEEN EURO-AMERICAN AND OTHER ETHNOCULTURAL GROUPS

| Euro-American Values | Values of Other Ethnocultural Groups |
| --- | --- |
| Mastery over Nature | Harmony with Nature |
| Personal Control Over the Environment | Fate |
| Doing—Activity | Being |
| Time Dominates | Personal Interaction Dominates |
| Human Equality | Hierarchy/Rank/Status |
| Individualism/Privacy | Group Welfare |
| Youth | Elders |
| Self-Help | Birthright inheritance |
| Competition | Cooperation |
| Future Orientation | Past or Present Orientation |
| Informality | Formality |
| Directness/Openness/Honesty | Indirectness/Ritual/"Face" |
| Practicality/Efficiency | Idealism |
| Materialism | Spiritualism |

Note: From *Towards a Culturally Competent System of Care* (Vol. II, p. 12), by M. R. Isaacs and M. P. Benjamin, 1991, Washington, DC: CAASP Technical Assistance Center—Center for Child Health and Mental Health Policy; based on *Strategies for Working with Culturally Diverse Communities and Clients*, by E. Randall-David, 1989, Washington, DC: Association for the Care of Children's Health.

the everyday life of many people of color. Spirituality is reflected in practices such as blessing food and calling on ancestors for guidance. Spiritual beliefs help people garner the strength needed to overcome adversity. People who have maintained a connection to their spiritual beliefs tend to be more satisfied with their lives than those who do not believe in a higher power (Coke, 1992; Martinez, 1988; Red Horse, 1982; Tooles-Walls and Zarit, 1991). When assessing the strengths and coping strategies of people of color, it is important to inquire about their spiritual beliefs, their involvement with religion, and whether they belong to an organized religion. This provides information not only about the source of their strength and guidance, but also about informal support that might be available to them.

We also need a basic understanding of the religious practices of people of color with whom we interact and how these practices influence our clients' behavior. For example, people of African descent may practice Christian religions but add African spiritual worship, such as Santeria, Voodoo, and other Yoruba-based religions (Black, 1996). Santeria and Espiritualism are also practiced in Cuba, Puerto Rico, and other islands with African, Spanish, and Indian influences (Brandon, 1997).

Many African and Asian people practice various forms of Islam. Islam is similar to Judeo-Christian religions in that it sees the individual as unique and responsible for his or her own actions (Smith, 1991). Confucianism plays a major role in the day-to-day lives of many Asian Americans of ethnic Chinese descent. Confucianism governs behavior, demands respect for authority, and teaches that the good of the whole is more important than personal beliefs (Philips, 1996; Smith, 1991). Hinduism has two basic tenets: karma (as you sow, so shall you reap) and reincarnation. The caste system is also a component of the Hindu way of life, but there have been attempts to end this system in India (Almeida, 1996; Smith, 1991). Buddhism is widely practiced by Asian Americans. Buddhists believe that an individual should seek nirvana or the highest point a human spirit can strive to attain (Smith, 1991). Taoism is noted for its emphasis on balance to enhance spiritual well-being. Practices such as acupuncture, herbal medicine, and the concepts of yin and yang emanate from Taoist beliefs (Philips, 1996; Smith, 1991).

You are not expected to learn all the tenets of each religious system. However, you must understand how religion and spirituality are intertwined with behavior, patterns of seeking help, health care, and family practices of clients. You are obligated to find out as much as possible about the religion or spiritual beliefs of clients. If your own beliefs were shaped by Judeo-Christian religions, you must be able to accept beliefs that run counter to your religious upbringing.

**Acceptance of Fate**   Practitioners often have a hard time accepting clients who do not act to improve their situation because they have accepted their fate. The American values of taking charge of one's life and individual responsibility run counter to the beliefs of many ethnocultural groups. Moving someone toward an action takes time, patience, and the development of trust. This is especially true in situations that have taken a long time to get to the point where social work intervention is needed.

The patience of First Nations peoples can be interpreted as lack of motivation and laziness. Their seeming inactivity contrasts with the "doing" nature of the American value system (Lewis and Ho, 1994). African Americans use phrases such as "Lord willing," "If God wanted me to do this," and "God only gives us as much as we can bear" to demonstrate their belief that their current situation will change when God is ready to change it. Sometimes practitioners can help people who believe in fate to understand that the actions they do or do not take in this life will affect the next life (Karnik and Suri, 1995; Philips, 1996).

Taking initiative and functioning autonomously are values of general American society. If they are not part of a client's belief system, negative labels often find their way into the assessment. Social work practice in a managed care environment requires practitioners to demonstrate their effectiveness in increasingly shorter time periods. Culturally competent practice, however, requires the opposite—slowing down and listening to the client's story to understand his or her perception of reality.

**Time**   In America, everything is fast. The world operates by appointments. This linear time runs counter to the concept of time used by people of color. People of color are often more focused on the present and the past than on the

## CASE 14.6 | THEY ARE NEVER THERE

Emily D., the social worker from a sectarian social service agency, had scheduled several appointments for the T. family, immigrants from Southeast Asia, to come to the office and discuss their need for alternate housing. The apartment building in which they lived was being sold, and they had to relocate. The family had arrived late for each appointment, and Emily had other appointments and did not see them. She scheduled a visit to their home, but when she arrived, they were out. Emily felt that she had given her best effort. She recommended closure, saying the family was "resistant to assistance." She felt that when the eviction was closer, they would be willing to accept help. The family, on the other hand, did not understand why they were not being helped. They have come to the agency several times, and no one has met with them. From their viewpoint, the agency and worker were not helpful, and the family did not know where to turn for help.

---

future. In some cultural groups, time is characterized as circular or tied to natural phenomena (Lewis and Ho, 1994). Social workers often resent people who show up late for appointments or are not home at a scheduled time. Clients and families do not like the fact that they cannot see workers whenever they wish, or that they have to plan their day around the time the worker wants to visit. The case example in Case 14.5 illustrates the conflict between different concepts of time.

In the following case, the agency wanted to help and the family wanted help. The barrier was the different values placed on time. Agencies and workers who wish to achieve a high level of cultural competency in a multicultural practice environment must be willing to expand their concept of time. Although agencies need to have set hours of operation, they must be flexible enough to respond to clients' time perceptions. Not doing so can be a major barrier to the delivery of services.

All communities of color have insider jokes about their concept of time and how it clashes with the dominant U.S. culture. Time is another concept about which communities of color are more similar to each other than they are to the majority culture. Social work practitioners who set long-range goals rather than attainable short-range goals will become frustrated in their attempts to push clients toward a future orientation.

## Working with Individuals and Families of Color

In working with people of color, if you are not a member of the group, you have a barrier to overcome. Because of the country's history of racism, the immigration experience of people of color, and the clash in cultures, practitioners and clients must educate one another and build a relationship before collaborative work can begin. U.S. history provides numerous examples of abuses of power, including the internment of the Japanese during World War II, the long history of African-American slavery, and the genocide of First

## CASE 14.7 | A CONFLICT OF ROLES

The P. family, who immigrated to the United States from India, have requested marital therapy. The family consists of a husband, wife, son, and daughter. The children both attend private school. The husband is a physician; the wife, a college professor. They are Hindu and of the Brahmin caste.

The husband's mother lives with the family and exerts a great deal of influence in the household. Although the daughter-in-law has tried to keep the peace by following the dictates of her husband's mother, she is having difficulty meeting everyone's expectations while still maintaining her own career. She helps with her husband's practice while also caring for her children and her mother-in-law. The wife has insisted that they seek outside help, but the husband is reluctant to participate. He has expressed shame about talking to an outsider about issues that should remain in the family. They have not discussed this with the mother-in-law.

Nations peoples and their subsequent segregation on reservations, so mistrust of authority by people of color should come as no surprise.

Although individuals of color do receive assistance through social work intervention, it is best to view practice with people of color from a collective rather than an individual perspective. The focus should be not only on the individual but also on the family systems, including extended family, immediate family, kinship networks, fictive kin (people considered nonblood relatives), and community organizations. The family has a major influence on whether an individual client will stay with the process. For example, many ethnocultural societies are male dominated. A worker may encourage a Latina client to be more assertive with her husband about her educational and work goals. But if the husband is not involved and does not support the wife's goals, the wife may feel torn between two cultures and leave treatment.

The households of people of color often are multigenerational, with extended family members living under the same roof or nearby. Because elder veneration is a value of every group of color in this country, elders have a great deal of influence over the middle and younger generations. This can cause tension in initial relationships and may cause some couples to seek social work help.

In the case described in Case 14.6, the worker must begin by learning about Indian culture. Some time needs to be spent allowing the wife to express her feelings of being trapped and to discuss the conflict between her role as prestigious and valuable college professor and her role as family member, where she does not feel valued by her husband and mother-in-law. The husband needs to be encouraged to discuss his feelings so he does not stop coming to subsequent sessions. At some point, there will need to be a discussion with the mother-in-law; she is key to the situation and must take part in family therapy for it to be effective. Involving the mother-in-law will take time, patience, and understanding of the cultural aspects of the situation.

## CASE 14.8 | MY HOME IS WITH MY FAMILY

Señora C. was born in Puerto Rico but has lived in the United States for 40 years. She lives in an urban area and speaks very little English. Her four children accompany her to places such as the Social Security office and the bank to help her transact business. She lives in a house with two of her children, their spouses, and five grandchildren. This home has only one bathroom and three bedrooms. It belongs to one of the children. Señora C. sleeps on a sofa bed in the living room.

The social worker has suggested that Señora C. relocate to senior citizen housing. Although Señora C. describes her situation as being "homeless with a home," she is reluctant to make changes. She is afraid that the family will abandon her if she leaves. She also fears that the family will suffer because she is the caretaker for the grandchildren after school. The family cannot afford to have another adult member leave a job to care for the children.

As social workers, we might push Señora C. to think of her own needs. But it is obvious that she cannot do so and that she will need time to weigh the positives and negatives of moving. Talking to the family to get their views and to gain their trust will be critical. Locating her as close to the family as possible is one solution. Another is helping the rest of the family work out alternative arrangements for child care and reviewing family income and expenses to determine whether they can afford to pay for child care. This case illustrates the importance of working with the entire family system instead of concentrating on the needs of the individual client.

In African-American, Asian, Latino, and First Nations cultures, life revolves around the family. People seek the guidance of their family before making major decisions. When help is needed, the family provides it. Families need to be helped to deal with the shame and guilt that is generated when they cannot provide needed assistance. The following guidelines, which were developed to use with Asian families, can be applied to work with other ethnic groups of color:

- When assessing Asian-American families, practitioners should gather information regarding specific families' ethnic backgrounds, languages, immigration and refugee experiences, acculturation levels, and community support systems.
- Attempt to maintain and, if appropriate, reestablish traditional family structures according to cultural norms. Respect the family hierarchy.
- Use extended family members for support systems; lines between nuclear families and extended families are not as rigid in Asian families as they are in Western culture.
- Allow families and their individual members opportunities to save face whenever possible.
- Avoid creating situations that may lead to conflict and confrontation. Rather, use indirect methods of communication, when appropriate, to make a point.

- Because Asians prefer to keep problems within the family, maintaining confidentiality is critical. Families must be assured that their problems will not become public knowledge.
- Service providers must be active and offer tangible interventions for Asian Americans. Passivity in the worker may be viewed as lack of expertise and authority. Many Asian-American families are seeking concrete, tangible solutions to their problems and are uncomfortable with process- and insight-oriented strategies. (Philips, 1996, p. 2)

Figure 14.1 illustrates assessment as a combination of inputs from the informal environment that affect individual factors, which in turn result in a response from formal systems. Informal inputs include the family and fictive kin or nonblood relatives as well as neighbors, friends, and community organizations such as religious institutions. These people and groups have their own knowledge and perceptions of formal services, and their views will influence whether individuals and their family systems engage in the helping process. Informal inputs have an effect on individual characteristics, which are shaped by such experiences as racism, immigration, and other biopsychosocial factors. The output is the formal response, which can be formal assistance the client is already using. The client may need to be connected to additional services or resources, or we may need to engage in resource mobilization to meet the identified needs. Many factors must be considered in conducting a comprehensive assessment of individuals and families of color.

## Group Work with People of Color

Although people of color are generally group centered, they are often reluctant to engage in therapeutic and support groups because they feel shame and do not want to talk to outsiders about problems. They are reluctant to trust the information they receive from social workers and may not readily understand the benefits of group approaches.

Group leaders should pay particular attention to the demographic composition of a group. Although there are no rules about how many people of color to have in a group, if is not a good idea to have only one category of persons (whether it is one gender, age, race, or physical ability).

People of color often cannot divorce themselves from the issue of race and racism. Therefore, the group leader, regardless of the purpose of the group, should raise the issue. Discussing race and racism may be initially difficult because of the volatility of such discussions (Davis, 1984). However, it is necessary for trust to develop and for the members to come together as a group.

Group leaders who work with groups of people of color must be willing to be active participants and to provide some information about themselves. The following are some suggestions for working with groups of African-American youth:

- Groups should not have a psychotherapeutic focus but rather should focus on the improvement of skills so members can function in society; in

FIGURE 14.1 | HOLISTIC ASSESSMENT

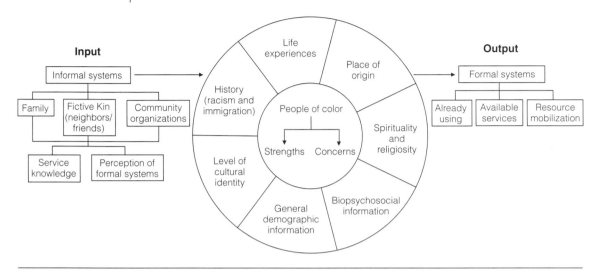

other words, groups should use action-oriented, not insight-oriented, techniques.

- Behavior in the group should be examined in terms of members' experiences in American society.
- Group leaders have to learn to deal with anger as well as be comfortable with the possibility that they may have to confront group members.
- Group leaders must be willing to self-disclose as well as understand the culture of members.
- The group leader is a role model who provides guidance and direction but should avoid telling people what to do.
- The group leader needs to be aware of nonverbal behavior as a component of communication patterns, including physical contact.
- Group workers must be prepared to be challenged before a relationship is established. (Brown, 1984, pp. 121–123)

The incorporation of culturally sensitive material as an integral part of the group process serves to help people of color recapture their past strengths and apply them to future situations (Harvey, 1997; Kunjufu, 1985). Groups that take members through rites of passage have helped African Americans of all ages gain a sense of self-esteem.

Group leaders can facilitate the success of groups with Latinos by understanding the natural support networks of the members and by being bilingual, if necessary, and bicultural (Delgado and Humm-Delgado, 1984). Being focused on the present rather than the past or the future and paying attention

| CASE 14.9 | YOU MAY BE BLACK, BUT YOU'RE FROM A DIFFERENT WORLD |
|---|---|

Ms. J., an African American, had never worked with high school students. She was assigned to work with a group of freshmen that would meet every week. The goal of the group was to prevent dropping out of school. At least 40 percent of freshmen did not complete high school. The group, made up entirely of African Americans, decided what areas they wanted to focus on. Because this was a morning group, breakfast was provided as an incentive to attend meetings.

These students described gang violence, police brutality, and sexual experiences that shocked Ms. J., whose life experiences were very different. When the students challenged her about her background and the expressions on her face when they talked about

events in their lives, Ms. J. felt free to talk about her own growing up, the generational differences between the students and herself, her feelings of being overwhelmed by their experiences, and her admiration of their strength in surmounting the obstacles.

Ms. J.'s self-disclosure provided the students with a view of the world that went beyond their neighborhoods. They learned that all African Americans are not the same, do not all live in the inner city, and do have the power to achieve. Ms. J. was then able to establish trust and serve as a role model for the young people in the group. All the group members finished high school, and one went on to a community college.

---

to location and access issues increase the likelihood that Latino clients will participate in the group. It is important to socialize the members about group rules, behavior, and self-disclosure.

In discussing group work with First Nations persons, Lewis and Ho (1994) emphasize the need for the leader to be bilingual and bicultural. They are pessimistic about obtaining positive results with First Nations persons in heterogeneous groups. Actions by the leader that call attention to lateness or silence may result in a member dropping out. Contrary to what was recommended for other groups of people of color, action-oriented steps are not a good idea.

The worker in the case described in Case 14.8 was not careful about her nonverbal behavior, and group members picked up on her discomfort about their self-disclosure and stories. As young people often will, they challenged her to engage them in a discussion about her own experiences. Once she did so, they were able to relate to her and trust her.

## Community Work with People of Color

When you begin work with a community with which you are unfamiliar, the first thing you and/or your organization needs to do is to become known. This takes time. Joining community groups as a member of an advisory committee or board member, going to community or public affairs meetings, meeting public officials, and volunteering for service all help you become known and trusted. Following through on your promises and commitments is necessary in building community relationships.

Doing outreach and program development in communities of color means being prepared to stay involved for a long period of time. Communities of color have been repeatedly studied and used for pilot programs, so much so that a great deal of distrust has developed among the residents of many communities. You need to be in it for the long run and have patience to engage in community work.

A Latino research center and a community mental health center designed an outreach project with the goal of increasing the use of mental health services by Puerto Rican clients. After three years, the use of outpatient mental health services increased and hospitalizations decreased. The outreach efforts had overcome cultural barriers to mental health service use (Vazquez, 1994). This experience emphasizes the need for long-term commitment. Programs that in the short run are viewed as failures may prove to be successful when measured over a long period of time. Another example is the Head Start program, which is one of the few surviving programs developed during the War On Poverty in the 1960s. Children participating in the program did benefit over time, even though initial program evaluations found no significant improvements (Johnson, 1998; Segal and Brzuzy, 1998).

In many ways, communities of color organize themselves to take care of their own needs because they are unable to access mainstream organizations and services. Communities of color have organized around societal injustice, such as inequality, economic and environmental injustice, community violence, and the current HIV and AIDS crises (Gutierrez et al., 1996).

To understand the functioning of a community and its support networks, you will need to become aware of community-based services provided by churches and other religious institutions, indigenous health care providers, and private organizations. Outsiders involved in organizing a community must be bicultural and bilingual or obtain the assistance of someone who can relate on a primary level to the members of the community (Rivera and Erlich, 1998). In order to avoid the mistakes made in the past, do not assume that all communities of color are identical and do not apply the same techniques to every community. The unique attributes of each population group and each community must be recognized and taken into consideration.

If the agency described in Case 14.9 is able to begin where the community is, it will honor their request for assistance. Once community members trust the agency, they may seek assistance in working on issues that are traditionally viewed as mental health issues. However, relieving the stress caused by not knowing English is the residents' primary concern.

Organization in communities of color requires getting to know key gatekeepers. These are people who can give legitimacy to your efforts or can put up roadblocks. Learning who has the power in the community and including those people in the process is critical for a community effort to succeed. To work effectively with communities, you must do the same things you do when working with smaller client systems. You must be patient and respectful, have some understanding of the culture, approach the work from a strengths per-

| CASE 14.10 | NO ONE CAME |
|---|---|

A local mental health agency wants to increase the numbers of Asian Americans who use its services. The Asian population has grown rapidly, but the agency still serves very few Asians. The first idea was to post flyers in the community to advertise the services. This did not get results, probably because the flyers were in English.

The program manager of the agency decided to put together a focus group and hold a meeting. Flyers were sent out to Asian community organizations that the agency had identified, but no one showed up the day of the meeting.

The program manager then contacted an Asian service provider who arranged the location of the meeting, printed signs in Chinese, and called every-

one who had indicated they would come to remind them of the meeting. The service provider also lined up several people to provide interpretation because the ethnic Chinese participants spoke different languages and dialects. On the day of the meeting, the provider met the focus group at the bus stop, provided Chinese pastries, and arranged for the agency to give each participant a small gift and monetary compensation. Although an agency official welcomed and thanked everyone for coming, the Asian community leader ran the focus group meeting. The agency expected the meeting to result in a list of issues to address, but the focus group participants' number one concern was learning English as a second language.

spective, enter the relationship as a partner, and remember that trust is earned, not automatically bestowed (Gutierrez et al., 1996).

## SUMMARY

All of us gravitate to people with whom we have something in common. It could be language, culture, field of employment, geographic origins, or other experiences. Likewise, people of color would like the social worker that engages with them to have a real understanding of their culture and experiences to increase the chances that a good relationship will develop. The reality is that most clients and workers are dissimilar in many ways, such as race, ethnicity, gender, sexual orientation, religion, age, and social class. In order for work to begin and progress, a relationship must develop that transcends differences. Unfortunately, barriers are all too often created in the initial meeting, and the result is that clients do not return to complete the social work process.

When social workers work with individuals, families, groups, or communities with whom they are unfamiliar, it is incumbent on them to learn as much as possible about the values, beliefs, and cultural traditions of the client system. We must suspend the notion that it is the client who has to adapt to the agency's method of providing service. Rather, we must learn to be flexible in our service delivery so that it fits the needs of the client group we are trying to engage.

In addition, we must continually explore who we are as cultural beings. We must learn our own history and culture in order to understand the importance of history and culture to others. It is very hard to walk in someone else's shoes unless we feel comfortable walking in our own shoes. As social workers, we must be open to the idea that each community of color has a uniqueness that cannot be ignored. The concept of the melting pot in the United States has never accurately depicted what happens to people who have come to this country.

Learning how to successfully work with people who are different from us takes considerable time and energy. It is not mastered by one or two training sessions or by reading the existing literature. It is a continuous learning process that, with commitment, can reap tremendous benefits for the clients, their community, and the social worker.

## CASE EXAMPLE

The final case example in this chapter took place at an Area Agency on Aging (Case 14.10). It illustrates culturally sensitive generalist practice and the importance of taking a client system's values and beliefs into consideration.

---

| CASE 14.11 | WE TAKE CARE OF OUR OWN |

Mrs. F. is 65 years of age and lives with her daughter, Miriam S. She came to this country from Cuba 20 years ago on a makeshift raft with her husband, 20-year-old son, and 18-year-old daughter. During the voyage, the raft capsized, and the son was lost at sea. Mrs. F.'s parents and siblings still reside in Cuba, and she has not seen them since she left. The F. family came to the United States because Mr. F. faced imprisonment because of his political views.

### Assessment

Mr. and Mrs. F. became U.S. citizens and owned a grocery store in a Cuban neighborhood in a large metropolitan area. The business was successful, but it closed when Mr. F. died of a heart attack 2 years ago when he was 68. He had no pension or life insurance. The proceeds from the sale of the business were invested in order to give Mrs. F. some financial security. Her only other income is from her husband's Social Security benefits.

Daughter Miriam persuaded Mrs. F. to sell her home and move in with her and her two daughters so that Mrs. F. would not be lonely and could stretch out her resources as long as possible. Mrs. F. went from a bustling urban Cuban neighborhood to a suburban area with no other Cuban families. The

move was stressful for both mother and daughter. For Mrs. F., it represented loss of independence, community, friends, and status. Miriam felt obligated to take her mother in, but at the same time was resentful.

Miriam is raising two children on her own. She was divorced right before her father's death. As devout Catholics, Miriam's parents fought bitterly with her about the divorce and the shame it would bring to the family. Miriam harbors guilt that she may have caused her father's heart attack.

The two granddaughters resent Mrs. F.'s coming to their home. They now have to share a bedroom. They see Grandma as overbearing and old-fashioned. She speaks to them in Spanish, a language they do not understand. They were not consulted about this change in living arrangements. They love and respect their grandmother but are embarrassed to introduce her to their friends, who are Caucasian and were born in this country.

Mrs. F. has chronic health problems for which she receives medical attention and takes medication. Her overall health is good, and she cares for herself with little assistance. Miriam describes her as having mood fluctuations from marked irritability to melancholia. Sometimes Mrs. F. will not accept telephone calls from her friends, who now live 45 minutes away. She does not go to church on a daily basis like she used to, even though the church is within walking distance. Mrs. F.'s own parents are in failing health in Cuba, and she sends money to help support them.

Miriam has talked about her home situation to her best friend, who is concerned that she is being pulled in too many directions and needs guidance. Miriam very reluctantly went to a family service agency to discuss her situation with a social worker.

### Intervention

At the initial meeting, the social worker let the daughter express her frustration about being the one in the middle and feeling guilty about her less-than-positive attitude about caring for her mother. The social worker was concerned about Miriam's level of stress. The worker convinced Miriam that the first course of action was to have an open discussion with all the household members to determine their views of the current living situation. Miriam wanted the meeting to take place in her home because she was convinced that her mother would never come to the agency, and the worker agreed.

It took several sessions before Mrs. F. and the children felt comfortable enough to express their honest feelings about the current living situation. Mrs. F. was feeling profound loss not only because of the move, but because she had not let herself grieve for the loss of her husband and because of her inability to care for her own parents. She no longer had access to the neighborhood support system that could relate to her past and present experiences. Miriam had her own guilt about her role as a parent and as a daughter. The teenage girls are experiencing their own issues of trying to fit in with their peers.

It was eventually decided that Mrs. F. would move to a small apartment in her old neighborhood. Miriam and the granddaughters would visit a few times a month, or more often if needed. Miriam and her children continued in therapy in order to help them adjust to the divorce and their own grief issues. Mrs. F. was reconnected with her church and community, and her spirits lifted.

### Termination

The worker terminated involvement with Mrs. F. after three months, when relocation was achieved and she was reestablished in her old community. The remaining family members stayed in therapy for an additional three months. Miriam and her children attend different support groups on the issues of divorce and grief.

---

## DISCUSSION QUESTIONS

1. Since Miriam S. has come to the agency reluctantly, what should the social worker do to develop the initial relationship (Case 14.10)? Assuming that the worker is not Cuban, what might he or she do before the interview to prepare for working with someone from another culture?

2. What additional interventions might be appropriate for Mrs. F after she moves back to her old neighborhood? Would reminiscence therapy be warranted? (For information on reminiscence therapy, see Dornat 1994.)

3. Miriam is sandwiched between two generations. How can the social worker help her discuss options within the cultural context of family obligation?

4. The family has experienced much grief and loss. What cultural strengths and coping skills might the social worker help Miriam and the rest of the family draw on?

5. What additional community resources might the social worker seek to provide the family with a support network? What additional options would you suggest for this family?

6. How has social work's approach to working with people of color changed over the history of the profession? In what ways has social work's approach mirrored the prevailing societal values?

7. How has racism affected people of color and their communities? How are racist beliefs institutionalized? How might generalist social workers combat institutional racism?

8. In what ways is the strengths model of practice similar to Afrocentric social work practice? In what ways is it different?

9. What are the major differences in communication style and values among African Americans, First Nations peoples, Latino Americans, Asian Americans, and Caucasian Americans?

# REFERENCES

Almeida, R. (1996). Hindu, Christian, and Muslim families. In M. McGoldrick, J. Giordano, and J. Pearce (Eds.), *Ethnicity and family therapy* (2nd ed., pp. 395–423). New York: Guilford.

Asante, M., (1990). The African essence in African-American language. In M. Asante and K. Asante. *African culture: The rhythms of unity* (pp. 233–252). Trenton, NJ: Africa World Press.

Asante, M. (1987). *The Afrocentric idea.* Philadelphia: Temple University Press.

Atkinson, D. R., Thomson, C. E., and Grant, S. K. (1993). A three-dimensional model for counseling racial/ethnic minorities. *The Counseling Psychologist, 21*, 257–277.

Attneave, C. (1969). Therapy in tribal settings and urban network intervention. *Family Process, 8*, 192–210.

Axinn, J., and Levin, H. (1997). *Social welfare: A history of the American response to need* (4th ed.). New York: Longman.

Baker, M. R., and Steiner, J. R. (1996). Solution-focused social work: Meta-messages to students in higher education opportunity programs. In P. L. Ewalt, E. M. Freeman, S. A. Kirk, and D. L. Poole (Eds.), *Multicultural issues in social work* (pp. 295–309). Washington, DC: NASW Press.

Barker, P. (1985). *Using metaphors in psychotherapy.* New York: Brunner Mazel.

Baynes, C. F. (Trans.). (1967). *I Ching.* Princeton, NJ: Princeton University Press.

Bibb, A., and Casimir, G. J. (1996). Haitian families. In M. McGoldrick, J. Giordano, and J. Pearce (Eds.), *Ethnicity and family therapy* (2nd ed., pp. 97–112). New York: Guilford.

Black, L. (1996). Families of African origin: An overview. In M. McGoldrick, J. Giordano, and J. Pearce (Eds.), *Ethnicity and family therapy* (2nd ed., pp. 57–65). New York: Guilford.

Boyd-Franklin, N. (1989). *Black families in therapy: A multisystems approach.* New York: Guilford.

Brandon, G. (1997). *Santeria from Africa to the New World: The dead sell memories.* Bloomington, IN: Indiana University Press.

Brown, J. A. (1984). Group work with low-income black youths. *Social Work with Groups, 7*(3), 111–124.

Chan, S. (1991). *Asian Americans: An interpretive history.* Boston: Twayne.

Charles, C. (1986). Mental health services for Haitians. In H. P. Lefley and P. B. Pederson (Eds.), *Cross-cultural training for mental health professionals* (pp. 183–198). Springfield, IL: Thomas.

Chong, N. (2002). *The Latino patient: A cultural guide for health care providers.* Yarmouth, ME: Intercultural Press.

Chung, D. (1991). Asian cultural commonalties: A comparison with mainstream American culture. In S. Furuto, R. Biswas, D. Chung, and F. Ross-Sheriff (Eds.), *Social work practice with Asian Americans* (pp. 27–44). Newbury Park, CA: Sage.

Coke, M. (1992). Correlates of life satisfaction among elderly African-Americans. *Journal of Gerontology, 47*(5), 316–320.

Cox, Mathew, and Associates, Inc. (2002). Black, Hispanic admissions up at University of California law, medical schools. *Black Issues in Higher Education 19*(19), 17.

Cross, T. L., Bazron, B. J., Dennis, K. W., and Isaacs, M. R. (1989). *Towards a culturally competent system of care: A monograph on effective services for minority children who are severely emotionally disturbed* (Volume 1). Washington, DC: Georgetown University Child Development Center, CAASP Technical Assistance Center.

Cuellar, I., Harris, L. C., and Jasso, R. (1980). An acculturation scale for Mexican American normal and clinical populations. *Hispanic Journal of Behavior Sciences, 2,* 199–217.

Davis, L. E. (1984). Essential components of group work with black Americans. *Social Work with Groups, 7*(3), 97–109.

Day, P. J. (1989). *A new history of social welfare.* Englewood Cliffs, NJ: Prentice-Hall.

De Jong, P., and Miller, S. (1995). How to interview for client strengths. *Social Work, 40*(6), 729–736.

Delgado, M., and Humm-Delgado, D. (1984). Hispanics and group work: A review of the literature. *Social Work with Groups, 7*(3), 85–95.

de Shazer, S. (1988). *Clues: Investigating solutions in brief therapy.* New York: Norton.

de Shazer, S. (1985). *Keys to solution in brief therapy.* New York: Norton.

Devore, W., and Schlesinger, E. G. (1999). *Ethnic-sensitive social work practice* (5th ed.). Needham Heights, MA: Allyn and Bacon.

Dornat, J. (Ed.), (1994). *Reminiscence reviewed: Perspectives, evalauton, achievements.* London: Taylor and Francis.

Ehrenreich, J. H. (1985). *The altruistic imagination: A history of social work and social policy in the United States.* Ithaca, NY: Cornell University Press.

Everett, F., Proctor, N., and Cartnell, B. (1983). Providing psychological services to American Indian children and families. *Professional Psychology, 14,* 588–603.

Fong, R., and Mokuau, N. (1996). Not simply "Asian Americans": Periodical literature on Asians and Pacific Islanders. In P. Ewalt, E. Freeman, S. Kirk, and D. Poole (Eds.), *Multicultural issues in social work* (pp. 269–281). Washington, DC: NASW Press.

Foreman, A. K., and Pressley, G. (1987). Ethnic culture and corporate culture: Using black styles in organizations. *Communication Quarterly, 35*(4), 293–307.

Freeman, E. (1990). Theoretical perspectives for practice with black families. In Logan, S., Freeman, E., and McRoy, R. *Social work practice with black families: A culturally specific perspective* (pp. 38–52). White Plains, NY: Longman.

Garcia-Preto, N. (1996). Latino families: An overview. In M. McGoldrick, J. Giordano, and J. Pearce (Eds.), *Ethnicity and family therapy* (2nd ed., 141–154). New York: Guilford.

Goldstein, H. (1990). The knowledge base of social work practice: Theory, wisdom, analogue, or art? *Families in*

*Society: The Journal of Contemporary Human Services, 71*(1), 32–43.

Gutierrez, L., Alvarez, A., Nemon, H., and Lewis, E. A. (1996). Multicultural community organizing: A strategy for change. *Social Work, 41*(5), 501–507.

Hardy, K. V. (1989). The theoretical myth of sameness: A critical issue in family therapy training and treatment. In G. E. Saba, B. M. Karrer, and K. V. Hardy (Eds.), *Minorities and family therapy* (pp. 17–33). New York: Haworth.

Harper, K. V., and Lantz, J. (1996). *Cross-cultural practice: Social work with diverse populations.* Chicago: Lyceum.

Harvey, A. (1997). Group work with African-American youth in the criminal justice system: A culturally competent model. In G. Grief and P. Ephross (1997). *Group work with populations at risk* (pp. 160–174). New York: Oxford University Press.

Hawkins, B. D. (1997). "Hostile environments": Reducing applications to medical schools nationwide. *Black Issues in Higher Education, 14*(20), 18–20.

Ivey, A. (1981). Counseling and psychotherapy: Toward a new perspective. In A. J. Marsella and P. Pedersen (Eds.), *Cross-cultural counseling and psychotherapy* (pp. 279–311). New York: Pergamon.

Jilek, W. (1982). *Indian healing: Shamanic ceremonialism in the Pacific Northwest today.* Laine: Hancock House.

Johnson, H. (1998). Public welfare and income maintenance. In H. Johnson (Ed.), *The social services: An introduction* (5th ed., pp. 45–74). Itasca, IL: F. E. Peacock Publishing, Inc.

Karger, J., and Stoesz, D. (1998). *American social welfare policy: A pluralist approach* (3rd ed.). New York: Longman.

Karnik, S., and Suri, K. (1995). The law of karma and social work considerations. *International Social Work, 38*, 365–377.

Kochman, T. (1981). *Black and white styles in conflict.* Chicago: University of Chicago Press.

Kunjufu, J. (1985). *Countering the conspiracy to destroy black boys* (Vol. II). Chicago: African-American Images.

Lewis, R. G., and Ho, M. K. (1994). Social work with Native Americans. In B. Compton and B. Galaway, *Social work processes* (pp. 167–172). Pacific Grove, CA: Brooks/Cole.

Locke, M. (1998, April). California's Proposition 209 takes effect: Minority admissions plummet. *The Associated Press News Service.*

Lorde, A. (1995). Age, race, class and sex: Women redefining difference. In M. Andersen and P. Collins (Eds.), *Race, class, and gender: An anthology* (2nd ed., pp. 532–540). Belmont, CA: Wadsworth.

Lum, D. (1996). *Social work practice and people of color: A process-stage approach.* Pacific Grove, CA: Brooks/Cole.

Marimba, A. (1994). *Yorugu: An Afrocentric critique of European cultural thought and behavior.* Trenton, NJ: Africa Free World Press.

Marin, G., and Marin, B. (1991). *Research with Hispanic populations.* Newbury Park, CA: Sage.

Martinez, C. (1988). Mexican-Americans. In L. Comas-Diaz and E. E. H. Griffith (Eds.), *Clinical guidelines in cross-cultural mental health* (pp. 182–203). New York: Wiley.

Maslow, A. H. (1968). *Toward a psychology of being.* New York: Van Nostrand.

Min, P. G. (Ed.). (1995). *Asian Americans: Contemporary trends and issues.* Thousand Oaks, CA: Sage.

Morales, A. T., and Sheafor, B. W. (2002). *The many faces of social work clients.* Boston: Allyn and Bacon.

Morales, A. T., and Sheafor, B. W. (1995). *Social work: A profession of many faces* (7th ed.). Boston: Allyn and Bacon.

O'Hanlon, W. H., and Weiner-Davis, M. (1989). *In search of solutions: A new direction in psychotherapy.* New York: Norton.

Patterson, O. (1995, August 9). Affirmative action on the merit system. *New York Times,* p. 13.

Perlman, H. (1957). *Social casework: A problem solving process.* Chicago: University of Chicago Press.

Philips, W. (1996). Understanding Asian family values. *Children's Voice—Child Welfare League of America, 6*(2), 1–2.

Pinderhughes, E. (1982). Family functioning of Afro-Americans. *Social Work, 27*(1), 91–98.

Pinderhughes, E. (1989). *Understanding race, ethnicity, and power: The key to efficacy in clinical practice.* New York: Free Press.

Proctor, B. D., and Dalaker, J. (Sept., 2002). *Current population reports, P60–219, Poverty in the United States: 2001.* Washington DC: U.S. Government Printing Office.

Proctor, E. K., and Davis, L. E. (1994). The challenge of racial difference: Skills for clinical practice. *Social Work, 39*(3), 314–323.

Red Horse, J. (1982). Clinical strategies for American Indian families in crisis. *Urban and Social Change Review, 15*(2), 17–19.

Reid, W. J. (1986). Task-centered social work. In F. J. Turner (Ed.), *Social work treatment* (3rd ed., pp. 267–295). New York: The Free Press.

Reid, W. J., and Epstein, L. (1972). *Task-centered casework.* New York: Columbia University Press.

Rivera, F. G., and Erlich, J. L. (1998). *Community organizing in a diverse society* (3rd ed.). Boston: Allyn and Bacon.

Roberson, E. (1995). *The Maafa and beyond: Remembrance, ancestral connectedness and nation building for the African global community.* Columbia, MD: Kujichagulia Press.

Roberts, J. M. (1964). The self-management of cultures. In W. H. Goodenough (Ed.), *Explorations in cultural anthropology* (pp. 433–454). New York: McGraw Hill.

Ross-Sheriff, F. (1991). Adaptation and integration into American society: Major issues affecting Asian Americans. In S. M. Furoto, R. Biswas, D. K. Chung, K. Murase, and F. Ross-Sheriff (Eds.), *Social work practice with Asian Americans* (pp. 45–64). Newbury Park, CA: Sage.

Ryan, W. (1976). *Blaming the victim.* New York: Vintage.

Saleebey, D. (1994). Culture, theory, and narrative: The intersection of meanings in practice. *Social Work, 39*(4), 352–361.

Saleebey, D. (1992). Introduction: Power in the people. In D. Saleebey (Ed.), *The strengths perspective in social work practice.* New York: Longman.

Samovar, L. A., and Porter, R. E. (1994). Intercultural communication: An introduction. In L. A. Samovar and R. E. Porter (Eds.), *Intercultural communication: A reader* (7th ed., pp. 4–36). Belmont: Wadsworth.

See, L. A. (Ed.). (1998). *Human behavior in the social environment from an African-American perspective.* New York: Haworth.

Segal, E., and Brzuzy, S. (1998). *Social welfare policy, programs and practice.* Itasca, IL: F.E. Peacock Publishing, Inc.

Smith, J. (1991). *The world's religions.* San Francisco: Harper.

Sue, D. W., and Sue, D. (1990). *Counseling the culturally different: Theory and practice* (2nd ed.). New York: Wiley.

Sue, S., and Morishima, J. K. (1989). *The mental health of Asian Americans*. San Francisco: Jossey-Bass.

Suinn, R. M., Rickard-Figuerora, D., Lew, S., and Vigil, P. (1987). The Suinn-Lew Asian self-identity acculturation scale: An initial report. *Educational and Psychological Measurement, 7*, 401–417.

Sutton, C. T., and Broken Nose, M. A. (1996). American Indian families: An overview. In M. McGoldrick, J. Giordano, and J. Pearce (Eds.), *Ethnicity and family therapy* (2nd ed., pp. 31–44). New York: Guilford.

Thomas, N., and Hayman-El, L. (2000). Cultural identity and African-American elderly: Implications for practice. Unpublished manuscript.

Tooles-Walls, C., and Zarit, S. (1991). Informal support from black churches and the well-being of elderly blacks. *The Gerontologist, 31*(4), 490–495.

Trattner, W. I. (1999). *From poor law to welfare state: A history of social welfare in America* (6th ed.). New York: Free Press.

U.S. Bureau of the Census (2000). *Projections of the resident population by race, Hispanic origin, and Nativity: Middle series, 2006–2110*. Washington DC: Census Bureau, Population Projections Program, Population Division.

U.S. Bureau of the Census. (2002). *Statistical abstract of the United States*. Washington DC: Census Bureau, Administrative and Customer Services Division. Statistical Compendia Branch.

Vazquez, R. G. (1994). *A study of program efforts to facilitate access and increase the utilization of community mental health services by Puerto Rican/Hispanic clients*. Unpublished doctoral dissertation, Hunter College.

Velasquez, J., Vigil, M., and Benavides, E. (1994). A framework for establishing social work relationships across racial/ethnic lines. In B. Compton and B. Galaway (Eds.), *Social work processes* (pp. 172–176). Pacific Grove, CA: Brooks/Cole.

Weber, S. N. (1994). The need to be: The socio-cultural significance of black language. In L. A. Samovar and R. E. Porter (Eds.), *Intercultural communication: A reader* (7th ed., pp. 221–225). Belmont, CA: Wadsworth.

Wehrly, B. (1995). *Pathways to multicultural counseling competence: A developmental journey*. Pacific Grove, CA: Brooks/Cole.

Whan, M.W. (1979). Accounts, narrative, and case history. *British Journal of Social Work, 9*, 489–499.

Whittler, T. E. Calantone, R. J., and Young, M. R. (1990). Strength of ethnic affiliation: Examining black identification with black culture. *The Journal of Social Psychology, 131*(4), 461–467.

Wilkinson, C. B., and Spurlock, J. (1986). The mental health of black Americans: Psychiatric diagnosis and treatment. In C. B. Wilkinson (Ed.). *Ethnic psychiatry* (pp. 13–59). New York: Plenum.

Wilson, W. J. (1980). *The declining significance of race: Blacks and changing American institutions*. Chicago: University of Chicago Press.

Yamamoto, J. (1986). Therapy for Asian Americans and Pacific Islanders. In C.B. Wilkinson (Ed.), *Ethnic psychiatry* (pp. 89–141). New York: Plenum.

Yellow Bird, M. (1999). Indian, American Indian and Native Americans: Counterfeit identities. *Winds of Change: A Magazine for American Indian Education and Opportunity, 14*(1), 86.

# GENERALIST PRACTICE WITH ABUSED AND NEGLECTED CHILDREN AND THEIR FAMILIES

*Martha Morrison Dore and Nancy Feldman*

Ricki M. is a senior BSW student who has a field placement with the county child protective services agency. Ricki is assigned to the unit that provides children and families with services in their own homes, the SCOH unit (Services to Children in Own Homes). SCOH services are designed to keep families together and to prevent the placement of children in foster care. Ricki is nervous about having to visit families in their own homes and about being able to develop helping relationships with involuntary clients. Her first visit is scheduled with Ms. J. and her 10-year-old daughter, Shanai, both of whom have diabetes. SCOH services are involved because of Ms. J.'s neglect of Shanai's medical condition.

In preparing for the home visit, Ricki researched diabetes. She also reviewed the family's case record and found that other workers had been relatively unsuccessful in getting Ms. J. to recognize the seriousness of the disease and to follow the recommendations for the care of her daughter. Ms. J. continually failed to keep Shanai's medical appointments, to follow up on scheduled tests, and to get Shanai to follow the prescribed diet. Ricki was perplexed. Why was Ms. J. unconcerned about her own and her daughter's health? Why was she unwilling to do what was expected of her in terms of caring for Shanai? Ricki wondered how to approach her work with Ms. J. What could she do that might be more effective? How could she develop a helping relationship with Ms. J?

This chapter presents information that a generalist practitioner needs to work effectively with families and children where there are issues of abuse and neglect. We first present an overview of the history of care for abused and neglected children in the United States, followed by a review of current public policy issues that define the delivery of services to this population. Next we discuss the causes of child abuse and neglect and the effect on the psychosocial functioning of the child. We also look briefly at the long-term effects of childhood abuse and its implications for perpetuating an intergenerational cycle of child maltreatment. The remainder of the chapter focuses on practice with families with issues of child abuse and neglect. We discuss developing a helping relationship with such families, particularly with parents who are often frightened and unresponsive to the offer of help from the generalist social worker. By becoming informed about the multiple factors that contribute to the maltreatment of children and the variety of effective interventions with such families and children, generalist social workers who find themselves confronted with these vulnerable families can see their strengths and build on them for the safety and benefit of the children. By the end of this chapter, you should be able to help Ricki

- Describe how the response to child abuse and neglect has changed over time
- Identify the current policy issues related to the prevention of child maltreatment and the care of abused and neglected children
- Understand the causes and consequences of child maltreatment

- Identify special issues in developing helping relationships with abusive and neglectful families
- Describe the types of interventions available for families dealing with child abuse and neglect

## SOCIAL RESPONSES TO CHILD MALTREATMENT

Child maltreatment is a pervasive social problem in this country. Each year, three million reports of suspected child abuse or neglect are filed with state and county **child protective services (CPS)**. About half of these reports are for neglect, a quarter for physical abuse, and a quarter for sexual, psychological, and other forms of abuse. Reports of suspected child maltreatment have tripled in the last 20 years, primarily because of better systems of reporting (Center for the Future of Children, 1998).

What makes parents and other caregivers abuse and neglect the children they are supposed to love and cherish? That question has been studied by generations of thoughtful people committed to the health and well-being of children. Not so long ago, it was believed that such behavior occurred only in immigrant families and among the poor. We know now that the maltreatment of children occurs at all levels of society and among all ethnic and racial groups. Certain factors make the risk of child abuse and neglect more likely, though not inevitable. These risk factors include poverty, unemployment, single parenthood, adolescent parenthood, parental mental illness, parental substance abuse, and low educational attainment by parents, and they combine to heighten stress in families. These stressors may push parents or caregivers into acting in ways that are characterized by society and experienced by children as abusive and neglectful.

As our beliefs about child development and our understanding of the role of children in society have changed, so too has our definition of and response to child abuse and neglect. Prior to the late 1800s, community authorities were primarily concerned with child neglect. Abuse of children was not an issue of social concern until the latter part of the nineteenth century.

## CARING FOR NEGLECTED CHILDREN

In the earliest years of this country's settlement, all hands were needed to ensure the survival of the family and the community. Children were expected to contribute in concrete ways from the time they were very young. Few families could afford to educate their children or otherwise provide them with the kind of freedom from work and want that many children experience today. In most families, a child of 6 or 7 was expected to work alongside his or her parent of the same sex, farming, engaging in a trade, or maintaining the household. Families could little afford special activities to ensure optimal growth and development. The early colonial settlers were primarily Protestants, whose religious beliefs viewed children as fundamentally flawed from birth and held parents responsible for breaking children's will through severe discipline and hard work.

In colonial times, when parents abandoned a child or when death or disability meant they were unable to adequately care for a child, community elders stepped in without hesitation. Children were most often placed with another family, who would agree to care for the child in return for the child's labor. Occasionally, in the best of situations, the new family would agree to teach the child a trade. These placements were not monitored, and no thought was given to the emotional or developmental needs of the child, only to providing for his or her survival. Alternatively, some communities built almshouses or workhouses for all indigent people, including mentally ill, mentally retarded, and aged persons, as well as children without resources. These facilities usually included a work program, often a farm, where children as young as 4 years of age labored for their keep.

As the population increased, particularly in larger cities, it became difficult to place all children without adequate support in families. During the late 1700s and early 1800s, concerned individuals of economic means founded orphanages to care for such children. Children whose parents could not afford to care for them and children deamed neglected by the authorities could be placed in these institutions. There was a similar trend toward institutional care in Europe during this time, sparked by the work of Catholic nuns, who often cared for dependent children in their convents. Indeed, the first children's institution in this country was founded by Catholic nuns in New Orleans in 1727. Its purpose was to care for children orphaned in an epidemic.

Most children's institutions founded in the beginning half of the nineteenth century were either secular or Protestant in origin. Not until the first large wave of Irish immigrants began arriving at midcentury did Catholic institutions begin appearing in any numbers. This reflected a growing concern among Catholics that Protestant child rescue organizations were taking in large numbers of Catholic children and converting them. Similarly, Jewish children's homes were established in large cities after the Civil War. By 1880, there were more than 600 orphanages nationally, caring for more than 50,000 children. Thirty years later, the number of children's institutions as well as the number of residents had nearly doubled (Smith, 1995).

The popular term for children living in orphanages and other children's homes during this period was "dependent and neglected." Most were not really orphans. The typical resident had one living parent who was unable to care for him or her financially and so placed the child in the care of others, contributing a small amount weekly to the child's upkeep. These were usually widowed or abandoned mothers for whom gainful employment was limited and day care nonexistent. In a 1902 book entitled *The Care of Destitute, Neglected, and Delinquent Children*, Homer Folks described conditions in orphanages as ranging from adequate to deplorable. He was particularly hard on communities that placed children in almshouses, painting a grim picture of life among adults with psychotic disorders, mental disabilities, severe physical impairments, and other debilitating conditions.

Although care for dependent and neglected children in congregate institutions became widespread in the second half of the nineteenth century, placement of children in the homes of unrelated families was still the preferred form of care in some communities. The Boston Children's Aid Society championed the use of substitute family care for children whose parents were unable to care for them, and its director was an outspoken opponent of institutional placement of children. Massachusetts agencies began experimenting with paying foster families in the late 1880s, thereby insuring that the younger children would not have to work for their keep (Tyor and Zainaldin, 1979).

One noteworthy program was that of the Children's Aid Society of New York, whose director argued that institutional care could not adequately prepare children to fulfill their social and community roles (Brace, 1880). Instead, he advocated putting children from the streets of New York aboard trains headed west and placing them in rural homes along the way:

> Children chosen to be placed out were considered orphaned, homeless, abandoned, dependent, or neglected. In reality, only a few were orphans, and many others had at least one living parent and housing of some sort. Unless children were actual orphans, parents were required to give their permission for the child's participation in the placement program. Children who were thought to be incorrigible, who appeared to be sickly, or who were physically or mentally handicapped were generally not accepted for participation (Cook, 1995, p. 183).

As the orphan trains wended their way west, crowds would gather at each station stop along the way in response to advance notices posted by Children's Aid Society agents. The children were arrayed along the train platform. Farmers who wanted an extra hand in the fields or farmer's wives who needed help in the kitchen would step forward to claim an appropriate candidate (Wheeler, 1983). Approximately 150,000 dependent and neglected children were placed this way between 1854 and 1930 (Cook, 1995).

Services to children of color were provided outside mainstream child welfare practice. As with other social services for African Americans, services for dependent and neglected African-American children were provided by churches and other voluntary and benevolent associations, particularly those organized by women of color (Billingsley and Giovannoni, 1972). The National Association of Colored Women, founded in 1896 and representing African-American clubwomen nationally, led the way in calling for its member organizations to respond to the needs of vulnerable children. One response was the Virginia Industrial School for Girls, founded by the Virginia Federation of Colored Women's Clubs in 1915 to care for dependent and delinquent African-American girls (Peebles-Wilkins, 1995). Other responses were more personal. For example, Carrie Steele Pitts, a woman of color who worked as a maid at the Atlanta Railroad Station, founded an institution in 1888 to care for the infants and young children she found abandoned there (Peebles-Wilkins, 1995).

# THE DISCOVERY OF CHILD ABUSE

Not until the second half of the nineteenth century was child abuse widely recognized as a separate issue that warranted active intervention in the private lives of families (Hacsi, 1995). Until this time, children did not have rights separate from those of their parents (actually, those of their fathers, since women had few legal rights independent of their husbands and fathers). Children were the property of their fathers, and a father could treat a child just about any way he wanted without fear of community intervention. There was more public concern about cruelty to animals than about cruelty to children.

In 1885, the American Humane Association (AHA), which had been founded as a federation of animal rescue groups, took on the cause of child rescue as well. Children were removed from situations determined to be dangerous to their well-being by AHA agents and placed in institutions or foster homes. The New York Society for the Prevention of Cruelty to Children was the first separate organization solely for the protection of children. By the early twentieth century, there were more than 300 Societies for the Prevention of Cruelty to Children across the United States, all under the purview of the AHA (Schene, 1998). These anticruelty societies acted as private policing agencies, with little regard for or interest in understanding family circumstances or dynamics; neither did they provide services to preserve families. Needless to say, they were viewed suspiciously and with some disdain by those in the newly emerging social work profession who were involved in **child helping,** as child welfare work was called in its early years.

Efforts to integrate child rescue with other approaches to child helping were met with intractable resistance by members of the AHA. Eventually, some progressive AHA member agencies split off from the organization and joined with other child-helping agencies to form the Child Welfare League of America (CWLA) in 1921. Its membership primarily included orphanages, child-placing agencies, and industrial schools (Anderson, 1989). These agencies viewed their work as child protection rather than child rescue. They defined child protection as a range of activities designed to prevent all forms of maltreatment:

> Child protection is a specialized service in the field of child welfare on behalf of children suffering from cruelty or abuse; or whose physical, mental or moral welfare is endangered through the neglect of their parents or custodians; or whose rights or welfare are violated or threatened. (Theodore Lothrop, quoted in Anderson, 1989, p. 231)

The difference between child rescue and child protection was more in quality than in kind. Those in the child protection movement identified less as policemen and more as social workers. Although they did remove children from situations of abuse and neglect, they often tried to work preventively with families to address problems that led to maltreatment of children. These usually had to do with poverty and unemployment or with alcoholism. Those in the child protection movement also gave more thought to the needs of the child and tried to find the most suitable placement rather than the most expedient one. Most believed that the birth family was really the best place for a child.

## CHILD PROTECTION IN THE TWENTIETH CENTURY

The Social Security Act of 1935 provided grants to rural communities that lacked privately funded children's services to establish public child welfare services, including child protection. Before public child welfare agencies were established under the Social Security Act, child protection was mostly in the hands of private child welfare agencies and the police. There was little public or legal oversight. By the 1940s, several states were using public child welfare agencies to provide child protection. However, it was not until 1956, when Congress passed the Home Life Amendment to the Social Security Act, that federal funding became available to establish public child protective services in all communities, rural and urban.

The 1935 Social Security Act also had a significant effect on the use of large congregate institutions for caring for dependent and neglected children. By providing universal entitlement to Aid to Dependent Children (later renamed Aid to Families with Dependent Children, or AFDC), the law allowed single parents who previously might have placed their children in care because they were unable to support them financially to receive public assistance to care for them at home. States expanded their use of foster homes as the preferred method of out-of-home care for children who could not remain with their biological families (Hacsi, 1995).

In the 1950s, radiologists who looked at x-rays of children's bones began to notice a pattern of numerous poorly mended fractures in some children. In discussing this phenomenon at professional meetings, these doctors realized they were seeing evidence of ongoing physical abuse of children. A widely noticed article published in 1962 in the *Journal of the American Medical Association* exposed these findings (Kempe et al., 1962) and heightened awareness of the prevalence of child abuse. The result was the passage in all states of laws requiring the mandatory reporting of child abuse by physicians and medical personnel as well as teachers, social workers, and other professionals who became aware of possible maltreatment of children by their parents or caretakers.

The 1950s and 1960s also saw a movement to close large congregate care facilities of all types and to substitute community-based care. This movement, which began in the field of institutional care for adults with mental illness and mental retardation, eventually resulted in the closing of many large congregate care institutions for children and adolescents as well.

In 1974, Congress passed the Child Abuse Prevention and Treatment Act (CAPTA). It provided federal funds to states to treat families identified as abusive and neglectful toward their children. It was the first federal recognition of the pervasive national problem of child abuse. It grew directly out of efforts by the American Humane Association and other advocates for maltreated children. CAPTA provided support for state reporting systems and increased the funds available to states for treating victims of child abuse and neglect.

Recognition of child maltreatment as an issue of national significance led to a call for more attention to prevention. In 1991, the U.S. Advisory Board on Child Abuse and Neglect recommended implementation of a national program of home visits to families of newborns to educate parents about infant care and to identify and target potentially vulnerable families for ongoing services (U.S. Advisory Board on Child Abuse and Neglect, 1991). Hawaii's successful Healthy Start program was the model for this initiative. The following year, the National Committee to Prevent Child Abuse began a nationwide campaign to develop prevention and early intervention services in all states. By 1996, 150 programs in which nurses, teachers, or social workers made home visits were in operation in 28 states and appeared likely to reduce the incidence of child maltreatment (Guterman, 1997).

Between 1974 and 1978, a subcommittee of the U.S. Senate held a series of hearings regarding placement of Native American children in families of other ethnocultural groups for foster care and adoption. In response to this committee's findings, Congress passed the Indian Child Welfare Act, which granted decision-making powers on child welfare issues to tribal authorities (Mannes, 1995). The act represents an important recognition of the hegemony of a minority group over the welfare of its own members.

Studies of foster care carried out in the 1960s and 1970s highlighted the lack of attention paid to planning for permanent futures for children in placement (Fanshel, 1971; Fanshel and Shinn, 1976). Many children seemed to drift for years in foster care, lost in a system that could only react to the next crisis. Little effort was made to ensure that families remained connected with their children and that they were working to address the problems that contributed to the removal of their children from home (Jenkins and Norman, 1975).

The publication in 1973 of *Beyond the Best Interests of the Child* (Goldstein, Solnit, and Freud) called public attention to the significance of psychological parenting in a child's life, that is, the importance of primary attachment. The **primary attachment figure** is usually a birth parent but may also be a grandparent, older sibling, foster parent, or adoptive parent. Goldstein and his colleagues stressed the importance of preserving these relational ties and called attention to the fact that a brief period of time in an adult's life is an essential period in a child's developmental time. So, for example, a child who is placed in foster care for six months or a year has often begun to form strong attachments to his or her foster parents. To move the child to a series of foster homes inhibits the formation of these important ties and may make it impossible for the child to form lasting attachments. Goldstein and his colleagues, all psychotherapists, were responding to a child welfare system that placed children in out-of-home care with little thought to the importance of psychological parenting. The effect of *Beyond the Best Interests of the Child* on child welfare policy was significant, particularly with regard to providing a theoretical basis for permanency planning.

The Adoption Assistance and Child Welfare Act of 1980, or P.L. 96-272 as it was popularly known, called on state and local child welfare agencies to review the status of all children in out-of-home care every 18 months and to make reasonable plans for permanency for each child. **Permanency options,** in order of preference, included

1. Returning the child to his or her birth or extended family
2. Terminating parental rights and placing the child for adoption
3. Establishing guardianship with relatives or others
4. Making a specific plan for long-term foster care

The law required the use of the least restrictive, most homelike setting possible for every child. It was an attempt to shift public policy away from breaking up families and placing children. Not only did it emphasize timely reunification or the development of alternative plans for permanency for the child, it also called on public child welfare agencies to prevent "the unnecessary separation of children from their families by identifying family problems, assisting families in resolving their problems, and preventing the breakup of the family where the prevention of child removal is desirable and possible" (Samantrai, 1992). Initially, P.L. 96-272 appeared to be effective in reducing the number of children entering the foster care system, with a nearly 50 percent reduction between 1977 and 1983.

One effect of the emphasis on permanency planning has been a substantial increase in **kinship care,** the placement of children with relatives. By the late 1990s, 29 percent of all foster children were in kinship placements (Urban Institute, 2001). A number of factors have contributed to growth in the use of kinship care. One is the shrinking supply of foster homes. Another is the increased demand for out-of-home placements for children affected by the drug epidemic, AIDS, and homelessness (Dubowitz et al., 1994). There has also been increased recognition of the importance of cultural ties and kinship support networks, particularly among minority families (Hornby, Zeller, and Karraker, 1996). Some practitioners feel that adjustment is easier and the psychological trauma of separation and placement is greatly reduced when a child is placed with a relative. Some also believe that relatives have a special commitment to the children of kin. Kinship care may facilitate ongoing contact between children and their birth parents (Dubowitz, Feigelman, and Zuravin, 1993). Kinship placements are also more stable and less apt to break down than other forms of foster care (Ehrle, Geen, and Clark, 2001).

Kinship care is not without controversy, however. There is some evidence that child welfare authorities are less careful in screening kinship care families for conditions that might present a threat to the child's safety or well-being. There is also likely to be less supervision by the child welfare agency of the child's ongoing adjustment in a kinship placement (Dubowitz, Feigelman, and Zuravin, 1993). These families are given fewer supports and services in managing the care of the children, even when the children have special needs. Many relatives who provide kinship care are elderly grandparents and great-grandparents with few resources for caring for additional family members. They may also lack the energy required to care for active young children. A number of recent studies have highlighted the need for more training and support of kinship caregivers (Berrick, 1998; Dubowitz et al., 1994; Urban Institute, 2001).

Another result of P.L. 96-272 was the development of **family preservation programs** to prevent family breakup and child placement (Edna McConnell Clark Foundation, 1985). One such program is the **HomeBuilders model**, developed in Tacoma, Washington, by clinicians at Catholic Family Services and described later in this chapter. In the early 1990s, a number of states passed legislation specifically calling for HomeBuilders-type family preservation services aimed at families with children at imminent risk of foster home placement. This activity culminated in a 1993 amendment to the Social Security Act entitled the Family Preservation and Support Services Program. This amendment provided federal funds to state child welfare agencies to develop family preservation and family support services nationwide (Early and Hawkins, 1994).

## CURRENT POLICY ISSUES

At the same time that child welfare advocates were calling for increased attention to preventing family breakup and out-of-home placement of children, a new threat to family stability and child safety was appearing on city streets and in suburban neighborhoods: **crack cocaine.** This inexpensive form of cocaine made its debut in the drug culture in the mid-1980s, and within a few years the number of children entering foster care increased dramatically, despite a decade of family preservation programs and policies. In some communities, testing positive for cocaine at birth was deemed sufficient evidence of neglect to remove an infant from its mother. In others, crack-addicted mothers, unable to provide even minimal parenting, lost their children to the foster care system. The number of infants and young children entering foster care skyrocketed, placing new demands on an already overburdened child welfare system. By 1989, there were 360,000 children in foster care nationally, up from 262,000 at the end of 1982 (Pelton, 1989). By the mid-1990s, this number had reached half a million.

Horror stories of crack-addicted mothers leaving young children alone for hours, even days, at a time as they pursued their drugs filled the media. Instances of severe maltreatment and even death of children at the hands of parents high on drugs made banner headlines across the country. Few drug treatment centers were equipped to treat women with children, and programs that accepted pregnant drug-involved women were rarer still. Thus, even parents who wanted help with their drug problems were hard-pressed to find it. By the mid-1990s, between 40 percent and 60 percent of children in foster care had parents who were involved with drugs or alcohol (Dore and Doris, 1997).

Drug-abusing parents were difficult to reach. Family preservation programs such as HomeBuilders were seldom successful in ameliorating their problems (Dore, 1993). Even parents who sought and received treatment often relapsed, thereby extending the stay of their children in foster care or requiring re-placement of those already reunified. The length of time children spent in foster care once again increased as addicted parents struggled to rebuild their lives.

In response to this shifting child welfare environment, Congress passed the **Adoption and Safe Families Act, P.L. 105-89,** in 1997. This legislation requires timely review of foster care cases and severance of parental rights of parents who fail to actively move toward reunification with their children. It requires permanency-planning hearings for children within 12 months of entry into out-of-home care. It also gives states the right to require even shorter periods for case review for children under 3 years of age. The law also stipulates that authorities may act within 30 days to terminate parental rights in certain circumstances, as when the parent's rights to a child's sibling have been terminated, when the parent has assaulted the child or a sibling, or when the child has been subjected to "aggravated circumstances" as defined by state law (Child Welfare League of America, 1998). Termination must be initiated for a child in the care of state child welfare authorities for 15 out of the most recent 22 months.

The Adoption and Safe Families Act of 1997 also places greater emphasis on adoption as an alternative to family reunification than did previous child welfare policies. States are required to document efforts to place children for adoption and are given bonus payments for exceeding previously established base levels of adoption of children in foster care.

Many concerns have been raised about the effect of this legislation in conjunction with the potential effects of abolishing AFDC. The Personal Responsibility and Reform Act of 1996 replaced AFDC with **Temporary Assistance to Needy Families (TANF),** which requires adults who receive public assistance to participate in some form of work or work-related activity. Adults may collect TANF for no longer than 5 years over their lifetimes, according to federal guidelines. Some states have reduced the eligibility period even further. Opponents fear that poor and minority families, who are most vulnerable to changes in the economy and instability in the labor market, are disproportionately affected by the provisions of TANF. They are quickly using up their lifetime eligibility for assistance and are forced to place their children in foster care because they cannot support them. Or, being forced to take jobs, these parents are unable to afford, or even find, appropriate child care, and their children are being neglected or placed in dangerous situations.

There is also concern that the many families affected by substance abuse and the lack of adequate treatment resources will be greatly disadvantaged under the Adoption and Safe Families Act (Courtney, 1998). Parents struggling to rebuild their lives can leave their children in foster care for no longer than 15 months within a 22-month period before their parental rights are terminated. Given the limited resources devoted to supporting reunified families, there are grave concerns about the vulnerability of this particular group to termination of parental rights.

There are also fears that adoption resources are woefully inadequate for all the children who may be released for adoption under this bill's provisions. Further, many children who come into foster care have been emotionally damaged by their experiences of abuse and neglect. It is far from clear that the child welfare system will be able to find adoptive homes for children with emotional and behavioral problems and whether it will provide ongoing services and supports to families that do adopt these children.

# CAUSES AND EFFECTS OF CHILD MALTREATMENT

Why do some parents abuse and neglect their children? What effects does maltreatment have on children? Do these effects last into adulthood?

## Causes of Maltreatment

Generally, parents who harm their children do so because of a combination of factors (Belsky, 1984, 1993). These factors include the parents' own personal characteristics, social factors such as a culture's belief in the use of corporal punishment, and child factors such as difficult temperament. The personal characteristics associated with abusive and neglectful behavior include clinical levels of depression, alcoholism, and drug addiction. Fifty percent or more of parents whose children come to the attention of child welfare authorities have substance abuse problems. Mothers who maltreat their children are significantly more likely to demonstrate symptoms of posttraumatic stress disorder (PTSD) than other mothers (Famularo, Kinshcherff, and Fenton, 1992). There are associations between PTSD symptoms and physical and sexual abuse in both children and adults (Carlson et al., 1997). The presence of this disorder in maltreating parents indicates that many parents who abuse and neglect their children may themselves have been abused and neglected in childhood (Kaufman and Zigler, 1987; Widom, 1989). There is also an association between childhood abuse, particularly sexual abuse, and symptoms of borderline personality disorder in women, a disorder that has been associated with maltreating behavior (Taylor et al., 1991).

About one-third of individuals who have been abused and neglected are likely to grow up to abuse and neglect their own children (Malinosky-Rummell and Hansen, 1993; Oliver, 1993). Another third are at heightened risk for maltreating their children and can be pushed into such behavior by high levels of environmental stress. The final third of such persons grow up to be competent parents who nurture and care for their children appropriately.

Among the child-related factors that appear to place children at higher risk of maltreatment are premature birth, being the first born, being male, having a physical disability, being under age 6, and having a difficult temperament, including being hard to soothe, restless, fussy, colicky, and a poor eater. One of these characteristics alone does not heighten the risk of maltreatment, but when several occur in combination, particularly when a parent is vulnerable or the environmental stressors are great, the probability of abuse or neglect greatly increases.

Environmental stressors include events or conditions that adversely affect the parent's functioning in his or her multiple roles. For example, unemployment or underemployment and the resulting poverty place stress on families when they are unable to meet daily living expenses. Increased hostility and conflict among family members often follow job loss and a subsequent decline in family income (Conger et al., 1994; McLoyd et al., 1994). Poverty is related to severe forms of violence against children when children are preschool age, the caretaker is under 25 years old, and the caretaker is a single parent (Gelles, 1992). This constellation of factors suggests a highly stressful environment interacting with a parent with few personal or interpersonal resources for coping.

Garbarino and Sherman (1980) studied community environments as factors in child maltreatment. They compared two inner-city neighborhoods that were equally economically depressed. One neighborhood had relatively low rates of child maltreatment, and the other had high rates. In the neighborhood with low rates of child maltreatment, there was a strong sense of community despite the poverty, residents knew one another, and most residents had lived there for several years. In the neighborhood with high rates of maltreatment, residents were isolated from one another even in the same building, there was no sense of community, and people moved in and out all the time.

This study highlights an important factor repeatedly observed in the environments of maltreating families: they are often socially isolated and have few social networks to offer them support in times of high stress. Although this isolation is frequently attributed to deficits in the family's ability to interact socially with others, it may also be a function of living in an environment that does not support the universal need of families and children for ongoing social supports. Families living in high-rise apartment buildings and surrounded by street violence are unlikely to feel safe enough to reach out to neighbors or make new acquaintances at the community playground. Alex Kotlowitz compellingly documents the fear and social isolation found in such communities in his book *There Are No Children Here* (1991).

## Effects of Maltreatment in Childhood

Although the physical effects of child abuse and neglect are most immediately apparent in bruises, broken bones, and failure to thrive, all forms of child maltreatment have serious adverse consequences for social and emotional development. Babies who are abused or neglected by their primary caregivers have difficulties forming the secure attachments to others that predict positive social and emotional functioning throughout childhood and into adulthood. Maltreated infants are often disorganized in their responses to their caregivers after a brief separation from them (Carlson et al., 1989; Lyons-Ruth, Connell, and Zoll, 1989). They are highly distressed during the separation and appear to want to establish physical contact with the returning caregiver, just like children who have not been maltreated. However, unlike most distressed infants, who go directly to their caregiver to be comforted, maltreated children appear anxious about what to do and generally avoid contact with the caregiver. Crittenden and Ainsworth (1989), who have conducted much of the research on attachment in abused and neglected children, attribute this response to the maltreating mothers' insensitivity to their child's affective state. Harsh, controlling, interfering, and negative interactions with infants and children mark this maternal insensitivity (Fagan and Dore, 1993; Pianta, Egeland, and Erickson, 1989).

A child who has experienced harsh treatment from a parent or other caregiver often treats others harshly in return. Preschool children who have been physically abused are less able to initiate positive interactions with peers than other children and, at the same time, are more likely to use aggression against others in their play (Haskett and Kistner, 1991; Mueller and Silverman, 1989).

As maltreated children enter the school years, their difficulties in learning become apparent. Physically abused children display "pervasive and severe academic and socio-emotional problems," while neglected children are similar to their nonmaltreated peers in social and emotional functioning but learn more slowly and are at high risk of school failure (Kurtz et al., 1993, p. 100). Stress in the family may not only contribute to child abuse and neglect but may also have an independent effect on the child's social, emotional, and academic functioning (Kurtz et al., 1993). For example, parents of neglected children have high rates of marital conflict and interpersonal problems, both of which affect children's functioning even when there is no evidence of maltreatment (Fincham, 1994; Kashani, et al. 1992). Substance abuse is also common in these families, another factor that independently places children at high risk of poor developmental outcomes (Dore, Nelson-Zlupko, and Kauffman, 1996).

Maltreated school-age children also have high rates of depression (Kaufman, 1991; Kazdin et al., 1985; Toth, Manly, and Cicchetti, 1992). This depression may be a consequence of the disrupted attachments experienced by maltreated children. Abused and neglected children may see themselves as unloved and unlovable, which in turn leads to pervasive feelings of sadness and hopelessness (Cummings and Cicchetti, 1990).

Child maltreatment is generally classified into five subtypes: physical abuse, sexual abuse, physical neglect, psychological maltreatment, and educational neglect (Wells and Tracy, 1996). Researchers have asked whether child neglect has a different effect on a child's psychosocial development than physical or sexual abuse. There is some evidence that neglect has particularly dire effects on academic performance (Kurtz et al., 1993). Emotional or psychological abuse, on the other hand, seems to be detrimental to a child's developing self-esteem and is closely associated with depression (Crittenden,

Claussen, and Sugarman, 1994). However, most forms of child maltreatment occur in combination; one study found that a single form of abuse or neglect occurs in isolation only 5 percent of the time, so it is difficult to determine differential effects (Ney, Fung, and Wickett, 1994).

One study found that physical abuse and verbal abuse are frequently associated, as are physical neglect and sexual abuse (Ney, Fung, and Wickett, 1994). This study also found a correlation between frequency of maltreatment and its severity. In addition, the earlier in a child's life maltreatment began, the greater its severity and frequency. Physical neglect was a precursor to abuse in many instances. These researchers determined that, from the child's perspective, physical neglect, physical abuse, emotional neglect, and verbal abuse have the greatest negative effect on the child's view of himself or herself and the world (p. 710).

Another study found that frequency of abuse was highly correlated with child functioning in a variety of dimensions, which included social competence and behavior problems (Manly, Cicchetti, and Barnett, 1994). The more frequent the abuse, the more impaired the child's functioning became. However, frequency and severity were interrelated, and if maltreatment was severe enough, its frequency did not matter. Even a relatively few instances of severe maltreatment could result in great damage to a child's psychosocial functioning. As in the study described above, the presence of physical neglect was key in determining the effect of other forms of maltreatment.

Children who were sexually abused but did not experience any other form of maltreatment functioned at a much higher level than other maltreated children and were indistinguishable from the children in the comparison group who had not been maltreated (Manly, Cicchetti, and Barnett, 1994). It may be that children that are sexually abused are more likely to receive counseling and other services than other maltreated children. Sexually abused children may experience serious impairments at later stages of psychosocial development, such as when they begin forming intimate relationships.

## Effects in Adulthood

Child abuse and neglect may negatively affect all aspects of a child's life, including emotional and psychological functioning, relationships with peers and adults, behavioral functioning, and capacity for learning. Some children are more resilient than others, but it is unlikely that any child escapes totally unscathed (Farber and Egeland, 1987). Even children who function well despite being maltreated are likely to experience latent effects that can inhibit adjustment in adulthood, particularly interpersonal relationships (Luthar, 1993). There is increasing evidence of a long-term negative effect on adult functioning.

There is an association between childhood maltreatment and antisocial behavior in men. One study found that 55 percent of a group of men who had been maltreated as youngsters 40 years earlier had a criminal record, were alcoholic or mentally ill, or had died before the age of 35 (McCord, 1983). A study of men incarcerated for violent crimes found that 41 percent had been physically or sexually abused or severely neglected in childhood (Dutton and Hart, 1992).

Most men appear to externalize their responses to childhood abuse and neglect, engaging in aggressive and violent behavior against others. Women, on the other hand, tend to internalize their responses, which are manifested in major depression, suicidal behaviors, self-mutilation, eating disorders, dissociation, and psychosis. Studies have consistently found rates of depression that far exceed those for women who were not sexually abused (Carlson et al., 1997). Women with a borderline personality and disassociative and other disorders have higher than expected rates of childhood physical and sexual abuse (Herman, Perry, and van der Kolk, 1989; Weaver and Clum, 1993). Women who were abused as children often turn to drugs or alcohol to cope with the effects of the trauma (Briere and Zaidi, 1989; Pribor and Dinwiddie, 1992). Because depression, personality disorders, and substance abuse are also associated with parenting behaviors that are abusive and neglectful, it is not hard to see how the maltreatment of children is transferred from one generation to the next.

# GENERALIST PRACTICE WITH MALTREATING PARENTS AND THEIR CHILDREN

In most states, child and protective service (CPS) investigators use specific criteria to assess whether abuse or neglect has taken place and whether there is a risk of future maltreatment. Often these criteria are contained in a standardized rating scale. There are seven primary areas of assessment (McDonald and Marks, 1991):

1.  Characteristics of the child
2.  Characteristics of the primary caretaker
3.  Environmental factors
4.  Characteristics of the maltreatment
5.  The alleged perpetrator's access to the child
6.  Family characteristics
7.  Parent–child interaction

Assessment of the child includes age, capacity for self-protection, developmental status (physical and social functioning relative to age), physical appearance, and reactions to the caretaker. The physical and mental health of the caretaker are assessed, along with any history of criminal behavior or substance abuse. The CPS worker also notes how the caretaker responds to the investigation. Is the caretaker aware of any problems? How motivated is the caretaker to solve the problems? How cooperative is the caretaker with the investigation? Environmental factors include the cleanliness, safety, and security of the general living environment and the presence or absence of social supports. The type, severity, and frequency of the alleged maltreatment would also be considered.

Family characteristics considered in a CPS investigation include whether there is an adult male present in the household and his relationship to the child. Unrelated adult males, such as the mother's boyfriend, are responsible for a high proportion of child deaths from physical abuse. Sexual abuse of young girls is also more often perpetrated by males with frequent access to the child, such as an uncle or a stepfather. A history of family violence is also considered. Clinicians in battered women's shelters have long observed a relationship between spousal abuse and child abuse. Research is beginning to document this relationship as well.

Evidence is found to substantiate the reported abuse or neglect in about a third of cases, meaning that parents or other caregivers have clearly violated state laws defining child abuse or neglect. Definitions of the various forms of child maltreatment are established in each state. Although there are similarities, there are also differences. Some states have established very narrow standards for abuse, often requiring physical evidence of maltreatment. Other states have broader standards that include less obvious forms of mistreatment, such as psychological abuse.

Once a CPS investigation has substantiated child maltreatment, child welfare authorities must decide whether to leave the child in the situation without additional services, to provide services to the entire family, or to remove the child from the home. Children are removed from their homes and placed in foster care in about one case in 10. In 25 percent of substantiated cases, no services are provided to the family at all. In the remaining 65 percent of cases, child welfare agencies either provide services themselves or, more often, refer the family to a community agency for family counseling, parenting education, individual therapy, or other appropriate services (Center for the Future of Children, 1998). In many communities, a type of program called **intensive family preservation services** would be mandated to try to prevent family breakup and out-of-home placement of the maltreated child. When the CPS investigation is complete, and abuse or neglect has been substantiated, the generalist social worker often becomes involved.

## Target Problems

Target problems related to abuse and neglect include

- Inadequate parenting skills
- Lack of effective strategies for problem solving
- Limited ability to cope with stress
- Mental health issues such as depression, anxiety, and substance abuse
- Difficulties in interpersonal relationships
- Lack of material resources

A parent's own history of abuse, neglect, or unmet nurturance needs may come into play as well. Difficulties with court, school, hospital, or child welfare personnel may also require intervention. It is equally important to respond directly to the child, who may be experiencing emotional or behavioral difficulties related to an insufficiently stable and nurturing environment. If the child has been placed out of the home, the trauma of separation and placement, fears of becoming attached to foster parents, and feelings of disloyalty to the birth family need to be addressed (Dore and Eisner, 1993).

## Types of Interventions

A variety of direct interventions are available for families dealing with child abuse or neglect. These include

1. Individual play therapy with the maltreated child
2. Individual therapy or counseling with the maltreating parent or parents
3. Family therapy for the entire family
4. Family groups in which several maltreating families participate
5. Group psychotherapy for parents or children
6. Parent support or mutual aid groups
7. Assistance in creating or enhancing support networks
8. Parent training or education on child management issues
9. Assistance for parents to make the home safe
10. Support for parents and children in school meetings, court proceedings, medical appointments, supervised foster care visits, and other situations

Indirect interventions may include referrals to after-school programs, supplementary or remedial education programs, recreation programs, camps, respite care, substance abuse treatment programs, income maintenance, and other concrete services; and advocating for, or creating, more or different services according to need.

In many communities, there are two primary types of agencies potentially involved with families dealing with child abuse or neglect. One is the preventive services agency, which may contract with the public child welfare agency to provide preplacement services to families and children to attempt to preserve the family, prevent further maltreatment, and keep the child out of the foster care system. The other is the agency that provides foster care, adoption, and reunification services to families whose children have been removed from the home by child welfare authorities after a protective services investigation.

A preventive services agency may serve families for as little as four to six weeks or as long as several years. One example of a short-term treatment model of preventive services is the **HomeBuilders model,** which has a well-developed treatment approach based on crisis intervention and cognitive-behavioral theories (Kinney, Haapala, and Booth, 1991). The practitioner works with one or two families at a time, for 4–8 weeks, and is available on call to the family 24 hours a day, 7 days a week. Most of the work is done in the family home with both the parents and the children. It includes basic environmental interventions, such as helping the family replace broken windows or plaster and paint walls in order to bring the housing up to code. The **fam-**

ily preservation workers, as they are called, also teach parents new behavior management techniques, such as using behavior charts and time-outs. The HomeBuilders approach is holistic; intervention includes whatever it takes to stabilize the family and prevent out-of-home placement. It has proved effective with certain types of families, particularly those with some personal and social resources who are committed to making the changes necessary to keep their children at home. It appears to be less effective with parents who are unable to follow through with the specific techniques they are taught, whether because of limited education or cognitive ability or mental health issues, such as severe depression or substance abuse. It also seems to be less effective with very poor families and with single-parent families, who may require longer-term, more extensive support services.

Another model of preplacement family preservation service is the **family-based treatment model** based on family systems theory (Lindblad-Goldberg, Dore, and Stern, 1998). Programs using this model usually last for three to six months or even longer. Services are delivered primarily in the family's home, and clinicians are on call 24-hours a day. Unlike the HomeBuilders-type models, which are based on cognitive and behavioral psychology, family-based models use family systems theories and techniques. They look beyond the family to its relationships with other social systems, such as the neighborhood and larger community. Treatment is not confined to the family; instead there is active intervention in the family's social network to identify and develop resources that can alleviate stress and enhance the family's ability to cope. Attention is also paid to intergenerational processes at work in the family. Genograms and ecomaps are used to help families identify patterns of relationships that may positively or negatively affect functioning (see Lindblad-Goldberg, Dore, and Stern, 1998, for a complete discussion of the family-based model).

Services for families whose children are placed in foster care focus primarily on addressing factors contributing to the abuse or neglect, with the goal of reunification or of making a determination that reunification is not possible and that termination of parental rights is necessary. Securing adequate housing is often a prevailing issue, particularly for families who have been homeless or who are living in housing hazardous to the health and well-being of the child. Unfortunately, many children are removed from the care and custody of their parents simply because their living environment is unsuitable. Severe federal cutbacks in funding for public housing programs have left many poor families homeless.

Substance abuse and spouse abuse frequently confront the generalist practitioner working with families in the child welfare system (Dore, Doris, and Wright, 1995). These are particularly difficult issues because of the lack of treatments available in most communities and the time constraints imposed by the Adoption and Safe Families Act of 1997. You will need to know how to do a substance abuse assessment with a parent and how to assess for spousal violence. Motivational interviewing techniques have proved to be effective in helping individuals with substance abuse problems accept treatment (see Hohman, 1998, for an excellent discussion of the use of motivational interviewing with child welfare clients). It is also important to know the treatment resources available in the community and the criteria for referral and admission to these programs. There is nothing more detrimental to substance-abusing parents who have acknowledged the need for treatment than to be referred to a program that is unable to accept them because of funding constraints or admission criteria. Achieving sobriety is a long and arduous process requiring a great deal of support and encouragement. Most people do not achieve sobriety on the first or even second try. Maintaining hope and a belief in the parent's ability to succeed is an important part of your role.

You also need to be familiar with shelters for battered women and to provide the mother with information on how to keep herself and her child safe in violent situations. Helping a woman recognize that she has options and developing a concrete plan to deal with violence are essential first steps in helping her move out of a violent relationship. Battered women's support groups can be valuable resources in treatment planning for mothers in abusive relationships.

Another type of intervention often used with parents who are working toward reunification is developing a network of social supports that are available on an ongoing basis. Do not overlook the role of religious institutions in this network; they can provide a community of warmth and acceptance for isolated parents and children. Many parents who have maltreated their children feel deeply ashamed of their behavior, particularly if it is associated with a substance-abusing lifestyle. Religious institutions can help these parents forgive themselves and find meaning in their lives.

Reconnecting parents with extended family members may also be a part of developing a social network. Often, maltreating parents have worn out their family relationships, particularly if they have had substance-abuse problems or have made poor choices in their intimate relationships. Helping them learn how to establish and sustain healthy interpersonal relationships may be an important aspect of the intervention process. Mutual aid and support groups can be effective ways for parents to learn new social skills (Otto, 1990). A recent approach has been to develop multifamily groups that include maltreating parents and their children (Meezan, O'Keefe, and Zarianai, 1997).

Parenting programs are frequently used with parents who have abused or neglected their children, but they need to be used with caution (Dore and Lee, 1999). Maltreating parents usually have other problems in addition to their lack of awareness of child management techniques, and parent programs that focus on teaching specific parenting skills, such as use of time-outs and positive reinforcements, are not effective with parents with multiple problems. Parenting programs should be part of an array of treatment activities and services, not the sole approach.

Children who have been maltreated by a parent or other caregiver have treatment needs as well. Individual **play therapy** is the traditional approach to addressing problems experienced by these children (Mann and McDermott, 1983). Some children who have been victims of abuse suffer from posttraumatic stress disorder. Play therapy can help these children work through and eventually gain some sense of control over stressful events. Play therapy can also serve to explore attachment issues, externalize fear, and widen the emotional and behavioral repertoire of maltreated children (see Gil, 1991, and Webb, 1999, for further discussion of the use of play therapy with traumatized and maltreated children). Therapeutic nurseries and play groups have been established to provide treatment for very young children (Oates and Bross, 1995). Group treatment is seen by some as the intervention of choice for children of school age or even younger (Steward et al., 1986). Group treatment often helps children overcome shame and self-blame by exposing them to other children's similar experiences. It also provides an opportunity to develop and expand interpersonal skills, including nonaggressive ways to express anger and being upset.

## Special Issues in Working with Abusive or Neglectful Families

There are numerous challenges in developing collaborative relationships with clients where child abuse and neglect is involved. Parents who are poor and parents of color have been particularly vulnerable to intrusion by a child welfare system in which inadequate attention has been paid to bolstering a family's ability to function as a unit (Pelton, 1989). Historically, children in these families have been more likely to be removed from their homes and the rights of their parents more readily terminated (Stehno, 1982). Families have less frequently been offered supports and services designed to enable them to resume caring for their children (Jones, 1993). Understandably, attempts to help are often perceived as investigatory and are met with mistrust and defensiveness.

Mistrust and suspicion are also exacerbated by the social worker's role as mandated reporter, someone who is required by law to report any suspicion of child abuse or neglect to a central state registry or hotline. Creating an effective helping relationship in this context demands forthrightness about the responsibility to provide services to the child and family while ensuring the safety and well-being of the child. Be clear with parents at the beginning of the work together that you are required by law to report possible abuse or neglect. If such a report becomes necessary, first inform the parent that it must be made and discuss the reasons for your concerns.

Practitioners are often fearful that making a report will severely damage the fragile trust built with maltreating families. The worker, often correctly, believes that the parent will end the relationship and that no further productive work can be done. There is no choice, however, but to make the report. Parents can be helped to understand this. If there is a positive working relationship, help the parent work through the feelings of anger, fear, and humiliation that present barriers to further work. If CPS investigators can be assured that the family is actively working to address the situation, continued services to the family without child placement may be recommended. If CPS makes a decision to place a child as a result of the report, the worker may have an opportunity to work with the family toward reunification or an extended kinship placement, or to help parents make a decision about terminating their rights and freeing the child for adoption.

Social workers working with families in which there are abuse or neglect issues are prone to siding with the child. Children are vulnerable and need protection. Protecting children is mandated by society and by the NASW code of ethics. However, working with the entire family system, while ensuring the protection of the child, helps protect fragile family bonds, which are, in the long run, important to the child.

Another potential barrier to developing a helping relationship with parents is raised by a client's questions about the social worker's own parenting status. "Do you have kids?" is a question that can be experienced as an attack, especially by a worker who is childless. And sometimes it is an attack, a defensive maneuver designed to convey the message, "You can't help me." But just as often, the parent is asking for reassurance that he or she will not be judged harshly as an inadequate parent. The supposition is that another parent can better understand the difficulties of being a parent. Or, the parent may simply want to know more about who the worker is. If that is the case, an answer is conveyed not only by the content of the response but also by the manner. A matter-of-fact, open, and honest response can reassure the parent that you are respectful of his or her concerns. Regardless of the parent's intent, a nondefensive, nonreactive posture goes far in establishing a productive worker–client relationship.

Parenting practices acceptable in some cultures may be considered abusive under current laws in the United States. This is particularly true for some forms of child discipline. For example, switching or striking a child with branches is a common practice in some cultures, but CPS workers may see it as abusive, particularly if it leaves welts. In communities with a large immigrant population or diverse cultural or ethnic groups, it is important to learn about the particular customs and practices of the various groups. Sources of information include professional literature, supervision, and formal immigrant organizations.

Some immigrant groups experience difficulty in coming from an environment in which children are raised communally to one in which nonfamily involvement in child rearing is seen as intrusion into family privacy. This may result in loneliness, isolation, and despair for immigrant families accustomed to receiving support from a large extended kinship system or a whole village.

Beware of feelings of urgency in responding to situations that appear to involve abuse or neglect. Sensationalist media coverage of some cases may encourage impulsive and otherwise reactive responses, making it difficult to weigh both confirming and contradictory evidence about what has occurred and what action is in the best interests of the child. Do not let fear of leaving a child in a potentially dangerous situation lead you to overestimate the threat to the child's safety and to remove the child from the family without considering less drastic measures such as temporary voluntary placement with a relative or close friend. Removing a child from familiar surroundings is nearly always traumatizing to the child, no matter how unsatisfactory those surroundings may appear to an adult. It is only when the risk to the child of remaining in the situation clearly outweighs the risk of damage from removal that such a step should be considered.

The current child welfare system has great potential for reabusing and neglecting already vulnerable children and families. Despite laws that mandate the use of methods to assess imminent danger and future risk of abuse and neglect, many child protective workers "remove first and ask questions later." They feel pressure from sensationalist media coverage of tragic events or from child welfare administrators who implicitly or explicitly convey that this is good practice. There are also fiscal incentives for leaving children in foster care longer than may be necessary. In some states, the contract agencies that provide placement prevention services also provide foster care services. They get paid at a higher rate for the latter than the former; this is an incentive to place children away from their families and to keep them in placement.

Child abuse and neglect also occur in foster homes. It is not just biological parents who maltreat children. Low boarding payments, inadequate screening of foster parents, lack of training in meeting the special emotional needs of foster children, and lack of supportive services, including frequent, routine home visits, all contribute to the potential for abuse and neglect by foster parents. It is a sad irony that children who are removed from their biological families because of maltreatment may be placed in substitute homes that are equally as abusive or neglectful, or more so.

Awareness of the potential for abuses in the child welfare system causes some social workers to avoid making use of the system even when it is necessary and appropriate. Concerns about the system's present inadequacies and history of racism and prejudiced attitudes against the poor may cloud our judgment. We may hesitate to remove children from situations that are clearly detrimental to their well-being because we are worried about how they will be treated by the system. If we have such concerns, we must ask ourselves what we are doing to advocate for changes in the system. We must clearly document instances of maltreatment perpetrated by the child welfare system and educate the community and lawmakers about these abuses. We should not wait until a child dies in foster care to speak out about the failures of the child welfare system and to propose changes that can make it more responsive to the needs of troubled families and their children.

## SUMMARY

The abuse and neglect of children is a significant social problem that appears to be growing, as indicated by the increasing number of reports to child protection agencies. At last count, at least half a million children were in out-of-home care in the child welfare system because of maltreatment by parents or other caregivers.

The response in the United States to child abuse and neglect has changed over time. In this country's earliest years, neglect drew greater attention than abuse. Town fathers did not hesitate to step in and remove children from families that were judged inadequate to care for them. Placing such children as unpaid laborers with other families in the community was the common response. As cities and towns grew larger and less able to manage all the children in their care, congregate care institutions were built to house them. These facilities were often constructed by religious groups to care for children of their faith. Most dependent and neglected children were cared for in this way, although there were also agencies that continued to place children with foster families, especially very young children. In the twentieth century, institutional care for children fell out of favor, and efforts were increasingly made to help families provide care to their own children. Throughout the twentieth century, public awareness of the existence and extent of child abuse has grown, particularly with the invention of the x-ray, which allowed doctors to see long-standing patterns of abuse.

Social concern with child maltreatment has led to varied public policy responses on the federal level. The first response was to fund public agencies to handle child protection and care. Federal legislative initiatives have funded programs of foster care, particularly for children living below the poverty level. In the 1970s, identification and reporting of child abuse and neglect was the predominant policy concern. Then, as the number of children entering out-of-home care soared, legislation was enacted to fund programs to preserve families and keep children in their own homes. As the drug epidemic in the 1980s began to affect families and the care of their children, the policy pendulum swung back again. Family preservation took a back seat to child protection. At the same time, however, Congress enacted legislation to limit the length of time a child could be in foster care without a permanent home. Concurrent planning, a mechanism whereby a permanent plan for a child is made at the time he or she enters care in the event that family reunification is not possible, is the focus of child welfare policy at the present time.

In the last 50 years, researchers and others concerned about the maltreatment of children have sought to develop an understanding of why some parents and caregivers abuse and neglect children in their care. The reasons seem to be complex and varied, having to do with the child, the family, and the social environment. Some children, such as those with disabilities, are particularly vulnerable to abuse. And some families, particularly those who are stressed by poverty, unemployment, racism and oppression, mental illness, and substance abuse, are more likely than others to maltreat their children. Some communities have unusually high rates of child abuse and neglect. These seem to be communities with transient populations and few social connections among inhabitants.

Child abuse and neglect raise intense reactions in almost everyone. Generalist social workers who work with maltreating families, or with families at high risk of child maltreatment, must be aware not only of the dynamics of abusive and neglectful families but also of the effects of the child welfare system on families. It is essential to base practice with these families on a thorough assessment of each situation, without a rush to judgment. Most parents want to do right by their children but may be unable to for a variety of reasons, often having to do with their own unmet needs for nurturing, difficulties in psychosocial functioning, or both. To identify and build on a family's strengths so that it can better cope with the stress of nurturing its children is at once more challenging and more gratifying for all concerned than severing a family's affectional ties and offering a child an unknown future.

## CASE EXAMPLE

The case example in Case 15.1 shows how one generalist social worker addressed the problems of a family experiencing many of the stressors found in families at high risk for child maltreatment. This case illustrates the kind of family situation that often results in intervention by child welfare authorities: a minority family, struggling financially, with many children and overworked, isolated, and depressed parents who have relinquished some of their authority to a child or children in the family. It also demonstrates how the generalist practitioner works with multiple systems in such cases and maintains a presence in the community and in the family home.

---

**CASE 15.1** | A VULNERABLE FAMILY

Manuel R., age 34, and his wife Maria, 28, had 5 children: Yvette, 9; Manuel Jr., 8; Carlos, 7; Connie, 4; and Angelique, 1. The R. family was referred to a family service agency for counseling by Maria R.'s physician. Maria was suffering from high blood pressure and anemia and reported feeling overwhelmed by her family responsibilities. Her husband had been working two jobs to make ends meet and did not have much time to spend with Maria and the children. In addition to meeting the daily needs of 5 children under the age of 10, Maria was dealing with school behavior problems that Yvette, age 9, had begun to exhibit. At the time of referral, Yvette was being recommended for special education. This disturbed Manuel and Maria, for they had always thought of her as a bright child, and they feared that special education would limit her opportunities to learn and develop.

At intake, members of the R. family appeared caring toward each other but highly stressed. Yvette often stepped in when one of the younger children approached Maria for attention or help. Manuel seemed uncomfortable, but he was able to speak openly about needing outside help, stating: "Our

pastor has always been able to help us. This time it is different." He spoke softly about his concern about his wife's health. Manuel said that his worries distracted him at work and made him snap at his young children at home. Maria said little during the session, responding only in monosyllables when addressed. She appeared to be sad and withdrawn. She cradled her youngest child, Angelique, in her lap, holding her tenderly but not interacting with her. The other children played with plastic blocks in a corner of the room.

In the first session, Jane F., the social worker, learned that the R. family's support network consisted of their church and extended families. The support was mainly spiritual and emotional and was extremely important to the family. However, concrete support, in the form of respite for Maria, for example, was not forthcoming because church and extended family members were also overburdened. Jane also determined that Maria had received prenatal care during all of her pregnancies and that the children had developed within the normal range in all areas (motor, cognitive, physical, and socioemotional).

*(continued)*

## CASE 15.1 | *continued*

### Assessment

Jane assessed the R. family as having many strengths. The parents were deeply committed to each other and to their children. The children were healthy and developing well physically. The family had strong spiritual values and beliefs and a network of supportive individuals. However, the family was currently experiencing a great deal of stress. Maria was overwhelmed with the responsibility of caring for five active young children alone. She had few social contacts with other mothers and little support in her parenting role from family and friends. There were few Latino families in the neighborhood, and their church was located several miles away, in their old neighborhood. Maria felt shy around the other young mothers in her building who gathered at the playground to chat while their children played.

Manuel tried to help out with the children when he could, but his work demands were great. The oldest daughter, 9-year-old Yvette, tried to alleviate some of the pressures on her mother by acting as a surrogate mother with the youngest children. But her anxieties about her mother and the family situation were being expressed in behavior problems in the classroom. This bright, formerly high achieving girl was being labeled as a problem child by school authorities and was about to be tracked into special education classes for children with learning and behavior difficulties.

### Intervention

Jane's initial interventions focused on reducing stress in the family. She invited Maria to a women's support group in which most of the women were mothers and several were Latina. The three older children began attending a neighborhood program after school five days a week. Connie, the 4-year-old, was put on a waiting list for Head Start. In family counseling sessions, efforts were made to strengthen the parental unit and relieve Yvette of the parenting role. Jane also assisted the family with Yvette's school problems. She attended a school-based support team meeting with Mr. and Mrs. R., in which the plan to put Yvette in special education was discussed. When

Jane suggested ways to include Yvette in classroom activities without focusing too much on her problem behavior, she was invited to work with Yvette's fourth grade class.

Jane, along with her supervisor, Carol W., focused on helping the children and teachers create a productive learning environment through the use of improvisational drama and games. For example, when two youngsters began to fight while Jane and Carol were working with the class, they were asked to create and direct a play about fighting. The two children became so engrossed in producing their play that their interactions with one another improved dramatically. Although Yvette was not in any way identified as the focus of attention for her problem behavior, her school behavior problems ceased after only a few weeks of participating in classroom activities with Jane and Carol.

However, during this period, the state hotline received an anonymous report claiming that Maria was abusing Angelique and that burns were seen on the baby's arms and hands. When questioned by a child protective service (CPS) caseworker, Maria asserted that Angelique had been playing close to the radiator and that she hadn't realized how hot it was until Angelique screamed after having been burned. When asked why she had not taken Angelique to the doctor, Maria replied that she was afraid they would blame her and take her baby away from her. Maria also stated that she knew how to take care of burns and that Angelique's burns were healing well, which was, in fact, the case.

Nevertheless, the CPS worker perceived that Angelique and 4-year-old Connie were in immediate danger of serious harm because there was no daily community oversight of them (that is, they were not in day care or school). The worker believed that Maria was covering up her actions. Maria's openness about the stress she had been feeling and the family's involvement with the family service agency backfired. The worker took it as evidence that Maria was a troubled woman and could not be trusted with the care of her youngest children. Without interviewing Manuel, the neighbors, Jane, or anyone else involved with the family, the CPS worker immediately removed Angelique and Connie from their family and placed them in separate foster homes.

Over the next several weeks, Jane helped the family negotiate a reunification plan with the CPS worker and foster care agency personnel and prepare for an upcoming court date. She educated Manuel and Maria about the hearing process and spoke to the court-appointed lawyer on their behalf. Maria plunged into a deep depression, and Yvette and Carlos began exhibiting behavioral difficulties in school. Manuel Jr. started having nightmares. The family system was under enormous stress. In family therapy sessions, the children talked about what the removal of their younger siblings meant for them and for the absent children. In individual sessions, Maria began to explore her emotional pain, including her frustration and despair about feeling and being powerless against the child welfare system and seeing herself as a failure as a wife and mother. Jane continued to support Manuel in his increasingly active role as father.

Support from the women's group, the family and individual therapy sessions, and a series of successful visits with Connie and Angelique at the foster care agency helped Maria feel less depressed and more hopeful. She became more actively involved in meeting the court's requirements. She had to complete a parent training program, and although she continued to feel that she had been wrongly accused of hurting her child, Maria was able to use the parent training sessions to learn alternative methods of disciplining and stress management techniques. After hearing the positive testimony of both Jane and the foster care worker, the judge in charge of the case ordered the return of the two youngest R. children to the home. The child welfare agency was to supervise the family for six months, at which time another decision would be made about the agency's involvement with the family.

The three older children continued attending the after-school program, and Connie began a full-day Head Start program. Maria and Angelique joined a mother–child play group that was initiated and organized by the women's support group. With support and encouragement from Jane, Maria made friends with one of the young mothers in her building, who then introduced Maria to the other mothers

at the playground. At Jane's suggestion, Maria and her new friend, Elise C., began exchanging child-care duties so that each mother had one free afternoon a week. Maria usually used her afternoon to shop for groceries at a big discount supermarket several bus transfers away, a trip that would have been stressful and exhausting with several children in tow.

Although Manuel continued to be absent for many hours because of his heavy work schedule, the time he spent with the family was qualitatively different than it had been before. Maria had previously served as a barrier between Manuel and the children in an attempt to "protect" the little time he had to relax. Now he played and talked with the children. The various school and sleep problems experienced by the children decreased and then disappeared as the family system became more stable. Family members were able to recognize ways they had grown individually and as a family.

### Termination

A year and a half after beginning at the family service agency, Maria and Manuel initiated termination. Maria's physical health had improved considerably; she was no longer anemic, and her blood pressure had returned to the normal range. Her depression had lifted, and her affect was brighter and livelier. Manuel commented that she seemed more like the young woman he had courted. Maria was also more responsive to the children in family sessions and during Jane's home visits. The children were doing well in school and at home, and they seemed to be in agreement that it was time for family sessions to end. The family's support network had been greatly enlarged with the addition of mothers from the women's support group, neighbors, parents from the Head Start program, and school personnel who had become allies when they realized how committed the R. parents were to the education of their children.

In addition to reviewing the work they had done together, Jane reassured the family that they could always come back if they needed to and that the older children's participation in the after-school program and Connie's participation in Head Start would not be affected by termination of counseling. Maria continued to participate in the women's support group.

# DISCUSSION QUESTIONS

1. How would you discuss your role as a mandated reporter with the R. family in order to help them continue the helping relationship (Case 15.1)?
2. What other interventions might be appropriate for Yvette? Could she benefit from a behavior modification intervention? (For more information on behavior modification, see Miltenberger, 2001, or Spiegler and Guevermont, 2003.)
3. What are the strengths of the R. family? How does Jane, the social worker, build on these in her work with the family?
4. What are some other ways Jane could have created or expanded social supports for the R. family?
5. How might the R. family's experiences have been different if they had not been working with Jane at the time Maria was reported for child abuse?
6. How can a family's spiritual values be identified and incorporated into treatment planning?
7. What have been the changes in response to child abuse and neglect over time in the United States? What caused these changes?
8. What effect might physical and emotional neglect have on an infant? On a 3-year-old? On a school-age child? On an adolescent?
9. What does it mean to say that child abuse is multiply determined?

# REFERENCES

Anderson, P. G. (1989). The origin, emergence, and professional recognition of child protection. *Social Service Review, 63*, 222–244.

Belsky, J. (1984). The determinants of parenting: A process model. *Child Development, 55*, 83–96.

Belsky, J. (1993). Etiology of child maltreatment: A developmental-ecological analysis. *Psychological Bulletin, 114*, 413–434.

Berrick, J. D. (1998). When children cannot return home: Foster family care and kinship care. *Futures for Children, 8*(1), 72–87.

Billingsley, A., and Giovannoni, J. M. (1972). *Children of the storm: Black children and American child welfare.* New York: Harcourt.

Brace, C. L. (1880). *The dangerous classes of New York, and twenty years' work among them* (3rd ed.). New York: Wynkoop and Hallenbeck.

Briere, J., and Zaidi, L. Y. (1989). Sexual abuse histories and sequelae in female psychiatric emergency patients. *American Journal of Psychiatry, 144*, 1426–1430.

Carlson, E. B., Furby, L., Armstrong, J., and Shales, J. (1997). A conceptual framework for the long-term psychological effects of traumatic child abuse. *Child Maltreatment, 2*, 272–295.

Carlson, V., Cicchetti, D., Barnett, D., and Braunwald, K. (1989). Disorganized/disoriented attachment relationships in maltreated infants. *Developmental Psychology, 25*, 525–531.

Center for the Future of Children. (1998). Protecting children from abuse and neglect: Analysis. *The Future of Children, 8*(1), 1–3.

Child Welfare League of America. (1998). The Adoption and Safe Families Act of 1997 (P.L. 105–89). Available on the Internet at http://www.childrensdefens.org/safestart_pass3.html

Conger, R. D., Ge, X., Elder, G. H., Lorenz, F. O., and Simons, R. L. (1994). Economic stress, coercive family process, and developmental problems of adolescence. *Child Development, 65,* 541–561.

Cook, J. F. (1995). A history of placing-out: The orphan trains. Child Welfare, 74, 181–197.

Courtney, M. E. (1998). The costs of child protection in the context of welfare reform. *The Future of Children, 8*(1), 88–103.

Crittenden, P. M., and Ainsworth, M. (1989). Child maltreatment and attachment theory. In D. Cicchetti and V. Carlson (Eds.), *Child maltreatment* (pp. 432–463). New York: Cambridge University Press.

Crittenden, P. M., Claussen, A. H., and Sugarman, D. B. (1994). Physical and psychological maltreatment in middle childhood and adolescence. *Development and Psychopathology, 6,* 145–164.

Cummings, E. M., and Cicchetti, D. (1990). Attachment, depression, and the transmission of depression. In M. T. Greenberg, D. Cicchetti, and E. M. Cummings (Eds.), *Attachment during the pre-school years* (pp. 339–372). Chicago: University of Chicago Press.

Dore, M. M. (1993). Family preservation and poor families: When "homebuilding" is not enough. *Families in Society, 74,* 545–556.

Dore, M. M., and Doris, J. M. (1997). Preventing child placement in substance-abusing families: Research-informed practice. *Child Welfare, 77*(4), 407–426.

Dore, M. M., Doris, J., and Wright, P. (1995). Identifying substance abuse in maltreating families: A child welfare challenge. *Child Abuse and Neglect: The International Journal, 19,* 531–543.

Dore, M. M., and Eisner, E. (1993). Child-related dimensions of placement stability in treatment foster care. *Child and Adolescent Social Work Journal, 10,* 301–317.

Dore, M. M., and Lee, J. W. (1999). The role of parent training with abusive and neglectful parents. *Family Relations, 48,* 1–13.

Dore, M. M., Nelson-Zlupko, L., and Kauffman, E. (1996). Psychosocial functioning and treatment needs of latency-aged children from drug-involved families. *Social Work, 44,* 179–190.

Dubowitz, H., Feigelman, S., Harrington, D., Starr, R., Zuravin, S., and Sawyer, R. (1994). Children in kinship care: How do they fare? *Children and Youth Services Review, 16*(1/2), 85–106.

Dubowitz, H., Feigelman, S., and Zuravin, S. (1993). A profile of kinship care. *Child Welfare, 72*(2), 153–169.

Dutton, D. G., and Hart, S. D. (1992). Evidence for long-term, specific effects of child abuse and neglect on criminal behavior in men. *International Journal of Offender Therapy and Comparative Criminology, 36,* 129–137.

Early, B. P., and Hawkins, M. J. (1994). Opportunity and risks in emerging family policy: An analysis of family preservation legislation. *Children and Youth Services Review, 16*(5/6), 309–318.

Edna McConnell Clark Foundation (1985). *Keeping families together: The case for family preservation.* New York: Author.

Ehrle, J., Geen, R., and Clark, R. (2001, February). *Children cared for by relatives: Who are they and how are they faring?* Document Series B, No. B-28. Washington, DC: The Urban Institute.

Fagan, J., and Dore, M. M. (1993). Mother-child play interactions in neglecting and non-neglecting mothers. *Early Child Development and Care, 87,* 59–68.

Famularo, R., Kinscherff, R., and Fenton, T. (1992). Psychiatric diagnoses of abusive mothers: A preliminary report. *The Journal of Nervous and Mental Disease, 180,* 658–661.

Fanshel, D. (1971). The exit of children from foster care: An interim research report. *Child Welfare, 50*(2), 65–81.

Fanshel, D., and Shinn, E. (1976). *Children in foster care.* New York: Columbia University Press.

Farber, E. A., and Egeland, B. (1987). Invulnerability among abused and neglected children. In E. J. Anthony and B. J. Cohler (Eds.), *The invulnerable child* (pp. 253–288). New York: Guilford.

Fincham, F. D. (1994). Understanding the association between marital conflict and child adjustment: Overview. *Journal of Family Psychology, 8,* 123–127.

Folks, H. (1902). *The care of destitute, neglected, and delinquent children.* New York: Macmillan.

Garbarino, J., and Sherman, D. (1980). High-risk neighborhoods and high-risk families: The human ecology of child maltreatment. *Child Development, 51,* 188–198.

Gelles, R. J. (1992). Poverty and violence toward children. *American Behavioral Scientist, 35,* 258–274.

Gil, E. (1991). *The healing power of play.* New York: Guilford.

Goldstein, J., Solnit, A., and Freud, A. (1973). *Beyond the best interests of the child.* New York: Free Press.

Guterman, N. B. (1997). Early prevention of physical child abuse and neglect: Existing evidence and future directions. *Child Maltreatment, 2*(1), 12–34.

Hacsi, T. (1995). From indenture to foster family care: A brief history of child placing. *Child Welfare, 74,* 162–180.

Haskett, M. E., and Kistner, J. A. (1991). Social interactions and peer perceptions of young physically abused children. *Child Development, 62,* 979–990.

Herman, J. L., Perry, J. C., and van der Kolk, B. A. (1989). Childhood trauma in borderline personality disorder. *American Journal of Psychiatry, 146,* 490–495.

Hohman, M. M. (1998). Motivational interviewing: An intervention tool for child welfare case workers working with substance-abusing parents. *Child Welfare, 77*(3), 275–290.

Hornby, H., Zeller, D., and Karraker, D. (1996). Kinship care in America: What outcomes should policy seek? *Child Welfare, 75*(5), 397–417.

Jenkins, S., and Norman, E. (1975). *Beyond placement: Mothers view foster care.* New York: Columbia University Press.

Jones, L. (1993). Decision making in child welfare: A critical review of the literature. *Child and Adolescent Social Work Journal, 10*(3), 241–262.

Kashani, J. H., Daniel, A. E., Dandoy, A. C., and Holcomb, W. R. (1992). Family violence: Impact on children. *Journal of the American Academy of Child and Adolescent Psychiatry, 31,* 181–189.

Kaufman, J. (1991). Depressive disorders in maltreated children. *Journal of the American Academy of Child and Adolescent Psychiatry, 30,* 257–265.

Kaufman, J., and Zigler, E. (1987). Do abused children become abusive parents? *American Journal of Orthopsychiatry, 57,* 186–192.

Kazdin, A. E., Moser, J., Colbus, D., and Bell, R. (1985). Depressive symptoms among physically abused and psychiatrically disturbed children. *Journal of Abnormal Psychology, 94,* 298–307.

Kempe, C. H., Silverman, F. N., Steele, B. F., Droegemueller, W., and Silver, H. K. (1962). The battered child syndrome. *Journal of the American Medical Association, 181,* 17–24.

Kinney, J., Haapala, D., and Booth, C. (1991). *Keeping families together: The homebuilders model.* New York: Aldine de Gruyter.

Kotlowitz, A. (1991). *There are no children here: The story of two boys growing up in the other America.* New York: Doubleday.

Kurtz, P. D., Gaudin, J. M., Howing, P. T., and Wodarski, J. S. (1993). The consequences of physical abuse and neglect on the school age child: Mediating factors. *Child and Youth Services Review, 15,* 85–104.

Lindblad-Goldberg, M., Dore, M. M., and Stern, L. (1998). *Creating competence from chaos: A comprehensive guide to home based services for children with serious emotional disturbances and their families.* New York: Norton.

Luthar, S. S. (1993). Annotation: Methodological and conceptual issues in research on childhood resilience. *Journal of Child Psychology and Psychiatry, 34,* 441–453.

Lyons-Ruth, K., Connell, D. B., and Zoll, D. (1989). Patterns of maternal behavior among infants at risk for abuse: Relations with infant attachment behavior and infant development at 12 months of age. In D. Cicchetti and V. Carlson (Eds.), *Child Maltreatment* (pp. 464–493). New York: Cambridge University Press.

Malinosky-Rummell, R., and Hansen, D. J. (1993). Long-term consequences of childhood physical abuse. *Psychological Bulletin, 114,* 68–79.

Manly, J. T., Cicchetti, D., and Barnett, D. (1994). The impact of subtype, frequency, chronicity, and severity of child maltreatment on social competence and behavior problems. *Development and Psychopathology, 6,* 121–143.

Mann, E., and McDermott, J. F. (1983). Play therapy for victims of child abuse and neglect. In C. E. Schaefer and K. J. O'Connor (Eds.), *Handbook of play therapy* (pp. 134–168). New York: Wiley.

Mannes, M. (1995). Factors and events leading to the passage of the Indian Child Welfare Act. *Child Welfare, 74*(1), 264–282.

McCord, J. (1983). A forty-year perspective on effects of child abuse and neglect. *Child Abuse and Neglect, 1,* 265–270.

McDonald, T., and Marks, J. (1991). A review of risk factors assessed in child protective services. *Social Service Review, 65,* 112–132.

McLoyd, V. C., Jayaratne, T. E., Ceballo, R., and Borquez, J. (1994). Unemployment and work interruption among African American single mothers: Effects on parenting and adolescent socioemotional functioning. *Child Development, 65,* 562–589.

Meezan, W., O'Keefe, M., and Zariani, M. (1997). A model of multi-family group therapy for abusive and neglectful parents and their children. *Social Work with Groups, 20*(2), 71–88.

Miltenberger, R. G. (2001). *Behavior modification: Principles and procedures* (2nd ed.). Belmont, CA: Wadsworth.

Mueller, N., and Silverman, N. (1989). Peer relations in maltreated children. In D. Cicchetti and V. Carlson (Eds.), *Handbook of child maltreatment* (pp. 529–578). New York: Cambridge University Press.

Ney, P. G., Fung, T., and Wickett, A. R. (1994). The worst combinations of child abuse and neglect. *Child Abuse and Neglect, 18,* 705–714.

Oates, R. K., and Bross, D. C. (1995). What have we learned about treating child physical abuse? A literature review of the last decade. *Child Abuse and Neglect, 19*(4), 463–473.

Oliver, J. E. (1993). Intergenerational transmission of child abuse: Rates, research, and clinical implications. *American Journal of Psychiatry, 150,* 1315–1324.

Otto, M. L. (1990). Treating abusive parents in outpatient settings. *Journal of Offender Counseling, Services, and Rehabilitation, 15,* 57–64.

Peebles-Wilkins, W. (1995). Janie Porter Barrett and the Virginia Industrial School for Colored Girls: Community response to the needs of African American children. *Child Welfare, 74*(1), 143–161.

Pelton, L. (1989). *For reasons of poverty: A critique of the child welfare system in the United States.* New York: Praeger.

Pianta, R., Egeland, B., and Erikson, M. F. (1989). The antecedents of maltreatment: Results of the Mother-Child Interaction Research Project. In D. Cicchetti and V. Carlson (Eds.), *Child maltreatment* (pp. 203–253). New York: Cambridge University Press.

Pribor, E. F., and Dinwiddie, S. H. (1992). Psychiatric correlates of incest in childhood. *American Journal of Psychiatry, 149,* 52–56.

Samantrai, K. (1992). To prevent unnecessary separation of children and families: Public Law 96–272 policy and practice. *Social Work, 37*(4), 295–302.

Schene, P. A. (1998). Past, present, and future roles of child protective services. *The Future of Children, 8*(1), 23–38.

Smith, E. P. (1995). Bring back the orphanages: What policymakers today can learn from the past. *Child Welfare, 74,* 115–142.

Spiegler, M. D., and Guevremont, D. C. (2003). *Contemporary behavior therapy* (4th ed.). Belmont, CA: Wadsworth.

Stehno, S. (1982). Differential treatment of minority children. *Social Work, 27*(1), 39–46.

Steward, M. S., Farquhar, L. C., Dicharry, D. C., Glick, D. R., and Martin, P. W. (1986). Group therapy: A treatment of choice for young victims of child abuse. *International Journal of Group Psychotherapy, 36*(2), 261–277.

Taylor, C. G., Norman, D. K., Murphy, J. M., Jellinek, M., Quinn, D., Poitrast, F. G., and Goshko, M. (1991). Diagnosed intellectual and emotional impairment among parents who seriously mistreat their children: Prevalence, type, and outcome in a court sample. *Child Abuse and Neglect, 15,* 389–401.

Toth, S. L., Manly, J. T., and Cicchetti, D. (1992). Child maltreatment and vulnerability to depression. *Development and Psychopathology, 4,* 97–112.

Tyor, P. L., and Zainaldin, J. S. (1979). Asylum and society: An approach to institutional change. *Journal of Social History, 13,* 23–48.

U.S. Advisory Board on Child Abuse and Neglect. (1991). *Creating caring communities: Blueprint for an effective federal policy on child abuse and neglect.* Washington, DC: U.S. Government Printing Office.

Urban Institute. (2001). *Report to Congress on Kinship Foster Care. Part I: Research Review.* Washington, DC: Department of Health and Human Services.

Weaver, T. L., and Clum, G. A. (1993). Early family environments and traumatic experiences associated with borderline personality disorder. *Journal of Counseling and Clinical Psychology, 61,* 1068–1075.

Webb, N. B. (1999). *Play therapy with children in crisis* (2nd ed.). New York: Guilford.

Wells, K., and Tracy, E. (1996). Reorienting intensive family preservation services in relation to public child welfare practice. *Child Welfare, 75*(6), 667–692.

Wheeler, L. (1983). The orphan trains. *American History Illustrated, 18,* 10–23.

Widom, C. (1989). Does violence beget violence? A critical examination of the literature. *Psychological Bulletin, 106,* 3–28.

# CREDITS

## PHOTO

# TEXT

This page constitutes an extension of the copyright page. We have made every effort to trace the ownership of all copyrighted material and to secure permission from copyright holders. In the event of any question arising as to the use of any material, we will be pleased to make the necessary corrections in future printings. Thanks are due to the following authors, publishers, and agents for permission to use the material indicated.

**Chapter 2. 30:** From Saleebey, Dennis (Ed.) Strengths Perspective in Social Work Practice, 3/e. Published by Allyn and Bacon, Boston, MA. Copyright © 2002 by Pearson Education. Reprinted by permission of the publisher.

**Chapter 3. 62, 63:** Originally published in "Development of a helping relationship for social work practice," by J. Poulin and T. Young, 1997, Research on Social Work Practice, 7, p. 463–489. Reprinted by permission of Sage Publications, Inc.

**Chapter 4. 76:** C. Cowger in Saleebey, Dennis (Ed.). "Assessing Client Strengths," in Strengths perspective in social work practice, 3rd ed. Published by Allyn and Bacon, Boston, MA. Copyright © 2002 by Pearson Education. Reprinted by permission of the publisher.

**Chapter 5. 105:** Clinical assessment for social workers: Quanititative and qualitative methods by C. Jordan and C. Franklin. Copyright © 1995, Lyceum Books. Reprinted with permission. 106: B. Carter and M. McGoldrick (Eds.), The changing family life cycle: A framework for family therapy (2nd ed.). Published by Allyn & Bacon, Boston, MA. Copyright © 1993 by Pearson Education. Reprinted by permission of the publisher. 123: From Groups: Interaction and performance by J. McGrath. Copyright © 1984, Prentice-Hall. Adapted with permission of Pearson Education, Inc., Upper Saddle River, NJ.

**Chapter 7. 167:** From B. W. Sheafor, C. R. Horejsi, and G. A. Horejsi, Techniques and guidelines for social work practice, 3rd ed. Published by Allyn & Bacon, MA. Copyright © 1994 by Pearson Education. Reprinted by permission of the publisher.

**Chapter 9. 241, 242, 243:** From M. Bloom, J. Fischer, and J. Orme, Evaluating practice: Guidelines for the accountable professional (2nd ed.). Published by Allyn & Bacon, Boston, MA. Copyright © 1995 by Pearson Education. Reprinted with permission of the publisher. 251: From A conceptualization and measure of argumentativeness, by D. A. Infante and D. S. Rancer, 1982, Journal of Personality Assessment, 46, 72–80. Copyright © 1982 by Lawrence Erlbaum Associates, Inc. Reprinted with permission. 257: From Fundamental approaches to single subject design and analysis by C. H. Krishef. Copyright © 1991 by Krieger Publishing Company. Reprinted with permission. 259, 262: From S. Berlin and J. Marsh, Informing practice decisions. Copyright © 1993 by Allyn & Bacon. Reprinted by permission of the publisher.

**Chapter 11. 304:** The Effects of Drugs chart was produced by CEIDA (Centre for Education and Information on Drugs and Alcohol) © CEIDA 1985, revised 1995. Reprinted with permission from the NSW Department of Health, Australia.

**Chapter 12. 333, 334:** Adapted with permission from "Healing from Cultural Victimization" by J. H. Neisen in Journal of Gay and Lesbian Psychotherapy, Vol. 2, No. 1. Copyright © 1993, The Haworth Press.

# INDEX

TO THE OWNER OF THIS BOOK:

I hope that you have found *Strengths-Based Generalist Practice: A Collaborative Approach*, Second Edition useful. So that this book can be improved in a future edition, would you take the time to complete this sheet and return it? Thank you.

School and address:_____

Department:_____

Instructor's name:_____

1. What I like most about this book is:_____

_____

_____

2. What I like least about this book is:

_____

_____

3. My general reaction to this book is:

_____

_____

4. The name of the course in which I used this book is:

_____

5. Were all of the chapters of the book assigned for you to read?_____

   If not, which ones weren't?_____

6. In the space below, or on a separate sheet of paper, please write specific suggestions for improving this book and anything else you'd care to share about your experience in using this book.

_____

_____

_____

Attn:  Lisa Gebo, Social Work Editor

BrooksCole/Thomson Learning
60 Garden Ct  Ste 205
Monterey CA  93940-9967

OPTIONAL:

Your name:_____ Date: _____

May we quote you, either in promotion for *Strengths-Based Generalist Practice: A Collaborative Approach*, Second Edition, or in future publishing ventures?

Yes: _____   No: _____

Sincerely yours,

John Poulin